second edition

NATIVE AMERICAN VOICES: A READER

Susan Lobo and Steve Talbot

Prentice
Hall

UPPER SADDLE RIVER, NEW JERSEY 07458

Library of Congress Cataloging-in-Publication Data

Native American Voices: A reader / [compiled by] Susan Lobo, Steve Talbot.—2nd ed.
    p. cm.
    Includes bibliographical references and index.
    ISBN 0–13–030732–7
    1. Indians of North America. 2. Indians of North America—Government relations.
3. Indigenous peoples—America. 4. Indians—Social conditions. 5. Indians—
Government relations. I. Lobo, Susan. II. Talbot, Steve.

E77 .N3517 2001
970.004'97—dc21   00-052873

VP, Editorial Director: Laura Pearson
AVP, Publisher: Nancy Roberts
Managing Editor: Sharon Chambliss
Director of Marketing: Beth Gillett Mejia
Interior Design and Project Management: Serena Hoffman
Prepress and Manufacturing Buyer: Benjamin Smith
Copy Editor: Margo Quinto
Line Art Manager: Guy Ruggiero

About the cover: Parris K. Butler (Mohave/Cherokee) created the cover art entitled "Icon Indigena—
    Locus #1," as well as the interior part opening art.

This book was set in 10/12 Palatino
by Interactive Composition Corporation
and was printed and bound by Hamilton Printing Company.
The cover was printed by Phoenix Color Corp.

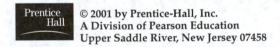

© 2001 by Prentice-Hall, Inc.
A Division of Pearson Education
Upper Saddle River, New Jersey 07458

10 9 8 7 6 5 4 3

ISBN 0-13-030732-7

Prentice-Hall International (UK) Limited, *London*
Prentice-Hall of Australia Pty. Limited, *Sydney*
Prentice-Hall Canada Inc., *Toronto*
Prentice-Hall Hispanoamericana, S.A., *Mexico*
Prentice-Hall of India Private Limited, *New Delhi*
Prentice-Hall of Japan, Inc., *Tokyo*
Pearson Education Asia Pte. Ltd., *Singapore*
Editora Prentice-Hall do Brasil, Ltda., *Rio de Janeiro*

CONTENTS

iii

FOREWORD

José Barreiro

In September 1977, at the first international conference of American Indigenous Peoples, held in Geneva, Switzerland, the nearly 150 indigenous delegates sat in concentric circles around five speakers who would give the major addresses for the group the next day. That gathering more than twenty years ago, the Conference on Discrimination Against the Indigenous Populations in the Americas, has come to be known as the first major touchstone of the movement that carried Indigenous Peoples' cases and perspectives into the United Nations. It occurred at a moment when the last wave of repression of Indian communities in the Americas was being unleashed and human rights violations of major intensity were terrifying Indians in a number of countries.

In Guatemala, the massacres of individual families were beginning. They would grow into the scorched earth policy of the 1980s, when 400 Indian communities were burned to the ground and their residents slaughtered. In Paraguay, Ache children were being yanked from their mothers and sold to white families. In Brazil, the miracle of development was eradicating one tribe after another as obstacles to progress, while in the United States the Federal Bureau of Investigation had launched the most intense persecution of Native leadership in over eighty years, resulting in some 400 court cases, several killings, and the incarceration of Leonard Peltier after an obviously biased and hostile trial.

But in Geneva, as the Indian elders from the various regions of the Western Hemisphere gave their advice to the selected speakers, something curious happened. One after another—from the Iroquois to the Mayan, to the Bolivian Quechua and Aymara, to the Ecuatorian Shuar and the Mapuche from Chile, and back north to the Lakota and the Hopi—each requested that the speakers, first of all, address the problems of Mother Earth. Leon Shenandoah, Iroquois Tadodaho, called her "Etanoha." "Yes, our Pachamama," said an ancient gentleman from the Andes. No matter how much of a problem we have as human beings, first of all, tell the world about the suffering of Mother Earth, said Corbett Sundown, Seneca. "I say the same as he," said the Maquiritari chief from Venezuela, Simeon Jimenez. Tell them first how the forests are being destroyed, how our rivers are made dirty by the gold mining.

It was a transferable sentiment, tellingly supported by all Indians in the room, and it fell to Oren Lyons, of the Iroquois, the following day, to ask the gathered

José Barreiro is author of the novel *The Indian Chronicles* and editor-in-chief of Akwe:kon Press/*Native Americas Journal,* at Cornell University. Of Guajiro ancestry from eastern Cuba, Barreiro is a member of the Taino Nation of the Antilles.

nations: "Where at the United Nations is the seat for the eagle? Who represents the trees? Who represents the fish? I ask you again: Who represents the eagle at the United Nations?"

That expression of world view opened the door for Native peoples to have an impact on international discourse. Within fifteen years, by the 1992 Earth Summit (the Rio de Janeiro United Nations Conference on the Environment and Development, UNCED), the centrality of indigenous knowledge systems for sustainable development had been written into Agenda 21, a major planning document. Two years later, delegates from the indigenous communities witnessed and consecrated the opening of the United Nations Decade of Indigenous Peoples (1994–2004), wherein the intellectual movement of the international community that endorses sustainability on environment and development issues declared the importance of the indigenous message to the world as we entered the new millenium.

Clearly, the vanishing American Indian of the 1890s, conquered and ostensibly destined for extinction, has persisted and has reemerged in the 1990s. The Native, or indigenous, peoples of the Americas did not only survive the twentieth century; they ended it on a note of protagonism never before possible. Steadily recovering population and reinvigorating community culture for over ninety years, Native peoples initiated a process in the 1970s that has inscribed recognition of indigenous peoples' traditional knowledge and community ways into international covenants; while in the home communities, efforts are being undertaken that will lead to cultural and political revitalization.

The old Mayan saying that the conquest cut the branches and even the trunks of the peoples but could not yank out the roots appears a truism. After forty years of terrifying war, "Mayan-ness" returns with elemental vigor in Guatemala and in Chiapas, Mexico. Also in Mexico and in the United States and Canada, autochthonous communities spring up to claim aboriginal jurisdiction. In Ecuador, the Native peoples shut down the country's markets with their demand to be heard and topple a government. A unique dialogue has followed. In Bolivia, the first Indian vice president, Aymara activist Victor Hugo Cardenas, broke a monumental race barrier with the swiftness of a reality whose time has come. In Chile, the Mapuches are a major factor now, constantly in the news, with land claims and environmental issues at the forefront of an intense cultural revival. Even in ultra-European Argentina, community cases, small and isolated, continue to emerge in international channels. And everywhere—Columbia, Guyana, Peru, Panama, Venezuela, Brazil, the Caribbean—indigenous voices and movements are active and pressing their cases.

In North America, the old Iroquois tradition of the White Roots of Peace, predicting that many scattered Native peoples would reawaken and find their way back to the Tree of Peace (to their aboriginal culture), appears to have life. Revitalization movements—in education, in language, in community healing—are making headway in Indian country. As cultures reconnect and communities recover, economic options based on retained and long-fought-for jurisdictional rights have been exercised. Then, too, interestingly, within this painful process of capital formation in Indian country, against prediction, traditional culture appears to persist and even to be reinvigorating. Thus, the Oneida people of both New York and Wisconsin, among others, persist, against economic advice, in buying land and supporting language programs with their casino profits—obvious imperatives that sustain their cultures.

This collection of readings in Native Studies, prepared by Professors Susan Lobo and Steve Talbot, is a significant step in the recognition of this contemporary reality. The perspective is hemispheric, rightfully assuming the universality of indigenousness in the Americas. The topics and voices are fully actualized, combating the most significant and mistaken stereotype of American Indians—that they belong in the past and are not part of the present or the future.

The study of Native peoples now has for the first time become grounded in a Native self-interpretation. This collection celebrates that reality. It is a masterly selection, carefully edited for maximum clarity, and it is a serious contribution to Native Studies. It posits that a Native Studies that would be useful and vital to its constituency must contribute to the improvement and strengthening of positive community life. Native peoples' traditions and cultural knowledge and the currency of their practice and usefulness can be the central and primary guiding factors.

For 500 hundred years, the approach to Native peoples hinged on one of two schools of thought: outright genocide—indigenous peoples were obstacles to progress that had to be eradicated—or defense of indigenous peoples as victim—the doctrine of human rights that was initially proposed by the Dominican friar Bartolomé de las Casas. At the turn of the century, however, a Native protagonism emerged—and it is evident in this volume. More and more Native voices are being directly heard. Native peoples of the Americas—attacked as savages, pagans, and primitives for over half a millenium and thought to be the vanishing Americans at the turn of the twentieth century—have now sustained an identity that is projected as a message of change and hope at the dawn of the twenty-first century.

The Native American world is as vibrantly traditional as it is modern. Divided by the many interplays of forces in the national societies, it nevertheless has internal cohesiveness—the kinship base of membership and cultural aboriginality—realities that do not fade. Strength and resilience are elemental qualities of American Indian peoples.

José Barreiro
Crows Hill, N.Y.

PREFACE

We are pleased by the very positive response to the first edition of this reader by students, colleagues, and the Native American community. The changes and additions to the new edition, we believe, will generate an even greater appreciation for the uniquely Indian-based perspective and hemispheric approach that characterize this volume and that clearly differentiate it from the standard, introductory works on Native Americans in the disciplines of anthropology and history.

The idea for this work grew out of the editors teaching an introductory level college course, The Indian Experience, for several years at the University of California at Davis in the late 1980s to the 1990s. This course and Introduction to Native American Studies were originally developed along with a dozen or so others in the late 1960s by Jack D. Forbes for the then new Native American Studies program at the University of California at Berkeley and at the University of California at Davis.[1] Steve Talbot, a co-editor of this reader, was a member of the faculty in the new Native American studies program at the University of California–Berkeley from 1971 to 1974 and consequently helped to develop these introductory courses. The Indian Experience became one of the core courses for the programs at these two institutions.

Other developing Native American Studies (or American Indian Studies) programs in colleges and universities during the 1970s created similar introductory courses.[2] These included the University of Minnesota, Washington State University, Humboldt State University, the University of California at Irvine, the University of California at Los Angeles, Dartmouth, the University of Wisconsin at Madison, and the University of Arizona.

The 1960s was the time of the "new Indian" movement and renewed activism signaled by the formation of the National Indian Youth Council, the American Indian Movement, and other Indian protest organizations, as well as by continued actions by the Iroquois and other traditional Indian peoples, the occupation of Alcatraz, the Trail of Broken Treaties to Washington, D.C., and Wounded Knee II and

---

[1] We will use the terms *Indian, American Indian, Native American,* and *Native* interchangeably throughout this volume, although scholars prefer the term *Native American* because it takes into account Aleuts and Eskimos as well as Indians. Sometimes the adjectives *indigenous* or *aboriginal* are used in reference to the peoples who are native to the Americas.

[2] In a recent work (*Studying Native America: Problems and Prospects,* University of Wisconsin Press, 1998, 79–107), Russell Thornton documents the historical background and development of Native American Studies. Although he writes that "the impetus for the development . . . came from new numbers of Native American students on campus" (p. 87), he understates the Indian student activism and contribution of the traditional Indian community that pressured mainstream institutions of higher learning into "establishing" the new Native American and American Indian Studies programs.

its aftermath of government repression. This was a time when urban-based Indians and their reservation counterparts joined forces under the guidance of traditional elders and religious leaders to press for treaty rights, sovereignty, and self-determination. It was also a time when hundreds of Indian young people were able to enter college under special admissions programs (affirmative action), receive financial aid, and bring the issues and demands of the larger Native American struggle to the university campus. The idea behind these introductory Native American studies classes was to bring the "Indian experience" into the classroom and thereby make the college curriculum relevant to the lives of the new population of Indian students on campus; they were also intended to correct misconceptions and stereotypes about Indian history, religion, and culture for the general student population and the larger society.

The Indian Experience course substituted for the more mainstream Introduction to North American Indians course traditionally taught in anthropology. The paradigms for the two courses differ substantially; indeed, there are profound differences in the respective paradigms of Native American studies and anthropology. Yet, although there are many introductory North American Indian books in anthropology and history, there are very few in Native American studies and virtually none, especially a reader, that are suitable as an introduction to Native American studies for the college student and the general public with an interest in American Indians. There are, of course, some excellent atlases, almanacs, and edited works, including various compilations of Indian literature and poetry, but, again, nothing that approximates a Native American studies reader such as we have compiled here. (See the Suggested Readings list in Part I.) Thus, we envision that this book will fill the void that we perceived from our teaching experience.

Unlike history, or even anthropology, the Native American studies theoretical perspective, or paradigm, is multidisciplinary by the very nature of its subject matter: that is, the experience of Indian peoples. Thus, a major aim of this reader is to provide a representative sampling of this experience. This reader, therefore, contains not only scholarly articles but also journalistic selections, documents, oral history and testimony, songs and poetry, maps and art. A related purpose here is to meet the needs of classes at the undergraduate level in the social sciences and related fields, particularly Native American studies, but also ethnic studies, anthropology, sociology, history, American studies, political science, and even law, education, and social welfare.

The book is divided into nine topical parts that encompass the major concerns and interests of Native American peoples and nations. Although we concentrate on Indian peoples of the United States, we have included representative selections from Canada and Latin America, especially those that indicate the linkages existing among all indigenous peoples of the Western Hemisphere. We believe that a hemispheric approach is not only appropriate theoretically but also is one that reflects the wider perspective, history, and reality of all of the indigenous peoples of the Americas.

The parts are arranged to focus on a series of interrelated themes. Parts I, II, and III lay the foundation, giving an overview of Native perspectives on history and heritage, as well as locations and demographics. The goal in Part IV is to facilitate an understanding of the values and stereotypes held by many non-Indians that have created, and in many instances served to maintain, a social context of racism and injustice with which Indian people must deal. Parts V, VI, and VII once again focus on Native strengths: that is, the individual, family, and community or tribal foundation based on relationships to spiritual truths and to the land. Part VIII deals with some of the specific problem areas that Native People face, many of these the legacy of generations of externally imposed conflict and injustice. The final section, Part IX, discusses the many ways that Native peoples have confronted, resisted, and struggled to survive as peoples and to once again thrive culturally.

At the end of each part are discussion questions that will assist the student or other readers of this book in understanding the salient points of each selection. These are followed by Key Terms and, finally, Suggested Readings. At the beginning of the book are maps of North and Central America and South America, which indicate the names and locations of the Indian peoples and nations discussed in this work, as well as some other important peoples. At the end of the volume there are appendixes for Native media, major indigenous peoples' organizations, a website guide to Native American Studies programs in the United States and Canada and a list of institutions that offer them.

Many people, in one way or another, contributed to this volume. They include our many colleagues, both Indian and non-Indian, who share our vision. Among them, however, we wish to mention José Barreiro (Guajiro/Taino), Victoria Bomberry (Muskogee/Lenape), Duane Champagne (Turtle Mountain Chippewa), Jack D. Forbes (Powhatan-Renape and Delaware-Lenape), Frank Lobo (Acjachemen), Kelina Lobo (Acjachemen), Jane Monden, Marcus Peters (Anishinabeg), Claudia Peters, Luana Ross (Salish), Mariechen C. Talbot, and Darryl Wilson (Pit River/ Ajuma/Atsuge). We thank also the several classes of students in Steve Talbot's Introduction to American Indians course at San Joaquin Delta College who provided valuable feedback to the first edition. Finally, we acknowledge the assistance and support of the following institutions and professional associations: Akwe:kon Press and *Native Americas* magazine; the American Friends Service Committee; the International Indian Treaty Council; Intertribal Friendship House in Oakland, California; the Native American Studies Department at the University of California at Davis; the American Indian Studies Center at the University of California at Los Angeles; the Anthropology Department at Oregon State University; and San Joaquin Delta College in Stockton, California.

We thank also our publisher, Prentice Hall, its Assistant Vice President, Nancy Roberts, and managing editor, Sharon Chambliss. They have been especially helpful and understanding during the production process. Special thanks go to our production editor, Serena Hoffman.

We dedicate this volume to the late Edward H. Spicer, social anthropologist and cultural historian, who was mentor for both of us at the University of Arizona in the 1960s. The theoretical and ethical grounding that we received under his tutelage has stood us in good stead in our academic pursuits, and his personal example of compassion and sensitivity in relating to our fellow human beings has also helped guide us in our relationships with Indian friends and relations.

ABOUT THE EDITORS

Susan Lobo is a consultant emphasizing research, advocacy, and project design, working primarily for American Indian tribes and community organizations in the United States and Central and South America. She has a Ph.D. in anthropology from the University of Arizona and has taught at the University of California at Berkeley, where she was the coordinator of the Center for Latin American Studies. She has also taught Native American studies at the University of California at Davis and environmental studies at Merritt College. Since 1978 she has been the coordinator of the Community History Project archive at Intertribal Friendship House, the American Indian Center in Oakland, California. She was also a producer for many years of the KPFA-FM radio series *Living on Indian Time*. Her publications include *A House of My Own: Social Organization in the Squatter Settlements of Lima, Peru* (1992); *American Indians and the Urban Experience*, co-editor (2000); *Pride of Place: The American Indian Community in the San Francisco Bay Area* (2001), and many articles in professional and popular journals.

Steve Talbot has written several books and many articles dealing with Native Americans, including *Roots of Oppression: The American Indian Question* (1981). Currently, he is a retired instructor of sociology, anthropology, and Native American Studies at San Joaquin Delta College in Stockton, California, and an adjunct professor of anthropology at Oregon State University, where he continues to teach part-time. He received his master's degree in anthropology and community development in 1967 from the University of Arizona and a Ph.D. in anthropology from the University of California, Berkeley in 1974. In the early 1960s he was a fieldworker in Indian community development for the American Friends Service Committee, and in that capacity he spent three years on the San Carlos Apache Reservation in Arizona. He then moved to the San Francisco Bay area, where he served on the board of Oakland's Intertribal Friendship House. Later, as a doctoral student at the University of California, Berkeley, he was closely associated with Indian student activism on campus, the Alcatraz occupation, and the founding of the Native American Studies program at the university. From 1971 to 1974 he was acting assistant professor of Native American Studies at the University of California, Berkeley. He has since lectured extensively and has taught Native American Studies courses in Europe and at various universities in the United States. From 1988 to 1990 he was a lecturer in Native American Studies at the University of California, Davis. His major interest today is producing text materials for Native American studies.

ABOUT THE ARTISTS

Parris K. Butler, whose art appears in this volume, on the cover and at the beginning of each part, works in a variety of two-dimensional media, including pen and ink, acrylic on canvas, and various printmaking techniques. In 1985 he received an Associate of Fine Arts Degree from the Institute of American Indian Arts in two-dimensional arts and creative writing. He currently resides in the San Francisco Bay area.

Leonard Chana (Tohono O'odham) was born in Burnt Seeds, now Santa Rosa village, Arizona. He specializes in a unique art form, stippling, in which images are formed with dots in pen and ink. He also paints in acrylics.

1

PEOPLES AND NATIONS: FOLLOWING IN THE FOOTSTEPS OF THE ANCESTORS

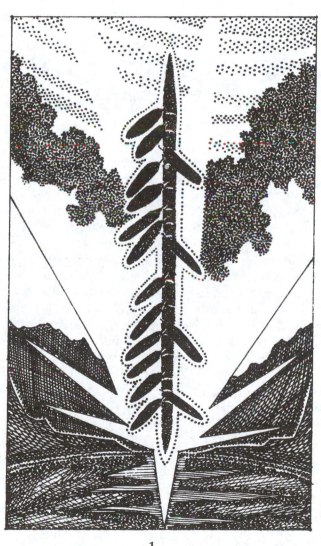

Hearing the Song
William Stafford

My father said, "Listen," and that subtle song
"Coyote" came to me; we heard it together.
The river slid by, its weight
moving like oil. "It comes at night,"
he said; "some people don't like it." "It sounds
dark," I said, "like midnight, rich. . . ."
His hand pressed my shoulder:
"Just listen." That's how I first heard the song.

This book takes a Native American studies perspective rather than that of mainstream anthropology, sociology, or even history. That perspective is what is meant by the subtitle to this part, "following in the footsteps of the ancestors." Our emphasis and perspective are those of the indigenous peoples of the Americas as peoples and nations, not as ethnic minorities. Native American studies (NAS) arose as an academic field of study in the late 1960s during the "new Indian" movement. As part of this development, forty-six undergraduate programs in Native American studies with either a major or a minor, or both, were founded, nineteen programs on college and university campuses in California alone.[1] By 1984, according to the Carnegie Foundation for the Advancement of Teaching, at least eighty-five non-Indian colleges and universities had organized Indian studies programs. A 1999 survey by the Association for the Study of American Literatures found thirteen programs and departments offering graduate degrees in Native American studies, at least four with Ph.D. programs.[2] Furthermore, more than 350 professors in more than 100 colleges and universities have identified themselves as Native American or Alaska Native, according to Elizabeth Cook-Lynn (Lakota), editor of *Wicazo Sa Review*.[3] Indian scholar Russell Thornton, in a recent work (see the Suggested Readings for Part I, on page 67), has written a useful essay on the historical development of Native American studies. Thornton, however, attributes the intellectual origins of NAS mainly to Anglo educational institutions.

Our perspective on this question finds a different line of development, one that is grounded in traditional indigenous history, culture, and struggle. An issue that emerged in the 1960s concerned the relationship of NAS to the already established academic departments such as anthropology, sociology, art, history, and literature, which are part of the Western scientific and humanities tradition. Professors in these mainstream departments sometimes saw themselves in an adversarial relationship with the new course offerings in NAS and American Indian studies in a kind of "turf war" mentality. Native American studies was not considered an academic discipline in its own right but, instead, was viewed as a nonserious "program" created by Indian ideologues who espoused a cultural nationalism. This is still the view in some quarters today.

Unlike the other disciplines, NAS is multidisciplinary in scope, whereas anthropology, for example, although holistic in context, is not. Native American studies also takes an indigenous rather than a Eurocentric or Western perspective. Native American studies often asks different theoretical questions than do the other academic disciplines, and it employs a variety of research techniques that are not unique to any single discipline. For example, in Part IV, we excerpt a portion of *Red Earth, White Lies*,[4] by Vine Deloria Jr. (Standing Rock Sioux). In this essay, he challenges the standard anthropological theories of the Bering Strait land bridge peopling of the Americas and the subsequent megafaunal extinction. A review of that work in the *American Anthropologist* makes the following insightful comment.

> Deloria's concern is the theory embraced by anthropology that, some 11,000 years ago, ancestors of contemporary American Indians crossed a land bridge which then connected Asia and Alaska and that they found a land with giant creatures who were unafraid of humans and therefore fell prey to skilled hunters. The Indians embarked on a slaughter of these animals, driving them to extinction. . . . Deloria argues the land bridge theory is far more problematic than the anthropology profession generally teaches, there is very little physical evidence and extremely fuzzy logic to support the extinction of the megafauna at the hands of Paleolithic Indians . . . that anthropologists should pay more attention to American Indian stories about what happened in the remote past for clues [i.e., Indian oral history].[5]

Historian Jack D. Forbes (Powhatan-Renape and Delaware-Lenape) critically examines some standard anthropological concepts and gives us an excellent guide to understanding Native history and culture (see Suggested Readings). He provides us with some crucial conceptual tools from a Native American studies perspective as a lens to view the "Indian experience." In his discussion of culture, for example, he explains the problems surrounding the anthropological "linguistic area" concept as a device for classifying Indian languages. Indians speak a specific language or a dialect of a language, not a language "family" like Algonkian any more than an Englishman speaks Indo-European. Nor do Indians identify themselves by "culture area." When meeting another Indian, one gives one's name and tribe or nation (sometimes clan affiliation) and not a culture area designation. Yet it is common for anthropology to begin a work on American Indians with a discussion of Indian culture and linguistic areas as if these were the most important things one needs to know to gain an introductory understanding of Indian peoples. This is not an Indian perspective, however, and even on empirical grounds it can be a faulty concept.

A culture area is defined by anthropologists as a geographic region in which a number of Indian "ethnographic groups" follow a similar way of life that can be identified by a list of similar cultural traits that correspond to the Indians' biotic or physical environment, such as the "Plains Indians" buffalo-hunting culture. Anthropologists identify ten to a dozen culture areas for North America alone, such as Eastern Woodlands, Southwest, Great Plains, Mesoamerica, California, and the Arctic. Today, even some anthropologists criticize the concept for its geographic determinism. And this system of classification also ignores more meaningful kinds of classifications, such as recognizing Indian peoples by the similarity of their nature of political organization, their military alliances, trade networks, ceremonial practices, or interethnic marriage customs. From an Indian perspective, the culture area concept focuses too much on the more esoteric and less politically strategic areas of "pre-Columbian" life rather than on flesh-and-blood peoples living in the crucible of Western conquest and neocolonialism.

Another criticism of the culture area concept is the time problem, the use of the "ethnographic present" in anthropological works regarding Indians. Ethnographic present is the cultural description of an indigenous people not as they are living in the contemporary world, but as they were thought to have lived in the past. In the first place, a culture area is a reconstruction, not reality itself, by nonnative anthropologists. The chief aim of the anthropologists studying Indians was not to produce a dynamic description of Native Americans as changing and enduring peoples, but, instead, to "reconstruct" Indian cultures as they were supposed to have existed in a pure stage or hypothetical Golden Age of their development before European conquest. Such reconstructions are based on an ahistorical concept, an "outside of time view," since the supposed Golden Age for an Indian people living in one part of North America will necessarily be a different time than for those living in another part of the continent. There is necessarily a 100- to 200-year or more time lag in terms of Indian–white contact as Europeans moved from east to west across the continent in the process of Western expansion along the Indian frontier. In the Native American studies paradigm, on the other hand, it is important to be "in time," or historical, since the focus is on the dialectics of conquest, the colonial pattern, resistance, cultural revitalization, and the struggle for sovereignty.

In promoting an indigenous perspective, Forbes points out that Native American studies is not a new discipline as is frequently thought.[6] He reminds us that it was a Quechua-speaking Inca scholar who made a scientific study of Spanish colonial society several centuries before most of the contemporary Western academic disciplines such as sociology and anthropology even existed. This scholar was Guaman Poma (Felipe de Ayala), who documented Peruvian customs and life under the seventeenth-century Spanish yoke.[7] (An example of his drawings is included in this part.) Poma's work was suppressed and remained unpublished for 300 years, but, even so, we might well consider him one of the founders of Native American

COREGIMIENTO

COREG.°₂ AFRENTAAI,

al cal se hor denauo por sos guebos que no le sa mi tay o.

probincias · como

This drawing by Guaman Poma reflects a scene after the coming of the Spanish in Peru. "The corregidor punishes the magistrate for failing to collect a couple of eggs from an Indian laborer."

From *Guaman Poma: Writing and Resistance in Colonial Peru* by Roleno Adorno (Austin: University of Texas Press, 1986). Reprinted by permission of Siglo XXI Editores.

studies long before the other modern academic disciplines, with the exception of history, came into being.

There have been other early Native American scholars, such as Titu Kusi, whose "Relación" in 1570 gave the Inca side of the Spanish conquest, and the Inca Garcilaso de la Vega, who wrote a history of Peru in 1609. Both the Mayan and Aztec cultures were highly literate civilizations before the European invasion burned thousands of their codices, or books. North America, too, had its Native American intellectuals. Pablo Tac, a Luiseño Indian, wrote in 1835 of his experiences and those of his people after the arrival of Spanish missionaries in California. And between 1809 and 1821, Sequoyah (Charles Gist) worked out a syllabary for writing the Cherokee language.

Even earlier, a number of North American Indian peoples made scientific observations and kept records. Many kept "sky charts," which are astronomical observations in connection with the planting cycle and the ceremonial calendar. The Hopi, for example, still maintain this ancient practice through their "sun watchers," or priests, who are able to calculate accurately the lunar and solar calendars. The Delaware had their "Walam Olum," a traditional history; the Tohono O'Odham (Papago) have their calendar stick; and the Kiowa had their ledger books. The Lakota (Teton Sioux) are known for their "winter counts," which utilize the Lakota concepts of "winters" (years) and generations (about 70 years). These serve as mnemonic devices to recall the event for which each winter was named. The Iroquois wampum belts serve a somewhat similar purpose. Wampum, made from white and purple sea shells, ratified treaties, opened government deliberations, confirmed leaders into office, registered the history of the Iroquois constitution, memorialized the dead, confessed the penitent, and aided prayer. "This belt preserves my words" is the frequent closing remark of Iroquois speeches today. Finally, even Western-trained scholars and ethnohistorians are coming to recognize the value of Indian oral history, the memories of the people, as a valid historical instrument in its own right.

In Part I, we have sought to lay the groundwork—the various names of Native American peoples and nations, as well as some important Indian concepts and issues. At the first international gathering of Native Peoples, the Conference on Discrimination Against the Indigenous Peoples of the Americas, which took place at the United Nations headquarters in Geneva, Switzerland, in 1977, Romesh Chandra, chairperson of the nongovernmental organizations sponsoring the conference, highlighted four concepts that the Native American delegates had brought to the attention of the United Nations and the international community. These were Nation, Land, Genocide, and Self-determination. First of all, the various Indian peoples of the Americas are not ethnic minorities in the generic sense of the term; rather, they are nations. Native Americans are the only "minority group" whose history and culture are rooted in land, whose identity as a people is defined by a traditional territory. In North America, "the right to the soil" is validated by the treaty relationship, and in Latin America it is affirmed by tradition and history. Nationhood is not determined by either population size or the extent of territory, however. Vine Deloria Jr. examined this question regarding the Native American right to sovereignty in *Behind the Trail of Broken Treaties,* in a chapter titled "The Size and Status of Nations" (see Suggested Readings). He pointed out that size of population or territory is not a precondition for sovereignty; in fact, a number of fully recognized nation-states that hold membership in the United Nations are as small as, or even smaller than, U.S. Indian peoples' such as the Navajo or Lakota.

Chief Oren Lyons (Onondaga Iroquois) once defined a nation as a group of people with a distinct language, a way of life, a territory, self-government, and, reflecting on the American genocide, "their children, their future generations."[8] Land, as José Barreiro in the foreword to this book points out, is more than territory or real estate; in the indigenous world it is a sacred thing—Mother Earth, or, as the Indians of Andean South America express it, Pachamama. Land and its resources were the "prize" of the Western conquest of the Americas, and genocide was the means by which the land and its riches were appropriated by the European colonists and non-Indian elites. Self-determination is the concept that provides an indigenous solution. Under international law, indigenous peoples as nations have inherent sovereignty and the right to self-determination: that is, the collective authority to govern themselves as separate states.

These are some of the concepts and issues addressed by journalist Phillip Wearne in "Definitions and Diversity," the first selection in this part, which is taken from his book *Return of the Indian.* The subtitle, *Conquest and Revival in the Americas,* tellingly sums up his thesis. A unique feature of Wearne's book is his hemispheric perspective, which is also the approach taken in this reader. He treats Native Peoples as a whole, throughout the Americas, thereby showing the linkage in traditions and current issues involving the land, cultural traditions, identity, and social justice. Wearne also describes in detail the great diversity of Native Peoples in the Americas, including their linguistic complexity. He points out that, today, hundreds of indigenous groups in Latin America can claim "separate nationhood" on the grounds of ethnicity and territory, even though the Portuguese or the Spanish, unlike the English, never recognized this inherent sovereignty.

Mesoamerica and South America contain approximately forty million indigenous people, many times the number found in the United States and Canada. The greatest concentrations of Indian people are found in Mexico, Guatemala, Ecuador, Peru, and Bolivia. In Guatemala 60 to 70 percent of the population are Indian, most of whom speak one of over two dozen native languages rather than Spanish. Furthermore, all over Latin America, as in the Mayan Indian rebellion in southern Mexico, an upsurge in cultural and ethnic identity and political organizing is testing the limits of established, non-Indian–controlled governments.

The box by Anthony Long and Catherine Beaty Chiste of the University of Lethbridge in Alberta is an excerpt from an excellent contribution on the Native American peoples of Canada. This all too brief selection will at least acquaint the reader with the three main ethnic categories of the Native Peoples in Canada—Indians, Métis, and Inuit—as well as the peculiarities of the Canadian system of governmental (or neocolonial) administration in its legal distinction between "treaty," "status," and "nonstatus" Indians. Although, for the most part, the Indian experience in Canada is similar to that of the United States, there are some important differ-ences in history and policy toward the First Nations (as Native Americans are fre-quently called in Canada).

The Inuit, commonly known as Eskimo in the United States, are a unique case because their population and homeland embrace not only Canada, where they number some thirty-five thousand persons, but also Alaska, Greenland, and Rus-sia—a total of 115,000 persons in all. In Canada, the Inuit in the Northwest Territo-ries have pressed successfully for land claims and political control over their vast aboriginal territory, which they call Nunavut, "Our Land." Today, Nunavut is an au-tonomous province of Canada. Greenland, by the way, even though colonized by Denmark, is geographically and ethnically part of North America.

An important development occurred in 1982 when the new Canadian Consti-tution recognized the "existing aboriginal and treaty rights of the aboriginal peo-ples of Canada." Throughout the decade of the 1980s important conferences were held in Canada between the government's First Ministers from the provinces and representatives of the Native peoples. The landmark Charlottetown Accord was hammered out, which would recognize Native American self-government. Unfor-tunately, this accord was defeated in 1992 by the Canadian electorate, but public sen-timent suggests that sometime in the near future Canadian Native Americans will achieve their constitutional right to self-government.

In the next selection, Ward Churchill (Keetoowah Cherokee) examines the thorny question of Indian identity politics, specifically the blood quantum stan-dard used by the U.S. government for determining who is a "legal" Indian and to whom the government is therefore obligated to give treaty-mandated services. He traces the history of the Indian identity question and attributes this governmental policy to "the racial dimension of divide and rule." What distinguishes Indians from ethnic minorities is the fact that Native Americans own property—a reserva-tion land base and valuable resources. The blood quantum device defines out of ex-istence many bona fide Native Americans and thereby deprives them of the right to land, resources, and treaty-obligated services that are mandated under federal Indian law. It also separates federally recognized Native Americans from relatives and neighbors who are unrecognized or who are not considered Indian because of the blood quantum device. As the interracial marriage rate increases, and as more and more Indian adults marry intertribally, fewer Native American children can claim enough "blood" of any one tribe or nation to qualify as federally recognized Indians. This trend has been termed *statistical genocide.*

Another kind of statistical bias that leads to discrimination is ethnic fraud (see Pavel et al. in the Suggested Readings). Because U.S. Indians are the only ethnic group who must prove their ethnicity, ethnic fraud occurs when individuals with slight or no Indian heritage nonetheless claim an Indian or Alaska Native identity to receive affirmative action status, employment or educational preference, or some other benefit. This is particularly a problem in higher education. The University of California at Davis as recently as 1989 recognized well over 100 students as Native American, yet the two dozen bona fide Indians on campus were at a loss to discover who those individuals were. The suspicions of the campus Indian community seemed confirmed when several cases came to light of non-Indian students either mistakenly or willfully claiming American Indian descent in order to gain admission as an ethnic minority person. Without a verification policy, the reported percentage of Native American students entering a college or university will be inflated. This inflation lets the institution off the hook, so to speak, relieving it from having to aggressively recruit bona fide Indians, whether in student or academic recruitment.

Ironically, since U.S. Native Americans are the only racial or ethnic group who must legally prove ethnicity, and since the present policy or custom promotes statistical genocide, Churchill predicts that Indian identity will increasingly become a cultural matter rather than a "pure blood" definition in the twenty-first century. He cites, as an example, the forward-looking policy of the Cherokee Nation of Oklahoma, which completely dispensed with blood quantum requirements for enrollment and substituted a more traditional method based on genealogy.

The way statistical genocide works in Canada is somewhat different. As the selection "The Canadian Natives," by Long and Chiste points out, Canadian law set up a "nonstatus" Indian category, which for decades illogically reduced the number of legal Indians. Until the Canadian Indian Act was changed in 1985, Indians could lose their Indian status if they received "half-breed lands or money scrip" or if an Indian woman married a person who was not an enrolled Indian. Tens of thousands of Indians "vanished" because of this law, and they are only now being reinstated.

In Latin America, on the other hand, "Indianness" is determined largely by cultural rather than racial standards. If one speaks the Spanish language instead of an Indian one and adopts a Ladino or mestizo way of life, he or she is no longer considered an Indian person. Even so, millions of people in Central and South America still speak an Indian language and maintain a Native American ethnic identity.

The article by John Anner points up the way "the numbers game"—that is, the U.S. census count of Indians—results in their invisibility as a viable ethnic minority. The ways in which the U.S. Census Bureau counts (or, in fact, does not count) Indians results, once again, in statistical genocide. The Census figures, taken every ten years, determine, among other things, the level of federal funding for Indian programs in the United States, not to mention the political nature of congressional representation in Indian country (see the box titled "Native American Statistics" for a definition of Indian country). Lobo believes that the census undercount is especially serious in large urban areas such as the San Francisco–East Bay of California, since the bulk of the Indian population in the country's most populous state is urban rather than reservation-based or rural. In the United States as a whole, more than half of the Native American population is now considered urban rather than rural and reservation-based, although the urban versus rural/reservation opposition is in many other respects a false dichotomy, since a high proportion of so-called urban Indians continue to relate strongly to their tribal roots in Indian country.

In the last selection, Susan Lobo examines the crucial question of what an Indian community is in an urban setting. She points out that an Indian community, whether rural or urban, is fundamentally the dynamic and complex interrelationships of people and place. The Indian community "is not a geographic location with clustered residency or neighborhoods, but rather it is fundamentally a widely scattered and frequently shifting network of relationships with locational nodes found in organizations and activity sites of special significance." Viewed in this light, the Indian urban, multitribal community embraces both the reservation and urban aspects of contemporary Indian life. The city is "our urban encampment out here." As Lobo notes, an understanding of the nature of community also leads to a knowledge of self and identity.

NOTES

1. Charlotte Heth and Susan Guyette, *Issues for the Future of American Indian Studies* (Los Angeles: UCLA American Indian Studies Center, 1984).

2. Robert M. Nelson, ed. *A Guide to Native American Studies Programs in the United States and Canada,* March 1999. (Web site is listed in Appendix C.)

3. *Wicazo Sa Review,* 9, no. 1 (Spring 1993): 57.

4. Vine Deloria Jr., *Red Earth, White Lies: Native Americans and the Myth of Scientific Fact* (New York: Scribner, 1995).

5. John Mohawk, "Review of Deloria's *Red Earth, White Lies,*" *American Anthropologist,* 98, no. 3, 1995: 650–651.

6. Jack D. Forbes, *Native American Studies Newsletter,* U.C. Davis 1, no. 1 (May 1990): 3, 7.

7. Guaman Poma (Felipe de Ayala), *Guaman Poma: Writing and Resistance in Colonial Peru* (Austin: University of Texas Press, 1986).

8. Steve Talbot, *Roots of Oppression: The American Indian Question* (New York: International Publishers, 1981) p. 51.

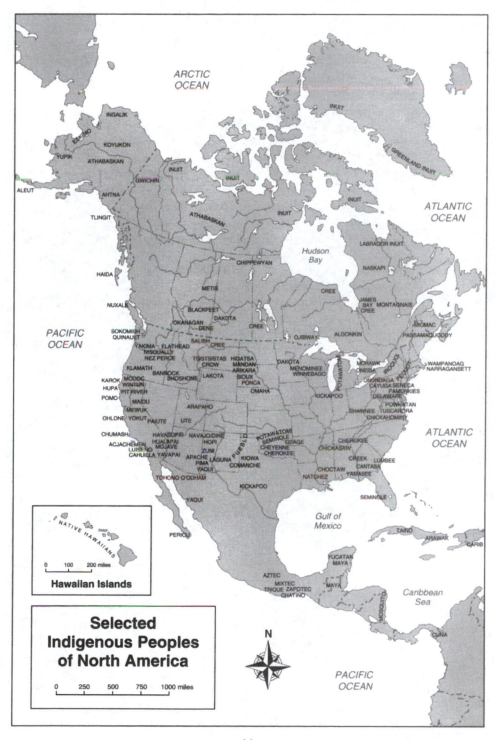

ARCTIC OCEAN

INGALIK
ESKIMO
YUPIK   KOYUKON
ATHABASKAN
ALEUT
AHTNA
GWICHIN
TLINGIT
INUIT
INUIT
ATHABASKAN

INUIT
INUIT
GREENLAND INUIT
ATLANTIC OCEAN

HAIDA
CHIPPEWYAN
Hudson Bay
LABRADOR INUIT
NASKAPI
METIS
CREE
JAMES BAY CREE   MONTAGNAIS
MICMAC

NUXALK
BLACKFEET
OKANAGAN   DAKOTA
DENE
CREE
ALGONKIN
PASSAMAQUODDY

PACIFIC OCEAN
SOKOMISH   SALISH
QUINAULT
YAKIMA   FLATHEAD
NISQUALLY
NEZ PERCE
CREE
OJIBWAY
MOHAWK
ONEIDA
WAMPANOAG
NARRAGANSETT

KLAMATH
KAROK   MODOC   BANNOCK
HUPA   WINTUN   SHOSHONE
PIT RIVER
POMO
MAIDU
MEWUK
OHLONE   YOKUT
TSTSTSISTAS   HIDATSA
CROW   MANDAN
ARIKARA
LAKOTA   SIOUX
PONCA
OMAHA
DAKOTA
MENOMINEE
WINNEBAGO
KICKAPOO
ONONDAGA
CAYUGA SENECA
PAMUNKIES
DELAWARE
POWHATAN
SHAWNEE   TUSCARORA
CHICKAHOMINY

ARAPAHO
PAIUTE   UTE
CHUMASH
HAVASUPAI   NAVAJO/DINE
HUALAPAI   HOPI
ACJACHEMEN   MOJAVE
LUISENO
CAHUILLA   YAVAPAI
ZUNI
PIMA   LAGUNA
APACHE
YAQUI
TOHONO O'ODHAM
POTAWATOMI
PUEBLO   SEMINOLE
CHEYENNE   OSAGE
CHEROKEE
KIOWA
COMANCHE
CHEROKEE
CHICKASAW
CHOCTAW
NATCHEZ
KICKAPOO
CHEROKEE
CREEK   LUMBEE
CANTABA
YAMASEE

ATLANTIC OCEAN

YAQUI
KICKAPOO
SEMINOLE
Gulf of Mexico
TAINO
ARAWAK
CARIB

PERIOU
YUCATAN MAYA
AZTEC
MIXTEC
TRIQUE ZAPOTEC
CHATINO
MAYA
MOSQUITO
Caribbean Sea
CUNA

NATIVE HAWAIIANS
0   100   200 miles
Hawaiian Islands

PACIFIC OCEAN

Selected Indigenous Peoples of North America

0   250   500   750   1000 miles

N

DEFINITIONS AND DIVERSITY

Phillip Wearne

- In Ecuador, tens of thousands of indigenous people block roads and refuse to supply city markets, shutting down the country for a week in what becomes known as "The Uprising."
- In Bolivia, Víctor Hugo Cárdenas, an Aymara activist, is inaugurated as vice-president, donning the vice-presidential sash over a vicuña scarf, a traditional badge of authority. He announces a "new era" in a speech in Aymara, Guaraní, and Quechua, the country's three main indigenous languages.
- In Mexico, a well-drilled Maya army takes over four towns and forces Latin America's longest-ruling party into protracted negotiations on indigenous rights and democratic principles.
- In Canada, Elijah Harper, a Cree-Ojibwa politician, blocks a constitutional agreement with Quebec, opening the way for a new deal for the country's indigenous people, including a constitution recognizing native peoples' "inherent right to self-rule."
- In Oslo, Rigoberta Menchú Tum, a 33-year-old K'iche' Maya woman, a one-time domestic servant and illiterate coffee-picker, becomes the youngest-ever winner of the Nobel Peace Prize.

Something is happening in the Americas. A tenacious resistance to the cultural onslaught that began in 1492 with the arrival of a lost Genoese sailor by the name of Christopher Columbus has begun to make sporadic appearances in international headlines. As it does, a myth has been exposed—the myth that the native peoples of the Americas were ever conquered, assimilated, wiped out, or that they never even existed. "As I go round the world many people I meet are surprised we indigenous peoples of the Americas still exist. They seem to think we died out years ago," observes Rigoberta Menchú.

The events listed above are as amorphous and diverse as indigenous culture itself, generic "Indianness" being as much a European imposition as the "discovery" and "conquest" of the Americas was a European invention. What seems to be a revival in ethnic consciousness in the Americas defies the categorization or empirical analysis scholars so relish. Moreover, it is ubiquitous, appearing anywhere and everywhere from Alaska and northern Canada to Chile and Argentina.

Although such events may represent nothing as cohesive as a movement across the two continents of the Americas, they do represent a growing clamour for justice. Ask those leading what one scholar, Javier Albó, has labeled the "return of the Indian" what

Excerpted and reprinted from the chapter titled "Definitions and Diversity" in *Return of the Indian: Conquest and Revival in the Americas,* by Phillip Wearne (Philadelphia: Temple University Press, 1996), pp. 1–31. Reprinted by permission of Temple University Press and Latin American Bureau. ©1996 by Phillip Wearne. All rights reserved. References omitted.

they are doing, and you receive only slight variations on a theme: "reclaiming our identity," "demanding our rights," "regaining our pride and self-worth," "recovering our spirit."

The greater prominence given to such events is at least partially a response to another set of stories appearing in the world's media in recent years, illustrating a darker side to the current fate of indigenous people:

- In Brazil, thousands of Yanomami have died as gold prospectors spread diseases and mercury poisoning throughout their Amazon territory. The Yanomami often have no resistance to diseases such as measles, chicken-pox, or even the common cold.
- In Guatemala, entire villages of Maya were massacred or displaced during the 1980s as the army unleashed a brutal counter-insurgency campaign in the highland mountain zones of the northwestern *altiplano*.
- In Canada, Hydro-Quebec is defying bitter opposition with its plans to flood tens of thousands of square miles of Cree lands as part of the US$12 billion Great Whale hydroelectric dam scheme, designed to produce cheap energy for export.
- In Paraguay, the New Tribes Mission seeks out uncontacted forest peoples, converts them to Christianity in mission bases, while "civilizing" them to adhere to its own narrow evangelical norms.

Disease, military conquest, multinational capitalism, religious conversion . . . the indigenous peoples of the Americas are today losing life and land to the same forces that have devastated their numbers and culture for more than five hundred years. For many indigenous peoples the threat has intensified markedly in recent years. "We have been pushed to the edge of the cliff . . . now they want to push us over," explains one Innu from Canada.

Growing land shortages have forced waves of settlers on to what were once marginal, indigenous lands. Free-market economics and state budget cuts have undermined subsistence economies and what little social provision indigenous communities enjoy. Civil wars have seen whole villages massacred, put to flight, caught in the cross-fire or forced to take sides. As an editorial in one indigenous publication, *Pueblo Indio,* puts it, "Only our patience has saved us from extermination, but even the patience of the Indian has its limit."

Yet stories about the renewed threats to indigenous peoples have at least served to expose other myths: that the conquest of the Americas, North, South and Centre, was all over within a few decades of the arrival of Europeans; that it was carried out by a few brutal brigands with a bloodlust and greed exceptional even by the standards of their own age; that there is no connection between what is happening today and what happened yesterday. The conquest is five hundred years old and continues today, but so is indigenous resistance. "There comes a point where you can't take any more. This is the message we're passing on to our children," says Sirionó leader Juana Irubi, whose tenth child, Anahi Dignidad, was born on a three-hundred-mile protest march by indigenous people to the Bolivian capital La Paz in 1990.

NUMBERS AND TYPES: INDIGENOUS PEOPLES TODAY

That both conquest and resistance are still going on comes as a shock to those who have always assumed that the indigenous peoples of the Americas are on their way out, set to disappear through assimilation as "modernity" and "progress" radiate out from the continents' cities. Vivid costumes in Mexican museums or pyramids in "lost" jungle cities in Peru are fine; the real thing in the form of protesting peasants, guerrilla fighters or slum dwellers' organizers is less palatable.

"Mexicans make no connection between their Aztec ancestors and the poor Indian selling vegetables on the pavement," notes one official in Mexico's National Indigenous Institute. "For most Mexicans one represents historic pride; the other contemporary shame." Ariel Araujo, a Mocoví leader from northern Argentina agrees. "According to Argentina's official history, we were exterminated at the beginning of the century. So why are there more than 1½ million of us today?"

In fact there are an estimated 40 million indigenous people in the Americas today, about 6 percent of the total population, and their numbers are growing faster than the rest of the population. They are the surviving descendants of what can only be called a holocaust: the events that followed the arrival of Europeans in the Americas at the end of the fifteenth century. The greatest killing, followed by the greatest plunder, following arguably the most important "discovery" in world history.

Estimates of the number of people living in the Americas in 1492 range as high as 112 million, about one-fifth of the world's entire population at the time. Estimates of how low their numbers fell as a result of disease, starvation, slave labour and post-conquest conflict go as low as 2 million. The continued existence and recovery of the indigenous peoples of the Americas in the face of what they and their ancestors have suffered is the best testimony to the tenacity of their resistance.

The indigenous peoples of today are concentrated in the same places as their distant ancestors, the sites of the Aztec, Inka and Maya civilizations. Guatemala (5.4 million) and Bolivia (about 5 million) have majority indigenous populations, with Peru

counting more than 8 million, Mexico at least 10.5 million and Ecuador about 3.8 million. The three largest countries have relatively small indigenous populations: Canada has an estimated 892,000, or 3.4 percent of its total, the United States just under 2 million, or 0.8 percent, and Brazil about 325,000, or 0.2 percent of its 165 million people.

Traditionally, the continents' indigenous peoples can be divided into two distinct cultural groups. Highland peoples tend to grow staples such as maize, beans, and potatoes on largely inadequate strips of land in the most mountainous, least fertile regions—the marginal "regions of refuge" into which they have been pushed over the centuries. They tend to live in villages or hamlets where there is little, if any, non-indigenous population. They predominate in the Andean countries and farther north in Guatemala and Mexico. Many highland people survive by supplementary seasonal work on export-crop plantations or paid work in the cities to which increasing numbers are being forced to migrate as they face the double squeeze of a contracting land base and growing numbers.

Lowland peoples account for less than 5 percent of the continents' total indigenous population, but perhaps 80 percent of the different ethno-linguistic groups. They too are confined to the remotest parts of the continent. They fish, hunt, and practise slash-and-burn farming or horticulture. They live in the Amazon basin, the remains of the forests of Central America, and to a lesser extent on the plains and sub-Arctic tundra of Canada and the United States.

In some areas the lifestyles of highland and lowland peoples overlap, but in any case another yardstick may be more useful: the level of contact with the dominant Hispanic, Anglophone, or Francophone cultures. Through their contact with representatives of the state, their dress, migration patterns, and proficiency in European languages, highland peoples tend to show a greater degree of association with the dominant groups. Governments, political parties, and trade unions have at times made concerted efforts to "incorporate" them into national institutions, often by redefining them as "peasants" rather than indigenous peoples.

Lowland peoples, on the other hand, tend, at least until relatively recently, to have had less, if any, contact with the outside world. Tribal, aboriginal, and fiercely independent, lowland peoples have led much of the recent growth in indigenous resistance and organization, attracting attention out of all proportion to their numbers. "Five centuries of contact has produced only marginalization, exploitation and misery for our highland colleagues. We're not volunteering for the same," says Evaristo Nugkuag, an Aguaruna leader from lowland Peru.

Such differences stem from pre-Columbian times. When Columbus first reached the Americas, highland peoples of the Andes, Mexico, and Central America had already experienced thousands of years of assimilation into urban-based indigenous civilizations, empires, and kingdoms, whose influence had been spread by conquest and trade. Adapting to life under the rule of outsiders was already part of their cultural baggage.

Most lowland peoples, on the other hand, had never been assimilated into broader political structures and had a profound sense of personal autonomy. Such differences helped determine their reaction to colonial rule, and to state power today.

LANGUAGES: SPEAKING IN MANY TONGUES

There are roughly 800 known ethno-linguistic groups in the Americas today, down from a total believed to have been more than 2,000 at the end of the fifteenth century. The largest single group today are those speaking Quechua, numbering about 11 million. They speak the language of the Inkas, *runasimi*, literally "mouth of the people" or "human speech" in Quechua, and live in the lands of their former empire, the *Tawantinsuyu*, comprising modern-day Peru, Bolivia, Ecuador, southern Columbia, and northern fractions of Chile and Argentina.

They are followed by the Maya, scattered throughout southern Mexico, Guatemala, Belize, and Honduras, numbering about 9 million but speaking more than 30 different, but related, languages in both highland and lowland areas. Aymara, spoken by about 2 million people centered around Lakes Titicaca and Poopo in Peru and Bolivia, as well as in Bolivia's capital, La Paz, is the third most widely spoken language. Nahuatl, the language of the Aztecs, spoken by about 1 million people today in Mexico City and central Mexico, is also significant. In North America, Cree, with an estimated 64,000 speakers mainly in Canada, along with Navaho, with about 130,000 speakers in the USA, are numerically the most important indigenous languages.

None of these languages or any others are recognized as official languages in the countries concerned, although Quechua assumed that status in Peru under a reformist government from 1969 before being downgraded later. The most curious exception is Guaraní, the native language of about 35,000 Guaraní Indians in Paraguay and tens of thousands more in Bolivia, Brazil, and Argentina. Guaraní became an official language in Paraguay in 1992 but has for centuries been a lingua franca, especially outside the capital, Asunción. Perhaps 90 percent of Paraguay's 4.2 million people speak it as their own language, reserving Spanish for public speech. This makes Guaraní the second most widely spoken indigenous language in the Americas, although most of its speakers would be horrified to be described as indigenous. The case illustrates the complexity of definition discussed in the following section.

History shows that the smallest language groups are those most in danger of extinction. Some 66 percent of the ethnolinguistic groups in the Americas have fewer than 5,000 speakers; some have just a handful. In North America, 80 percent of indigenous languages are no longer taught to children, according to University of Alaska linguist Michael Krauss. Unless something changes fast, he believes, such languages are doomed.

Brazil is the most ethno-linguistically diverse country in the region, although figures for the number of groups vary from 200 to 300. The most complete survey to date, *Indigenous Peoples of Brazil* by the Ecumenical Documentation and Information Centre (CEDI), puts the figure at just over 200. Of these, 84 groups (40 percent of the total) have populations of less than 200, 45 groups have populations of between 200 and 500 people, and 30 groups have between 500 and 1,000 members. This means that a staggering 77 percent of the Indian peoples of Brazil have populations of less than 1,000. Only four groups (the Guajajára, Potiguára, Xavánte, and Yanomami) have populations of between 5,000 and 10,000; another four (the Terêna, Makuxí, Ticuna, and Kaingang) have populations between 10,000 and 20,000. The Guaraní are the only people above this number. The numerical vulnerability explains why Latin America's largest country has "lost" an average of one indigenous group per year since 1900, amounting to one-third of its cultures.

However, the United States and Canada are not far behind in either diversity or vulnerability. According to *Ethnologue: Languages of the World*, the United States has more than 170 known language groups, more than two-thirds of which have fewer than 5,000 speakers. In Canada, 56 of the more than 70 indigenous languages fall into the same category. Unsurprisingly, 90 percent of Canada's indigenous languages are considered declining or endangered, nearly 30 percent of them on the brink of extinction.

Despite phenomenal variety, Indian languages throughout the Americas show common features that distinguish them markedly from European tongues. These include glottal stops—as in k'iche', for example—an interruption of breath caused by suddenly closing the vocal cords; reduplication, the doubling or trebling of part or all of a word in order to change meaning; and polysynthesis, the conglomeration of many words into a single word to carry the meaning of what might be a whole sentence in a European language.

The complexity and flexibility of indigenous languages were complemented by the way in which they universally mirrored the speakers' view of the universe and their immediate world. Cultural norms were reflected in many languages' distinction between inalienable relationships like those with relatives or even animals and less fundamental possessions such as tools or other objects. Both major Inuit languages, Yupik and Inupik, have dozens of words for snow and ice; Amazonian Indians have words that make subtle distinctions between the age and size of important rain forest plants.

Today, the indigenous languages of the Americas are written in a variety of forms. Cree, for instance, is still written in a system of syllabic symbols produced by a Protestant missionary in 1840. Cherokee is today written in an unchanged 86-character syllabary completed by Sequoyah (George Guess) in 1821. Convinced that the white man's power sprang from his mastery of the written word, Sequoyah, an untrained craftsman, laboured for 12 years at a task normally restricted to highly trained linguists. But most indigenous languages are written in the Roman alphabet, with their clusters of consonants and glottal stop marks (') being the most distinguishing features to those speaking only European languages.

NAMES AND IDENTITIES: CULTURE AND LANGUAGE FIRST

Who are these people? Natives, tribals, First Peoples, Amerindians, Indians, Native Americans, indigenous peoples? How should we define or identify them? How do they identify themselves? Columbus called them "Indians," dying convinced that he had sailed around the world to reach Asia. Ironically, a label that stuck and became a term of contempt throughout the Americas was probably not so far from the truth. Genetics and archaeology suggest that 30,000 years before the arrival of Europeans, the ancestors of today's indigenous peoples crossed the neck of land that linked Asia to the Americas across the Bering Straits, although the origin myths of many native Americans tell a variety of different tales.

The first peoples who set foot in the Americas spread throughout the continents, surviving in every environment from desert to jungle in one of history's most successful tales of adaptation and evolution. Initially they were hunter-gatherers, but many settled, raised livestock and crops and, in the case of empires such as those of the Inkas, Aztecs, and Mayas, founded civilizations that rivalled ancient Greece and Egypt in architecture, agriculture, mathematics, and astronomy. The main objection to the term "Indian" today is its colonial, external imposition. As a Eurocentric error, it perpetuates the myth that there was or is such a thing as generic "Indianness." Indigenous

American societies in the sixteenth century were more varied than the European nationalities invading their continent. They remain so today.

A universal term denies indigenous peoples the chance to identify themselves by their own names in their own languages. As such it can be a barrier. "How I loathe the term 'Indian.' . . . 'Indian' is used to sell things—souvenirs, cigars, cigarettes, gasoline, cars. . . . 'Indian' is a figment of the white man's imagination," says Lenore Keeshig-Tobias, an Ojibwa from Canada.

Stripping someone of his or her name and identity, then redefining them in your own terms, is the first step towards dehumanizing people, an essential part of the conquest and colonization of the Americas. It happened throughout the Americas on both a collective and individual basis, as many indigenous people were given European names as part of their conversion to Christianity.

Although there is no universally accepted definition of indigenous peoples, it is worth remembering that, like the term "Indian," it is an externally imposed and relative term. The indigenous peoples of the Americas are only indigenous because they and their territories were colonized by others. Most of their own terms for themselves mean simply "people"—*Runa* in Quechua, *Shuar* in Shuar, *Eenou* in Cree.

Historically, it is clear that the continents' indigenous peoples are the pure-blooded descendants of its original inhabitants. In that, they are different from the white European invaders and the *mestizos, ladinos, mistis,* or mixed-bloods who were the product of conquest and who now predominate in Peru, Mexico, Ecuador, and elsewhere. Yet many people defined today as *ladinos* or *mestizos* are in fact racially indigenous. Racially at least, they are "de-ethnicized" indigenous people.

Although social classification has hinged on different criteria over the centuries, today culture remains the best means of defining status. Anyone who is considered culturally Hispanic, Anglo, or French is non-indigenous, whatever their ancestry. Yet throughout the Americas, culture has become intertwined with race and class, so that classifications are often considered interchangeable. Indians tend to be poor, rural peasants or hunters, under- or unemployed; "whites" (in Latin America at least) tend to be rich, urban, professional or in business.

Knowing what we mean by culture is one thing; defining it is another. A common set of values, beliefs, and practices that bind a group of people together in a common perception or understanding of life might be one theoretical definition. A lifestyle or common way of life might be a more practical definition. Culture as a means of making sense of life, giving it meaning, might be a more spiritual interpretation.

Although cultural diversity is the norm in the Americas, there are common threads. Traditionally, indigenous culture has been based on peasant farming or hunting in an often marginal rural area in a monolingual community with a collective identity. Such a community is governed by a strong ceremonial understanding of life based on ancestors, traditions, and deities embedded within the immediate environment of mountains, rivers, forests, and the earth. Its culture is rooted in the traditions of co-operation, community, consensus, and above all continuity, the ground rules that have ensured the survival of individual peoples. "Listen to your mother and you will live long," as one Dene adage puts it.

But culture is intangible. Europeans and *mestizos* have found it easier to define indigenous peoples by externals such as racial features, dress, and language. Although none of these is definitive, language or first language remains arguably the most important tangible indicator.

An indigenous language is nearly always unique to the people that speak it, although some distinct groups share a language. Yet some individuals who are clearly culturally indigenous do not speak an indigenous language and in some cases whole peoples have adopted another language (European or indigenous) as their own.

Despite such caveats, language is the main means of conveying culture and values—what one indigenous leader described as "accessing self." It is the essential means of transmitting myth, history, and song in cultures that remain largely oral. "It captures the ideas of a people and the feelings and values of their existence," says Robert St. Clair in his study *Language Renewal among American Indian Tribes.* "To deny one his or her native language is comparable to more blatant forms of genocide. When the language goes so does the culture."

One good example of both points comes from the Odawa language, whose speakers live in northern Michigan in the United States. There are five hundred ways to say "love" in the Odawa language yet by 1992 there was only one person, Kenny Pheasant, who could say them all. For Odawa, read any one of scores of other threatened or extinct indigenous tongues in the Americas today.

Eli Taylor, a Sioux, has captured what indigenous linguistic expression and the threat to it can mean culturally. "Our native language gives a name to relations among kin, to roles and responsibilities among family members, to ties within the broader clan group. . . . There are no English words for these relationships. . . . if you destroy our languages you break down not only those relationships but those that describe man's connection with nature, the Great Spirit and the order of things. Without languages we will cease to exist as separate people.". . .

NATIONS AND PEOPLES:
SELF-IDENTIFICATION,
SELF-DETERMINATION

In the offices of umbrella organizations such as ONIC, the National Organization of Colombian Indigenous Peoples in Bogotá, indigenous activists define themselves today as "peoples" in terms of their "nationality," be it Páez, Guambiano, or Guajiro. It sounds revolutionary and it is. First, it challenges the image of the centralized, dominant nation-state that found one of its most brutal forms of expression in the Americas, with indigenous peoples its major victim. Secondly, it recognizes that the term "nation" has traditionally been defined by ethnicity and territory. Today, hundreds of different ethnic groups in the Americas can claim separate nationhood on both grounds.

Until independence came to the Americas in the late eighteenth and early nineteenth centuries, the word "nation" had always referred to the continents' native peoples. The indigenous nations of the Americas first gave meaning to nationality in the continents, a meaning later expropriated by the "patriots" who fought for independence from Spain, Portugal, and Britain. Today, indigenous organizations are defining the term "nation" by reclaiming such history, just as they are reclaiming their identity, their "ethnicity." The key to both is territory: control of and access to the soil, subsoil, air, waters, sea ice, and other natural assets that compose indigenous peoples' resource base from Antarctica to the North Pole.

The right to a territory implies the right to a way of life: the right to hunt, fish, and practise slash-and-burn agriculture in the case of lowland peoples and, in embracing the right to land, the concept of territory also implies the right to practise communal agriculture in the case of highland peoples. But it implies more: in particular, the right of indigenous peoples to exercise their own legal jurisdiction, including the observance of customary law.

Controlling territory thus gives indigenous peoples the chance of "self-determination"—the right to determine their own future development and thus the right to nationhood. This issue lies at the heart of the recent rise on indigenous consciousness in the Americas. It is also the root of the hostility of governments in the Americas to the terms "territory," "self-determination," peoples," and "nations." Such terms challenge governments' definition of sovereignty and the nation-state. This challenge is what has become known as the "national question" in the Americas and beyond. If Chile is a state, can the Mapuche call themselves a nation? Can the Navaho in the United States, the Cree in Canada, or the K'iche' in Guatemala?

While colonial domination shared many characteristics across the Americas, there were marked differences between the indigenous experience under the British, Spanish, and Portuguese. One of the most important was the British practice of recognizing indigenous peoples as sovereign nations capable of entering into treaties with the English authorities as equals. Whether the treaties were then respected or not is another matter; the important point was the recognition of indigenous sovereignty, a practice continued by both Canada and the USA until the second half of the nineteenth century.

Neither the Spanish nor the Portuguese recognized such sovereignty for the indigenous Americans they faced, and as a result few treaties were ever signed. Both the different nature of the conquest, and their hierarchical mentality, led the conquerors to see all Indians as vanquished and therefore subjects of a new crown and sword.

As a result, Indian peoples coming out of the English colonial experience have fought for treaty rights and sovereignty as a priority, whereas indigenous groups in Latin America have more traditionally demanded their rights as subjects of Latin American nation-states. Such historical differences can produce chasms of misunderstanding when indigenous peoples from north and south America meet.

Ironically, indigenous peoples' claims to territory have come to be based on the concept of eminent domain, the legal provision under which states have traditionally argued in favour of the inalienable nature of national territory and their right to occupy such territory in the national interest. Indigenous nations have reinterpreted the concept, arguing that it applies more appropriately to them as they occupied the land before colonization. Their rights, they argue, pre-date and take precedence over laws subsequently passed by nation-states.

The issue is how "nations" can share sovereignty within a single territory, or even more contentiously across existing frontiers, as in the case of the Yanomami in Brazil and Venezuela. Many indigenous peoples remain mystified as to why this should be a problem. "In the Amazon, in a province created in 1964, we are being told we must have land titles . . . we who have been the owners of these lands for thousands of years!" complains Ampam Karakras of CONAIE, Ecuador's indigenous confederation. "We have become exiles in our own lands. This is why we say we must have more authority."

Some indigenous leaders have distinguished between what might be termed internal self-determination—the right to control education, social affairs, health care, religion, and cultural activities—and external self-determination, covering areas such as defence, foreign relations, and external trade, which should be left in the hands of a larger political entity, such as a federal state. But for many this is nothing less than the distinction between autonomy and genuine self-determination. For them, internal self-determination can become a stepping-stone to external self-determination if the nation in question so chooses. Some have already made that choice and are in the process of implementing it. Shoshone people from the southwest of the United States already carry their own passports, and the Mohawk nation boasts an embassy in the Dutch capital, The Hague.

Almost without exception, indigenous peoples and organizations in the Americas are striving for a plural "multinational" society that rejects assimilation and integration but for the most part rejects complete separation as well. Their aim, in the words of the Aymara vice-president of Bolivia, Víctor Hugo Cárdenas, is "to construct a pluricultural, pluriethnic and plurinational society." As one Maya activist puts it, "We want a role in the states from which we have been so long excluded, rather than their overthrow or break-up."

"Multinational" describes the Americas before the arrival of the Europeans. Ever since the conquest, indigenous peoples have been baffled by the colonists' need to superimpose an alien identity on them. To them it demonstrated a lack of respect, and statement after statement from indigenous leaders has called for the mutual tolerance and acceptance that would allow all to live together. "We only ask an even chance to live as other men live. We ask to be recognized as men," Chief Joseph of the Nez Percé pleaded to US congressmen in 1879.

"You say, 'Why do not the Indians till the ground and live as we do?' May we, with equal propriety, ask why the white people do not hunt and live as we do?," Corn Tassel, a Cherokee statesman asked U.S. commissioners in 1785. "We are a separate people!" Plural, multiethnic diversity was not only possible but natural to indigenous people, a reflection of the natural world around them. As Tatanka Yotanka (Sitting Bull), the great nineteenth-century Sioux chief, said, "It is not necessary that eagles should be crows."

It is vital for indigenous peoples to be seen as "nations" and "peoples" rather than simply "ethnic groups" and "people." The terminology has a specific connotation in international law associated with collective rights and self-determination. "Peoples" have a right to self-determination; ethnic groups merely the right to minority rights.

There is one more serious problem for any outsider trying to define indigenous identity: it is a moving target. From the Inuit of the Canadian Arctic to the Mapuche of southern Chile, indigenous people in the Americas are constantly redefining their identity. In the past, they were almost universally subsistence farmers, day labourers, or hunters—monolingual, illiterate, rural, and marginalized. Today millions of indigenous people live in towns and cities; hundreds of thousands work in commerce or factories; tens of thousands are completely bilingual or even trilingual, and thousands have university degrees and professional jobs. They are exhibiting one of the most outstanding qualities of their ancestors, the ability to find ways to live in new, often hostile environments without losing their identities or values.

In their offices, at their newspapers or radio stations, in their government departments, many of the new "urban Indians" are at the forefront of the struggle for indigenous rights. So are they any less indigenous? Many would argue exactly the opposite, on the grounds that experience of the wider world has made them more culturally aware and more political, even if outsiders have yet to recognize this. "Only Western anthropologists would want to freeze us in some noble-savage state," complains Valerio Grefa in his office in downtown Quito, Ecuador. "Who says I can't be Quichua running COICA, the largest multinational indigenous organization in the Americas, in a big city like Quito? Who best defines me—them or me?"

Culture has never been static; to survive, it must evolve. Many of the designs woven into indigenous textiles or clothes by women today would not be recognized by their great-grandparents as being Maya, Mixtec, Mapuche, or Mohawk, but they are just as much a part of indigenous culture.

The mobile phones, short-wave radios, computers, modems, faxes, and videos you see and hear in indigenous organizations' offices throughout the region are part of the solution, not the problem, a means of defending and campaigning rather than subverting and destroying. "Culture is how we survive. And adjusting and changing is part of survival," explains Mohawk leader Kenneth Deer.

RECOVERING IDENTITY: A MOVING TARGET

Identity is a moving target in another sense: it can be different things at different times. It is quite possible for an indigenous person to take on different identities simultaneously or at different times, to move in and out of different cultures at will. "Indigenous people have begun to use their ethnic identity strategically and opportunistically," notes Tomás Huanca, an Aymara ethnohistorian. "But no one is less Aymara, Quechua or anything else for using his or her ethnicity in an intelligent way."

Circumstances, interests, and motives can all be crucial in determining what identity someone might choose to take at any one time. "It's quite common to hear a Peruvian lowland Indian declaim, 'We Peruvians must all stick together' when claiming some right of citizenship, then hear the same person curse 'those damned Peruvians!' when their jungle river valley is being invaded by settlers," observes one anthropologist.

The Americas are full of examples like that of the Cree, who hunt occasionally on the frozen plains of Quebec not because they need to hunt for food but because they consider it part of themselves and their cultural heritage; of Maya who wear nylon trousers and shirts in Guatemala City but homespun indigenous dress when they return to their highland village; of Aymara who leave jobs in La Paz at planting or harvest time to tend the family plot they retain in their native village.

The difficulties involved in identification are perfectly illustrated in El Salvador, the most densely populated country in the Americas, sandwiched between Guatemala and Honduras in Central America. Anthropologists have concluded that the country has about 500,000 people, just under 10 percent of the total population, who call themselves and are identified by others as *indios* or *naturales*. Yet these people have lost virtually all the hallmarks of their identity, including their language, dress, and most of their culture and customs. They are in anthropological terms almost completely "acculturated."

How then are they identified as *indios?* How do they identify themselves? Poorer Spanish, poverty, low self-worth and being "closer to God" than their *mestizo* counterparts, believes anthropologist Mac Chapin, on the basis of extensive fieldwork in El Salvador. Chapin concludes that "it may be argued that the Salvadorean Indians'

collective identity as victims of injustice and crushing exploitation is the main ingredient that holds them together as an ethnic group." History within what might be called "a culture of poverty" or a "culture of oppression" is perhaps all they have in common, a cultural feature by no means unique to El Salvador, whatever indigenous traits other groups may retain.

The work on El Salvador illustrates the perils of terms like "acculturation" or "assimilation" as well as those of identification. Defining peoples as acculturated or assimilated precludes defining them as indigenous, which they often remain.

Mestizaje, the Spanish term for the mixing of races which is often taken to mean cultural mixing, is used quite generally, often politically. The phenomenon produces *mestizos, mistis, ladinos,* or *cholos,* according to country, who may have a number of indigenous traits or none at all and may in any case define themselves very differently from any anthropologist.

A more accurate description is "syncretism," the blending together of cultures as they absorb and reinterpret elements drawn from each other. It is a term usually applied to religious beliefs, nowhere more pertinently than in the blending of Christian and traditional beliefs that has taken place in the Americas. After the arrival of the Europeans, cultures in the Americas interacted with each other to a much greater extent than is often acknowledged. No cultural conquest ever completed the conquistadores' military victory. Instead, cultural cross-fertilization became a fact of life. It took place in varying degrees in different places, but it was always a two-way process. The concept of "syncretism" helps correct some of the bias of history. It recognizes the words, place-names, foodstuffs, medicines, traditions, environmental knowledge, biochemical expertise, and philosophy that the indigenous peoples of the Americas retain and continue to give to the world beyond their shores.

With so many different cultures in the Americas, it is hardly surprising that recovering identity means different things to different ethno-linguistic groups or individuals. For some it is simply rediscovering history, traditions, names, and languages that seemed lost; for others it means adapting technology that once seemed alien; others want control of economic development within their communities. For still others, such objectives can only stem from a deeper recovery of self-esteem. "We need to concentrate on internal healing: to cure ourselves of prejudices, feelings of inferiority, self-marginalization," says Quechua leader Tarcila Rivera Zea. "We must regain our dignity. Without it we cannot help ourselves, let alone others."

All these efforts are part of the same cultural struggle for economic and political self-determination. The battle is as much practical as spiritual. In many communities traditional forms of communal landholding, working, and farming have become the basis for renewed economic development. "Cultural rescue is impossible without development at the community level, and the converse is also true," notes Ecuadorean Quichua activist Juan García.

Although culture is the obvious vehicle, self-identification, followed by self-determination, is clearly the aim. What these two terms mean in theory has been set out respectively by two agencies of the United Nations: self-identification by the International Labour Organization (ILO), self-determination by the UN Working Group on Indigenous Populations in its proposed Universal Declaration on Indigenous Rights. In practice both principles are being interpreted in different ways by different peoples in different regions of the Americas. In some cases, vociferous, well-organized indigenous nations are securing considerable autonomy. In an age when the concept of the nation-state seems increasingly outdated, they may go on to secede in name or practice. At the other end of the scale, many indigenous communities would be content just to be listened to or be able to prevent outside authorities blocking the democratic decisions of their traditional councils or elders.

The struggle of indigenous people is evolving all the time with a dynamism and momentum of its own. Securing some rights often gives people the weapons and confidence with which to fight for more. "At the moment it's about forcing governments to recognize that they are plurinational, pluri-ethnic states," says Evaristo Nugkuag, a leading Aguaruna activist from Peru. "In the future who knows? This is uncharted territory."

MOTHER EARTH: THE FIGHT FOR LAND

However diverse the struggles waged by indigenous peoples, all have in common the fight for land. The struggle for possession, legal recognition, and demarcation of land and territory may involve demanding the recognition of hundreds of square miles of forest territory in the case of lowland peoples; the fight for a legal title to a few square yards of steep, eroded mountainside in the case of highland peoples; or a concerted effort to get state, provincial, or federal governments to recognize communal rights to land enshrined in treaties signed more than a century ago.

The continents' indigenous peoples define themselves primarily through their relationship to the land. Whereas the names they give themselves—Inuit, Kayapó, Runa (Quechua)—often mean simply "people," the names they give their territories usually translate simply as "land." The two are inseparable. As the World Council of Indigenous Peoples, a global federation based in Canada, noted in 1985, "Next to shooting indigenous peoples, the surest way to kill us is to separate us from our part of the earth."

For most indigenous peoples land is "Mother Earth"; the Pacha Mama of the Andes. It feeds, supports, and teaches; it is a sentient being that has to be apologized to before being tilled, thanked for its harvests, and nourished with sacrificial offerings. Many ethnic groups believe it or its fruit gave them birth. The *Popul Vuh* (Book from the Seat of Authority or Book of Counsel) is a sacred K'iche' Maya text whose lengthy tale of genesis tells how the first people were created out of maize flour, the clay of Adam having proved unsuitable.

Something of that genesis survives today in Latin America in the traditional belief amongst some indigenous peoples that if they do not eat the potatoes, maize, or game that form their staples, they will somehow lose their identity. The literal belief that you are what you eat and that what you eat should come from the land nurtured by previous generations, prevails throughout the Americas. "A person is born with animals. He has to eat animals. That is why animals and people are as one," observes one Inuit hunter.

Land is identity—past, present, and future. The earth is literally and figuratively the home of the ancestors, the people who gave the current generations life and who demand veneration in traditional rituals and custom. Land represents, in one indigenous activist's words, "the living pages of our un-written history." Such history is more important than legal ownership. "The bones of our grandparents' grandparents, resting in the ground, are our titles to the ownership of the land," explains one Guajiro elder from Colombia.

Land on which to raise crops or hunt both is essential to provide for immediate material needs and represents the future, the inheritance held in trust for children and grandchildren. More than any other facet of indigenous life, culture revolves around land and land around culture. "Culture is like a tree. If the green branches—language, legends and customs—are carelessly lopped off, then the roots that bind people of their place on the earth and to each other begin to wither. The wind and the rain carry the topsoil away; the land becomes desert," says Mariano López, a Tzotzil leader from Chiapas, Mexico.

This sense of place and connection to the land extends to all living things. Plants, animals, and human beings are all mutually dependent on the earth, rivers, mountains, and forest. What outsiders call environmental awareness is for indigenous people simply the logic of observation and interdependence. The material and spiritual worlds are interwoven. "The land is a part of our body and we are part of the land," says Buffalo Tiger, a Miccosukee.

In most indigenous societies, land traditionally could not be privately owned, but was held communally for use by each village or family group according to need. The seizure of such land was the basis of the conquest and the key to the fundamental clash of two irreconcilable philosophies. Indigenous land contained the mineral wealth, gold, silver, and more recently oil, plus the forest resources, timber, and now biotechnology, that the conquistadores and their descendants coveted.

From the prairies to the pampas, indigenous land has grown the cash crops such as sugar-cane, coffee, bananas, wheat, and soya beans that have made the Americas a massively profitable enterprise for a few and a place of malnutrition and hunger for many. The expansion of commercial crops has meant less or no land for hunting game or planting staples for people who knew no other way of life.

Ultimately, nothing has undermined indigenous cultures like the loss of their land. Expropriation, enclosure, expulsion—land grabs have happened in different ways in different areas at different times, but they remain the most important aspect of the continuing conquest. From mass marches to land occupations, most indigenous mobilization has centered on securing title, demarcation, and protection of land. Seminal protests such as the 1990 uprising in Ecuador and the "March for Land and Dignity" in Bolivia the same year have won presidential decrees guaranteeing large tracts and have forced the international community to acknowledge the importance of land rights to the maintenance of indigenous culture.

As the struggle for land has evolved, so has an indigenous strategy to protect it or secure it. Armed struggle has always been an option for some. Comando Quintín Lame in Colombia was an armed indigenous movement designed to protect farmers and their lands, while guerrilla armies in Mexico, Guatemala, and Peru have recruited large numbers of indigenous fighters to their ranks.

Favourable national and international circumstances have been vital to the progress indigenous peoples have made in winning land rights in recent years. In Latin America, the eclipse of military dictatorships has created at least a limited level of democratic space in which to organize. The worldwide growth in the environmental and development lobbies has allowed indigenous grass-roots organizations on the ground to forge powerful international alliances.

The first step has been legal registration to replace the oral tradition and historic claims that have been the basis of indigenous land tenure to date. "In the past, indigenous peoples have lost their land simply because they couldn't prove they owned it," says Mac Chapin, an anthropologist who heads Native Lands, a Washington-based organization that helps indigenous communities to map their territory.

In many areas, legal titles to both swathes of lowland forest and tiny highland plots have been successfully established, but that simply raises another problem: enforcement. "Many of the rights we have on paper now are excellent. It's the impunity with which they are violated that's our principal problem," says Antonio Jacanamijoy, deputy president of ONIC in his office in downtown Bogotá, Colombia.

Throughout the Amazon basin and expanses of North America, indigenous guards now patrol the frontiers of huge tracts of land on foot, by canoe, snow-mobile, or four-wheel-drive jeep. In some places, short-wave radios link these foot soldiers to the nearest community centres from which faxes, computer networks, and telephones can alert national security forces and international support networks.

In many areas these front-line activists continue to pay the same price as their warrior ancestors did years ago. Since 1974, more than 400 indigenous leaders have been killed in Colombia. Up to 3,500 Ashaninka have died or disappeared during 15 years of violence in Peru; another 10,000 have had to flee their homes. Thousands of Maya community activists, lay preachers, and organizers—anyone showing leadership ability or potential—have been murdered or "disappeared" in Guatemala over the same period.

POVERTY AND RESISTANCE:
THE WEAPONS OF THE WEAK

The loss of indigenous peoples' lands combines with lack of access to social services such as health and education to ensure that throughout the continent they are the most marginalized segment of the population. Without exception, they have the lowest incomes, the highest rates of infant mortality, the lowest life expectancies, the highest malnutrition rates, and the lowest rates of literacy and secondary school education. Indeed, as the evidence from El Salvador cited above illustrates, being poor, marginalized, and overworked is frequently part of the definition of being indigenous in the eyes of both indigenous and non-indigenous peoples.

The statistics are so stark that they glare through imponderables such as the problems of determining ethnicity or making cultural allowances for attitudes to paid employment or social services. According to a study by George Psacharopoulos and Harry A. Patrinos, *Indigenous People and Poverty in Latin America: An Empirical Analysis*, 48.1 percent of the non-indigenous population in Bolivia in 1989 was classified as poor, but the figure rose to 63.7 percent of the bilingual indigenous population and 73.5 percent of those speaking only an indigenous language.

In Mexico, municipal districts which are less than 10 percent indigenous have a poverty headcount index of 18 percent; in districts 10–40 percent indigenous, 46 per-

cent of the population is poor, and in those over 70 percent indigenous, more than 80 percent of the population is poor. In the United States, seven of the ten poorest counties in the country contain Indian reservations.

But caution is advisable. Poverty, illiteracy, and mortality are Western indices. There are no equivalents to measure cultural vitality, spiritual well-being, or ethnic consciousness. After five hundred years of supposed domination, the weakness and dependence of most nation-states in the Americas contrasts starkly with the strength and self-sufficiency of indigenous culture. Five hundred years after Europeans set out to conquer, assimilate, and convert the continent, indigenous peoples remain distinct. They speak their own languages, follow their own traditions, farm and hunt much as their ancestors did. Moreover, they are increasing in number and becoming steadily more vociferous in demanding their rights.

Sheer survival is the best evidence of the scale and success of ethnic resistance. It is not just the noted resistance of some relatively well-known indigenous leaders over the past five hundred years, although the rebellions they led are often at best footnotes in Western history, but the ordinary, everyday resistance of ordinary, everyday peasants. Foot-dragging, false compliance, dissimulation, feigned ignorance, even sabotage and isolated acts of violence—these are what James Scott, the Eugene Meyer Professor of Political Science at Yale University, has termed "the weapons of the weak" in his book of the same name. These are the tactics of the ruled in their low-key, daily struggle against their rulers. As an Ethiopian, but universally applicable proverb quoted by Scott runs, "When the great lord passes, the wise peasant bows deeply and farts silently."

Indigenizing useful Western imports, ejecting the assimilated from their communities, diversifying economically wherever possible—indigenous peoples in the Americas have rarely sought direct confrontation with the state. That, they know from bitter experience, is likely to be met with genocidal repression and the occupation of their communities. This has not prevented them testing the limits of the possible at every available opportunity and constantly developing new ideas to dilute and divert whatever power the state may exercise over their lives. Amorphous, unseen and rooted in the smallest mountain village or remotest river valley, indigenous resistance acts like a gas released into the atmosphere: it fills every space available. Today, such resistance shows itself best in the cultural redoubts that are indigenous villages, reservations, or protected areas, ironically the areas indigenous people were confined to as transit camps on their road to "disappearance". These areas have now become centers of cultural revival: primary health care promoters have been trained to combat preventable disease, bilingual community teachers to reduce illiteracy, young shamans to revive traditional medicine and oral tradition.

The recent surge in such community development is as diverse as indigenous culture itself, ranging from pig- or chicken-breeding co-operatives designed to offset the worst effects of inflation and government budget cuts, to literacy classes designed to help migrants find work in the cities. Once the generic "Indian" myth is rejected, indigenous society in the Americas emerges as plural and localized rather than uniform and homogeneous, and the state as weak and dysfunctional rather than omnipotent and hegemonic. Just like the conquest itself, nation-states in the Americas have never been all they were made out to be.

In the "New World", the nation-state, a European import, has never been the integrated, centralized model it became in the Old World. The continents' indigenous peoples, their communities and culture, have played a leading role in keeping these nation-states weak through the skill and effectiveness of their resistance. "I will die, but I will rise again and I will be millions," said Tupaq Katari, the Aymara chief, moments before his execution for rebellion against colonial rule in 1781. His words must seem prophetic to many governments in the Americas today, besieged by indigenous demands from all sides.

To the many indigenous peoples of the Americas who share a cyclical or oscillating sense of the flow of time, everything that happens is balanced or redressed by an opposite at some point in the future. The only surprise to them is that non-indigenous peoples are taken aback by the upsurge in indigenous consciousness. "What did you expect?", asks Valerio Grefa, the head of COICA in Ecuador. "Our people have always expected nothing less." Indian legends throughout the Americas reveal a belief in change, role reversal, a renewal which will turn the tables. "When the new world comes, the white people will be Indians, and the Indians will be white people," says one Apache fable.

Action breeding reaction, conquest leading to reconquest, ups causing downs; such cycles are part of the everyday indigenous world. Many in the Andes are convinced that the *pachakut'i*, literally the "balance upheaval" that legends and oral history have prophesied for centuries, has finally arrived.

THE CANADIAN NATIVES

Anthony Long and Katherine Beaty Chiste

Although the aboriginal peoples of Canada are a small segment of the total population, they have always played a significant role in Canadian history. Their historic and contemporary importance is now acknowledged in Section 35, Parts 1 and 2, of the Canadian *Constitution Act, 1982,* which states,

> 35(1) The existing aboriginal and treaty rights of the aboriginal peoples of Canada are hereby recognized and affirmed.

> 35(2) In this Act, "aboriginal peoples of Canada" includes the Indian, Inuit and Métis peoples of Canada.

The constitutional recognition of aboriginal peoples and their rights, however, occurred only after a protracted struggle on the part of aboriginal leaders to convince federal and provincial government officials of the legitimacy of their claims. While constitutional recognition signifies a landmark achievement for Canadian Indians, Inuit, and Métis, it is only one step in their quest for an enlarged political and legal status within the Canadian confederation that will give them a greater degree of control over their future. Moreover, significant strides must be taken in the social and economic development of aboriginal peoples. The legacies of past government policies have left aboriginal peoples as the most disadvantaged group in Canadian society. The rates of social pathology among aboriginal peoples as evidenced by the degree of alcohol abuse, crime, incarceration, and suicide, as well as other indicators, are well over the levels of non-aboriginals. In addition, unemployment rates for aboriginal peoples far exceed those for the remainder of the Canadian population. Increasingly, aboriginal leaders see self-government for their peoples as the only way to escape these deplorable conditions. The mounting pressure by aboriginal leaders for the constitutional recognition of their right to self-government, coupled with an increased awareness among other Canadians of their plight, continues to give aboriginal issues a prominent place on the Canadian political agenda.

Aboriginal Peoples: A Profile

Although Indians, Métis, and Inuit are now collectively recognized as aboriginal peoples, their cultural, legal, and political differences remain very important as the Canadian state attempts to accommodate their respective demands. Indians in Canada have traditionally been subdivided into three groups: status, treaty, and non-status Indians. A status Indian is a person registered or entitled to be registered as an Indian for purposes of the Indian Act, which was first passed in 1876, setting forth a policy of assimilating Natives into Canadian society. Status Indians are members of the 633 bands across Canada; "bands" are legal administrative bodies established under the Indian Act that correspond generally to traditional tribal and kinship group affinities. In the establishment of the Canadian reserve system, unlike that of the United States, different tribes were not placed together on the same reserve; nor were groups of Indians relocated to reservations far from their ancestral homelands. Most bands are located south of the sixtieth parallel on reserves, numbering 2,281, within the provinces. The Indian "register" (1990) estimates that there are 500,000 status Indians in Canada.

Treaty Indians are those persons who are registered members of, or can prove descent from, a band that signed a treaty. Most status Indians are treaty Indians, except those living in areas not covered by treaties, such as most of the province of British Columbia.

Non-status Indians are those persons of Indian ancestry and cultural affiliation who have lost their right to be registered under the Indian Act. The most common reason for loss of status was marriage of a registered Indian woman to a non-Indian. Loss of status has also occurred in other ways, such as voluntary renunciation, compulsory enfranchisement to non-Indian status, and failure of government officials to include some Indian families in the registry. Indians who served in the military during the world wars, for example, usually became enfranchised, losing their status as Indians. Non-status Indians do not have a distinct constitutional standing but are grouped with the Métis for jurisdictional and public policy purposes. The situation for many non-status Indians changed in 1985, when the federal government amended the Indian Act with Bill C-31 to restore registered Indian status to those women and their children who had lost it through marriage. Aboriginal women's groups welcomed this change. However, the response of Indian communities to Bill C-31 was not uniformly favorable; many Indian bands saw the bill as an unwarranted intrusion on their right to control band membership. The reinstatement process was largely completed by 1991, adding approximately 92,000 Indians to the registry.

The Inuit are those aboriginal people who inhabit Canada's northernmost regions, including the Mackenzie Delta, the Northwest Territories, the northern coasts of Hudson Bay, the Arctic Islands, Labrador, and parts of northern Quebec. The Inuit were classified with registered Indians for program and jurisdictional purposes in 1939, by a decision of the Supreme Court of Canada. They are the smallest group of Canadian aboriginal people, numbering around 35,000 (1990).

The Métis are people of mixed Indian and non-Indian ancestry. The term *Métis* originally referred to people of mixed ancestry living on the prairies. This is the definition now generally endorsed by the Métis National Council, which considers the contemporary Métis to be the descendants of the Métis community that developed on the prairies in the 1800s, and of individuals who received land grants and/or scrip under the Manitoba Act, 1870, or the Dominion Lands Act, 1879. Statistics Canada now includes in the category of Métis all people living in any part of Canada who claim mixed Indian and non-Indian ancestry. This classification corresponds to the definition of the Native Council of Canada, an umbrella group representing Métis and non-status Indians and now also identifying itself as the voice of urban Indians. The 1986 census set Canada's Métis and non-status Indian population at 400,000. Métis spokesmen themselves dispute the census figure and suggest the combined population of Métis and non-status Indians is close to one million. Approximately two-thirds of the Métis live in the provinces of Manitoba, Saskatchewan, and Alberta and in the Northwest Territories; the remainder are scattered throughout the rest of the country.

Finally, although aboriginal peoples remain widely distributed throughout rural Canada, recent decades have witnessed a growing migration of aboriginal peoples to urban areas. In western urban centers such as Vancouver, Edmonton, Calgary, Regina, Saskatoon, and Winnipeg, aboriginal peoples comprise a substantial portion of the population. The Department of Indian Affairs and Northern Development (DIAND) estimates that approximately one-third of status Indians now live off their reserves.

From *Native America: Portrait of the Peoples,* edited by Duane Champagne. Copyright 1995 by Visible Ink Press. Reprinted with permission of the Gale Group.

2

THE CRUCIBLE OF AMERICAN INDIAN IDENTITY
NATIVE TRADITION VERSUS COLONIAL IMPOSITION IN POSTCONQUEST NORTH AMERICA

Ward Churchill

Don't we have enough headaches trying to unite without . . . additional headaches? Why must people be categorized as full-bloods, mixed-bloods, etc.? Many years ago, the Bureau of Indian Affairs decided to establish blood quanta for the purpose of [tribal] enrollment. At the time, blood quantum was set at one-quarter degree, [a matter which] caused many people on the reservation to be categorized and labeled. The situation was caused solely by the BIA, with the able assistance of the Interior Department.

—Tim Giago

Among the most vexing issues afflicting Native North America at the dawn of the twenty-first century are the questions of who does or does not hold a legitimate right to say he or she is American Indian, and by what criteria—whose definition—this may or may not be true. Such queries, and the answers to them, hold an obvious and deeply important bearing not only upon the personal sense of identity inhering in millions of individuals scattered throughout the continent, but in terms of the degree to which some form of genuine self-determination can be exercised by indigenous nations in coming years. Conversely, they represent both an accurate gauge of the extent to which the sovereignty of North America's Native peoples has been historically eroded or usurped by the continent's two preeminent settler-states, the United States and Canada, and a preview of how the remainder stands to be eradicated altogether in the not so distant future.

Defining for itself the composition of its membership (citizenry), in whatever terms and in accordance with whatever standards it freely chooses, is, of course, the very bedrock expression of self-determination by any nation or people. The ability to maintain this prerogative is thus a vital measure of its sovereign standing. By the same token, intervention in or preemption of this plainly internal function by an external entity may be taken as signifying the abridgment of a nation's right to self-determination and a corresponding diminishment of its sovereignty. For that very reason, under conditions of

"The Crucible of American Identity" by Ward Churchill. Reprinted from the *American Indian Culture and Research Journal*, Volume 23, number 1, by permission of the American Indian Studies Center, UCLA. © Regents of the University of California.

colonialism—where one nation is directly subordinated to the politico-economic or strategic interests of another, and most especially in the kind of "internal colonial" systems prevailing in North America, where the colonizing powers have quite literally subsumed the territoriality of the colonized within their own claimed geographies—such domination assumes the weight of a structural imperative.

Things cannot be put so straightforwardly in contemporary practice, however, since colonialism in all forms has been flatly prohibited by international law since at least as early as 1960. In these circumstances, the kinds of subterfuge designed to create false appearances are an essential aspect of colonial technique. Hence, it is necessary for the colonizer not merely to preempt the sovereignty of the colonized, but to co-opt it, inculcating a comprador consciousness among some segment of the subaltern population in which the forms of dominion imposed by colonization will be advocated as a self-determining expression of will emanating from the colonized themselves.

At this point, with the codes of colonial domination embraced by many Native people as comprising their own traditions, and articulation of the latter often perceived as a contravention of indigenous sovereignty, the colonized become for all practical intents and purposes self-colonizing. In this most advanced and refined iteration of imperialism, confusion accomplishes much more cheaply, quietly, and efficiently what raw force was once required to achieve. In these circumstances, the kinds of subterfuge designed to create false appearances are an essential aspect of maintaining and perfecting the order of colonial rule. Meaningful resistance, never mind decolonization, among those so thoroughly indoctrinated and deluded as to accept and enforce the terms of their own subjugation in the name

of liberation is, on its face, quite impossible. Yet both resistance and decolonization are not simply rights but obligations under international law and most other recent philosophical and moral schemas of justice.

The situation presents a serious dilemma. Resolving it, and thereby actualizing the potential for a coherent and constructive indigenous response to the realities which now confront us, and which will confront our future generations, requires a systematic unraveling of the web of mystification through which North America's Native peoples have been bound ever more tightly into the carefully crafted mechanisms of oppression and eventual negation. The purpose of the present essay is to make a contribution in this regard by sorting out that which has traditionally been part of the "Indian way" of identifying member/citizens from that which has not, and to sketch the mechanisms through which the latter has supplanted the former. From the resulting vantage point it should prove possible to ascertain with some clarity the methods that must be (re)asserted if we are ever to throw off the yoke of colonial bondage.

THE TRADITIONAL WAY

There is not, and has never been, much of a genetic ("hereditary") distinction to be drawn between indigenous peoples in the Americas. In part, this devolves upon the probability that the great proliferation of culturally distinct groups evident in the hemisphere by the time the European invasions commenced around 1500 had all evolved from three, or perhaps four, discernible gene stocks, figures correlating rather well to the evident number of root linguistic variants. More to the point, Native peoples have for the most part always maintained relatively high degrees of sociocultural inclusiveness and consequent reproductive interactivity (interbreeding) among one another.

Since time immemorial, the Cheyenne (or their precursors) have intermarried with Arapaho, Ojibwa with Cree, Cayuga with Onondaga, Yaquis with Turamara, Choctaw with Chickasaw, and so on. In such instances, depending on whether the cultures in question were matrilinear or patrilinear, either the male or female spouse would become a part of the other's society, as would their offspring. Genealogy rather than genetics was the core component of societal composition, although procedures for incorporation of individuals and sometimes whole groups by adoption, naturalization, and occasional merger were similarly well established and practiced with varying degrees of scale and frequency by most peoples, either periodically or continuously.

Whatever else may be said of such processes, they served over time to erase any meaningful genetic distinctions between the groups involved. Indeed, there are recorded instances—as when the Mohawk absorbed significant portions of both the Huron and the Susquahannock during the seventeenth century—in which the number of outsiders incorporated into a given society noticeably exceeded that of the original members. Given these historical circumstances, the contemporary notion of somehow being Mohawk "by blood" is self-evidently ludicrous, albeit no more so than similar claims advanced with respect to the Pawnee, Cherokee, Apache, Paiute, or virtually any other Native people.

Once non-Indians began to appear in substantial numbers across the hemisphere, the same time-honored principles prevailed. Probably the earliest group of English to have simply melted into a Native society were the inhabitants of Raleigh's "lost colony" of Roanoak in 1590. A century later, there were literally thousands of "white Indians"—mostly English and French, but also Swedes, Scots, Irish, Dutch, and others as well—who, diseased with aspects of their own cultures, had either married into, been adopted by, or petitioned for naturalization as member/citizens of indigenous nations. By then, the phenomenon had become pronounced enough that it had long since precipitated a crisis among the Puritans of Plymouth Colony and figured in their waging of a war of extermination against the Pequots in 1637.

The attraction of "going native" remained so strong, and the willingness of indigenous peoples to accept Europeans into their societies so apparent, that it prevailed even among those captured in Indian–white warfare. During the 1770s, George Croghan and Guy Johnson, both acknowledged authorities on the Native peoples of the mid-Atlantic region, estimated that the great bulk of the several hundred English prisoners of all ages and both genders taken by the Indians had been adopted by them rather than being put to death. At about the same time, Benjamin Franklin lamented that:

> [W]hen white persons of either sex have been taken prisoners young by the Indians, and lived a while among them, tho' ransomed by their Friends, and treated with all imaginable tenderness to prevail with them to stay among the English, yet in a Short time they become disgusted with our manner of life, and the care and pains that are necessary to support it, and take the first good Opportunity of escaping again into the Woods, from thence there is no reclaiming them.

The literature of the period is filled with similar observations. Virginia's Lieutenant Governor Francis Fauquier, for example, noted that whites "recovered" from Indians had to be "closely watched [lest] they will certainly return to the Barbarians. Colonel Henry Bouquet, who headed a 1764 expedition to take charge of "captives" returned under terms of a treaty with England by the Shawnee, Miami, and other peoples of the Ohio River Valley, issued orders that "they are to be closely watched and well Secured [as] most of them, particularly those who have been a long time among the Indians, will take the first Opportunity to run away." The Reverend William Smith, chaplain and chronicler of Bouquet's foray, noted that most younger whites seemed to view their "liberators" as captors and "parted from the savages with tears."

Some, like fourteen-year-old John McCullough, managed to escape Bouquet's column and quickly reunited himself with his Native family. Adults often expressed the same sentiments, as with the English wife of a Native leader who shortly slipped away to rejoin her husband and their children.

> Although most of the returned captives did not try to escape, the emotional torment caused by the separation from their adopted families deeply impressed the colonists. The Indians "delivered up their beloved captives with the utmost reluctance; shed torrents of tears over them, recommending them to the care and protection of the commanding officer." One young woman "cryed and roared when asked to come and begged to Stay a little longer." "Some, who could not make their escape, clung to their savage acquaintance at parting, and continued many days in bitter lamentations, even refusing sustenance." Children "cried as if they would die when they were presented to us." With only small exaggeration an observer . . . could report that "every captive left the Indians with regret."

Many Indians reciprocated by refusing to surrender those they had married, adopted, or otherwise accepted, especially children, under any but the most coercive circumstances. In cases where there was no viable alternative, the record is replete with examples of adoptive Native parents regularly visiting and otherwise maintaining familial relations with such children for the remainder of their own lives. And, of course, children born of a union between Indian and non-Indian were almost invariably never relinquished at all (not least because whites, not Indians, tended to frown upon such mixed-blood offspring and thus made little or no effort to claim them). One upshot is a marked proliferation of European surnames among indigenous peoples, not only in the East but the West as well; witness such sizable contemporary mixed-blood families as Morriseau, Robideau, Peltier, and Bellecourt among the Chippewa, and the Pourier, Garnier, Amiott, Roubideaux, Archambault, and Mousseau among the Lakota.

With respect to blacks—mostly Africans brought to the southeastern quadrant of North America as chattel slaves, but the occasional free man as well—the situation was not dissimilar, albeit the imperative for them to reject a return to Euro-American society was obviously greater than for whites, and a much larger proportion of adults was involved. Escaped slaves were typically accepted among the Native peoples they encountered, marrying and producing children who were fully integrated into indigenous societies. So prominent was this process of intermingling that at some point around 1750 an entire people, the Seminole, was constituted as an amalgamation of the remnants of several thoroughly decimated indigenous nations and a very substantial element, about one-third of the whole, of blacks.

Hence, by 1830 at the latest, the notion of defining "Indianness" in terms of race had been rendered patently absurd. It has been reliably estimated that something approaching half of all Native people still residing east of the Mississippi River were at that point genetically intermixed not only with one another, but with "Negroid and Caucasoid racial stock," a demographic pattern which would spread rapidly westward during the next half-century. There is little if any indication, moreover, that most indigenous societies viewed this increasing admixture as untoward or peculiar, much less threatening, in and of itself (this is as opposed to their often bitter resistance to the cultural, political, and material encroachments of Euro-American "civilization").

ON THE MATTER OF FIDELITY

It has become an article of faith among historical interpreters that mixed-bloods served as something of a Trojan Horse within indigenous societies during the era of Euro-American conquest, undermining their cohesion and thereby eroding their ability to resist the onslaught effectively. While it is true that the colonizing powers, especially the United States, often sought to use those of mixed ancestry in precisely this fashion, the realities of mixed-blood performance were rather different. Indeed, their aggregate record in mounting a defense of Native rights is not only equal in most respects to those who were of the "pure" variety, it was plainly stronger in certain instances. Examples abound, beginning with the above-mentioned Seminole, who proved to be the U.S. army's most successful adversaries east of the Mississippi.

During the twenty-year period leading up to the Cherokee Removal of 1838, it was John Ross, a man "seven-eighths Scotch-Irish and one-eighth Cherokee by descent," who served as the primary leader of his people's effort to revitalize their traditional culture, prevent the loss of their homelands in the Georgia-Tennessee area, and thereby avert mass relocation to Oklahoma Territory. On the other hand, it was John Ridge—son of a full-blood leader called "Major" Ridge by whites, and himself only one-eighth white by pedigree—who headed the accommodationist ("sell-out") faction of Cherokee

society. The dilution of unity that weakened Cherokee resistance, as well as the internal strife plaguing this nation for generations after its Trail of Tears, were thus demonstrably attributable to Ridge and his generally well-blooded followers rather than the "genetically marginal" Ross.

Far to the west, a comparable example may be found in Quanah (Parker), "half-breed" son of Peta Nacona, principal leader of the Quahadi Comanche, and Cynthia Ann Parker, a white captive who was his wife. Beginning in the late 1860s, after his father had been killed and his mother "recovered" by white raiders, Quanah emerged as a major galvanizer of military resistance to the United States, not just among the Quahadi but with respect to all Comanche and allied Kiowa, Kiowa Apache, Southern Cheyenne, and Arapaho. After consummation of the U.S. conquest of the Southern Plains during the mid-1870s—the Quahadis were last to lay down their arms—Quanah shifted to a position of political leadership, a role which included introduction of the peyote religion, charting the Comanche course through the perilous waters of the early reservation period and on into the twentieth century.

Among the Cheyenne were the brothers George, Robert, and Charlie Bent, sons of William Bent, a noted white trader, and his Cheyenne wife. While each struggled for their people's rights in his own way— George, for instance, fought briefly against the white invaders and testified on three separate occasions against perpetrators of the Colorado militia's infamous 1864 massacre of noncombatant Cheyennes and Arapahos at Sand Creek—Charlie is the better example (or at least the most reviled among mainstream commentators). Accepted into the Cheyenne elite Crazy Dog Society (or Dog Soldiers), he acquired an almost legendary status because of his courage in physically defending his homeland. Ultimately, Charlie

Bent gave his all, dying an agonizing, lingering death in 1868 of wounds suffered during a skirmish with Pawnees fighting for the United States.

To the north, among the Oglala Lakota, there was the all but mythic figure of Crazy Horse, the man who vanquished both Crook and Custer, establishing himself in the process as perhaps the preeminent symbol of Native valor and integrity, both to his own people and to many others as well. Slight, pale-complexioned, with fair, wavy hair—he was actually named Curly as a Youth—the "strange man of the Oglalas" may well have been of mixed racial descent. Regardless of Crazy Horse's ancestry, it is clear that men like Red Cloud, who figured most prominently in undercutting his ability to sustain the Lakota resistance, were themselves full-bloods. So too was Little Big Man, the former friend who pinned Crazy Horse's arms, allowing William Gentles, a U.S. army private, to get close enough to bayonet him to death during the fall of 1877.

The same could be said of Bull Head and the rest of the contingent of Indian police who murdered Sitting Bull in December 1890, the Arikara, Crow, and Pawnee scouts who guided Custer and Colonel Ranald Mackenzie on their bloody paths across the plains, and the bulk of those who finally ran Geronimo to ground in the upper Sonora Desert. Nor was it a question of genetics that prompted Crow Dog, a noted "recalcitrant," to kill the government-sponsored Brûlé Lakota chief, Spotted Tail, whom the former viewed as having sacrificed his people's interest in favor of personal gain (both materially and in terms of imagined prestige). The list goes on and on, with deadly repetition.

At the same time, it wasn't necessarily required that one be of any part Indian blood to assume a position of importance within an indigenous society. A salient example is that of Jim Beckwourth (variously spelled as Beckworth or Beckwith), who was by all accounts of exclusively African descent. Having been adopted by the Crow during the mid-1820s and marrying a woman named Still Water shortly thereafter, he was elevated first to the station of counselor to the headmen and eventually to serving as a headman in his own right. Although he left the Crow for a time after the death of his second wife, he remained unstinting in his defense of Indian rights and returned in 1866 to die among the people who had accepted him as a naturalized leader.

On balance, then, it is both fair and accurate to observe that questions concerning the likelihood an individual might display a strong loyalty to Indian interests never devolved upon his or her genetic makeup. Unquestionably, mixed-bloods and persons lacking even the pretense of a Native gene stood among the foremost exemplars of patriotism in a number of indigenous nations during the nineteenth century (and earlier). By the same token, many Native people "untainted" by any hint of admixture with whites or blacks conducted themselves with all the fidelity of Vidkun Quisling. Such matters were well understood in traditional societies, which is precisely why they never considered blood quantum to be a useful factor in determining citizenship or cultural identity.

THE RACIAL DIMENSION OF DIVIDE AND RULE

The intellectual establishment of the United States played a major role in pioneering such pseudoscientific "disciplines" as ethnology, craniometry, phrenology, and eugenics from the early nineteenth century onwards. In essence, although it has evidenced a variety of offshoots and subtexts over the years, the entire project—which has lasted into the present moment—has been devoted to devising "objective" criteria by which the human species may be subdivided into races according to certain "heritable" and "empirically demonstrable" characteristics. Values are then assigned to these genetically transmitted attributes in order to create the appearance of a natural hierarchy of humanity, ranging upward from Negroid at the lowest level to Caucasoid at the highest.

With publication of Samuel George Morton's *Crania Americana* in 1839, it is no overstatement to suggest that the Euro-American intelligentsia stood at the cutting edge of "scholarly" efforts to lend both a patina of academic respectability and an aura of sheer inevitability to the white supremacist ideology attending European imperialism. While it was put to various uses abroad, such material was utilized in the United States to justify both a domestic order of which black chattel slavery was an integral aspect and a continental trajectory of national expansion—America's "manifest destiny" to extend uninterruptedly "from sea to shining sea"—which could be consummated only at the direct expense of North America's indigenous population.

It is instructive that while U.S. policymakers professed to embrace racism on both scientific and philosophical grounds, standpoints implying an at least minimal consistency in application, their implementation of its principles was at once transparently self-serving and utterly contradictory. Since blacks were considered to be property, yielding value not only in their labor but as commodities which could be bought and sold, it was profitable not only to employ but to breed them in ever larger numbers. To this end, an elaborate system of quantifying their racial admixture was devised—classifications such as maroon, quadroon, and octoroon—by which to assess their relative worth. The overriding premise, however, was the one-drop rule: A person with

any amount of "Negroid blood" could be considered black for purposes of law, even if computation of their quantum revealed them to be 127/128 white.

Native people, by contrast, were legally understood to own property—mainly land, and minerals within that land—coveted by whites. It followed then, as it still does, that reductions in the number of Indians at large in North America corresponded directly to diminishment of the cloud surrounding the dominant society's claims of clear title to, and jurisdictional rights over, its purported land base. Hence, any racial admixture at all, especially with blacks, was often deemed sufficient to warrant individuals, and sometimes entire groups to be legally classified as non-Indians, regardless of their actual standing in indigenous society. On this basis, most noticeably in the South but elsewhere as well, whole Native peoples were declared extinct via the expedient of simply reclassifying them as mulattos or coloreds.

While the intermingling of Natives with blacks was invariably cast in a negative light, the mixing of Indian with white "stock" came to be viewed more favorably. As no less than Thomas Jefferson observed in 1803, a calculated policy of subsuming Native genetics within a much larger white gene pool might serve as an alternative to outright extermination in answering what he termed the "Indian Question."

> In truth, the ultimate point of rest and happiness for them is to let our settlements and theirs meet and blend together, to intermix, and become one people. Incorporating themselves with us as citizens of the United States, this is what the natural progress of things will, of course, bring on, and it will be better to promote than retard it.

Completely oblivious to the reality of North America's abundant indigenous agriculture, and to the fact that whites had learned to cultivate corn and other crops from Indians rather than the other way round, America's "most admired . . . slave-holding philosopher of freedom" actually urged a delegation of Munsee, Lenni Lenape, and Mohican leaders to adopt a farming way of life when they visited him in 1808. "You will become one people with us," he went on to tell the astonished Indians, "your blood will mix with ours, and will spread with ours across this great land."

The sentiments underlying Jefferson's "humanitarian" strategy were framed less pleasantly, but with remarkable clarity, by J. C. Nott, a racial theorist whose views were endorsed by Morton and other prominent scientists of the day. With reference to the idea that at least five southern peoples—Cherokee, Choctaw, Chickasaw, Creek, and Seminole—had become "civilized" in their own right before being forcibly evicted from their homelands during the 1830s, he argued:

> It has been falsely asserted that the Choctaw and Cherokee Indians have made great progress in civilization. I assert positively, after the most ample investigation of the facts, that the pure-blooded Indians are everywhere unchanged in their habits. Many white persons, settling among the above tribes, have intermarried with them; and all such trumpeted progress exists among these whites and their mixed breeds alone. The pure-blooded savage still skulks untamed through the forest, or gallops athwart the prairie. Can any one call the name of a single pure Indian of the Barbarous tribes who—except in death, like a wild cat—has done anything worthy of remembrance?

It followed, according to the noted phrenologist Charles Caldwell, that the "only efficient scheme to civilize the Indians is to cross the breed. Attempt any other and you [will have no alternative] but to *extinguish the race* [emphasis in the original]." Such views, posing the alternative of genetic and cultural absorption to literal extirpation, were avidly embraced by Lewis Henry Morgan, the "founding giant" of American anthropology. Indeed, Morgan was of the express opinion that the former option was preferable to the latter mainly because a blending of minute quantities of Indian blood into that of the white "mainstream" would serve to "toughen our race" even while it "painlessly" eradicated the indigenous population as such.

All told, by 1860 or shortly thereafter, Euro-American academicians had forged the full range of conceptual tools necessary for their government to use the traditionally inclusive structures of Native societies in a manner that would facilitate their rapid division, fragmentation, and, so it was thought at the time, ultimate dissipation. Slowly but steadily, a national consensus was emerging to the effect that this represented the most appropriate (and final) solution to what was by then being called "The Indian Problem." What remained necessary was for these tools to be applied systematically, through the design and implementation of a comprehensive set of policies. And, to this end, experimentation had long since begun.

THE IMPOSITIONS OF U.S. POLICY

Probably the first concerted effort by U.S. officialdom to use the incorporation of whites and their mixed-blood offspring as a wedge with which to pry indigenous societies apart began in the late 1700s, when Moravian missionaries were asked to serve as de facto federal emissaries to the Cherokee Nation. Imbued with the mystical notion that Aryan genetics correlated to such innate endowments as intellect and moral capacity—which in their minds corresponded with the potential to adopt "civilized" (Christian) outlooks and values—the Moravians and, after 1803, their Presbyterian colleagues "went out of their way to befriend" mixed-bloods rather than "pure" Indians while pursuing their goals of obtaining religious converts cum political allies.

Predictably, this racial bias translated into a privileging of mixed-bloods in both political and material terms, regardless of their rank within the Cherokee polity and irrespective of whether they desired such "benefits," a situation which was quite reasonably resented by other Cherokees (most especially those whose authority was undermined or supplanted by such external manipulation). The result, obviously intended by the United States, was the opening of deep cleavages among Cherokees that greatly weakened them in military as well as political and cultural terms, circumstances which amplified considerably the decisive advantages the United States already enjoyed in its drive to dispossess them of their property. Meanwhile, similar initiatives had been undertaken vis-à-vis the Creek, Choctaw, Chickasaw, and others.

The United States largely refrained from attempting such maneuvers in a more formal sense during the first thirty years of its treaty making with indigenous nations. This interval roughly corresponds to the period in which the young republic, a veritable revolutionary outlaw state, desperately required the legitimation which could be bestowed through Native recognition of its sovereign status (indigenous sovereignty having already been recognized through treaties with the European powers). Nonetheless, special provisions pertaining to mixed-bloods soon entered U.S. diplomacy with Indians, beginning with an 1817 treaty with the Wyandot and several other peoples of the Ohio-Pennsylvania region. Thereafter, the performance was repeated in compact after compact, at least fifty-three times by 1868.

In only a few instances—such as the 1847 treaty with the Chippewa of the Mississippi and Lake Superior, in which it is recognized by the United States that "half of mixed bloods of the Chippewas residing with them [should simply] be considered Chippewas"—is there acknowledgment of the right of indigenous nations to naturalize citizens as they saw fit. In most cases, such treaty provisions are plainly designed to accomplish the opposite effect, distinguishing those of mixed ancestry from the rest of their people, almost always by unilaterally privileging them in a material fashion. Usually this followed upon the model established in the 1817 treaty, the eighth article of which provided that while the Indians themselves would hold certain lands in common, those "connected with said Indians, by blood or adoption" would receive individual tracts averaging 640 acres each.

There were several variations on the theme. In one, exemplified by the 1818 treaty with the Miami, chiefs as well as mixed-bloods and intermarried whites were assigned individual parcels, one to six sections each in this case, while the rest of the people were assigned a tract in common. Thus, not only were mixed-bloods figuratively elevated to the same standing as chiefs by external fiat, but the Miamis' actual leaders were implicitly linked to them rather than to their people as a whole. On other occasions, as in the 1855 treaty with the Winnebago, missionaries were substituted for chiefs. On still others, as in the 1837 treaty with the Sioux, money and/or other special provisions were substituted for land. Even in cases like that of the 1861 treaty with the Cheyenne and Arapaho, where full-bloods and mixed-bloods were nominally treated the same (i.e., everyone was allotted a parcel and/or monetary award), mixed-bloods were singled out to receive larger quantities.

In a number of instances, as in the 1857 treaty with the Pawnee, provisions were explicitly designed to induce an outright physical separation of mixed-bloods from their people, a particularly odious practice in cases such as that addressed by the 1865 treaty with the Osage where "breeds" were the only group allowed (or coerced) to remain within a traditional homeland from which the rest of their nation was removed. In the 1831 treaty with the Shawnee, the notion of blood quantum was first applied in a formal way to determine who would—or, more importantly, who would not—be recognized by the United States as a "real" Indian.

And, racism aside, the treaties often employed a virulent sexist bias, tracing descent, acknowledging authority, and bestowing land titles along decidedly patriarchal lines even (or especially) in contexts where female property ownership, political leadership, and matrilinearity were the indigenous norms. When combined with the usual racial manipulations, such gender criteria represented an extraordinarily potent means of subverting the integrity of Native cultures, undermining their sociopolitical cohesion, and confusing or nullifying their procedures for identifying member/citizens.

In 1871, sensing that the capacity of most indigenous nations to offer effective military resistance was nearing an end, Congress suspended further treaty making with Indians. There then followed a decade of reorganization during which the government shifted from what had been primarily a policy of subjugating Native peoples to an emphasis upon assimilating what remained of them, both geographically and demographically. There were a number of aspects to this transition, notably the extension of U.S. criminal jurisdiction over reserved Native territories via the Major Crimes Act of 1885. Its hallmark, however, was passage of the 1887 General Allotment Act, a measure expressly intended to dissolve the collective relationship to land that was the fundament of traditional cultures by imposing the allegedly superior Anglo-Saxon system of individuated property ownership.

The main ingredient of the allotment act was that each Indian recognized as such by the United States would be assigned an individually deeded parcel of land within existing reservation boundaries. These varied in size, depending on whether the Indian was a child (40 acres), unmarried adult (80 acres), or head of a family (160 acres). Once each Indian had received his or her personal allotment, becoming a U.S. citizen in the process, the law prescribed that the balance of reserved territory be declared surplus and opened up to homesteading by non-Indians, corporate usage, or placed in some form of perpetual federal trust status (e.g., designated as national parks and forests, military installations, etc.). In this manner, about two-thirds of the approximately 150 million acres of land still retained by indigenous nations at the outset passed to whites by 1934.

The bedrock upon which the allotment process was built was the compilation of formal rolls listing those belonging to each reservation-based Native people. While the act itself posited no specific criteria by which this would be accomplished, responsibility for completing the task was ultimately vested in the individual federal agents assigned to preside over the reservations. Endowed as they were with staunchly racialist perspectives, and fully aware that whatever definitional constraints might be applied in determining the overall number of Indians would translate directly into an increased availability of property to their own society, it was predictable that these men would rely heavily upon the sort of blood quantum standards already evident in treaty language.

In practice, it was typically required that potential enrollees or allottees be able to demonstrate that they possessed "not less than one-half degree of blood" in the particular group in which they wished to be enrolled (intertribal pedigrees were seldom accepted, even for ostensible full-bloods, and the overall standard was almost never allowed to slip below quarter-blood). The upshot was that anywhere from one-third to two-thirds of all those who might otherwise have been eligible to receive allotments were denied not only land but federal recognition as member/citizens of their nations. In sum, government functionaries admitted to the existence of only 237,196 Native people within U.S. borders by the late 1890s, of whom only a small percentage were less than half-blood members of specific groups.

To complete this racist reshaping of Indian identity, the act provided that those enrolled as full-bloods would be placed under the legal presumption of being genetically incompetent to manage their own affairs. Hence, they were issued "trust patents" for their allotments, to be "administered in their behalf by the Secretary of the Interior of his delegate" (local Indian agents) for a quarter-century. Mixed-bloods, by virtue of their white genetics, were deemed to be competent and issued patents in fee simple. This, along with other blatantly preferential treatment bestowed as a matter of policy upon those of mixed ancestry, drove the final wedges into many once harmonious indigenous societies. In the more extreme instances, such as that of the Kaw in Kansas, the full-bloods' visceral response was to repudiate mixed-bloods altogether, demanding their elimination from the tribal roll and seeking to expel them as a body from their society.

By the turn of the century, virtually every indigenous nation within the United States had, by way of an unrelenting substitution of federal definitions for their own, been stripped of the ability to determine for themselves in any meaningful way the internal composition of their polities. The manner in which this had been accomplished, moreover, ensured that rifts even among those still acknowledged as being Indians were of a nature that would all but guarantee eventual dissolution of Native societies, at least in the sense they had traditionally understood themselves. Allotment and the broader assimilation policy of which it was part had truly proven to be, in the words of Indian Commissioner Francis E. Leupp, "a mighty pulverizing engine for breaking up the tribal mass."

INTERNALIZATION

The break-up and diminishment of the reservation land base were not the only factors leading to confident predictions that there would be no Indians culturally recognizable as such in the United States by some point around 1935. Beginning in the 1860s, there had been an increasing emphasis on educating Native youth in the ways of the dominant society, a trend that was consolidated in the 1880s as a key aspect of assimilationist technique. While there were several other options available, all of them less expensive and more humane, the mode selected for delivery of such instruction was primarily that of off-reservation boarding schools located in places as remote as possible from Native communities.

The model for what became an entire system was Pennsylvania's Carlisle Indian School, established in 1875 by Captain Richard Henry Pratt, a man whose main qualification for the task seems to have been that he had earlier served as warden of a military prison at Fort Marion, Florida. Following Pratt's stated objective of "killing the Indian" in each student, Carlisle and other such facilities—Chilocco, Albuquerque, Phoenix, Haskell, Riverside (by 1902, there were two dozen of them)—systematically "deculturated" their pupils. Children brought to the schools as young as age six were denied most or all direct contact with their families and societies for years on end. They were shorn of their hair and required to dress in the manner of Euro-America, forbidden to speak their languages or practice their religions, and prevented from learning their own histories or being in any other way socialized among their people.

Simultaneously, all students were subjected to a grueling regimen of indoctrination in Christian morality, mainly the "virtues" of private property, sexual repression, and patriarchy; "proper" English and arithmetic; and officially approved versions of history, civics, and natural science, the latter devoted mostly to inculcating prevailing notions of racial hierarchy. To instill the work ethic—that is, to prepare students for the lot assigned their racial group once it had been fully digested by Euro-America—they were also required to spend half of each day during the school year engaged in "industrial vocational training" (i.e., uncompensated manual labor). During the summers, most of the older boys were "jobbed out" at very low wages to work on white-owned farms or local businesses; girls were assigned as domestics and the like.

Individual Native families and often whole societies resisted the process. As a result, in 1891 and again in 1893, Congress authorized the use of police, troops, and other forcible means to compel the transfer of children from reservations to boarding schools and to keep them there once they'd arrived. Hence, despite the best efforts of their elders, and not infrequently of the students themselves, a total of 21,568 indigenous children— about a third of the targeted age group—were confined in the schools in 1900. As of the late 1920s, the system had been diversified and expanded to the point that upwards of 80 percent of each successive generation

of Native youth was being comprehensively "acculturated" in a more or less uniform fashion.

By 1924, assimilation had progressed to the point that a "clean-up bill" was passed through which the responsibilities, though not necessarily the rights, of U.S. citizenship were imposed upon all Indians who had not already been naturalized under the allotment act or other federal initiatives. Although it appeared that this might represent the culminating statutory ingredient necessary to bring about a final absorption of Native America, fate intervened in a most unexpected fashion to avert any such outcome (formally, if not in terms of more practical cultural, political, and economic realities). This, rather ironically, took the form of resources: The mostly barren tracts of land left to Indians after allotment, thought to be worthless by nineteenth-century policymakers, had by the late 1920s been revealed as some of the more mineral-rich territory in the world.

Loath to see these newfound assets thrown into the public domain (many had strategic value, real or potential), the more forward-looking federal economic planners quickly perceived the utility of retaining them in trust, where they might be exploited at controlled rates by preferred corporations for designated purposes. This resulted, in 1925, in the recommendation by a committee of one hundred officially selected academic experts and business leaders that allotment and the more draconian objectives of assimilation policy be abandoned in favor of preserving the reservations in some permanently subordinated capacity and inaugurating a policy of carefully calibrated economic development therein.

This, in turn, led to passage of the 1934 Indian Reorganization Act (IRA), through which what remained of traditional Native governments were for the most part supplanted by federally designed tribal councils meant to serve as the medium for long-term administration of the freshly conceived internal colonial domain. Although the IRA was imposed behind the democratic façade of reservation-by-reservation referenda, the record reveals that BIA field representatives obtained favorable results by presenting skewed or patently false information to voters in a number of instances, flatly rigging the outcomes in others. And, while democratic appearances were reinforced by the fact that the government of each reorganized reservation functioned on the basis of its own "tribal constitution," the reality is that these "founding" documents were essentially boilerplate contraptions resembling corporate charters hammered out on an assembly line basis by bureau personnel.

Nowhere is this last more obvious than in the language of the IRA constitutions pertaining to criteria of tribal membership. While there are certain variations between instruments, most simply aped the prevailing federal quantum standard of quarter-blood minimum, while all of them, regardless of the degree of blood required, advanced genetics as the linchpin of identity. That there was no noteworthy resistance among Native supporters of the IRA to this conspicuous usurpation of indigenous tradition is unsurprising, given that such persons were all but invariably drawn from the ranks of those indoctrinated in the boarding schools to see themselves in racial rather than national, political, or cultural terms.

With the embrace of the IRA constitutions by what were proclaimed as solid majorities on most reservations, Euro-American definitions of and constraints upon Indian identity were formally as well as psychologically and intellectually internalized by Native America. From there on, the government could increasingly rely upon Indians themselves to enforce its race codes. Consequently, whenever racial formulations of Native identity have been challenged, Washington has been able to lay the onus of responsibility directly at the feet of the IRA councils it not only invented and installed, but which remain utterly and perpetually dependent upon federal patronage for their base funding and whatever limited authority they might wield. In turn, the councils defend Washington's negation of indigenous sovereignty in the name of maintaining it. A more perfect shell game is impossible to imagine.

ENTER THE "PURITY POLICE"

The reconfiguration and structural assimilation of the mechanisms of indigenous governance—by the early 1990s, IRA-style councils were openly referred to as a "third level" of the federal government itself—were facilitated and reinforced, through both the increasingly pervasive indoctrination of Native students via the educational system and by lingering effects of allotment. Foremost in this respect was the "heirship problem" created by the fact that the reserved Native land base had been reduced to a size corresponding to the number of Indians recognized as existing during the 1890s. No provision was made for a population rebound of any sort. As the matter was politely explained in 1994:

> Upon the death of the original allottees the allotments, or portions of them, have descended to heirs or devisees. As these heirs in turn have died, their holdings have been subdivided among their heirs or devisees, and so on through the years. As a result, about half of the allotted Indian lands are in heirship status. The authors of the original legislation failed to anticipate the problems that would be caused by the partitioning of an individual's land following his death. Thousands of the allotments in an heirship status are subject to so many undivided interests that they can be utilized

only with great difficulty by their Indian owners. . . . Undivided interests in a single allotment can often be expressed by fractions with a common denominator of 1,000,000 or more [by this point].

In other words, there was no reservation land available to accommodate the 50 percent increase in the number of recognized Indians recorded by the U.S. Census between 1900 and 1950. Rather than correcting the problem by transferring some portion of the territory unlawfully stripped from Native people back to its rightful owners, the government launched a massive and sustained program to relocate the Native "population surplus" from the land altogether, dispersing them for the most part into major urban areas. At the same time, as an incentive for them to leave, funding for on-reservation programming of all sorts was sliced to the bone and sometimes deeper. One result is that, while well over 90 percent of federally recognized Indians lived on the reservations in 1900, fewer than 45 percent do so today.

Another cost-cutting measure, inaugurated in the mid-1950s, was for the Congress to simply "terminate" its recognition of entire nations whose reservations were found to be devoid of minerals, or who were deemed to be too small and insignificant to warrant the expenditures necessary to administer them. A total of 103 peoples, ranging from large groups like the Menominee in Wisconsin and [the] Klamath in Oregon to the tiny "mission bands" of Southern California—[all] were thereby dissolved, their remaining lands absorbed into the U.S. territorial corpus and their population effectively declared to be non-Indians before the process ran its course in the early sixties. Only a handful, including the Menominee but not the Klamath, were ever reinstated.

Predictably, far from seeking to combat such trends, federally installed and supported tribal councils amplified them. In the face of declining federal appropriations to the BIA, the councils by and large set out to reduce the number of Indians eligible to draw upon them. Arguing that the fewer people entitled to receive benefits such as health care and commodity foodstuffs—or to receive per-capita payments against mineral extraction, water diversions, and past land transfers—the larger the share for those who remained, the councils were able to peddle their bill of goods to many of their increasingly impoverished reservation constituents. In short order, the IRA constitutions on many reservations were amended or rewritten to reflect higher blood quantum requirements for tribal enrollment. In a number of instances, reservation residency was required as well, a stipulation that excluded the children of relocatees, regardless of their documentable degree of Indian blood.

The council heads, through a federally funded lobbying organization dubbed the National Tribal Chairmen's Association (NTCA), then launched an aggressive campaign to once again recast the definition of "Indian" in the public consciousness—and, they made it clear, in law—this time as being only those "enrolled in a federally recognized tribe. "Consigned to the status of non-Indians in this perverse scenario was everyone from terminated peoples like the Klamath to the unenrolled traditionals still living on and about many reservations, from nations like the Abnaki of Vermont who had never consented to a treaty with the United States—and who were thus officially unrecognized—to the NTCA members' own nieces and nephews residing in cities. Also sacrificed in the proposed ethnic purge were thousands of hapless children, orphaned and otherwise, whom federal welfare agencies had caused to be adopted by non-Indian families.

The government initially declined to accept the NTCA's simplistic nomenclature of Indianness. Instead, it conjured up a proliferation of what by now amount to at least eighty different and often conflicting definitions of its own, each of them conforming to some particular bureaucratic or policy agenda and sporting a larger or smaller claque of Indian subscribers queued up to defend it under the presumption they will somehow benefit by their endorsement. Under such conditions, it is possible to challenge the legitimacy of virtually anyone identifying as Indian on one or several grounds (often having little or nothing to do with genuine concerns about identity, per se). The result has been a steadily rising tide of infighting, occasioned in most instances by outright race-baiting, between and among Native peoples during the past forty years.

Things did not become truly pathological until 1990, however, when the NTCA's reactionary vision was at least partially realized at the federal level. With passage of the so-called Act for the Protection of American Indian Arts and Crafts in this year, it became a criminal offense punishable by fines of $250,000 to $1 million and imprisonment of up to fifteen years for anyone not enrolled in a federally recognized tribe to identify as an Indian "for purposes of selling artwork." Although Congress did not provide the statute an enabling clause to allow its enforcement until 1996—not least because of concerns that to do so might technically require the arrest and prosecution of individuals deemed to be Indian under other elements of federal law—its very existence unleashed an utter frenzy of witch-hunting among Indians themselves.

Within months, ad hoc patrols of "identity monitors" were prowling selected museums and galleries, demanding to see documentation of the pedigrees of the Native artists exhibited therein, while freelance Indian spokespersons advocated that comparable legislation pertaining to "ethnic fraud" should be enacted with respect to writers, educators, filmmakers, and journalists, among many others. The theme was quickly picked up, tabloid-style, by papers like *Indian Country Today* and *News from Indian Country*, while the Internet came figuratively alive with a swarm of essentially anonymous rumors that dozens of Native America's most distinguished artists, authors, thinkers, and activists weren't "really" Indians after all.

Perhaps most disgustingly, a literal flying squad of self-appointed "purity police" in the San Francisco Bay Area took it upon itself to systematically disrupt the functioning of all manner of community service organizations in 1992 and 1993—their targets ranged from Native programming on radio station KPFA, to an AIDS clinic administered by the Indian Health Service, to the local school district's Indian education project—to ensure that everyone involved fit their particular notion of what an Indian should be (children as young as eight years of age were buttonholed and ordered to prove they were "genuine" Indians). Meanwhile, back on the "rez," at least some IRA leaders were arguing that the tribal constitutions should be amended yet again, this time to disenroll members who married non-Indians, on the premise that such measures had become vital "to protect the purity of our Indian blood."

THE WAY AHEAD

The internalization of Euro-Americans' conception of race by Native peoples, the virulence with which it is now manifested in all too many sectors of the indigenous community, and the ubiquity of the confusion and divisiveness it has generated among Indians and their potential supporters represent a culmination of federal policy initiatives originating nearly two hundred years ago. To all appearances, Native North America has been rendered effectively self-colonizing and, if present attitudes persist, it stands to become self-liquidating as well. The tale is told in the demographic data pertaining to those who are federally recognized. [As reported by Russell Thornton in *American Indian Holocaust and Survival: A Population History Since 1492* (Norman: University of Oklahoma Press, 1987): 174–175.]

> During the twentieth century population recovery of American Indians there has been an increasing mixture between them and non-Indian peoples. Data concerning this may be obtained from the 1910 and 1930 U.S. censuses of American Indians. . . . [In 1910] 56.5 percent of American Indians enumerated in the United States were full-blood—150,053 out of 265,682—with the blood quantum of 8.4 percent (22,207) not reported. . . . In the U.S. census of 1930, however, 46.3 percent—153,933 out of 332,397—were enumerated as full-bloods and 42.4 percent (141,101) were enumerated as mixed-bloods, with the degree of Indian blood of 11.2 percent (37,363) not reported. Thus, whereas the American Indian population size increased by slightly over 66,000 from 1910 to 1930, the number of full-blood American Indians increased by only 4,000; most of the increase was among mixed-blood Indians.

Such trends have not only continued but accelerated. By 1970, approximately two-thirds of the marriages of those on the tribal rolls were to people who were not, with the result that only 59 percent of births reflected a situation in which both parents registered themselves as possessing any Indian blood at all. The number of supposed full-bloods has correspondingly dropped to almost nothing—among populous peoples like the Minnesota-Wisconsin Chippewa, they now represent only 5 percent of the whole—while the proportion and composition of mixed-bloods have climbed dramatically. At present rates of intermarriage, the segment of the federally recognized Native population evidencing less than one-quarter-degree blood quantum, presently about 4 percent, will have climbed to 59 percent or more by 2080. To tighten or even adhere to quantum requirements in the face of such realities is to engage in a sort of autogenocide by definitional and statistical extermination. As historian Patricia Nelson Limerick has observed in this connection:

> Set the blood quantum at one-quarter, hold to it as a rigid definition of Indians, let intermarriage proceed as it [has] for centuries, and eventually Indians will be defined out of existence. When that happens, the federal government will be freed of its persistent "Indian problem."

Cognizant of this, some peoples with smaller numbers, like the Umatilla in Oregon, have already undertaken to preserve racial cant while offsetting the consequent prospect of definitional self-extinguishment by proposing revision of their constitutions to require that future enrollees demonstrate some degree of Umatilla blood, no matter how minute, in addition to "at least one-quarter degree of blood . . . in another federally recognized tribe or tribes." Left conspicuously unexplained in such convoluted formulations is exactly how being a quarter-blood Lakota or Mohawk supposedly makes a person one whit more Umatilla than does being a full-blood Irishman, Ibo, or Han. Nor is it explained why a person genealogically connected to the group should be less Umatilla in orientation, absent some sort of generic "Indian" genetic structure, than a person who has it.

The implications of such nonsense become most striking when it is considered in juxtaposition to the actual—rather than federally recognized—size of the present indigenous population of the United States, and the potential power deriving from its scale. Jack Forbes, perhaps the closest examiner of the issue, has noted that since 1969,

> The Bureau of the Census, conspiring with the Office of Management and Budget and political special interests, has [deliberately obfuscated] the "racial" character of the U.S. population and, as part of the process, has "lost" some six to eight million persons of Native American ancestry and appearance with a scientifically useless "Hispanic/Spanish" category. In addition, [seven million or more] persons of mixed African and Native American ancestry remain uncounted as such because of the way census questions were asked and the answers tallied.

Forbes estimates that, even using standard blood-quantum criteria, the actual Native population of the "lower 48" in 1980 was well over 15 million rather than the 1.4 million officially admitted by the census bureau. Employing traditional indigenous methods of identifying population rather than racial criteria would have resulted in an even higher number. And, as of 1990, when the official count reached nearly 2 million, inclusion of these most rapidly growing sectors of the Native population results in an aggregate of as many as 30 million persons overall. The ability to wield political and economic clout inherent to the latter tally, as opposed to the former—which comes to less than 0.5 percent of the overall U.S. population—is self-evident.

Fortunately, there is at least one concrete example of how things might be taken in the direction of realizing this potential. The Cherokee Nation of Oklahoma (CNO), in its 1975 constitution, took the unprecedented step, . . . unparalleled by other twentieth-century indigenous governments, of completely dispensing with blood-quantum requirements in its enrollment procedures. Instead, the CNO placed its reliance upon the more traditional genealogical mode of determining citizenship. This had the effect

of increasing the number of persons formally identified as Cherokee from fewer than 10,000 during the late 1950s to slightly over 232,000 by 1980 (and about 300,000 today).

On this basis, the Cherokee, whose reservation was dissolved pursuant to the 1898 Curtis Act, have been able to assert what amounts to a split jurisdiction over their former territory. Moreover, while much has been made by assorted race mongers about how this course of action was "diluting" whatever was left of "real" Cherokee culture and society, the precise opposite result has obtained in practice. [As stated by Thornton, op. cit., 200]:

> The Oklahoma Cherokee, without a reservation landbase, have been able to survive tribally by an inclusive definition of what it is to be Cherokee. Their definition allowed relatively large numbers of people with Cherokee lineage but relatively small amounts of Cherokee blood into the tribe. This allowed the tribe to reestablish itself after virtual "dissolution" and to achieve political power in Oklahoma. The tribe, in turn, has protected a smaller group of full-blood, more traditional Cherokee from American non-Indian ways of life.

Plainly, in and of itself, the CNO initiative has neither ended the internecine bickering over identity which has precluded anything resembling unity among Native people, much less established the basis upon which to free even the Cherokee from internal colonial domination by the United States. It does, however, represent a substantial stride in the right direction. If the model it embodies is ultimately seized and acted upon by a broadening spectrum of indigenous nations in the years ahead, the tools required for liberating Native North America may at long last be forged. In the alternative, should the currently predominating racialist perspectives associated with the IRA regimes prevail, the road to extinction can be traversed rather quickly.

3

TO THE U.S. CENSUS BUREAU, NATIVE AMERICANS ARE PRACTICALLY INVISIBLE

John Anner

"Statistical genocide," says Dr. Susan Lobo, who works with the Intertribal Friendship House in Oakland, California, "relates to the ways in which figures and statistics are used to determine programs and set policies." The most important source of these figures and statistics is the once-a-decade national census. Census figures are used to determine, among other things, who gets what in terms of federal funding and congressional representation. If you are not counted by the census, then, in the eyes of government agencies, you don't count. In fact, you don't exist at all.

For Native Americans, the last U.S. census—which science writer James Gleick says "seems certain to stand as a bleak landmark in the annals of arithmetic"—deserves the name "statistical genocide." It has made a lot of people vanish, for the most part people of color. Native Americans, however, claim that their communities are undercounted much more than other races or ethnicities, and the process has made them all but invisible in urban America. "Demography," writes University of California at Davis Professor Jack Forbes, "for Native Americans, has always pointed towards a struggle against disappearance, or, more precisely, against being forced to vanish!"

As census officials readily admit, the national count always misses people of color

more often than whites, due to mistrust of agents of the federal government, cultural and language communication problems, and so on. Depending on the area and ethnic group in question, this undercount is variously estimated at three to fifteen percent. Whites are generally undercounted by approximately one percent, according to the Census Bureau. Some Native American leaders, however, feel that their urban constituencies are undercounted by as much as 60 percent. And in some ways, an accurate count is even more important to Native Americans than it is to other people of color, for reasons having to do with federal recognition of various tribes and new proposals regarding how Bureau of Indian Affairs (BIA) money is allocated.

Despite the magnitude of the problem and the importance of the outcome, however, the 1990 U.S. Census will be tabulated without much attention to Native American objections to the way it was conducted, or protests about the severity of the undercount. In part, this has to do with size of the census project; it is difficult to change the overall direction of a massive bureaucracy that at its height employed some 350,000 workers in 487 field offices around the country. As Ramona Wilson, coordinator of the Urban Indian Child Resource Center said in an interview, "the census machinery is very rigid. Populations are put into the machinery and have to accommodate themselves to it, rather than the machinery accommodating itself to people."

The census is also an undertaking involving the abilities of a horde of statisticians and other "number-crunchers" who are not trained to be aware of cultural biases, and whose general attitude is, according to Lobo, "don't worry, we have sophisticated techniques—which you wouldn't understand—for correcting any problems." But the Native American community also failed to mobilize around the census in a way that could have changed the outcome, which reflects a lack of political clout on the national level and a scarcity of organizing in the local arena. In part, this failure to mobilize around the census is due to the barriers to organizing a community that lives dispersed, and is composed of numerous tribes that speak different languages and have different cultures. As explained below, the census undercounts Native Americans in part because they generally do not live in clustered residential communities. This same geographical scattering makes it more difficult to use traditional community organizing techniques with Native Americans than with other people of color, who tend to settle in a more homogenous pattern in urban areas.

SURVIVAL TACTICS

But Native Americans, according to Lobo, are also loathe to get involved with the federal government on any level, especially one that involves being counted—which brings back memories of being registered in federal programs that relocated and dispossessed Indian people from their traditional lands. "For Indian people," said Lobo, "being invisible is a survival tactic that has proved its worth in the past." Thus, although the benefits of being counted by the census were clear to many organizers and service providers, on the whole there was little enthusiasm on the part of their Native American constituency. Lobo also said that, for many Native American organizations, the census was a "new issue" around which they had not yet learned to organize effectively.

According to the organizations contacted for this article, there are three main changes they would like to see the Census Bureau make to better count Native Americans:

1. Change the way the census questions are worded to make it easier to self-identify as Native American;
2. Change the way the census is conducted in some areas to account for the dispersed living patterns of Native Americans;
3. Hire more outreach workers to work in Native American communities (there were only two for all of California in 1990).

Oakland, California, was one of several sites chosen around the country in which to do "post-enumeration surveys" (PES) to determine why certain populations were missed by census counters. (According to John Reader, Western Regional Census Director, the Census Bureau always does these surveys, and has until July 15, 1991, to decide if it wants to adjust the census figures based on the results of the PES.) The Bureau hired Dr. Susan Lobo and the Intertribal Friendship House to do follow-up, indepth interviews with 100 Native American families to determine what characteristics

Native Americans have that cause them to be undercounted by the census.

CENSUS COVER-UP

Framing the question in this way, says Lobo, automatically puts the blame for being missed on the people, not on the Census Bureau. "The more we got into the project," Lobo said in an interview, "the more we realized that . . . this study was something they created to cover their tracks. The real reason for the undercount is problems with the census process itself, not because people move too much or because they don't have recognizable housing."

Despite their sophisticated statistical techniques, according to Lobo, the census count is based on flawed assumptions about urban Native Americans, who now make up over half of all Native Americans in the U.S. The most important of these is the premise that all people of color live in homogeneous residential communities, i.e. that Latinos will tend to live near other Latinos, Asians near other Asians from similar geographic background, etc. This is important because in areas where large percentages of mailed-out census forms are not sent back—estimated at over 50% in many communities of color—census takers must go door-to-door to count people. If people are not home or refuse to answer the door, census takers must resort to "last resort information," i.e. asking the neighbors for information about others who live nearby. If no information is available, a residence is "coded as previously coded household"; in other words entered exactly as the prior household from which information was obtained.

This approach can work fairly well in ethnically homogeneous neighborhoods. For Native Americans, however, it is fundamentally flawed. Native Americans tend not to live in clustered residential communities, as

do other people of color. Using the "coded as previously coded household" technique will thus miss many Native Americans. In addition, "a lot of Indian people will keep a real low profile," says Lobo, and when people are asked for the ethnic background of Native American neighbors they are likely to guess that they are Latino or Filipino, rather than American Indian.

"I think the real reason why Indian people are so undercounted is due to the insensitivity and ignorance of the census people," Lobo said, "at one point, after explaining again why census assumptions about people living in congregated communities does not hold for Indian people, one of the census officials in Washington told me 'well, your information does not fit in with our profile of immigrant communities!'"

Lobo also found that once census information is collected, it is then coded in ways that can discriminate against people who don't fit the Census Bureau's assumptions. The census computer is programmed to reject census forms that indicate, for example, that the person who filled it out is 175 years old, or is an 11-year old widow. According to one story, the census coding system was at one point set to reject any form that indicated that the person was American Indian, lived in a high-income urban area and had an educational degree of Master's level or better. The census officials were apparently more ready to believe that the person in question accidently marked "American Indian" than that a Native American could reach such levels.

Luckily, this particular example of census bias was dropped following strenuous objections from a sociologist who happened to be in the room when the question was being discussed. Since the coding process is not made public, however, it is difficult to determine what other kinds of programmed bias might exist in the census computers.

Lobo and Intertribal Friendship House eventually decided that the census evaluation they were being asked to perform was rigged from the start, and they removed themselves from the study.

The census numbers—whether accurate or inaccurate—are important on a number of different levels. The *New York Times* reports that more than 400 programs covering everything from transportation to health and housing are funded based on census figures. Every single person counted in the census is worth between $125 and $400 in federal aid to cities, making an undercount a matter of intense concern to city officials, social service organizations, and community groups in an era of rapidly declining federal assistance and constantly rising needs.

Political influence is also a function of census statistics. Congressional and state legislative apportionment are both determined by census figures. A study conducted by the Joint Center for Political Studies, for example, indicates that three seats currently held by African-American Democrats (Reps. George Crockett and John Conyers of Michigan and William Gray of Philadelphia) may be lost when congressional districts are redrawn based on the 1990 census.

Latino political leaders also claim that significant numbers of people in their communities were missed by census enumerators; the *Guardian* cites congressional testimony by representatives from Texas who dispute figures showing declines in the population of Latino neighborhoods, and steep rises in the populations of mostly white suburbs. Asian political leaders have also complained bitterly about being undercounted; by some estimates Asian communities lost $50 to $110 million in federal revenue over the past ten years based on a 4 to 6 percent undercount in the 1980 census.

Being undercounted, for all people of color, means losing out both on government funding for various programs and on political representation, but for Native Americans there are two other potentially serious repercussions. First, there are a number of new proposals being floated in Congress that would allocate Bureau of Indian Affairs (BIA) money to Native American tribes to administer. Called "New Federalism" by proponents, it would decentralize the funding allocation process. Both total money allocated and the proportions that are allocated to each tribe will be determined by census figures.

Second, in order to get access to BIA funding in the first place (and to get access to a number of other federal programs), a tribe has to be officially recognized by the federal government. When a tribe applies for recognition, census figures are often used as a determining factor. If only a small number can be identified from census figures, the chances of being recognized are correspondingly small.

FIGHTING TOOTH AND NAIL

Despite how important the census figures are to Native Americans, and regardless of the extent of the undercount, there is little that can be done now to change the census figures. The census will give its final collected statistics to the White House on December 15. "At this point," Sally Gallego, director of the Consortium of Indian Nations (CUIN) told the *Trendsletter*, "there is really no recourse." Wilson of the Indian Education Center concurs: "The best we can hope for is that this experience will make [the census process] easier and better the next time."

However, it is likely that much could have been done earlier on to improve the way the census was conducted. Asians, for example, who were upset with the way the census questions were set up in the 1980 census, have a relatively strong presence in Congress, and were willing "to fight tooth and nail" (according to an article in *Asian Week*) to get the Census Bureau to add extra categories to the 1990 census to better define and count the Asian community. After strong pressure by Rep. Robert Matsui (D. California) and others, the Census Bureau added nine Asian subgroups to the census questionnaire. Clearly, the way the census is written and conducted is susceptible to pressure.

In fact, as Forbes makes clear in his writing, the process of making up the census questions carrying out the count is based first and foremost on political considerations. For example, people originally from Latin America, Puerto Rico, and Cuba can only classify themselves as Latino; the category of "Native American" is limited only to North Americans, despite the fact that the majority of Latin Americans are partially or wholly Native American. This is done, suggests Forbes, to subordinate Native American cultures and reduce their political presence—as well as to limit the numbers of people qualifying for federal assistance. A stronger national political presence may have given Native Americans the ability to influence the way the questionnaire is structured; it remains for Native Americans to build the constituency and alliances and develop the tactics necessary for that presence.

POLITICAL LEVERAGE NEEDED

Like the census itself, the post-enumeration survey can also be "adjusted" (with sufficient political leverage). According to Reader, the PES does not include urban Native Americans as a category that could be adjusted. By contrast, Asian Week reported that "[i]n response to months of pressure from Asian American groups, the U.S. Census Bureau announced October 18 that it would make a special

count of Asians and Pacific Islanders in its post-enumeration survey (PES)" to see how many the original census may have missed. Urban Native Americans, therefore, will be the only category of "minority population" not specifically counted by the PES.

Census officials told the Trendsletter that this is more a scientific problem than a political one, and that Native Americans lack sufficient numbers to make a statistically significant sample size, but it seems odd that the census should be so sure of how many there are before counting them. Most observers familiar with the census process readily agree that the whole operation is, in fact, highly political, rather than based on any purely scientific considerations.

On the local level, it is up to cities to sue the Census Bureau if they feel their populations were undercounted. While in many cities Native Americans did participate in so-called "full-count committees," Native American leaders admit that in general their communities had little visibility or political presence. Gallegos, for example, said that CUIN did not attempt to put constant pressure on city governments to recognize the extent of the Native American undercount. Organized local political pressure could conceivably have forced cities to sue the Census Bureau on behalf of their undercounted Native American populations. At best, says Wilson, Native Americans might get an official acknowledgement that the count is inaccurate (census officials contacted by the Trendsletter said this was unlikely). If the Census Bureau is forced to issue such a statement, however, it would at least give Native Americans room to argue that other methods need to be used to determine how their people's needs are met when questions of federal funding arise.

REFERENCES

"Census Outrage: Counting Asians As Caucasians," Asian Week, 7/6/90.

"Census Relents. Will Do Asian Survey," Asian Week, 10/26/90.

"Census Shows City 'Depopulation,'" *Guardian*, 10/10/90.

"Census Takers Recall Resistance and Lies in New York City Tally," *New York Times*, 9/3/90.

"Director Defends Census. Challenging Cities on the Uncounted," *New York Times*, 9/12/90.

Forbes, Jack. "Undercounting Native Americans" (unpublished study).

Gleick, James. "The Census That Doesn't Add Up," *This World*, 7/22/90.

"Many Cities Expected to Challenge Census," *San Francisco Chronicle*, 8/3/90.

"Matsui: Census Pits Asians against Black and Latinos," *Asian Week*, 9/14/90.

NATIVE AMERICAN STATISTICS—
UNITED STATES, 1990

Population

- Over 2 million Indians, Eskimos, and Aleuts. (The 1990 Census found 1.96 million self-identified Indians, up 37.9 percent since 1980.)
- 1.2 million are tribally enrolled (federally recognized). Millions of others have a significant degree of indigenous racial heritage but identify, or are classified, as African American, Chicano, or Latino.
- Of the 85,698 Native Americans in Alaska (termed "Alaska Natives"), more than half are Eskimo, about 36 percent are Indian, and about 12 percent are Aleut.

U.S. Citizenship

- Granted citizenship in 1924 under the Synder Act, although several western states did not allow Indians to vote until much later, for example, not until 1962 in New Mexico.
- Some Indians, such as the traditional Hopi and Iroquois, reject U.S. citizenship in favor of their own Indian citizenship under tribal sovereignty.

Tribes and Nations

- Over 500 federally recognized tribes and nations, including 200 Native villages in Alaska.

- At least 30 tribes are state recognized and are located mainly in the eastern United States and California.
- Many other groups remain unrecognized, and well over a hundred have petitioned for federal recognition.

Identity

- Indians are the only U.S. minority group that must legally prove its minority status (race or ethnicity).
- Most tribes require a one-fourth blood quantum for membership, although the Cherokee of Oklahoma accept anyone who can trace ancestry to their 1906 membership roles. The trend today is for tribes to relax the blood quantum requirement.

Ten Largest Tribes

1. Cherokee, 308,000
2. Navajo, 219,000
3. Chipewa (Ojibwe), 104,000
4. Sioux, 103,000
5. Choctaw, 82,000
6. Pueblo, 53,000
7. Apache, 50,000
8. Iroquois, 49,000
9. Lumbee, 48,000
10. Creek, 44,000

Top Ten Reservations by Size of Indian Population

1. Navajo (Arizona, New Mexico, Utah)
2. Pine Ridge (South Dakota)
3. Ft. Apache (Arizona)
4. Gila River (Arizona)
5. Tohono O'Odahm [Papago] (Arizona)
6. Rosebud (South Dakota)
7. San Carlos Apache (Arizona)
8. Zuni Pueblo (Arizona, New Mexico)
9. Hopi (Arizona)
10. Blackfeet (Montana)

Reservation/Nonreservation Distribution

- 62.3 percent live off-reservation, mostly in urban areas, with 37.7 percent living on reservation lands.
- Most off-reservation people maintain contact with their home areas and reservations, rancherias, villages, or Native communities.
- There are only two reservations in Alaska, and none in Oklahoma, although both states have significantly large Native American populations.

Size—Population and Land Base

- The spectrum ranges from groups of only several hundred members, such as the California Chumash, to the more than 300,000 Cherokee.
- There are over 300 federally recognized reservations, totaling 55 million acres; 44 million acres are held in trust for Indians by the federal government, and 11 million acres are individually owned. This is less than 3 percent of their former territory.
- Indian-held land ranges in size from the 3-acre Chicken Rancheria in California, with 10 Indians, to the 17-million-acre Navajo Nation, with 219,000 tribal members.

Indian Country

- Indian country is a legal concept and is defined as Indian reservations, the Pueblo villages of Arizona and New Mexico, the Native villages of Alaska, and the historical Indian areas of Oklahoma. The term is also used to denote everywhere that Indian people live or refer to as their home.

- Although Native Americans constitute less than 1 percent of the total U.S. population, there are large geographic areas of the United States where Native Americans are the majority, such as the Four Corners region of the Southwest (Arizona, New Mexico, Utah, and Colorado) and rural Alaska.

State Ranking

- The 1990 Census found Oklahoma to have the largest Indian population (252,420), followed by California (242,164), Arizona (203,527), and New Mexico (134,355). Alaska, Washington, North Carolina, Texas, New York, Michigan, and South Dakota all have more than 50,000 but fewer than 100,000 Native Americans.
- 15.6 percent of the population in Alaska is Alaska Native (Indian, Eskimo, or Aleut), followed by New Mexico (8.9 percent), South Dakota (7.3 percent), Montana (6.0 percent), Arizona (5.6 percent), and North Dakota (4.1 percent).

Reservation Resources

- Indian reservations contain 44 million acres in valuable range grazing lands; 5.3 million acres of commercial forest lands; 2.5 million acres of crop lands; 4 percent of all U.S. gas and oil reserves; 40 percent of all U.S. uranium deposits; and over 30 percent of western strippable coal.
- Alaska, alone, has more natural resources than all the rest of the nation put together, and Alaska Natives have title to 44 million acres of this vast state.
- The 1975 American Indian Policy Review Commission of the U.S. Congress found that most Indian reservations have enough economic resources to become self-supporting if Indians fully controlled resource development.

Health

- Although the Indian birth rate is higher than the national average, the death rate is 571.7 per 100,000, as compared with 435.5 nationally. The median age is 23.5 years for Indians, as compared with 30 years for the United States as a whole.
- The rate of tuberculosis is 7.4 times greater than in the non-Indian population.
- The rate of diabetes is 6.8 times greater.

- The rate of alcohol-related deaths is 10 times greater, although fewer Indians drink than do non-Indians.
- The rate of fetal alcohol syndrome is 33 times greater.
- The suicide rate is 15 per 100,000, as compared with 11.7 nationally. The suicide rate among Indian teenagers is 4 times greater than among non-Indian teenagers.
- Many reservation and rural communities do not have running water or adequate sanitation or housing. In the Navajo Nation, 46 percent have no electricity, 54 percent have no indoor plumbing, and 82 percent have no telephone.

Education

- Only 52 percent of Indians finish high school. The dropout rate is 35.5 percent, as compared with 28.8 nationally.
- About 250 tribal languages are still spoken, but their use is discouraged in the classroom. Native American languages and cultures are undervalued by mainstream institutions.
- Only 17 percent of Indians attend college (89,000 are currently enrolled).
- Only 4 percent of Indians graduate from college.
- Only 2 percent of Indians attend graduate school, and Native Americans are grossly underrepresented in the sciences and professions.

Economic Welfare

- The average household income is $20,025, as compared with $30,056 nationally, but the majority of those in the work force earn less than $7,000 per year.
- The poverty rate is 23.7 percent for Indian families, as compared with 10.3 percent nationally.
- Unemployment averages 14.4 percent for Native Americans nationally but is closer to 45 percent for Indians on, or adjacent to, reservations. Unemployment on some reservations approaches 90 percent. For example, Shannon County, South Dakota, where the Pine Ridge Reservation is located, is one of the two poorest counties in the nation.
- Third World living conditions are typical of Indian country.

Note: The results of the 2000 Census of Population were not yet available for this edition of the Reader. The statistics cited above are therefore drawn from the 1990 Census.

1990 U.S. Census; Karen D. Harvey and Lisa D. Harjo, Indian Country: A History of Native People in America (Golden, Colo.: North American Press, 1994), Appendix L (used by permission); Native American Connections, 4, no. 1 (1996–97); American Indian Digest: Contemporary Demographics of the American Indian (Phoenix, Ariz. Thunderbird Enterprises, 1995).

IS URBAN A PERSON OR A PLACE?
CHARACTERISTICS OF URBAN INDIAN COUNTRY

Susan Lobo

Is urban a person or a place? Urban is a place, a setting in which many Indian people at some time in their lives visit, "establish an encampment," or settle, into. Urban doesn't determine self-identity, yet the urban area and urban experiences are the context and some of the factors that contribute to defining identity. The intent of this chapter is to delineate some of the general structural characteristics of urban Indian communities in the United States and to indicate the ways that urban communities interplay with individual and group identity. While most of the focused research for this discussion has been carried out since 1978 in the San Francisco Bay Area, and the principal examples given here are specific to that region, many of the comments also are applicable on a general level to other urban Indian communities such as those found in Seattle, Los Angeles, and Chicago. The works, for example, of Garbarino and Straus in Chicago, Liebow in Phoenix, Shoemaker in Minneapolis, Bramstedt and Weibel-Orlando in Los Angeles, Danziger in Detroit, and

An earlier version of this chapter appeared in the *American Indian Culture and Research Journal*, 22, no. 4 (1998) 89–102 and this version appeared in the *American Indian Urban Experience*, edited by Susan Lobo and Kurt Peters (Walnut Creek, California: Altamira Press, 2000).

Guillemin in Boston indicate parallels and counterpoints to the regional focus of this chapter.[1]

Each Indian community throughout the United States and Canada has its unique character. Yet, traveling from one to another, visiting friends and family, and participating in events around the country; one notices many underlying similarities that characterize urban Indian country, and these fundamental similarities create a setting that is "like home" in the city. Some of the significant factors influencing the parallels among different urban Indian communities, as well as each community's unique qualities, include the historical role played by the relocation program and other types of policy-driven external influences; the degree of proximity and ease of travel and communication between cities and tribal areas, reservations, and homelands; and the availability of employment, housing, and educational opportunities in urban areas. An in-depth comparative study of various urban Indian communities is long, long overdue.

This chapter is based on long-term applied work, research, and personal engagement in the San Francisco Bay Area American Indian community. I began in 1978, as a co-founder of, and have continued as the coordinator of, the Community

History Project located at the Oakland American Indian Center, Intertribal Friendship House (IFH). The center was established in 1955 and, along with the Chicago Indian Center, is one of the oldest urban Indian centers in the United States. It was founded in response to the federal relocation program and to the incipient demographic shift by Indian people from rural to urban areas that was then getting under way.

Intertribal Friendship House, as one of the early urban Indian institutions nationally, and the Bay Area Indian community overall continues to loom large in the Indian country cognitive map. Many Bay Area Indian residents remark that wherever one goes, no matter how remote, how seemingly unlikely, you can bet that whomever you may be talking to will say, "Sure I know Oakland. We used to go to the Wednesday night dinners at IFH all the time," or "We were there for a while when I was young and I remember my Mom took me over to see the buffalos at the San Francisco zoo when I was six, for my birthday. Boy, they were sure in bad shape. I still remember her saying that they didn't know how to really take care of them." IFH is identified by many as the emotional "heart" of the Bay Area Indian community. It is the ideal urban Indian community crossroads, where the Community History Project, a photographic and oral history archive, has developed. This is a collection of contemporary urban-focused historical materials that is referred to as a community resource archive because of the active involvement of "the community" in both formulating and building the archives and in using it for purposes identified by the community itself.

The IFH Community History Project, which started as a narrowly defined oral history project, has grown into an extensive Indian-controlled and community-based research unit and archive of taped oral histories, photographs, videos and films, documents, and ephemera focusing on the Bay Area American Indian community from the 1940s to the present. This is, to my knowledge, one of the very few, and also the most extensive, archive emphasizing Indian history within an urban area. It is also a working archive, open to the Indian community as well as to outside researchers, and it is actively circulated, added to, reformulated, interpreted, and used for a wide array of educational and advocacy purposes. Immersion in this material, participation in the continual flow of community events and activities, and working jointly with Indian community members on an ongoing basis on a variety of community projects are the foundations for the description and analysis that follows.

Methodologically, this kind of deep, long-term, and unabashedly personal involvement in a community allows for an understanding of both those aspects of the community that shift and those aspects that persist over time, sometimes stretching across generations. For example, there are those delicate balances of power, informed by kinship and tribal affiliation, or the routes that leadership and alliance formation take, all unfolding fluidly over long periods of time.

THE COMMUNITY

For American Indians living in the Bay Area and for our definitional purposes here, the Indian community is not a geographic location with clustered residency or neighborhoods, but rather it is fundamentally a widely scattered and frequently shifting network of relationships with locational nodes found in organizations and activity sites of special significance. It is a distinct community that answers needs for affirming and activating identity; it creates contexts for carrying out the necessary activities of community life; and it provides a wide range of circumstances and symbols that encourage "Indian" relationships at the family and community levels.

The American Indian community in the San Francisco Bay Area is characterized here on a general level as a social group in which:

1. Community members recognize a shared identity.
2. There are shared values, symbols and history.
3. Basic institutions have been created and sustained.
4. There have emerged consistent features of social organization such as those related to social control and the definition of distinctive and specialized gender-related and age-related roles.

There are geographic markers around the Bay that set the stage for community activities: the enclosing hills, the Bay, and the bridges that connect the East Bay with San Francisco and San Francisco with Marin County. However, these geographic features only set the stage for the "Indian map" of the area of shared abstract connotations, where people speak of "going to the Healing Center," a residential treatment center for women and their children, or nodding with the head to the north of downtown Oakland and saying, "over by CRC," an American Indian family and child assistance agency. People in the Indian community know where these points of reference are; those not participating in the community would not know. Or, for exam-

ple, when an Indian person comments, quite possibly totally out of context, "You going to Stanford?" the question is not, "Do you attend Stanford University?" but rather, "Will I see you at the Stanford Pow-wow this May?" Or when someone says "I saw your niece up at Hilltop," the reference is to a high-profile Indian bar, not to be confused with a shopping mall of the same name. Each of these examples illustrates one of the ways that Indian people in the Bay Area talk about or interpret their environment, which is both a setting for community as a place and is also deeply intertwined with the network of relatedness that ties the community members together. Theodoratus and LaPena express this idea well in reference to Wintu sacred geography, "It [this paper] is about topographical features that are the embodiment of Wintu expression of an ordinary and nonordinary world. It is about a concept of land and interpretations of that natural universe that translate into a coherent world."[2] In the case of the Bay Area Indian community vision of community, it is both the topographical features and the built environment that are a part of creating this "coherent world."

This physical environment, while the backdrop and the grounding for much of the community activity, is not "the community," which instead finds its focus in relationship dynamics and in the more abstract realm of shared knowledge that informs and shapes actions. Nor is an urban Indian community situated in an immutable, bounded territory as is a reservation, but rather it exists within a fluidly defined region with niches of resources and boundaries that respond to needs and activities, perhaps reflecting a reality closer to the way Native homelands were before the imposition of reservation borders. For example, with the development and flourishing of D-Q University, an Indian-controlled community college, the conceptualization of the Bay Area Indian community extended sixty miles to the north to include this institution as an outlaying entity.

On tribal homelands, a major source of identity is embodied in the land and, often, the old stories and songs that tie personal reality to time and place. As Basso notes, "Knowledge of place is therefore closely linked to knowledge of the self, to grasping one's position in the larger scheme of things, including one's own community, and to securing a confident sense of who one is as a person."[3] Yet, in an urban community there essentially is no land base, except for a few recently purchased buildings and properties. Or, on the other hand, as someone recently pointed out to me, "All of it is our urban territory." In this urban context, the Indian organizations come to powerfully represent Indian "space" or "a place that is Indian" and are intimately tied to identity. Consequently, the control, the programs, and the guiding values of these organizations are under constant scrutiny, negotiation, and adjustment by core community members who act as community arbitrators.

To many outside the urban Indian community, it is an invisible population, not only because of the abstract and nongeographically clustered nature of the community but also because of the continued existence of a series of stereotypes regarding Indian people. A widespread and mistaken assumption held by the general public is that American Indians have "vanished" or live overwhelmingly on reservations in rural areas. In reality, this is an expanding population, and the majority of Indian people now live in urban areas. From the perspective of much of the social science literature, as reflected in federal and state policies, as well as in criteria frequently utilized by funding sources, there is an oft-cited mindset that imposes a dichotomy between urban and rural, based on the lingering stereotype that *Indian* is synonymous with rural and that urban is somehow not genuinely Indian. Although there are certainly differences in these two types of settings, establishing rural/urban as the defining characteristic of identity is not realistic from an Indian point of view and serves to further officially alienate Indian people from homelands. One of the most notorious recent policies reflecting this attitude was relocation, initiated in the 1950s and based on government assumptions that Indian people, once removed or relocated from tribal homelands, would become urban . . . definitively. Conversely, for many Indian people the urban areas are visualized at one level more as an extension of home territory or, as one person put it, "our urban encampment out here." For those living in the city, even those a few generations removed from tribal homelands, these strong linkages to "back home" are, for the most part, not broken. One simply extends the sense of territory, often keenly aware, for example, that sacred places are found at home and that after death one will very likely be buried there. With third- and fourth-generation urban people, this connection to home may change and take new forms, but it nevertheless continues.

The underlying Native sense of community—if viewed fundamentally as a network of relatedness that has become structured in many tribal homelands into formalized, federally prescribed tribes—reemerges in the city, as the rigid, bounded "tribe" demanded of federally recognized tribalness falls away. The federal

government's image of tribes as social entities within a geographically rigid demarcat-
ed territory or reservation, governed by a
body of elected officials, and with stringent-
ly designated criteria for membership is not
transferred to urban Indian communities.
Here in cities, in contrast, the social entity is
reconstituted with a structuring based on a
network of relatedness; the fluid territory
has changing outer limits; there is no
overarching formalized governing body; and
membership is defined by a series of strongly situational and to some degree negotiable
criteria.

The most striking urban parallel to the
tribal political structuring found on rural
reservations is the legal not-for-profit status
of many urban Indian organizations, in
which there are a governing board of directors, by-laws, and possibly membership lists.
However, Indian people in the city, in contrast to the situation in a reservation tribal
setting, are not governed by these
organizations, nor do the organizations
establish and enforce criteria for community membership. Also in the city, people may
choose whether to become active in any
particular organization at any specific time.

Although structured differently, the
urban community comes to hold many connotations for Indian people that are similar
to those of the tribe. The urban community
gives a sense of belonging, a need to look in-
ward to this social entity, and a feeling of
responsibility to contribute to the well-being
of the members, via support of the continuity and flourishing of urban institutions. In
the Bay Area, one occasionally hears joking
reference to the Indian community as "The
Urban Tribe."

One of the underlying objectives of the
federal relocation program initiated in the
1950s was the assimilation of American
Indians into an envisioned mainstream. Yet,
to many Indian people in the Bay Area, the
existence and resiliency of the Indian community are expressions of resistance to pressure and domination by the non-Indian
world. One factor in this persistence is the
fluid network-based social structure. As
Indian people often explain it, the community itself has the potential for regeneration.
The community is ephemeral in nature, as
the trickster Coyote has taught people to
appreciate, with the power to continually
take new forms and thus endure. Or it is
described as being like the old-time warriors'
strategy to disperse, vanish, become invisible, and then regroup to fight again another
day. This dynamic is a familiar one to Indian
people, who throughout the history of
Indian–white relations and before have
sought ways to persist as individuals and as
Peoples. The institutions in the Indian community are in continual flux, able to disas-
semble and reassemble. Yet through all of
this motion, there is an underlying network
structure that allows for persistence.

The urban community in addition to
having become the doorway to urban jobs
and education also functions as a refuge for
those who have unsolvable problems or who
are deemed undesirable in their home reservation area. The villain Emo, in Silko's classic novel *Ceremony*, is last mentioned leaving
New Mexico: "They told him to never come
back around here. The old man said that. I
heard he went to California. . . . 'California,'
Tayo repeated softly, 'that's a good place for
him.'"[4] The urban community is also a gateway for those such as Jackson discusses who
have been alienated from their tribal roots
and who wish to reidentify as Indian.[5]

There are also those with hazily defined distant Indian ancestry who create a
niche for themselves in the urban Indian
community and who are generally accepted
if they make a substantial contribution to the

community well-being. Increasingly, the urban community is a doorway into Indian country for Indian people who were "adopted out" in infancy or childhood—that is, were raised in foster care or adopted by non-Indian families—and who seek to reestablish their Indianness in adulthood. Some of these mechanisms of reidentification have been discussed by Snipp in regard to the increasing U.S. census count of American Indians.[6]

Also, the American Indian community is characterized by a geographic mobility as people move into and out of the city, make return visits to their rural home territories or reservations, or sometimes return there for good. People speak of circulating through or of establishing a temporary urban living situation as a way of indicating that living in the Bay Area is viewed by some as an extension of their original territory. At the same time, people often speak longingly of "back home," and there are shared in-group and tribally specific understandings of the connotations that "back home" holds. These are expressed in jokes ("You know that one about the Doggy Diner down on East 12th and the two Sioux guys who just come into town?"), in music (WithOut Rezervation—WOR, the name of a rap group whose CD cover speaks of the group's tie to "the mean streets of Oakland"), and in reference to aspects of the natural world. Movement through space, as movement through time, is a part of living.

In addition to increasing dramatically in population over the past fifty years, the Bay Area Indian community, as characteristic of many urban Indian communities, has become increasingly diverse and complex in the following ways:

1. *There has been a proliferation of organizations,* the crucial nodes on the network of community. This array of organizations has become increasingly specialized as community needs become apparent and funding and human resources become available. For example, the generalized multiservice Indian Center has spawned a now-separate preschool and a number of other educational efforts as well as many specialized cultural arts and social activities and social service–focused organizations and projects.

2. *The community is now multigenerational.* Whereas those first to come into the Bay Area through relocation in the 1950s were primarily young single people and young families, the infant fourth generation since relocation is now often seen playing at their mothers' feet during meetings. This generational layering means that experiences, urban personal histories, and orientation toward both urban and rural contexts have become increasingly varied. The urban angst expressed in the now-classic and still-enjoyed Floyd Red Crow Westerman songs of the 1970s such as "Quiet Desperation" and "Going Home" are contrasted with the more hardhitting contemporary urban Indian music.

3. *The community is multitribal,* and as intertribal marriages continue to occur, the children and grandchildren are themselves often multitribal. Being multitribal has the potential to enrich each child's identity but also to create complexities related to tribal enrollment and tribally based cultural knowledge. Recent research in the Bay Area in which 290 women were interviewed indicated ninety-two tribes represented, thirty-five in-state tribes and fifty-seven from out of state.[7]

4. *The community is linked* in increasingly diverse ways to often geographically distant people and places in Indian homelands. The term *Indian country* has come to include the urban communities.

Family members visit from home, and visits to home are made to attend funerals, visit relatives, or take children there for the summer. Many people return home for personal and spiritual renewal. Some return home to avoid problems with the law. Some older people decide to retire back home. Medicine people frequently come out to the city for ceremonies, or people return home for ceremonies. There is the recent and increasing presence in the city of the nearby "Casino Tribes" via their in-town offices and staff. There are also those living on the streets who follow an annual seasonal route between various cities and rural areas.

5. *There is increased economic and class diversity in the Bay Area Indian community*, some resulting from educational opportunities that first became available in the late 1960s and some that are the result of business and professional successes. There are those living hand to mouth on the streets, and there are those arriving in splendor at the gala annual American Indian Film Festival at the Palace of Fine Arts in San Francisco. Those living on the streets are not excluded from the community, nor are those living in the hills of Berkeley. In fact they may all sit at the same long table at the Indian Center during a community feast. There are the many whose education does not include high school graduation, and there are those completing their doctorates in ethnic studies, anthropology, or education at the University of California at Berkeley or Stanford, or those taking advanced computer courses at the community-based United Indian Nations in Oakland.

6. *There is now a recognized urban history,* and a community persona, that is frequently referenced and that creates a framework for shared identity. A series of events and people, tied to dates, is shared in the minds of community members as being symbolically significant. For example, particularly memorable are the occupation of Alcatraz, the Bay Area Princess competitions, the old Intertribal Friendship House Music Festivals, and the annual Stanford Pow-wow. Everyone knows who is being referred to when there is mention of Floyd or Bill within specific contexts. And the old-timers have full recollections of Walter and Mrs. Carnes. Remembrances are filled with shared connotations. "Remember when they drew the ticket for that raffled car, there was standing room only, and it was the director's girlfriend who got it!" Ah, yes. And what about the meeting twenty-three years ago, "And your grandmother stood up and in front of everyone said that about my aunt at that board meeting." Everyone gives "that look," remembering this event well; if they weren't there they certainly heard about it in detail. A well-known activist leader recalled recently to a group, "And we started right here. We started the Longest Walk to Washington, D.C., right at this door." Many nodded in agreement and remembrance. These are parables of life in the city and a means of validating the shared historical content of urban living as a community.

IDENTITY

The defining of "Who is Indian?" and the issue of who does the identifying are emotion-laden topics anywhere in Indian country, with implications of inclusion and exclusion. For example, there is self-identity; there is identity externally imposed; there are the situationally appropriate shifts in identity; and there are the shifts in identity that may occur over a lifetime. In urban areas, although no role exists comparable to tribal roles, there are a number of other ways that one is identified by self and others as a community member and as Indian. The urban Indian community is most frequently invisible to the non-Indian world, both informally in the general public mind that has not discarded the stereotype that everything Indian is rural and in the past, and formally via institutions such as the U.S. Census Bureau, which has yet to adequately count urban Indian people.[8] Likewise the federal emphasis on ancestry as the outstanding defining criteria, represented in a blood quantum model, is a much narrower and limiting criterion than that found in urban Indian communities.

From within the urban community, there is a very different perspective regarding membership than that found on those tribal homelands that are structured by federally imposed criteria. As is defining the urban "territory," defining membership in the urban Indian community and the link to Indianness, as defined by the community, is fluid. Membership in the Indian community is known and agreed upon through informal consensus. Indian people feel comfortable with this approach. This is the way it is, through consensus, rather than written on a piece of paper, a document. There is a shared understanding by participants of the social boundaries of the American Indian community as well as of membership within the community. These boundaries and the community membership are fluid, however, and always under review and negotiation. Those non-Indians who do not participate, who are external to the community, are not aware of these dynamics that tie the community together and mark who is "in the community," and who is not. Defining Indianness in the city is therefore essentially released from the burden of the formalized documentation

imposed on federally recognized tribes. For example, recently, in preparation for the board election at one of the urban organizations in the Bay Area, a board member, as a strategy to channel the election outcome, sent out a letter indicating that, in order to vote, community members should bring documentation proving they were Indian. Many people, those who could bring forward documentation and those who could not, were acutely offended; the strategy backfired, and the board member was roundly criticized for taking an inappropriate stance. Her request was ignored at the polls.

Another example in an urban setting of the rejection and disdain for a federally imposed tribal formula emanating from governmental demands for enrollment numbers was demonstrated by a group of Bay Area Indian artists in protest of laws requiring proof of Indianness in order to exhibit their art as Indian artists. One artist, Hulleah Tsinhnahjinnie, took a series of defiant photographs of herself with numbers painted across her forehead. In essence, these people are asserting, "I am Indian because I say I am." "I am Indian because you know me and my family and see me participate in the community." "And I am Indian because I know what it is to be Indian: the protocols, the jokes, the knowledge of shared history, the racism and struggle that are part of who we all are." "Trying to identify me as a number is fucked."

Thus, in urban areas Indian identity is defined through:

1. *Ancestry:* Does a person have Indian relatives and ancestors and function as a member of an Indian extended family?
2. *Appearance:* Does a person "look Indian"?
3. *Cultural elements:* Is the person knowledgeable of the culture of his or her People and of those pan-Indian values and

social expectations shared within the urban Indian community?

4. *Indian community participation:* Does the person "come out" for Indian events and activities in the Indian community and contribute to the community well-being?

The weight and combination given to these elements vary situationally to determine Indian identity and to some extent are always under community assessment, shifting with the changing times. For example, there are many people well accepted in the Bay Area Indian community who may not "look very Indian" or who may not have verifiable documented Indian ancestry, yet through a long history of active participation in and contribution to the community well-being, as well as by demonstrating a thorough understanding of Indian values and protocols, will be deemed without hesitation to be a member of the Indian community . . . until a conflict arises, then this combination may be critically scrutinized.

Also in an urban area there is an element of choice as each individual determines to what degree and in what circumstances tribal membership and urban Indian community participation are actualized. Thus, situationally, individuals may choose which criteria of Indianness may be activated and when. Some Indian people living in the Bay Area are affiliated with a home tribe but do not choose to participate in or identify with the urban Indian community during a particular time in their life. Others are actively engaged as members of their home tribe and are also participants in, and identify with, the Bay Area American Indian community. Others may not be enrolled and may not be active participants in their home tribe, yet they may be very involved and active in the urban community. There are also some

people who, though identifying as Indian, neither participate in nor identify with the urban community or a home tribe. There are some people who have chosen at some point in their life, as a result of racism, assimilation pressures, or out-marrying, to pass as a non-Indian, for example as Mexican, Italian, or white. Increasingly, many of these individuals are choosing to reevaluate their racial self-identity and often to reestablish their American Indian identity by reintegrating into and becoming active in an urban Indian community.[9]

The position of children in the urban community is a telling one. In an urban community as tribally diverse as the Bay Area, there may come to be, after two or three generations, a number of children who, while undeniably Indian genetically may have difficulty becoming enrolled in any one particular tribe because of their mixed tribal ancestry and tribally specific criteria for enrollment. There is also the consideration that some children with a mother from a patrilineal tribe and a father from a matrilineal tribe may not be recognized by, or enrolled in, either tribe. These children of mixed tribal heritage and those of Indian–non-Indian heritage who may have difficulties related to formal tribal enrollment, often, nevertheless are active and accepted participants in the urban Indian community. Indian parents who are involved in the Bay Area community, and whose children for one of the reasons sketched here do not have strong ties to a home tribe, often express concern that their children will lose their identity as American Indians and they agonize over the problems for their children that may be associated with tribal enrollment. A major theme of activities in the Bay Area Indian community is that participation validates and heightens Indian identity, and parents frequently facilitate their children's participation, knowing that this participation will foster a strong sense of Indian identity, as well as acceptance by the community. For example, children may join in special educational efforts such as attending Hintil Kuu Ca's preschool and after-school programs, may participate with the family in pow-wows and other activities, or may come with their families to events such as the Wednesday Night Dinner at Intertribal Friendship House.

CONCLUDING REMARKS

This chapter raises the caution that a much-used concept such as "community" may not be as simple, or as one-dimensional, as it appears. It is important to pay close attention to the ways that people, and communities of people, perceive and define their environment, both the physical and social aspects.

Some of the fundamental ways that the complex urban Indian community in the San Francisco Bay Area has constituted itself and, in turn, how this community structuring is related to identity have been delineated here. Conceptually, the community here is primarily abstract, based as it is on a series of dynamic relationships and shared meanings, history, and symbols rather than on the more commonly assumed clustered residential and commercial neighborhood. Although most Indian people living in the San Francisco Bay Area are by and large adept users of the roads and freeways, take advantage of the recreational opportunities the parks offer, and live in a wide range of apartments and houses, this physical environment, while the backdrop and the physical grounding for much of the community activity, is not "the community," which instead finds its focus in relationship dynamics and the more abstract realm of shared knowledge that informs and shapes actions.

NOTES

1. Merwyn S. Garbarino, "Life in the City: Chicago," in *American Indian in Urban Society,* ed. J. Waddell and R. Watson (Boston: Little, Brown and Co., 1971); Terry Straus, *Retribalization in Urban Indian Communities* (San Francisco, paper presented at the American Anthropological Association Meetings, 1996) and *Native Chicago* (Chicago, University of Chicago Press, 1998); Edward B. Liebow, "Urban Indian Institutions in Phoenix: Transformation from Headquarters City to Community," *Journal of Ethnic Studies,* 18; no. 4 (1991); Nancy Shoemaker, "Urban Indians and Ethnic Choices: American Indian Organizations in Minneapolis, 1920–1950," *Western History Quarterly* (November 1988); Wayne G. Bramstedt, *Corporate Adaptations of Urban Migrants: American Indian Voluntary Associations in the Los Angeles Metropolitan Area* (Ph.D. diss., University of California, 1977); Joan Weibel-Orlando, *Indian Country, L.A.: Maintaining Ethnic Community in Complex Society* (Urbana: University of Illinois Press, 1991); Edmund Jefferson Danziger Jr., *Survival and Regeneration: Detroit's American Indian Community* (Detroit: Wayne State Press, 1991); Jeanne Guillemin,

Urban Renegades: The Cultural Strategy of American Indians (New York: Columbia University Press, 1975).

2. Dorothea J. Theodoratus and Frank LaPena, "Wintu Sacred Geography," in *California Indian Shamanism,* ed. Lowell Bean (Menlo Park, Calif.: Ballena Press, 1992), 211.

3. Keith H. Basso, *Wisdom Sits in Places: Landscape and Language among the Western Apache* (Albuquerque: University of New Mexico Press, 1996), 34.

4. Leslie Marmon Silko, *Ceremony* (New York: Viking Press, 1977), 260.

5. Deborah Jackson, *Urban Indian Identity and the Violence of Silence* (San Francisco, paper presented at the American Anthropological Association Meetings, 1996). Another version of this paper appeared in the *American Indian Culture and Research Journal,* 22, no. 4 (1998).

6. C. Matthew Snipp, *American Indians: The First of This Land* (New York: Russell Sage Foundation, 1989).

7. Dorie Klein, Elaine Zahnd, Bohdan Kolody, Sue Holtby, and Loraine T. Midanik, *Pregnant and Parenting American Indian Study* (Berkeley: Western Consortium for Public Health and San Diego State University Foundation, 1995).

8. For discussion of the Indian undercount in the Bay Area, see Susan Lobo, *Oakland's American Indian Community: History, Social Organization and Factors That Contribute to Census Undercount* (Washington, D.C.: Center for Survey Methods Research, Bureau of the Census, 1990) and Susan Lobo, *American Indians in the San Francisco Bay Area and the 1990 Census: Ethnographic Exploratory Research Report no. 18* (Washington, D.C.: Center for Survey Methods Research, Bureau of the Census, 1992).

9. Snipp, *American Indians.*

PART REVIEW

DISCUSSION QUESTIONS

Introduction

1. From the information presented in this part introduction, how would you describe Native American studies? How does it differ from the academic disciplines of anthropology and history?

2. Who is Guaman Poma? Why might one conclude that Native American studies is not an entirely new field?

Phillip Wearne, *Definitions and Diversity*

1. How many indigenous people live in the Americas today? Enumerate some of the main peoples or nations and their geographic location. Describe their linguistic diversity.

2. How is the concept of *nation* defined, and what is its relevance to Native American peoples in their struggle for self-determination?

3. What is the significance of land, or Mother Earth, to Native Americans?

Anthony Long and Katherine Beaty Chiste, *The Canadian Natives*

1. What are the three major kinds of Native American peoples in Canada? What is the difference between status Indians, treaty Indians, and non-status Indians?

Ward Churchill, *The Crucible of American Indian Identity*

1. Explain the blood quantum principle that is used by the federal government, and most contemporary tribal governments, to determine Indian tribal identity. How does this differ from the way that Indian communities traditionally determined tribal membership in the past?

2. How has the blood quantum method of determining Indianness led to statistical genocide and land alienation?

3. What, according to Churchill, is the solution in "the way ahead?"

John Anner, *To the U.S. Census Bureau, Native Americans Are Practically Invisible*

1. Why are Native Americans practically invisible to the U.S. Census Bureau?

2. Why does the census process regarding Indian people deserve the name *statistical genocide?*

Native American Statistics— United States, 1990

1. In view of what you read in Anner's chapter about the U.S. Census count of Indians, how accurate do you think the information is in this box?

2. How many people in the United States claimed Native American identity in the 1990 census? Which three tribes or nations had the largest population? Name the two largest reservations.

Susan Lobo, *Is Urban a Person or a Place?*

1. Explain why the term *urban Indian* inaccurately defines Indian identity.

2. Describe the characteristics of the "Indian community," and explain why is it a more meaningful concept in understanding the urban experience than is geographic location. How has the Indian community in urban areas become increasingly diverse and complex?

KEY TERMS

assimilation
Bering Strait land bridge theory
Charlottetown Accord
culture area
ethnic fraud
ethnographic present
First Nations
General Allotment Act of 1887
Guaman Poma
identity politics
IFH Community History Project
Indian country

Indian Reorganization Act of 1934
Lakota "winter counts"
mestizo
Metis
"new Indian" movement
Nunavut
Pachamama
Quechua
relocation
statistical genocide
urban Indian community
wampum

SUGGESTED READINGS

CAMPBELL, GREGORY R. "The Politics of Counting: Critical Reflections on the Depopulation Question of Native North America." Pages 67–131 in *The Unheard Voices: American Indian Responses to the Columbian Quincentenary 1492–1992*. Ed. CAROLE M. GENTRY and DONALD A. GRINDE JR. *Los Angeles:* UCLA American Indian Studies Center, 1994. 67–131.

CHAMPAGNE, DUANE, ed. *Native America: Portrait of the Peoples*. Foreword by DENNIS BANKS. Detroit: Visible Ink Press, 1995. [This is an abbreviated version of *The Native North American Almanac*. Ed. Champagne. Detroit: Gale Research, 1994.]

CROZIER-HOGLE, LOIS, and DARRYL BABE WILSON. *Surviving in Two Worlds: Contemporary Native American Voices*. Austin: University of Texas Press, 1997.

DAVIS, MARY B., ed. *Native America in the Twentieth Century: An Encyclopedia*. New York: Garland Publishing, 1994.

DELORIA, VINE, JR. *Behind the Trail of Broken Treaties: An American Declaration of Independence*. Austin: University of Texas Press, 1984.

FORBES, JACK D. "Basic Concepts for Understanding Native History and Culture." In *Native Americans of California and Nevada*. Happy Camp, Calif.: Naturegraph Publishers, 1982.

ISMAELILLO and ROBIN WRIGHT, eds. *Native Peoples in Struggle: Cases from the Fourth Russell Tribunal & Other International Forums*. Bombay, N.Y.:

Anthropology Resource Center and E.R.I.N. Publications, 1982.

KROUSE, SUSAN APPLEGATE. "Kinship and Identity: Mixed Bloods in Urban Indian Communities." *American Indian Culture and Research Journal*, 23, no. 1 (1999): 73–89.

MORRISON, BRUCE R., and C. RODERICK Wilson, eds. *Native Peoples: The Canadian Experience*. 2d ed. Toronto: McClelland & Stewart, 1995.

ORTIZ, SIMON. *Woven Stone*. Tucson: University of Arizona Press, 1992.

OSWALT, WENDELL H., and SHARLOTTE NEELY. *This Land Was Theirs*. Mountain View, Calif. Mayfield Publishing, 1996.

PAVEL, D. MICHAEL, TIMOTHY SANCHEZ, and AMBER MACHAMER. "Ethnic Fraud, Native Peoples, and Higher Education." *Thought Land Action*, 10, no. 1 (Spring 1994): 91–100.

PRICE, JOHN. *Indians of Canada: Cultural Dynamics*. Salem, Wis. Sheffield Publishing, 1970.

PRUCHA, FRANCIS PAUL. *Atlas of American Indian Affairs*. Lincoln: University of Nebraska Press, 1990.

SPICER, EDWARD H. *The American Indians: Dimensions of Ethnicity*. Cambridge, Mass. Belnap Press, 1980.

STIFFARM, LENORE A., with PHIL LANE JR. "The Demography of Native North America: A Question of American Indian Survival." Pages 23–53 in *The State of Native North America:*

Genocide, Colonization, and Resistance. Ed. M. ANNETTE JAIMES. Boston: South End Press, 1992.

TALBOT, STEVE. "Anthropology versus Native American Studies: Theoretical and Ethical Implications." Pages 133–155 in *The Unheard Voices: American Indian Responses to the Columbian Quincentenary 1492–1992.* Ed. CAROLE M. GENTRY and DONALD A. GRINDE JR. Los Angeles: UCLA American Indian Studies Center, 1994.

TAYLOR, DREW HAYDEN. *Funny, You Don't Look Like One: Observations from a Blue-Eyed Ojibway.* Penticton B.C., Canada: Theytus Books, 1996.

THORNTON, RUSSELL, ed. "Institutional and Intellectual Histories of Native American Studies," and "The Demography of Colonialism and 'Old' and 'New' Native Americans." In *Studying Native America: Problems and Prospects.* Madison: University of Wisconsin Press, 1998.

WALDMAN, CARL. *Atlas of the North American Indian.* New York: Facts on File, 1985.

II
THE HIDDEN HERITAGE

I don't imagine the turquoise bracelet the dusky wash makes,
or the red hills circling the dreaming eye of this sacred land.
I don't imagine anything but the bracelet around my wrist,
the red scarf around my neck as I urge my pretty horse home.

Joy Harjo "The Hidden Heritage"*

The Native American heritage is the cultural foundation of the Americas. Whereas the European, African, Asian, and Latino/Chicano heritages are important to a plural society, it is nonetheless the heritage of indigenous America that is common to us all. It is this heritage, that of the First Americans, which makes all of us uniquely American with respect to the rest of the world, whether we reside in North, Central, or South America. This heritage is made up of two parts. First, there is the biological or genetic legacy of indigenous America, which forms the major racial ancestry of most Latin American populations. Second, there is the Native American historical and cultural legacy, in which, to an even larger degree, all citizens of the Americas share, regardless of their specific racial or ethnic or national background.[1]

In Part I we examined the tremendous indigenous ethnic diversity of the Americas. Indigenous peoples today number at least 40 million; most of them live in Central and South America. Yet, when European colonists first invaded, there were perhaps as many as 100 million Native people in the Western Hemisphere. At that time, population density was greatest in the highlands of Peru, Colombia, Yucatan, and the Valley of Mexico. Linguists estimate that there were originally at least fifty-six language families and many more totally distinct languages. Although many languages were lost in the years following the European invasion, others continue to flourish. For example, today, Runasimi ("language of the people"), or Quechua, is the indigenous language of a large portion of the populations in the South American highlands, with about 10 million speakers in all. Millions more speak Aymara, and still several million more in southern Mexico and Guatemala speak one of the many Mayan languages. The oral traditions of these many indigenous linguistic groups find expression in many contemporary cultural forms, such as music and oratory. Also, several thousand words in Spanish and English derive from languages native to this hemisphere.

In terms of the cultural heritage, there exists today some knowledge and appreciation for the Aztec, Mayan, and Incan civilizations of Central and South America—the monumental architecture, urbanism, astronomy, mathematics, food and mining technology, government, religious ceremonialism, and other cultural contributions. Yet, how many people are aware that a thousand years before the founding of Christianity in the Middle East there was a thriving Mound Builder civilization in what is the present-day eastern United States? The Temple Mound Builders rivaled Egypt in terms of their urban, social complexity and monumental

*"The Hidden Heritage," from *Secrets from the Center of the World* by Joy Harjo and Stephen Strom. © 1989 the Arizona Board of Regents. Reprinted with permission of the University of Arizona Press.
[1]Portions of the following discussion are taken from Jack D. Forbes, *Native Americans of the Far West: A Handbook* (Berkeley, Calif.: Far West Laboratory for Research and Educational Development, 1969); and Steve Talbot, "Why the Native American Heritage Should Be Taught in College," *Indian Historian*, 17, no. 1 (January 1974).

architecture. Yet this impressive cultural development is almost never mentioned in U.S. history and humanities texts and remains a part of the hidden heritage of North America.

Even though a relatively small population in the United States, Native Americans continue to be an indirect but vital factor in the many political, economic, and moral issues of American life, such as protecting the environment and fostering gender equality, grassroots democracy and a sense of community, respect for elders, family values, spiritual life, and the struggle against multinational corporations. In short, these and other aspects of the hidden heritage of indigenous America make the continuing Indian contribution to the United States an important one, far beyond the number of tribal Americans in the general population. It is simply impossible on empirical grounds to understand history, government and political science, art, social studies, and the humanities without recognizing that a fundamental part of the American heritage is Native American.

The way of life of the majority population in the United States is often referred to as "Western" (i.e., a part of Western civilization). In point of fact, however, much that is basic to this way of life originated in the Middle East and North Africa. Consider, for example, the Moorish influence in the Iberian Peninsula, which North African peoples occupied for seven centuries before the Spanish conquest of the Americas. Islamic scholar Ibn-Khaldoun (born in Tunisia in A.D. 1312) studied and taught chemistry, engineering, geography, literature, mathematics, physics, psychology, and sociology. One could contend that the European Renaissance was the result, at least in part, of this North African influence. Thus, the culture of the dominant Spanish and Anglo-American populations of the Americas is, from its European foundation, a very mixed or heterogeneous one.

Once in the Americas, the commingling with the indigenous cultures made the sum total even more of an amalgam. An acknowledgment of these cultural roots is exemplified by *La Plaza de las Trés Culturas* (Plaza of the Three Cultures) found in Mexico City, which celebrates the Spanish heritage, the Indian heritage, and the resulting Mexican "race" with its mestizo culture.

A mixed cultural heritage also became the common legacy of North American people, which derives a significant part of its character from contributions made by Native American groups, although this fact is poorly understood and seldom acknowledged. Even as the seventeenth- and eighteenth-century English way of life was being modified by forest warfare tactics, the fur trade, the Indian slave trade, dressed deerskin clothing (such as that worn by Daniel Boone), the canoe, the toboggan, the political influence of the Iroquois confederation, thousands of native place names, hundreds of Indian words, mining and food technologies, and numerous other items, Anglo-Americans persisted in obscuring the origin of these cultural changes. Each trait borrowed from the Indians by Euro-Americans was emotionally assimilated and thereby became, in the popular mind, a "frontier" or "American" trait.

From a Native perspective, an understanding of heritage comes from knowing about the beginning of time, when the cosmos was taking form and life came into being. Often this understanding is based on Old Stories and the songs that are intimately linked to the land. Pultizer Prize–winning Kiowa author Scott Momaday in *The Way to Rainy Mountain* referred to his homeland, the western plains of Oklahoma, in this way: "All things in the plain are isolate; there is no confusion of objects in the eye, but one hill or one tree, or one man. To look upon that landscape in the early morning, with the sun at your back is to lose the sense of proportion. Your imagination comes to life and this you think, is where Creation was begun."

In the first selection, Pit River Nation writer Darryl Babe Wilson explains the deep significance that *Akoo-Yet* (Mount Shasta) in northern California has had for Indian people for countless generations. Yet, how many non-Indian people have heard about Mis Misa, the tiny, yet powerful spirit that lives within the mountain, which "balances the earth with the universe and the universe with the earth"? To mainstream society this mountain appears as real estate, a resource to be developed; a place to stop for food on the way north or south along Interstate 5; a ski resort for winter holidays. Wilson, however, explains that Akoo-Yet is a sacred mountain and that there is an important message in Mis Misa that everyone in today's world needs to heed.

All peoples in the world, indigenous peoples included, have stories and traditions of their ethnogenesis. Nancy Parezo, in "The Gathering of the Clans," recounts the origin of the Diné (Navajo) clans. The kinship networks, lineages ("where we came from"), and supernatural origins (clans), are a vital part of the indigenous heritage.

In the next selection, Donald Grinde Jr. (Yamasee) and Bruce Johansen uncover the story of how the U.S. form of government was influenced in major ways by the Six Nations Iroquois Confederacy. This fact can be easily demonstrated by observing the back or green side of a one dollar bill and noting the "American" eagle clutching thirteen arrows in one talon and an olive branch in the other. The olive branch is related to the Greco-Roman heritage. The "American" eagle, it turns out, was borrowed as a symbol from the Iroquois Confederacy, the ever-vigilant eagle against the Confederacy's enemies, and the arrows originally represented the bunched strength of the Iroquois nations. But, as the two historians explain, the Indian influence was much more significant than just these symbols; Iroquois traditions are at the roots of U.S. democratic ideals and the U.S. form of government.

John Mohawk continues the story begun by Grinde and Johansen in the box titled "Origins of Iroquois Political Thought." He traces the role of the White Roots of Peace and the Peacemaker in founding the League of the Haudenosaunee and the fundamental contributions to Iroquois political thought. This thought, "the power of righteousness," continues to influence native peoples throughout the Americas and in the larger indigenous struggle today. In fact, it is a timely message for all the peoples of the world.

Not the least of the Indian heritage of the Americas is humor. Older Americans know that one of the greatest U.S. humorists was satirist Will Rogers, a Cherokee Indian. The white stereotype of the "silent, stoic Indian" is just that, a myth, because Indian people love to joke and tease. One important function of humor is that it is a social leveler. No one can get too puffed up without some Indian wit cutting him or her down in an easy, teasing but pointed way. Hopi author Emory Sekaquaptewa, in our third selection, describes another important function when he explains the world of Hopi clowns. Clowns are an important aspect of many Indian religions: they provide fun and laughter, but they also serve as an ethical and moral compass for the participants in the tribal culture. For example, whether they imitate lewd and mischievous behavior or punish the errant, they are nonetheless demonstrating the mores of an Indian society.

Gaming and sports are other important components of the Native American heritage. The box titled "Jim Thorpe: All-American (Indian) Athlete" features Indian athlete Jim Thorpe, who epitomizes the indigenous sports hero.

The fourth selection deals with Latin America's indigenous peoples as enduring ethnic communities. Rather than acculturating to the non-Indian world and disappearing as ethnic entities, the Indian peoples are now growing in numbers and developing effective political organizations in their struggle for self-government. After providing historical background to explain the differences between the Spanish and English conquests of the Americas, Michael Kearney and Stefano Varese detail the essential forms of "ethnic resilience and opposition" that characterize Latin American Indian peoples for whom rebellion and various forms of resistance are essential parts of the cultural and historical legacy. The nature of political organization for self-government and autonomy, however, is markedly different from political rebellions of the non-Indian society due to the indigenous concern for the integrity of the land, the traditional indigenous territories. Of special interest is the authors' discussion of the dramatic growth of Indian refugee populations in California, which are not officially acknowledged by U.S. immigration officials. We are reminded of the following story. Several years ago before the Zapatista rebellion in Chiapas, Mexico, the governor of Oaxaca visited Santa Rosa, California, where he gave a public address to the local "Mexican" constituents. However, most of the people in the audience identified primarily as Mixteca Indians, not as Mexicans, and were speaking in the Mixtec Indian language, not in Spanish!

The final selection, by Alexander Ewen (Perepeche), focuses on the various ways that native ethnic and racial identity has been defined through time and in distinct regions. In most Latin American countries, including Mexico, the emphasis in externally imposed ethnic identity has historically been on cultural traits such as language and dress. In contrast, the emphasis within the United States has been on biological ancestry, including the concept of blood quantum. Ewen also points out some of the negative consequences for native people on political, economic, and cultural levels as a result of these imposed means of determining ethnic identity. For example, in Mexico, the ethos of *mestizaje* becomes a means of assimilation to a national norm, often reducing the political power of native peoples or denying their existence altogether. As Ewen emphasizes, there is a long and varied history in Mexico of indigenous peoples' identifying ways to resist these and other pressures of assimilation or even annihilation. One of the most recent is the Zapatista movement in Chiapas. This and many other indigenous forms of resistance and confrontation have deep cultural and historical roots and are linked, as Ewen shows, to events that are widespread throughout the hemisphere.

L. FRANK MANRIQUEZ

long ago black bears
sang around our lodge fires
tonight they dance
alive through our dreams

MIS MISA

THE POWER WITHIN AKOO-YET THAT PROTECTS THE WORLD

Darryl Babe Wilson

In the legends of my people there are many events of "our history" that have precise meaning and are completely understandable in our society. Our lessons are from oral "historians." As a people we have been taught, for all seasons, to listen to these stories and to apply the lessons within the stories to everyday life. This is one way to gather spiritual and mental "power" and to maintain emotional as well as physical human strength—to somehow balance our being with the awesome velocity of the churning, continuous universe.

Mis Misa is the tiny, yet powerful spirit that lives within *Akoo-Yet* (Mount Shasta) and balances the earth with the universe and the universe with the earth. Its assigned duty makes Akoo-Yet the most necessary of all of the mountains upon earth, for Mis Misa keeps the earth the proper distance from the sun and keeps everything in its proper place when Wonder and Power stir the universe with a giant yet invisible *ja-pilo-o* (canoe paddle). Mis Misa keeps the earth from wandering away from the rest of the universe. It maintains the proper seasons and the proper atmosphere for life to flourish as earth changes seasons on its journey around the sun.

The lesson establishes that Akoo-Yet was the first mountain created long ago and that it is a seat of power, a spiritual place. It is a mountain that must be worshipped not only for its special beauty and its unique power, but also because it holds Mis Misa deep within it. My old people of wisdom may have identified the mountain as *wiumjoji se-la elam-ji* (living place spirit), or *wiumjoji elam-ji se-la* (living spirit place).

In the "old" lessons and according to the "old" laws, to ascend this mountain with a pure heart and a real purpose, and to communicate with all of the lights and all of the darkness of the universe is to place your spirit in a direct line from the songs of Mis Misa to *hataji* (the heart) of the universe. While in this posture, the spirit of man/woman is in perfect balance and harmony. Few people are able to accomplish this mission. The person must be born for making and maintaining the "connection" between his/her nation and all that there is—and for no other purpose. This is one way nature has of ensuring the health of the whole earth.

In a balanced society that experiences few interruptions, "long range plans" are maintained that will ensure the continuation of the society and the honoring of Mis Misa. The people will continue to live, it is said, for as long as the instructions from the spirit of the universe are honestly obeyed.

When the season approaches that the person who has been assigned this duty prepares to enter the "other" world, a child is dreamed of and born. The planning is intricate since the person "departing" must have sufficient time to train the child to maturity in order that the many lessons and songs are understood as they were created—and are learned with unaltered purity. The most important of all of the lessons, it is said, is to be so quiet in your being that you constantly hear the soft singing of Mis Misa.

To not keep this "appointment" between the society and the powers of the world is to break the delicate umbilical cord between the spirit of the society and the awesome wisdom of the universe. To not listen, intently, to the song coming from Mis Misa is to allow the song to fade. Should the song cease, then Mis Misa will "depart" and the earth and all of the societies upon earth will be out of balance, and the life therein vulnerable to extinction—as the moon was.

It is, therefore, imperative that the practice of communicating with Mis Misa be maintained. Now that "civilization" has entered our native homeland and permeated our people with half-truths, there are few Original People who think in this manner. The linear thought patterns of "education" have brought some of us to be ashamed of our language, our songs, our traditions.

But, the imposing Euro-American intrusion into this hemisphere will not dominate the native societies with enough velocity to cause us to forget our songs and to forget to think beautiful thoughts of all of the precious life that surrounds us—or to forget the ceremony that must be maintained in order for that precious life to flourish.

Akoo-Yet and Mis Misa are little known and may never be sacred to "civilization," to which Akoo-Yet is known as Mt. Shasta. There are no songs coming from it. It is a natural resource. It is property of the United States. It is a piece of real estate that contains animals and varmints upon its slopes that must be "harvested" and "controlled" with guns and poisons. The timber is a valuable resource and it must be subject to political gymnastics as individuals within the American government and the corporate society connive to manipulate the income from the sale of the forests to their personal advantage.

Neither the individuals of the American government nor the individuals of the corporate state "see" the thousands of life forms that are a part of that forest. They do not "see" the bacteria necessary to grow the forest, they do not "see" the animals and birds that are displaced or destroyed as the mountains are shaved clean of forests. They do not "see" the insects and the butterflies of the forest as an element in balance with the universe.

However, they do see this mountain as an object that can be "developed" to entertain the skier and the mountaineer. They dream of constructing villages upon its beautiful slopes and of constructing roads around it. In their "land use" plans, civilization intends to create a circus of this majestic mountain of softly singing beauty.

A letter from Grandfather Craven Gibson always arrived with a sense of urgency. He always claimed that he was born on Alcatraz Island in San Francisco Bay around 1860—during the time when the U.S. government was using that rock as a detention center for Original Native People of the west.

While I could barely decipher his broken spelling and the individual letters that he had labored over (as he wrote "in American"), the fact that it came from him demanded immediate attention, as the elders of my Nation are the keepers of truths and treasures, keepers of wisdom and knowledge.

My brother and I arrived at Grandfather Craven's home in *Atwam* (Big Valley, California) in the early evening. After a cup of bitter coffee from his stained mugs, we went outside to study the clear and perfect night sky. Grandfather did not talk about the universe, he talked about the moon. His was a message given in a controlled panic—as one who knows a disaster is about to occur but also understands that it would be more damaging to try to warn the people. The early night was solemn. There was a hush, a quiet. Not even a coyote howled. Wind, still. Wild, silent.

With a gnarled hand, our ninety year old grandfather pointed to the full moon of August, 1973 and said, "Can you see the scars upon the face of the moon, the injured land? That is what my grandmother spoke of long ago. When I was a child long ago, she said there was a war. It was a big war between the people—a war between the thinkings. There was a terrible war. It was between those people who did not care about life and did not care if the moon remained a dwelling place, and those others who wanted the moon to remain a good place to live. That war used up the moon. When the moon caught fire there wasn't even enough water to put it out. It was all used up. The moon burned. It cooked everything. That huge fire cooked everything. Just everything."

We went back into his old and crooked shack and he talked until breaking light about the eroding condition of earth and the eroding condition of the spirit of humanity.

Because Grandfather wanted us to observe the moon, we went outside and stood with him in the early chill. The old people call it *Lok-mhe*, the light just before the silver of dawn. He told us of his fears of how this earth could be *itamji-uw* (all used up) if all of the people of all of the world do not correct their manner of wasting resources and amend their arrogant disregard for all of life.

There was a thickness under the brilliance of a million dancing stars in the moments before first light. Thirty miles to the north, Akoo-Yet shivered white against the velvet cold black. We were surrounded by the immense silence upon the ancient land of our people of the Pit River Nation, on the flat land of Atwam where the Pit River meanders towards the sea.

(According to legend, the moon bumped earth at Atwam, making a huge circular indentation—as if the surrounding mountains were pushed out by an immense pressure. The mole people, it is said, dug under the moon and with a united thrust, shoved the moon back into its present orbit).

Our talk turned to Akoo-Yet. "The power that balances the universe, Mis Misa, dwells there," Grandfather said, nodding a white head in the direction of the shining mountain. We knew that we were about to hear another story so old that time could not erode it and so real that only truth and understanding could recognize it.

An old coyote howled in a black canyon somewhere to the south. An owl glided nearby, wings whispering upon the darkness, huge eyes searching for slight movements in the sea of darkness. Over near the mountains there was a soft roaring sound of falling waters as the winds brushed the thousand pines. The perfume of sage moved all around us. A meteor streaked across the night sky, a white arrow—vanished—as if it were but a part of an imagination.

In our custom, one is not supposed to intrude into the silence created while someone who is telling a story hesitates to either search for proper words or to allow the listener time to comprehend. At this moment, however, I thought Grandfather should be aware of some plans for the most precious mountain of all of the mountains of his life. "Grandfather, did you know the white man wants to make buildings upon Akoo-Yet?"

After a deliberate silence Grandfather's frozen posture relaxed. His hands made an outward gesture, showing his worn palms for an instant. Then he said, "Can you say why the white man wants to make buildings there?"

Sometimes I explained things to him like he was a child, but he was a wise, old person. "It is for money and entertainment. They have a ski lift on the mountain now so the people who want to slide down the slopes don't have to climb up there. They ride on a chair. The chairs are pulled to the highest point by huge cables. The cables are held up in the air by towers much like those used by PG&E to move electricity through huge wires from here to San Francisco. Now they want to make a town on the mountain—a city."

There was another silence. Then, with the tired motions of an old grizzly bear, Grandfather said, "It must be time to tell the white people the story of Mis Misa." His story began when the present universe was made:

"When *Quon* (Silver-gray Fox), the power that created all that we know, and *Jamol* (the coyote power that *still* wants to change all that Quon has created) were through with making this land, it is said, Great Power made a law, a rule. It is hard to say. It is a rule or a law or something like that. I will call it a 'law,' but somebody else will call it a 'rule.'

"This 'law,' Great Power placed it within Akoo-Yet. But before, that mountain was just another mountain. By placing the 'law' in there, *Quon* made Akoo-Yet the most powerful of all mountains. He gave the mountain a real job. My Grandmother told me of this 'law.' It is known as Mis Misa by our people. I have never heard it called anything else. It is a small thing. You cannot see it, but you can hear it singing—if you listen carefully."

There was a long pause. We waited. Often much of the meaning of the message that our elders offer is in the quiet between sentences, sometimes it is just a hesitation. But, again, the silence could last for an unbearably long time. It is certain, however, that when you are in the presence of the old ones and they feel it is time for them to continue they simply proceed and you must not forget where they left off—even if the story is continued a year later.

In these long moments of silence I thought of how delicate and intricate the universe really is. Sun shines. Rain falls. Trees grow. Fish swim. Birds fly. Rainbows arch. Earth turns. Seasons change. Grass turns green. But what immense knowledge stirs the universe and yet holds life in a manzanita seed for years before it is heated, dampened, then sprouts?

I reasoned that there probably is not an explanation for the phenomenon of all of existence within the psyche of humanity when there is a "belief" involved because "belief" indicates that the next acceptable argument could replace the present "belief." (I would have to agree with anybody who said that Coyote fashioned "belief" from a "truth" made by Quon but altered, just a little—to make it better).

All of nature seems to be in balance with some completeness, some wholeness that most humans are denied access to.

Breaking the silence Grandfather continued, "We are told to be careful. Be careful while near this mountain. Always come to this mountain with a good heart. Mis Misa knows what you are thinking—always think good thoughts. Listen. If you do not listen you will not hear the singing and this is not respectful. It is like breaking a command-ment of the white man's God, they say. You could be punished. Your whole family could be punished—even the children, the babies. That's what they say.

"The purpose of Mis Misa is but one: *To balance the earth with the universe and the uni-verse with the earth.* When Quon created earth and universe long ago, that power under-stood many things. Also, that power knew that it could not make everything just right. That's a wise power. For this reason power made Mis Misa and put Mis Misa within the mountain. It lives there. You can hear it singing. Remember always this power. It bal-ances the universe. It is a 'law.' It knows what you are thinking."

Grandfather continued to explain how Mis Misa works. It is like a free-swinging pendulum combined with a gyroscope. If the earth wanders slightly off course, Mis Misa adjusts itself to that change. If the stars are slightly off course, Mis Misa ad-justs itself to that change also. It is never at rest. It is constantly adjusting. It is forever singing.

Grandfather continued, "My Grand-mother was born there (on the moon), so I know. I know because she told me. She told me many things. Many things she told me. That's how I know. My Grandmother was born on the moon. She knew many things and she told me.

"She told how *chool* (the moon) was the last 'earth' but it was *itamji-uw* (all used up). At one time it was pretty. At one time it was cute. There was life everywhere. Just every-where there was life. There was happiness. Happiness everywhere. But a wrongful power come. I don't know where it come from . . . but it come. From somewhere it come and it denied the people.

"It used *chool*. That wrongful power, it used it up.

"My Grandmother said it, that's how I know the moon was the last earth."

We again studied *chool* glowing full and strong in the silver of dawn.

"Look for signs of war and destruction," Grandfather said. "Do you see there, the rip-ping as with a flint knife? Over there a bruise. Over there a long scar. There was aches and there was pains. Do you see what my Grandmother said? Can you see the place there where there was war and de-struction? Do you now know why *chool* is scarred and bruised and scratched?"

In silence we studied the moon. We wondered about it. I longed to know the exact reason why it is no longer an earth, why there no longer is life dwelling there. My mind raced backwards through an un-known measurement of time until it "saw" the moon, green and blue and covered with life—then my focus returned to the shim-mering moon turning around earth and sun in some magnetic loneliness today. Some-thing inside my spirit, a bell or an alarm went off! With a trembling voice, Grandfa-ther's words pierced my thoughts once more as he pursued the story.

"It is said that the power that created earth and the universe made one mistake. It made 'vanty.' 'Vanty' makes a person love himself and nothing else. Nothing else. It is said, we must constantly guard against be-coming a part of that wrong, that no good. We must be good to one another. It is easy to be bad to one another. We must not be bad to one another. We must be good to earth. We must be good to life. Do not kill life. We have no choice. This earth is the last place. We call it *atas-p-im mukuya* (to stop, last place). We have no place else to go. We must go back to the stars.

"Mt. Shasta," by Frank LaPena, © 1987.

"When *chool* was close to being all used up," Grandfather continued, "the people threw their songs out into the vastness. Out there. It was a long time. Our people were in a big hurry, but it was a long time. Then, earth began to be made by that song. Just by that song! It was prepared. It was green and brown and blue.

"One day during the last war, the war between the thinkings, chool caught on fire. There was fire everywhere. It was flames. People were cooking to death. Everything was cooking to death. Earth was the closest. The people jumped. We landed here in our nation. The other people landed in their nation." *Weet-la* (the demon spirit) landed on an island beyond east salt waters, it is said. "The last to jump was frog. Frog jumped here because he was afraid if he stayed on chool he would have to walk like *weet-la,* so frog came, too."

It was not many seasons later when we found Grandfather. His spirit had proceeded to its rendezvous with destiny. He was looking up into forever with clouded eyes. How I longed to seek more answers from his wisdom, but he could not hear mortal beings, now. There were so many "whys" that I needed answers to. There were so many "whys" the whole earth needed answers to.

Once he showed us where he was going if he died. There was a small spot near the handle of the big dipper that appeared to be unoccupied. That was his destination. There is a glint there now.

I had a dream. Grandfather had departed. At least his spirit had. He was no longer in his little shack on the flatlands of Atwam.

In that dream I watched Grandfather as he fashioned another "earth" from the "star" that he had created with his power. He labored and labored. He did not see me watching him. He hammered and chiseled. He planted and trimmed. He watered and molded. He stopped a moment to survey his work then smiled and labored again. His old and crooked hands were worn thin with a new employment, a new purpose. He did this and he did that as he prepared a new earth.

Then the light of the "star" hesitated. It glimmered like the light bulb in his ancient lamp. It flickered. It went out. Grandfather yet toiled. "Star" turned green and blue and brown. It turned green with trees and spring. It turned blue with water and with clouds of singing birds. It turned brown with herds of deer and mounds of earth. There were bears and flowers. There was soft drumming and happiness. There was life dancing, dancing in a new sunshine.

From his star, Grandfather turned and pointed his index finger at the top of Akoo-Yet. In my dream I felt Mis Misa shift ever so slightly. Perhaps it wasn't a dream. Maybe Grandfather is, at this moment, laboring to make another "earth" so that we might have a place to go if life is again *itamji-wu* (used up).

I look across the earth seeing so much unnecessary destruction. Forests are being erased throughout this entire hemisphere and around the world. Most rivers are sick and dying. The sky is gray over the huge cities. The air stinks. Pavement covers the meadows where flowers are supposed to grow. Mountains are being moved and removed. Rivers are diverted and the water terribly polluted. Earth is being drilled into and her heart and her guts and her blood are being used as private property for private gain.

There is an immense vacuum where the spiritual connection between human beings and nature is supposed to be—that umbilical cord that we inherited long before our birth and we were instructed to nurture and to protect for all of the existence of our nations. It seems as though too many people think that nature is an element that they are not a part of. They, like the old Coyote, think that nature, life, must be tamed, must be challenged, must be conquered, must be changed in order to make it better.

History has unveiled many battles and many wars. In this era, we can look back through the pages of time like changing channels on the TV. Yes, there have been some terrible wars. Yes, there has been much destruction. Yes, some wars have engaged the entire world.

But those conflicts were over human supremacy—which king or which governing entity would rule the masses and control the bounty of earth. Who would be the master over all of the people and who would control the wealth. Whose gnarled dreams would be unleashed at which time in history to make an indelible mark urged through vanity.

In these conflicts mother earth was treated as a woman slave. She had to yield the materials that were needed to continue the conflagration. She had to yield the waters for the thirsty battalions. She had to yield fruit and food to feed the armies that marched. She had to provide the medicine to heal the wounded. She had to provide the bounty that was the crown for the victor!

These are new times. The whole earth is threatened with extinction. No longer is it acceptable for human beings to contend for the supreme pinnacle of the various societies of earth; from this moment forward there must be a battle, there must be an intense war.

But this time for the salvaging of earth. This time to see whether or not there will be only a "moon" left here one day after all of the products are used up, after the balance of existence has turned for the worse, and after vanity has led us down a time-path that has an absolute expiration date (and, before we discover that my dream of Grandfather was simply that).

Yes, Grandfather's story is *only an Indian story.* But it is a story with evidence—the moon. It is a story that has endured time and maintains its direction and its solemn concern. There is a moon—there is also Mis Misa. Not once have I encountered a reference to that beautiful power within that sacred mountain—while "constructionists" and "progressives" plot the future of development of Akoo-Yet. The "constructionists" see Akoo-Yet as a piece of valuable real estate. They fail to see its sacred value. For how many more seasons can these mistakes find pardon within nature?

My thoughts lead me to walk among the stars every morning during the silver just before dawn, *lok-mhe.* Ringing in my ears the worried words of Grandfather: "When I was a child long ago, my Grandmother said there was a war. It was a big war between the people—a war between thinkings. There was a terrible war. That war used up the moon. When the moon caught fire there wasn't enough water to put it out. It was all used up."

I look upon the moon and worry. I look upon earth and see the corporate entities exercising greed and profit as their reasons for their existence. I see children crying and hungry all around the world. I see the land of my Grandmother and Grandfather being used up.

Yes, there is a callousness in the manner that people have abused the world. Yes, environmentally oriented people must oppose that irresponsibility. Yes, children have a right to live in respect and harmony. Yes, Grandmothers and Grandfathers have an absolute right to peace and protection. Yes, we, the able and capable, have an absolute duty to defend our loved ones in their journey through life.

Yes, there will be a terrible and great war again. There must be, for the silver of dawn, first light, belongs to us all, equally. We must not deny its panorama to anybody—especially those we are, by our spirit, bound to protect forever. We should not fear. Besides the dawn of day and the strength of the power that turns earth around the sun and the sun around a greater wonder, we have, as an ally, Mis Misa.

CREATION STORY: THE GATHERING OF THE CLANS

Nancy J. Parezo

When Changing Woman left for the west, her younger sister, White Shell Woman, returned to her home in the San Juan Mountains. But after five days White Shell Woman longed for company. Talking God saw her plight and brought all the Holy People to her house. Changing Woman brought two sacred blankets of dark embroidery and white embroidery. Talking God brought two buckskins, and First Man and First Woman brought two perfect ears of female and male corn.

With ceremony and prayer, Talking God pointed the corn in the four cardinal directions. He placed them on the blanket under the buckskins. The Wind breathed on the corn four times, and the white corn changed into a man and the yellow into a woman. Rock Crystal Boy gave them minds, and Yellow Corn Girl gave them voices. When the Holy People were finished forming these Earth Surface People, they went into White Shell Woman's home, and the Holy People departed for their homes.

In four days, Talking God brought Ground Mist Girl and Mirage Boy to marry the first siblings. Each couple had one boy and one girl. From these people are descended the Tséní-jíkiní clan, the Honeycombed Rock People. Because Talking God pointed the corn in the four directions, the Navajo people never live like the Pueblo people. They migrate constantly from place to place and are scattered across the land.

One day, the Honeycombed Rock People saw a fire far off in the distance. They searched for the source for many days, and with the help of the Wind they found a small encampment of Earth Surface People. The people rejoiced and asked, "Where do you come from?"

"We come from Tséłigaii íí'ahí, the Place Where the White Rock Stands," the newcomers answered. "We have survived only on ducks and snakes, prairie dogs, and whatever berries and seeds our women and children have been able to gather."

The people of the Honeycombed Rock clan asked them to live with them because they had food. "You are welcome to travel the path we travel, to rest where we rest, to hunt where we hunt, and to share that which we have." So they brought the people to White Shell Woman, who named them Tsétłáhnii, or Rock Corner Place People, after the place where they had met. She called all of them her children.

Soon other clans came and were named. Then Talking God took White Shell Woman to live in Tsegi Canyon at the Place of the Mountain Sheep. The people did not want to see her go, but she told them not to be sad: "I will come often to see you and I shall watch over you. Your need for me is no longer great. You are growing stronger as a people and learning to control the things of this world. Look for me when you see the gentle showers of female rain."

Now when new people came, they named themselves. Some came from other groups—Ute, Zuni, Pueblo, Mexican, and Apache. Some were formed by Changing Woman when she was lonely. Others had no known history, having survived the monsters. All had long journeys and faced many hardships and adventures before finding the right place to live. Sometimes they dwelled apart for a while, but eventually they joined the Diné and behaved as if they were one. Each brought new skills, which they shared. From that time on, the Diné flourished as they hunted and grew food, living simply here on the surface of the Fifth World.

Adapted from Paul Zobrod's *Diné Behane: The Navajo Creation Story,* by Nancy Parezo from *Paths of Life: American Indians of the Southwest and Northern Mexico,* edited by Thomas E. Sheridan and Nancy J. Parezo. Copyright © 1996 The Arizona Board of Regents. Reprinted by permission of the University of Arizona Press.

PERCEPTIONS OF AMERICA'S NATIVE DEMOCRACIES

THE SOCIETIES COLONIAL AMERICANS OBSERVED

Donald A. Grinde Jr. and Bruce E. Johansen

This is reversing the natural order of things. A tractable people may be governed in large bodies but, in proportion as they depart from this character, the extent of their government must be less. We see into what small divisions the Indians are obliged to reduce their societies.
—Thomas Jefferson, disputing proposals to enlarge
the size of states to be admitted to the Union

All along the Atlantic seaboard, Indian nations had already formed confederacies by the time they first encountered European immigrants—from the "federated republic" of the Creeks in what is now Georgia and Florida; to the Cherokees and Choctaws in the Carolinas; to the Iroquois and their allies, the Hurons, in the Saint Lawrence Valley; to the Penacook federation of New England, among many others. According to Anthony F. C. Wallace, "Ethnic confederacies were common among all the Indian tribes of the Northeast."

Village bands, and tribes speaking similar languages, holding similar customs, and sharing a tradition of similar origin usually combined into a loose union that at least minimized warfare among themselves. The Illinois Confederacy, the "Three Fires" of the Chippewa, Ottawa and Pottawatomi, the Wapenaki Confederacy, the Powhatan Confederacies, the tripartite Miami—all the neighbors of the Iroquois—were members of one confederation or another.[1]

By the late eighteenth century, as resentment against England's taxation flared into open rebellion, the colonists' formative ideology displayed widespread knowledge of native governmental systems. Thomas Jefferson, Benjamin Franklin, James Adair, Father Le Jeune, and others—from framers to farmers along the length of the coast and into the Saint Lawrence Valley—all saw governmental systems that were remarkably similar in broad outline but had their own variations on the common theme of democracy in councils. These systems had evolved to coordinate governance—across geographic distances that must have seemed huge to these transplanted Europeans—and permit maximum freedom to nations within confederations and individuals within nations.

The colonists forming the United States were charged with similar tasks in molding their own emerging nation, so it should not be surprising that early government in the United States (especially under the Articles of Confederation) greatly resembled native systems in many respects. This is not to say that the founders copied Indian societies—if they had, we would have evolved precincts along family lines, and our senators and representatives would be nominated solely by women—but to say that the native systems of governance, along with European precedents, were factored into a new ideological equation.

The Iroquois' system was the best known to the colonists (in large part because of their pivotal position in diplomacy, not only between the English and French but also among other native confederacies); therefore, we begin our examination of how native confederacies governed themselves with their example. Called the Iroquois by the French and the Five (later Six) Nations by the English, the Haudenosaunee controlled the only relatively level overland passage (the later route of the Erie Canal) between the English colonies on the coast and the French settlements in the Saint Lawrence Valley; their diplomatic influence permeated the entire eastern half of North America.

Cadwallader Colden, who was regarded as "the best-informed man in the New World on the affairs of the British-American colonies," provided the first systematic study of the Haudenosaunee in 1727, which he augmented in 1747. Franklin read Colden's *The History of the Five Indian Nations Depending on the Province of New York in America* before he began his diplomatic career by representing Pennsylvania in meetings with the Iroquois and their allies. After drawing up his Albany Plan of Union in 1754, which in some respects greatly resembled the Iroquois Confederacy's governmental structure, Franklin's first stop was Colden's estate. Colden held several colonial offices, including lieutenant governor of New York.

He also carried on extensive research in various natural sciences and was an anthropologist before the field had a name. Colden was also an adopted Mohawk.

Because of their skills at oratory, warfare, and diplomacy, as well as the republican nature of their government, Colden compared the Iroquois to the Romans. "When Life and Liberty came in competition, indeed, I think our Indians have outdone the Romans in this particular. . . . The Five Nations consisted of men whose courage could not be shaken." Colden's belief that the Indians, particularly the Iroquois, provided the new Americans with a window on their own antiquity was shared by Franklin, Jefferson, and Thomas Paine and, a century later, by Karl Marx and Frederick Engels as well as the founders of modern feminism. For two centuries of revolutionaries and reformers, this belief provided a crucial link between Indian societies and their own as well as a counterpoint by which to judge society's contemporary ills.

Elaborating on his belief, Colden wrote, "We are fond of searching into remote Antiquity to know the manners of our earliest progenitors; if I be not mistaken, the Indians are living images of them," an assumption held in common with many other writers about the New World and its peoples—from Peter Martyr in the sixteenth century to Engels in the late nineteenth century.

> The present state of the Indian Nations exactly shows the most Ancient and Original Condition of almost every Nation; so, I believe that here we may with more certainty see the original form of all government, than in the most curious Speculations of the Learned; and that the Patriarchial and other Schemes in Politicks are no better than Hypotheses in Philosophy, and as prejudicial to real Knowledge.[2]

Colden provided an extensive description of the Iroquois' form of government, which had "continued so long that the

Christians know nothing of the original of it."

> Each Nation is an Absolute Republick by its self, governed in all Publick affairs of War and Peace by the Sachems of Old Men, whose Authority and Power is gained by and consists wholly in the opinions of the rest of the Nation in their Wisdom and Integrity. They never execute their Resolutions by Compulsion or Force Upon any of their People.[3]

> The Five Nations have such absolute Notions of Liberty that they allow no Kind of Superiority of one over another, and banish all Servitude from their Territories.[4]

Although some twentieth-century anthropologists maintain that the Iroquois League was only fully formed after Europeans made landfall in North America, the historical records of Europeans such as Colden contained no hint that the Confederacy was in formation at that time. The consensus of seventeenth- and eighteenth-century writers, who saw the Confederacy in its full flower, was that it had formed sometime before colonization. The oral history of the Iroquois indicated a founding date somewhere between A.D. 1000 and 1450. Lewis Henry Morgan and Horatio E. Hale estimated the founding date to be toward the end of that spectrum, although William N. Fenton has placed his estimate even later. What united all these estimates and educated guesses was their agreement that the League was firmly in place before the coming of the Europeans.

According to Iroquois oral history, the Confederacy was formed by the Huron prophet Deganawidah (called "the Peacemaker" in oral discourse), who, because he stuttered so badly he could hardly speak, decided to enlist the aid of Aiowantha (sometimes called Hiawatha) in order to spread his vision of a united Haudenosaunee confederacy. The oral history attributed the Peacemaker's stuttering to a double row of teeth.

The Confederacy originally included the Mohawks, Oneidas, Onondagas, Cayugas, and Senecas; the sixth nation, the Tuscaroras, migrated into Iroquois country in the early eighteenth century.

Peace among the formerly antagonistic nations was procured and maintained through the Haudenosaunee's Great Law of Peace [*Kaianerekowa*], which was passed from generation to generation by the use of wampum, a form of written communication that outlined a complex system of checks and balances between nations and sexes. Although a complete oral recitation of the Great Law can take several days, encapsulated versions of it have been translated into English for more than a hundred years and provide one reason why the Iroquois are cited so often today in debates regarding the origins of fundamental law in the United States. While many other native confederacies existed along the borders of the British colonies, most records of the specific provisions of their governments have been lost.

To understand the provisions of the Great Law, one must first understand some of the symbols it used to represent the Confederacy. The Confederacy itself was likened to an extended, traditional longhouse, with the Mohawks guarding the "eastern door," the Senecas at the "western door," and the Onondagas tending the ceremonial council fire in the middle. The primary national symbol of the Haudenosaunee was the Great White Pine, which served throughout the Great Law as a metaphor for the Confederacy. Its branches sheltered the people of the Five Nations, and its roots spread to the four directions, inviting other peoples, regardless of race or nationality, to take refuge under the tree. The Haudenosaunee recognized no bars to dual citizenship; in fact, many influential figures in the English colonies and early United States, Colden among them, were adopted into Iroquois nations.

Each of the five nations maintained its own council, whose sachems were nominated by the clan mothers of families holding hereditary rights to office titles. The Grand Council at Onondaga was drawn from the individual national councils, but could also nominate sachems outside the local hereditary structures based on merit alone. These sachems, called "pine tree chiefs," were said to have sprung from the body of the people much as the symbolic Great White Pine had grown from the earth.

The rights, duties, and qualifications of sachems were explicitly outlined, and the clan mothers could remove (or impeach) a sachem who was found guilty of any of a number of abuses of office—from missed meetings to murder. An errant chief was summoned to face charges by the war chiefs, who, in peacetime, acted as the peoples' eyes and ears in the council (somewhat as the role of the press was envisioned by Jefferson and other founders of the United States). A sachem was given three warnings, then removed from the council if he did not mend his ways. A sachem found guilty of murder not only lost his title, but his entire family also was deprived of its right to representation. His women relatives who held the rights to office were "buried," and their title was transferred to a sister family. Iroquois law also provided for the removal from office of sachems who could no longer adequately function (a measure remarkably similar to the twenty-fifth amendment to the United States Constitution, adopted in 1967, which detailed procedures for the removal of an incapacitated president). Sachems were not allowed to name their own successors, nor could they carry their titles to the grave—the Great Law even provided a ceremony for removing the title from a dying chief.

The Great Law stipulated that sachems' skins must be seven spans thick, so that they would be able to withstand the criticism of their constituents. The law pointed out that sachems should take pains not to become angry when people scrutinized their conduct in governmental affairs. Such a point of view pervades the writings of Jefferson and Franklin, although it was not fully codified into United States law until the Supreme Court decision *New York Times v. Sullivan* (1964), which made it virtually impossible for public officials to sue for libel.

The Great Law also included provisions guaranteeing freedom of religion and the right of redress before the Grand Council. It even forbade unauthorized entry into homes—measures which sound familiar to United States citizens through the Bill of Rights.

As was mentioned earlier, women played a profound role in Iroquois political life. Although the Iroquois were bound together by a clan and chieftain system, which was buttressed by a similar linguistic base, the League of the Iroquois was much more than simply a kinship state. The basic unit of government was the "hearth," which consisted of a mother and her children. Each hearth was part of a wider group called an *otiianer,* and two or more *otiianers* constituted a clan. The word *otiianer* specifically referred to the female heirs to the chieftainship titles of the League. The *otiianer* women selected one of the males within their group to fill any of the fifty seats in the League.

All the sons and daughters of a particular clan were related through uterine families that often lived far apart. In this system, a husband went to live with his wife's family, and their children became members of the mother's clan by right of birth. Through matrilineal descent, the Iroquois formed cohesive political groups—headed by the "clan mothers"—that had little to do with where people lived or from what village the hearths originated. All authority sprang from the people of the various clans that made up the Iroquois Confederacy. The clan mothers appointed the male delegates and deputies who, after consultation within the clan, spoke for them at tribal meetings where issues and questions were formulated and subsequently debated in council.

Iroquois political philosophy was rooted in the concept that all life was spiritually unified with the natural environment and other forces surrounding people. The Iroquois believed that the spiritual power of one person was limited, but was enhanced when combined with other individuals in a hearth, *otiianer*, or clan. Whenever a person died, whether of natural causes or by force, the "public" power was diminished. To maintain the strength of the group, the dead were replaced either by natural increase or by adopting captives of war. This practice insured the continued power and durability of the matrilineal system as well as the kinship state.

Instead of formal instruments of authority, the Iroquois governed behavior by instilling a sense of pride and belonging to the group through common rituals and the careful rearing of children. Iroquois youth were trained to enter a society that was egalitarian, with power more evenly distributed between male and female, young and old, than was common in Euro-American society. Iroquois culture could be loosely called a "shame culture" because of its emphasis on honor, duty, and collaborative behavior, while European culture was more "guilt-oriented," since it emphasized an authoritarian hierarchy and advancement through the acquisition of property, status, and material possessions. Because the Iroquois prized competence as a protector/provider more than material wealth, their children

were trained to think for themselves as well as provide for others. The Iroquois did not respect submissive people who were cowed by authority. With this approach, Iroquois society had no use for the elaborate European mechanisms of control to direct the lives of its citizenry. Ostracism and shame were the primary punishments for transgressors, until they had atoned for their actions and demonstrated that they had undergone a purification process.

The League of the Iroquois arose out of the desire to resolve the problem of the blood feud. Before the tribal councils had the Great Law of Peace to sanctify and buttress their society, blood revenge caused strife. Once a clan was reduced by murder or kidnapping, the victim's kinfolk were bound by clan law to avenge the loss of their relative, resulting in endless recriminations. As long as justice and the monopoly on violence resided in the clans, there was no hope of peace and goodwill.

Visionaries among the Iroquois such as Hiawatha (who lived among the Onondagas) tried to call councils to eliminate the blood feud, but all attempts were thwarted by the evil and twisted wizard Tadodaho, an Onondaga who used magic and spies to rule by fear and intimidation. After having failed to defeat the wizard, Hiawatha traveled to countless Mohawk, Oneida, and Cayuga villages with his message of peace and brotherhood. He found acceptance everywhere he went, with the proviso that he first persuade the formidable Tadodaho and the Onondagas to embrace the covenant of peace. Just as Hiawatha was despairing, the prophet Deganawidah entered his life and changed the nature of things among the Iroquois; together, they developed a powerful message of peace. Deganawidah's vision gave substance to Hiawatha's oratory, and so the Constitution of the Iroquois was formulated.

"The Peace Tree" from *Migration of the Iroquois,* 2nd edition, by Aren Wkweks. Illustration by John Kahionhes Fadden. Copyright © 1971 by White Roots of Peace, Mohawk Nation at Akwesasne via Rooseveltown, NY 13683. Reprinted with permission.

In his vision, Deganawidah saw a giant evergreen (the Great White Pine) reaching to the sky and gaining strength from three counterbalancing principles of life. The first law of nature was that a stable mind and healthy body must be in balance so that peace between individuals and groups could occur. Secondly, Deganawidah believed that humane conduct, thought, and speech were requirements for equity and justice among peoples. Finally, he divined a society in which physical strength and civil authority would reinforce the power of the clan system.

Deganawidah's tree had four white roots that stretched to the four directions of the earth. A snow-white carpet of thistledown spread out from the base of the tree, covering the surrounding countryside and protecting the peoples who embraced the three life-affirming principles. Deganawidah explained that this tree was humanity, living within the principles governing relations among human beings, and the eagle perched on top of the giant pine was humanity's lookout against enemies who would disturb the peace. He postulated that the white carpet could cover the entire earth and provide a shelter of peace and brotherhood for all mankind. His vision was a message from the Creator, bringing harmony to human existence and uniting all peoples into a single family guided by three principles.

With such a powerful vision, Deganawidah and Hiawatha were able to subdue Tadodaho and transform his mind. Deganawidah removed the evil feelings and thoughts from the head of Tadodaho and commanded him to "strive . . . to make reason and the peaceful mind prevail." The evil wizard was reborn as a humane person, charged with implementing the message of Deganawidah. After Tadodaho's redemption, Onondaga became the central fire of the Haudenosaunee and the Onondagas the "firekeepers" of the new Confederacy. (To this day, the Great Council Fire of the Iroquois Confederacy is kept in the land of the Onondagas.)

Deganawidah then gathered together the clan leaders of the Five Nations (Mohawk, Oneida, Onondaga, Cayuga, and Seneca) around the council fire at Onondaga to hear the laws and government of the Confederacy, which espoused peace, brotherhood, and unity, a balance of power, the natural rights of all people, and sharing of resources, as well as provisions for impeachment or removal of leaders. Moreover, the blood feud was outlawed and replaced by a Condolence Ceremony. Under this new law, when a man was killed, his grieving family could forego the option of exacting clan revenge (the taking of the life of the murderer or a member of the murderer's clan) and, instead, could accept twenty strings of wampum (freshwater shells strung together) from the slayer's family (ten for the dead person and ten for the murderer's own life). In the case of the murder of a woman, the price became thirty wampum strings. Through this ceremony, the monopoly on legally sanctioned violence was enlarged from the clan to the League.

Deganawidah gave strict instructions governing the conduct of the League and its deliberations. Tadodaho was to maintain the fire and call the Onondaga chiefs together to determine if an issue brought before him was pressing enough to call to the attention of the Council of the Confederacy. If the proposed issue merited council consideration, it would assemble and Tadodaho would kindle a fire and announce the purpose of the meeting. The rising smoke penetrating the sky was a signal to the Iroquois allies that the council was in session. The Onondaga chiefs and Tadodaho were charged with keeping the council area free from distractions.

The Confederacy's legislative process began with a policy debate by the Keepers of the Eastern Door (Mohawks) and the Keepers of the Western Door (Senecas). The question was then thrown across the fire to the Oneida and Cayuga statesmen (the younger brothers) for discussion in much the same manner. Once consensus was achieved among the Oneidas and the Cayugas, the discussion returned to the elder brothers—first to the Senecas and

Mohawks for confirmation and finally to the Onondagas for their decision. At this stage, the Onondagas had a power similar to judicial review; that is, they could raise objections to the proposed measure if they believed it was inconsistent with the Great Law. Essentially, the legislators could rewrite the proposed law on the spot so as to be in accord with the Constitution of the Iroquois. Once the Onondaga sachems had reached consensus, Tadodaho gave the decision to Honowireton (an Onondaga chief who presided over debates between the delegations) for confirmation. Finally, Honowireton or Tadodaho returned the legislation to the Mohawks and the Senecas for announcement to the Grand Council.

The overall intent of such a parliamentary procedure was to encourage unity at each step by emphasizing checks and balances, public debate, and consensus. The League's legislative process was similar to the mechanisms of the Albany Plan of Union, the Articles of Confederation, and the United States Constitution.

The rights of the Iroquois citizenry were protected by portions of the Great Law. According to Section 93,

> Whenever an especially important matter . . . is presented before the League Council . . . threatening their utter ruin, then the chiefs of the League must submit the matter to the decision of their people.[5]

Public opinion played an important role. Within the League of the Iroquois, people could have a direct say in the formulation of government policy even if the sachems chose to ignore the will of the people. According to Section 16 of the Great Law of Peace, "If the conditions . . . arise . . . to . . . change . . . this law, the case shall be . . . considered and if the new beam seems . . . beneficial, the . . . change . . . if adopted, shall be called, "Added to the Rafters." This law resembles provisions for popular initiative in several states of the United States, as well as the mechanisms by which the federal and many state constitutions may be amended.

The people of the League could also initiate impeachment proceedings and treason charges as well as alert the council to public opinion on a specific matter. The Iroquois people also had the power to remove the "hereditary" sachems of the League's Council. Upon the death or removal of a Confederacy chief, his title reverted to the women in his clan, who had "inherited the right" to appoint and remove peace chiefs to the Confederacy. After the clan mothers had nominated the next chief (who was always a male), their proposal was put before the men of the clan. The nomination was then forwarded to the council of the League, where the new chief was installed.

The League of the Iroquois was a family-oriented government, which had a constitution with a fixed corpus of laws concerned with mutual defense. Through the elimination of the clan blood feud, the state was given a monopoly on legally sanctioned violence, which brought peace through a fundamental social contract. But the Iroquois were not inclined to give much power to authorities because of their basic psychological and social attitudes. Thus, unity, peace, and brotherhood were balanced against the natural rights of all people and the necessity of sharing resources equitably. Unity for mutual defense was an abiding concept within the League and was represented by a bundle of five arrows tied together to symbolize the complete union of the nations and the unbroken strength that such a unity provides (Section 57 of the Great Law of the Iroquois). With the strength of many came peace for future generations.

The notion of federalism was strictly adhered to by the Iroquois. The hereditary Iroquois sachems were interested only in external matters such as war, peace, and treaty-making. The Grand Council could not interfere in the internal affairs of the tribe. Each tribe had its own sachems, but their role was limited to matters between themselves and other tribes; they had no say in matters that were traditionally the concern of the clan.

Through public opinion and debate, the Great Law gave basic rights to the Iroquois people within a distinctive and representative governmental framework. The Great Law solved disputes by giving all parties an equal hearing. The Grand Council often functioned as a think tank, for thinking was the primary activity that went on underneath the Great Tree. The Iroquois believed that the more thinkers there were beneath the tree, the better. The Iroquois League accorded prestige to the peace chiefs and thus sought to reduce conflict between war and peace chiefs and the generations. The middle-aged peace chiefs were the firekeepers, encircled by warrior/providers, women, and, finally, the public-at-large. Although the tribes had unequal representation, this was irrelevant, since each tribe voted as one. At the level of village, tribe, and Grand Council, consensus devices were used to obtain unanimity and to report up and down the governmental structure. The League was not able to centralize power in matters other than mutual defense, but it was effective in diminishing friction among the Five Nations. The kinship state, with its imagery of a longhouse spread afar, was clearly comprehended by the Iroquois people. Iroquois power rested upon the consent of the governed and was not coercive in areas of military service, taxation, and police powers.

To the colonial Americans chafing under British authority, such a government and attitude toward freedom were powerful examples that could be used in resisting British sovereignty and tyranny. Certainly, the imagery and concepts of the League had a powerful influence on the hearts and minds of the founders and the American people. Likewise, the Iroquois leaders took an active interest in teaching colonial leaders about the tenets of the Iroquois constitution.

The system of the Hurons was remarkably similar to that of their neighbors, the Iroquois. According to Bruce J. Trigger's *Children of the Aataentsic: A History of the Huron People,* the Hurons' polity, like the Iroquois', was rooted in family structure. Leaders of the various clans used public opinion and consensus to shape decisions, and issues "were usually decided upon by majority vote" and "discussed until a general consensus was reached." No human being would be expected to be bound by a decision to which conscious consent had not been given.

As with the Iroquois, the Huron clans—Porcupine, Snake, Deer, Beaver, Hawk, Turtle, Bear, and Wolf—created familial affinity across the boundaries of their four confederated nations. Members of each clan could trace their ancestry to a common origin through the female line. In each village, clan members elected a civil chief and a war chief. The titles were carried through the female family line, but bestowed on men. While the titles were hereditary in the same sense as in the Iroquois tradition, they did not pass from head to head of a particular family as in most European monarchies. When the time came to choose a leader, members of each clan segment in a particular village had a choice of several candidates, whose personal qualities—"intelligence, oratorical ability, reputation for generosity, and, above all, performance as a warrior"—counted most heavily.

If a village included more than one clan segment (most did, but not all), the elected leaders of each segment formed a village council, which met on purely local issues. The council resolved issues through debate that led to consensus. Each of the four nations, including several villages, held councils that included all the village civil and war chiefs. The four nations—the Attignawantan, Arendarhonon, Attigneenongahac, and Tahontaeanrat—also held a central council, which, according to Trigger, probably consisted of all the village chiefs, representing all the clans. Compared to the Iroquois Grand Council, very little documentation exists regarding this council's operations. It is likely that the Huron Confederacy had a looser structure, since its central council met only once a year, usually for several weeks in the spring (although emergency meetings could be called at any time). The meeting of the central council was meant to bind the four nations and served as much as a social occasion as it was a legislative session. Its proceedings were embellished with feasts to install new village headmen, reunions among old friends, singing, dancing, and war feasts. The central council dealt with issues that affected all four nations in common, such as treaty negotiations and trade with Europeans.

When the Huron central council met, the Attignawantan (by far the largest of the four nations) sat on one side of a ceremonial longhouse, across the council fire from the representatives of the other three nations. The speaker, always an Attignawantan, presided over the speeches of welcome and thanksgiving, which were followed by recitation of the agenda. As each item of the agenda was taken up, the representatives stated their opinions in turn, without interruption. Speaking in council called for a special oratorical style, "full of metaphors, circumlocutions, and other rhetorical devices that were uncommon in everyday speech." Members of the council were expected to retain their composure, even during severe disagreement, in order to guide the debate toward eventual consensus. Many procedures, such as those governing debate among the nations on each side of the council fire or those regarding desirable qualities for sachems or grounds for impeachment, probably existed but have been lost to history.

In the early eighteenth century, the Cherokee Nation was composed of sixty villages, averaging three to four hundred persons each, in five regions. Each village controlled its own affairs and sent delegates to a national council only in times of national emergency. The Cherokees took public opinion so seriously that, if a village became too large (about five hundred people) to permit each adult a voice in council, it was usually split in two. It may have been this kind of political organization that Jefferson had in mind when he penned the following comment regarding a proposal to make the states several times larger than the original colonies:

> This is reversing the natural order of things. A tractable people may be governed in large bodies but, in proportion as they depart from this character, the extent of their government must be less. We see into what small divisions the Indians are obliged to reduce their societies.[6]

In Cherokee society, each adult was regarded as an equal in political matters, and leadership titles were few and informal. Therefore, when Europeans sought "kings" or "chiefs" with whom to negotiate treaties, they usually did not understand that the individuals holding these titles could not compel the allegiance or obedience of others. The Cherokees made a conscious effort to keep government to a minimum, in the belief that personal freedom would be enhanced. George Milliken Johnson, a surgeon who lived with the Cherokees during the middle of the eighteenth century, remarked that "subjugation is what they are unacquainted with . . . there being no such thing as coercive Power among them." Another observer commented that it was "by native politeness alone" that Cherokee chiefs were able to "bind the hearts of their subjects, and carry them wherever they will."

As with many other confederacies, a clan system bound the individual Cherokee villages together. A man or woman, traveling outside his or her own village, knew that members of the same clan awaited them to provide hospitality and other support. The clan system cemented the Confederacy, giving it enough strength and endurance to prevent such a high degree of local autonomy from degenerating into anarchy. In village councils, each clan met in caucus before consensus decisions were reached in a general session. In the new United States, the clan system was replaced by the formation of a large number of voluntary organizations that were national in scope. Franklin, for instance, encouraged these kinds of affiliations in order to tie together people in a geographical area that must have seemed vast—not only to immigrants who were accustomed to the smaller scale of Western Europe, but also to their sons and daughters.

The Cherokees also frowned on acquisition of material wealth. Henry Timberlake speculated that the Cherokees buried valuables with the dead to prevent the development of a class structure based on inherited wealth, thereby making "merit the sole means of acquiring power, honor and riches." One cannot help but wonder how this native example affected the ongoing debate in the colonies and early United States over primogeniture—the right of the first-born son to all or most of his father's estate, a European custom bitterly opposed by Jefferson. According to Timberlake's account, the Cherokees maintained a ceremony meant to provide for the poor. During a special war dance, as each warrior was called upon to recount the taking of his first scalp, anyone with something to spare—"a string of wampum" or a piece of silver "plate, wire, paint," or lead—heaped the goods on a blanket or animal skin that had been placed on the ground. The collection was later divided among the poor of the community, with a share reserved for the musicians who had provided entertainment during the ceremony.

The Choctaws, like the Cherokees, elected leaders from each town or village and sent them to a central council. Their system has been characterized as "amazingly efficient," combining "elected officials, unlimited debate, civilian rule, and local self-government."

Some of the similarities among the political systems of the Iroquois, Hurons, and Cherokees probably were not accidental, since all three groups were linked by a common ancestry. Floyd G. Lounsbury, a linguist, traced the Iroquois and Cherokee linguistic base to a shared language, which split about thirty-five to thirty-eight hundred years ago. There is evidence that the Cherokees migrated southeastward from the Ohio valley and shared the basics of their language with both the Iroquois and the Hurons; this migration continued as late as 1700. In fact, it was about that time that the Tuscaroras moved from an area near Cherokee country to become the sixth nation of the Iroquois.

The similarities in the ways in which colonial observers described native societies, whether or not the native polities actually operated similarly, may have been due to the purpose of their study. As noted earlier, the observers' perceptions of these societies often were incomplete and profoundly reshaped by their own struggle for liberty; therefore, it is likely that native political reality was much more varied, and differences more pronounced, than many contemporary observers believed. However, their beliefs shaped their perceptions of reality; so, even if this knowledge is deemed incomplete or inaccurate by present-day standards, it does not mean that those who drew an image of liberty from native societies got nothing from their endeavors. Quite the opposite was true. Views and visions of America also profoundly affected debate and the course of empire in Europe, as knowledge of native political structures became crucial to the conduct of trade and diplomacy in North America.

NOTES

1. Anthony F. C. Wallace, *The Death and Rebirth of the Seneca* (New York: Vintage Books, 1969), p. 42.

2. Cadwallader Colden, *The History of the Five Indian Nations Depending on the Province of New York in America* [1727 and 1747] (Ithaca: Cornell University Press, 1968), p. xx.

3. Colden, Ibid., p. xx.

4. Colden, Ibid., p. xix.

5. Paul A. W. Wallace, *The White Roots of Peace* (Philadelphia: University of Pennsylvania Press, 1946), sec. 93.

6. Adrienne Koch and William Peden, eds., *The Life and Selected Writings of Thomas Jefferson* (New York: The Modern Library, 1944), p. 408.

ORIGINS OF IROQUOIS POLITICAL THOUGHT

John Mohawk

The story of the White Roots of Peace is the story of the thinking around the events which led to the founding of the League of the Haudenosaunee (as the Six Nations Iroquois call themselves).

This was a time of great sorrow and terror for the Haudenosaunee. All order and safety had broken down completely and the rule of the headhunter dominated the culture.

The Peacemaker sought out the most remarkable survivors of this random and undeclared war and he initiated discussions with them. He offered the idea that all human beings possess the power of rational thought and that in the belief in rational thought is to be found the power to create peace.

The Peacemaker laid forth a promise of a hopeful future, a future in which there would be no wars, a future in which human beings would gather together to use their minds to create peace. He raised the idea of rational thinking to the status of a political principle. He promoted clear thinking as the highest human potential, and he preached it in the spiritual language of his contemporaries.

The Peacemaker spent considerable time moving from individual to individual among the leadership of the peoples who much later would come to be known as the Mohawk, the Oneida, the Onondaga, the Cayuga, and the Seneca nations.

It was not possible to take action to bring about a solution of the blood feuds because people simply could not think clearly in an environment dominated by revenge and death, fear and hatred. The Peacemaker brought a process of clear thinking to that reality.

He promised them power. Not military power, but the power of righteousness. He defined righteousness as the result of the best thinking of collective minds operating from principles which assume that a sane world requires that we provide a safe environment for our children seven generations into the future.

A people living in fear cannot apply their potentially best thinking to solving their problems. A people living under terror can barely think at all.

The weapons may change, the distinct situations may change, but warfare and human needs remain the same. Human beings, in order to function at their very best, need to believe in a future. To motivate them, they need a vision of that future which they can help to create. They need to believe they have the potential to do what must be done in order to reach that future, and they need to have a collective identity which supports them in doing that.

The White Roots continue to represent a tradition of thinking about ourselves as a species, and the responsibility to use our minds that we will continue to survive and to create a good world for our children seven generations into the future.

Excerpted with permission of the author from *Northeast Indian Quarterly* (Summer 1986). Reprinted by permission of Akwe:kon Press.

ONE MORE SMILE FOR A HOPI CLOWN

Emory Sekaquaptewa

The heart of the Hopi concept of clowning is that we are all clowns. This was established at the very beginning when people first emerged from the lower world. In spite of the belief that this was a new world in which no corruption and immorality would be present, the people nevertheless took as their own all things that they saw in the new world. Seeing that the people still carried with them many of the ways of the corrupted underworld, the Spirit Being divided them into groups and laid out a life-pattern for each of them, so that each would follow its own life-way.

Before the Hopi people left from the emergence place, one man chosen by them as their leader went up on a hill. I can just imagine the throng of his people around him who were excited and eager in getting ready to be led out to the adventures of a new world. The leader gets up on this hill and calls out, "yaahahay!" four times. Thus gaining their attention he said. "Now you heard me cry out to you in this way. You will hear me cry in this way when we have reached the end of our life-way. It will be a sign that we have reached the end of the world. We will know then whether we have fulfilled our destiny. If we have not we will see how it is to be done." The leader who

was a visionary man chose this way of reminding his people that they have only their worldly ambition and aspirations by which to gain a spiritual world of eternity. He was showing them that we cannot be perfect in this world after all and if we are reminded that we are clowns, maybe we can have, from time to time, introspection as a guide to lead us right. From this beginning when we have been resembled to clowns we know that this is to be a trying life and that we will try to fulfill our destiny by mimicry, by mockery, by copying, by whatever.

This whole idea of clowning is reenacted at the time of the *katsina* dances. When they are dancing in the plaza the *katsinas* represent the spiritual life toward which Hopi destiny is bent. The *katsinas* dance in the plaza at intervals throughout the day and sometimes for two days. When the clowns come they represent man today who is trying to reach this place of paradise. That is why the clowns always arrive at the plaza from the rooftops of the houses facing the plaza where the *katsinas* are dancing. The rooftops signify that even though we have reached the end, we are not necessarily ready to walk easily into the spiritual world. The difficulties by which clowns gain the place of the *katsinas* make for fun and laughter, but also show that we may not all be able to make it from the rooftop because it is too difficult. We are going to clown our way

From "One More Smile for a Hopi Clown," by Emory Sekaquaptewa, as appeared in *The South Corner of Time,* 1980, edited by Larry Ivers. Reprinted with permission of Larry Ivers.

through life making believe that we know everything and when the time comes, possibly no one will be prepared after all to enter the next world. We will still find the way difficult with obstacles in front of us. Maybe some of us won't make it.

The clowns come to the edge of the housetops around noon and they announce themselves with the cry "yaahahay!" four times. This announces as foretold at emergence the arrival at the end of the life-way journey. And then they make their way into the plaza with all sorts of antics and buffoonery representing the Hopi life quest. In their actions they reveal that we haven't yet fulfilled our destiny after all. By arriving at the late hour, noon, they show that we are lagging behind because we think we have many things to do.

Once in the plaza they act just as people did when they emerged in this world. They presume that they are in a new world, clean and pure. They are where they can finally have eternal life like the *katsinas*; indeed, this is the day all Hopi look forward to. But as they are remarking on the beauty of this place filled with plants and good things they hear the *katsina* songs. They grope around the plaza looking for someone. They pretend they cannot see them because they are spirits. Finally, one of the clowns touches a *katsina* and upon his discovery of these beautiful beings, the clowns immediately try to take possession of them. "This is mine!" "This is mine!" They even fight each other over the possession of the *katsinas* and over the food and things they find.

The remainder of the afternoon is filled with all sorts of clown performances, many of which are planned in advance. Others just happen. These are satires focused on almost anything whether it be in the Hopi world or in the non-Hopi world. Clowns make fun of life and thereby cause people to look at themselves.

Imagination is important to the clown. There are good clowns and not so good clowns when it comes to being funny and witty. But all clowns perform for the smiles and laughter they hope to inspire in the people. When the clowns leave the kiva on their way to the plaza the last request by each is a prayer something to the effect, "If it be so, may I gain at least one smile."

The clown skits and satiric performances done throughout the afternoon are reminiscent of the corruption that we experienced in the underworld, where we presumably had Conscience as a guide. We chose not to follow the Conscience and it comes into play during the clown performances in the form of *katsinas* that visit the plaza. The Owl *katsina* on his first visit comes with a handful of pebbles, carrying a switch. He appears at each corner of the plaza presumably unseen by the clowns and throws little pebbles at the clowns, occasionally hitting them. These pangs of Conscience are felt but not heeded by the clowns. Owl *katsina* returns to the plaza later accompanied by several threatening *katsinas* carrying whips. And this time, instead of pebbles, he may brush up against one of the clowns. He may even knock him down. Conscience keeps getting stronger and more demanding and insistent. On Owl's third visit, the clowns begin to realize that they may suffer consequences if they don't change their ways. Still, they try to buy their safety by offering Owl a bribe. On the sly, the head clown approaches Owl, presumably unseen by anyone, but, of course, they are in the middle of the plaza and are witnessed by all the spectators. Those two kneel together in an archaic conversation modeled upon an ancient meeting.

Owl finally accepts the bribe of a string of beads and thus leads the clown to believe that he has bought his safety. The head clown asks Owl to discipline the other clowns so as to get them back on the right road, but he thinks he will be safe.

With each of Owl's visits more and more *katsinas* accompany him. They do not come as one big group, but in groups of two or three. Throughout the afternoon the tension builds with the threatening presence of the whip-carrying *katsinas*. All of the spectators begin to identify with the plight of the clowns. You feel like you are the one who is now being judged for all these things.

Owl's fourth visit may not come until the next day. On this visit he brings with him a whole lot of warrior *katsinas*. The atmosphere is one of impending catastrophe. They move closer and closer, finally attacking the clowns, who are stripped and whipped for all they have done. In this way they force the clowns to take responsibility for their actions. After they are whipped, water is poured on them and sprinkled about the audience to signify purification.

When it is all over the threatening *katsinas* come back to the plaza again, but this time they are friendly. They shake hands with the clowns signifying that they have been purified. Then they take each clown the length of the plaza and form a semi-circle around him. At this time the clowns make confessions, but even here they are clowns for their confessions are all made in jest. Having worked up satires for the occasion they jump and sing before the *katsinas*. Their confessions usually are focused on their clan, who, by way of being satirized, are actually honored.

I'll tell you one I heard not long ago. When it was time for this young clown man to make his confession he jumps up and down in front of the *katsina* and says, "Ah ii geology, geology, ah ii." Then he made a beautiful little breakdown of this word so that it has Hopi meaning. "You probably think I am talking about this geology which is a white man's study about something or

other. Well, that's not it," he says. "What it really is is that I have a grandmother, and you know she being poor and ugly, nobody would have anything to do with her. She is running around all summer long out in the fields doing a man's job. It breaks her down. She would go out there every day with no shoes and so her feet were not very dainty and not very feminine. If you pick up her foot and look at her sole, it is all cracked and that's what I am talking about when I say geology." Every Hopi can put that together. *Tsiya* means "to crack" and *leetsi* means things placed "in a row," so these cracks are in a row on the bottom of the feet, geology. Things like that are what the confessions are like.

There is a story about the last wish of a Hopi man who died many years ago that shows the character of clowning.

In those days the clown society was very much formalized. It was a practice for men who had great devotion for their ritual society to be buried in the full costume of their office. Of course, this was not seen by the general public since Hopi funerals are rather private affairs.

This story is about a man who had gained great respect for his resourcefulness and performance as a clown. Clowning had become a major part of his life and he was constantly attending to his work as a clown by thinking up new skits and perfecting his performance. As he reached old age he decided that clowning had made his place in this world and he wanted to be remembered as a clown. So he made a special request for what was to be done with him at his death as he realized his time was short. He made his request to his family very firmly.

When he died his nephews and sons began to carry out his request. In preparation for burial the body was dressed in his clown costume. Then the body was carried around to the west side of the plaza and taken up on a roof. While this was being done the town crier's voice rang out through the village calling all the people to the plaza. Everybody was prompt in gathering there. I can just see the women, as with any such occasion, grabbing their best shawl on their way to the plaza. It didn't matter whether they were dressed well underneath the shawl.

When the people arrived they saw this unusual sight on the roof of the house on the west side of the plaza, men standing around a person lying down. When all of the people had gathered, the attendants—pallbearers I guess you could call them—simply, quietly, picked up the body and took it to the edge of the house near the plaza. They picked it up by the hands and legs and swung it out over the plaza as if to throw it and they hollered, "Yaahahay!" And they'd swing it back. Then they'd swing it once more. "Yaahahay!" Four times! On the fourth time they let the body go and it fell down, plop, in the plaza. As they threw the body the pallbearers hollered and laughed as they were supposed to. It took the people by surprise. But then everybody laughed.

© 1997 H.J. Tsinhnahjinnie

JIM THORPE: ALL-AMERICAN (INDIAN) ATHLETE

Steve Talbot

An important part of the Native American heritage is athletics and sports heroes. Unquestionably, the greatest Indian athlete in the United States was Jim Thorpe, a Sac and Fox from Oklahoma, who won gold medals in the pentathlon and the decathlon in the 1912 Stockholm Olympics. With 8,412 points, he broke the decathlon world record by an incredible 998 points. King Gustav of Sweden described him as "the greatest athlete in the world." Thorpe attended Carlisle Indian School in Pennsylvania from 1908 to 1912, where he played football. In a memorable game against Harvard University, he scored a touchdown and kicked four field goals. Carlisle won with a score of 18 to 15. He held world records in track and field and was an All-American college athlete in lacrosse and basketball as well as football. He also excelled in golf, swimming, rowing, hockey, and boxing.

After his Olympic triumph he was stripped of his medals and his records were expunged when it was learned that he had played semiprofessional, summer baseball in 1909 for fifteen dollars a week. Under the Olympic rules in 1912, his semiprofessional status disqualified him from further amateur sports and eligibility for participation in the Olympic games. This narrow interpretation of Olympic rules has been widely viewed by Native Americans and fair-minded sports enthusiasts as grossly unfair and discriminatory. Thorpe nevertheless went on to play major league baseball with the New York Giants and later became the first president of the National Football League in 1920. In 1950, the Associated Press poll of sportswriters and sportscasters voted him the greatest football player of the half century, beating out Red Grange. He was also voted the best all-round male athlete. He surpassed Babe Ruth, Jack Dempsey, and other outstanding athletes in this poll.

In 1984, after a national campaign, his Olympic medals were finally returned to the Thorpe family.

SOURCES: Duane Champagne, ed., *The Native North American Almanac* (Detroit: Gale Research, 1994), 1177; Mary B. Davis, ed., *Native America in the Twentieth Century: An Encyclopedia* (New York: Garland, 1996), 613; Brendan White (bfw2@cornell.edu), "Vote for Jim Thorpe As Athlete of the Century," 1-11-2000.

4

LATIN AMERICA'S INDIGENOUS PEOPLES
CHANGING IDENTITIES AND FORMS OF RESISTANCE

Michael Kearney and Stefano Varese

Any attempt to make meaningful and valid generalizations about the contemporary indigenous peoples of the Americas is a daunting task given their vast geographical extension and wide variation in social forms and living conditions. There are tens of millions of indigenous peoples, or *indígenas*, in

Latin America. Their distribution today generally follows that of pre-Columbian population patterns. Thus, they range from a majority of the population in Bolivia, Peru, and Guatemala to large minorities in Mexico, Colombia, Venezuela, Ecuador, Paraguay, and Chile. A small minority in the vastness of Brazil, *indígenas* nevertheless have acquired unanticipated importance in the politics of their country.

Contemporary indigenous identities are best understood through historical examination. Several major epochs have shaped the economic and political conditions affecting indigenous communities. Furthermore, these conditions continue to change, just as anthropological understandings about indigenous identity have evolved. Therefore, in reviewing the status of the contemporary *indígenas* in Latin America, we must also comment on the development of the concepts that have been used to interpret these identities.

There are various ways to approach the history and identity of indigenous peoples. Anthropological thinking was dominated until recently by the assimilation model. In this view, the *indígenas* possess traditional social forms and cultures that will eventually give way to modern society, a process that is thought to occur through the acceptance of modern technology and cultural forms whereby *indígenas* are supposed to be acculturated into modern society. This perspective sees contemporary indigenous identities largely as survivals from earlier periods, especially pre-Columbian times. One implication of this acculturation perspective is that indigenous communities are destined to disappear as successive generations lose their traditional traits and assimilate into modern society. To be sure, there has been much acculturation and assimilation of *indígenas* who have retained few traits stemming from their original cultures. Hundreds of local indigenous communities and their languages have completely disappeared over the past five hundred years. But at the same time, many *indígenas* have displayed a remarkable staying power, and in recent years their presence has become ever more notable.

The durability of the *indígenas* called for a different theoretical perspective. The working notion of this theory is that social identity is formed largely in opposition to others in a dialectic of what are called "othering" and "self-attribution." The rest of this chapter explores this twofold phenomenon of leveling and differentiation and assumes that it is inherent not only in local but also in global economic and cultural relations.

FROM PRE-COLUMBIAN TO COLONIAL SOCIETIES

At the end of the fifteenth century, when the first appreciable numbers of Europeans came into their midst, the native peoples of what is now Latin America were arrayed in numerous and diverse types of societies ranging from nomadic foraging bands to complex state civilizations comparable to those of Asia and Europe. In the two centuries after the arrival of Columbus, the destinies of *indígenas* of the region were overwhelmingly shaped by the devastating impact of this encounter; numerous communities disappeared completely while others suffered population declines of 80 to 100 percent (for an overview of the human tragedy associated with the Conquest, see Galeano 1973). During the ensuing three hundred years the identity of *indígenas* was shaped by their subordinate position as colonized subjects and, later, as subordinated ethnic groups within the postcolonial nation-states dominated by non-*indígenas*.

The Conquest irrevocably incorporated the indigenous peoples into global relationships with European states in what was becoming a world capitalist system (Wolf 1982). As the logic of that new world order was understood by the political leaders of the time, European nations, to prosper and to be strong vis-à-vis other nations, needed colonies as sources of wealth. According to the theory of mercantilism that gained favor in sixteenth-century Europe and influenced economic thought through the eighteenth, the ideal colonies possessed both natural resources and the native populations needed to extract them. The resources produced by cheap labor in the colonies could supply industries in the home countries, which in turn would produce merchandise for sale back to the colonies and on the world market in general.

The identity of the *indígenas* during the Conquest and colonial periods was shaped mainly by Spanish, Portuguese, French, and English policies designed, first, to maintain distinctions between the European nations and their colonies in what was called the New World and, second, to maintain, within the colonies, the distinctions between Europeans and the non-Europeans found there. Spanish occupation of the Americas and Spanish colonial policies regarding the *indígenas* contrasted sharply with those of the English in their colonial project in North America, which was effected largely through the migration of prosperous dissident religious communities consisting of entire families. Imbued with notions of religious and economic freedom, they sought worldly and spiritual salvation through industry and commerce in which the indigenous peoples were seen as having no significant role. Indeed, the English colonists of North America saw the *indígenas* more as obstacles to their projects than as resources.

At the time of its conquest of the Americas, Spain had emerged from several hundred years of military struggle against the (non-European) Moors on the Iberian Peninsula. Indeed, the final episode in that long war, the fall of Grenada in 1492, coincided with Columbus's first voyage to the islands of the Caribbean. To a great extent the subsequent conquest of what became Spanish America was a continuation of Spain's reconquest of the peninsula and was carried out largely as a military and religious crusade. Whereas English settlement in North America sought to clone the communities of England, Spanish America was occupied by battle-hardened military men, for the most part unaccompanied by women and children. Furthermore, whereas the English settlers went to North America to stay, the first waves of Spanish into the Western Hemisphere went to acquire wealth with which to improve their status upon their return to Europe. Unlike the English in North America, who generally viewed the natives as obstacles to their enterprises, the Spanish regarded indigenous labor as essential to extract wealth from the gold and silver mines and from plantations that produced commodities such as sugar, silk, indigo, and cochineal for the world market.

In Spanish America, the indigenous peoples were an essential economic resource that needed to be protected so that it might be perpetually exploited. To this end many existing indigenous communities were legally recognized and given resources so that they might endure as sources of labor and other forms of wealth for the Spanish crown, the Spanish colonists, the church, and various Catholic religious orders. The catastrophic post-Conquest population declines noted above made labor scarce, however, and necessitated stronger policies for the husbandry of these communities. The subsequent social identities and destinies of the *indígenas* and their communities in Spanish America thus developed under markedly different conditions from the English colonies.

Whereas in North America the indigenous peoples were not greatly valued as an economic resource and were mostly exterminated outright or forced onto reservations, in Spanish Latin America the larger populations of *indígenas* were concentrated in communities that were in effect internal colonies. By way of contrast, the Portuguese colonists in Brazil regarded the *indígenas* much as the English (and subsequently the Americans) had the *indígenas* in North America. Although many *indígenas* were incorporated into rubber tapping and mining, African slaves assumed a much more important role in the overall economy of Brazil than they did in most of Spanish America.

FROM INDEPENDENCE
TO THE MID-TWENTIETH CENTURY

By the early nineteenth century criollos throughout Spanish America had come to think of themselves as more American than Spanish; that is, as residents of the regions in which they were born and with which they identified. When these sentiments culminated in successful independence movements, the independent criollos were faced with the challenge of building nation-states out of the former colonies. Central to the concept of a modern nation-state was the idea of a common national cultural identity. The postcolonial nation-states, striving as they were to create more or less culturally homogeneous citizenries, swept away colonial laws that defined peoples as members of racial castes such as "Indian," "white," "black," and combinations thereof. Although racism did not disappear, it now became imbricated more in a social structure based on class. The main distinctions in this class structure grew out of how one earned a living, and the major divide was between those who did manual labor and those who did not. Of course, the *indígenas* fell almost exclusively into the former category. Thus, although the formal structure of the caste system was dismantled, the position of the *indígenas* on the bottom rung of the social hierarchy was perpetuated.

The architects of the Latin American nation-states assumed that the *indígenas* would disappear from history along with the system of castes. And toward this end some of them enacted reform programs in the mid-eighteenth century aimed at eliminating the colonial laws that protected the indigenous communities. In Mexico, for example, the liberal procapitalist elements that enacted the 1857 constitution dissolved the corporate legal basis of the indigenous communities that had prevailed during the colonial period. The assumption was that exposure of the communal resources (primarily communal lands) of the *indígenas* to market forces would break down the backwardness of these communities. Thus, they ceased to be regarded as primarily economic resources and were now seen as barriers to the development of the types of modern agriculture and manufacturing taking place to the north in the United States. Indeed, the liberals saw development in the United States as due in large part to the absence of large indigenous peasant communities such as those in Latin America. In contrast to the colonial period, therefore, in which the *indígenas* were seen as sources of wealth, the indigenous communities were now regarded as pockets of backwardness that were inhibiting progress.

This situation prevailed for the most part until after World War II, when the United States took a renewed interest in Latin America in the context of the cold war. Concerned to maintain its hegemony in the Western Hemisphere in the face of a presumed communist threat, the United States and various international agencies such as the World Bank sought to promote economic development in Latin America. Indeed, the policies and projects of this period were variations on nineteenth-century developmental goals, except they were now promoted in the cold war context, with the U.S. government and international agencies assuming considerable responsibility for the economic and political development of "backward" communities. In this period the Indians were largely identified as peasants. That is to say, they were seen according to economic and developmental criteria rather than for their identity as indigenous peoples. The assumption was that "underdeveloped" communities would be transformed into modern developed ones.

During this period the population growth rate in many countries of the hemisphere exceeded the rates of socioeconomic development measured in terms of job creation and improved standards of living. The population growth also affected indigenous communities, and earlier prognostications about their demise were shown to be inaccurate. Indeed, the simultaneous growth in poverty and numbers of the indigenous peoples suggested that modern history was taking a turn other than that predicted by the architects of the modern Latin American states and the theorists of development.

THE PERSISTENCE OF THE *"INDÍGENAS"*

After the disastrous biological holocaust caused by the epidemics of the "Columbian exchange" (Crosby 1972), which produced probably the greatest population decline in human history (Denevan 1976; Borah and Cook 1963; Dobyns 1966), the indigenous peoples of colonial Spanish and Portuguese America began a slow demographic recuperation that by the early 1990s had brought their population to the vicinity of 40 million (Mayer and Masferrer 1979; World Bank 1991). This number, however, is far below the estimates of the hemisphere's original indigenous population.

There is an intriguing paradox in regard to this obstinate biological and cultural perseverance of the Native American people: How could they outlast the European military invasion, the resulting biological disaster, the systematic "ecological imperialism" (Crosby 1986), the meticulous destruction of their institutions, and still undergo a cultural, social, and political recuperation that has allowed for their continuous and increasing presence in the social and biological history of the continent? The answer to this question has to be sought in the complex forms of resistance and adaptation of the various indigenous peoples over the past five centuries.

Four fundamental forms of ethnic resilience and opposition recur in this long history. The first is what we may call the "moral management" of the cosmos, a type of environmental ethic and practice found in the majority of indigenous societies (Varese 1995). The second is an economic rationality and a social philosophy that contrasts with the individualism and market-based economies of modern societies. This "moral economy," as Scott (1976, 1985) refers to it, occurs among some peasant societies and operates with a logic informed by the ecological cosmology noted above. It seeks to preserve the common resources of the community and minimize internal economic differentiation. Basic economic resources are held in common, and access to them is determined by good citizenship, defined by one's willingness to serve the community in ways that often involve considerable self-sacrifice. Such an economy is centered more on use-value than exchange-value, and economic transactions are mediated primarily by reciprocity rather than by market or profit considerations.

Related to the specifically indigenous nature of these two factors is a third: the tendency of *indígenas* to conceal their ethnobiological knowledge while maintaining an active exploration, investigation, experimentation, and conservation of biodiversity. Finally, indigenous peoples have been extremely adaptable in restructuring their political action to respond to a constantly changing world.

Latin America's indigenous communities were able to establish a new, decolonized institutional, political, and cultural relationship not only among themselves but also with the nonindigenous peoples of the Americas in a number of ways. A reconfiguration of this nature implies a demise of nineteenth-century nationalistic ideology and practices and the negotiation of autonomy and sovereignty with national and international entities (the nation-states, intergovernmental organisms, the transnational corporations, etc.).

Since the European invasion of the Americas, indigenous societies have attempted to conceal their biotic and biotechnological knowledge, well aware that such knowledge was among the most contested cultural domains of the colonial mercantile and evangelical enterprise. For most of the indigenous peoples, agricultural and food production, as well as environmental management, were suffused with religious significance. As such, these social practices were extremely vulnerable to repression by the colonial authorities.

It is well documented that the Spaniards' early ambiguous attitudes toward the Native American biotic heritage induced a series of repressive measures against the cultivation and use of certain plants and resources. The most notorious example is the Mesoamerican *alegría* (amaranth—called *tzoalli* and *huautli* by the Mexicans), whose cultivation, trade, and consumption were banned throughout New Spain during the early colonial period with the argument that it was a pagan sacrificial plant. However, use of medicinal and psychotropic plants and substances, use of stimulants like coca and of animal and insect foods, techniques of preparation of food and fermented beverages, and techniques of food production (e.g., various types of swidden cultivation) have been contentious areas of cultural and political control throughout the colonial period and up to the present.

In Mexico, Bishop Zumarraga, "wished to outlaw pulque [fermented maguey juice] in 1529 because it smacked of idolatry," and for the missionary "drinking, with its ritual vestiges, was a major obstacle to evangelical expansion" (Super 1988:75). But similar aspirations are still at the core of various types of evangelical fundamentalism practiced, for example, by the Summer Institute of Linguistics or a number of Protestant missionaries working with the *indígenas* (Stoll 1985). In sum, European colonialism brought to the Americas definite ideas about food and food production that are still very much part of the hegemonic culture and the ideology that informs most development planning and policy affecting the indigenous regions.

The indigenous peoples did not simply react to colonial impositions. Their responses reflected a variety of strategic accommodations and initiatives. For example, immediately following the Spanish invasion of Mexico, the Maya people of Yucatan repeatedly resisted the invaders—actions that often turned into armed insurrections. These rebellions were motivated by a call to reconstitute the precolonial order and to restore the world's sacredness: to purify a nature contaminated by foreign oppressors. In 1546 the *chilam* (prophet-diviner) Anbal brought together a coalition of the Maya people. On the calendar date of Death and End (November 9), they initiated a war of liberation that sought to kill the invaders, end colonial domination, and purify the earth. The rebels killed Spaniards and their Maya slaves in sacrificial rites and meted out the same fate to all the plants and domesticated animals brought by the Europeans (Barabas 1987; Bartolomé 1984).

In 1786 the Totonacs of Papantla, in southeastern Mexico, rose in rebellion against the Spanish authorities in defense of their threatened trees. A Spanish source observed that "the trees give shade to people and help them to persevere, are useful to tie animals, protect houses from fires, and the branches and leaves are used as fodder for animals" (cited in Taylor 1979:137).

Earlier, in 1742, in the Amazon jungle of Peru, a Quechua messiah, Juan Santos Atahualpa Apu Capac Huayna, fomented a rebellion that mobilized thousands of Ashaninka, Quechua, and a dozen other ethnic groups and kept the Spaniards and Creoles out of the region for a century. Some of the insurgents' revolutionary demands and proposals were informed by an ecologically based morality: the right to live in dispersed villages and households to allow a rational use of the tropical rain forest; the eradication of European pigs considered harmful to farming and human health; the right to freely cultivate and use coca, known as the "the herb of God"; and the right to produce and ceremonially drink *masato,* a fermented manioc beverage of substantial nutritional value (Brown forthcoming; Varese 1973; Zarzar 1989).

Two centuries later, in 1973, among the Chinantecs of Oaxaca, Mexico, an intense messianic movement flared up in opposition to a proposed dam that would flood their territory and force them into exile to distant lands (Barabas and Bartolomé 1973; Barabas 1987). To defend the ecological integrity of their territory, which they considered sacred, the Chinantecs resorted to a diversified strategy that ranged from legal and bureaucratic negotiations with the government and alliance-building with poor mestizo peasants to the mobilization of shamans, the "caretakers of the lines" (the ethnic borders) whose "lightning" or *nahuals* would kill the president of Mexico, Luis Echeverría Alvarez. The Chinantec messianic movement gained cultural and social legitimacy with the sacred appearance of the Virgin of Guadalupe and the "Engineer Great God," who ordered the performance of a series of rituals to strengthen the physical and spiritual integrity of certain ecocultural features such as rivers, mountains, trees, springs, caves, and trails.

On January 1, 1994, Tzeltal, Tzotzil, Chol, Tojolabal, and Zoque Maya *indígenas* organized into the Zapatista National Liberation Army (*Ejército Zapatista de Liberación Nacional,* or EZLN) and declared war on the government, quickly establishing the military occupation of four major municipalities in Chiapas, Mexico. An *indígena* army of eight hundred combatants occupied the city of San Cristobal de las Casas, seized the municipal palace, and proclaimed their opposition to the "undeclared genocidal war against our people by the dictators," and described their "struggle for work, land, shelter, food, health, education, independence, freedom, democracy, justice, and peace" (EZLN 1994).

Of the six points stated in the EZLN's Declaration of War, the first five spelled out their rules of engagement; the sixth stated that the EZLN would "suspend the looting of our natural resources" in the areas the rebels controlled. This armed movement of an estimated two thousand persons was essentially composed of the Mayan ethnic groups noted above. A fundamental objective of the insurrection was the defense of their lands and natural resources. In other public declarations and communiqués, the EZLN also stressed its opposition to the North American Free Trade Agreement (NAFTA), which it considered a "death certificate" for the indigenous peasants, and to the modification of Article 27 of the Mexican Constitution, which permits the privatization of indigenous and peasant collective and communal lands. "This article 27 of the Constitution, they changed it without asking us, without requesting our input. Now it is time for them to listen to us, because to take our land is to take our life" (IATP 1994). These are but a few examples taken from innumerable historical and contemporary cases illustrating the moral economy that has guided indigenous resistance to economic exploitation and political oppression.

Nevertheless, since at least the mid-seventeenth century, local indigenous communities have participated in an economic system in which part of the production satisfies subsistence needs while the rest, the surplus, enters circuits of commercial exchange (Varese 1991a). Contemporary indigenous communities are thus not uncontaminated citadels of precapitalist economy. They are ruled first by the basic principles of moral economy founded on the logic of reciprocity and on the "right to subsistence," and, second, by the necessity of exchange with the surrounding capitalist market. Both principles permeate the social life of prepeasant, peasant, and even some postpeasant *indígenas* who, self-exiled from their communities because of poverty, partially reconstitute this moral economy as urban subproletarian or transnational migrant workers in the agricultural fields of California (Kearney and Nagengast 1989; Zabin et al. 1993). . . .

BUILDING INDIAN SOVEREIGNTY IN THE AMAZON

The creation of the Federation of Shuar Centers in 1964 is a benchmark in the development of new forms of resistance by indigenous peoples in Latin America. This surprising form of political organization had by 1987 incorporated 240 centers and more than 40,000 Shuar people into a unique social program of economic and cultural self-determination. Four years after the Shuar Federation was formed, the Amuesha people (Yanesha) of the Peruvian Upper Amazon convened the first Amuesha Congress, which was later transformed into a permanent political body called the Amuesha Federation.

Between 1970 and 1974, in an intense series of mobilizations, Colombian *indígenas* organized the Indian Regional Council of Cauca and several other organizations. During the 1970s in Peru, the indigenous people of the Amazon region formed many local organizations and regional federations—for instance, the Ashaninka Congress of the Central Jungle, the Shipibo Congress and Defense Front, and the Aguaruna Huambisa Council. In the highlands of Bolivia the organized expressions of a strong Aymara and Quechua nationalism were initially shaped by the Katarist movement. To the south in Chile, under the safeguard of Salvador Allende's socialist government, the Mapuches participated in the elaboration and implementation of a *Ley de Indígenas* (Law of the Indígenas). This short-lived taste of multiethnicity ended in 1973 with General Augusto Pinochet's military dictatorship and the death, imprisonment, and exile of the Mapuche leadership.

In March 1984 representatives of five indigenous organizations from the Amazonian countries of Brazil, Bolivia, Colombia, Ecuador, and Peru met in Lima and founded the international organization called the Coordinating Body of Indigenous Peoples' Organizations of the Amazon Basin (*Coordinadora de las Organizaciones Indígenas de la Cuenca Amazónica*, or COICA). COICA's main political objective was to became a coordinating body that would present a common policy position for all the organized *indígenas* of the Greater Amazon Basin before the region's governments and the international community. COICA's origins can be traced to the three regional, community-based organizations of the early 1960s noted above: the Shuar Federation in Ecuador, the Congress of Amuesha Communities in Peru, and the Regional Indigenous Council of the Cauca in Colombia (Smith 1993). These local organizations, initially unknown to one another, established a model of social mobilization that gave voice to each local community's problems of territorial loss, human rights abuses, and cultural oppression. Throughout the 1970s, numerous other organizations emerged among the Amazonian peoples and began to establish contacts facilitated by the solidarity of various nonindigenous groups, such as sympathetic Catholic missionaries, proindigenous NGOs, and environmentalists.

COICA has primarily been concerned with territorial and environmental rights; human, cultural, and linguistic rights; and rights to economic and political self-determination (Smith 1993; Varese 1991a). Today COICA comprises more than one hundred interethnic confederations of Amazonian groups from Bolivia, Brazil, Colombia, Ecuador, Guyana, French Guyana, Peru, Suriname, and Venezuela, which represent approximately 1.5 million indigenous people (Chirif et al. 1991; Smith 1993).

COICA's active involvement in the U.N. Working Group on Indigenous Peoples' Rights, in the discussions concerning the ILO's Covenant 169 on Indigenous and Tribal People approved in 1989, and in various committees of the Amazon Treaty Cooperation sponsored by the Inter-American Indigenous Institute brought the members of the organization in contact with an increasing number of international bureaucrats, advocates, indigenous support groups, the leaders of other ethnic minorities, parties, labor organizations, the European Green movement, and funding agencies. In 1986 COICA won an ecological prize, the Right Livelihood award, which gave the organization front-page international coverage and major exposure to official circles. During 1989 COICA was recognized by the World Bank and had established official contact with the European Community (now the European Union). In 1991 COICA gained official advisory status with the Indigenous Commission of the Amazon Cooperation Treaty. Moreover, between 1990 and 1991, it was one of the founding members of the Alliance for Protecting the Forest and Climate, formed with representatives from more than one hundred cities in five European countries (Smith 1993).

This relatively rapid success brought strains to COICA, revealing its structural limitations in representing its constituencies and its lack of means and methods for efficient communications between its community-based units, the regional and national federations, and its central administrative body. And, finally, the central administration had become somewhat autocratic (Smith 1993). By 1992 a general congress of COICA unanimously decided to create a less hierarchical structure and to facilitate communications and accountability by decentralizing decision-making. COICA headquarters were also moved from Lima to Quito.

MESOAMERICAN INDIGENOUS PEOPLES IN THE UNITED STATES

The activities of migrants from Guatemala and southern Mexico to the United States have been one of the most notable developments in the recent history of new Latin American indigenous movements. Since the outbreak of war in Guatemala during the late 1970s between several indigenous-based guerrilla groups and the government, some tens of thousands of *indígenas* have been killed, and many thousands more have fled the country to seek sanctuary either in Mexico or in the United States. Those who sought refuge in the United States in the past fifteen or so years have settled mainly in Los Angeles. Within the Guatemalan indigenous community in Los Angeles, many different ethnic groups are represented, each of which is from a distinct community that speaks its own Mayan language. Whereas these refugees were isolated by distance and culture in

Guatemala, they have been thrown together in the city's sprawling Latino neighborhoods, where they found common cultural and political bonds. On the basis of this shared heritage, the need to defend themselves as aliens in a strange and often hostile land has motivated them to form several interethnic associations. The largest of these, known as "Ixim," takes its name from the Mayan word for maize, which in cognate forms is found in the languages of all the Guatemalan indigenous peoples in Los Angeles.

Comparable to the presence of indigenous Guatemalan refugees in Los Angeles is the presence in California of tens of thousands of *indígenas* from the state of Oaxaca in southern Mexico. At any given time there are some 25,000 to 40,000 Mixtec migrant farm workers in California (Runsten and Kearney 1994). Whereas the Guatemalan *indígenas* are refugees from a horrendous war waged against them, the Mixtecs are mainly economic refugees from a region in which the environment has been steadily deteriorating, undermining the subsistence farming that is their primary livelihood. In the 1980s, Mixtec migrants from various towns formed self-help associations based on their communities of origin, and by the early 1990s these local groups had come together to form a common Mixtec front.

Since the 1960s, uncounted thousands of Zapotecs from Oaxaca have migrated to California to work temporarily or to settle, primarily in the Los Angeles area. As in the Mixtec case, the Zapotecs have formed migrant associations based on their communities of origin, some twenty of which came together in the late 1980s to create a coordinating body, the Oaxacan Regional Organization (ORO).

The objectives of the Zapotec and the Mixtec federations are binational in scope in that they seek to protect and promote the well-being of their members in the United States and also to defend and otherwise support their communities of origin in Oaxaca through financial and symbolic support and by intervening in government policies directed at the indigenous communities. A major milestone in Oaxacan political evolution in California was the coming together in 1991 of most of the Mixtec and Zapotec groups to form the Mixtec-Zapotec Binational Front, which has since acquired considerable legitimacy with the Mexican government and international agencies. In 1994 other indigenous groups in Oaxaca asked to join the front. These groups represent Mixe, Triques, and Chatinos, thus occasioning another name change, this time to the all-inclusive Frente Indígena Oaxaqueña Binacional (FIOB), which can without terminological inconsistency now accept groups representing any of the sixteen indigenous peoples of Oaxaca.

The history of the formation of the Guatemalan and Oaxacan indigenous groups in California is perhaps the most notable example of the transnationalization of Latin American indigenous politics in that the primary locus of these international groups has been outside not only their home territories but also Latin America. In their organizational forms, as in their personal lives, the members of these groups transcend the boundaries between the United States, Guatemala, and Mexico, and also between the so-called industrial and developing worlds, a distinction that has become largely obsolete as Mesoamerican indigenous peoples increasingly live transnational lives.

LESSONS FROM EXPERIENCE AND FUTURE PERSPECTIVES

An assessment of the Latin American indigenous movement in the 1990s reveals two crucial concerns of the indigenous people. The first is the right of self-government and autonomy. These rights are becoming an increasingly prominent part of the democratization process in various Latin American countries. The demands of the Mayan rebels of Chiapas presented to the Mexican government in 1994 are a good example. As mentioned above, the indigenous insurgents demanded communal and regional autonomy, free elections, self-rule, and guarantees of nonintervention on the part of the government in their internal affairs. The second concern is their right to territorial and resource sovereignty. Their demands for ethnic self-determination and autonomy include full control over the lands, water, and resources that fall within their newly defined ethnic boundaries.

The recuperation of ethnic territories and political autonomy is based on three principles, the first of which is the historical depth of the claim. The current territorial fragmentation and reduction in Latin America is the result of centuries of colonial and postcolonial expropriation; therefore, restitution of land and/or reparations are major issues.

The second principle is based on the ethnobiological integrity of territories traditionally occupied by specific indigenous groups. In other words, bioregions and ethnoregions were largely coincident before the territorial disturbances of the Europeans. There is no such thing in the contemporary period as natural, untouched landscape: Rational intervention by *indígenas* over the millennia has shaped and molded the environment and its biotic resources (see Chirif et al. 1991).

The third principle is the repudiation of any solution to territorial and environmental claims that would involve the commoditization of nature. As one indigenous leader is reported to have stated in objection to the celebrated debt-for-nature swaps promoted by some Northern environmentalists: "It is our nature—and it's not our debt" (Brysk 1992).

Recognition of and respect for these three principles must constitute the ethical framework for any political and economic negotiations between the indigenous peoples and national and international entities regarding political, territorial, and resource sovereignty. Some of the specific practical aspects of ethno-sovereignty rights that will have to be jointly addressed by *indígenas* and nonindigenous peoples are briefly mentioned below.

First of all, there is the important question of the social and spatial definition of indigenous peoples and groups. According to the indigenistic legislation of various national governments, the indigenous ethnic groups are legally defined by their respective constituent communities (e.g., the *resguardo* in Colombia, the *comunidad nativa* and *comunidad campesina* in Peru, the *comunidad indígena* and *ejido* in Mexico, etc.). The whole ethnic group, even if legally recognized in some capacity by the state, does not constitute a juridical subject. Nevertheless, the indigenous organizations of Ecuador have succeeded in obtaining the state's recognition of the term "nationalities" for the various indigenous ethnic communities, but this is a definitive exception in Latin America.

In view of the disagreement and confusion throughout the continent about ethnosocial definitions and boundaries, indigenous intellectuals and leaders are addressing two levels of sovereignty that are rather complementary: One is "communal sovereignty," which is usually legally recognized by the state. At this level there are local indigenous institutions and authorities and clear social-ethnic boundaries; the rather murky and more complicated biotic boundaries therefore pose a more complex problem of genetic and resource sovereignty.

In contrast, the concept of "ethnic sovereignty" is legally rare or nonexistent from the state's point of view. However, some groups are beginning to define this type of sovereignty (Varese 1988). Total ethnic sovereignty is represented in the numerous indigenous ethnic organizations that have a legal and fully institutional existence. In this case, negotiated restitutions and formal interinstitutional agreements are required at various organizational levels, including the local community, the ethnic organization, local and central government agencies, and external investors and/or scientific parties. In instances of this type, the issue of biotic, cultural, and resource boundaries is easiest to resolve since there may be an approximate coincidence between ethnopolitical and ethnobiotic boundaries. By "ethnopolitical

boundaries," the indigenous people mean the historically traceable ethnic frontiers, even if they are not actually under ethnic control and are not being reclaimed by the organization as a political objective.

Finally, there is the challenge of further developing organizational and legal forms that recognize and meet the needs of the ever-growing numbers of de-territorialized indigenous peoples who reside in cities and in nations far removed from their traditional homelands and modes of existence. These issues of boundaries and identities, of sovereignty and self-determination, promise to be increasingly salient issues to the indigenous peoples of Latin America in the twenty-first century.

REFERENCES

Barabas, Alicia M. *Utopias Indias: Movimientos Socio-religiosos en México.* Mexico City: Grijalbo, 1987.

Barabas, Alicia M., and Miguel A. Bartolomé. *Hydraulic Development and Ethnocide: The Mazatec and Chinantec People of Oaxaca, Mexico,* IWGIA Document No. 15. Copenhagen: IWGIA, 1973.

Bartolomé, Miguel A. "La dinámica social de los mayas de Yucatán." Ph.D. diss., Facultad de Ciencias Políticas y Sociales de la UNAM, 1984.

Borah, Woodrow, and S. F. Cook. *The Aboriginal Population of Central Mexico on the Eve of the Spanish Conquest.* Berkeley: University of California Press, 1963.

Brown, Michael F. "Facing the State, Facing the World: Amazonia's Native Leaders and the New Politics of Identity," in Philippe Descola and Anne-Christine Taylor, eds., *L'Homme: Anthopologie et histoire des sociétés amazoníennes.* Forthcoming.

Brysk, Alison. "Acting Globally: International Relations and the Indian Rights in Latin America." Paper presented at the Seventeenth International Congress of the Latin American Studies Association, Los Angeles, September 24–27, 1992.

Chirif Tirado, Alberto, Pedro Garcia Hierro, and Robert C. Smith. *El Indígena y su territorio son uno solo: Estrategia para la defensa de los pueblos y territorios indígenas en la cuenca amazónica.* Lima: Oxfam America, 1991.

Crosby, Alfred W. *The Columbian Exchange: Biological and Cultural Consequences of 1492.* Westport, CT: Greenwood, 1972.

————. *Ecological Imperialism: The Biological Expansion of Europe, 900–1900.* Cambridge: Cambridge University Press, 1986.

Denevan, William M., ed. *The Native Population of the Americas in 1492.* Madison: University of Wisconsin Press, 1976.

Dobyns, Henry F. "Estimating Aboriginal American Populations: An Appraisal of Techniques with a New Hemispheric Estimate." *Current Anthropology,* no. 7 (1966):395–416.

EZLN. *Comunicados del Ejército Zapatista de Liberación Nacional,* January 1, 6, 11, 12, and 13, 1994.

Galeano, Eduardo. *The Open Veins of Latin America.* New York: Monthly Review Press, 1973.

IATP (Institute for Agriculture and Trade Policy). "Chiapas Digest." 1994. Via E-mail.

Kearney, Michael, and Carole Nagengast. "Anthropological Perspective on Transnational Communities in Rural California." Working Paper No. 3 of the Working Group on Farm Labor and Rural Poverty. Davis: California Institute for Rural Studies, 1989.

Mayer, Enrique, and E. Masferrer. "La población indígena de América en 1978." *América Indígena,* 39, 2 (1979).

Runsten, David, and Michael Kearney. *A Survey of Oaxacan Village Networks in California Agriculture.* Davis: California Institute for Rural Studies, 1994.

Scott, James. *The Moral Economy of the Peasant: Rebellion and Subsistence in Southeast Asia*. New Haven, CT: Yale University Press, 1976.

————. *Weapons of the Weak: Everyday Forms of Peasant Resistance*. New Haven, CT: Yale University Press, 1985.

————. "COICA and the Amazon Basin: The Internationalization of Indigenous Peoples' Demands." Paper presented at the Thirteenth International Congress of Anthropological and Ethnological Sciences, Mexico City, July 29–August 5, 1993.

Stoll, David. *Pescadores de hombres o fundadores de Imperio?* Lima: DESCO, 1985.

Super, John C. *Food, Conquest, and Colonization in Sixteenth-Century Spanish America*. Albuquerque: University of New Mexico Press, 1988.

Taylor, William B. *Drinking, Homicide, and Rebellion in Colonial Mexican Villages*. Stanford, CA: Stanford University Press, 1979.

Varese, Stefano. *La sal de los cerros: Una aproximación al mundo campa*. Lima: Ediciones Retablo de Papel, 1973.

————. "Multi-ethnicity and Hegemonic Construction: Indian Plans and the Future," in Remo Guidieri, Francisco Pellizzi, and Stanley J. Tambiah, eds., *Ethnicities and Nations*. Austin: University of Texas Press, 1988.

————. "The Ethnopolitics of Indian Resistance in Latin America." Working Paper. Cambridge: M.I.T. Center for International Studies, 1991a.

————. "The Ethnopolitics of Indian Resistance in Latin America." *Latin American Perspectives* (1995).

Wolf, Eric R. *Europe and the People without History*. Berkeley: University of California Press, 1982.

World Bank. *Informe sobre el desarrollo mundial*. Washington, DC: World Bank, 1991.

Zabin, Carol, Michael Kearney, Anna Garcia, David Runsten, and Carole Nagengast. *Mixtec Migrants in California Agriculture: A New Cycle of Poverty*. Davis: California Institute for Rural Studies, 1993.

Zarzar, Alonso. *Apo Capac Huayna, Jesús Sacramentado: Mito, utopia y milenarismo en el pensamiento de Juan Santos Atahualpa*. Lima: Ediciones CAAP, 1989.

Copyright 1996, Paul Conrad. Distributed by Los Angeles Times Syndicate. Reprinted with permission.

MEXICO
THE CRISIS OF IDENTITY

Alexander Ewen

For many, the proof that what has occurred in Chiapas is not an Indigenous uprising is the high degree of political articulation in the communiqués and social actions of the EZLN. Any action above a childlike and inarticulate level is no longer considered Indigenous. From this point of view, when an Indian ceases to be wretched, he ceases to be Indian.

—Eugenio Bermejillo

The political earthquake that rocked Mexico on the first of January [1994] continues to reverberate across the country's complex social landscape. Powerful national currents have been unleashed, and the status quo, which has held for more than half a century, is clearly shaken. That a few armed Indians in the most remote and impoverished state in the nation could possibly bring down the Mexican house of cards may seem unlikely at first, yet it looms as a foretaste of the displacement and unrest that Mexico could be forced to see before the decade is out.

That it is Indigenous people who have seized the initiative is not surprising, given the lack of choices facing the large Indian populations in Mexico today. Yet the Zapatista movement would have quickly dissipated had it not struck deep chords inside of Mexico and bells of alarm internationally. By blowing out the candles on the NAFTA cake, the uprising was well timed to receive the largest amount of international media coverage and enlist the sympathy of the powerful anti-NAFTA coalition in the United States. It exposed deep divisions among the Mexican elite and marked the Indians and the rural poor as a political force still to be reckoned with. It also tore into the carefully constructed façade of political stability and allowed the world a glimpse of the vast contradictions within Mexican society.

Mexico, a country marked by fatalism and tied to strong traditional roots, living under a glorious and ambiguous ideal called *la Revolución,* has been undergoing as profound a transformation as any in its history. Shifting slowly but surely since the 1940s, this metamorphosis has accelerated at an exponential rate as the last two Mexican administrations cast their lots with the newly emerging global economy. The consequences of this political decision threaten to leave no corner of Mexican life untouched. To this vast transformation have come the Zapatistas and the Indians, raising the stark question. "What is the place of Indian people in this modern Mexico?"—a question the Mexican leadership had hoped it would not have to address.

Alexander Ewen, "Mexico: The Crisis of Identity," from *Akwe:kon Journal,* Vol. XI, no. 2 (Summer 1994). Copyright 1994 by Akwe:kon Press. Reprinted with permission.

WHO IS AN INDIAN?

Mexico is home to the largest population of Indigenous people in the Western Hemisphere. Before the European conquest, the Indigenous population reflected in their cultures the vast diversity of the land that would become Mexico. From the authoritarian empires and city-states to the unfettered nomadic hunter-gatherers, virtually every lifestyle and form of government was represented at the time of contact in 1492. The number of Indians was astounding, estimated to be over twenty-five million—a figure that would not be reached again in Mexico until 1950. Today the Mexican Indigenous population is still the most diverse in the hemisphere, with over 230 different languages still spoken.

Unlike the United States, where the question of who is an Indian is largely a matter of ethnicity, in Mexico it is much more a question of social class. According to the 1990 Mexican census, seven and a half percent, or approximately seven million of Mexico's ninety-two million people, are Indians. Yet this is only the number of Indians who continue to speak their Indigenous language. Mexicans who speak only Spanish, no matter how pure their Indian blood, are considered *mestizo*. Under the same criterion the number of Indians in the United States would drop from two million to only 350,000. Moreover, this system of identifying Indians excludes small children, who would only become Indians when they learn how to speak. Pure-blooded whites are thus given a greater share of the Mexican population than Indians, a remarkable turn of demographics from the beginning of the century.

Using an ethnic basis, estimates for the number of Indians who belong to a distinct cultural group range as high as forty percent of the total Mexican population. Using the wider criteria of the United States, almost ninety percent of Mexico's population has some Indian blood and might well be considered Indigenous if they desired. The general, non-official consensus is that there are more than twenty-five million Indians in Mexico, making up approximately thirty percent of the total population, who are clearly descended from one of Mexico's 230 distinct Indian tribes.

THE MYTH AND REALITY OF "MESTIZAJE"

The reason for limiting the number of Indians in Mexico is due in part to a Mexican political policy that furthers the Mexican ideal of *mestizaje*, that of the egalitarian mixed-race Mexican nation. Today, Mexico considers almost nine out of ten members of its population to be *mestizo*. Originally, a *mestizo* was a person of mixed Spanish and Indian descent, a category within the complex system of assigning pedigree depending on the mix of Spanish, Indian, African, or Asian blood. This system was necessary during the colonial period of Mexico's history in order to help preserve the rigid racial hierarchy that prevailed at the time. At the top of the hierarchy were the pure-blooded whites, known as the *peninsulares* if they came from Spain and *criollos* if born in Mexico. *Mestizos,* though far from the elite, were considered *gente de razón,* a people of reason. *Indios* were peons, and blacks were slaves.

The slaves are long gone, their descendants largely mixed into the *mestizo* world, and the old system of rigid hierarchy has been replaced by *mestizaje*. This ideal is a uniting force in Mexico, similar to the way the "American Dream" has bound disparate groups of immigrants together in the common quest of finding a new and better life in America. *Mestizaje* combines a tremendous pride in the legendary Indian ancestry with a yearning for white material advantages. The myth dilutes any other ethnic identity and effectively subsumes the citizen to Mexican nationalism. A *mestizo* is one who is neither Indian nor white, but a new race, the prototypical Mexican. Therefore according to Mexico, the definition of who is an Indian depends on whether or not they have succumbed to this myth—whether or not they are acculturated into the Mexican system. If they have, no matter how pure the Indian blood, they are *mestizo.*

After independence, Mexico's colonial heritage of strict racial hierarchy became a structure of racial equality, encouraging all Mexicans to reject their backgrounds and become *mestizo.* All legal distinctions of class and privilege were abolished, and "Indian" as a legal entity disappeared. Any pride in Indian ancestry was tempered by the notion that Indians were backward, primitive, and not fully Mexican. Indeed, by remaining Indian, one was holding back Mexico from its true potential; for Mexico to achieve its glorious destiny, all would have to march through the gate of *mestizaje.* This perspective did little to abate prejudice against Indians, and *indio* remained a pejorative term. Expressions such as *"feo como un indio"* ("ugly as an Indian") are still common throughout much of the country.

Despite the philosophy of egalitarianism, it is white Mexicans that are a model that *mestizos* aspire to. Whites continue to be the elite, and dominate the media, finance, and politics. It is they who are the fashion models and television stars. As a population, whites show a remarkable resistance to the mixing tendencies of the rest of Mexico, and in real terms their population has increased in the past ten years. Though many *mestizos* have now moved into the elite class, they often come to think of themselves as *criollos,* and prefer to be distinguished from the majority of *mestizos.*

Yet to a large extent, *mestizaje* is more than a myth, it is a very real and tangible force, deeply entwined with the heart of Mexico. The *mestizo* class has become the huge middle spectrum of the population, sandwiched between the elite and the Indian and ranging from the upper middle class to the very poor. The pull of *mestizaje* is extremely strong and effective outside of Indian communities. Indians who are relocated or lose their land quickly discard their languages and traditions and embrace the *mestizo* world. They tend to reject the fact that they are Indians, and do not identify as such. To remain Indian would mean repudiating a unifying foundation of the current Mexican identity, an identity that recognizes Indianness, but not Indians. While in the United States it is fashionable to identify oneself as an Indian, in Mexico, one does not do so lightly.

THE CONQUEST

The experience of the Indigenous people of Mexico was, from the inception of Spanish colonial rule, vastly different from that of the United States. The Catholic church, through the encyclicals of Pope Paul III and the advocacy of Bartolomé de Las Casas, established a long lasting Catholic and Spanish policy of assimilating Indians and making them a part of the national culture. The early arrival of the Franciscans, in 1524, and the Jesuits, in 1572, was an acknowledgment by the Spanish Empire that the conquest of New Spain was justified on the grounds of bringing Christianity to the Indigenous populations.

Unlike the Catholics, the early Pilgrims in New England had no illusions of worldwide religious hegemony and concerned themselves more with maintaining their religious and moral purity than proselytizing. English political policy viewed Indians as distinct and separate peoples with which political alliances could be forged, a perspective which would be maintained by the United States until the 19th century.

Except for the most isolated areas, by the time of national independence in 1821. Mexican Indians were overwhelmingly Catholic. In contrast, the United States would wait another sixty years before embarking on a national policy of cultural, religious, and social assimilation. Early Spanish colonists followed the example of Cortés and his Indian mistress, *la Malinche,* and readily settled down with Indian women. The colonial Puritans and their followers were not so inclined, and north of Spanish settlement strict separation of the races was the norm.

The historical demographic profile of both countries was vastly different. The catastrophic declines in Indian populations abated in Mexico by 1650 and by the late 18th century their populations were showing natural rates of increase. There were many restrictions on immigration to New Spain and to Mexico after independence. It would take until 1800, 300 years after the conquest, for the white population of Mexico to exceed one million, assuring an Indian majority well into the 19th century. Indians were always a small minority within the boundaries of the United States. By the time westward expansion began in earnest in 1850, the non-Indian population of the States was twenty-three million, far greater than the Indian population.

The differences between the English and Spanish economies has also played a strong role in shaping the differing Indigenous experiences. Unlike Spain and Mexico, the English and French settlers from the very beginning were practicing a form of free-market enterprise that enlisted Indians as trade partners, suppliers of raw material, and consumers of trade goods. England and France liberally supplied their Indian friends with guns, gunpowder, and horses in return for goods and services. Devastating trade wars that resulted between Indian nations became a significant factor in the expansion of British power into the frontier. On the other hand, the Spanish Empire was interested in incorporation and tribute, not alliance. The fabulous gold and silver treasures taken from the Mexican and Peruvian Indians fueled the world's most powerful military machine, which easily subdued most Native resistance. Still a feudal society, Spain transferred from Europe her system of strictly regulated trading and an economy based on vast landed estates. Indian towns were forced to pay tribute to Spanish lords or gentlemen under the *encomienda* system and the Church under *repartimientos.* In contrast to the Indians north of Spanish settlement, where peonage was virtually unknown, Indians in Mexico were quickly forced to work for the new owners of their lands.

While resistance to Spanish rule continued sporadically through Independence, the subjugation and terrible exploitation of the vast majority of Indians was most characteristic of the colonial period. Subsumed to a dominant Spanish and Catholic culture. Indigenous cultures showed a remarkable ability to retain many of their original features, including religious ceremonies, by subtly blending them with Catholicism. More importantly, as the *encomienda* and *repartimiento* systems did not force them off their lands, Natives managed to keep much of their *ejido* system of land management intact. The Indian wars sparked by the pioneers' insatiable demand for land in America by and large did not find their counterpart in New Spain. Once the conquest was complete. Indians in Mexico found themselves under an oppressive yoke, but at least they could stay on their ancestral lands.

In American history, Indians played a role only to the extent that they engaged the United States in war or were forcibly removed out of the country's way. In Mexico, Indians quickly became an integral part of the social fabric, though starting on the lowest rung of the ladder. The strong interaction between the races began forging a new Mexican society which was to destroy the colonial way of life.

THE INDIAN MASSES

By the time of the Mexican War for Independence in 1810, the Indian majority had become a powerful—and angry—political force, waiting to be unleashed. The war is characterized to a large degree as a struggle for power within the ruling Spanish elite, largely setting the *criollos* against the *peninsulares*, and arising out of the Spanish empire's declining power. Among the dominant factors in organizing the revolt was the political instability arising from Napoleon's overthrow of the Spanish monarchy, disaffection among the *criollos*, and the liberalizing social currents of the Enlightenment. However, once begun, the revolt quickly took on aspects of an Indian war against Spanish and clerical oppression. Both Hidalgo and Morelos were dependent on Indian support for their abortive attempts at independence. Indeed, Hidalgo mobilized almost 50,000 Indians to march on Mexico City, a show of Indian power not seen since the Aztec and Tarascan empires, and the Spanish viceroy was forced to abolish the centuries-old system of Indian tribute in an attempt to keep Indians loyal to the Crown.

Independence for Mexico in 1821 degenerated into a half century of uninterrupted civil war between the reactionary old hierarchy and a new breed of republican reformers. Indians fared badly no matter which ruled. The theft of Mexican lands by Texas and the United States and the punishing wars they began pushed Mexico to the brink of anarchy. Indians took the opportunity to mete out some punishment of their own, such as in the Yucatán, Papantla, and the Sierra Gorda of San Luis Potosí. The liberal administrations of Ignacio Comonfort and Benito Juarez, while abolishing the brutal class system, created as many problems as they solved. The *Ley Lerdo,* enacted in 1856, was intended to dissolve the huge Church estates, which covered almost half of Mexico by mandating the sale of all surplus property. However, the net effect of the law was to transfer these lands to wealthy speculators and ranchers, who quickly expelled the thousands of Indians living on them. In an attempt to create small Indian property holders, the law also forced the sale of *ejidos* next to Indian villages, which were also bought up by speculators. The bitter war over *la Reforma* found Indians divided between those following *caciques* such as Thomás Mejía, who was opposed to the new laws, and Benito Juarez, the first Indian president in the hemisphere. Ultimately, the *Ley Lerdo* set in motion a pattern of economic modernization, culminating with the dictatorship of Porfirio Díaz, that by 1910 had transferred most Indian subsistence lands to wealthy plantation owners and ranchers.

La Revolución, begun once again as a struggle for power between elites, unleashed once more the suppressed anger and bitterness of the Mexican Indians. Conditions among Indians had reached new lows. In 1910 there were more than four million landless Indians in the country, most of them serfs to the 834 *hacendados* who owned ninety percent of Mexico's rural land. Since the Mexican population was still eighty percent rural, they were joined in their plight by an equal number of landless *mestizos*. The feudal order of New Spain had given way to the new feudal world of the *hacienda*.

Unlike the wars for independence, where the non-Indian leadership failed to grasp Indian aspirations and consequently failed to appeal to most of the Indian communities, during *la Revolución* the Indian ideal finally found its voice in the person of Emiliano Zapata. To the universal desire for liberty, Zapata had added the magical word—land!

This hunger for the return of ancestral lands, the simple desire to grow corn on small plots without a crushing tribute, transcended the disintegration of the Revolution and the assassination of Zapata. Despite the lack of participation by Indians and *campesinos* in the drafting of the Mexican Constitution of 1917, the constitutional assembly acquiesced to the seething pressures for agrarian reform. Article 27 became the centerpiece of the new constitution—as remarkable a synthesis of human aspirations as the First Amendment is to the United States. Embodied in the new laws was the belief that the lands in Mexico belonged to the people, for the use of the people. It brought back the ancient Indian landholding system, the *ejido,* as an inalienable part of the national structure and mandated the return of stolen lands. After 400 years, the dreams of Mexico and the dreams of Indians had finally come together.

"INDIGENISMO" AND "INDIANISMO"

The great Mexican champion of Indian rights, Lázaro Cárdenas, who realized many of the unfulfilled promises of the Revolution, was also the great proponent of *indigenismo,* the philosophy of assimilating Indians into the Mexican body politic. In the historic, 1940 Inter-American Indian Conference of Pátzcuaro, Cárdenas acknowledged the political and cultural importance of Mexican Indians, yet urged Indians to subsume themselves to the greater Mexican nationalism, a nationalism evolving into the modern expression of *mestizaje.*

The political philosophy of Indian acculturation had a long history in Mexico, beginning, of course, with the Spanish. Yet in New Spain Indians were acculturated only to the extent that they joined, as a separate and distinct group, the deeply stratified Spanish society. Mixed-breeds would lose their Indian identity, yet simply move up another social layer. The republican period of Mexican independence, dominated by the figure of Benito Juarez, demanded an end to the unjust system of social classes, and as a consequence the end of the distinction between Indians and non-Indians. There was therefore no legal definition in his liberal constitution of 1857 of Indians as a people, nor was one added to the constitution of 1917.

For Cárdenas, *indigenismo* would solve, once and for all, the inherent problems associated with racism and inequality in Mexican society. The means for this gradual, peaceful acculturation would be national organizations such as the Instituto Nacional Indigenista (INI), formed in 1948. The expansion of education, the building of roads and modern infrastructure in the countryside, and the transformation and commercialization of Indian cultures into a folklore were extremely effective in dramatically reducing the sense of Indian identity among Mexican Indians. The tremendous expansion of commercial opportunities as Mexico modernized and restructured its economy created a new urban class with a different conception of Mexico. Mexico, sixty-five percent rural in 1940, had become almost sixty percent urban by 1970.

Most Mexican Indians, moreover, did not have cultures that precluded acculturation. Many of their American counterparts could call on ancient traditions such as the Two Row Wampum or national heroes such as Crazy Horse to help them resist white culture. In Mexico, however, Indian resistance was frequently led by radical Catholic priests—often Jesuits, until their expulsion in 1768. After Independence the national Indian political position had been almost exclusively represented by large agrarian movements, which by the time of the Revolution, included as many *mestizos* as Indians. After the Revolution Indians continued to put pressure on the government for their rights through large *campesino* organizations such as Confederación Nacional Campesina (CNC). National Indigenous political forces were hamstrung by the lack of pan-Indian identity in Mexico, due to the variety of Indian cultures and their differing situations.

A small break in this long slide to *mestizaje* was organized in Chiapas by the same Samuel Ruíz who today continues to champion Indigenous people. In 1974, in the Native stronghold of San Cristóbal de Las Casas, the seat of the great Bishop Bartolomé de Las Casas, the Indian Congress of San Cristóbal broke from the traditional *campesino* demands and began the process of formulating and pursuing Indian-specific issues. To a large extent the sparks to this movement, known as *indianismo,* ignited during the social upheavals of the late '60s. The formation of the Confederación Nacional de Comunidades Indígenas (CNCI) in 1968 marked a break from Indian organizations in the past, putting forward a platform that for the first time advocated political

autonomy for Indian peoples in Mexico. The general anti-authoritarian climate of the late '60s and early '70s, the political liberalization (*apertura democrática*) of the Echeverría regime, and a crisis in the agricultural sector began to shift Indian mobilizing towards the more "radical," Indian-oriented groups. The Congress of San Cristóbal brought many of these new philosophies together, along with a strong turnout of Indians in the region. Many differing organizing currents sprang from this Congress, including the present day Zapatistas, working separately yet united in the spirit of *indianismo,* the Indian way.

The radicalization of Indian movements did not go unnoticed by the Mexican government. Indeed, Echeverría's liberal and nationalistic rhetoric and political actions inspired a wave of land takeovers by *campesinos* tired of waiting for the land reform promises of the Revolution. True to its past behavior, Mexico moved to try to co-opt these radicalizing strains by making them a part of the official platform. The First Congress of Indigenous People, held in Pátzcuaro in 1975, was presided by Echeverría himself, who called for an *"indigenismo de participación."* The creation from this conference of the Consejo Nacional de Pueblos Indios (CNPI) was designed to take the steam out of a movement that was becoming more assertive about land rights.

Not only did the Indian movement get stronger, the CNPI quickly showed its independence by directly criticizing the policies of Echeverría's successor, José López Portillo. In particular the CNPI denounced the *Ley de Desarrollo Agropecuario,* the centerpiece of Portillo's overhaul of Mexico's faltering agricultural sector, and it repudiated the administration's increasingly anti-Indian development policy. The president responded by dissolving the CNPI and stepping up repression in the countryside.

Under Portillo, corruption in Mexico, always endemic, became a full-scale looting of the country, whipped into a feeding frenzy by the tapping of Mexico's vast offshore oil riches and the heavy international oil prices and the subsequent collapse or Mexico's economy greeted Portillo's replacement, Miguel de la Madrid Hurtado in 1982. The Mexican peso lost half its value overnight and effectively wiped out any economic gains Indians and *campesinos* may have made after the Revolution. As rural conditions became desperate, militant *campesino* movements such as the national Coordinadora Nacional Plan de Ayala and the Chiapas-based Organización Campesina Emiliano Zapata became the new voices of *indianismo*. As the Mexican infrastructure crumbled, its leaders turned to the global markets in an attempt to stop the free fall.

THE TROUBLED PRESENT

In 1989, Mexico created the Commission of Justice for Indian People in order to draft a proposal to amend Article 4 of the Mexican Constitution. This part of the Constitution, which assures the equality of all Mexicans, was modified to acknowledge "Mexico's multicultural composition based upon Indigenous people" and would "protect and promote the development of their language, cultures, traditional ways, customs, specific means and forms of social organization, and would guarantee to their members true access to the laws of the state." For the first time, Indians were formally recognized by the Mexican government. The new amendment, signed into law in 1990, was immediately attacked by Indigenous organizations as having little practical value and being simply *"indigenismo* with a new set of clothes."

For most observers, changes in Article 4 of the Constitution were simply a way for the Salinas administration to take the sting out of the amendments to Article 27, the symbol of Indian aspirations since the Revolution. Salinas, as economic czar under De la Madrid, had come to the conclusion that "land for the people" was not working and that the Mexican government could no longer afford to subsidize what was an increasingly costly relic of the past. The *ejido* system could not keep up with the tremendous explosion in Mexico's population. Its yield per acre of corn, Mexico's staple grain, was only one-third that of American producers. Yet to protect the *ejidos,* importation of cheaper American corn was allowed only under the most regulated circumstances. Moreover, in lieu of a welfare system, the government had been artificially holding down the national price of Mexico's basic foods, depleting a national treasury that was little more than bankrupt.

While not publicly acknowledged, the real problem was Mexican corruption. It had not only made the state-controlled economic system unviable, it precluded any real solutions without sweeping change in the political order. Yet Carlos Salinas de Gortari was a product of this political order, and had come to power as a result of the backroom machinations of the ruling party, the PRI. For Salinas and his fellow *tecnócratas,* it was therefore easier, and philosophically more desirable, to remove the public sector from its role in running the economy than to directly confront many of the powerfully entrenched PRI interests. Privatization of Mexico's huge apparatus of state-run businesses, co-opting or dismantling the powerful Mexican unions, and increasing foreign investment were to be the underlying principles of his economic policy. NAFTA and GATT [General Agreement on Tariffs and Trade] would provide the investment opportunities and make the country a full-fledged member of the international economic market. Mexican lands and subsoil riches, protected by Article 27, would have to be opened up or sold off to allow more efficient means of exploitation and to fulfill international obligations. Mexico's traditionally closed, state-managed economy was undergoing a sweeping about-face. Nevertheless, mired in a deep economic crisis since 1982, the Mexican people, it seemed, took no notice.

For Indians and *campesinos*, the Revolution, no matter how unfulfilled or poorly applied, was over. The dream of Zapata, and the dream of Indians, was no longer the dream of modern Mexico. The changes to Article 27 effectively inaugurated the breakup of the *ejido* system, which covers nearly half of Mexico's agricultural lands and directly supports more than a quarter of its people. The mechanism for breakup is, in many ways, similar to the American system of allotment of Indian lands in the 1880s, a measure which cost U.S. Indians over two-thirds of their remaining land base before it was repealed. Indian and *campesino* organizations condemned the changes to Article 27, but given the political stranglehold of the Salinas administration, the objections achieved nothing.

Onto this stage have wandered the Zapatistas, upsetting the applecart in a way no one could have predicted. Armed and dangerous, yet charming and reasonable, they called for reform, not revolution, and they rekindled the dying embers of *la Revolución*. For a few months they mesmerized the Mexican public and put the Salinas administration badly on the defensive. It took the assassination of PRI presidential candidate Donaldo Colosio on March 23 to break

the Zapatista spell, raising fears among Indians that the deadly act might mean a harder line was taking over.

The Zapatista influence has not been translated into a national political movement largely because the one man who might have the ability to shoulder the aspirations of Indian people has declined to do so. Cuauhtémoc Cárdenas has remained more of a symbol than an alternative, and judging from the unenthusiastic reception he received among the Zapatistas in May, his potential constituents are tired of the lack of charisma, the lack of decisiveness, and most importantly, the lack of a viable platform that takes into account the Indian and *campesino* demands. His traditional urban-leftist perspective has had little in common with the agrarian demands of the Indians and *campesinos*. In the six years since his powerful showing in the presidential elections, he has seen his strength sapped by a never ending series of political miscalculations. His initial coolness to the Zapatistas in an attempt to quell any notion that he supported violence followed by his ill-conceived attempts to curry their support, seems like more of the same. Nor does it appear that he, nor any political alternative, has the strength to buck the new economic order, as voters in Canada found to their chagrin last year. The perennial politician, Cárdenas has now softened his tone and no longer rejects the free trade agreement, his platform more closely resembling [that of] PRI candidate Ernesto Zedillo than that of the Zapatistas.

At this point, in early June, the election is wide open, a scenario unthinkable before January 1st. The conservative PAN has the only candidate with strong personal appeal and is sure to capture the vote of a large share of the growing entrepreneurial class. There is a national sense of dissatisfaction with the PRI and it has become highly unpopular among vast sectors of the electorate, in particular Mexico's ruined middle class. Moreover, there is tremendous pressure from political forces in the United States to keep the election clean, a difficult problem to overcome, given the power of the local party bosses. From the perspective of international finance, it also appears that the PRI is no longer a prerequisite for stable investment and has become dispensable. Indeed, the election of an opposition candidate might be more favorable for releasing the pent-up pressures that the Zapatistas have shown are ever present. Far from monolithic, the PRI has spent a considerable amount of its energy in internal political battles, rather than displaying a unified front.

Yet despite these signs, Zedillo and the PRI are still the favorites to win the election. They certainly have no intention of losing. The PRI has a preponderance of resources and it spends far more on presidential elections than any political party in the United States. If their ability to buy votes falters, they still may try to alter the election results, international pressure notwithstanding.

None of this bodes well for the Zapatistas and for Indian and *campesino* movements in Mexico. Whichever political party takes office in August, it is highly unlikely that they will reverse the current modernization trends that threaten Indian sustainability. The most that Indians can hope for is government aid to soften what will be a very hard landing. With more than twenty million Mexicans dependent on the *ejido* system or living on communal Indian lands, the potential for social upheaval as these lands are lost is frightening. It has the possibility of becoming the largest forced migration of Indian people since the conquest. These people would have no place to go to except to join their impoverished brethren in the crowded Mexican cities and across the American border. However, the policies of the *tecnócratas*, represented by Salinas and Zedillo, seem to have become an irresistible force.

Yet the Zapatistas have clearly tapped into a strong national current. The Indians and the rural poor still remain a powerful bloc and the uprising has given a significant boost to Mexican Indian identity and their will to resist. It helps that the Zapatistas show an intelligence and political savvy rarely seen in a modern Indian movement, or any modern popular movement, for that matter. Subcomandante Marcos has become a celebrity in Mexico, and if he can stay alive, he could well become a national leader. While the Zapatistas have clearly captured the imagination of the Mexican people, whether this will translate into political gains hinges on the strength and unity of the Indians and the *campesinos*.

For Mexico, the future is full of grim possibilities. A quarter of a century of mismanagement and corruption has left a wealthy country bankrupt and unstable. The solutions currently offered by the *tecnócratas* represent a dramatic break from Mexico's traditional past, and yet are based upon purely theoretical economic formulas. The extent to which they can transform Mexico peacefully and successfully will depend to a large degree on the character and strength of the mass of Mexican people.

It can be argued that the crisis Mexico faces today is a crisis of identity. In many ways Mexico is a tortured transforming soul, not fully ready for the leap into the modern order, not fully rid of its rich past. This deep crisis is represented by Salinas, NAFTA, and a culture of modernity on the one hand, and by Indians, representing *la Revolución*, tradition, and anti-modernity on the other. It is a crisis stripped of its cover by a ragtag Indian army, which raised the question no one had thought to ask, "where is our place, where is the place of Indian people, in this modern Mexico?"

PART REVIEW

DISCUSSION QUESTIONS

Introduction

1. Why should the Native American heritage be known to everyone?

Darryl Wilson, *Mis Misa*

1. In the selection by Darryl Wilson, who or what is Mis Misa? What is its central purpose or function?
2. How is the Indian's view of Mt. Shasta different from that of many non-Indians?

Donald A. Grinde Jr. and Bruce E. Johansen, *Perceptions of America's Native Democracies*

1. Who are the two founders of the Six Nations Iroquois Confederacy? Name the six nations of the confederacy.
2. How did the Iroquois League function? Briefly describe its legislative process.

John Mohawk, *Origins of Iroquois Political Thought*

1. What was the Peacemaker's message to the Haudenosaunee?
2. What did he mean by "the power of righteousness"?

Emory Sekaquaptewa, *One More Smile for a Hopi Clown*

1. Sekaquaptewa states that "the heart of the Hopi concept of clowning is that we are all clowns." Explain what he means by this statement.

Michael Kearney and Stefano Varese, *Latin America's Indigenous Peoples*

1. According to the article by Kearney and Varese, how did the Spanish occupation of the Americas and Spanish colonial policies regarding the Indian peoples differ from those of the English?
2. What are the "four fundamental forms of ethnic resilience and opposition" that have occurred in indigenous Latin American history?
3. As demonstrated by the demands of the Mayan rebels of Chiapas, Mexico, in 1994, what are the two central concerns of the indigenous peoples of Latin America?

Alexander Ewen, *Mexico: The Crisis of Identity*

1. What is the difference between *indigenismo* and *indianismo,* and why is this distinction important to Native peoples?
2. In Mexico, who are *mestizo*?
3. Explain the relationship between NAFTA and the Zapatista movement in Chiapas.

KEY TERMS

Aiowantha (Hiawatha)
Anglo-American, Euro-American
clan
Cortés, Hernando
Deganawidah, or Peacemaker
ethnic confederacies
Great Law of Peace
Haudenosaunee
Indian clown
indianismo
indígenas
Iroquois Six Nations Confederacy

katsinas
longhouse
mestizaje
Mis misa
Mixtec
Mound Builders
NAFTA, North American Free Trade Agreement
power of righteousness
sachem
White Roots of Peace
Zapatistas

SUGGESTED READINGS

BALLANTINE, BETTY, and IAN BALLANTINE, ed. *The Native Americans: An Illustrated History.* Atlanta: Turner Publishing, 1993.

CHAMPAGNE, DUANE. *American Indian Societies: Strategies and Conditions of Political and Cultural Survival.* Cambridge, Mass.: Cultural Survival, 1989.

Council on Interracial Books for Children. *Chronicles of American Indian Protest.* Greenwich, Conn.: Fawcett-Premier, 1971.

CRUM, STEVEN J. *The Road on Which We Came: A History of the Western Shoshone.* Salt Lake City: University of Utah Press, 1994.

EASTON, ROBERT. "Humor of the American Indian." Pages 177–206 in *The American Indian.* Ed. Raymond Friday Locke. Los Angeles: Mankind Publishing, 1970.

FORBES, JACK D. "Undercounting Native Americans: The 1990 Census and the Manipulation of Racial Identity in the United States." *Wicazo Sa Review,* 6, no. 1 (Spring 1990): 2–26.

GRINDE, DONALD. *The Iroquois and the Founding of the American Nation.* San Francisco: Indian Historian Press, 1977.

GRINDE, DONALD, A. and BRUCE E. JOHANSEN. *Exemplar of Liberty: Native America and the Evolution of Democracy.* Los Angeles: UCLA American Indian Studies Center, 1991.

JOHANSEN, BRUCE. *Forgotten Founders: Benjamin Franklin, the Iroquois and the Rationale for the American Revolution.* Ipswich, Mass.: Gambit, 1992.

LEON-PORTILLA, MIGEL, ed. *The Broken Spears: The Aztec Account of the Conquest of Mexico.* Boston: Beacon Press, 1962.

LEON-PORTILLA, MIGEL. *Pre-Columbian Literature of Mexico.* Norman: University of Oklahoma Press, 1969.

MACLEOD, WILLIAM CHRISTIE. *The American Indian Frontier.* New York: Alfred A. Knopf, 1928.

MOMADAY, N. SCOTT. *The Way to Rainy Mountain.* Albuquerque: University of New Mexico Press, 1969.

SHERIDAN, THOMAS E. and NANCY J. PAREZO (eds.) *Paths of Life: American Indians of the Southwest.* Tucson: The University of Arizona Press, 1996.

SILKO, LESLIE MARMON. *Storyteller.* New York: Arcade Publishing, 1981.

SPICER, EDWARD H. *The American Indians.* Cambridge, Mass.: Harvard University Press, 1980.

WEARNE, PHILLIP. *Return of the Indian: Conquest and Revival in the Americas.* Philadelphia: Temple University Press, 1996.

WEATHERFORD, JACK. Indian Givers: *How the Indians of the Americas Transformed the World.* New York: Fawcett Columbine, 1988.

WEATHERFORD, JACK. Native Roots: *How the Indians Enriched America.* New York: Fawcett Columbine, 1991.

WILSON, DARRYL BABE. *The Morning the Sun Went Down.* Berkeley, Calif.: Heyday Books, 1998.

VLAHOS, OLIVIA. *New World Beginnings: Indian Cultures in the Americas.* New York: Viking Press, 1970.

THE AMERICAN INDIAN STORY (HISTORY)

Was He a Fool?

[About Christopher Columbus]

Was he a fool or was he a hero?
The motherf____er was lost, that makes him a zero in
my book! cuz of the lives he took, cuz of the land he
stole, all in the hopes of gold!
trick him, put him down in American mythology as a
hero that never really could be.
You see, his claim to fame was discovering a land
already claimed by 10 million redmen!

he comes to MY land thinking it's India?
I got news for you, you don't have a clue
of where you are, but they still gave you a holiday! the
lie is up, now it's time to pay!
in 1999, whatcha gonna do? people pushed up
so consider yourself through: your name, your fame,
your game, consider it over! when I'm done with you,
you'll be rolling over in your grave, yeah it's just like
that! cuz if you were alive, I'd have to get the gat and
blast your ass outta this atmosphere
a hero to me? You could never be!

I'm not from India, don't call me an Indian!
I'm not American, cuz we got our own land,
or what's left of it,
they took it, stole it, raped it,
and now they're destroying it!
They left my people in poverty, they starve me!
a genocidal catastrophe, how can it be? they say they
got a plan, but they don't understand, they're the damn
reason we're sinking in quicksand!

But those days of sinking are over!
and we know you ain't nothing but a rover.
We had enough of this. We're coming back with fist!
Telling truths about things that are ludicrous.
They take a man like Christopher Columbus, they mold
him, shape him and make him their hero. but the bottom
line is The Facts are simple. you might as well be
honoring a pimple.

"What!?!" A pimple's a thing, disgusting white and
dirty. It's okay to say you heard it from me!
(the comparison) Oh, how embarrassing! To honor a
man who was just on a scam plan!
How the hell did he think this was his land?
"but, that's what they teach us in school?"
it's their plan to fill a land full of fools that think

"Was He a Fool?" from WithOut Reservation, Native Rap Group. Lyrics by Chris LaMarr. Reprinted by permission.

only whatcha tell'em.
but not me, I won't stop yelling about the truth.
just leave the simple facts to me.
Listen! Open your eyes so you can see
about Columbus and what he did to us
and then you'll see why
we're raising such a damn fuss.

Columbus, The Modern-Day Scenario: unbearable,
incomparable! Suppose some punk
walked straight up in your house, and
yelled out, "Get the Hell Out!"
raped your wife and beat your kids
(that's what he did, God forbid!)
Then to make matters worse, they throw him a party!
a celebration? what a nation, to honor the man who
led to the onslaught! They forgot? I won't let'em.

What is historical truth? Does the story of Indian–white relations taught in our history books accurately reflect the American Indian experience? Or is the history of the Americas actually "his-story"—i.e., white, male, and Eurocentric? These questions came to a head in 1992 in the controversy surrounding the Columbian Quincentennial, the five hundredth year anniversary of the voyage of Christopher Columbus across the Atlantic Ocean and the "discovery and conquest of America." How to "celebrate" or observe the Quincentennial became the profound question for many Native Americans.

As 1992 approached, the indigenous peoples of the Americas viewed with alarm the many official declarations and events being planned for the Columbian Quincentennial, which not only excluded them in the planning process but also took on a carnival atmosphere. Spain launched an imitation flotilla of the *Niña*, *Pinta*, and *Santa Maria* for a reinvasion of America, as if the first invasion in 1492 that signaled the beginning of the American holocaust in which tens of millions of Native people lost their lives was not tragic enough. In the United States, the city of Columbus, Ohio, enthusiastically organized its AmeriFlora exhibition, which "included everything from an African-American Heritage Consortium to 'Discover Columbus' international soccer tournaments, an air show, a marathon, even a world horseshoe tournament—but no Indians."[1] Enormous sums were earmarked for the Quincentennial; Spain alone budgeted U.S. $14 billion, and the U.S. government set aside $28 million.

The Quincentennial controversy and Indian reaction to it, however, did have some important positive outcomes. In the first place, Indian people and their supporters all over the Americas organized counter demonstrations and special events to tell the other side of the story. For example, Indian delegates representing 120 indigenous nations and organizations met in Quito, Ecuador, in July 1990 to organize a hemispheric response. A similar conference took place in Guatemala in October 1992. The many counteractions and Indian protests also nurtured the major "revisionist" movement already under way among anthropologists, historians, and other scholars to produce more complete information and a broader interpretation of the European invasion and colonization of the Americas. For example, the UCLA American Indian Studies Center sponsored a conference of scholars on the American Indian responses to the Columbian Quincentenary and published the conference proceedings as *The Unheard Voices* (see Gentry and Grinde in Suggested Readings).

Contributing to this need for a revisionist movement, or truth in history, has been the fact that most scholars who write history are the products of their own particular ethnic past. They have "recorded" and interpreted historical events through the eyes of the "pioneers" and "empire builders," who were almost entirely white males of property and influence. Thus, most general histories of the Western Hemisphere are not histories of the region, nor are they histories of all of the many peoples who reside there, that is, a people's history. Rather, most such works are essentially chronicles of the European conquest and the subsequent national development of English-, Spanish-, and Portuguese-speaking white people during the succeeding centuries. In the same manner, history courses, because of ethnocentric and racial biases, have all but eliminated the Native American heritage, except negatively, from the scene and therefore fail to explain historical events fully.

An accurate understanding of the history and culture of the entire hemisphere includes a consideration of the role of the Indian nations in colonial history and their decisive influence on the course of subsequent historical developments: the fact that the Spanish based much of their colonial organization on existing Incan, Aztec, and Mayan social organization; the importance of the eastern Indian confederacies in the United States, which were co-equal if not superior in power and influence to the thirteen English colonies; the fact that the U.S. Constitution and governmental structure were modeled, at least in part, on the League of the Iroquois; the fact that Rousseau and other philosophers who inspired Europeans to oppose feudal tyranny and oppression based their views on the personal freedom they found in North American Indian societies; the fact that many outstanding statesmen, generals, and religious leaders throughout the hemisphere were Native American.

Part of the revisionist movement among scholars, especially in history, is the growing interest in ethnohistory. Ethnohistory combines the use of data from several fields, including geography, archival records and reports, diary entries, oral history and biography, archaeology, folklore, and ethnography, in order to construct an integrated picture of the social and ethnic processes taking place among a particular people (in this case, Native Americans) during a particular historical period. The ethnohistorian attempts to get as close to the actual event as possible, for instance through eyewitness accounts and on-the-scene reports, rather than to interpret the event some years afterward. When this approach is taken, for example, the Battle of Wounded Knee, so named by U.S. military historians, becomes the Massacre of Wounded Knee, since eyewitnesses describe the ruthless atrocities of white troops in 1890 against unarmed women and children in which upward of 300 Indians were slaughtered.

A common device used by historians is to divide history into periods differentiated by significant events or historical processes. Mainstream historians, for example, most often divide U.S. history into "colonial," "early years of the republic," "Civil War," and similar historical compartments that perhaps make sense from an Anglo-American perspective. But to call the period in North American Indian–white relations from 1540 to the U.S. Revolution the "colonial period" is misleading and ethnocentric. Although colonialism may have been the situation for the English colonists at the time, the term does not accurately describe the situation of the even more numerous Indian peoples, who were not living as politically subordinated and culturally dominated people. By the 1790s only some of the smaller Indian nations had been eliminated or reduced to colonial dependency. Throughout most of the region between the Atlantic Ocean and the Mississippi River, Indians remained as independent nations. From an Indian viewpoint it was a period of many competing nations (both European and Indian), a period of trade competition, of forced migration of tribes such as the Kickapoo and the Delaware, of shifting alliances, especially among the imperial European powers, of political instability, and, of course, of rapid cultural change on the part of both Europeans and the Native peoples.

An integral part of Native American ethnohistory is the question of sovereignty. Native Americans in the United States are the only ethnic group who retain the legal right to territory and whose political status is governed by treaty relations and the concept of sovereignty. Hank Adams, a 1960s Indian activist, defined sovereignty as "the collective authority of a people to govern themselves." Nevertheless, Indian sovereignty has been steadily chipped away over the last century by the plenary power of the U.S. Congress. The plenary power doctrine gives Congress the power to pass any law it pleases to unilaterally limit the sovereignty of Indian nations. For example, in 1988, Congress passed the Indian Gaming Regulatory Act to promote tribal economic development even though it violates the Interstate Commerce clause of the U.S. Constitution, which states that only the federal government can "treat with Indian tribes" (see "The Dealer's Edge," by Tim Johnson in Part VII.) Thus, part of the act was struck down by the U.S. Supreme Court in 1996, and the legislation is now in turmoil. Sovereignty issues, especially land claims, and hunting and fishing rights, continue to occupy North American Indian concerns and legal actions. After a 12-year-long quest, Venetie Village (Athabascan) in Alaska received a negative judgment in 1998, when the U.S. Supreme Court reversed a favorable decision by a lower court that had allowed the village to tax and govern its own land. The Cayuga and other Iroquois nations have been pursuing land claims against the state of New York for ancestral land taken illegally in the past. But even an anti-Indian organization opposing the Cayuga claim has publicly stated that "sovereignty is the main issue."

The struggle for sovereign rights that Indian nations in the United States (and the treaty Indians in Canada) continue to pursue gives hope to the indigenous peoples and nations of Latin America, and Hawai'i for that matter, in their struggle for self-determination. In Chiapas, Mexico, the Zapatista Indian movement was organized in direct protest to the ending of Mexican national legislation, which formerly protected Indian and peasant land tenure through the *ejido* law, as well as to the deleterious impact of the passage of the North American Free Trade Agreement (NAFTA) on indigenous economic self-sufficiency. These are the very problems often ignored by mainstream scholars. Indian ethnohistory, on the other hand, focuses on these and related issues.

These perspectives and developments in the documentation and depiction of the history of Indian and white relations, a Native American perspective and ethnohistory, are reflected in the articles chosen for this part. In the first selection, Indian attorney Mario Gonzalez (Oglala Lakota) explains the legal case for the claim of the Lakota (Sioux) and Tsistsistas (Cheyenne) to the Black Hills, which border the western edge of South Dakota. In 1980 the U.S. Supreme Court ruled that the Black Hills, sacred to Indian people, had been illegally taken by the U.S. government in the previous century when it broke the 1868 Ft. Laramie Treaty. But rather than return the region to its Indian owners, the Court awarded a $102 million monetary compensation. This outcome has been compared to a situation in which a thief (in this case, the United States) who, after confessing the crime, refuses to return what was stolen and also sets the terms of his own punishment and restitution to the victim. Gonzalez also explains the sacred nature of the Black Hills, with its many holy places, such as Bear Butte, that figure prominently in the Lakota and Tsistsistas religions. Paha Sapa, or the Black Hills, is "the heart of everything that lives," and its sacredness forms the linchpin of the Northern Plains Indian cultures.

In the second selection, Poka Laenui (Native Hawaiian), president of the Pacific-Asia Council of Indigenous Peoples, reexamines Hawaiian history and lays out the historical justification for an independent native Hawaiian nation. Few Americans realize that Hawai'i was a thriving, internationally recognized nation before Western imperialist interests, backed by U.S. Marines, overthrew the constitutional Hawaiian monarchy in 1893. Exploited economically and culturally as a territory for the next sixty years, Hawai'i became a state in 1959. Yet, in that statehood referendum the question of independence was never raised, and the opinions of native Hawaiians were never solicited. In the past decades, however, there has been a cultural and political revitalization among native people with a growing demand for Hawaiian sovereignty. The most recent expression in the quest for justice in the Hawaiian case is the discovery of the 1897–1898 'Aina Anti-Annexation Petitions uncovered recently in the National Archives in Washington, D.C. These contain the signatures of all those Hawaiians opposed to the annexation of the islands by the United States. This petition, combined with the signatories of a second 1897 petition conducted by Hui Kulai'aina, prove that almost forty thousand people, nearly all of the Hawaiians living at the time, opposed the July 7, 1898, annexation. The newly discovered petitions convincingly demonstrate that the Hawaiian people were overwhelmingly opposed to the U.S. takeover in the last century and that the treaty of annexation should have been overturned by Congress. Today, the history and true meaning of the petitions are being taught to Hawaiian children.

When Rupert Costo (Cahuilla) and Jeannette Henry Costo (Eastern Cherokee) of the American Indian Historical Society rushed their book on California missions into print in 1987, it was to counteract a racist trend on the part of some church scholars to rationalize the genocide of tens of thousands of Indians under the Spanish mission system. There was a serious attempt by some in the Catholic Church hierarchy to canonize the eighteenth-century head of the Franciscan missions in California, Fr. Junipero Serra, in conjunction with the anniversary of the signing of the U.S. Constitution. Rather than "the defender, protector, and father" of Indian people, Serra is viewed by many Indian people as the personification of a barbaric mission system that embodied starvation, enslavement, untold physical abuse and suffering, and that led to the rapid population decline of California Indians. In today's context, the United Nations would define the mission practices as an act of genocide, as illustrated in the box titled "The Crime of Genocide."

A different kind of history, "visual history," is discussed by Theresa Harlan (Laguna Pueblo) in the next selection. She examines how Native photographers depict their own history and concludes that Native people have a very different perspective than do non-Indian observers. Euro-American image making that focuses on the "proud" and the "primitive," she writes, does not "carry messages for survival." Native image makers, on the other hand, depict the everyday world and actions of Indian people in images that "recognize the origin, nature, and direction of their Native existence and communities."

Iroquois scholar John Mohawk rounds out the history selection with an overview of the past hundred years of Indian policy in the United States and the Indian reaction to it. The names of Indian policies and laws that are totally foreign to non-Indian Americans (for example, the 1887 Dawes Act, in which half of the tribal land base was lost to Indian people, or the 1934 Indian Reorganization Act, which stopped the land loss but ushered in the policies of neocolonialism) are, on the other hand, household words for most Indian people in the United States. At the same time, Indians in the United States are also cognizant of important political and social movements and activities, all a part of a long struggle. These include the 1969 Alcatraz occupation, the Trail of Broken Treaties caravan to Washington, D.C., in 1972, the 1973 protest at Wounded Knee, the worldwide effort to free Indian political prisoner Leonard Peltier (Turtle Mountain Chippewa), the many efforts to create and enforce the 1978 American Indian Religious Freedom Act and its amendments, participation in the United Nations Working Group of Indigenous Peoples, and the many activities aimed at repatriation of ancestral remains from museums and archaeological sites, as well as cultural and language restoration projects and programs.

The last selection is the box titled "The 20-Point Program," which was developed by a broad coalition of Indian organizations and presented to the U.S. government in 1972 during the Trail of Broken Treaties caravan. Although pushed aside and forgotten by federal authorities, it remains one of the most important solution proposals to the U.S. "Indian question" ever formulated and therefore deserves serious study.

NOTE

1. C. Patrick Morris, "Who Are These Gentle People?" *American Indian Culture and Research Journal*, 17, no. 1 (1993): 15n.

THE BLACK HILLS
THE SACRED LAND OF THE LAKOTA AND TSISTSISTAS

Mario Gonzalez

The Black Hills are the Sacred Land of the Lakota (Sioux) and their friends and allies, the Tsistsistas (Cheyenne). Lakota and Tsistsistas claims to the Black Hills are based on the following legal concepts:

Aboriginal Indian Title: Aboriginal title depends on the law of nations, not upon municipal right. It recognizes the right of tribes as the rightful occupants of the soil, with a legal as well as just claim to retain possession. Exclusive use and occupation "for a long time" prior to the loss of the property by a tribe is sufficient to establish aboriginal title. It entitles the tribes to full use and enjoyment of the surface and mineral estates, and to resources (such as timber) on the land. The right of possession is valid against all but the sovereign and can be terminated only by sovereign act.

"For a long time" can be interpreted as from time immemorial to a given number of years. Both Lakota and Tsistsistas tribes used and occupied the Black Hills for periods sufficient to establish aboriginal title.

Recognized Indian Title: For Indian title to be recognized. Congress, acting through a treaty or statute, must grant legal rights of permanent occupancy within a sufficiently defined territory. There must be an intention to accord or recognize a legal interest in the land.

Only the Lakota claim recognized title to the Black Hills based on land grants under the 1851 and 1868 Ft. Laramie Treaties. (This places Lakota tribes in the anomalous position of having the United States "grant" them title to land they already own under aboriginal title.)

A grant of title under United States law has its advantages, however. The federal courts have ruled that tribal lands held under aboriginal title are not protected by the Fifth Amendment; therefore, Congress can confiscate these lands without payment of compensation. On the other hand, the federal courts have also ruled that confiscation of lands held under recognized title are protected by the Fifth Amendment and require the payment of just compensation.

Religious Liens: Congress recognized religious liens in the American Indian Religious Freedom Act (1978) by acknowledging native peoples' "right of access" to religious sites on federal lands. Since all land titles in the United States derive from federal grants, it follows that federal grants to states and individuals were made subject to these religious liens.

In *Sequoyah v. Tennessee Valley Authority* (1980), the sixth Circuit Court of Appeals stated that: "while [lack of a property interest in the land] is a factor to be considered, we feel it should not be conclusive in view of the history of the Cherokee expulsion from South Appalachia followed by the 'Trail of Tears' to Oklahoma and the unique nature of [their] religion." This reasoning suggested that religious liens are strongest on lands from which tribes were forcibly removed, such as the Black Hills.

Today, the total Black Hills area remains sacred to the Lakota and Tsistsistas. Although Lakota ownership of the Black Hills is still in dispute, the Lakota and Tsistsistas still possess religious liens to sacred sites located on federal, state and private lands, including: Devil's Tower, Iyan Kara Mountain, Harney Peak, Wind Cave, Hell's Canyon and Craven's Canyon (which contain petroglyphs), Hot Springs (now called Evan's Plunge) and Bear Butte.

THE POWDER RIVER WAR
AND 1868 FT. LARAMIE TREATY

The Lakota and Tsistsistas tribes used and occupied vast territories on the northern plains. Some of their territories (such as the Black Hills) overlapped.

The 1851 Ft. Laramie Treaty (Art. 5) recognized Lakota title to 60 million acres of territory, including the Black Hills. The same treaty recognized Tsistsistas title to 51 million acres southwest of Lakota territory.

In 1866–1868, the Lakota fought a war with the United States called the "Powder River War." The War culminated with the signing of the 1868 Ft. Laramie Treaty (and was the first military conflict that the United States ever lost). Under the treaty (Art. 16), the United States agreed to remove its forts along the "Bozeman Trail" which was established to protect hordes of miners and settlers involved in the Montana Gold Rush. The gold rush forced the Lakota tribes to go

to war to protect buffalo herds on 1851 Treaty lands from trespassing miners. The very existence of the Lakota people and their way of life depended on the buffalo (which were their source of food, shelter and clothing), and any interference with the tribes' buffalo by U.S. citizens resulted in warfare.

The 1868 Treaty also modified the 1851 Treaty in the following respects:

- Article 2 created a 26 million-acre reservation from the Lakota tribes' 1851 Treaty territory (all of present day South Dakota west of the Missouri River—including the Black Hills) ". . . for the absolute and undisturbed use and occupation . . ." of the Lakota and ". . . other friendly tribes and individuals . . . they may be willing, with the consent of the United States, to admit amongst them." Article 2 also provided that "no persons except those designated and authorized so to do . . . shall ever be permitted to pass over, settle upon, or reside in the territory described. . . ."
- Article 12 provided that no future cession of the permanent reservation (sometimes referred to as the "Great Sioux Reservation") would be valid without the consent of three-fourths ($\frac{3}{4}$) of the adult male Indians, occupying or interested in the permanent reservation.
- Articles 11 and 16 recognized Lakota hunting rights over the remaining 34 million acres of 1851 Treaty territory and an expanded hunting right northwestward to the Bighorn Mountains and southwestward to the Republican River, ". . . so long as the buffalo may range thereon in such numbers as to justify the chase."

In 1874, Lt. Col. George Armstrong Custer led a military expedition into the Black Hills in violation of the 1868 treaty, and sent out glowing reports of gold deposits.

The news resulted in a gold rush and a demand that the Lakota sell the Black Hills.

On June 25, 1876, Lakota and Tsistsistas tribes defeated Custer at the Battle of the Little Bighorn. Congress responded by passing the "sell or starve" act, which provided that no further appropriations would be made for the subsistence of the Lakota (as required by the 1868 treaty) unless they first agreed to cede the Black Hills and Articles 11 and 16 hunting rights.

Thereafter, President Grant appointed the "Manypenny Commission" to negotiate the cession of the Black Hills and Articles 11 and 16 hunting rights. When the Commission could not obtain the requisite three-fourths adult male signatures to effectuate a cession, Congress broke the "impasse" by enacting the proposed "agreement" into law on February 28, 1877. (See map showing 1851 and 1868 treaty areas and the 1877 Black Hills confiscated area.)

INDIAN CLAIMS COMMISSION— DOCKET 74-B

In 1946, Congress passed the Indian Claims Commission Act and mandated that tribes file their claims with the Indian Claims Commission (ICC) within five years or lose them. The jurisdiction of the ICC was limited to monetary compensation only, thus, preventing tribes from suing for a return of their ancestral lands.

The Lakota tribes filed their treaty claims with the ICC on August 15, 1950, as "Docket 74." In 1960, the ICC bifurcated Docket 74 and placed all Fifth Amendment claims (i.e., property confiscated by the 1877 Act) in Docket 74-B. The Docket 74-B claims included:

- The Black Hills: On June 30, 1980, the U.S. Supreme Court affirmed a 1974 ICC ruling that the Lakota tribes were entitled to $102 million for the Black Hills.

In support of its ruling, the Court found that "a more ripe and rank case of dishonorable dealings will never, in all probability, be found in our history."

- Lakota Hunting Rights: Article 16 hunting rights included two categories—those rights already owned under the 1851 treaty, plus new rights granted west of 1851 treaty lands to the Bighorn mountains. Article 11 hunting rights included new rights granted south of the 1851 treaty lands to the Republican River.

In 1970, the ICC ruled that the new hunting rights constituted "consideration" under the 1868 treaty thereby entitling the Lakota tribes to compensation for these rights if they could prove that they had a higher value in 1877 when they were confiscated than in 1868 when they were created. The U.S. Government, of course, argued that the new rights were worthless because there were less buffalo in 1877 than in 1868 (caused in large part by the Government's policy of eliminating the Lakota tribes' source of subsistence by exterminating the buffalo).

The ICC also ruled that in its final 1974 opinion in Docket 74-B that "[o]n December 29, 1970, [the Lakota tribes through their claims attorneys] notified the Commission that they did not intend to pursue their claims for loss of Article 11 and 16 hunting rights." The Lakota tribes, therefore, ended up with no compensation for their hunting rights.

- Black Hills Gold: The ICC also ruled in its 1974 opinion that the Lakota tribes were entitled to only $450,000 for placer (surface) gold stolen by trespassing miners prior to the passage of the 1877 Act. This ruling was based on the rationale that the 1868 treaty forbade miners to trespass in the Black Hills, and that "[i]n November 1875 the President ... knowing that such action was in violation of the

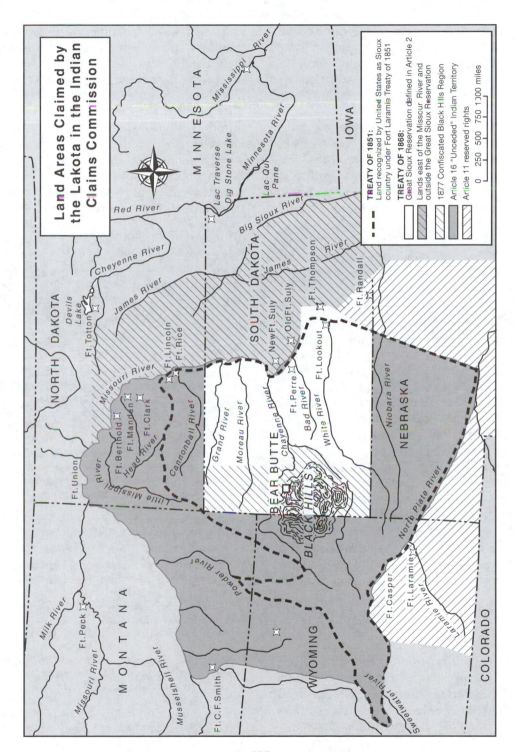

Land Areas Claimed by the Lakota in the Indian Claims Commission

TREATY OF 1851:
Land recognized by United States as Sioux country under Fort Laramie Treaty of 1851

TREATY OF 1868:
Great Sioux Reservation defined in Article 2

Lands east of the Missouri River and outside the Great Sioux Reservation

1877 Confiscated Black Hills Region

Article 16 "Unceded" Indian Territory

Article 11 reserved rights

0   250   500   750   1000 miles

Government's treaty obligation and that such action would certainly result in thousands of non-Indians entering the Great Sioux Reservation to prospect for minerals, ordered the Army to withdraw from the Black Hills and to cease interfering with miners attempting to enter the reservation. As a direct result . . . thousands of non-Indians entered the Sioux reservation, established towns, organized mining districts, filed and developed mining claims, and mined and removed gold from the reservation." The ICC ruled that this Government action resulted in a "taking" of private property in violation of the Fifth Amendment, even though the beneficiaries were private parties.

No compensation was awarded for the billions of dollars worth of gold and other precious metals contained in the Black Hills even though the U.S. Government was aware of their existence in 1877. Today, the Lakota's sacred lands are commercialized. Homestake Mine, the largest gold mine in North America, alone has earned more than $14 billion from gold and silver revenues since 1876.

In stark contrast, the Lakota people live in abject poverty on nearby reservations while the U.S. Government and its citizens continue to plunder their land and natural resources year after year.

It is not surprising, then, that one Lakota tribe (the Oglala Sioux tribe) rejected the Supreme Court's 1980 decision and demanded fidelity to Lakota treaties; the tribe filed suit in U.S. District Court at Rapid City, South Dakota, on July 18, 1980, to quit title to the Black Hills and for $11 billion in damages for the denial of the "absolute and undisturbed use and occupation" of the hills for 103 years. U.S. District Judge Albert G. Schatz slammed the court-house doors in the Tribe's face, however, ruling that the United States was immune from suit in land recovery cases, and that if the tribe wanted to sue for the Black Hills, the ICC was its exclusive remedy.

Other Lakota tribes subsequently joined the Oglala Sioux Tribe in rejecting the $100 million ICC award and getting two bills introduced in Congress to resolve the Black Hills claim.

BROWN HAT'S 1856 VISION OF THE SALE OF THE BLACK HILLS FOR $100 MILLION IN THE YEAR 2000

Brown Hat (also known as Baptiste Good) was a Lakota who kept a traditional calendar known as a "winter count." The Tenth Annual Report of the U.S. Bureau of Ethnology (1888–89) contains the following account of his visit to the southern Black Hills in 1856:

In the year 1856, I went to the Black Hills and cried, and cried, and cried, and suddenly I saw a bird above me, which said: "Stop crying; I am a woman, but I will tell you something: My Great-Father, Father God, who made this place, gave it to me for a home and told me to watch over it. He put a blue sky over my head and gave me a blue flag to have with this beautiful green country. ***My Great-Father, Father God . . . grew, and his flesh was part earth and part stone and part metal and part wood and part water; he took from them all and placed them here for me, and told me to watch over them. I am the Eagle-Woman who tells you this.

The whites know that there are four black flags of God; that is, four divisions of earth. He first made the earth soft by wetting it, then cut it into four parts, one of which, containing the Black Hills, he gave to the [L]akotas, and, because I am a woman, I shall not consent to the pouring of blood on this chief house . . . , the Black Hills. The time will come when you will remember my words; for after many years you shall grow up one with the white people." She then circled round and round and gradually passed out of my sight. I also saw prints of a man's hands and horse's hoofs on the rocks (here he brings in petroglyphs), and two thousand years, and one hundred million dollars ($100,000,000).

Prints of a man's hands and horse's hoofs had significance in 1856. It was a message of death. A dying warrior would leave his bloody hand print on his horse to let his family know that he died in battle.

The message in Brown Hat's vision is a message of death to all the Lakota tribes. It says that the Lakota tribes, and their culture and governments, will cease to exist on earth if they allow the United States Government to force the $100 million ICC award on them in the Year 2000.

What Brown Hat's vision failed to foresee, however, was the determination of the current generation of Lakota to carry on the fight for the Black Hills, not in the battlefields, but through the White men's own legal institutions. It failed to reveal that the Spirit of Crazy Horse would still be alive in 1980, when the Lakota people rejected the $100 million award and declared that "the Black Hills are not for sale." The current generation of Lakota will never allow the U.S. Government to force the $100 million ICC award on them in the year 2000. [*Note by editors of this volume:* The Lakota continue to litigate, refusing to accept the monetary settlement proposed by the government.]

PETE CATCHES' EXPLANATION OF WHY THE BLACK HILLS ARE SACRED TO THE LAKOTA

The religious significance of the Black Hills to the Lakota tribes was described by medicine man Pete Catches in 1993 as follows:

To the Indian spiritual way of life, the Black Hills is the center of the Lakota people. There, ages ago, before Columbus came over the sea, seven spirits came to the Black Hills. They selected that area, the beginning of sacredness to the Lakota people. Each spirit brought a gift to the Lakota people.

The first spirit gave the whole of the Black Hills to the Lakota people forever and ever, from this life until the great hereafter life.

The next spirit that came told the Lakota people there is an eternal fire deep in the bowels of the earth, which we know as volcanoes—the fire, the everlasting fire—so the Black Hills belong to the Lakota people, and from it, that eternal fire in the bowels of the Black Hills is the life-giving heat.

The next spirit brought water, commonly known to us now as 'Hot Springs.' We went there ages ago, together healing—which became eventually Evans Plunge, commercialized—where we, Indians, go for our healing in the healing waters of life.

The third spirit brought the air that we breathe. You'll see that—you go to Wind Cave and the Earth breathes air in and out. That's very sacred. It's needed for life. Without it, we cannot live, nothing can live. The plants need the air, all creation needs air.

The fourth spirit brought the rock people, which includes the gold, as mentioned here a while ago, and the minerals. That is why the Black Hills [are] sacred to the Oval Office.

The fifth spirit brought medicine. In the area of the Black Hills—that today's pain and disease has to do with AIDS—if we were left alone and if we can go there, we can develop our way of healing—even to the end of time, which is AIDS now, today. We can do that because the Black Hills [are] sacred, because that is life itself.

The next spirit brought animals, the buffalo, the deer, all the small animals from which we get body parts. From the eagle, we get eagle feathers, from many of the smaller animals, we get parts of their body, transform it into our way of life—because all of creation is one unit, one life. We are them and they are us. This is his creation.

The seventh spirit brought the Black Hills as a whole—brought it to give it to the Lakota forever, for all eternity, not only in this life, but in the life hereafter. The two are tied together. Our people that have passed on, their spirits are contained in the Black Hills. This is why it is the center of the universe, and this is why it is sacred to the Oglala Sioux. In this life and the life hereafter, the two are together.

Why should we part with the Black Hills? Land is not for sale.

I'd like a life to look forward to after this life. Generations and generations ago, our people have looked upon the Black Hills as the center of the world, and it's a circle. We began from there and we make a complete circle of life, and we go there after our demise from this world. That is why it is sacred to us.

Today Lakota people are desperately struggling to protect their religious sites in the Black Hills from desecration. Lakota elders recently stopped mountain climbing at Devil's Tower. And the struggle to protect Bear Butte—the most sacred site of all—continues.

BEAR BUTTE: THE SACRED MOUNTAIN OF THE LAKOTA AND TSISTSISTAS

Bear Butte is located on the eastern edge of the Black Hills near Sturgis, South Dakota. It is a place where Lakota and Tsistsistas come each year for vision quests. Traditional leader Larry Red Shirt described the importance of the Sacred Mountain in 1982 as follows:

[E]ven before the Sacred Pipe was given to us, the vision quest was the oldest ceremony of our people and the original instructions of the Lakota was given by the Creator on a sacred mountain similar to the way the Ten Commandments were given to Moses on a mountain. . . . [T]he Lakota originated in the Black Hills and [the] sacred instructions given to us by the Creator were given to us on Bear Butte. This makes Bear Butte the central and most sacred mountain to the Lakota people. . . . The sacred calf pipe is the most sacred object with which to pray with in Lakota religion. Bear Butte is the most sacred place to pray with that pipe. Bear Butte and the sacred calf pipe hold the secret to the past, present and future of the Lakota people in this life cycle.

Although similar, Tsistsistas' use of Bear Butte is not identical to that of the Lakota. Elder Walter R. Hamilton described the

importance of the Sacred Mountain to the Tsistsistas as follows:

The four sacred arrows of the [Tsistsistas] came from within Bear Butte as a covenant with the Almighty God/Maheo . . . [and the mountain, therefore, is] . . . the holiest place to the [Tsistsistas] people, who use the mountain regularly for pilgrimages, and who think about it every day, and who mention it in their prayers.

Even though Congress confiscated Bear Butte (along with the rest of the Black Hills) in 1877 and granted it to private parties under the Homestead laws, Lakota and Tsistsistas religious practitioners have used the Sacred Mountain for religious ceremonies continuously up to the present time.

In 1962, the State of South Dakota purchased the traditional ceremonial grounds from a private landowner, turned it into "Bear Butte State Park," and began to physically alter the natural topography of the mountain by constructing roads, hiking trails, machine shops, wooden walkways, parking lots, camp grounds and a permanent visitor center for tourists. As a natural and intended consequence, tourist visitation has increased to over 100,000 people per year, while over 4,000 Native Americans participate in religious ceremonies there.

State officials intended some of the construction projects, such as service roads, to benefit Native American worshippers. These officious inter-meddlers, however, failed to comprehend that a religious shrine is desecrated by changing its natural features, and that this is the same as destroying it. Desecration denies access by destroying what makes a holy place holy, and renders worship ineffective.

Moreover, the principal ceremony conducted at Bear Butte, the "Vision Quest," takes up to four days to complete and requires solitude and extreme concentration before a worshipper can achieve a vision. It is difficult to concentrate, however, because the growing number of tourists each year has greatly infringed on the ability of Lakota and Tsistsistas people to conduct religious ceremonies. Tourists have intruded on religious ceremonies by riding up to the visitor center on loud motorcycles, walking up the hiking paths with radios blaring; standing on overlook platforms along hiking trails and photographing worshippers as they pray; taking offerings left by worshippers as souvenirs; taking food and water on the mountain; and allowing non-Native American women on the mountain during their menstrual period in violation of traditional religious practice.

In 1982, the state of South Dakota closed the ceremonial grounds for one month for construction and required worshippers to camp two miles away at Bear Butte Lake. The state even required one worshipper to pay a fee to camp and conduct her ceremonies. This prompted traditional Lakota and Tsistsistas religious practitioners to initiate a lawsuit in federal court (*Fools Crow v. Gullet* 1982) for violations of the Free Exercise Clause of the First Amendment of the U.S. Constitution, the 1978 American Indian Religious Freedom Act and Article 18 of the International Covenant on Civil and Political Rights.

The worshippers asked the court to declare their right to full, unrestricted and uninterrupted religious use of Bear Butte and injunctive relief from construction projects altering the Butte's natural features. U.S. District Judge Andrew Bogue rejected their claims, and suggested that the State might be establishing religion by protecting Native Americans' religious practices at the Butte.

Although permit and registration requirements have often been held per se unconstitutional when applied to exercise of freedom of speech and religion in cases such as *Shuttlesworth v. City of Birmingham* (1969), the state of South Dakota still restricts access to the Butte by requiring worshippers to obtain a permit to conduct religious ceremonies there. This places state officials in a position to arbitrarily approve or deny the exercise of religious freedoms.

Lakota and Tsistsistas religious practitioners ask only that their religious sites and ceremonies be protected to the same degree that mainstream religious sites and ceremonies are protected. If an establishment clause problem exists, it is the failure of the federal courts to provide Native American worshippers the same protection in conducting ceremonies at sacred sites as provided to worshippers at churches and synagogues. This failure to protect Native American worshippers effectively establishes mainstream religions over Native American religions in the United States.

CONCLUSION

The Lakota tribes' rejection of the $100 million ICC award for the Black Hills in 1980 has come to symbolize Native American resistance in North America. The tribes have two primary concerns in rejecting the claim: (1) the protection of the religious sanctity of the Black Hills and (2) the protection of the culture, sovereignty and economic self-sufficiency of the Lakota people.

First, no one would ever expect Christians, Jews and Muslims to accept monetary compensation for their sacred sites and shrines in the Middle East. Yet, these same Christians, Jews and Muslims residing in the United States have no objection to forcing a monetary settlement on the Lakota tribes for their Sacred Black Hills. No amount of money in the world can compensate the Lakota tribes for their religious property.

Secondly, Article 5 of the 1877 Act, in pertinent part, provides as follows:

> In consideration of the foregoing cession of territory and [hunting] rights . . . , the United States does agree to provide all necessary aid to assist the Indians in the work of civilization.

***Also, to provide said Indians with subsistence consisting of a ration for each individual . . . , or in lieu of said articles the equivalent thereof. Such rations, or so much thereof as may be necessary, shall be continued until the Indians are able to support themselves.

The "aid for civilization" and "subsistence rations" received by the Lakota tribes today are part of the quid pro quo for the illegal confiscation of the Black Hills and Lakota hunting rights in 1877. The Lakota tribes currently receive over $300 million annually in Article 5 benefits (although many Lakota feel that this is inadequate consideration when compared to the billions of dollars plundered from their treaty lands each year; a substantial portion of these funds are also used to cover the costs of the federal administrative agencies that oversee Indian affairs). The dollar value of these benefits, multiplied over the next 100 years, would be in excess of $30 billion!

The Lakota tribes are concerned that acceptance of the $100 million ICC award will extinguish not only their title to the Black Hills, but their benefits under Article 5 of the 1877 Act as well. They fear that the United States Government will argue that payment of the award results in a "full discharge of the United States of all claims and demands touching any of the matters involved in the controversy" under Section 22 of the Indian Claims Commission Act.

Thus, the long-term survival of the Lakota people depends on how the Black Hills claim is ultimately resolved. In the meantime, the $100 million ICC award for the Black Hills has grown (with compound interest) to over $380 million since 1980. Still the tribes reject it, insisting that the U.S. Government return the federally held lands to the tribes and settle their claims for the remaining lands held by private parties in a fair and honorable manner, consistent with their religious beliefs.

Should the U.S. Government attempt to force the $100 million ICC award on the Lakota tribes in the year 2000, the Oglala Sioux Tribe is prepared to initiate a new round of litigation in the federal courts to stop payment of the award based on untested legal theories. [*Note by editors of this volume:* Following 2000 a new round of litigation was initiated.]

REFERENCES

Fletcher v. Peck, 10 U.S. (6 Cranch) 87 (1810).

[Fools] Crow v. Gullet, 541 F.Supp. 785 (D.S.D. 1982); See Affidavits of Larry Red Shirt and Walter R. Hamilton.

Johnson v. M'Intosh, 21 U.S. (8 Wheat.) 543 (1823).

Oglala Sioux Tribe v. United States, 650 F.2d 140 (8th Cir. 1981).

Sac and Fox Tribe v. United States, 315 F.2d 896 (Ct. Cl. 1963).

Sequoyah v. Tennessee Valley Authority, 620 F.2d 1159 (6th Cir. 1980).

Shuttlesworth v. City of Birmingham, 394 U.S. 147 (1969).

Sioux Nation of Indians v. United States, 33 Indian Claims Commission 151 (Feb. 15, 1974).

Tee-Hit-Ton Indians v. United States, 348 U.S. 272 (1958).

United States v. Sioux Nation of Indians, 448 U.S. 371 (1980).

United States Ex Rel Chunie v. Ringrose, 788 F.2d 638 (9th Cir. 1986).

1851 Ft. Laramie Treaty, 10 Stat. 969.

1868 Ft. Laramie Treaty, 15 Stat. 635.

1876 Appropriation Act (Sell or Starve Act), 19 Stat. 176.

1877 Black Hills Act, 19 Stat. 254.

1946 Indian Claims Commission Act, 60 Stat. 1055.

1978 American Indian Religious Freedom Act, 42 U.S.C. 1996.

Hearing before the Committee on Indian Affairs: Oversight Hearing on the Need For Amendments to the Religious Freedom Act, S. Hrg. 103–6, Part 3 (103rd Cong., 1st Sess.); see Testimony of Peter Catches.

International Covenant on Civil and Political Rights, Article 18, General Assembly Resolution No. 2200A (XXI), 16 Dec. 1966, signed by President Carter on Oct. 5, 1977.

Tenth Annual Report of the U.S. Bureau of Ethnology (GPO 1888–1889); See Brown Hat's account of his 1856 visit to the Black Hills.

THE REDISCOVERY OF HAWAIIAN SOVEREIGNTY

Poka Laenui

INTRODUCTION

On January 16, 1893, American marines landed in peaceful Hawai'i armed with Gatling guns, Howitzer cannons, carbines, and other instruments of war, as well as double cartridge belts filled with ammunition. The United States troops marched along the streets of Honolulu, rifles facing Iolani palace, the seat of Hawai'i's sovereignty.

The following day, resident conspirators numbering eighteen, mostly Americans, sneaked to the back steps of a government building a few yards from where the American troops had lodged the night before. There, Henry Cooper, an American lawyer and resident of Hawai'i for less than a year, proclaimed that he and seventeen others were now the government of Hawai'i. Calling themselves the "provisional government" and selecting Sanford Dole president, they were to exist for the explicit purpose of annexing Hawai'i to the United States. American minister plenipotentiary John L. Stevens immediately recognized the "provisional government" as the government of Hawai'i. He then joined in their

"The Rediscovery of Hawaiian Sovereignty," by Poka Laenui, in *American Indian Culture and Research Journal*, 17, no. 1(1993): 79–101. Copyright 1993 by Regents of the University of California, American Indian Studies Center. Reprinted with permission. Portions of the article and the endnotes have been omitted.

demand that Queen Lili'uokalani, the constitutional monarch of the Hawaiian nation, surrender under threat of war with the United States. Faced with such a threat, the queen eventually capitulated, but not without protest. These are her words:

> I, Lili'uokalani, by the grace of God and under the constitution of the Hawaiian Kingdom, Queen, do hereby solemnly protest against any and all acts done against myself and the constitutional Government of the Hawaiian Kingdom by certain persons claiming to have established a Provisional Government of and for this Kingdom.

> That I yield to the superior force of the United States of America, whose minister plenipotentiary, his excellency John L. Stevens, has caused United States troops to be landed at Honolulu and declared that he would support the Provisional Government.

> Now, to avoid any collision of armed forces and perhaps the loss of life, I do, under this protest, and impelled by said force, yield my authority until such time as the Government of the United States shall, upon the facts being presented to it, undo the action of its representative and reinstate me and the authority which I claim as the constitutional sovereign of the Hawaiian Islands.

Rather than undoing its actions, the United States continued in its conspiracy to deprive an independent people of their right to self-determination, forcing Hawai'i to serve as the command headquarters of its

Pacific military forces as well as an important finger of the American economic hand reaching into Asia. The United States had "discovered" Hawai'i and extended by force its sovereignty over this once independent Pacific nation.

EARLY HISTORY

Hawai'i's early inhabitants journeyed throughout the vast Pacific, guided by stars, the rising sun, clouds, birds, wave formation, and flashing lights from the water's depth. They touched on many lands, including the most isolated land mass in the world—Hawai'i. As seafarers, they continued commerce with cousins of the South Pacific many years after arriving in Hawai'i. They had occasional contacts with Japan, Great Turtle Island (today North America), and other Pacific Rim places.

Hawai'i remained virtually unknown to Europeans until the arrival, in 1778, of James Cook, captain of the British navy ships *Resolution* and *Discovery*. Cook found a highly developed Hawaiian society and was welcomed in friendship. In an unfortunate misunderstanding, however, Cook initiated violence against the Hawaiian people. The Hawaiian response resulted in his blood flowing into the waters of Kealakekua Bay, Hawai'i, and he journeyed no further.

Soon after contact with Cook, Hawai'i was cast into world attention and was accepted quickly as a member of the international community. During the reign of Kamehameha I (1779–1819), Hawai'i traded with China, England, the United States, and other nations on a regular basis. On November 28, 1843, Great Britain and France joined in a declaration recognizing Hawaii's independence and pledged never to take it as a possession. When the United States was invited to join this declaration, J. C. Calhoun,

secretary of state, replied that the president adhered completely to the spirit of disinterestedness and self-denial that breathed in the declaration. "He had already, for his part taken a similar engagement in the message which he had already addressed to Congress on December 31, 1842."

By 1887, Hawai'i had treaties and conventions with Belgium, Bremen, Denmark, France, the German Empire, Great Britain, Hamburg, Hong Kong, Italy, Japan, the Netherlands, New South Wales, Portugal, Russia, Samoa, Spain, the Swiss Confederation, Sweden, Norway, Tahiti, and the United States. Hawai'i was a member of one of the first international organizations, the Universal Postal Union. Approximately one hundred diplomatic and consular posts around the world were established.

Over the years, many immigrants came to Hawai'i from all parts of the world, many renouncing their former national allegiance and taking up Hawaiian citizenship. The nation of Hawai'i had a literacy rate that was among the highest in the world. It had telephones and electricity built into its governing palace, "Iolani," before the White House had such technology. Multilingual citizens abounded. Hawaiian leaders had excellent comprehension of world and political geography; King Kalakaua was the first head of state to circle the world as part of his plan to weave a tapestry of international economic and political alliances to assure Hawaiian independence. By 1892, Hawai'i was a vibrant, multiracial, multicultural nation engaged in intellectual and economic commerce with the world.

Christian Missionaries Arrive

Early in its exposure to the Western world, Hawai'i became the focus of Christian zeal. The first flock of missionaries arrived from Boston in 1820. Many remained, established homes and families, and were welcomed into Hawaiian society. They became a strong influence over the people.

Over time, many children of missionaries left the pulpits of the church and entered business and politics. After several decades, an alliance arose of missionary offspring and developing business interests. Growing and selling sugar comprised the principal interest of this alliance. Land, labor, and market were its major concerns, and it addressed those concerns through political and social control. The new alliance called itself the "missionary party."

Land Assault

The missionary party drastically changed land relationships in Hawai'i. Formerly land was under the care of the ruling chiefs. They allotted the use of the lands to their subchiefs, who reallotted the remaining lands to their supporters. By 1839, these distributions were revocable only for cause (Bill of Rights of 1839). Land "ownership" in the Western sense did not exist. Land was an integral part of the life of Hawai'i, along with the air, the sunlight, the winds, the waters, and the people. None of these parts was to dominate the others. This was a basic philosophy of existence for Hawai'i's early inhabitants.

Under the influence of the missionary party, however, less than thirty years after missionary arrival, this land relationship was overturned. Land was parceled out in fee simple estates along the traditions of England and the United States. Foreigners could now be permanent landowners in Hawai'i.

Labor Assault

Many of the indigenous people refused to work at low plantation wages. In response, the missionary party influenced immigration policies, importing laborers to perform the exhausting sugar plantation work on the lands now controlled by them. The sugar industry spread across Hawai'i with easily available lands and cheap imported labor.

Market Assault

With land and labor under control, the missionary party applied itself to the last step in this commercial cycle—securing a market for its sugar. The United States was the logical market, because it was geographically closer to Hawai'i than any other market. Most members of the missionary party were citizens of the United States and had been in constant communication and trade with their mainland. The United States military was hungry for a naval armada in the Pacific, so it was a willing partner for close relationships with Hawai'i.

To secure the American market, the missionary party saw two alternative solutions: reciprocity agreements or annexation. Reciprocity would permit Hawaiian sugar importation into the United States duty-free. In return, products would be imported into Hawai'i duty free. However, reciprocity agreements were temporary. Annexation offered greater security. Under annexation, Hawaiian sugar would be considered domestic rather than foreign and thus not subject to tariff as it entered the American market.

Initial reciprocity arrangements between Hawai'i and the United States were tried but did not last long. The United States soon wanted more than just an exchange of trade rights. It wanted sovereignty over Pearl Harbor in order to extend its commercial and military arm into the Pacific.

King Kalakaua and Queen Lili'uokalani Under Attack

Kalakaua, previously elected Hawai'i's Mo'i (ruling sovereign 1874–91), refused to cede Pearl Harbor. The missionary party attacked

Kalakaua by slander, rumors, and attempts on his life. They accused him of being a drunk and a heathen because he attempted to revitalize the hula and preserve the religious practices of his ancestors. They branded him a womanizer. His character and his activities were continually berated in the press. Yet the people rallied around him and remained loyal in the face of these attacks. The missionary party, so intent on wresting power from Kalakaua, drew lots to decide which of five conspirators would murder him. The one selected was so horrified by his selection that he refused to act.

Following numerous public attacks on Kalakaua's reputation and esteem, the missionary party secretly formed a league, armed themselves, and forced the king at gunpoint to turn the powers of government over to them. In 1887, Kalakaua signed the "bayonet" constitution, the name reflecting the method of adoption. This constitution stripped Kalakaua of power.

Once in power, the missionary party granted the United States exclusive right to use Pearl Harbor. In return, it received an extension of seven years on the existing reciprocity treaty, which would soon have expired. The sugar market was temporarily secure.

Kalakaua died in 1891 in San Francisco, on a trip that was intended to help him recuperate from illness advanced by the activities in Hawai'i. Rumors still abound in Hawai'i that his death was caused by the missionary party's agents in the United States. Lili'uokalani succeeded him.

Quite soon upon her accession, Queen Lili'uokalani received a petition of two-thirds of the registered voters imploring her to do away with the bayonet constitution and return the powers of government to the Hawaiian people. By January 14, 1893, she had completed a draft of a new constitution and had informed her cabinet of her intention to institute it immediately. She was persuaded by the cabinet, which, under the bayonet constitution, was controlled by the missionary party, to put off the constitutional change for a short time, and she acceded to this request. Members of her cabinet rushed to report the queen's intentions to the leaders of the missionary party.

Mr. Thurston, Mr. Dole, and United States Minister Stevens

It is important to identify two men in particular who were at the head of the missionary party. Lorrin Thurston was the grandson of Asa Thurston, one of the first missionaries. Sanford Dole was the son of Daniel Dole, another early missionary. As early as 1882, Lorrin Thurston had already exchanged confidences with leading American officials on the matter of the takeover of Hawai'i. In fact, the United States secretary of the navy assured Thurston that the administration of Chester A. Arthur would look with favor on a takeover. In 1892, in another visit to the United States, Thurston again received the same assurance from the administration of Benjamin Harrison.

When Thurston received word of the queen's intention, he declared that she had no business attempting to institute a new constitution by fiat. Along with twelve others, he formed a "Committee of Public Safety" and arranged an immediate visit to the American minister plenipotentiary in Hawai'i, John L. Stevens, to conspire for the overthrow of Lili'uokalani.

Little convincing was necessary, for Stevens was already one of the foremost advocates for a United States takeover of Hawai'i. Appointed in June 1889 as the United States minister plenipotentiary, he regarded himself as having a mission to bring about the annexation of Hawai'i by the United States. His letters to secretary of state James G. Blaine, beginning less than a month after his arrival, reflect his passion to take Hawai'i for the United States. On March 8, 1892, after three years of promoting the annexation, he writes to ask how far he may *deviate from established international rules and precedents* in the event of an orderly and peaceful revolutionary movement and sets forth a step-by-step prediction of future events. In later letters, he argues that those favoring annexation in Hawai'i are qualified to carry on good government, "provided they have the support of the Government of the United States." He continues, "[H]awaii must now take the road which leads to Asia, or the other, which outlets her in America, gives her an American civilization, and binds her to the care of American destiny. . . . To postpone American action many years is only to add to present unfavorable tendencies and to make future possession more difficult." He calls for "bold and vigorous measures for annexation. I cannot refrain from expressing the opinion with emphasis that the golden hour is near at hand. . . . So long as the islands retain their own independent government there remains the possibility that England or the Canadian Dominion might secure one of the Hawaiian harbors for a coaling station. Annexation excludes all dangers of this kind."

Thus, when Thurston met with Stevens on January 15, 1893, the "golden hour" was at hand. It was agreed that the United States marines would land under the guise of protecting American (missionary party) lives. The missionary party then would declare itself the provisional government and immediately would turn Hawai'i over to the United States in an annexation treaty. As a reward, the missionary party would officially be appointed the local rulers of Hawai'i. The United States would obtain the choicest lands and harbors for its Pacific armada.

The landing of the marines is now a matter of history. The queen yielded her authority, trusting to the "enlightened justice" of the United States, expecting a full investigation to be conducted and the United States government to restore the constitutional government of Hawai'i.

On January 18, 1893, the day after Lili'uokalani yielded, the provisional government forbade any of the queen's supporters from boarding the only ship leaving Hawai'i. The new leaders then rushed off to Washington to obtain annexation. By February 16, 1893, a treaty of annexation had been hurriedly negotiated, signed, and presented by President Harrison to the United States Senate for ratification.

President Grover Cleveland

However, Grover Cleveland replaced Harrison before the Senate voted. Meanwhile, traveling as businessmen, the queen's emissaries had managed to sneak to the United States. Upon reaching Washington, they pleaded with Cleveland to withdraw the treaty and conduct the promised investigation. Cleveland agreed and appointed as special investigator the former chairman of the House Foreign Relations Committee, James H. Blount.

After several months of investigation, Blount exposed the conspiracy. Cleveland subsequently addressed Congress, declaring,

By an act of war, committed with the participation of a diplomatic representative of the United States and without authority of Congress, the Government of a feeble but friendly and confiding people has been overthrown. A substantial wrong has thus been done which a due regard for our national character as well as the rights of the injured people requires we should endeavor to repair. . . .

[Lili'uokalani] knew that she could not withstand the power of the United States, but believed that she might safely trust to its justice. [S]he surrendered not to the provisional government, but to the United States. She surrendered not absolutely and permanently, but temporarily and conditionally until such time as the facts could be considered by the United States [and it could] undo the action of its representative and reinstate her in the authority she claimed as the constitutional sovereign of the Hawaiian Islands.

In summarizing the events, Cleveland concluded:

The lawful Government of Hawai'i was overthrown without the drawing of a sword or the firing of a shot by a process every step of which, it may be safely asserted, is directly traceable to and dependent for its success upon the agency of the United States acting through its diplomatic and naval representatives.

But for the notorious predilections of the United States Minister for annexation, the Committee of Safety, which should be called the Committee of Annexation, would never have existed.

But for the landing of the United States forces upon false pretexts respecting the danger to life and property the committee would never have exposed themselves to the pains and penalties of treason by undertaking the subversion of the Queen's Government.

But for the presence of the United States forces in the immediate vicinity and in position to afford all needed protection and support the committee would not have proclaimed the provisional government from the steps of the Government building.

And finally, but for the lawless occupation of Honolulu under false pretexts by the United States forces, and but for Minister Stevens' recognition of the provisional government when the United States forces were its sole support and constituted its only military strength, the Queen and her Government would never have yielded to the provisional government, even for a time and for the sole purpose of submitting her case to the enlightened justice of the United States.

[T]he law of nations is founded upon reason and justice, and the rules of conduct governing individual relations between citizens or subjects of a civilized state are equally applicable as between enlightened nations. The considerations

that international law is without a court for its enforcement, and that obedience to its commands practically depends upon good faith, instead of upon the mandate of a superior tribunal, only give additional sanction to the law itself and brand any deliberate infraction of it not merely as a wrong but as a disgrace.[1]

As long as he remained president, Cleveland refused to forward the treaty to the Senate. Lili'uokalani was advised of the president's desire to aid in the restoration of the status existing before the lawless landing of the United States forces at Honolulu, if such restoration could be effected in terms providing for clemency as well as justice to all parties. In short, the past should be buried and the restored government should reassume its authority as if its continuity had not been interrupted. The queen first protested that such a promise from her would constitute an unconstitutional act and was therefore beyond her powers to grant, but she later acceded to the demands for general amnesty upon the return of the powers of government.

The provisional government was informed of this decision immediately and was asked to abide by Cleveland's decision, yielding to the queen her constitutional authority. It refused. In doing so, the members protested Cleveland's attempt to "interfere in the internal affairs" of their nation, declaring themselves citizens of the provisional government and thus beyond Cleveland's authority. Only a short time before, they had relied on their American citizenship and thus had justified the landing of United States marines to protect their lives! Cleveland, though filled with principled words, left the United States troops in Hawai'i's harbors to protect American lives.

The Puppet Government Changes Clothes

The provisional government was under international criticism for being a government without the support of its people—existing, in fact, without even a constitution or other fundamental document to afford even the appearance of legitimacy. Faced with an American administration that would not condone the conspiracy yet kept American warships in Honolulu harbor, the conspirators devised a plan to restructure themselves so they would appear to be a permanent rather than a provisional government. When a new American president came to office, the "permanent" government would place the conspiracy back on course.

A constitution giving them permanence and validity had to be drafted. Sanford Dole, acting as president of the provisional government, announced a constitutional convention of thirty-seven delegates: eighteen elected and the remaining nineteen selected by him. The candidates and voters for the eighteen elected positions were first required to renounce Queen Lili'uokalani and swear allegiance to the provisional government. Less than 20 percent of the voting population participated in the election.

The constitutional convention was held, and the document that was adopted was substantially the same as the one submitted by Dole and Thurston. The constitution of the "Republic of Hawai'i" claimed dominion over all lands and waters of Hawai'i and claimed all of Hawai'i's citizens as its own. Foreigners who supported the new regime could vote; citizens loyal to the queen could not. Because the Japanese and especially the Chinese supported Lili'uokalani, they were, as a group, disenfranchised. Further, only those who could speak, read, and write English or Hawaiian and could explain the constitution, *written in English,* to the satisfaction of Dole's supporters could vote.

On July 4, 1894, while Americans were celebrating their independence day by firing the cannons on their warships in Honolulu harbor, Dole proclaimed the constitution and thus the Republic of Hawai'i into existence.

Lili'uokalani had lost her throne because she had considered altering the constitution by fiat. Now, circumstances having altered the players, the conspirators invoked the name of liberty and did substantially the same thing.

McKinley: Sleight of Constitutional Hand

When William McKinley replaced Cleveland as president, Dole's group rushed to Washington to complete the conspiracy. With a constitution in hand declaring them the legal government, the new administration of Hawai'i ceded "absolutely and without reserve to the United States of America all rights of sovereignty of whatsoever kind in and over the Hawaiian Islands. . . ." A treaty of annexation was signed.

Realizing the treaty would not get the two-thirds Senate approval required in the United States Constitution, the conspirators circumvented that requirement and settled for only a joint resolution of Congress. The Newlands Resolution of July 7, 1898 was passed. Following this congressional resolution, the United States assumed authority and soon established the government of the "Territory of Hawai'i."

As these events were happening, Lili'uokalani engraved her plea to the American people:

> Oh, honest Americans, as Christians hear me for my downtrodden people! Their form of government is as dear to them as yours is precious to you. Quite as warmly as you love your country, so they love theirs. [D]o not covet the little vineyards of Naboth's so far from your shores, lest the punishment of Ahab fall upon you, if not in your day in that of your children, for "be not deceived, God is not mocked." The people to whom your fathers told of the living God, and taught to call "Father," and whom the sons now seek to despoil and destroy, are crying aloud to Him in their time of trouble; and He will keep His promise, and will listen to the voices of His Hawaiian children lamenting for their homes.[2]

Her plea fell on deaf congressional ears. And so we close the chapter on Hawai'i as a free and unoccupied nation. Hawai'i was now to undergo years of American brainwashing, colonization, and military occupation. These were to be the payoff years for the conspirators.

THE RECYCLING OF HAWAI'I 1900–1959

Hawai'i now underwent traumatic changes affecting every aspect of life. Sanford Dole, appointed territorial governor, provided government positions and lucrative government contracts for his friends. Monopolies in shipping, finance, and communications developed. The Big Five, a coalition of five business entities with roots in the Missionary Party, controlled every aspect of business, media, and politics in Hawai'i. Beginning with sugar, they took steps to control transportation, hotels, utilities, banks, insurance agencies, and many small wholesale and retail businesses. When they teamed up with McKinley's Republican party and the United States Navy, there was virtually nothing left unexploited.

While the Big Five were taking over Hawai'i, they were propagating the myth of the superiority of the Anglo-Saxon race. In addition, a massive brainwashing program was begun to convince Hawaiians that the United States was the legitimate ruler and that Hawaiians were no longer Hawaiians but Americans. The term Hawaiian was redefined as a racial rather than a national term. Large numbers of citizens were identified no longer as Hawaiians but as Chinese, Japanese, Korean, English, Samoan, and Filipino. The divide-and-conquer tactic was employed even with the Hawaiian race, when Congress declared that "native Hawaiians" (at least 50 percent aboriginal blood) were entitled to special land privileges while others of lesser "blood" were not.

Children were forced to attend American schools and were taught to pledge their allegiance to the United States. They were trained in the foreign laws, told to adopt foreign morality, to speak no language but the foreign (English) and to adopt the foreign (American) lifestyle. Official government proceedings were to be conducted in English and not the Hawaiian language. In the schools and colleges, if the language of Hawai'i was taught at all, it was only in the foreign language departments.

The customs and traditions, and even the cultural names of the people, were suppressed in this recycling effort. The great *makahiki* celebrations honoring Lono, an important god of peace, harvest, agriculture, and medicine, were never observed or mentioned in the schools. Instead, Christmas was celebrated with plays and pageants. People were coaxed into giving children American names that had no ties with their ancestors— names that described no physical substance, spiritual sense, or human mood; names that could not call upon the winds or waters, the soil or the heat; names totally irrelevant to the surroundings.

The arts and sciences of Hawai'i's ancestors were driven to near extinction. The advanced practice of healing through the medicines of plants, water, or massage, or just the uttered words, were driven into the back countryside. The science of predicting the future through animal behaviors, cloud colors, shapes and formations of leaves on trees was discounted as superstition and ridiculed as a collection of old folktales. The Hawaiian culture was being ground to dust.

Massive immigration took place, controlled by the United States. Hawai'i witnessed an influx of Americans, bringing with them a barrage of cultural, moral, religious, and political concepts. Hawaiians were "persuaded" to mimic American ways, to idolize American heroes, and to adopt American lifestyles. As Americans infiltrated, they took choice jobs with government agencies and management positions with business interests. They bought up or stole, through the manipulation of laws applied by them, much of the land and resources of Hawai'i. They gained power in Hawai'i, controlled greater chunks of the economy, controlled the public media, entrenched themselves in politics, and joined in the brainwashing of the Hawaiians to believe they were Americans.

The military turned Hawai'i into its Pacific fortress, converting Pearl Harbor from a coaling and fueling station to a major naval port. It bombed valleys and took a major island (Kaho'olawe) for its exclusive use as a target range. At will, the military tossed families out of their homes and destroyed sacred Hawaiian heirlooms (Lualualei, Oahu), building, in their place, naval communication towers that emitted radiation and ammunition depots that hid nuclear weapons. It declared martial law at will, violating the United States Constitution, and imposed military conscription on Hawaiian citizens. Freedom of trade was stopped. Congress assumed control over foreign relations. Hawaiians could buy only American goods or foreign goods the United States approved. The Big Five controlled all shipping. Every aspect of Hawai'i was Americanized. Military strength was constantly on display. Trade was totally controlled. Education and media were regulated. The secret ballot was a farce.

Hawai'i, that melting pot of cultures, races, languages, and lore, changed from a reality to an advertising slogan for politicians and merchants.

HAWAIIAN STATEHOOD, 1959

Finally, after three generations of brainwashing, Hawaiians were given the opportunity to be equal Americans! The United States placed the following question to the qualified voters in Hawai'i: *Shall Hawai'i immediately be admitted into the Union as a State?* "Qualified" voters were Americans who had been residents of Hawai'i for at least one year. The United States had already assured the vote with the thousands of American citizens brought in through its immigration program and through military assignments, as well as with generations of socialization of Hawaiian citizens. Those who resisted American domination and insisted on their Hawaiian citizenship could not vote.

In posing the statehood question so adeptly, the United States government precluded any real self-determination by limiting the choice to Hawai'i's either remaining a territory of the United States or becoming a state within its Union. The question, Should Hawai'i be free? was never asked. The Americans chose statehood overwhelmingly. . . .

Cultural Rejuvenation

. . . During the 1960s, Hawai'i witnessed the unfolding drama in the United States of the Black struggle for equality, including the riots in Watts, the marches and the bus boycotts, the voter registration drives, and the massive rallies in Washington, D.C. The American Indian Movement's activities also caught the attention of Hawaiians. The Black and American Indian movements, however, were soon overshadowed by the Vietnam War. Many Hawaiian citizens became directly involved in that war. By the end of the 1960s, attitudes toward the United States government had changed; its image had become tarnished.

Many in Hawai'i came out of the 1960s with greater sensitivity toward racial identity and pride in the cultural heritage of Hawai'i. Hawaiians were more willing to challenge governments, either individually or in organizations. Hawaiian music took on new vigor. Hula *halaus* (training schools and repositories of Hawaiian dance) gained wider prestige and membership, canoe clubs became more popular, interest in the Hawaiian language took hold, as well as practice in the natural medicines of Hawai'i and interest in Hawai'i's history. Hawaiian names were used prominently and with greater insistence. People of many different races joined this cultural rejuvenation in Hawai'i.

For native Hawaiians, land soon became another focus of contention. The eviction of farmers in the Kalama Valley on Oahu sparked a wave of challenges to the system. The movement to protect another island, Kahoolawe, from military bombing expanded the target of protest to the previously "sacred" military establishment. Soon a plethora of new Hawaiian organizations came into being. The issue of Hawaiian sovereignty and self-determination was a natural outgrowth of the disenchantment with Hawaiian social and economic conditions. The combination of all of these factors brought about a new consciousness of injustice—the denial of the Hawaiian nation.

By the second half of the 1970s, the sovereignty challenges were becoming more explicit. In a highly publicized trial of a reputed Hawaiian underworld leader, the defense raised the question of the state court's jurisdiction over a Hawaiian citizen. The Blount Report, President Cleveland's address to Congress, the Newlands Resolution annexing Hawai'i to the United States, and other historical documents and events were made part of the case record. Then the attorney, arguing that he was not a United States citizen but a Hawaiian, challenged the authority of the United States district court to force him to participate as a juror. The case drew wide public attention.

Soon after these events, the evictions of predominantly native Hawaiians from Sand Island, then from Makua Beach, then from Waimanalo all challenged the jurisdiction of the courts to try Hawaiian citizens. Those eviction cases reflected another direction of growing Hawaiian consciousness. The lands in question, originally in the inventory of the government of Hawai'i or owned by the Crown and subsequently ceded to the United States by the Republic of Hawai'i, were viewed by Hawaiians not as ceded but stolen lands. However, when asked, before a packed courtroom, to trace the title of those lands, the state's expert witness in the Makua Beach eviction case stated that it was simply state policy that no such tracing was necessary. The court then ruled that the evidence was conclusive that the Republic of Hawai'i had held proper title to cede these lands to the United States.

The Office of Hawaiian Affairs

As part of the awakening consciousness of native Hawaiians toward the historical injustices perpetrated against them, they incorporated into the state constitution in 1978 the Office of Hawaiian Affairs. The creation of the OHA marked a first in organizational representation for native Hawaiians. Indeed, it is a response to indigenous peoples that appears to be unique in the world.

Unlike the Office of Maori Affairs of Aotearoa (New Zealand) or the Office of Aboriginal Affairs of Australia or the Bureau of Indian Affairs of the United States, the OHA is composed of trustees who are directly elected by the indigenous people. As a result, in theory at least, they answer to no one but their Hawaiian constituents. However, the OHA is still seen as an organization of limited scope, unable to grasp the full sense of decolonization, since its very existence is dependent on the colonial constitutional regime in Hawai'i. Furthermore, it is based on a race constituency and therefore is unable to expand to include all potential Hawaiian citizens. Its current position on Hawaiian sovereignty is that native Hawaiians should be treated as a tribal nation, as the colonial government treats the American Indian nations.

Re-emergence As a Sovereign, Independent Nation

Today, there is a growing vision of Hawai'i becoming an independent nation, rejoining the ranks of other nations of the world. Within this vision, the question of citizenship and residence would be settled not by racial extraction but by one's relationship to Hawai'i—measured by some standard of acculturation, vows of loyalty to Hawai'i, ancestry from Hawaiian citizens prior to the American invasion of 1893, and other similar means. The native Hawaiians' position in this nation is still being considered. Some possibilities are

1. A weighted voting system for public officials, within an electoral process such that the native vote would not be less than 50 percent of the total votes cast;
2. A bicameral legislature in which the members of one body would be selected exclusively by native Hawaiian voters;
3. The creation of a council of customs, protocol, and 'aina (land), within which certain matters would be controlled by native Hawaiians; and
4. Special provisions for land rights, access and gathering rights, and other rights recognized by developing international organizations such as the International Labour Office and the United Nations.

Many more challenges to United States rule in Hawai'i are coming to public notice. In the schools, children are refusing to join in the morning pledge of allegiance to the United States and to stand for the national anthem. Other Hawaiians are refusing to file tax returns or to pay income taxes. More and more people charged with criminal offenses are denying the jurisdiction of American courts over them. A groundswell of protest is being felt in Hawai'i. This groundswell has even affected the Hawai'i State Legislature. The joint houses of the legislature made the following statement:

Recognizing the Year 1993 as the 100th Year Since the Overthrow of the Independent Nation of Hawai'i

Whereas, the year 1993 holds special significance for everyone who has been a part of Hawai'i over the last 100 years for it marks the century point after the United States military committed the first overt act to overthrow the independent nation of Hawai'i; and

Whereas, the Legislature recognizes the increasing discussions and debate here in Hawai'i and at the Congress of the United States of the consequence such an overt act of military aggression against a peaceful and independent nation has to the citizens and descendants of that nation today; and

Whereas, the Legislature believes that the proper status of Hawai'i's indigenous people within the political regime of the State of Hawai'i and the United States of America has still not reached its final stage and is still in the process of evolution; and

Whereas, the Legislature recognizes the even broader issue of the proper status of all people, irrespective of race, to exercise the right to self-determination; and

Whereas, the Legislature believes that the full range of consideration of Hawai'i's people's rights and freedoms must be completely explored in order to bring about harmony within Hawai'i's society; . . . now, therefore,

BE IT RESOLVED by the House of Representatives of the Sixteenth Legislature of the State of Hawai'i, Regular Session of 1991, the Senate concurring, that the Legislature determines that the year 1993 should serve Hawai'i as a year of special reflection to the rights and dignities of the native Hawaiians within the Hawaiian and the American societies; and

BE IT FURTHER RESOLVED that the Hawai'i Legislature determines that the year 1993 be a special time for Hawai'i, not only for special reflection of native Hawaiians, but for questioning the present and future role of

people of every race who today constitute the "Hawai'i society"; and

BE IT FURTHER RESOLVED that the Legislature encourages the promotion of debate revolving around the future of Hawai'i as a Pacific Island society, *within or without the United States of America* [italics added].

NOTES

1. See President Cleveland's address to the U.S. Congress on 18 December 1893: Executive Doc. no. 47, 53d Congress, 2d session, House of Representatives (Washington, DC: U.S. Government Printing Office, 1893).

2. Lili'uokalani, *Hawai'i's Story by Hawai'i's Queen* (Rutland, VT: Charles E. Tuttle Co., 1964).

THE SWORD AND THE CROSS
THE MISSIONS OF CALIFORNIA

Jeannette Henry Costo

Fresh from their campaign of terror and devastation of Mexico, the Spanish legions of the Inquisition set their sights on the "Californias" beginning with explorations of Lower California in 1535. Hernando Cortés (1485–1547) commanded the army of Span-

"The Sword and the Cross: The Missions of California," by Jeannette Henry Costo, as appeared in *The Missions of California: A Legacy of Genocide*, edited by Rupert Costo and Jeannette Henry Costo. Copyright 1987 by the Indian Historian Press for the American Indian Historical Society. Reprinted with permission. Portions of the article have been omitted.

ish mercenaries and priests of the Holy Tribunal. It was an evil omen for the lands known only as "the Californias" when the first expedition into Lower California arrived in May, 1535. What happened in Mexico and all the nations of that continent was to be repeated in many different ways in Lower California and later in Alta California. It is therefore appropriate, as we begin this story of the missions in Alta California, to note what inspired the representatives of the Sword and the Crown in their lust for lands, gold and jewels, a trade route to the fabled East, and an ample supply of free labor to carry out their goals.

LAS CASAS

A long neglected Catholic priest has left a story of such horror and mayhem that reading it stirs up the utmost disbelief. This was Bartalomé de las Casas (1474–1566) who carried on a life long crusade on behalf of the Indian people of those lands which Cortés and his legions depopulated. His writings were banned for a long time in Spain and most of Europe, but interest is now being awakened in the life of this priest, and a movement has begun to declare him a saint by the Roman Catholic Church, if a saint they must have. In a book published after his death, Las Casas tells the harrowing and gruesome story of massacres and wanton killing of women and children by the Spaniards.

Titled *The Tears of the Indians* . . . the book relates the story of the holocaust endured by the native peoples of the West Indies, Mexico, Guatemala, Cuba, Peru "and other places of the hemisphere," as Las Casas writes:

> In the year 1517, New Spain was discovered; after the discovery of which they did nothing first or second, but immediately fell to their old practices of cruelty and slaughter; for in the following year the Spaniards (who call themselves Christians) went thither to rob and kill. Though they gave out that they went to people the country. From that year unto this present year 1542, the violent injustice and tyrannies of the Spaniards came to their full height.

Rape of women and the murder of children were ordinary occurrences for the Spanish soldiers. It was to be repeated in the Californias. Plunder of the native cities and the ensuing depopulation of the land came next. A system was put into practice whereby the sons of upper class natives were taken from the families when very young and educated to despise their parents and act as spies upon them for the benefit of the Spanish government.

THE SPANISH INQUISITION

Both Las Casas and Cortés lived during the time of the Spanish Inquisition. Immediately following the occupation of Mexico, the Holy Tribunal of the Inquisition was set in motion. The occupation of Mexico and the following genocidal attack upon the people followed the interests of Spain, then making a vigorous advance into the New World. It was the Spanish Inquisition that unified Spain's aristocracy and made possible the ambitious campaign to overcome and take possession of the New World. The 16th century, when a dynamic Spain established its hegemony over Europe, America and the Atlantic and Pacific Oceans, was the era of Spain's greatest expansion. The Inquisition, although it functioned long before the 15th century, was established formally by Papal decree in 1478. Its stated object was to examine the genuineness of the Jewish "conversos," those who had converted to Catholicism. In fact, this arm of the church, part of the Spanish Crown, and for some time under the control of Spain, was instituted for economic reasons, not solely religious. The aim of the Inquisition was to obliterate the Jews, who were the great financiers of Spain.

The Moors, who had held Spain for more than five hundred years, were another target of the Inquisition. During the next fifty years the Jews would be subjected to genocide, and the Moors were all but wiped out in bloody pogroms against them and the Jews. Most of both peoples had by then been converted to Catholicism usually unwillingly, and many had Catholic spouses and children of mixed blood. These were called "conversos," and under the Inquisition they were compelled to prove that their conversions were genuine. For this purpose tribunals were set up, with priests and bishops officiating, as well as representatives of the Spanish monarchs. This "bloody institution," as it became known, was transferred to the New World, where it became the handmaiden of the holocaust.

AN IMPERIAL THREAT

The Inquisition had the power and it used that power to bring before its secret tribunals any person who was deemed a danger to Catholicism. It lasted well into the 19th century. In 1802, for example, the crown was issuing threats against those of its subjects who were shielding Jews against the Inquisition.

In 1713 there was born on the island of Majorca a Spanish child who was destined to play an ominous role in Alta California. He was Junipero Serra, later to become a Franciscan priest. Majorca was occupied by the Moors until driven out by the Spanish monarchs in the 15th century. The Inquisition existed even in the universities of Spain, where it outdid the vilest of tribunals in attacks against scholars of distinguished attainments. It also existed in the Catholic university in Majorca, where Serra was educated and later became a professor and librarian of the monastery before he was sent to Mexico.

The Inquisition was brought to the Americas by the Spaniards, and the tribunals began to function. It was introduced into Lima, capital of Peru, and followed by the founding of a tribunal in Mexico City in 1571, and Cartagena de Indias in 1610. Following the gruesome details of the Spanish conquest of Mexico, and the activities of the Inquisition in the New World, the tribunal functioned persistently, issuing a decree banning the Las Casas book exposing the Spanish atrocities, on pain of punishment.

Thus the ideology, the structure and the power of the Spanish Inquisition held sway throughout the rise and decline of the Jesuit Missions in Baja California, and then in Alta California, until the Mexican revolution and the ensuing secularization of the missions in 1834.

NATIVE REVOLT

In Baja California the Inquisition and the massacres it inflicted led to revolts among the natives. In Alta California, the Cross was held somewhat more carefully in the hands of such as Junipero Serra and his colleagues, but the structure, and the philosophy of the Inquisition were responsible for the forced labor, the forced conversion, and the racial genocide that took place following missionization in California.

A period of earnest incubation by the Inquisition took place for Serra. He entered the Franciscan order in 1730; was sent to Mexico City in 1749; became a missionary to Indians in the northeast of Queretaro from 1750 to 1759; then was sent to Lower California in 1767, and cooperated with the government to establish missions in Upper California, founding missions in nine coastal areas of Alta California. Thus, it was Serra who led the invasion and the foreign occupation of California. The fact that the Indians of Baja California suffered severe hunger was known to him, but he claimed he could do nothing about it.

His diary relates at least two incidents when, on his way to Alta California, he was met by natives of the Peninsula who complained they had nothing to eat even though they were part of the mission establishment in the region. Serra kept his diary during the journey from Lower California to Alta California and the San Diego area, where he was Father-President of the mission system. On January 6 and February 7, short entries are made noting his joy at bringing the faith to the "pagans." But on April 7 and 8 he relates that he met with a group of Indians who complained they were hungry and had not eaten. They had waited for him on the road he was expected to travel. They said that the "Fathers for lack of food had sent them to the mountains. They belonged to the Guadalupe Mission." The next day he met again with a "greater number of Indians of the said principal village, who made the same complaint."

Continuing his journey to San Diego, he is given an introduction to the Indians who are "pagans," or "gentiles" (unconverted natives). He notes that they are followed surreptitiously by natives who do not show themselves. They are confronted by hostile demonstrations, are threatened with being shot with bows and arrows, and the natives at one point, attempting to frighten the strangers into going away, begin to shout and cavort in a vain effort to make them leave. Finally, the commanding officer "instructed the soldiers, on horses, to line up and shoot" at the Indians. When this is done, the Indians flee. They have never heard the sound of guns.

Serra makes the observation continually that they are meeting "a great number of gentiles" along the way, causing him to realize they are in a well populated region.

Serra had an academic life as well as one of missionary activities. He was a university professor in Majorca, accredited at Lullian University in 1744, and was also librarian at the monastery. When, in 1767, the Spanish monarch banished the Jesuit Society from Lower California, Serra was chosen to head the missionary campaign in Alta California. Mexico had been New Spain for more than two hundred years when Serra took up his post as Father-President of the mission sys-

tem. Then, in the middle of the 18th century, there were more than four thousand friars working in the colonies of New Spain alone. The Jesuits, who considered they had been ill-treated, had founded thirteen missions in Baja California, and in the course of time there had been at least eight revolts, and two priests had been killed by the natives who wanted the Spaniards to leave their country.

In receiving the post of Father-President, Serra was expected to minister to the spiritual needs of the natives. He was also an advisor to the civil and military authorities, not only for Alta California missions "but also the colonies, hundreds of leagues beyond the settled Mexican frontier."

Historians of later years do not see Serra as the foremost leader in the occupation of Alta California. Chapman states that:

> (Serra) . . . would not have distinguished (himself) from Portolá on the one hand or Father Lasuén on the other. Much more important as affecting his fame was the publication of a biography prepared by his life-long friend, ardent admirer, and co-worker Francisco Palou.[1]

Contending that the proposed sanctification of Serra originated two hundred years before the American Franciscans brought it to light, Chapman states:

> Palou's volume was written to prove the great work of Father Serra. It seems probable, as has been asserted, that the author hoped it might help to procure the beatification of his revered brother-Franciscan. In accord with the extravagant style of the period, the book displayed a tendency to colorful writing and was replete with miraculous happenings.[2]

As Chapman points out, Father Serra has "walked through" many thousand pages of print, with the advantage, too, of having his tale presented under the most favorable circumstances.

"Is it any wonder, then," the author asks, "that there sprang up a veritable 'Serra legend?'"

MORE THAN A PRIEST?

The Palou biography recited various "miracles" supposed to have been performed by Serra, and relates that Serra himself was the ruler of the province, not merely the mission priest. The Palou biography, in fact, gives credence to the claim made by the authors that it was Serra, not the soldiers of the military establishment, nor the civil governors, who ruled the missions, the presidios and the towns that began as pueblos in Alta California.

In the process of building the missions, Serra frequently had conflicts with the civil authorities. Historians utilize this fact in an attempt to prove that the priest was solicitous for the care of "his" neophytes. This appears to be a fable. The controversy with Governor Neve centered around the question of mission structure and purpose. Neve insisted that the missions ought to be built further inland, that they should not hold power over the converted natives, and that there should not be animals attached to the missions for grazing and butchering. He did not want "factories" to be established, and he objected to the punishment and the flogging for infractions of religious instruction that were meted out to the neophytes. The friars, Neve contended, must cease their monopoly on the economy and the fruits of the economic ventures accomplished by the Indians. This conflict, of course, also had economic overtones of power. Neve wanted control of the economy. Serra would not give it up, and so the conflict quietly ran on, emerging now and then into open conflict. In most if not all cases, Serra was the winner.

Considering the history of the Serra legend, the tasks he was given as one worthy of complete trust by the Spanish monarch and the Inquisition, as well as Serra's oft-recognized capacity as an administrator, it would appear logical to believe that he was indeed the architect of the mission system in Alta California. In that capacity he set the rules; he laid down the laws; he compelled (by whatever mild means but by benign coercion as well) obedience, as indeed did the Holy Tribunals wherever they existed.

As one example of the events soon after the founding of the first mission at San Diego, we note the long-forgotten Letter of Fray Luis Jayme, a Franciscan who was delegated as missionary to the new mission. In 1772, Fr. Jayme, in frustration over an incredibly tragic situation at the mission, wrote a personal letter to the Father Guardian of the College of San Fernando in Mexico:

> At one of these Indian villages near this mission of San Diego, which said village is very large, and which is on the road to Monterey, the gentiles therein many times have been on the point of coming here to kill us all, and the reason for this is that some soldiers went there and raped their women, and other soldiers who were carrying the mail to Monterey turned their animals into their fields and they ate up their crops. Three other Indian villages have reported the same thing to me, several times.[3]

Father Jayme presented evidence to his superior about three other incidents in which the soldiers gang-raped women, one a blind woman who was carried screaming and beaten into the woods to be raped. The Indians were so afraid of these soldiers and tried so hard to protect their wives and daughters, that they "leave their huts and the crops which they gather from the lands around their villages, and go to the woods and experience hunger. They do this so that the soldiers will not rape their women as they have already done so many times in the past."

The problem of rape was endemic. But this is not mentioned in the historical works about the missions. Jayme informs his superior further that:

> I have heard it said that they (the Indians) are given to sexual vices, but among them here I have not been able to discover a single fault of that nature. Some of the first adults whom we baptized, when we pointed out to them that sexual intercourse with a woman to whom they were not married, (was bad) told me that they already knew that, and that among them it was considered to be very bad, and so they did not do so at all.[4]

However, in a report to the superior, dated July 1, 1785, and dealing with the years from 1770 through 1774, Serra never mentioned the problem of rape of Indian women, which was general at all the missions. It was believed by the native people, that the priests could have stopped it, had they been as concerned about the welfare of their neophytes as they protested. Some natives, sophisticated beyond any believed of them by the civil authorities or the priests, believed that the priests allowed the rapes to occur, to "keep the soldiers content." Such suggestions come down through the years by way of family beliefs and, by this time, by tradition. Who is to believe otherwise, when the rapes continued until the end of the mission period?

Thus, the same Father Luis Jayme, who raised the question with his superior at San Fernando, and opened up the subject (or so he thought), was himself killed in the revolt of the natives of San Diego in November, 1772. The mission itself was burned down in 1775, the Indians at last having decided to stop the rapes and the destruction of their crops, by the only means left to them.

Abuse at the missions was general. Catholic historians such as Fr. Zephyrin Engelhardt explain it this way:

> As those Indians are accustomed to live in the plains and the hills like beasts, they are informed in advance that, if they wish to be Christians, they can no longer go to the mountains, but have to live at the Mission, that if then they leave the rancheria (thus they call the huts and dwelling place of the convert Indians) they will be followed and sought and then will be punished.[5]

That there was forced labor in the missions, without exception, is borne out by reports of scholars, anthropologists, ethnologists, and historians, who have studied the matter and accumulated considerable evidence.

"There can be no serious denial," said Cook, "that the mission system, in its economics, was built upon forced labor."

Wrote the historian George Harwood Phillips, about the Indians, "They were, indeed, the economic backbone of the mission system." In the same article, Phillips states, "The documentation clearly demonstrates that Indian discontent with mission life was prevalent from the very inception of the system and was often manifested in fugitivism."

The burden of excessive confining work is described by Fr. Maynard Geiger who writes, about the Santa Barbara Mission, that:

> Women helped to carry adobes. Women also aided in transporting bricks and tiles. They rarely carried stones . . . Children were employed in combing wool and at looms assisting weavers. Others guarded freshly made tiles and adobes to prevent them being trampled on by animals. The weaving of cloth was one of the principal mission industries, which was already in full operation by 1796.[6]

Geiger advises that all were employed and that weaving was a very lucrative vocation for the mission. Here one may perceive perhaps the first indication of the piece-work system in the west. The mission women and children worked at piece-work rates, as did the men in making adobe bricks. Payment was "in kind," Geiger states, and the amount of work expected was specifically set. Thus, Geiger reports "spinners spun a pound a day to the width of a foot for clothing and one-and-a-half pounds a foot in width for blankets."

Treatment of the Indians at this very Santa Barbara Mission is described by a traveler in 1829, who stated that:

> (At Santa Barbara) Another door of the church opened upon the cemetery, where were buried the deceased Christians of the Mission and Presidio surrounded by a thick wall, and having in one corner the charnel house, crowded with a ghastly array of skulls and bones.[7]

These were Indian bones, for, instead of either the Christian or native religious burial, the natives were allowed to rot and then thrust into the charnel house.

MISERABLE CONDITIONS

At San Luis Rey, Robinson finds "The condition of these Indians is miserable indeed; and it is not to be wondered at that many attempt to escape from the severity of the religious discipline at the mission. They are pursued, and generally taken; when they are flogged and an iron clog is fastened to their legs, serving as additional punishment and a warning to others."

Abuse at the missions was general, as can be found in a study of such reports, but more can be learned from *The Indian Testimony*. Furthermore, as the historian Chapman solemnly states:

> Ultimately, too, the Indians would become a source of profit to the crown, for those who had submitted to Spanish authority were required by law to pay an annual tribute, though this was remitted for the Indians still in missions.[8]

The impact of missionization upon the Indians of California took many adverse forms. First of these was the forcing of Indians into structures that were larger and in larger aggregates. As compared with the normal group of the Indian village, that of 30–100, the mission population averaged 50–600 and frequently was made even greater. Aggregates of population of one thousand were common and occasionally a population of two thousand and more was reached. (Cook)

Abuse, forced conversion, destruction of Indian crops and property—these were the effects of missionization. There was mindless control of the missions. Some missions continued to prevent foodgathering in aboriginal sources, but when the missions were hard-pressed for food, the neophytes were actually sent out, returning in most cases with good stores of the natural foods. The only exceptions to this result were the areas that had been destroyed by cattle grazing or plowing the ground for unsuccessful mission (European) crops, or digging and destroying Indian crops for building mission structures. (Cook)

Thus, "in 1806 the crops failed in San Diego and there was scarcely enough food to maintain the neophytes." In 1819 the crops were destroyed at Santa Ynes and the missionary feared there would be a famine. In the same year the Bay region suffered. The minister at San Francisco reported that the stock were dying and the crops poor. He undertook to plant crops in the region of San Jose "to alleviate the great misery in which these unfortunate neophytes find themselves." (Cook)

Genocide came early in California, soon to be followed by more of the same in other regions of the state. But the destruction of the native people took a different form in southern California. First among the policies of the Franciscan missionaries was to gather the Indians together, locate them in a mission in the very center of highest Indian population, and put them to work after conversion to Catholicism. This might have been considered efficient by the mendicant priests, but it resulted in an almost instantaneous destruction of the Indians as a race, and would have continued had it not been for the native stubborness in clinging to whatever was left of his culture, his language, and the traditions and religion of the people.

RACIAL GENOCIDE

San Gabriel mission is a classic example of this process. Here, in the very midst of what is believed to have been Cahuilla land, there was built a mission to which were taken Indians of various other tribes. One could find Serrano, Kumeyaay, even Mohave and Yuma people. In time there were thousands of tribal people—none of whom had the possibility of retaining their practices of tribal authority, tribal laws, and tribal religious rituals. There was immediate confusion. Tribes that had observed rigid systems of territorial ownership, suddenly found themselves without territory at all. This was confiscation of their land, without the fact being recognized by the Indians. They came, were treated to a ceremonial show of which they had no knowledge. It interested them, and they were told that no longer would they be subjected to the laws of their tribes. They would have such ceremonies, colorful and with a strange new kind of music, all the time. Only they must abide by certain different rules and must promise to remain in the missions so that they could be educated and taught new skills.

They were fascinated. They believed they could go home at any time they wished. And there were those who submitted quietly at first. Until they discovered what the mission system meant, and then there was dismay, followed by unrest, followed by fugitivism, and if it was found possible, it was followed by revolt.

That there was forced conversion is the conclusion of scholars who have examined the record. Jack D. Forbes, a historian and author, wrote: "No matter what means were used to entice Indians into a mission, however, force had to be used to keep them there and to coerce them into abandoning their native customs." In the same study Forbes also observes a significant result of missionization, stating: "The effects of missionization varied from region to region. In general, however, the natives frequently became depressed and lethargic, giving the impression of dull-wittedness."[9]

The destruction of tribal identity went hand-in-hand with the destruction of Indian economy. Cattle raising was a popular feature of the mission economy. From the very beginning of contact with the missionaries and the soldiers, the cattle posed a major problem for the Indians. Immediately, their food stores were broken into. Their plants which they had carefully cherished and protected, and watched during the growth period, were often ready to be harvested. But the cattle, the horses and sheep destroyed or ate the food which the Indians had depended upon for their livelihood.

Population decline in the missions has been studied and many reports have been made on the matter. In the aboriginal state, coastal and valley Indians were spaced very exactly in conformity with the food supply. In regions of prolific sustenance the general density of population was high, whereas in barren areas it was low. Thus, Cook explains, "Condensations of population were found along rivers in coast lowlands, and in small fertile valleys."

This was the natural system of population use of the land and the native concept of population growth . . . or decrease, for that matter. For, as soon as it became clear that population was increasing faster than the resources would be capable of sustaining such growth, there was a natural split of the extended family, or even the tribe, which found another area in which to build a livelihood, within the territory of the tribe as a whole.

NATURAL LAND USE

In the memories of some old-timers it is told how the people would gather, those of the same tribe, in their families and clans, and discuss whether it would be best for a certain group to take up residence in another part of their territory. And one might tell the other "Go ahead and take that corner where I have my place." It was shared, and there was no problem about property within the tribe. This was a natural use of land and control of population growth in relation to the use of the land and the economy.

Cook explains the complex way in which population declines in relation to the birth factor in his study.

"In the brief span of 65 years of mission operation, extending from the first founding 1769 to the secularization of the missions in 1834, 81,000 Indians were baptized in the missions and 60,000 deaths were recorded to 1834. In 1834 there remained about 15,000 resident neophytes in the 21 missions, who were then released from the care of the mission fathers." (Heizer and Elsasser)[10]

There is a general myth, probably encouraged by mission historians, that the Indians were docile, passive, did not revolt and make war upon the mendicant orders or the civil authorities as the natives did in the east and the Plains. This is untrue. There were revolts from the very beginning of missionization. San Diego is a point to consider, where there were uprisings so often that it ceased to be considered a measure of the discontent felt by the natives in the missions. Unreported and often undocumented uprisings were known, however, to the natives in every area of the state. In several articles, historian Jack Holterman has dealt with the history of revolts in the San Francisco Bay area.

Working in the California State Archives, and with access to several elderly people who had knowledge of such matters, Holterman was able to piece together the story of leaders of revolts against the missions around the San Francisco Bay area, such as Yozcolo, Estanislao, Marin and Quintin. These uprisings took place from 1820 through the 1830s.

In southern California a woman, (not named in the records but is believed to have been Taypurina) led an uprising in 1785 at Mission San Gabriel. Four were arrested in that revolt. They received twenty lashes each and were released. Two years later, General Ugarte's order came, condemning one native named Nicolai, to six years of work at the presidio, followed by exile to a distant mission. The woman was sent into perpetual exile, and the other two were dismissed with two years' imprisonment.

THE INQUISITION RIDES AGAIN

The Indian leader Yozcolo was finally captured, beheaded and his head hung on a pole for all to see. It was the Inquisition in American dress. Two famous uprisings should be described in separate articles, as the Indians experienced these events. They were the uprising at Santa Barbara, which spread like wildfire through the five missions. Conditions were so terrifying, and restraints were so unbearable that it took only a final thread to break the back of passivity and lead to active resistance. This occurred when one Indian was flogged so badly that he died of his wounds. We have already related the events at San Diego. In all cases the Indians were led to resist when they understood that there was no way out of the mission system for them except to escape. Many were willing to die to get out of that barbaric system of servitude, duress and privation.

No Indian can forget the exploits of Pomponio of San Rafael Mission, originally from Mission Dolores in San Francisco. For several years (1821–24) he ranged up and down the coast between San Rafael and Santa Cruz and probably further, in a guerrilla war of attrition against the Spaniards. He fought against the natives who succumbed to the missions as well. He is thought to have been Coast Miwuk.

The historian Jack Forbes explains it this way: "The California missions were also authoritarian, coercive institutions (totalitarian best describes it) . . . From the native viewpoint, the missions were a catastrophe of indescribable proportions."

The mission system began to break down following the Mexican revolution, and the Mexican government held sway over California from 1822 until 1848, when the state passed into the hands of the United States.

The history of the Mexican period in California is not as simple, so far as the Indian condition is concerned, as it has been made to appear in simplistic historical tales. It is stated usually that secularization came to the Indians, who were thrust into the outside world, their mission life taken away from them and leaving them without the leadership of the priests. Much is made of the ensuing poverty among the Indians, but little has been said or known of the fact that the Indians were not passive participants even in the process of secularization. It is true that secularization brought homelessness in large degree to those who had lived as converts in the missions. But they did have several options, as historian George H. Phillips explains:[11]

> They could drift into the Mexican towns in search of domestic or agricultural employment; they could petition the government for land grants; they could seek work on the ranchos; or they could withdraw into the interior

The Franciscan Missions in California

San Diego de Alcalá, Fr. Serra	July 16, 1769
San Carlos Barromeo, Monterey, Fr. Serra	June 3, 1770
San Antonio de Padua, Frs. Serra, Pieras, Sitiar	July 14, 1771
San Gabriel Arcangel, Frs. Somera, Cambón	Sept. 8, 1771
San Luis Obispo de Tolosa, Fr. Serra	Sept., 1772
San Francisco de Asis (Dolores) Frs. Palóu, Cambón, Peña	Oct. 9, 1776
San Juan Capistrano, Fr. Serra	Nov. 10, 1776
Santa Clara, Fr. Peña	Jan. 12, 1777
San Buenaventura, Frs. Serra, Cambón	March 31, 1782
Santa Barbara, Fr. Lasuén	Dec. 4, 1786
La Purissima Concepcion, Fr. Lasuén	Dec. 8, 1787
Santa Cruz, Frs. Salazar, Lopez	Sept. 25, 1791
Nuestra Señora de la Soledad, Fr. Lasuén	Oct. 9, 1791
San José, Fr. Lasuén	June 11, 1797
San Juan Bautista, Fr. Lasuén	June 24, 1797
San Miguel Arcangel, Frs. Lasuén, Sitiar	July 25, 1797
San Fernando Rey de España, Frs. Lasuén, Dometz	Sept. 8, 1797
San Luis Rey de Francis, Frs. Lasuén, Santiago, Peyri	June 13, 1798
Santa Inez, virgin and martyr, Frs. Tápis, Cipres	Sept. 17, 1804
San Rafael Arcangel, Frs. Vicente, Sarria	Dec. 14, 1817
San Francisco Solano, Sonoma, Fr. Altimera	July 4, 1823

with the intent of joining kinsmen or establishing new sociopolitical groups.

It is not generally understood that the Indian people are very adaptive, and the will to live is great within them. They had learned how to cope with earthquake, accident, weather, and finally the strangers who came and took their land and their heritage. As to those options, they took one or all three as they found it possible. They worked. They endured, and they survived.

One other element remained (and remains) for the Indians of California. For despite the most intensive moral pressures and persuasion, "the Indians retained the basic pattern of their culture intrinsically unaltered. Indeed they went so far as to conform to their own manner of thought. In this one respect, therefore, the Indian achieved an adaptational success, which stands unique in their history."

AMERICA TAKES CALIFORNIA

The United States became the formal owner of the state of California when the Treaty of Guadalupe Hidalgo with Mexico was signed in 1848. This treaty was ratified by the Senate and signed into law by the president in 1850. (Treaty Series No. 207–9 Statutes 922-43, 13 pt 2 Public Treaties 492-503)

And so ended the tenure of the mission system in California. What is left now are some historic structures open to the public. In some, one can still see the cells in which Indians were incarcerated, as well as the cramped space where the women were allowed to live with tiny windows too high to reach and no air. What also remains is the romance of the missions, the sentimental notion and the myth that here was the beginning of California civilization. If this can be accepted, pray for this state, for the legend is fouled, and the history has been distorted beyond recognition of the facts.

What also remains is the fond belief that in Fr. Junipero Serra, the people of this state have a fable and a heroic figure to emulate, both in life and in spirit. Serra has been lauded as a humanitarian. No commissioner of the Inquisition could possibly be considered a humanitarian. But these claims for Serra's good works on behalf of the Indians rest upon a failure to understand Indian life and culture. . . .

NOTES

1. Chapman, Charles E. *A History of California: The Spanish Period* (New York: The Macmillan Co., 1921): 352.

2. *Ibid.:* 353.

3. Jayme, Luis, O.F.M. *Letter. Oct. 1, 1772.* Maynard Geiger, tr. (San Diego: Dawson's Book Shop, 1970), rept.

4. *Ibid.:* 42.

5. Englehardt, Zephryin. *San Gabriel Mission and the Beginning of Los Angeles* (San Gabriel Herald Press, 1927): 34.

6. Geiger, Maynard, O.F.M. *Mission Santa Barbara 1782–1965* (Santa Barbara: Francisan Fathers of California, 1965): 61–65.

7. Robinson, Alfred. *Life in California* (San Francisco: William Doxey, 1981): 57.

8. Chapman, *Ibid.:* 151.

9. Forbes, Jack D. ed. *The Indian in America's Past* (Englewood Cliffs, N.J.: Prentice Hall, 1964): 75, 76.

10. Heizer, Robert F., and Albert Elsasser. *The Natural World of the California Indians* (University of California Press, 1980): 226.

11. Phillips, George H. *The Enduring Struggle* (San Francisco: Boyd & Fraser, 1981): 33.

From *Acorn Soup* by L. Frank. Copyright © 1999 by L. Frank. Reprinted by permission of Heyday Books. All rights reserved.

THE CRIME OF GENOCIDE
A UNITED NATIONS CONVENTION AIMED AT PREVENTING
DESTRUCTION OF GROUPS AND AT PUNISHING THOSE RESPONSIBLE

Rupert Costo and Jeannette Henry Costo

Genocide is a modern word for an old crime. It means the deliberate destruction of national, racial, religious or ethnic groups.

History had long been a grim witness to such acts, but it remained for the twentieth century to see those acts carried out on the largest and most inhuman scale known when the Nazi Government of Germany systematically annihilated millions of people because of their religion or ethnic origin. A shocked world then rejected any contention that such crimes were the exclusive concern of the State perpetrating them, and punishment of the guilty became one of the principal war aims of the Allied nations. The charter of the International Military Tribunal at Nuremberg, approved by the Allies

in 1945, recognized that war criminals were not only those who had committed crimes against peace, and violations of the laws or customs of war, but those who had carried out "crimes against humanity;" whether or not such crimes violated the domestic law of the country in which they took place.

During its first session in 1946, the United Nations General Assembly approved two resolutions. In the first, the Assembly affirmed the principles of the charter of the Nuremberg Tribunal. In the second—the basic resolution on genocide— the Assembly affirmed that genocide was a crime under international law and that those guilty of it, whoever they were and for whatever reason they committed it, were punishable. It asked for inter-national cooperation in preventing and punishing genocide and it invited Member States to enact the necessary national legislation. In a final provision, the Assembly called for studies aimed at creating an international legal instrument to deal with the crime. That was the origin of the Convention on the Prevention and Punishment of the Crime of Genocide unanimously adopted by the Assembly on 9 December 1948.

The term "convention" in international law means an agreement among sovereign nations. It is a legal compact which pledges every Contracting Party to accept certain obligations.

How the Convention Was Prepared

In 1946 the General Assembly requested the Eco-nomic and Social Council to undertake the neces-sary studies for drawing up a draft Convention on the crime of genocide. In 1947 the Secretary-General, at the request of the Economic and Social Council, prepared a first draft of the Convention and circulated it to Member States for comments. At that stage, the Secretary-General was assisted by a group of international law experts, among them the late Dr. Raphael Lemkin, who in 1944 had coined the term "genocide." In 1948 the Eco-nomic and Social Council appointed an ad hoc Committee of seven members to submit to it a re-vised draft. That the Committee did, and after a gen-eral debate, the Council decided on 26 August to transmit the draft to the General Assembly. At the Paris session of the General Assembly the draft was debated by the legal Committee and adopted by the Assembly on 9 December 1948.

The Definition of Genocide in the Convention

Genocide, the Convention declares, is the com-mitting of certain acts with intent to destroy—wholly or in part—a national, ethnic, racial or religious group as such.

What are the acts? First, actual killing. But it is possible to destroy a group of human beings without direct physical extermination. So the Con-vention includes in the definition of genocide the acts of causing serious bodily or mental harm; deliberate infliction of conditions of life "calculat-ed to bring about" physical destruction; imposing measures to prevent birth and, finally, forcibly transferring children of one group to another group.

Those acts, the Convention states, constitute "geno-cide." In accordance with the Convention, related acts are also punishable: conspiracy to commit genocide, direct and public incitement to com-mit genocide, an attempt to commit the crime and complicity in its commission.

To Prevent and to Punish

The Convention first declares that genocide "whether committed in time of peace or in time of war" is a crime under international law which the contracting States "undertake to prevent and to punish."

Main principles established by the Conven-tion are:

1. Contracting States are bound to enact the laws needed to give effect to the provisions of the Convention, in particular to provide effective penalties.
2. States undertake to try persons charged with those offenses in their competent national courts.
3. Parties to the Convention agree that the acts listed shall not be considered as political crimes. Therefore, they pledge to grant extra-dition in accordance with their laws and treaties.

All those pledges are for national action. The Convention also envisages trial by an internation-al penal tribunal should one be set up and should the Contracting Parties accept its jurisdiction. Fur-thermore, it provides that any of the contracting States may bring a charge of genocide, or of any of the related acts, before the competent organs of the United Nations and ask for appropriate action under the Charter.

If there is any dispute between one country and another on the interpretation, application or ful-fillment of the Convention, the dispute must be submitted to the International Court of Justice at the request of any of the Parties.

Genocide in California

The patterns of genocide in southern California dif-fered from that of the American Gold Rush, and the modern Holocaust of Nazis in Germany.

In southern California the genocide was prac-ticed against the entire race—the Native people of the land. It is not possible to condone the near extinction of this people through the notion that the missionaries believed the Indians were "civilized," or that they were children who must be brought to the true religion of Roman Catholicism in the garb of the Spanish monarchy.

The truth is that the evidence of native culture and lifeways, of land use and natural development of a peoples' economy were all about the Franciscans. The land itself, by all appearances, was one in which people, human beings, had cared for, nurtured, and protected its beauty for all to enjoy.

They must have known they were exterminating a race. They did know it. And it was done with utter heartlessness, with utter disregard for the human individual. It was done by trickery, by cajolery, by enticement.

It must not be repeated. Together with the victims of the Nazi genocide, we must say "Never again! Never again!"

"The Crime of Genocide," pp. 126–129 in *The Missions of California: A Legacy of Genocide,* ed. Rupert Costo and Jeannette Henry Costo. Copyright 1987 by the Indian Historian Press for the American Indian Historical Society. Reprinted with permission.

"Obey" by Mike S. Rodriguez, © 1988.

CREATING A VISUAL HISTORY:
A QUESTION OF OWNERSHIP

Theresa Harlan

In 1992 I guest-curated "Message Carriers: Native Photographic Messages" for the Photographic Resource Center at Boston University.[1] When invited, I could not accept without careful consideration of significant issues such as: ghettoization, opportunism (mine and theirs), and exploitation. Mainstream museums and publications often set apart "artists of color," "multicultural artists," and "ethnic artists," thereby designating us as the "other" or "different." The art and writings of these "other"artists are locked into discussions of "their" art, "their" people, and "their" issues. While there are still few opportunities to exhibit works by Native artists, there are even fewer exhibitions that treat these works in terms of their intellectual and critical contributions. Contemporary Native art is often characterized as angry, created from the voices of the defeated, and confined to the realm of the emotions.

Native people have—but are not perceived as having—diverse histories, cultures, languages, economics, politics, and worldviews. As Native people, we must claim rights to, and ownership of, strategic and intellectual space for our works. We must reject the re-

duction of Native images to sentimental portraits, such as those depicted by Marcia Keegan in her book *Enduring Culture: A Century of Photography of the Southwest Indians.*[2] Keegan writes, "From the beginning of my acquaintance with them, it was the Indians' confidence and attunement to the eternal verities that inspired my wonder and admiration. Thus it became my enduring commitment to try to experience, imagine, and document that more elusive subject, the traditional Indian way of life."[3] This type of thinking reduces Native survival to a matter of nostalgia, and precludes discussion of the political strategies that enabled Native survival. The writer bell hooks refers to nostalgia as "that longing for something to be as once it was, a kind of useless act. . . ."[4] and calls for the recognition of the politicized state of memory as ". . . that remembering that serves to illuminate and transform the present."[5]

Native survival was and remains a contest over life, humanity, land, systems of knowledge, memory, and representations. Native memories and representations are persistently pushed aside to make way for constructed Western myths and their representations of Native people. Ownership of Native representations is a critical arena of this contest, for there are those who insist on following the tired, romantic formulas used to depict Native people. Those myths ensure

From *Strong Hearts: Native American Visions and Voices*, edited by Peggy Roalf (New York: Aperture Foundation, 1995), pp. 20–33. Reprinted by permission of the author. Photographs originally included in this article have been replaced.

an existence without context, without history, without a reality. An existence that allows for the combing of hair with yucca brushes in the light of a Southwest sunset; competition powwow dancing reborn as a spiritual ceremony; or the drunken Indian asleep on cement city sidewalks unable to cope with the white man's world. These are the representations constantly paraded before us by non-Native photographic publications such as Keegan's *Enduring Culture,* or *National Geographic's* 1994 issue on American Indians, or Marc Gaede's *Border Towns.* Such constructed myths and representations are given institutional validation in the classroom and are continually supported by popular culture and media.

American classrooms are usually the first site of contest for Native children. In her essay, "Constructing Images, Constructing Reality: American Indian Photography and Representation," Gail Tremblay writes, "When Native children are taught that they are not equal, that their cultures are incapable of surviving in a modern world, they suffer from the pain that has haunted their parents' lives, that haunts their own lives. For an indigenous person, choosing not to vanish, not to feel inferior, not to hate oneself, becomes an intensely political act. A Native photographer coming to image-making in this climate must ask, 'What shall I take pictures of, who shall I take pictures for, what will my images communicate to the world?' "[6]

Photographer and filmmaker Victor Masayesva, Jr., has described the camera as a weapon. "As Hopi photographers, we are indeed in a dangerous time. The camera which is available to us is a weapon that will violate the silences and secrets so essential to our group survival."[7] Writer, curator, and photographer Richard Hill, Jr. of the Tuscarora nation, also named the camera as a weapon, but a weapon for "art

confrontation rather than military confrontation. Indians themselves now have taken the power of the image and begun to use it for their own enjoyment as well as for its potential power as a political weapon."[8] Artist Hulleah Tsinhnahjinnie declared, "No longer is the camera held by an outsider looking in; the camera is now held with brown hands opening familiar worlds. We document ourselves with a humanizing eye, we create new visions with ease, and we can turn the camera and show how we see you. The power of the image is not a new concept to the Native photographer—look at petroglyphs and ledger drawings. What has changed is the process."[9]

Masayesva, Hill, and Tsinhnahjinnie speak from the experience of seeing themselves spoken for by outsiders, of seeing the surreal positioned as the real. As Trinh T. Minh-ha says, Native image-makers "understand the dehumanization of forced-removal/relocation/reeducation/redefinition, the humiliation of having to falsify your own reality, your voice—you know. And often cannot say it. You try and keep on trying to unsay it, for if you don't they will not fail to fill in the blanks on your behalf, and you will be said."[10]

When Native people do pick up the camera, often their image-making is greeted with a patronizing welcome. The "Indian" no longer sits passively before the camera, but now operates the camera—a symbol of the white man's technology. The voices and images of Native photographers must be understood as rooted in and informed by Native experiences and knowledge.

Lee Marmon has created, and continues to create, photographic representations of Native people that affirm Native memories, self-knowledge, and presence. Upon his return from World War II, Marmon began taking photographs of the old people in the villages at Laguna Pueblo—so that there

"1491" from the "Feather" series by Larry McNeil, © 1992.

would be something to remember them by. Marmon's photographic remembrances are of a generation of people who had to devise ways to affirm and protect Laguna knowledge despite the pernicious attempts—beginning in the sixteenth century—of the Spanish, Mexican, and later, the United States governments to strip them of land, culture, religion, and the memory of that existence. Thus, these are not merely images of cute old people. The presence of Juana Scott Piño; of Jeff Sousea in *White Man's Moccasins;* or of Bennie at the sheep camp might at first seem ironic or contradictory, as some are dressed in "traditional" clothing and others not. Marmon's photography is not confined to any strict notion of Indianness. It differs vastly from Keegan's inspired commitment to document the "elusive traditional way of life," as these images include the context of Laguna lives and experiences. Marmon did not drive around seeking the best adobe wall to use as a background; he photographed his community while delivering groceries for his family's store.[11] What we see through Marmon's photographs are images of people living and working as they are—and without an im-

plied mystical "elusiveness." Marmon's title, *White Man's Moccasins,* is more than the irony of an old Laguna man wearing high-tops. It is Pueblo objectification of Western society through the appropriation of a popular Western icon.

Marmon's images are of people who do not perceive themselves as confined to any mythic or imagined concepts held by others. They remain fresh because they are not restricted by essentialist notions that Native people must dress as Natives in order to look Native and to be Native. Even some Native documentary photographers fall prey to expressing Native thinking and traditions through what is worn. By doing this, they risk entering into the same trap of only being able to recognize themselves through the eyes of non-Natives.

Zig Jackson provides ethnographic material about non-Native practices in photographing Native people in his series "Indian Photographing Tourist Photographing Indian." The tourists he records are so intent on their subjects and the drama of the moment that they are unaware of Jackson's presence. They exhibit a fascination usually reserved for movie stars, rock stars, scandalized politicians, or famous athletes. For these photographers, the value of Native images is based strictly on appearance. But would they clamor to take pictures of Native people wearing the clothes they wear at school, work, or home? No. Because when Native people wear bright colors, fringe, beads, leather, and feathers, they are "real" Indians. When they are dressed in everyday clothes they are not. Robert Berkhofer, Jr., discussed this in *The White Man's Indian: Images of the American Indian from Columbus to the Present.* "Since Whites primarily understood the Indian as an antithesis to themselves, then civilization and Indianness as they defined them would forever be opposites. Only civilization had history and dynamics in this view, so therefore

Indianness must be conceived as ahistorical and static. If the Indian changed through the adoption of civilization as defined by Whites, then he/she was no longer truly Indian according to the image, because the Indian was judged by what Whites were not. Change toward what Whites were made him [her] ipso facto less Indian."[12]

Larry McNeil deliberately avoids representations of the "feathered" Indian and instead chooses a single feather to discuss Native survival. Some critics have described this work as relying on an easily recognized symbol, even a cliché. In fact, to reduce McNeil's use of feathers to a cliché is to accept the dominant thinking that is continually wielded against Native people. (Dominant thinking prevails when Native symbols are reduced to cliché while American colonization continues to be described as Manifest Destiny.) In McNeil's series, Native survival deliberately is not shown through full-color images of powwow dancers. Instead, he keeps to the visceral side of survival through black-and-white depictions of worn and broken feathers set against a dark background. Here, the Native memory of survival is neither romantic nor nostalgic.

James Luna's photo-essay "I've Always Wanted to Be an American Indian," is a satirical jab at those who at some point discover a thread of Native ancestry in their past and then draw on myths of Indian identity to realize their ancestral inheritance. Luna's wake-up call is for these individuals to realize the reach of racist, political, and economic subordination of Native people, who cannot pick and choose their Native circumstances. Luna escorts the wake-up Indian on a guided tour of his La Jolla reservation, pointing out interesting sites and bits of information. His snapshot photographs of the mission church, schoolchildren, and a disintegrating adobe building are combined with positive and negative snips of information. Statements such as "During the last five years on the

"Would I Have Been a Member of the Nighthawk, Snake Society or Would I Have Been a Half Breed Leading the Whites to the Full-Bloods. . . .?" by Hulleah Tsinhnahjinnie, © 1991.

Reservation there have been and/or are now: three murders, an average unemployment rate of 47 percent, . . . twenty-one divorces and/or separations . . . thirty-nine births, forty-five government homes built . . . an increase in the percentage of high school graduates."[13] At the end of the tour, Luna asks "Hey, do you still want to be an Indian?"

Hulleah Tsinhnahjinnie reveals the current dispute among Native people over who, in fact, is "Indian." Tsinhnahjinnie's *Would I Have Been a Member of the Nighthawk, Snake Society or Would I Have Been a Half-Breed Leading the Whites to the Full-Bloods*, signed "111–390" (her issued tribal enrollment number) uses self-portraiture to discuss identity politics within a historical context. These graphic, 40-by-30-inch, black-and-white head-and-shoulder shots, which resemble passport or police photographs, support her discussion of the use of photography to identify and control the "other." The reference to the Nighthawk, Snake Societies, and half-breeds comes from a 1920 statement made by Eufala Harjo regarding the practice of the Bureau of Indian Affairs of securing names of Creek, Chickasaw, Choctaw, and Cherokee resistance-group members from "half-breed" informants.[14] Societies were formed to resist tribal leaders' decisions to ignore previous treaty agreements and to accept the 1887 Dawes Allotment Act, which reallocated parcels of lands to individual ownership—thereby overturning tribal practices of land collectively held through the maternal line.

Tsinhnahjinnie is one of the few artists who have taken a public stand on the 1990 Indian Arts and Crafts Act, which requires tribal enrollment numbers, state census roll numbers, or a special "Indian artist" status to be provided by an artist's tribal council in order for Native artists to sell their work as "Indian" art. Tsinhnahjinnie reminds us that we, as Native people, must recognize and understand identity politics as the invention of the United States government.

Jolene Rickard's *Sweka and PCBs* calls our attention to the fact that we may be ignoring or underestimating the dangers that accompany moneyed solicitations of tribal land use for toxic dump sites that contaminate food sources. Rickard draws a connecting line from toxic contamination to the gathering, collecting, fishing, and hunting of foods, and the ritual ceremonies that emanate from those sources. Rickard warns us, "If Indians no longer have a material and spiritual relationship with 'land,' then certain teachings and ceremonies cannot take place. Even when it is possible to transform these teachings into abstract space, without the geographic place of community, experience has shown that the teachings increasingly dissipate."[15]

Sweka and PCBs is not a romantic representation of an Indian man and his relationship to the natural world. It is a warning for all of us to confront our own threatened survival as human beings. We may become our own endangered species along with the salmon and the eagle that feeds on the salmon.

In Pamela Shields Carroll's *Footprints*, family images are printed on cut-out soles of baby moccasins, along with porcupine quills, collected in a small wooden box. *Footprints* evokes family memories that ultimately inform the next generation. The image on the left sole is of Carroll's brother celebrating his third birthday, dressed as a cowboy, sitting on a pony. The right sole depicts Carroll's great-aunt's Sun Dance tipi. *Footprints* is layered with personal memories, but also speaks from historical experience. It is a sister's quiet memory of her brother—and a statement about non-Native influences. The complexity of growing up Native is revealed in a family snapshot, in which her brother, as a child, adopts the dress of those who were part of the conquest of his larger Blackfoot family. It is also a memory of family participation and responsibility in ceremony, and the health of a com-

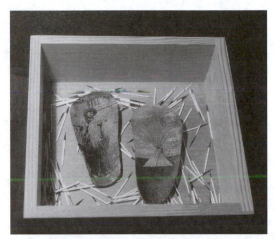

"Footprint" from the "Imprints" series by Pamela Shields, © 1994.

munity through the Sun Dance. Yet together the moccasin soles represent diverse paths: the left, reflective of outside influences and future generations; the right, inside sources of knowledge and the integrity of Blackfoot culture.

Creating a visual history—and its representations—from Native memories or from Western myths: this is the question before Native image-makers and photographers today. The contest remains over who will image—and own—this history. Before too many assumptions are made, we must define history, define whose history it is, and define its purpose, as well as the tools used for the telling of it. The intent of history is to help us keep our bearings. That is, to know what is significant and, most importantly, to teach us *how* to recognize the significant. What happens when history is skewed, or when we no longer have the same skills of recognition? We as human beings become disabled by the

inability to distinguish what is real from what is not. Gerald Vizenor, in his book *Manifest Manners: Postindian Warriors of Survivance,* calls this "Postindian simulations [which] are the absence of shades, shadows, and consciousness; simulations are mere traces of common metaphors in the stories of survivance and the manners of domination."[16] . . .

What Native photographers provide is the possibility of a Native perspective unclouded by White liberal guilt or allegiance to Western heroes. Yet these possibilities are not guaranteed by race or genetics. For if the photographer picks up his or her camera and approaches image-making with the same notions of capturing a "proud/primitive" moment, then we are not getting a Native perspective. We are seeing Euro-American image-making traditions in action in Native hands. Those images do not carry messages of survival. In fact they are an ominous signal that colonization has been effective, in that the "Indian" can now recognize him- or herself only through the outside, as an outsider.

Native image-makers who contribute to self-knowledge and survival create messages and remembrances that recognize the origin, nature, and direction of their Native existence and communities. They understand that their point of origin began before the formation of the United States and is directly rooted to the land. These Native image-makers understand that the images they create may either subvert or support existing representations of Native people. They understand that they must create the intellectual space for their images to be understood, and free themselves from the contest over visual history and its representations of Native people.

NOTES

1. Gail Tremblay, "Constructing Images, Constructing Reality: American Indian Photography and Representation" in *Views: A Journal of Photography in New England* (Vol. 13–14, Winter 1993), p. 30.

2. "Message Carriers: Native Photographic Messages" was at the Boston Photographic Resource Center at Boston University in October, 1992. The exhibition included the works of Patricia Deadman, Zig

Jackson, Carm Little Turtle, James Luna, Larry McNeil, Jolene Rickard, Hulleah Tsinhnahjinnie, and Richard Ray Whitman. Then staff curator Anita Douthat initiated the exhibition. The PRC was instrumental in the success of the exhibition.

3. Marcia K. Keegan, *Enduring Culture: A Century of Photography of the Southwest Indians* (Santa Fe: Clear Light Publishers, 1990), p. 11.

4. bell hooks, *Yearning, Race, Gender, and Cultural Politics* (Boston: South End Press, 1990), p. 147.

5. Ibid

6. Tremblay, p. 30.

7. Victor Masayesva, Jr., "Kwikwilyaqua: Hopi Photography," in *Hopi Photographers/Hopi Images,* edited by Larry Evers (Tucson: *Sun Tracks,* University of Arizona Press, 1983), pp. 10–11.

8. Richard Hill, Jr. quoted in Susan R Dixon, "Images of Indians: Controlling the Camera," in *North East Indian Quarterly* (Spring/Summer, 1987), p. 25.

9. Hulleah J. Tsinhnahjinnie, "Compensating Imbalances," in *Exposure 29* (Fall 1993), p. 30.

10. Trinh T. Minh-ha, *Women Native Other: Writing Post-coloniality and Feminism* (Indianapolis: Indiana University Press, 1989), p. 80.

11. Lee Marmon owns and manages the Blue Eyed Indian Bookshop at Laguana Pueblo.

12. Robert Berkhofer, Jr., *The White Man's Indian: Images of the American Indian from Columbus to the Present* (New York: First Vintage Books Edition, A Division of Random House, 1979), p. 29.

13. James Luna, *Art Journal* (Vol. 51, No. 3, Fall 1992), pp. 23–25.

14. For further discussion see Angie Debo's *A History of the Indians of the United States* (Norman: University of Oklahoma Press, 1990).

15. Jolene Rickard, "Frozen in the White Light," in *Watchful Eyes: Native Women Artists* (Phoenix: Heard Museum, 1994), p. 16.

16. Gerald Vizenor, *Manifest Manners: Postindian Warriors of Survivance* (Hanover, N.H. and London: Wesleyan University Press, University Press of New England, 1994), p. 53.

5

DIRECTIONS IN PEOPLE'S MOVEMENTS

John Mohawk

The Indian plays much the same role in our American society that the Jews played in Germany. Like the miner's canary, the Indian marks the shift from fresh air to poison gas in our political atmosphere. Our treatment of Indians, even more than our treatment of other minorities, reflects the rise and fall in our democratic faith. . . .
—Felix Cohen, father of the study of American Indian Law

Helen Hunt Jackson wrote about injustice to Native peoples a century ago. European writers wrote about it before that, and some have written about it since then. The American Indian people have been abused, disinherited, their nations shamelessly attacked, their rights ignored or abused, their lands taken, their people killed or driven into exile on marginal lands. Jackson called it "A Century of Dishonor" and decried the fact that the United States had been carrying on a policy of deliberate aggression against the Indian peoples—a policy which had led the U.S. to break every treaty ever made with Indian people which contained any recognition of their rights as distinct peoples.

Generations of people, especially in North America and Europe, have known of these horrible injustices. In fact, the injustices have become almost a part of Americana, and are generally presented to school children as the unfortunate results of "cultures in conflict," sometimes which shouldn't have happened but did happen in the past and now it's too late to do anything about it.

The Indian people, of course, are also aware of the nature of these injustices. On many Indian territories, the people have spoken of the day when they will receive justice from the Americans or the Canadians—the day the Black Hills will be returned, the day the fraudulent treaties will be exposed and the people will get their lands back in the Cayuga or Oneida country, the Ojibway or the Cherokee lands. If it has become legendary among European peoples that the American Indians have been wronged, it has also been a kind of "reservation legend" that those wrongs would somehow be brought right someday, that somebody would find a way to bring the Indian people justice.

For years (perhaps for something nearing two centuries) people have sought legal remedies to these problems. There arose among some of the people the thought that what was needed was an Indian lawyer who really understood the law—someone who could champion the Indian peoples' cause through the courts and bring justice where none was ever found before. That line of thinking was fairly strong in many communities during the first half of this century.

The U.S. policies toward Native peoples have been consistent in one respect—they have moved to destroy the Native peoples. Following the American Revolution, the United States embarked on a series of wars of extermination, and the extermination policy was a dominant theme until after the War of 1812. Then came the removal period—the U.S. policy which attempted to remove all the Native peoples to lands in the "INDIAN TERRITORIES" west of the Mississippi. There were some horrible chapters in that period . . . the Trail of Tears, which removed the Cherokee Nation from their lands in Georgia, was the most widely known, but there were other horrors of that period, many of them, which are less well-known to the public.

The Removal Policy was interspersed with more wars of extermination as the United States enacted its famous (or infamous) Manifest Destiny, and the wars which ensued continued until the 1880s and [were] officially terminated in 1890, a convenient date because of the Wounded Knee massacre of men, women and children at a place which is now known on the maps as the Pine Ridge Reservation.

By that time (1890) the U.S. was in the serious process of taking Indian lands by fair means or foul. Congress passed The Dawes Act in 1887, an act which was said to be in the best interest of the Indians because it provided Indian families with "allotments" but which was argued on the floor of Congress to be the largest land rip-off in history. Land rip-off it was. The Dawes Act caused millions of acres of Indian land to be transferred to the hands of non-Indians, many of whom were speculators. It was another shameful chapter in a history with consistently little but shameful chapters.

But even the Dawes Act, the armies, the wars and other assorted swindles failed to fully exterminate the Indian peoples. As the 20th century dawned, Native peoples still occupied some valuable lands—lands made more valuable as the need for natural resources of a growing industrial society expanded. At the period following World War I, the policy of disinheritance and alienation of Native peoples took a new turn. The new idea was that Indian people would be legally absorbed into the mainstream American society. The hidden agenda of that policy was that Indian peoples' remaining resources would also be absorbed, a fact which made the policy much more attractive to those who had little or no interest in making Native peoples into American citizens.

In 1924 the American Indian Citizenship Act was passed. It was not an act intended to convey benefits to the Indians, but one intended to convey benefits to the people who had interests in Indian lands and resources. It was Step One in the Plot to Take Indian Lands, though the public relations campaign which accompanied the act heralded it as a new step in "righting the wrongs" done to the Indian peoples.

Step Two (in the twentieth century) came in 1934. The federal government was very consistent in its objectives to the extent that, decade by decade, it enacted what it perceived needed to be enacted to disinherit the Indian people of all power over their lives and, not incidentally, their resources. In 1934, the Indian Reorganization Act was passed. This was heralded by the propagandists of the day as an act which reorganized Indian government in such a way that it was more "democratic," as though a government set up by Washington under Washington's rules and with the support of Washington's military and with moneys controlled by Washington could somehow be more democratic. Indian people were induced to accept the Indian Reorganization Act by promises that IRA governments would more likely be successful in applying for government funds, an inducement which continues to this day. There was, of course, a catch. To get the government funding, Indian people had to agree to do what the federal government wanted of them. It is a system called neocolonialism.

The next step in this process came to light in 1946 when Congress passed the Indian Claims Commission Act. The idea behind this act, according to the publicists, was to correct the wrongs done to Indian people when their lands were stolen either with the complicity of the federal government or when the federal government failed to act to protect Indian interests. It was not an entirely charitable act. It provided that Indian people could sue for recovery of damages for takings of land, but that they could only recover the value of the land in dollars at the time of the taking, and they could not recover any of the land irregardless of the enormity of the injustice at the time of the taking. As a legal policy, it was unique in the annals of U.S. law. The hidden agenda of that act was that it enabled a small cadre of law firms which specialized in Indian claims work to become very wealthy while at the same time it effectively and forever quieted title to lands which, through the corrupt proceedings, the U.S. had admitted were illegally taken.

The need to quiet titles forever came about because the U.S. was in the process of enacting another policy which came to light in the 1950s—the Termination Policy. During the 1950s (under a Republican Congress) laws were enacted which had the effect of simply declaring that Indian peoples, nations, tribes or whatever, simply no longer existed, and that their lands were, in a word, forfeited. The Termination Policy was intended to achieve the long-held objective of the United States to destroy, once and for all, the Indian peoples.

Those legal policies, which for many Indian peoples were in fact life-threatening policies, were accompanied by social policies which shared the same agenda. The reservations had suffered a two-centuries long assault by social policy agents which intended to destroy the cultures of the peoples and thus, the ability of the Indian people to act as a people. Thus, while the wars of extermination were in full swing, there were intensive missionary penetrations of Indian communities which had the effect of creating divisions and disunities in the Indian Country. The missionaries stayed on through the Removal Policy period and were joined during the 19th century with "educators," whose objective, as one famous educator once said, was to "destroy the tribe." Education has political objectives. The educators moved with a zeal equal to that of the missionaries to destroy the social fabric of the Indian peoples. It has been, sadly, a tremendously effective campaign. One of the things that the education policy set out to do was to acquaint, at least on a rudimentary level, the Indian people with the culture and legal processes of the United States. The idea was to present the United States as a just society with a "system" which, if allowed to work, could set right grievous wrongs. Armed with that ideology, Indian people in this century set out to set right the wrongs done to them through the political and legal processes which their "education" told them existed at the heart of the U.S. system of government and laws.

During the 20th century, the people on the Indian territories talked extensively of legal remedies to regain their lands and their self-government. That approach actually was strengthened and expanded during the period following World War II even though U.S. policy was growing increasingly hostile to Indian peoples everywhere.

The whole process reached a crisis in the 1960s. In 1968, Congress passed an act called the Indian Civil Rights Act. Much can be said about the intent of that act, but in fact many Indian people read the act in such a way that it seemed to them to protect their rights, at least against the neo-colonial governments erected by the Indian Reorganization Act. Within a short time, however, the courts moved to interpret the act in such a way that it did not protect their rights against the Tribal governments (which were and are in major ways controlled by the Bureau of Indian Affairs and the Interior Department) in anything but a habeas corpus provision. The Indian Civil Rights Act was a diversion, a promise without substance. It did not protect Indian rights, but merely individuals' rights in certain situations involving arrests by tribal authorities. By 1972, conditions on some of the Indian reservations were indeed intolerable, especially at Pine Ridge Reservation in South Dakota. On that reservation, the BIA had set up a land tenure system which effectively denied the Lakota people any say in the use of huge parts of their land base. It was a complicated policy of land-use swindle which existed (and exists) there. The plight of the Oglalas is a good place to look for an understanding of the situations under which Native peoples live and the role of the BIA in their everyday lives.

The BIA has set up land tenure (land use) rules on Pine Ridge which are quite complicated but which serve a definite end. According to these rules, there are lands which are "allocated" to certain families. When the heads of those families died, the lands were divided among the heirs. Since a person has two parents, it is seen that one might inherit rights in two parcels of land. By the third generation, one might inherit rights to very small parcels of land from eight landholdings, each parcel of which might be too small to support [a family], especially in situations where people had large families.

The BIA provides rules that amount to a dictum that in cases where the landholdings of an individual are too small and/or too scattered to provide an individual's support, the BIA would step in and manage the allotments (power they seem to derive under their "trust" responsibility). Thus the BIA steps in and then leases the lands of individuals to large ranchers, paying the proceeds to the individual landowners. That policy, almost without saying, causes large-scale injustices. In some cases, the BIA was leasing the lands of Oglalas to large ranchers for as little as $1 per acre per year. The rental moneys were then deducted from the family allowances of the landowners. Effectively, the "landowners" were dispossessed from their lands, and in effect, received no compensation and had no rights or power over the disposition of those lands. It has been a situation unique in U.S. law, but not unique in "Indian" law.

In 1972, the Oglala people organized an entity they called the Oglala Sioux Landowners' Association. This group tried to effect what amounts to a land reform policy under which they would reacquire control over their own lands. They ran head-on into IRA Tribal Chairman Dick Wilson whose job (and whose interests) lies in maintaining the status quo. His resistance to reform caused the people to organize the Oglala Sioux Civil Rights Organization which soon had as its objective the impeachment of Wilson.

There was much general discontent in the Indian Country by 1972. Indian peoples in the urban areas had begun to respond to the experience of racism during the 1960s. In 1968, Indian people had occupied Alcatraz as a move to demonstrate their general discontent and as a statement of their intent to survive as a people. Alcatraz was the birth of a new movement in the sense that it served as a touchpost for Native people who were seeking change and it demonstrated to them that concerted action could have some results, however faltering those efforts may seem to us now. Also in 1968, the American Indian Movement was organized in the St. Paul-Minneapolis area, originally as a kind of citizens action group to protect Indian people from police violence.

That movement gained great popularity among an Indian population which had suffered decades of abuse. Native people who had been victims of the organization policies of the federal government which accompanied the Termination Era joined the movement *en masse*. AIM, meanwhile, reached out to the Indian communities to oppose the injustices suffered by individuals at the hands of police agencies, championing the causes of men and women who had been ravaged by racist court systems. Their efforts, which brought both publicity and the feeling of power which accompanies organization, generated widespread support among the Indian people. As the summer of 1972 wore on, word that AIM was organizing a protest march on Washington and the BIA on the eve of the 1972 Presidential Election spread throughout the Indian communities. When the caravans began arriving in Washington in October of 1972, there were several thousand supporters.

Dubbed the Trail of Broken Treaties, the march on the BIA evolved into an occupation of the BIA building at the very moment that the country was suffering through the national election which reseated Richard Nixon as president of the United States. The country was also going through the agonies of the social disintegration being felt as a result of the Vietnam War. The "BIA Takeover," although it was not a planned event and could hardly have been interpreted as a threat to the United States, apparently set in motion the federal response which declared a domestic war on the American Indian Movement and its supporters.

The situation on the Pine Ridge Reservation coincided with the rise of the American Indian Movement, although the two were hardly of the same roots and in the beginning had somewhat different objectives. The leadership of the opposition to Wilson at Pine Ridge called upon the leadership of the American Indian Movement for help, and in February 1973 the two groups initiated the occupation of Wounded Knee, an event which occupied the front pages of newspapers in the United States and Europe for nearly three months. It is interesting that through all that time, the root causes of the Wounded Knee action were never articulated through the press—i.e., the basic injustices which were the reason that the Oglala Sioux Landowners' Association and the Oglala Sioux Civil Rights Organization had been formed.

DISCIPLINE—RESPECT—ENDURANCE

The events of Wounded Knee may not have done much to educate the American or the European public about the injustices suffered by the Indian people, but it did much to educate many young Indian people, and it did form at least the appearance of a leadership potential among the Indian people. The "Reign of Terror" conducted by the FBI and other military operations after the Wounded Knee occupation, the emergence of Cable Splicer and Garden Plot (domestic paramilitary counterinsurgency programs), the exposure of spies and infiltrators such as Doug Durham and the political assassinations conducted by the BIA police and other law-and-order factions ended for all time the question of whether or not there could be a peace movement toward justice for Indians in the United States. The "Wounded Knee trials" which followed saw FBI agents perjure themselves on the witness stand, witnesses who were coerced into perjuring themselves, and a federal judge actually publicly denounce the FBI's activities as an outrage to the American concept of justice. The trials also did much to educate the movement leadership to the nature of the system they were facing. There was a lot more resistance to reform than people had been taught. The legal systems consistently failed to protect peoples' rights in court against the abuses of power which were enacted in the name of the United States.

Those years (1973 to the present) have been a wild and tumultuous time for Native people. Movement people challenged the U.S. policies which prescribe the extinction of the Indian peoples through legal strategies designed to disempower and to disinherit and they were met by the paramilitary and military forces of the United States. It became clear that, to the Right Wing, Wounded Knee was used as a training ground for domestic war. Military groups were mobilized from all over the country. Information about secret paramilitary organizations—private police forces which were not under the control of the government—emerged, painting a picture of an underground Right Wing army, similar in character to the "Death Squads" of Argentina, which had access to official police and intelligence agency files [and which] not only existed but was in a position to act. It was a frightening spectre.

Movement leaders were indicted and persecuted relentlessly by the State of South Dakota and by the federal government. People were arrested, assaulted, and forced underground. Many spent time in jail. Murder convictions were obtained against people on the flimsiest of circumstantial evidence, and those convictions resulted in long jail sentences. Those who were present,

those who experienced that time, could not fail to understand that the United States and the people in power in the United States intended to suppress all opposition through whatever means necessary. Those who saw the Wounded Knee trials and the aftermath of the occupation of Wounded Knee would not easily be persuaded that there was any hope for justice for the Indian people.

By 1974, the movement leadership was in a position to call a meeting at Wakpala on the Standing Rock Reservation in South Dakota. At that meeting, several thousand people approved a plan to create an organization (called the International Indian Treaty Council) to take the problems of the Indian people to the United Nations and other international forums. The Indian people within the movement had learned a real lesson—there is no justice for the Indian people under the domestic laws of the United States. There never will be.

It was a major stepping stone, a major landmark in the strategy of the people who had set out to struggle for the survival of the Indian peoples and nations. It was a strategy which emerged at a fateful time for the movement. The Indian people were under a concerted attack on all fronts. The following summer, FBI agents attacked the Jumping Bull Ranch on Pine Ridge and a gun battle ensued. Two agents and one Indian man were killed in that incident, and the largest manhunt in history (up to that time) followed as the FBI and U.S. Marshalls invaded Pine Ridge in search of those who were suspected participants in the shootout. Eventually warrants were obtained for four men, three were brought to trial and the other, Leonard Peltier, escaped to Canada. The others were effectively exonerated for their part in the incident, some jurors calling what happened at Jumping Bull an act of self-defense. Peltier was extradicted from Canada on the testimony of Myrtle Poor Bear, testimony which the FBI knew to be false and which Poor Bear later recanted. Peltier was then tried and convicted of complicity in the deaths of the two agents. He remains incarcerated in the federal penitentiary at Marion, Illinois, one of the political prisoners whose history and plight truly sheds light on the American judicial system, and on the U.S. policies toward Indian people.

The Peltier story is particularly enlightening. At about the same time as the shooting FBI assault on the Jumping Bull Ranch, Tribal Chairman Dickie Wilson was signing over to the federal government a large tract of the Pine Ridge Reservation. Later, it was announced that minerals had been discovered on that tract of land. . . . It would stretch the credibility of all concerned to believe that this sequence of events was mere "coincidence." The United States had announced that there was a critical need for "energy" for the future, and reports surfaced which indicated that there were plans at high levels to create "national energy sacrifice areas" as sources of that energy.

In 1977, a large delegation from North America travelled to Geneva and gave testimony to the acts of the United States, charging that the United States was and is committing the crime of genocide against the Native peoples. This event sparked a new round of international outreach by Native peoples, and educated the movement about the global nature of the struggle. Native peoples claiming their rights to land, culture, political sovereignty and survival continue to emerge. It is a movement, as a result, which represents the interests of millions and millions of people.

The Longest Walk in 1978 provided some evidence that the people in the movement had learned a great deal about the nature of the enemy. The Longest Walk attracted the largest gathering of Native people of this century—perhaps, according to one eyewitness estimate, as many as thirty thousand people. The statement which ensued from that event was insightful. The people demanded an end to the most evil of the U.S. policies and specifically cited the Rule of TeeHitTon by which the courts have claimed that the U.S. can take Indian lands not protected by treaty without due process of law or compensation. The Longest Walk manifesto also attacked U.S. colonialism and neo-colonialism, and gave support to Indian political prisoners. The message to the United States from that gathering was clear: The Indian people demanded justice, and an end to exploitation. They supported the Navajo people who faced removal in this century, and denounced the genocidal policies of the United States.

Incredibly, the story of the Indian peoples' struggle for survival is largely a story untold. There can be little doubt that the United States is continuing in pursuit of a policy which has as it goals the destruction of the Indian peoples and communities. They have said as much. There can be little doubt that those plans are motivated by the desire to exploit Indian people, and to dispossess them of their land and water. The largest dispossession of a people in North America is at this writing taking place on the Navajo country, a dispossession which will destroy a huge part of the Traditional Navajo people just as surely as the persecution of the Jewish people in Europe destroyed their communities four decades ago. There is practically no coverage of this momentous event in the press or other mass media. While the Chairman of the Navajo Nation flies to Washington in his Lear jet, poor Navajos are being driven from their lands in order that the energy companies and a few wealthy Hopi families can use the lands to enrich themselves. Such is the U.S. policy relative to the Navajos and the Hopis. And just as surely as that policy is destroying those people today, just as surely as that policy initiated the Reign of Terror which blanketed the Pine Ridge Reservation in 1973–1977, just as surely as that policy resulted in the near-massacre of a large number of people in the Mohawk Nation in 1980, that policy will come home to each and every one of the Indian communities, one at a time. The Native peoples of this land are under attack. That fact cannot be ignored, and it cannot be resolved in courts, because the courts are one of the instruments of the attack.

The Native peoples are under attack in a number of areas, and the road to survival is a complex path. There is no single solution. Many things need to be organized. Some of these things are economic in nature, some are spiritual, some are political. The clearest lesson of the past is that no one and no single strategy will "save" the Indian people from extinction.

The move toward an access to the international community which might provide some publicity or perhaps even some international action is one of the steps which might lead to a small bit of relief from the worst abuses of the United States. The movement, which has also taken shape in recent years, toward the self-sufficiency of Native communities and peoples is also an important aspect of the overall struggle. But the largest move needs to take place among the Native peoples. There is not enough information reaching the communities to raise the consciousness of the Native people about the nature of the attack which they are under.

THE 20-POINT PROGRAM

Below is a condensation of the 20-point position paper formulated in St. Paul, Minnesota, October 22–29, 1972, by the Trail of Broken Treaties caravan and presented to the U.S. Government in Washington, D.C., in November of that year:

1. RESTORATION OF CONSTITUTIONAL TREATY-MAKING AUTHORITY: Repeal the provision in the 1871 Indian Appropriations Act to enable the President to resume the exercise of his full constitutional authority in the matter of Indian affairs.
2. ESTABLISHMENT OF A TREATY COMMISSION TO MAKE NEW TREATIES: The President and Congress would establish this body to contract a security and assistance treaty with Indian tribes and negotiate a national commitment to Indians for the future.

3. ADDRESS TO THE AMERICAN PEOPLE AND JOINT SESSION OF CONGRESS: Selection of four Indians—selected by Indians—to appear with the President and Congressmen to address a joint session of Congress regarding the future of Indians in America.
4. COMMISSION TO REVIEW TREATY COMMITMENTS AND VIOLATIONS: The President should create an Indian and non-Indian commission to review domestic treaty commitments and violation complaints and recommend corrective action.
5. RESUBMISSION OF UNRATIFIED TREATIES TO THE SENATE: The President should resubmit to the U.S. Senate treaties negotiated with Indian Nations or their representatives but never before ratified nor rendered moot.

6. ALL INDIANS GOVERNED BY TREATY RELATIONS: The Congress should enact a joint resolution to this effect.

7. MANDATORY RELIEF AGAINST TREATY RIGHTS VIOLATIONS: The Congress should add a new section to Title 28 of the United States Code to provide for the judicial enforcement and protection of Indian treaty rights.

8. JUDICIAL RECOGNITION OF INDIAN RIGHT TO INTERPRET TREATIES: The Congress should provide a new system of federal court jurisdiction and procedure when Indian treaty or governmental rights are at issue.

9. CREATION OF JOINT CONGRESSIONAL COMMITTEE ON RECONSTRUCTING INDIAN RELATIONS: The Congress should agree to withdraw jurisdiction over Indian affairs and Indian-related program authorizations from all existing committees except appropiations and create a joint committee.

10. LAND REFORM AND RESTORATION OF 110-MILLION ACRE LAND BASE: Congress and the Administration should implement by statutes or administrative actions a nondiminishing Native American land base to be owned and controlled by Native Americans. Included are: priorities in restoration of Indian land base; consolidation of Indian land, water, natural and economic resources; termination of leases and condemnation of non-Indian land title; and repeal of Menominee, Klamath, and other termination acts.

11. REVISION OF 25 USC 163: Restoration of rights to Indians terminated by enrollment and revocation of prohibitions against "dual benefits"—Congress should enact new measures in support of the doctrine that an Indian Nation has complete power to govern and control its own membership.

12. REPEAL OF STATE LAWS ENACTED UNDER PUBLIC LAW 280: Congress should nullify state statutes that pose a serious threat to Indian sovereignty and local self-government.

13. RESUME FEDERAL PROTECTIVE JURISDICTION FOR OFFENSES AGAINST INDIANS: Congress should support and seek passage of new provisions to extend protective jurisdiction of the United States over Indian persons, including: establishment of a national federal Indian grand jury; jurisdiction over non-Indians within Indian reservations; and accelerated rehabilitation and release program for state and federal Indian prisoners.

14. ABOLITION OF THE BUREAU OF INDIAN AFFAIRS BY 1976: A new Indian Reconstruction Act would create a new structure and remove the present BIA, providing an alternative structure of government for federal–Indian relations.

15. OFFICE OF FEDERAL INDIAN RELATIONS AND COMMUNITY RECONSTRUCTION: This new agency would replace the present BIA.

16. PRIORITIES AND PURPOSE OF THE PROPOSED NEW OFFICE: The central purpose of the new office would be to remedy the breakdown in constitutionally prescribed relations between the U.S. and Indian Nations.

17. INDIAN COMMERCE AND TAX IMMUNITIES: Congress would enact a statute certifying that trade, commerce and transportation of Indians remain outside the authority and control of the several states.

18. PROTECTION OF INDIAN RELIGIOUS FREEDOM AND CULTURAL INTEGRITY: Congress should insist on religious freedom and cultural integrity to be protected by penalty of law.

19. NATIONAL REFERENDUMS, LOCAL OPTIONS, AND FORMS OF INDIAN ORGANIZATION: Complete consolidation of Indian resources and restoration of purpose as the Indian population is small enough to be amenable to voting and elective processes of national referendums, local option referendums and other elections for rendering decisions on many issues and matters.

20. HEALTH, HOUSING, EMPLOYMENT, ECONOMIC DEVELOPMENT AND EDUCATION: The Congress, the Administration and the proposed Indian Community Reconstruction Office must allow for the most creative— if demanding and disciplined—forms of community development and purposeful initiatives.

PART REVIEW

DISCUSSION QUESTIONS

Mario Gonzalez, *The Black Hills*

1. If the 1851 and 1868 Ft. Laramie treaties recognized Lakota (Sioux) title to the Black Hills, how did the Lakota come to lose the Black Hills?

2. Explain why the Black Hills are sacred to the Lakota (Sioux) and Tsistsistas (Cheyenne).

3. In 1980 the U.S. Supreme Court affirmed a lower court ruling that the Lakota tribes were entitled to a $102 million compensation for the Black Hills. Why did the Indians refuse it?

Poka Laenui, *The Rediscovery of Hawaiian Sovereignty*

1. What were the circumstances that led the Hawaiian people to lose their sovereignty over the islands to the United States in 1893?

2. What harmful changes took place from 1900 to 1959 during the "recycling of Hawai'i" as a U.S. territory?

3. What are some of the developments that have occurred since the 1960s that have led to cultural rejuvenation and the demand for an independent Hawaiian nation?

Jeannette Henry Costo, *The Sword and the Cross*

1. Who was Father Junipero Serra, and on what grounds does the author oppose the efforts of some Catholic authorities to make him a saint?

Rupert Costo and Jeannette Henry Costo, *The Crime of Genocide*

1. How can the United Nations definition of genocide be applied to the history of the Franciscan missions in California, as described in Costo's chapter?

Theresa Harlan, *Creating a Visual History*

1. Why must we reject the reduction of Native images to sentimental portraits and stereotypes?

2. What does the author mean by "ownership of Native representations" from Native memories?

John Mohawk, *Directions in People's Movements*

1. List and briefly explain some of the important policies and laws that have had an impact on U.S. Indian peoples in the past two centuries.

2. What were the developments that led up to the 1973 protest at Wounded Knee on the Pine Ridge Reservation in South Dakota?

3. What are some of the recent protests and political developments in the U.S. Indian struggle?

The 20-Point Program

1. How many of the twenty points have to do with treaty rights or the treaty process? Which ones are they, and what aspects of treaties are covered?

KEY TERMS

American Indian Movement (AIM)
Bear Butte
Black Hills
Columbian Quincentennial
de las Casas, Bartalomé
genocide
Hawaiian bayonet constitution
Indian Claims Commission Act of 1946
The Longest Walk (1978)
Native image-making

Peltier, Leonard
Queen Lili'uokalani
Removal and Relocation Policies (relocation)
Serra, Fr. Junipero
Spanish Inquisition
Termination Policy
The Trail of Broken Treaties (1972)
20-Point Program
Wounded Knee occupation (1973)

SUGGESTED READINGS

COSTO, RUPERT, and JEANNETTE HENRY, ed. *The Missions of California: A Legacy of Genocide.* San Francisco: Indian Historian Press, 1987.

DUDLEY, MICHAEL KIONI, and KEONI KEALOHA AGARD. *A Hawaiian Nation II: A Call for Hawaiian Sovereignty.* Honolulu: Naa Kaane O Ka Malo Press, 1990.

GENTRY, CAROLE M., and DONALD A. GRINDE Jr. *The Unheard Voices: American Indian Responses to the Columbian Quincentenary 1492–1992.* Los Angeles: UCLA American Indian Studies Center, 1994.

KIRCH, PATRICK V., and MARSHALL SAHLINS. *Anahulu: The Anthropology of History in the Kingdom of Hawai'i.* (Chicago: University of Chicago Press, 1992.)

KOHLHOFF, DEAN. *When the Wind Was a River: Aleut Evacuation in World War II.* Seattle: University of Washington Press, 1995.

LYONS, OREN, and JOHN MOHAWK, ed. *Exiled in the Land of the Free: Democracy, Indian Nations, and the U.S. Constitution.* Santa Fe: Clear Light Publishers, 1992.

NABOKOV, PETER, ed. *Native American Testimony: A Chronicle of Indian-White Relations from Prophecy to the Present, 1492–1992.* With a foreword by Vine Deloria Jr. New York: Penguin Books, 1991.

Rethinking Columbus. A special edition of *Rethinking Schools,* an urban education journal. Milwaukee: Rethinking Schools, 1991.

SPICER, EDWARD H. *Cycles of Conquest: The Impact of Spain, Mexico, and the United States on the Indians of the Southwest, 1533–1960.* Tucson: University of Arizona Press, 1962.

TALBOT, STEVE. *Roots of Oppression: The American Indian Question.* New York: Internationv al Publishers, 1981.

WRIGHT, RONALD. *Stolen Continents: The "New World" through Indian Eyes.* New York: Houghton Mifflin, 1992.

IV
"THE ONLY GOOD INDIAN . . .": RACISM, STEREOTYPES, AND DISCRIMINATION

Incantation to Dispel New Age Dogma
Parris Butler

don't go cosmic on me baby
i don't wanna be your
native american experience
your five minute sound bite
your oppressed native reality bite
your catharsis
your true life experience a la
all the hollywood stereotypes you ever
absorbed off the silver screen
(this includes all john wayne era renditions
as well as the more recent native
intellectualism/spiritualism varieties)
don't go cosmic on me baby
'cause i don't wanna
indian guide you to, into, or through
a vortex
nor do i wish to provide for you
any form of pan-indian
political dogma
exorcism of karma
or blah blah blah blah
don't go cosmic on me baby
don't recite for me your alleged pedigree
your liberal humanism philosophy
'cause baby i don't wanna be
authentic for your approval
traditional for your perusal
political while you refuse all
actions speaking louder than words
don't go cosmic on me baby
'cause i do not necessarily relate
to your recollection of the native
military vet you once knew
the alcohol addict you once partied with
the traditional native artisan
(probably a jeweler) from whom you
collected whatever
or any other indigenous tribal person
you may have met known read about
heard about fantasized or otherwise
conjured baby
don't go cosmic on me

One of the means by which Native peoples are dominated and exploited is through creating and maintaining widespread attitudes of racial inferiority and negative racial and ethnic stereotyping. These pejorative beliefs and sentiments often become so routinized, so deeply entwined with a nation's popular culture and legal system, that they come to be viewed as "normal," everyday beliefs, which are continually revalidated through thoughts and actions that often operate at an unconscious level in the general psyche of the society. In turn, this circular logic then becomes a self-fulfilling rationalization to justify genocide, ethnocide, social and economic injustice, and discrimination. In the Americas, this rationalization justified, among other things, murder, assassination, and massacre; the imprisonment of political leaders; the destruction of native food sources; the dispossession of lands and resources; the destruction of Indian economies; the suppression of indigenous political systems; and forced acculturation through religious missionization and white-run educational institutions. It is to the question of racism and discriminatory stereotypes that we now turn our attention.

At the outset, we need to make a conceptual distinction between the terms *prejudice* and *discrimination*. Prejudice is an attitude of mind in which one holds members of a group to be inferior while one's own "race," ethnicity, culture, gender, or class is supposedly superior. Discrimination, on the other hand, is an overt act based on prejudice. Discrimination can be committed by either individuals or institutions, whether government, church, business, the criminal justice system, or other parts of the social structure. We call discrimination carried out by institutions *institutional* or *structural discrimination*. Institutional discrimination is almost always more damaging than individual acts of discrimination, but the eradication of institutional discrimination has an almost immediate democratizing effect on society. Racial segregation in the U.S. South is a case in point. Once racist Jim Crow laws were overturned in 1954, racial segregationists, regardless of their own personal prejudicial views toward African Americans, were forced to comply with the Supreme Court decision ending the most blatant forms of white privilege based on discriminatory practices.

"Redlining" is another example of institutional discrimination. Classic redlining occurs, for example, when a bank or loan agency draws a line around a low-income, minority community on a map and then denies loans to all of the residents within the red-penciled area regardless of their personal credit history. In April 1996, the U.S. Justice Department filed a complaint against a Nebraska bank for allegedly charging higher interest rates to American Indian borrowers, predominantly from the Pine Ridge Reservation of South Dakota, than to non-Indian borrowers. Such practices, although illegal, are not uncommon.

Another recent example is the negative ruling by the U.S. Supreme Court on the voting issue regarding the Office of Hawaiian Affairs. The OHA is a state agency that dispenses millions of dollars each year on behalf of native Hawaiians, who constitute at least 20 percent of the state's population. The money is derived from a trust of native land title that was retained by the Hawaiian people when the United States unilaterally annexed Hawai'i in 1898. At issue is the fact that under the state's constitution only native and part-native Hawaiians are permitted to vote for the

OHA trustees who administer the income from native Hawaiian lands. The recent decision by the Supreme Court, however, violated native sovereignty when it ruled that allowing only native Hawaiians to vote for OHA trustees discriminates against white people and is therefore unconstitutional.

One of the worst cases of institutional discrimination against Native Americans is without a doubt the scandal surrounding the U.S. Department of the Interior's mismanagement of the Individual Indian Money (IIM) trust fund accounts. By law, the accounts are held in trust and are composed primarily of money earned by Native Americans through leasing of their land for oil, gas, timber, ranching, and farming. There are no records for more than $100 million, and $2.4 billion remains unreconciled. A Federal District Court judge ruled that "the federal government has breached its fiduciary duties to 500,000 individual Indian fund beneficiaries, and cannot be trusted to carry out trust fund mismanagement reform without continued oversight by the Court."

In the case of indigenous peoples, the most extreme form of discrimination has been the legacy of racial murder and wanton killing. Until very recently, South American Indians were being killed by gold miners and other exploiters of the Amazon rain forest. In the United States in earlier years, such killing was condoned by slogans such as "The only good Indian is a dead Indian," coined by General Philip Sheridan in 1868 after celebrating the massacre of Black Kettle's southern Cheyenne on the Washita, and "Nits make lice," as justification for killing Indian children in massacres such as those at Sand Creek in 1864 and at Wounded Knee in 1890. A primary motive for the slaughter to the point of extinction of the great buffalo herds on the western plains was to eradicate the resident Indian populations in order to make room for white settlement and commercial "development." A medal coined at the time pictured a buffalo on one side and an Indian on the other, with the slogan "Every buffalo killed is an Indian gone." The era of the California '49ers (the Anglo-American 1849 gold rush and the Anglicization of California) was marked by the brutal massacres of Indian people, some at "hatcheting grounds." Even in this century, racist murders of Indians in the United States have persisted and, in fact, fueled widespread protests in the 1960s and 1970s by the American Indian Movement and other Indian protest groups. As recently as the year 2000, Lakota Indians were protesting the racial murders of Indians from the Pine Ridge Reservation. Stigmatizing and singling out a single racial or ethnic group for such widespread murder, backed by an elaborate mythology of racist stereotypes about that group, is called genocide.

In 1999, the Indigenous Alliance without Borders (*Alianza Indigena Sin Fronteras*) called for an investigation of the U.S. military role in the torture and killing of Indians by Central American death squads. It is well documented that the U.S. government, in the name of containing a supposed communist insurgency, has trained paramilitary and military forces to "neutralize" indigenous peoples who raise a cry for social and economic justice. Training manuals used by the U.S. Army School of the Americas at Fort Benning, Georgia, encouraged the use of extortion, blackmail, beatings, and executions. The Alliance charged, also, that Indian women were routinely shocked, burned, starved, exposed, stripped, and sexually molested during torture by U.S.-trained military and paramilitary groups.

In the public mind, genocide connotes the outright killing of a national, religious, or ethnic group, but, as we saw from an examination of the United Nations definition of genocide in Part III, it has a much broader meaning under international law. Peonage in the southern United States under the crop-lien system entrapped not only African Americans but also many Indians as recently as the first quarter of the twentieth century. Involuntary servitude of young Indian women is still widespread in parts of South America. The forcible relocation in the United States of Indian people from their homes under the 1974 Navajo–Hopi Land Settlement Act, in which 12,000 traditional Dineh (Navajo) lost their lands, homes, and livestock, and the earlier northward Inuit relocation by the Canadian government in the 1950s, are within the bounds of the United Nations genocide definition. So is the removal of Indian children from their homes, which occurred up to the 1990s under the Canadian Indian residential and U.S. Indian boarding school systems. The sterilization of Indian women without their informed consent, which took place at the hands of physicians under the Indian Health Service in the United States as recently as the 1970s, can also be considered genocide. Forced sterilization, which reduces the Indian birth rate, must be viewed within the context of the precipitous decline of the indigenous population caused by the extermination policies of the United States in earlier centuries.

The concept of cultural genocide, or ethnocide, on the other hand, refers to measures taken by the oppressor group to stamp out indigenous culture and its social institutions. The assimilationist slogan "Kill the Indian but save the man," which was coined by "friends of the Indian" (missionaries and reformers) in the 1880s, epitomizes this concept. The practicing of Indian cultural traditions was criminalized on U.S. reservations from 1883 to 1934 under the Courts of Indian Offenses set up by the Indian Office in the United States. These Indian "crimes" included not only Indian religious practices but also other customs deemed offensive to Christian missionaries. For example, in 1902 Indian Commissioner W. A. Jones issued his "short-hair" order, which banned not only long hair but also body painting by both sexes, the wearing of Indian clothing, religious dances, and "giveaway" ceremonies, which is the custom of giving away goods and possessions on important ritual occasions. These policies were not reversed until 1934, under the Roosevelt New Deal. Nevertheless, some important Indian religious ceremonies and other customs have continued to be banned or subtly discouraged by non-Indian individuals and institutions up to the present.

Historically, the two main stereotypes that have victimized North American Indians and have formed the justification for their genocide and ethnocide are the polar terms *Noble Redman* and *Red Savage.* The concept of stereotype connotes the idea of untrue or misleading generalizations about a group. *Noble Redman* is a romanticization of the Indian as a "wild creature" of the forest, akin to the animals, admired but uncivilized and subhuman. Many myths flow from the Noble Redman image, not the least of which is the mistaken belief that all Native peoples were nomadic hunters and gatherers wandering aimlessly across the land. If they did not utilize the land, then the European colonists who were agrarian had the

God-given right to "go forth and multiply" and "to make the land fruitful." As a matter of record, most of the larger indigenous populations of the Americas, including those in what is now the eastern and southwestern United States, lived in settled communities and were horticulturists. As Jack Weatherford points out in his best-selling work *Indian Givers,* Native Americans had impressive food technology, and over half of the world's foods (including the "Irish" potato) are the result of this development.[1] Those Native peoples who moved did so within their traditional territories and with an extensive understanding of the seasonal utilization of resources in ways defined appropriate by their cultural and ecological traditions so that no natural food source would become depleted.

The Noble Redman stereotype nurtured governmental paternalism and its bureaucratic overadministration through the Bureau of Indian Affairs that treated U.S. Indians as "Red children" living under wardship. This treatment foreclosed the possibility of Indian nations' becoming self-governing communities, a status that began to be regained only within the last half of the twentieth century.

The stereotype of the Red Savage, conversely, portrayed Native peoples as barbaric killers, "looting, burning, pillaging," who had to be eradicated by any means possible. The most horrible depredations were committed in the name of stamping out the Red Savage. Thus, the genocide of past centuries in North America went hand in hand with land and resource dispossession so that, today, Native Americans who once possessed 100 percent of the land base, now retain only 3 to 4 percent of North America in ownership title. Throughout Latin America, Native Americans retain little or no rights to the land base, even though in some countries they constitute an appreciable percentage of the national population.

The Red Savage stereotype, unfortunately, still lingers, but it has been modified to become the "drunken, incompetent" Indian. In Oklahoma, the state containing the United States' largest Indian population, the negative stereotype of the "four Ds" ("dark, dumb, drunk, and dirty") still plagued Indian young people as recently as the 1960s.

Derogatory terms such as *squaw* and *redskin* continue to do harm in their denigration of Native Americans.[2] According to the U.S. Geological Survey's Board on Geographic names, the word *squaw* is part of 1,050 geographic names in the United States, most of them in the Midwest and the West, such as Squaw Valley. The term *Redskin* was first used by the captain-general and governor-in-chief of the Province of Massachusetts Bay in a 1755 proclamation promoting the murder of American Indians by placing a bounty on their heads, scalps, and skins. For every male Indian prisoner above the age of twelve taken captive and brought to the town of Boston, 50 pounds in currency was offered on "Red Skins"; for every male Indian scalp brought in as evidence of their having been killed, 40 pounds was paid. In 1884 the governor of Pennsylvania also offered bounties on male and female Indians. During the Revolutionary War, the British commandant of Detroit became known as the "hair buyer" because he, too, paid bounties for Indian scalps. Signs on the walls of early trading posts announced bounties on "Red Skins," or bounty scalps, along with those on "Otter Skins" and "Beaver Skins." Thus, it is important for non-Indian Americans to know the historical origins of terms that they otherwise might believe to be harmless and inoffensive. Stereotypes such as these do real damage to the self-image of young Indian men and women in today's world.

Fortunately, Native Americans in the United States are beginning to have some success in pressuring states to eliminate derogatory Indian epithets. Maine, Minnesota, and Montana have recently enacted laws to eliminate the word *squaw* from state lands, maps, signs, and markers. Indian sports mascots, which communicate grotesque and negative images, must also be examined in this light. There is an old saying: "Sticks and stones can break my bones, but words can never hurt me." But as the readings in this chapter demonstrate, words *can* hurt. Racial and ethnic stereotypes, through words and images, set a tone and create a context in which prejudice and discrimination are seemingly justified.

The first selection in this part is by Vine Deloria Jr. (Standing Rock Sioux), dean of Native American scholarship and letters. This selection is taken from *Red Earth, White Lies*, in which he critically examines several of the more prominent "scientific" theories about American Indians and concludes that they are more myth than science. (On the other hand, what Western scientists term Indian myths may actually provide important clues from Indian oral accounts and remembrances regarding Native American origins and prehistory.) A case in point is the widely held assumption that Native Americans were somehow responsible for the megafaunal extinction, termed the "Pleistocene overkill" by some academic scholars, that took place 12,000 to 15,000 years ago. Did Native Americans actually kill and eat up the mammoth, mastodon, giant ground sloth, giant beaver, and other large creatures? Deloria doesn't think so. He scathingly examines the many logical contradictions and unfounded assumptions in this so-called scientific theory.

In the second selection, Cherokee folklorist Rayna Green examines what she terms the "Pocahontas perplex," the national cult and its pre-American origins surrounding the Pocahontas–John Smith legend as celebrated in paintings, poems, plays, movies, and literature. The Indian princess stereotype plays to the notion of the Noble Redman or good Indian who "rescues and helps white men" and becomes Christianized and acculturated. This stereotype, in turn, is counterpoised to its polar opposite, the "savage" Indian, or, in the case of Indian women, the "squaw"—a dull, unattractive beast of burden or whore.

The rap lyrics "Growin' Up on the Rez," found in the box on pages 211–212, are a strong expression of sentiments shared by many Indians, in both urban and rural areas in response to societal racism.

The third selection is by historian Bruce Johansen, Robert T. Reilly Professor of Communication and Native American Studies at the University of Nebraska at Omaha. He relates the tragic record of the coerced sterilizations of Indian women, some as young as fifteen years, by health authorities during the last several decades. One of the facts documented: the U.S. government's General Accounting

Office (GAO) examined only four of twelve Indian Health Service regions and found that 3,406 Native American women had been sterilized during the 1970s. Other estimates indicate a much higher total. Johansen places this governmental policy within the context of the eugenics movement and its racist, social Darwinist philosophy. The tragic implications for the U.S. Native American population are significant, not only because the overall Indian population of fewer than two million is small when compared with other ethnic minorities but also because the population is composed of many different mininationalities with small gene pools. As researcher Sally Torpy states and is quoted by Johansen: "A 200 million population could support voluntary sterilization and survive, but for Native Americans it cannot be a preferred method of birth control. While other minorities might have a gene pool in Africa or Asia, Native Americans do not: when we are gone, that's it."

The box titled "Indian-Named Mascots: An Assault on Self-Esteem" examines the issue of Indian sports mascots, such as the Atlanta Braves and the Cleveland Indians. Tim Giago (Nanwica Kciji; Oglala Lakota), the former editor of *Indian Country Today*, demonstrates the ways in which this practice is demeaning.

Currently, the most virulent form of discrimination is terrorism at the hands of vigilante groups, or even by the state itself. Since the bombing of the federal building in Oklahoma City, citizens of the United States have been alerted to the ominous rise of the "Patriot" or militia movement, but, as Indian historian Jack Forbes reminds us, the militia movement is nothing new. "Terrorism by bands of armed white men was the primary means used by the United States to harass, weaken, and then to almost wipe out tribe after tribe in the far west. The U.S. Army was usually brought in after irregular armed militias had done the dirty work."[2] Terrorism can not exist unless the targeted group is dehumanized through negative stereotyping. One need not turn to the 1800s to find an example of vigilante attacks on Indian people. In 1973, during the occupation-protest on the Pine Ridge Reservation at Wounded Knee, the federal government armed and abetted what became known as the "GOON squad" to attack and kill members and sympathizers of the militant American Indian Movement (AIM). Likewise, in Central and South America, armed, government-supported vigilante groups often threaten and terrorize indigenous communities. Guatemala is a case in point; tens of thousands of Indian people have been killed or "disappeared" in the past forty years of militarist rule and civil strife.

Ward Churchill (Creek/Cherokee/Métis) takes up this theme in the fourth selection, in which he charges that the U.S. government illegally sought to destroy or neutralize AIM. The government sent a federal army to quash the 1973 protest at Wounded Knee and later tied up the AIM leadership in long, costly trials in an attempt to destroy the Indian rights organization. Ironically, the courts later judged the government's actions at Wounded Knee illegal, but the damage to AIM and its supporters had already been done.

Finally, in the box titled "Free Leonard Peltier," we document the case of Indian political prisoner Leonard Peltier. Most U.S. citizens are unaware that there are racial and ethnic minority "prisoners of conscience" in U.S. jails who were either framed or wrongly convicted because of their ethnicity and political advocacy. Peltier's conviction grew out of Indian protests and the FBI vendetta against the American Indian Movement. The U.S. government's wrongful conviction of Peltier is protested throughout the world and casts an ugly pall on the concept of democracy and the protection of human rights in the United States.

NOTES

1. Jack Weatherford, *Indian Givers: How the Indians of the Americas Transformed the World* (New York: Fawcett Columbine, 1988).

2. Jack D. Forbes, "Irregular Militias Rooted in American History," *Windspeaker,* 13, no. 6 (October 1995): 6.

MYTHICAL PLEISTOCENE HIT MEN

Vine Deloria Jr.

[*Editor's Note:* The first three paragraphs that follow come from the chapter in *Red Earth, White Lies* entitled "Low Bridge, Everybody Cross," which lays the foundation for a reassment and rejection of the Bering Strait land bridge theory. Your editors suggest that you consult this chapter for a fuller discussion.]

... It may appear that I have sufficiently discussed the origins of man and thereby eliminated the Bering Strait theory as a possible explanation of the source of the occupancy of the Western Hemisphere by American Indians and that devoting more time to this idea is superfluous. Nothing could be farther from the truth. Most Americans do not see the connection between the different scientific theories, nor do they understand that a shift or collapse of a major scientific doctrine requires a significant adjustment of all subsidiary doctrines that relied on it for their validity. Thus, people accepting the idea that outmoded explanations of human evolution have been modified substantially will continue to hold with the Bering Strait theory, even though to do so is the great inconsistency. But another point must be made which requires a chapter of discussion—and that is whether or not the Bering Strait is simply shorthand scientific language for "I don't know, but it sounds good and no one will check."

There are immense contemporary political implications to this theory which make it difficult for many people to surrender. Considerable residual guilt remains over the manner in which the Western Hemisphere was invaded and settled by Europeans. Five centuries of brutality lie uneasily on the conscience, and consequently two beliefs have arisen which are used to explain away this dreadful history. People want to believe that the Western Hemisphere, and more particularly North America, was a vacant, unexploited, fertile land waiting to be put under cultivation according to God's holy dictates. As Woody Guthrie put it: "This Land is your land, this Land is my land." The hemisphere thus belonged to whoever was able to rescue it from its wilderness state.

Coupled with this belief is the idea that American Indians were not original inhabitants of the Western Hemisphere but latecomers who had barely unpacked before Columbus came knocking on the door. If Indians had arrived only a few centuries earlier, they had no *real* claim to land that could not be swept away by European discovery. Aleš Hrdlička of the Smithsonian devoted his life to the discrediting of any early occupancy of North America, and a whole generation of scholars, fearfully following the master, rejected the claims of their peers rather than offend this powerful scholar.

Finally, the embarrassing discovery that Clovis and Folsom points abounded in the western states forced the admission that the Indians might have beaten Columbus by quite a few centuries.

These ideas have great impact on how non-Indians view the claims for justice made by Indians.

. . . The theory of Pleistocene overkill originated as an effort to explain the extinction or disappearance of a significant number of Pleistocene animals, most specifically the megafauna over fifty kilograms in weight, during or at the end of the Pleistocene era, a geological period which is in itself a complex and suspect classification. We thus move from the question of the validity of land bridges, which are sacrosanct for many scholars, to extinctions which are a great puzzle for most scholars, since geological strata from the first signs of life show sudden and mysterious terminations of planetary biota and fauna.

This "overkill" idea originated in a form approaching its contemporary expression when Carl Sauer, then one of the premier scholars on the environment, suggested more than half a century ago that Paleo-Indian hunters had killed all the big-game animals which became extinct in the late Pleistocene era. Sauer thought that through the use of fire drives in which they both cleared large tracts of land for prairie grazing and eliminated the mammoth, mastodon, and a variety of other creatures, Indians had been responsible for the demise of the mammoth and mastodon. Sauer cited no large kill sites, mixed forest and plains animals indiscriminately, and could only point to the practices of some historic Indian tribes in burning grasses to encourage new growth the following year as evidence that Indians had even burned areas.

Sauer was easily routed in his efforts to gain acceptance for this thesis by Loren C. Eiseley, who wrote two articles raising questions that were never satisfactorily answered. Eiseley's criticisms were as follows:

1. Many kinds of smaller fauna also died during this period who could not have been killed by either fire drives or spears and atlatls—most specifically birds and freshwater creatures such as mollusks and frogs.
2. The larger species of bison, most probably *Bison taylori,* a giant version of our present *Bison bison,* became extinct along with many other large grazing animals but our bison, antelope, deer, elk, moose, and other familiar modern game animals did not.
3. Many animals were in fact forest dwellers and could not have been affected by grassland fires. It would have been impossible, given forest environments, to have exterminated whole species under any conditions.
4. There is no evidence, comparing modern examples of tribal hunting groups with *possible* ancient techniques, for any group to exterminate or even significantly affect an animal population unless the hunters and prey are restricted to a very small area.
5. Prey–predator ratios almost always adjust to conditions and do not get out of alignment unless there is a catastrophic decline of predators—the Grand Canyon Kaibab deer is always cited as an example.

With fundamental criticisms such as these, the thesis was rejected by most scholars and was forgotten until it was revived in another form by Paul Martin of the University of Arizona and his colleagues in a 1967 book of essays entitled *Pleistocene Extinctions.*

Since these events, if they did indeed occur, happened some 12,000 to 15,000 years ago, why should it matter? It matters immensely because the image which science has given American Indians is such that modern Indians are blamed for the extinction of these creatures. Conservative newspaper columnists, right-wing fanatics, sportsmen's groups, and scholars in general tend to see the "overkill" hypothesis as symptomatic of a lack of moral fiber and ethical concern for the Earth among Indians. Some people are offended by the idea that many people believe that Indians were more concerned and thoughtful ecologists than modern industrial users. Advocating the extinction theory is a good way to support continued despoilation of the environment by suggesting that at *no* time were human beings careful of the lands upon which they lived.

I can speak here from firsthand personal knowledge. In 1990, I was invited to speak at Stanford University, trumpeted as the "Harvard of the West," to celebrate its one hundredth anniversary. I was asked to speak on the Indian relationship with the land, and I tried as best I could to outline the philosophical principles I thought would be meaningful to the audience and the values I thought were involved in the Indian perspective on the natural world. The first question from the audience when I finished was a person asking whether I didn't think running hundreds of buffalo over a cliff was wasteful. The tone of the question implied that the previous weekend myself and other invited Indian speakers had destroyed hundreds of bison somewhere in Wyoming. Since the only recent slaughter of buffalo that I could remember was the Super Bowl, I took offense and refused to answer any more questions.

Lest the reader think I am overly sensitive, let us see what some of the respected science writers say about this thesis. They have, as a rule, accepted it wholeheartedly. Robert Bakker, whom we met in the previous chapter, casually noted that ". . . once

they got going, our primordial forefathers cut a wide swath through both the Old World and the New, exterminating dozens of big species of mammal—mammoths, mastodons, sabre-toothed cats, giant ground sloths, to name but a few. And they killed tortoises." Robert Ardrey, in *The Hunting Hypothesis*, waxes eloquently about the subject. "And so it is," he writes, "that every fossil record points to the probability that within a thousand years after our arrival in America across the land bridge we similarly exterminated the mammoths." Writing in such absolute terms encourages the layperson to believe that these questions have been proven beyond doubt, when they never have been, and it is wholly irresponsible.

Ardrey is not talking about "we" in the generic human sense. "The new hunters, who would father the American Indian, left an unmistakable record: within a few thousand years they and their descendants, armed with only throwing spears and Asian sophistication, exterminated all the large game in both North and South America." Thus while there is the pretense of speaking in general terms, it is American Indians, still living today, who are the object of the accusation. And how are Europeans treated? Some scholars find them as wasteful, but generally they are excused from blame. Kazimierz Kowalski writes, "Man was present at that time in Europe, but there is almost no evidence for his role in extermination of animals; at such a primitive stage of culture he was probably not a real danger for animals as large as an elephant or rhinoceros. The disappearance of these large mammals at the end of the last interglacial is the last episode in the great extinction of European fauna caused by Quaternary climatic changes in conjunction with the geographical configuration of the continent." In other words, Europeans can blame the weather; Indians cannot even suggest it as a cause.

Robert Ebisch of the *Seattle Times* published a story on the overkill thesis in May 1990 and secured comments from a number of people. Stephen Pyne, a professor of American Studies at Arizona State University, expanded the thesis enthusiastically. Without realizing the background of the issue, Pyne was quoted as saying: "It wasn't just the spears. They also had torches, and fire is a pretty powerful tool. The largest source of ozone and nitrous oxide in the world today is coming from the savannas in Africa that are burned annually, for hunting, slash and burn agriculture, etc.," thereby unwittingly bringing the debate full circle to Sauer's discredited thesis.

Jared Diamond has written one article on the so-called big game hunters and mentions the overkill thesis favorably in another article which was generally slanted in a pro–exploitation-of-environments alignment. He is enthusiastically in favor of blaming the big game hunters, as they have come to be called, and likens them to the people who exterminated the giant moa in Australia but not to the British colonists who eliminated the Tasmanians. I will save his comments for the in-depth discussion of Martin's thesis, since he offers additional arguments on its behalf.

So what are we really talking about? Let us look first at Paul Martin's original compilation of papers discussing the extinction of animals, then at comments made by fellow writers in the book. Having established the basic framework, we will then look at some of Martin's later elaborations on the idea. And we will raise some questions about the viability of the idea in rebuttal and critique.

Pleistocene Extinctions is roughly divided into three parts: introductory statements, a set of essays under the rubric of "Facets of the Problem," and a set of essays under the classification of "Regional Aspects and Case Histories." Before we examine Martin's argument, however, it is a good idea to list a representative sample of the species that [did] become extinct at some point in the recent past (perhaps 50,000 years ago) so readers will have some idea of the scope of the thesis and what it tries to cover. There is a process of selection that occurs when Martin develops his thesis that should not be missed. The species who became extinct that would most easily fit into his framework were:

Artodus—giant short-faced bears
Bootherium—extinct bovid
Boreostracon—glyptodon
Bos—yak
Brachyostracon—glyptodon
Camelops—extinct camels
Castorides—giant beaver
Cervalces—extinct moose
Chlamytherium—giant armadillos
Cuvieronius—extinct mastodons
Dinobastis—saber-toothed cat
Equus—horses
Eremotherium—giant ground sloth
Euceratherium—shrub oxen
Glyptodon—an armadillo-like creature
Glyptotherium—glyptodons
Hayoceros—extinct pronghorn
Hydrocherus—capybaras sloths
Mammut—American mastodons
Mammuthus—mammoths
Megalonyx—ground sloths
Mylohyus—woodland peccaries
Neochoerus—extinct capybara
Nothrotherium—small ground sloths
Paramylodon—ground sloths
Platyerabos—extinct bovid
Platygonus—extinct peccary
Preptoceras—shrub oxen
Sangamona—caribou
Siaga—Asian antelope
Smilodon—saber-toothed cat
Stockoceros—extinct pronghorn

Symbos—woodland musk ox
Tanupolama—extinct llamas
Tapirus—tapirs
Tetrameryx—extinct pronghorns
Tremarctos—spectacled bears

This list is not complete, but it is certainly representative of the loss of species. There are still a good variety of grazing herbivores who became extinct to be considered, and the popular carnivores, including the dire wolves, also suffered extinction during this period of time but have not been mentioned.

Martin more or less stacks the deck in his essay because his list of smaller species which became extinct is drawn primarily from the Pliocene era, not the Pleistocene, which makes it appear that megafauna alone suddenly vanished and that smaller fauna had already passed from the scene at an earlier date. No mention is made of avian species, who could not have been exterminated by hunters under any circumstances. So the question of extinction in the late Pleistocene has already been restricted to those species, and those species only, that Martin believes will make his case, leaving to others the necessity of accounting for the demise of the remaining species.

The basic problem is posed as follows. Martin's thesis is that thirty-one species of herbivores weighing over 50 kilograms became extinct *sometime* during the late Pleistocene. He rejects climate change as a possible source of their demise, pointing out that a lesser number of megafauna species became extinct on other continents. But he does not say how many species of megafauna actually inhabited other continents and also became extinct, thereby magnifying the scope of disaster in North America. If, for example, Europe had a small number of megafauna originally, percentage-wise the depletion might have been as severe.

As herbivore megafauna became extinct, so also did the mega-carnivores that once fed upon them. Martin avoids the question of how carnivores became extinct by confining his inquiry to the loss of herbivores. Presumably with prey declining precipitously, the mega-carnivores first reduced their population and then suffered radical and permanent decline for lack of food supply. Thus carnivores do not receive blame for the extinction of mega-herbivores even though they would probably have been the prime users of the grazing animals.

Martin's case becomes one of suggesting, without clearly stating, that the only remaining possible factor in the extinction of mega-herbivores would have been Paleo-Indian hunters, who he believes came into North America at this time and ruthlessly slaughtered the grazing mega-herbivores. The slaughter was made possible by the fact that these creatures had never seen human beings and were therefore helpless to protect themselves. Inherent in this proposition is the belief that herbivores could not or did not recognize danger when it approached them, whether in the form of a saber-toothed cat or a few hunters waving spears and stone clubs.

Since most American anthropologists accepted the Neanderthal to Cro-Magnon evolution, the late entrance of man into North America was a given. Clovis-point locations, which incidentally are scattered all over the western United States on the surface as much as buried, and which by the common agreement of scholars date to around 12,000 years ago, then enabled Martin to argue that "the Indians did it" by linking a few sites which had bones of extinct megafauna and were also dated at that time.

The thesis is really applicable only to the herbivores, however, because almost every advocate of the idea cites those locations where mammoth bones are associated with evidence of human activity. From the list above we never hear about the giant rhinoceros, giant beaver, or giant armadillo, nor do the scholars refer to carnivore extinction except by indirection, assuming that the extinction of herbivores doomed meat-eating predators. Can we imagine hungry saber-toothed tigers and other carnivores unable to feed upon the smaller species of deer, moose, and bison when they discovered that the mega-animals had been destroyed?

When the Europeans came to North America the land was filled to overflowing with all manner of edible grazing game. The bison are conservatively estimated at a population of nearly 60 million creatures at the time of discovery. Since no species could evolve in 12,000 years, we must assume that the game animals we see today were here in their present form at the time when Martin suggests the Paleo-Indians were ruthlessly slaughtering the mammoth and mastodon.

So we have actually two questions. Why did the mega-carnivores not pounce upon the smaller, weaker herbivores and maintain themselves in grand style? Why did the Paleo-Indian hunters not begin with smaller-sized animals, which would have been easier to kill, less dangerous to be around, and which themselves might be relegated to the fringes of the good grazing places by the larger and certainly more dangerous mega-herbivores? Martin made a feeble effort to answer the second question by admitting that "we must beg the question of just how and why prehistoric man obliterated his prey. We may speculate but we cannot determine how moose, elk, and caribou managed to survive while horse, ground sloth, and mastodon did not." He begged people not to ask him for specifics about the second question and was not even aware of the complexity of the first question.

Martin did, strangely, provide an opening for criticism of his idea by admitting:

"What would upset the hypothesis of overkill would be clear-cut cases on the continent of many of the extinct animals surviving beyond the time of the big-game hunters, or clear-cut cases of massive unbalanced Pleistocene extinction anywhere before man." I will provide evidence on this point in a later chapter, but it is sufficient here to note that Indian traditions and very late sites for some of the mega-herbivores are rejected by most scholars as being too late. That is to say, very early and very late dates for mammoth and other creatures are cast out when citing evidence for the theory, apparently because of doctrinal considerations.

Martin is no exception to this scholarly rule. In some areas of Alaska are deposits, politely termed "muck," which are simply large piles of broken animal bones, trees, some volcanic ash, and gravels. They played hell with hydraulic mining because they would give off a terrible stench akin to ammonia when they were melted. Martin deals with this evidence in a peremptory way: "Stratigraphic chaos, apparently the result of intense solifluction, has thus far defeated attempts at direct radiocarbon dating of the abundant remains of extinct horse, bison and mammoth in Alaskan muck. . . . The dates, on wood associated with the bones, appear much too young to represent the true age of the fauna and are thought to be intrusive."

"Intrusive" is a favorite concept for scientists who find that the data do not conform to theory. It means that you argue that *after* the deposits you are examining have been laid down, trees, coins, artifacts, and bones which were later deposited on the surface begin to worm their way into the soil and burrow until they become jarring discrepancies in the strata you are considering. If the muck deposits are a twisted mixture of intertwined bones, trees, and gravels, how can the wood be intrusive? Thus Martin explains away evidence that would conflict with his theory by a spurious argument phrased in traditional scientific lingo.

Another source of megafauna bones which have a relationship to the big-game hunter thesis once existed at Big Bone Lick, Kentucky. With respect to this evidence Martin writes: "In the case of Big Bone Lick, Kentucky, one of the richest late-Pleistocene deposits in eastern North America, two samples of wood initially thought to be associated with bones of extinct species proved modern." So what? Maybe they were modern; maybe these creatures weren't exterminated by hunters at all and survived until modern times. Fortunately, we have evidence of this survival recorded. George Gaylord Simpson discussed this site in an essay on fossils, and this site will be seen to have significance for our discussion:

> In 1762 John Bartram, the Philadelphia Quaker who supplied Linnaeus and other European naturalists with descriptions and specimens of American plants and animals, heard that a large tooth and a fragment of a tusk had been brought to Fort Pitt by some Indians. He requested his friend James Wright to make inquiries among the Indians concerning the place where these objects had been found. Through an interpreter, Wright secured an account of the site which came to be known as Big Bone Lick. According to Wright's informants, the lick contained five entire skeletons, the heads pointing toward a common center. The bones were of enormous size and were accompanied by tusks ten or twelve feet long. No such creatures as these had ever been seen alive by the Indians, but legend said that they had once been hunted through the forests by men of gigantic stature and that when the last of these men had died, God had destroyed their mighty prey in order to protect the present race of Indians.

We cannot date the giant men and we cannot say when these giant animals were finally destroyed, but we know that the Indians did not have a hand in their demise. If the bones are fresh, then Martin's rejection of them as modern is simply silly. They might be modern.

Ashley Montagu and others published articles in the 1940s suggesting that mammoths were still alive when white men began to move west across the Ohio River and early colonists collected some stories suggestive of mastodons. It would seem logical that if these animals were killed thousands, or even hundreds, of years ago, their bones would have decayed and disappeared. How bones of extinct animals could lie on the ground for any period of time without disintegrating is an objection that cannot easily be dismissed.

Other essayists in *Pleistocene Extinctions* generally seem to be sympathetic to Martin's thesis, but they admit points so discordant with his ideas that we must note them. James Hester attempted to deal with the question of mammoth extermination and his analysis is worthy of note. "The staple food during the Llano period consisted of the mammoth; during the later periods it was the bison. All other animals are poorly represented. The size of the kills varies from site to site, and it is not always possible to determine if the animals present were killed at one time or on several occasions. In addition it is not always possible to determine if the animals present at the site were killed by man or some other agency." There is, consequently, no clear and irrefutable evidence that Paleo-Indians ever killed more than one animal at a time, or that kills were numerous enough to even attract the attention of scholars.

Hester also pointed out that Folsom hunters generally chose small herds of bison to hunt, without discrimination as to age and gender. Clovis hunters would probably have followed the same general procedure. "In three separate kills at the Clovis site, the kills took place while the animals were knee deep in a pond, presumably drinking." This tenuous form of hunting is a far cry from massive herd extermination. N. K. Vereshchagin, in his essay, pointed out that Paleo humans were capable of killing large animals but we know nothing of their weapons. "Stone instruments of the Lower Paleolithic, large hand points (ovates) and rough narrow-pointed stones, were unsuitable for killing and cutting up large animals. A sleepy cave bear could be killed with a huge wooden cudgel or boar spring . . . but certainly not a mammoth or European Bison." We can imagine Paleo-Indians swarming into caves to dispatch sleepy cave bears and perhaps even saber-toothed cats, but in our wildest dreams we cannot see how they could exterminate a species by this method of depredation.

So, then, how did Paleo-Siberians hunt mammoth? According to Vereshchagin, "usually, communities of hunters armed with spears hunted for solitary mammoth or small groups of females with young, as African Negroes now hunt elephants. The hunters pierced the abdominal wall of the mammoth and then pursued them, sometimes for many kilometers; but hunters could obtain only single specimens at a time. They hunted woolly rhinoceros in the same manner." Surrounding a solitary mammoth, trying to pierce the abdominal wall with a spear to induce internal bleeding, and then chasing the creature until hemorrhage weakens or kills it would not seem to induce a massive destruction of species—certainly not cause the extinction of the thirty-one herbivore species that we lost somewhere in the Pleistocene.

Vereshchagin describes the effect of a hunting group traversing lands occupied by herds of grazing animals. He says that "after great but short-term migration of nomads, the population of large animals in steppe and forest-steppe did not disappear but relatively quickly returned to their former numbers. In the southern part of eastern

Europe the abundance of steppe and forest animals was maintained through the Middle Ages." So while hunting groups can temporarily reduce the numbers of a specific animal, what we know of hunting practices suggests that hunters cannot exterminate a single species, let alone a large number of species.

Vereshchagin also deals with the massive numbers of animals in the Siberian frozen wastes, but he does so directly and not by dismissing them. He notes that "the accumulations of mammoth bones and carcasses of mammoth, rhinoceros, and bison found in frozen ground in Indigirka, Kolyma, and Novosibirsk islands bear no trace of hunting or activity of primitive man. Here large herbivorous animals perished and became extinct because of climatic and geomorphic changes, especially changes in the regime of winter snow and increase in depth of snow cover." If we follow the Martin scenario, these Paleo-Indian hunters could have and should have exterminated the mammoths, the woolly rhinoceros, and the ground sloth, among others, in Siberia without having to travel across the Bering Strait but did not do so. *On their arrival in Alaska, we are asked to believe, an incredible blood lust appeared and Paleo-Indians changed their hunting techniques in order to slaughter herds of mammoth, bison, armadillos, for example, with great efficiency.*

Arthur Jelinek, Martin's colleague at the University of Arizona, suggested that the Paleo hunters did have great efficiency and that this "is attested by such sites as Solutre in east-central France, where a late-Perigordian level is estimated to contain the remains of over 100,000 horses." Other scholars give much lower estimates of the number killed, but generally this European site is believed to provide evidence of the blood lust of Paleo people at this time. But a much larger question arises: How in the world could primitive hunters, or anyone else, gather together 100,000 horses for any purpose? And would not these Paleo people have littered Europe with carcasses even before they traveled to Siberia? Scholars credit these ancients with feats that modern people would be hard pressed to duplicate.

Jelinek, although very supportive of Martin, noted a glaring lack of evidence for the theory, a defect that Diamond, Ardrey, and Bakker apparently did not catch. Jelinek admitted: "Throughout the New World one major puzzle exists with regard to linking man with the extinctions. *This is the absence of direct evidence of human activity associated with the remains of extinct animals. In fact we have kill sites with implements in association with partially articulated skeletons for only one of the many genera that disappeared in western North America and Mexico—Mammuthus.*" (Emphasis added.) So why is this "theory" an explanation for the loss of many species of animals, including but not strictly limited to megafauna, in the Pleistocene? Is it simply because Martin is a tenured academic in good standing with his peers? Does *anything* that a member of the scientific establishment says receive uncritical acceptance by his peers as scientific even if it doesn't make any sense at all? If there are so few sites linking ancient man with extinct animals, what are we talking about?

In 1990, Paul Martin published yet another article on his energetic and mischievous hunters entitled "Who or What Destroyed Our Mammoths?" It had been twenty-three years since his first essay, and, while he had published a variety of papers in the interim advocating his ideas, in this essay he waxed poetic. Instead of filling in the immense gaps in evidence that characterized the first and subsequent articulations of the theory, Martin devised a scenario which he believed gave a better description of his theory. The latest version of the tale will unquestionably be cited as a serious elaboration and perhaps final proof of the overkill thesis by the many popular science writers, although Martin himself couches it in terms of his "best guess" and calls it a scientist's "bedtime story." We will look at portions of the most recent Martin scientific venture.

> Once upon a time 12,000 years ago, a small band of people physically very like us and speaking a common language trekked farther east than anyone had ever gone before. . . .
>
> In autumn they followed their prey—mammoth, bison, and caribou—to wintering grounds. Helped in the hunt by opportunistic wolves or wolfish dogs, the hunters were expert at locating and tracking game, at killing it in excess of their needs, at butchering the carcass, and preserving the meat. . . . At 60° below, they dressed in warm furs and slept in bearskin bags. . . . By sharing food, there was always more than enough to eat and large animals were easily killed just for the fun of it, although wise elders spoke against this. . . .
>
> Spreading southward, the unwitting explorers found that they were in a hunter's paradise, a Garden of Eden vastly rich in resources of the kind they were so expert in hunting. Some of the animals they discovered were new to their experience and some of these, three great ground sloths, were slow-moving and extraordinarily easy to dispatch. The children of the hunters could use them for target practice.

I need not repeat any more of this dreadfully silly scientific scenario, but I can comment on these few points without fear of losing my bearings.

Hunters, in Europe, Asia, Siberia, and presumably even North America, moved south to north along river valleys. Northern Siberia already had megafauna in profusion which never felt the spear or butchering tools, so we know that the scenario of extinction of so many species is unlikely at best. If these hunters were going on a large-scale program of extermination they could have done it in Siberia; they did not need to travel to Alaska to do it.

Martin's hunters move from autumnal regions to wintering grounds which have temperatures of 60° [Fahrenheit] below zero. Now, Martin is from Arizona and consequently may have no firsthand knowledge of cold, so we can provide him with some helpful hints on how to improve his theory. At 60° below zero you are not out hunting mammoths, bison, and caribou. Everything is pretty much stationary and even a short exposure to these kinds of temperatures on bare flesh will give a pretty bad case of frostbite. Thus, to imagine hunters who have killed a mammoth deliberately going back out into this freezing cold to kill several more "just for the fun of it" is difficult at best when we consider that the method used to dispatch the beast is that of piercing the animal's abdominal cavity and chasing it until it bleeds to death. It is useful also to note that the coldest place on Earth today is Antarctica, which has temperatures of 70° below zero.

We are not told in this new Martin scenario what these animals are eating, but we can assume that there is some kind of grass in the area even at 60° below. But what about the helpful wolves and wolfish dogs? They are also predators and hence competitors of man, and it is unlikely that they are working in concert with these happy late Pleistocene hunters. More likely, if they are around at all, they are lurking in the hills waiting for humans to finish their hunt and hoping for leftovers. In the alternative, Martin would have to have these animals already domesticated, since without man they would have a terrible time scaring up a meal in that weather.

Why also do these hunters even bother to preserve food? At 60° below you have a reasonably good fast-freeze environment so that preserving food should be the least of your worries. Indeed, the problem would be finding enough fuel to keep a fire going to defrost supper. And if the hunters wastefully kill mammoths and never worry about having food, exactly what kind of food is being preserved?

We move southward with these hunters and discover new kinds of animals, and the kids use giant ground sloths as targets because they are so slow. Martin here shows an abysmal lack of knowledge of hunting societies. Children matured, or took on adult kinds of responsibilities, reasonably early in life, especially in Indian tribes. Luther Standing Bear in his books relates that by the age of ten he had killed a buffalo, gone on a war party, and been inducted into the Fox Society, an honorary group that performed a charitable function in Sioux society.

If boys were performing some adult functions by age ten, then the children who were knocking off the ground sloths must have been between five and nine years old. Since some of these ground sloths were the size of modern adult giraffes, we can conclude that these hunters' children were among the more precocious and ambitious youngsters any society has ever raised.

Martin has his hunters moving two hundred miles in a generation and he figures that the hunters reached Tierra del Fuego within five hundred years. The distance between Alaska and Tierra del Fuego must be in the neighborhood of eight thousand miles, so figuring two hundred miles per generation, we must have had around forty generations of people within a five-hundred-year period, or a generation every twelve and a half years. So not only were these people expert hunters, they were something to behold in those bearskin bags.

Martin's scenario is simply preposterous. There is no point at which it makes any sense at all. No convincing evidence is cited except that he believes something happened at 10,000 or 12,000 B.C. that eliminated the megafauna; he looks only at the evidence he has amassed in support of his theory and then insists that the Indians did it. Bakker, Diamond, Ardrey, and Ebisch and a good many others cannot have read the original essay or the updated scenario of helpful wolves and gigantic target sloths. If they had read it, surely they would not so casually endorse the overkill hypothesis. . . .

THE POCAHONTAS PERPLEX
THE IMAGE OF INDIAN WOMEN
IN AMERICAN CULTURE

Rayna Green

In one of the best known old Scottish ballads, "Young Beichan" or "Lord Bateman and the Turkish King's Daughter" as it is often known in America, a young English adventurer travels to a strange, foreign land. The natives are of a darker color than he, and they practice a pagan religion. The man is captured by the King (Pasha, Moor, Sultan) and thrown in a dungeon to await death. Before he is executed, however, the pasha's beautiful daughter—smitten with the elegant and wealthy visitor—rescues him and sends him homeward. But she pines away for love of the now remote stranger who has gone home, apparently forgotten her, and

contracted a marriage with a "noble" "lady" of his own kind. In all the versions, she follows him to his own land, and in most, she arrives on his wedding day whereupon he throws over his bride-to-be for the darker but more beautiful Princess. In most versions, she becomes a Christian, and she and Lord Beichan live happily ever after.

In an article called "The Mother of Us All," Philip Young suggests the parallel between the ballad story and the Pocahontas–John Smith rescue tale.[1] With the exception of Pocahontas' marriage to John Rolfe (still, after all, a Christian stranger), the tale should indeed sound familiar to most Americans nurtured on Smith's salvation by the Indian Princess. Actually, Europeans were familiar with the motif before John Smith offered his particular variant in the *Generall Historie of Virginie* (1624).

Francis James Child, the famous ballad collector, tells us in his *English and Scottish Popular Ballads* that "Young Beichan" (Child #40) matches the tale of Gilbert Beket, St. Thomas Aquinas' father, as well as a legend recounted in the *Gesta Romanorum*, one of the oldest collections of popular tales. So the frame story was printed before 1300 and was, no doubt, well distributed in oral tradition before then. Whether or not our rakish adventurer-hero, John Smith, had heard the stories or the ballad, we cannot say, but we must admire how life mirrors art since his story follows the outlines of the traditional tale most admirably. What we do know is that the elements of the tale appealed to Europeans long before Americans had the opportunity to attach their affection for it onto Pocahontas. Whether or not we believe Smith's tale—and there are many reasons not to—we cannot ignore the impact the story has had on the American imagination.

"The Mother of Us All" became our first aristocrat, and perhaps our first saint, as Young implies. Certainly, the image of her body flung over the endangered head of our hero constitutes a major scene in national myth. Many paintings and drawings of this scene exist, and it appears in popular art on everything from wooden fire engine side panels to calendars. Some renderings betray such ignorance about the Powhatan Indians of Virginia—often portraying them in Plains dress—that one quickly comes to understand that it is the mythical scene, not the accuracy of detail that moved artists. The most famous portrait of Pocahontas, the only one said to be done from life (at John Rolfe's request), shows the Princess in Elizabethan dress, complete with ruff and velvet hat—the Christian, English lady the ballad expects her to become and the lady she indeed became for her English husband and her faithful audience for all time. The earliest literary efforts in America, intended to give us American rather than European topics, featured Pocahontas in plenty. Poems and plays—like James Nelson Barber's *The Indian Princess; or, La Belle Sauvage* (1808) and George Washington Custis' *The Settlers of Virginia* (1827), as well as contemporary American novels, discussed by Leslie Fiedler in *The Return of the Vanishing American*—dealt with her presence, or sang her praises from the pages of literary magazines and from the stages of popular playhouses throughout the east.[2] Traditional American ballads like "Jonathan Smith" retold the thrilling story; schoolbook histories included it in the first pages of every text; nineteenth century commercial products like cigars, perfume and even flour used Pocahontas' name as come-on; and she appeared as the figurehead for American warships and clippers. Whether or not she saved John Smith, her actions as recounted by Smith set up one kind of model for Indian-White relations that persists—long after most Indians and Anglos ceased to have face-to-face relationships. Moreover, as a model for the national understanding of Indian women, her significance is undeniable. With her darker, negatively viewed sister, the Squaw—or, the anti-Pocahontas, as Fiedler calls her—the Princess intrudes on the national consciousness, and a potential cult waits to be resurrected when our anxieties about who we are make us recall her from her woodland retreat.[3]

Americans had a Pocahontas Perplex even before the teenage Princess offered us a real figure to hang the iconography on. The powerfully symbolic Indian woman, as Queen and Princess, has been with us since 1575 when she appeared to stand for the New World. Artists, explorers, writers and political leaders found the Indian as they cast about for some symbol with which to identify this earthly, frightening, and beautiful paradise; E. McClung Fleming has given one of the most complete explications of these images.[4] The misnamed Indian was the native dweller, who fit conveniently into the various traditional folkloric, philosophical and literary patterns characteristic of European thought at the time.[5] Europeans easily adopted the Indian as the iconographic representative of the Americas. At first, Caribbean and Brazilian (Tupinamba) Indians, portrayed amidst exotic flora and fauna, stood for the New World's promises and dangers. The famous and much-reproduced "Four Continents" illustrations (circa, early 16th century) executed by artists who had seen Indians and ones who had not, ordinarily pictured a male and female pair in America's place.[6] But the paired symbol apparently did not satisfy the need for a personified figure, and the Indian Queen began to appear as the sole representation for the Americas in 1575. And until 1765 or thereabouts, the barebreasted, Amazonian Native American Queen reigned. Draped in leaves, feathers, and animal skins as well as in heavy Caribbean jewelry, she appeared aggressive, militant, and armed with spears and arrows. Often, she rode on an armadillo, and stood with her foot on the slain body of an animal or human enemy. She was the familiar Mother-Goddess figure—full-bodied, powerful, nurturing but dangerous— embodying the opulence and peril of the New World. Her environment was rich and colorful, and that, with the allusions to Classical Europe through the Renaissance portrayal of her large, naked body, attached her to Old World History as well as to New World virtue.

Her daughter, the Princess, enters the scene when the colonies begin to move toward independence, and she becomes more "American" and less Latin than her mother. She seems less barbarous than the Queen; the rattlesnake (Jones' "Dont Tread On Me" sign) defends her, and her enemies are defeated by male warriors rather than by her own armed hand. She is Britannia's daughter as well as that of the Carib Queen, and she wears the triangular Phrygian cap and holds the liberty pole of her later, metamorphosed sister, Miss Liberty (the figure on the Statue of Liberty and the Liberty dime). She is young, leaner in the Romanesque rather than Greek mode, and distinctly Caucasian, though her skin remains slightly tinted in some renderings. She wears the loose, flowing gowns of classical statuary rather than animal skins, and Roman sandals grace her feet. She is armed, usually with a spear, but she also carries a peace pipe, a flag, or the starred and striped shield of Colonial America. She often stands with The Sons of Liberty, or later, with George Washington.

Thus, the Indian woman began her symbolic, many-faceted life as a Mother figure—exotic, powerful, dangerous, and beautiful—and as a representative of American liberty and European classical virtue translated into New World terms. She represented, even defended America. But when real Indian women—Pocahontas and her sisters—intruded into the needs bound up in symbols and the desires inherent in daily life, the responses to the symbol became more complex, and the Pocahontas perplex emerged as a controlling metaphor in the American experience. The Indian woman, along with her male counterparts, continued to stand for the New World and for rude native nobility, but the image of the savage remained as well. The dark side of the Mother-Queen figure is the savage Squaw, and even Pocahontas, as John Barth suggests in *The Sotweed Factor*, is motivated by lust.

Both her nobility as a Princess and her savagery as a Squaw are defined in terms of her relationships with male figures. If she wishes to be called a Princess, she must save or give aid to white men. The only good Indian—male or female, Squanto, Pocahontas, Sacagawea, Cochise, the Little Mohee or the Indian Doctor—rescues and helps white men. But the Indian woman is even more burdened by this narrow definition of a "good Indian," for it is she, not the males, whom white men desire sexually. Because her image is so tied up with abstract virtue—indeed, with America—she must remain the Mother Goddess-Queen. But acting as a real female, she must be a partner and lover of Indian men, a mother to Indian children, and an object of lust for white men. To be Mother, Queen and lover is, as Oedipus' mother, Jocasta, discovered, difficult and perhaps impossible. The paradox so often noted in Latin/Catholic countries where men revere their mothers and sisters, but use prostitutes so that their "good" women can stay pure is to the point here. Both race conflict and national identity, however, make this particular Virgin-Whore paradox more complicated than others. The Indian woman finds herself burdened with an image that can only be understood as dysfunctional, even though the Pocahontas perplex affects us all. Some examination of the complicated dimensions of that image might help us move toward change.

In songs like "Jonathan Smith," "Chipeta's Ride" and others sung in oral tradition, the Indian woman saves white men.[7] In "Chipeta's Ride," she even saves a white woman from lust-enraged Indian males. Ordinarily, however, she rescues her white lover or an anonymous male captive. Always called a Princess (or Chieftain's Daughter), she, like Pocahontas, has to violate the wishes and customs of her own "barbarous" people to make good the rescue, saving the man out of love and often out of "Christian sympathy." Nearly all the "good" Princess figures are converts, and they cannot bear to see their fellow Christians slain by "savages." The Princess is "civilized"; to illustrate her native nobility, most pictures portray her as white, darker than the Europeans, but more Caucasian than her fellow natives.

If unable to make the grand gesture of saving her captive lover or if thwarted from marrying him by her cruel father, the Chieftain, the Princess is allowed the even grander gesture of committing suicide when her lover is slain or fails to return to her after she rescues him. In the hundreds of "Lover's Leap" legends which abound throughout the country, and in traditional songs like "The Indian Bride's Lament," our heroine leaps over a precipice, unable to live without her loved one. In this movement from political symbolism (where the Indian woman defends America) to psychosexual symbolism (where she defends or dies for white lovers), we can see part of the Indian woman's dilemma. To be "good," she must defy her own people, exile herself from them, become white, and perhaps suffer death.

Those who did not leap for love continued to fall in love with white men by the scores, and here the sacrifices are several. The women in songs like "The Little Mohea," "Little Red Wing," and "Juanita, the Sachem's Daughter" fall in love with white travellers, often inviting them to share their blissful, idyllic, woodland paradise. If their lovers leave them, they often pine away, die of grief, or leap off a cliff, but in a number of songs, the white man remains with the maiden, preferring her life to his own, "civilized" way.

"Pocahontas Saving Captain John Smith," steel engraving, mid-nineteenth century.

"The Little Mohea" is a prime example of such a song.

As I went out walking for pleasure one
    day,
In the sweet recollection, to dwell time
    away.
As I sat amusing myself on the grass,
Oh, who should I spy but a fair Indian lass.

She walked up behind me, taking hold of
    my hand,
She said, "You are a stranger and in a
    strange land,
But if you will follow, you're welcome to
    come
And dwell in my cottage that I call my
    home."

My Mohea was gentle, my Mohea was kind.
She took me when a stranger and clothed
    me when cold.
She learned me the language of the lass of
    Mohea.

"I'm going to leave you, so farewell my dear.
The ship's sails are spreading and home I
    must steer."
The last time I saw her she was standing
    on the strand,
And as my boat passed her she waved me
    her hand.

Saying "when you have landed and with
    the one you love,
Think of pretty Mohea in the coconut
    grove."
I am home but no one comes near me nor
    none do I see,
That would equal compare with the lass of
    Mohea.

Oh, the girl that I loved proved untrue to me.
I'll turn my course backward far over the
    sea.
I'll turn my course backward, from this
    land I'll go free,
And go spend my days with the little
    Mohea.

Such songs add to the exotic and sexual, yet maternal and contradictorily virginal image of the Indian Princess, and are reminiscent of the contemporary white soldier's attachments to "submissive," "sacrificial," "exotic" Asian women.

As long as Indian women keep their exotic distance or die (even occasionally for love of Indian men), they are permitted to remain on the positive side of the image. They can help, stand by, sacrifice for, and aid white men. They can, like their native brothers, heal white men, and the Indian reputation as healer dominated the nineteenth century patent medicine business. In the ads for such medicines, the Indian woman appears either as a helpmate to her "doctor" husband or partner or as a healer herself. In several ads (and the little dime novels often accompanying the patent medicine products), she is the mysterious witch-healer. Thus, she shares in the Caucasian or European female's reputation for potential evil. The references here to power, knowledge, and sexuality remain on the good side of the image. In this incarnation, the Princess offers help in the form of medicine rather than love.

The tobacco industry also capitalized on the Princess' image, and the cigar-store figures and ads associated with the tobacco business replicate the Princess figures to sell its products. Cigar-store Princesses smile and beckon men into tobacco shops. They hold a rose, a bundle of cigars, or some tobacco leaves (a sign of welcome in the colonial days), and they smile invitingly with their Caucasian lips. They also sell the product from tobacco packages, and here, like some of the figures in front of the shops, Diana-like or more militant Minerva (Wonder-Woman)-like heroines offer the comforts of the "Indian weed." They have either the rounded, infantile, semi-naked (indicating innocence) bodies of Renaissance angels or the bodies and clothes of classical heroines. The Mother Goddess and Miss Liberty peddle their more abstract wares, as Indian Princesses, along with those of the manufacturer. Once again, the Princess comforts white men, and while she promises much, she remains aloof.

But who becomes the white man's sexual partner? Who forms liaisons with him? It cannot be the Princess, for she is sacrosanct. Her sexuality can be hinted at but never realized. The Princess' darker twin, the Squaw, must serve this side of the image, and again, relationships with males determine what the image will be. In the case of the Squaw, the presence of overt and realized sexuality converts the image from positive to negative. White men cannot share sex with the Princess, but once they do so with a real Indian woman, she cannot follow the required love-and-rescue pattern. She does what white men want for money or lust. In the traditional songs, stories, obscene jokes, contemporary literary works and popular and pictorializations of the Squaw, no heroines are allowed. Squaws share in the same vices attributed to Indian men—drunkenness, stupidity, thievery, venality of every kind—and they live in shacks on the edge of town rather than in a woodland paradise.

Here, Squaws are shamed for their relationships with white men, and the males who share their beds—the "squaw men"—or "bucks," if they are Indian—share their shame. When they live with Indian males, Squaws work for their lazy bucks and bear large numbers of fat "papooses." In one joke, a white visitor to a reservation sees an overburdened squaw with ten children hanging on her skirts. "Where's your husband?" the visitor demands. "He ought to be hung!" "Ugh," says the squaw, "pretty well-hung!" They too are fat, and unlike their Princess sisters, dark and possessed of cruder, more "Indian" features. When stories and songs describe relationships with white men,

Squaws are understood as mere economic and sexual conveniences for the men who— unlike John Smith or a "brave"—are tainted by association with her. Tale after tale describes the Indian whores, their alcoholic and sexual excesses with white trappers and hunters. A parody of the beautiful-maiden song, "Little Red Wing," speaks of her lewd sister who "lays on her back in a cowboy shack, and lets cowboys poke her in the crack." The result of this cowboy-squaw liaison is a "brat in a cowboy hat with his asshole between his eyes." This Squaw is dark, and squat, and even the cigar-store Indians show the changes in conception. No Roman sandals grace their feet, and their features are more "Indian" and "primitive" than even their male counterparts. The cigar-store squaws often had papooses on their backs, and some had corrugated places on their hips to light the store patrons' matches. When realities intrude on mythos, even Princesses can become Squaws as the text of the ragtime song, "On an Indian Reservation," illustrates.

A cigar-store figure.

An old chewing tobacco advertisement, mid-nineteenth century.

On an Indian reservation, far from home
   and civilization,
Where the foot of Whiteman seldom trod.
Whiteman went to fish one summer,
Met an Indian maid—a hummer,
Daughter of Big-Chief-Spare-the-rod.
Whiteman threw some loving glances, took
   this maid to Indian dances,
Smoked his pipe of peace, took chances
   living in a teepee made of fur.
Rode with her on Indian ponies, bought
   her diamond rings, all phonies,
And he sang these loving words to her:
Chorus:
   You're my pretty little Indian Napanee.
   Won't you take a chance and marry me.
   Your Daddy Chief, 'tis my belief,
   To a very merry wedding will agree.

True, you're a dark little Indian maid,
But I'll sunburn to a darker shade,
I'll wear feathers on my head,
Paint my skin an Indian red,
    If you will be my Napanee.
With his contact soon he caught her,
Soon he married this big chief's daughter,
Happiest couple that you ever saw.
But his dreams of love soon faded,
Napanee looked old and jaded,
Just about like any other squaw.
Soon there came papoose in numbers,
    redskin yells disturbed his slumbers,
Whiteman wonders at his blunders—now
    the feathers drop upon his head.
Sorry to say it, but he's a-wishing, that
    he'd never gone a-fishing,
Or had met this Indian maid and said:
Chorus:

The Indian woman is between a rock and a hard place. Like that of her male counterpart, her image is freighted with such ambivalence that she has little room to move. He, however, has many more modes in which to participate though he is still severely handicapped by the prevailing stereotypes. They are both tied to definition by relationships with white men, but she is especially burdened by the narrowness of that definition. Obviously, her image is one that is troublesome to all women, but, tied as it is to a national mythos, its complexity has a special piquance. As Vine Deloria points out in *Custer Died For Your Sins*, many whites claim kinship with some distant Indian Princess grandmother, and thus try to resolve their "Indian problem" with such sincere affirmations of relationship.[8]

Such claims make it impossible for the Indian woman to be seen as real. She does not have the power to evoke feeling as a real mother figure, like the black woman, even though *that* image has a burdensome negative side. American children play with no red mammy dolls. She cannot even evoke the

terror the "castrating (white) bitch" inspires. Only the male, with upraised tomahawk, does that. The many expressions which treat of her image remove her from consideration as more than an image. As some abstract, noble Princess tied to "America" and to sacrificial zeal, she has power as a symbol. As the Squaw, a depersonalized object of scornful convenience, she is powerless. Like her male relatives she may be easily destroyed without reference to her humanity. (When asked why he killed women and children at Sand Creek, the commanding general of the U.S. Cavalry was said to have replied, "nits make lice.") As the Squaw, her physical removal or destruction can be understood as necessary to the progress of civilization even though her abstracted sister, the Princess, stands for that very civilization. Perhaps the Princess had to be removed from her powerful symbolic place, and replaced with the male Uncle Sam because she confronted America with too many contradictions. As symbol and reality, the Indian woman suffers from our needs, and by both race and sex stands damned.

Since the Indian so much represents America's attachment to a romantic past and to a far distant nobility, it is predictable but horrible that the Indian woman should symbolize the paradoxical entity once embodied for the European in the Princess in the tower and the old crone in the cave. It is time that the Princess herself is rescued and the Squaw relieved of her obligatory service. The Native American woman, like all women, needs a definition that stands apart from that of males, red or white. Certainly, the Native woman needs to be defined as Indian, in Indian terms. Delightful and interesting as Pocahontas' story may be, she offers an intolerable metaphor for the Indian-White experience. She and the Squaw offer unendurable metaphors for the lives of Indian women. Perhaps if we give up the need for John Smith's fantasy and the trappers' harsher realities, we will find, for each of us, an image that does not haunt and perplex us. Perhaps if we explore the meaning of Native American lives outside the boundaries of the stories, songs, and pictures given us in tradition, we will find a more humane truth.

NOTES

1. "The Mother of Us All," *Kenyon Review* 24 (Summer 1962), 391–441.

2. See Jay B. Hubbell, "The Smith-Pocahontas Story in Literature," *The Virginia Magazine of History and Biography* 65 (July 1957), 275–300.

3. The many models, stereotypes and images operative for the Indian in Anglo-American vernacular culture are discussed in my dissertation, "The Only Good Indian: The Image of the Indian in Vernacular American Culture," Indiana University, 1973.

4. E. McClung Fleming, "Symbols of the United States; From Indian Queen to Uncle Sam," in Ray B. Browne et al., eds. *The Frontiers of American Culture* (Lafayette, IN: Purdue University Press, 1967), pp. 1–24; "The American Image As Indian Princess, 1765–1783." *Winterthur Portfolio* 2 (1968), 65–81.

5. For a summary of the philosophical backgrounds of the "Noble Savage" complex of beliefs and ideas, see Roy Harvey Pearce, *Savagism and Civilization: A Study of the Indian and the American Mind* (rpt. 1953, Baltimore: Johns Hopkins University Press, 1967). For references to folk motifs in Indo-European tradition, see Stith Thompson, *The Motif Index of Folk Literature*, 6 vols. (rpt. 1932–36, Bloomington, IN: Indiana University Press, 1955–58).

6. See Clare de Corbellier, "Miss America and Her Sisters: Personification of the Four Parts of the World," *Bulletin of the Metropolitan Museum of Art* 19 (1961), pp. 209–223; James Hazen Hyde, *L'Iconographie des quatre parties du monde dans les tapisseries de Gazette des Beaux Arts* (Paris: Beaux Arts, 1924).

7. Austin Fife and Francesca Redden, "The Pseudo-Indian Folksongs of the Anglo-Americans and French-Canadians," *The Journal of American Folklore* 67, no. 266 (1954), 381; Olive Wooley Burt, *American Murder Ballads and Their Stories* (rpt. 1958, New York: Citadel Press, 1964), pp. 146–49.

8. Vine Deloria, *Custer Died For Your Sins* (New York: Avon Books, 1968), p. 11.

GROWIN' UP ON THE REZ

Growin' up on the rez, just like a ghetto or hood cuz the man claims my people are always up to no good. but let me take you for a ride to my side. check out my people that's filled with red pride! and I gotta kick it down for them, no reason to
   pretend.
see, we're in it 'til the end. see I got their back and they got mine! this just happens to be our way
   of life.

and it couldn't be any other way see. cuz the man keeps trying to waste me, and my future, my present, my past. but you know we're good to go. we'll see who lasts longer, cuz we're coming much stronger!

they'll have to wonder when they feel our red thunder! we'll never die, we'll never ever fade away! and the rez makes damn sure we're here to stay.

(Hook)
we'll never die, we'll never ever fade away
we'll never die, we'll never ever fade away.
cuz that's life on the rez. cuz that's life on the rez!

Take a walk through my hood, looking around every single face is brown. and you know that it's damn good to be down. everything is all good it's all'ight! this here's the hood that made the
   Hiddesee.

and even though in the O—I'm without, when I hit the rez I'm back home without a doubt! and they claim what we got is negative. it's the system dissin' the way we live. cuz positive is what I see! cuz they know with the rez they can never get me! so I'll flow it out to the fools who dis our old ways, this is OUR old school, and OUR land and OUR ways and OUR laws! and you know that we'll fight the fight for the just cause! that's how it is, on the rez as long as we have it, yo we'll never be dead.

(Hook)
A red child is born, and you know we go on and on. can't stop until we're strong, like we were way back in
the days. Indian people have me amazed, we'll never
die, simply multiply
and we survived their attempted genocide!

and since we stood the test, my ancestors rest in peace.
and thank you for allowing me to survive with my red
pride. and for that WOR will never ever switch sides! cuz we got the rez and we got the people and that's stronger than the white man's evil. so don't fade my hood, cuz you know what? I think my people are just too damn good to be played out or fade out.
people like us were simply made to survive any situation given.
When you live your life on the rez, that's
how you live it. fool, see it's all good! and all the way live with our pride in our rez, you know we'll survive!

"Growing Up on the Rez." From WithOut Reservation, Native Rap Group. Lyrics by Chris La Marr. Reprinted by permission.

REPRISE/FORCED STERILIZATIONS
NATIVE AMERICANS
AND THE "LAST GASP OF EUGENICS"

Bruce E. Johansen

On the phone, during long marches, occupying federal surplus property, in court fighting for treaty rights—wherever Native activists

"Reprise/Forced Sterilizations: Native Americans and the 'Last Gasp of Eugenics,'" by Bruce E. Johansen, in *Native Americas* (Winter 1998), pp. 44–47. Reprinted by permission of Native Americas Journal.

gathered during the Red Power years of the 1970s—conversation inevitably turned to the number of women whose tubes were tied or ovaries removed by the Indian Health Service, a department of the U.S. government. This was, as one woman joked bitterly, a "fringe benefit of living in a domestic, dependent nation."

Communication spurred by activism provoked a growing number of Native American women to piece together an understanding of what amounted to a national eugenic policy, translated into social reality by copious federal funding. They organized Women of All Red Nations (WARN) at Rapid City, S. Dak., as Native women from more than 30 nations met and decided, among other things, that "truth and communication are among our most valuable tools in the liberation of our lands, people and four-legged and winged creations."

WARN and other women's organizations publicized the sterilizations, which were performed after pro-forma consent of the women being sterilized. Explanations sometimes were not offered in the women's languages, or followed threats that the women would die or lose welfare benefits if they had more children. At least two 15-year-old girls whose ovaries were removed were originally told that they were having their tonsils out.

The enormity of information on government-funded sterilizations had been compiled by Sally Torpy, a graduate student in history at the University of Nebraska at Omaha. Her thesis, "Endangered Species: Native American Women's Struggle for Their Reproductive Rights and Racial Identity, 1970s–1990s," which was defended during the summer of 1998, placed the sterilization campaign in the context of the eugenics movement.

No one knows, even today, exactly how many Native American women were sterilized during the 1970s. The General Accounting Office (GAO) provided one base for calculation, whose study covered only 4 of 12 Indian Health Service (IHS) regions from 1973 to 1976. Within that time frame, 3,406 Native American women were sterilized, according to the GAO.

Lehman Brightman, Lakota, who has devoted much of his life to this issue, including suffering a libel suit from doctors, provided another estimate. He estimated that 40 percent of Native American women and 10 percent of Native American men were sterilized during the decade. Brightman figures that number to be between 60,000 and 70,000 Native women sterilized during the decade.

According to Torpy, anecdotal evidence of the surge in sterilization began to accumulate as early as 1970. Torpy noted the case of Norma Jean Serena, Creek/Shawnee. Welfare caseworkers in Apollo, Pa., had removed Serena's daughter Lisa, 3, and son, Gary, 4, from her home before she underwent a tubal ligation after the birth of another son, Shawn, in 1970. One day after Shawn was removed to a foster home, Serena, emotionally battered by accusations from caseworkers that she was an unfit mother, signed consent forms for the surgery.

Three years later, with legal assistance from the Council of Three Rivers Indian Center in Pittsburgh, Serena sued Armstrong County for the return of her children from foster care. She also sued a number of area hospitals for damages related to her sterilization. A jury found that the children had been taken from her under false pretenses.

During the trial, Serena's attorneys questioned the evidence welfare caseworkers used to take her children and recommend Serena's sterilization. The main complaint seemed to have centered around Serena's black friends who visited her home, said neighbors who preferred to remain anonymous to protect their own children. One caseworker described Serena's apartment as "dirty and unkempt," and her children as "undernourished and dazed," unable to walk, speak or hold eating utensils. A doctor who examined the children shortly afterwards, however, found them "alert and in good health." According to Torpy, Serena was awarded $17,000 by a jury, and her children were ordered released to her. The Armstrong County child welfare bureaucracy stalled several months before returning the children, according to Torpy, and did so only after officials were confronted with a contempt-of-court citation.

In 1979, several doctors and a social worker were acquitted of having violated Serena's civil rights by taking part in her sterilization. The key issue was whether she had consented to the operation. Serena said she could not recall having signed a consent form; the attending physician said he had explained the operation to Serena and that he was convinced she understood him.

Another Torpy anecdote: A 26-year-old Native American woman entered the office of a Los Angeles physician in 1970 seeking a "womb transplant" because she had been having trouble getting pregnant. The doctor, who never asked the woman her name, told her that her ovaries had been removed. The [ovariectomy had been performed with the] hysterectomy, an operation that cannot be reversed. [These] had been performed under false pretenses. The woman, who was engaged to be married and had hoped to raise a family, was "devastated," Torpy said.

The last vestiges of legally sanctioned eugenics began to play out during the late 1960s, when concern about overpopulation became official federal policy—with massive spending to back it up—under President Richard Nixon's administration. Sterilization for the poor and minorities was officially sanctioned in 1970, and reservation populations became targets of a policy that was being advocated nationally, especially for poor and minority women. In 1969, the American College of Obstetricians and Gynecologists also relaxed its own restrictions on sterilizations.

In 1970, when the Indian Health Service initiated its 100 percent, federally funded sterilization campaign, the Department of Health, Education and Welfare (HEW) vastly accelerated programs that paid 90 percent of the costs to sterilize non-Native poor women, following enactment of the Family Planning Act

of 1970. The rate of sterilization for women as a whole in the United States jumped 350 percent in five years, according to Torpy's research.

Before 1969, the government banned the use of federal funds for sterilization, or abortion. Between 1969 and 1974, HEW increased its family planning budget from $51 million to more than $250 million, Torpy reported. HEW records reveal that between 192,000 and 548,000 women were sterilized each year between 1970 and 1977, compared to an average of 63,000 a year between 1907 and 1964, a period that included the zenith of the eugenics movement.

Torpy found that during 1977, Dr. R. T. Ravenholt, director of the U.S. Agency for International Development Office for Population Control, said the United States had hoped to sterilize 25 percent of the world's roughly 570 million fertile women. Ravenholt linked such control measures to the ". . . normal operation of U.S. commercial interests around the world." These statements were published in a news story in the *St. Louis Dispatch*.

During this wave of sterilizations, no other medical structure had the captive clientele of the IHS, however. "Native American women represented a unique class of victims among the larger population that faced sterilization and abuses of reproductive rights," Torpy wrote in her thesis. "They had, and continue to have, a dependent relationship with the federal government which has put them at greater risk. . . ."

Within half a decade, Indian Health Service doctors had sterilized so many reservation women that, according to Torpy, one Native American woman was sterilized for every seven babies born.

Outside of occasional anecdotal reports in a few major newspapers, the mainstream media generally ignored the wave of sterilizations as it was happening. The first large-audience, detailed description of the sterilizations was not published in the United States, but in Germany. Torpy tapped sources of information in small, specialized, often leftist or health-related journals of opinion that, taken together, sketched a history of the sterilization campaign. She credited Brightman and the International Indian Treaty Council and others, including Constance Redbird Pinkerton-Uri, Choctaw/Cherokee, for keeping the issue alive enough to spark the interest of Sen. James Abourezk of South Dakota. This led to a General Accounting Office report and congressional oversight hearings that eventually curbed the practice.

By 1974, IHS doctors who were critical of the sterilizations began their own investigation. Pinkerton-Uri, a physician and law student, started her own inquiry after Native patients lodged complaints against the Claremore, Okla., IHS hospital. Taking publicity about the Serena cases, what she found at Claremore, and other evidence, Pinkerton-Uri called Sen. Abourezk's office. The office had also received inquiries from Charlie McCarthy, an IHS employee in Albuquerque, N. Mex., regarding sterilizations of Native American women.

Torpy followed the trail of Abourezk's investigation, beginning with an intern in his office, Joan Adams, who took the initiative to investigate whether Native women were being sterilized "without their consent and under duress." This preliminary investigation convinced Adams, and, later, Abourezk, that further study was needed. Abourezk, using Adams' research, then called for a GAO investigation.

Torpy described the findings of the GAO report, which surveyed IHS records in one-third of the Bureau of Indian Affairs regions. The study covered 46 months, between 1973 and 1976. Within this sample, the GAO found evidence that the IHS or its contractors had sterilized 3,406 women, 3,001 of them of child-bearing age.

Since the GAO study did not even begin to arrive at a total number of sterilizations, opponents of the practice looked at the data in another way, as a percentage of the women of child-bearing age in each examined area who were sterilized. In Oklahoma, using the GAO study's numbers, 1,761 of roughly 17,000 women of child-bearing age were sterilized. In Phoenix, the number was lower, 78 of 8,000; in Aberdeen, the figure was 740 of 9,000. They began to make a case that, with only 100,000 fertile Native women of child-bearing age in the United States, the sterilizations put a significant dent in the gene pools of many individual Native American nations.

Regarding the threat to the Native American gene pool, Torpy quoted Pinkerton-Uri:

> A 200 million population could support voluntary sterilization and survive, but for Native Americans it cannot be a preferred method of birth control. While other minorities might have a gene pool in Africa or Asia, Native Americans do not; when we are gone, that's it.

At times, the battle over sterilization became localized and quite heated. In response to Pinkerton-Uri's charges against the Claremore Hospital, physicians threatened to close the facility. "In response," wrote Torpy, "an unidentified group of Native Americans erected a tipi on the hospital lawn alongside the American Indian Movement [AIM] flag."

By the mid-to-late 1970s, the sterilization program was well known on the Native movement circuit. By 1974, *Akwesasne Notes*, the major Native newspaper at the time, carried reports describing sterilizations, and Native American women's attempts to mobilize against them. As a doctoral student in Seattle who had become involved in Native American issues beginning with fishing rights, I requested an airing of the sterilization program in *The Nation*, the magazine that, in 1977, had allowed me to present the first nationally published account of Leonard Peltier's case. An editor at *The Nation* told me the magazine would publish the story only if I could supply a written statement from the IHS that genocide was its policy. No statement, the editor said, no story. I was unable to find such a tidy admission, although I could see a wave of sterilizations as I combined the GAO findings with case-study materials from my files.

By 1977, three Northern Cheyenne women had filed a class action suit in Montana. The names were not released publicly out of fear that the Cheyenne would condemn the three women. The class action suit never went to court, and never directly affected anyone other than the three claimants. Attorneys for the defendants offered a cash settlement on condition that the case remain sealed. The women accepted the settlement.

About the same time, Marie Sanchez, the Northern Cheyenne's chief tribal judge, conducted her own informal poll. Sanchez found that at least 30 women she contacted had been sterilized between 1973 and 1976. It was Sanchez who found the two 15-year-old girls who said they had been told they were having their tonsils out, only to emerge from a local IHS hospital without their ovaries.

Torpy's account brought what became a general pattern down to a personal level:

> Another woman who had complained to a physician about migraine headaches was told that her condition was a female problem, and was advised that a hysterectomy would alleviate the problem. Her headaches continued, however, until she was diagnosed with a brain tumor.

Also during 1977, the American Indian Policy Review Commission found that the IHS lacked adequate policies, appropriations, delivery services and oversight for provision of health services to Native Americans. Even in 1977, the rate of infant mortality on reservations was three times that of the general population in the United States; the tuberculosis rate was still eight times as high. The average life span of a Native American living on a reservation was 47 years, compared with almost 71 years in the general population. The IHS seemed to be short of personnel and equipment to treat many things, but the agency always had enough doctors, nurses, equipment and money to tie fallopian tubes and remove ovaries.

By the late 1970s, sterilizations continued at some IHS hospitals despite protests and suits. Brightman visited Claremore's IHS facility for six months during late 1978 and early 1979, collecting records, and found evidence of 81 sterilizations. Brightman later related his findings as part of a speech on the U.S. Capitol steps which was recorded and played for some of the Claremore nurses. According to Torpy those nurses "validated that sterilizations were occurring and with greater frequency."

Many Native women looked at the battle against sterilization as part of a broader, older, struggle to retain their families in a culturally appropriate context. The battle against sterilizations brought back memories of having children taken from their homes, beginning with the establishment of Carlisle Indian School at Carlisle, Pa., in 1879, and the gauntlet of forced assimilation in a factory model of education. By 1973, there were 33,672 Native American children living in federal boarding schools rather than at home, according to Torpy. In 1977, roughly one-third of reservation children still attended the same system of boarding schools that had become a principal part of the assimilative model of a century earlier.

Many women were also reminded of the Native children taken into foster care by non-Natives. In the mid-1970s, the proportion of Native children placed into foster care in Western states, compared to the general population, ranged from 640 percent in Idaho to 2,000 percent in North Dakota. This disparity was diminished, but not eliminated, by legislative measures in the 1980s that demanded social workers to appreciate Native ways of raising children.

On many reservations today, Native American midwives, or nurses, advise women on whether sterilization is appropriate. The number of births to Native women had risen to 45,871 in 1988, compared with 27,542 in 1975, according to census records cited in Torpy's thesis.

Although the cruder abuses of the sterilization wave in the 1970s seem to have abated, "Even today," wrote Torpy, "there remains a need for constant and close surveillance over physicians and health facilities so that all poor women and women of color are allowed to make their own reproductive choices."

INDIAN-NAMED MASCOTS:
AN ASSAULT ON SELF-ESTEEM

Tim Giago

It's shaping up to be quite a week. Two baseball teams with American Indian symbols and mascots are into the World Series, and the national media is giving the Indians a chance to respond.

This would not have happened five years ago.

Only in recent years, with the advent of a national forum and a national newspaper have the media doors finally opened to us.

My newspaper, *Indian Country Today,* started the campaign against Indians as mascots more than 13 years ago. My Knight Ridder-Tribune syndicated column opened more windows on the subject.

Out in Indian country some of the more than 20 Indian-operated radio stations have begun to use the airways to get across a point of view.

And yet, with all of this evidence that the majority of Indian people detest being used as mascots, the conservative *Arizona Republic* of Phoenix is still pushing the idea that Indians don't really care one way or the other. By referring to local Indian students—many of whom attend reservation schools with Indian symbols or names—the *Republic* is convinced this is a non-news subject.

Fact is, the Indian people operating or attending reservation schools with team names like Braves, Warriors or Chiefs do not act like your typical non-Indian sports fan.

They do not desecrate sacred Indian objects. They do not perform horrendous portrayals of what they suppose an Indian to be. They do not sing Hollywood war songs or make Hollywood whooping sounds just to prove they are Indian pretenders.

Indian reservation schools with Indian names treat their symbols and subject matter with respect and dignity.

If there is an Indian in America who can watch a Washington Redskin game or an Atlanta Braves game and see the actions of the mostly white, often inebriated sports fan, head adorned with turkey feathers, faces painted with streaks, and not feel insulted, they are not true Indians.

This morning, as I did a talk show for Wisconsin Public Radio, two callers made my day. They tuned in with the idea they were going to give me hell for questioning their right to behave as Indian mascots. After they listened and heard the other side of the story, they called to say they had changed their minds and they now understand why I feel the way I do about mascots.

It all boils down to self-esteem and self-respect.

Everything in life begins or ends with these two emotions. If we cannot respect ourselves or if we have low self-esteem, we turn to things that make us forget. Drugs and alcohol have been

Thom Little Moon. October 26, 1995. © Indian Country Today. Reprinted by permission.

the bane of Indian society. What's more, if the white society thinks of us as nothing more than mascots for their fun and games, they will not respect us on matters that are more important to our lives.

A few weeks back several parents watched a "Redskin" football game with their children at a reservation home. Shortly into the game the children became noticeably upset.

"Mom, why are those people acting crazy like that?" asked one child.

"Dad, why are those *wasicus* (white people) making fun of us?" said another.

"Mom, are all Indians bad people?" asked one six-year-old.

Sports fans just don't get it.

If even one Indian in America feels insulted by being used as a mascot, that should be enough. We don't have anything to prove, but we certainly have plenty to be angry about.

Sure, there are many important issues we need to address, but self-respect and self-esteem should be near the top of the list because without these two emotions firmly in tow, what else do we have?

So watch the World Series and have a good time. But, just for the moment of one game, put your feet into our moccasins.

Watch the red-painted faces. Watch the fanatics in the stands wearing turkey and chicken feathers in their hair. Watch the fools doing the tomahawk chop and singing that horrible chant.

Then picture that section of fans as people supporting a team called the African Americans. Imagine them doing the same things to black Americans as they are doing to Native Americans.

That's all I ask.

Just watch this spectacle and then put yourselves in our place just this once. If that doesn't register with you, nothing will.

Bigotry against one American is bigotry against all.

Self-respect and self-esteem: Give them back to the American Indian.

Is that so much to ask? After all, you have taken so much from us. Please return these two important things. America will be a better place if you do.

Editorial by Tim Giago, in *Indian Country Today,* October 26, 1995. Copyright 1995 by Indian Country Today. Reprinted with permission.

RENEGADES, TERRORISTS, AND REVOLUTIONARIES

THE GOVERNMENT'S PROPAGANDA WAR AGAINST THE AMERICAN INDIAN MOVEMENT

Ward Churchill

The bigger the lie, the more likely it is to be believed.
—Joseph Goebbels, Nazi Propaganda Minister

During the 1970s, the U.S. government conducted what amounted to a counterinsurgency war against the American Indian Movement. The campaign was designed to "neutralize" that organization's ability to pursue an agenda of Indian treaty rights, land recovery, and national sovereignty in North America. While many of the federal tactics took a directly physical form—assassinations, fabrication of evidence in criminal cases, and the like—a major propaganda effort was also integral to the government's strategy of repression. The motives for this lay not only in an official desire to deny AIM broad public support, but in a need to condition the citizenry to accept as "justified" the harsh and often extralegal nature of what authorities were otherwise doing to the group.

OPENING ROUNDS

The first substantial anti-AIM propaganda operation appears to have begun during the spectacular "Trail of Broken Treaties" occupation of the Bureau of Indian Affairs (BIA) building in Washington, D.C., on the eve of the 1972 presidential election. The incumbent Nixon administration, eager to avoid the impression of a serious "Indian uprising" at such a critical moment, went far out of its way to prevent statements by the occupiers from surfacing in the media. Simultaneously, it spent more than $100,000 importing selected "representative Indian spokesmen" to discredit the AIM leadership. A star performer in this regard was Webster Two Hawks, president of the federally sponsored National Tribal Chairmen's Association, who flamboyantly parroted the government line that AIM was composed of "renegades" and "irresponsible self-styled revolutionaries" who held no real standing in "Indian Country." Two Hawks's well-subsidized views were, of course, carried verbatim on national TV and splattered liberally across the front pages of the *Washington Post* and *New York Times*.

It is worth noting that Two Hawks, Nixon's hand-picked "leader" of American Indians, barely had time to return home to the Rosebud Reservation in western South Dakota before being unseated as tribal chairman by AIM supporter Robert Burnette. But by then federal media manipulators were at work against "the militants" even in this remote region. Solid evidence of this came on February 5, 1973, as AIM was organizing a demonstration at the Custer (S.D.) County Courthouse to protest the levying of mere manslaughter charges against a non-Indian who had brutally murdered a young Indian, Wesley Bad Heart Bull. On that date, an FBI agent impersonating an organizer called reporter Lyn Gladstone, causing a story stating the action had been cancelled to appear in the *Rapid City Journal*. Consequently, when AIM members showed up as planned at the courthouse the next day, very few supporters joined them. Few supporters at the scene meant few witnesses, and so when AIM was promptly attacked by a specially assembled force of riot police, "official spokesmen" were able to make it appear the other way around in the media.

WOUNDED KNEE

The ink was barely dry on the government's disinformation concerning "AIM violence" in Custer when federal forces laid siege to a group of organization members and supporters at Wounded Knee, on the nearby Pine Ridge Reservation. Contrary to the official line, immediately promulgated by the Justice Department and accepted by the press, that what was going on in the isolated hamlet was an "AIM occupation," the Indians had actually gone to Wounded Knee on the evening of February 27 in order to prepare for a press conference called for the following morning. Their purpose was to try and draw public attention to the corruption of Dick Wilson, the local tribal chairman, and the fact that federal authorities had blocked attempts by reservation residents to obtain even elementary due process in the matter. For instance. Wilson had been appointed by the BIA to preside over his own impeachment process, he had been funded to create a *de facto* private army calling itself the "GOON squad" with which to suppress his opposition, and a 65-man SWAT team of U.S. marshals had been sent to further back him up. Came the morning of February 28, the AIM group at Wounded Knee found itself completely surrounded by GOONs and marshals who were quickly reinforced by FBI. BIA police, non-Indian vigilante groups, and advisors from the army's élite 82nd Airborne Division.

Needless to say, the desired press conference never occurred. Instead, there began a 71-day confrontation during which numerous federal procedures were implemented by which to "regulate" (restrict) media access to those trapped inside the AIM perimeter. These rapidly manifested themselves in an outright barring of mainstream reporters from the scene of activity, and the issuance of threats of criminal prosecution to alternative press personnel who had essentially moved into Wounded Knee for the duration. "Press briefings" conducted by authorities were then substituted for direct coverage of what was happening. With this handy mechanism in place, the government was in a position to deliberately misrepresent reality in a number of ways. For example, when FBI agent Curtis Fitzpatrick was slightly wounded in the wrist by a spent rifle round on March 11, 1973, federal propagandists were able to arrange an extravaganza wherein reporters were allowed to witness his arrival at a nearby air force base in a military "med-evac" helicopter with his *head* swathed in bandages. Similarly, this eloquent (if utterly contrived) testament to "AIM violence" was still making the rounds nationally when federal "public relations officers" began announcing that individuals arrested for attempting to transport food and medical supplies into the AIM positions had actually been apprehended while smuggling "arms and ammunition." At one point, it was even announced that AIM was firing state-of-the-art M-60 machine guns at federal personnel despite the fact that the FBI was later revealed to have been fully aware that the Indians possessed no armaments other than an array of hunting rifles and shotguns.

In addition to allowing AIM to be tarred with the brush of fiction, barring the media from Wounded Knee allowed the government to cover up many of its own actions. For instance, the burning of several buildings inside the hamlet—widely attributed to AIM "vandalism"—was actually caused by the profuse use of heavy-calibre military tracer ammunition and the repeated firing of magnesium flares directly at the wooden structures. Nor was any mainstream reporter in a position to observe exactly who initiated the massive firefights—federal forces fired more than 500,000 rounds into Wounded Knee during the siege—which frequently lit up the nights. Or, to take another example, when AIM member Buddy Lamont was killed at Wounded Knee on April 27, no mention was made of the fact that he had bled to death because FBI commander Joseph Trimbach deliberately delayed his being placed in an ambulance for 45 minutes. Perhaps most importantly, a

steadily increasing intimacy between the FBI and the GOONs—with the former providing the latter with automatic weapons and stores of ammunition, military communications gear and other material support, as well as intelligence information and virtual immunity from prosecution—was also obscured.

THE "REIGN OF TERROR"

During the three years following Wounded Knee, more than 300 AIM members and supporters were physically assaulted on Pine Ridge. Of these, at least 69 died, giving the reservation a political murder rate precisely comparable to that prevailing in Chile during the three years immediately following the 1973 Pinochet coup. In virtually every instance, this "Third World" level of violence was plainly attributable to the GOONs, often on the basis of multiple eyewitness accounts. Yet the FBI—which held primary jurisdiction on the reservation, and which had thereon deployed the greatest concentration of agents to citizens in history—pled "lack of manpower" in solving or in most cases even investigating the homicides. Instead, despite the absence of casualties among the GOONs and police personnel, and the fact that the U.S. Commission on Civil Rights had formally concluded that the FBI and its GOON surrogate, rather than AIM, were fostering a "reign of terror" on Pine Ridge, Bureau publicists maintained a national media drumbeat proclaiming it was *AIM* which was "violence-prone." This aspect of the government's disinformation campaign culminated during the spring of 1975 when Douglass Durham, an FBI infiltrator/ *provocateur* who had worked himself into the position of AIM security chief, was allowed to testify as the sole witness before the Senate Committee on Internal Security. His uncorroborated, unsubstantiated, and in most cases utterly false testimony was then used as the basis for a widely disseminated official report branding AIM as a "revolutionary organization" committed to "the violent overthrow of the federal government."

At this juncture, FBI strategists appear to have felt that the public had been sufficiently conditioned to accept a final stroke which would physically destroy AIM once and for all. Hence, on June 26, 1975, two agents—Ron Williams and Jack Coler— were sent to an AIM compound located on the Harry and Cecilia Jumping Bull property, near the reservation village of Oglala. Ostensibly, the agents were attempting to arrest a seventeen-year-old AIM member named Jimmy Eagle on the charge of stealing a pair of used cowboy boots. Given that some 150 FBI and BIA SWAT personnel were prepositioned in the immediate area as "back up," it seems that Coler's and Williams's real mission was to provoke an armed confrontation which would justify the use of overwhelming force to crush the AIM encampment. In the event, having precipitated a firefight, the agents were cut off from their intended support. They, along with an AIM member named Joe Stuntz Killsright, were killed. The rest of the Indians escaped.

With their plan for a "quick kill" of AIM thus seriously off track, Bureau officials immediately rushed an additional 250 SWAT personnel to Pine Ridge. They also dispatched Tom Coll, a propaganda specialist, to "explain" why the FBI was suddenly conducting Vietnam-style search and destroy operations—complete with armored personnel carriers and attack helicopters—on an obscure South Dakota Indian reservation. The reason, according to Coll, was that the "terrorist American Indian Movement" had initiated "guerrilla warfare" on Pine Ridge. Agents Williams and Coler, he said, had been "lured into an ambush" where they were "attacked from a sophisticated bunker complex." After being wounded, he continued, they had been "dragged from their cars," "stripped," and "riddled with 15–20 bullets" apiece, the ammunition fired from "automatic weapons." In one account, they had also been "scalped." It had been "cold-blooded murder," said Coll, and agent Williams had been "executed" while lying on the ground "pleading with his killers to think of his wife and children."

None of this was true, as Coll knew at the time he fed it to the media. Each agent had been hit only three times, and from long rather than close range. The fabled "bunkers" were actually old root cellars and animal shelters—common to any rural area—which had *not* been used as AIM positions during the firefight. There was no evidence that AIM had utilized automatic weapons. Neither agent had been stripped, scalped, or otherwise mutilated. Far from being "lured" to the firefight site, the agents had been sent there by their own superiors. Still, it was nearly a week before FBI director Clarence Kelley openly admitted these facts, and by then a wave of sensational headlines and TV "news" reports had firmly established a public sentiment supporting the Bureau in its massive campaign of kicking in the doors of reservation houses, conducting "air assaults" on the properties of known AIM supporters, and generally terrorizing the entire reservation population. Even a few of the GOONs are known to have protested what was going on at this point, but under such circumstances the FBI was able to continue its invasion of Pine Ridge for three solid months without appreciable public outcry.

END GAME MOVES

It would probably be fair to say that the capstone of the federal propaganda war on AIM came a year later, in June of 1976, during the trial of Bob Robideau and Dino Butler in the deaths of Williams and Coler. In a bald attempt to influence the jury (and the public at large) against the defendants, the FBI suddenly announced that it had evidence that a force of "2,000 AIM warriors" known as "Dog Soldiers" and "trained in the Northwest" were about to arrive in South Dakota. Once there, they planned to "kill a cop a day . . . burn farmers . . . snipe at tourists . . . assassinate the governor . . . blow up the Bureau of Indian Affairs . . . blow up turbines at the Ft. Randall Dam . . . and destroy Mt. Rushmore National Monument," among other things. The "Dog Soldier Teletypes," as the FBI communiques quickly became known, also contended that this AIM activity was part of a multiracial venture in terrorism, planned jointly with a Denver-based Chicano group known as the Crusade for Justice, and Students for a Democratic Society (SDS; a long-defunct white radical organization). The information again brought on splashy headlines nationally, a situation which lasted until FBI director Kelley was cross-examined under oath by Butler/ Robideau defense attorney William Kunstler. When asked whether there was a "shred of evidence" to support the allegations trumpeted in his Bureau's teletypes, Kelley responded: "I know of none." The jury ultimately acquitted Butler and Robideau of the murder charges brought against them on the basis that they had killed the two FBI agents in self-defense. Nonetheless, the misimpression of AIM as a bunch of renegades,

terrorists, and revolutionaries had once again been deliberately inculcated among the general public. Cumulatively, the combination of sustained physical hammering, judicial railroading, and persistent public misrepresentation had proven sufficient to enable the government to attain its objective of neutralizing most of AIM's political effectiveness.

CONCLUSION

As Malcolm X once put it, "If you're not careful, the newspapers will have you hating the people who are being oppressed, and loving the people who are doing the oppressing." Certain particularities notwithstanding, the experience of the American Indian Movement as a domestic target of federal propaganda is hardly unique. As Malcolm knew, entirely comparable disinformation campaigns were being conducted during the early '60s, not only against the Nation of Islam, but also against groups such as the Student Nonviolent Coordinating Committee, Socialist Workers Party, and the Fair Play for Cuba Committee. By the latter part of the decade, the list had been expanded to include organizations such as the Revolutionary Action Movement, Black Panther Party, Young Lords Party, Student Mobilization, and SDS. During the '70s, the Weather Underground, prison liberation movement and Black Liberation Army were targeted. More recently, we see the same tactics employed to varying extents against entities like the Palestine Solidarity Committee, Silo Plowshares, CISPES, and *Puertorriqueño Independentista* formations such as *los Macheteros* and the FALN. In this sense, the government's anti-AIM propaganda effort can serve as something of a textbook illustration of a much wider technique of political repression.

FREE LEONARD PELTIER

Steve Talbot

Since 1977 Ojibway/Lakota Indian Leonard Pelti-er has been serving two consecutive life sentences in a federal prison for "aiding and abetting" the deaths of two FBI agents in a firefight on the Pine Ridge Reservation in 1975. Yet, there is no credi-ble evidence that Peltier fired the fatal shots, and the case has all the earmarks of a political frame-up; he is imprisoned falsely and solely for his de-fense of Indian treaty rights. Peter Worthington, a former publisher of the *Toronto Sun,* writes that Peltier "was railroaded into prison with the use of fabricated and manipulated and suppressed evi-dence." Subsequent to his imprisonment, Amnesty International became convinced that he had received an unfair trial. It listed Peltier as "a prisoner of conscience" and is now calling for Leonard's im-mediate and unconditional release. The European Parliament passed a resolution in February of 1999 calling for his release, and Labor MP Tony Benn in-troduced a motion in the British Parliament calling for all means of diplomatic pressure in support of Executive Clemency. A similar motion was intro-duced to the French Parliament.

It is now almost six years since former Attorney General Ramsey Clark filed a brief for Executive Clemency, a process which should have taken six to nine months. This earlier request for Execu-tive Clemency was endorsed by 55 members of the U.S. Congress, 60 members of the Parliament of Canada, 202 members of the European Parliament, Archbishop Desmond Tutu, Nobel Prize recipient Rigoberta Menchu Tum, President Nelson Mandela of South Africa, the Reverend Jesse Jackson, and Mother Teresa. His release is now also supported by the Kennedy Memorial Center for Human Rights, the Dalai Lama, and the Archibishop of Canterbury, among many others.

On a June morning in 1975, in a remote corner of the Pine Ridge Reservation near Wounded Knee, there was a fatal shoot-out in which two FBI agents and an American Indian died. The death of the Indian went uninvestigated, but the deaths of the agents inspired one of the biggest manhunts in FBI history. More than 150 armed agents in a shoot-first-ask-questions-later search swarmed over the poverty-stricken land of the Oglala Lakota Indians. Eventual-ly, four members of the American Indian Movement (AIM) were indicted on murder charges. One was later released for insufficient evidence, and two oth-ers were acquitted after a jury found that they had fired in self-defense. The fourth was Leonard Peltier.

Peltier was in charge of an AIM self-defense team of Indian warriors who sought to protect Lakota elders and their families from the assault by feder-al and vigilante forces that raged out of control fol-lowing the stand-off at Wounded Knee in 1973. In the months following Wounded Knee, dozens of AIM members and their supporters were killed or "disappeared," and the FBI, which is federally responsible for investigating homicides on Indian reservations, did nothing. Furthermore, new evi-dence now suggests that the FBI itself was indirectly involved in these murders of Oglala citizens.

In March 1996, the U.S. Parole Commission again denied parole to Peltier, even though the pre-siding parole officer had made a favorable recom-mendation for a retrial or parole based on the fact that no direct evidence exists against Peltier. He is not eligible for a rehearing until the year 2008, which is 17 years in excess of the commission's ap-plicable guidelines and six years after the date set by Congress for the abolition of the Parole Com-mission itself. The matter now rests with the U.S. Attorney General and President Clinton. The pres-ident can override the decision of the Parole Com-mission by granting Leonard Peltier an executive pardon. The year 1999 saw a redoubling of effort to free the imprisoned activist. Leonard is now 55 years of age and in deteriorating health. November 1999 was declared "Freedom Month for Leonard Peltier," and supporters protested in front of the U.S. White House and throughout the world. The National Congress of American Indians and the Assembly of First Nations in Canada joined with the Leonard Peltier Defense Committee in call-ing on President Clinton to grant clemency.

The late U.S. Representative Joe Kennedy summed up the case with the following words: "This government has the moral duty to correct this injustice. Seeing that justice is upheld for Leonard Peltier would amount to a major act of reconciliation for past injustices done to Native American peoples." Noted author Peter Matthiessen, whose book *In the Spirit of Crazy Horse* (1983) is the most authoritative account of the Peltier case, makes this telling comment: "The ruthless persecution of Leonard Peltier had less to do with his own actions than with underlying issues of history, racism, and economics. . . . Leonard Peltier's experience reflects more than most of us wish to know about the realities of Indian existence in America." Perhaps Leonard himself, in his book *Prison Writings: My Life Is My Sun Dance* (p. 203), has said it best:

This is the twenty-third year of my imprisonment for a crime I did not commit. . . . I can tell you this. We don't ask for vengeance, or even want it. I set aside all accusations because I know all too well what it is to be the accused. I set aside all condemnations because I know all too well what it is to be the condemned. We seek not revenge but reconciliation and mutual respect

among our peoples. We may be of different nations, but we are still of the same society, and we share the same land. We all want justice, equality, fairness . . . the very principles on which America is founded and by its own Constitution supposedly bestows on all within its borders, even Indians. Is that too much to ask?

Leonard Peltier, *Prison Writings: My Life Is My Sun Dance*, ed. Harvey Arden (St. Martin's Press, 1999). Compiled from the following sources: Jane Ayers, "Leonard Peltier Should Be Freed," Open Forum, *San Francisco Chronicle*, June 5, 1996; Peter Mathiessen, *In the Spirit of Crazy Horse* (New York: Viking Press, 1983); Jim Messerschmidt, *The Trial of Leonard Peltier* (New York: South End Press, 1983); Amnesty International U.S.A., "Prisoner Profile: Leonard Peltier," n.d.; Peter Worthington, "Commentary on Peltier—Still in Prison, and Still Innocent," *News From Indian Country* (Mid-April, 1996); Bruce Johansen, "Will Clinton Pardon Him? Leonard Peltier's Continuing Bid for Freedom," *Native Americas*, 14, no. 3 (Fall 1997): 55–57; "Peltier! International Pressure Mounts for Native America's Mandela," *AIM 4 Awareness* (Double Issue: Spring/Summer 1999): 11; Leonard Peltier Defense Committee, P.O. Box 583, Lawrence, Kans. 66044.

PART REVIEW

DISCUSSION QUESTIONS

Vine Deloria Jr., *Mythical Pleistocene Hit Men*
1. What is the theory of Pleistocene overkill, and what does it have to do with Native Americans?
2. Summarize Deloria's criticism of this theory from a Native American perspective.

Rayna Green, *The Pocahontas Perplex*
1. Outline the origin and development of the Pocahontas perplex in the national literature and art of the United States.
2. Discuss the meaning and function of the "Indian squaw" image and its relationship to the "Indian princess" stereotype.

WOR, *Growin' Up on the Rez*
1. Reservations are ususally viewed negatively by non-Native Americans. In what ways does the Indian rap artist view the reservation in a positive light?

Bruce E. Johansen, *Reprise/Forced Sterilizations*
1. Describe the nature and extent of sterilization of Indian women in the United States during

the 1970s. Why is sterilization a source of concern to the Native American community?
2. What does the author mean by the subtitle the "last gasp of eugenics"?

Tim Giago, *Indian-Named Mascots*
1. Why does the editorial writer find Indian-named sports mascots demeaning?
2. Were you aware that the subject of Indian-named mascots is a volatile issue in Indian country? Having read the material presented in this box, have you changed your opinion?

Ward Churchill, *Renegades, Terrorists, and Revolutionaries*
1. What was the purpose of the U.S. government's propaganda war against the American Indian Movement, and how was it manifested during the 1972 Trail of Broken Treaties protest in Washington, D.C., and at Wounded Knee in 1973?
2. During the "reign of terror" on the Pine Ridge Reservation following the Wounded Knee protest, there was an exchange of gunfire in

which an Indian man and two FBI agents were killed. How did the Federal Bureau of Investigation portray this event to the public media, and what, according to the author, is the truth of the matter?

Steve Talbot, *Free Leonard Peltier*

1. Who is Leonard Peltier, and what is the political significance of his legal case to Native Americans?

KEY TERMS

American Indian Movement (AIM)
Courts of Indian Offenses
ethnocide
eugenics
goon squad
herbivore megafauna
Indian sports mascots
institutional or structural discrimination
Peltier, Leonard

Pleistocene overkill
Pocahontas perplex
prejudice
prisoner of conscience
the Rez
stereotype
sterilization
Wounded Knee (1973)

SUGGESTED READINGS

BERKHOFER, ROBERT, JR. *The White Man's Indian: Images of the American Indian from Columbus to the Present.* New York: Vintage Books, 1978.

BRAND, JOHANNA. *The Life and Death of Anna Mae Aquash.* Toronto: James Lorimer & Company, 1978.

BURGOS-DUBRAY, ELISABETH, ed. *I, Rigoberta Menchú: An Indian Woman in Guatemala.* Trans. Ann Wright. New York: Verso, 1984.

CHARTRAND, PAUL. "'Terms of Division': Problems of 'Outside Naming' for Aboriginal People of Canada." *Journal of Indigenous Studies,* 2, no. 2 (Summer 1991): 1–22.

CHURCHILL, WARD. *Indians Are Us? Culture and Genocide in Native North America.* Monroe, Maine: Common Courage Press, 1994.

HARJO, SUSAN SHOWN. "Chief Offenders." *Native Americas,* 12, no. 4 (Summer 1999): 34–37.

HINTON, LEANNE. "Ishi's Brain." *News from Native California* (Fall 1999): 4–9.

MATTHIESSEN, PETER. *In the Spirit of Crazy Horse.* New York: Viking Press. 1983.

MARCUS, ALAN RUDOLPH. *Relocating Eden: The Image and Politics of Inuit Exile in the Canadian Arctic.* (Hanover, N.H.: University Press of New England, 1995.

MOHAWK, JOHN. "Epilogue: Looking for Columbus. Thoughts on the Past, Present and Future of Humanity." Pages 439–444 in *The State of Native America: Genocide, Colonization, and Resistance.* Ed. M. Annette Jaimes. Boston: South End Press, 1992.

Native Voices Public Television, Montana State University. *Without Reservations: Notes on Racism in Montana.* A film by Dave Wheelock et al.

NORTON, JACK. *Genocide in Northwestern California: When Our Worlds Cried.* San Francisco: Indian Historian Press, 1979.

PELTIER, LEONARD. *Prison Writings: My Life Is My Sun Dance.* Ed. Harvey Arden. New York: St. Martin's Press, 1999.

ROSENSTEIN, JAY. ed. *In Whose Honor?* Video documentary on American Indian mascots in sports. New Day Films, © 1997.

STEDMAN, RAYMOND WILLIAM. *Shadows of the Indian: Stereotypes in American Culture.* Norman: University of Oklahoma Press, 1982.

STILMAN, JANET. "Enough Is Enough." In *Aboriginal Women Speak Out.* Toronto: Women's Press, 1987.

THORNTON, RUSSELL. *American Indian Holocaust and Survival: A Population History Since 1492.* Norman: University of Oklahoma Press, 1987.

WEINBERG, BILL. "Requiem for Big Mountain: The Road to Relocation Is Unrelenting." *Native Americas,* 14, no. 3 (Fall 1997): 30–39.

WRONE, DAVID R., and RUSSELL S. NELSON JR., eds. *Who's the Savage? Documentary History of the Mistreatment of the Native North Americans.* Greenwich, Conn.: Fawcett Publications, 1973.

V

ALL MY RELATIONS: FAMILY AND EDUCATION

Indian Education Blues
Ed Edmo

I sit in your
crowded classrooms
& learn how to
read about dick,
jane & spot
but

    I remember
    how to get a deer

    I remember
    how to do beadwork

    I remember
how to fish

I remember
the stories told by the old

but

    spot keeps
    showing up
    &

        my report card
        is bad

The Apache Indians say that a rich person is one who has many relatives. This philosophy epitomizes the Indian world throughout the Americas: an indigenous person always positions himself or herself in a nexus of kin relationships.

For the Siouxan Indians of the United States, the ties that bind each one to another are composed of five interlocking social units: *otonwe, ospaye, ti-ospaye, wico-tipi,* and *ti-ognaka.*[1] The Western, or Teton, Sioux are the principal otonwe. They, in turn, are divided into Seven Council Fires, or divisions, the Oglala being the main ospaye of these. The ospaye are further divided into seven tipi-divisions, or bands, and each of these ti-ospaye is composed of one or more camps, or wico-tipi. Finally, each camp is made up of two or more ti-ognakapi (husbanded-tipis). The Mohawk can always find clan relatives (Deer, Turtle, Snipe, and so on) among any of the other five Iroquoian nations. If a traditional Dineh (Navajo) young man encounters a Dineh woman he fancies, he must find out her clan. If it turns out that they are of the same clan, then they are considered "brother" and "sister," and all thoughts of romantic love must be put aside. In fact, when one Indian meets another Indian, it is traditional that she or he gives a family name and a village or tribal affiliation or both. These last names, whether from an original Indian language or of European derivation, are well known to other tribal members and even to many Indians of other tribes. The new person can be located spatially in terms of tribal origin and often even genealogically. Indeed, the bonds of consanguinity remain strong in Indian country, whether one resides in a small Indian community or a large metropolitan area.

One is also related to the natural world. Christianity, which is derived from European peoples, ends prayer with "Amen," but Lakota Indians say "All My Relations," because all creatures great and small are one's brothers and sisters. In fact, as an extension of this kin principle of respect and mutual obligations, an underlying philosophical principle of many Indian cultures is that "the earth is our mother."

The family and child-bearing roles of women are highly valued in traditional Indian society, and women hold special spiritual power in terms of creating and balancing life in both the human and natural worlds. Author-poet Paula Gunn Allen (Laguna Pueblo/Sioux) contends that most North American Indian societies were originally women-centered, or gynocentric (see Suggested Readings). Among some indigenous nations, such as the traditional Iroquois, clan mothers hold an executive function in which they both choose and remove male clan chiefs and advise them in their decisions. Despite European-imposed laws and policies supporting patriarchy, women continue to play a central role in the Indian family and, often, in tribal political life and community affairs as well.

Elders, too, are revered. *grandmother, grandfather, aunt,* and *uncle* are terms not only of endearment but also of respect. Among most Indian peoples throughout the Western Hemisphere it is a common practice to address persons of older generations by these kinship terms, even when they are not blood kin. For example, one would respectfully address a non-blood-related person of one's grandparents' generation as "Grandfather," or "*Abuelo.*" Or a non-blood-related person of one's parents' generation might address a younger person as "nephew" or "niece." By inference, such non-blood-related persons become as kin.

Many Native peoples practice adoption. The Iroquois Indians in earlier times routinely replaced dead or killed members by adopting enemies taken in battle. The nineteenth-century Apaches raided Spanish settlements for captured women and children whom they then made their own. Ritual adoption, or *Hunka,* is still a solemn custom for the Lakota, who regard such "relatives" as even closer than blood kin. One of the emotionally traumatic events for the Lakota was when they were forced to give up their white relatives by U.S. authorities at the close of the nineteenth century after they were reduced to the status of captured nations under the reservation system.

The Indian extended family was the center of assimilationist attack during the worst years of federal assault on Indian culture, from the 1880s until the 1930s. The Christian mission school and the federal boarding school were designed to "kill the Indian but save the man," a form of cultural genocide. If the ties to the family, the primary socialization institution for tribal culture, could be broken, so the assimilationists reasoned, then Indian children would grow up "white" and the "Indian problem" would be solved. Following this line of reasoning, in the early years federal Indian agents in the United States, backed up by the reservation police, made raids on Indian communities to force children to attend boarding schools. The Sioux medicine man John (Fire) Lame Deer recalls that the worst threat that his grandparents could say to make him behave as a child was "Shh, *wasicun anigni kte*" ("be quiet or the white man will take you away").[2]

The film *Where the Spirit Lives* vividly portrays the tragic consequences of this system in Canada's residential schools, where Indian children were seized by the Indian agents and parceled out to the various Christian mission schools (see Suggested Readings). The Anglican Church ran twenty-six of the church-operated residential schools for native children throughout Canada, beginning in the 1800s and continuing into the late 1980s. In 1999, Floyd Mowatt, a former resident of one of these schools won a court case in his suit against the Anglican Church and the Canadian government for sexual abuse that took place as recently as the early 1970s. In a 106-page ruling, British Columbia's highest court found both parties "jointly liable" for assaults that included fondling, oral sex, and sodomy upon Mowatt and several other boys.

The brutal treatment and military discipline in these schools contrasted dramatically with the personal freedom and love that Indian children traditionally received at home, and this negative treatment resulted in severe mental and emotional problems. That sexual abuse was not uncommon in a number of these schools may account for some of the pathology of child abuse (virtually unknown in the past) found in today's generation of Indian families. For many years, attending boarding schools was the only way American Indians could get a high school education, such as it was. They were not allowed in California's public schools until 1935, and as recently as 1955, 81 percent of Navajo children were in boarding schools. Boarding schools were the defining experience for generations of Native Americans. One of the unexpected consequences, however, was the thousands of intertribal marriages that produced generations of "mixed-tribal" Indian people. Although Indian boarding and day school conditions have improved in recent years, many Indian children continue to be "adopted out." *Indian Country Today* reports that in both Canada and the United States, from the 1950s to the 1980s, 35 to 40 percent of all Native children were placed in foster care, adoptive homes, or similar non-Indian institutions.

In the first selection in this part, Wilma Mankiller, recent past Principal Chief of the Cherokee Nation in Oklahoma, explains the deep cultural significance of personal names and that of her own genealogical heritage in Cherokee culture and history. (The Cherokees have the largest indigenous population of any Native American peoples in the United States.) She also recounts the evolution of Sequoyah Training School, which started out as an orphan asylum, then became an asylum for Indian people with severe mental or physical problems, then a federal boarding school, and finally, today, a high school. Sequoyah was the famed Cherokee intellectual who is widely credited for devising a writing system that led to Cherokee literacy in the early 1820s. (Frequently overlooked is the fact that he was later treacherously killed by U.S. authorities when returning from a trip to Mexico.)

Deanna Kingston is an Inupiaq Eskimo anthropologist who has been documenting the stories, songs, and dances of her people, the King Island Inupiaq of the Bering Strait in Alaska. In the second selection in this part, she describes the ways in which Inupiaq people continue to maintain their traditions and cultural identity, even when they are living and rearing families in the Lower 48, away from King Island. Kingston, herself, grew up in Oregon. Nevertheless, one of the mechanisms by which she and her cross-cousin (mother's brother's children, or father's sister's children) continue to claim their identity as Inupiaq people is to engage in the practice of a "teasing" or "joking" relationship. She explains that teasing cousins engage in behavior designed to embarrass one another, but they are not to be offended or to get angry at one another when teased, because "if a person misbehaved or acted inappropriately, it was the teasing cousin's job or tell him to change his behavior." Teasing relationships, which are frequently found among indigenous peoples as an alternative to the coercive institutions of police forces and prisons, illustrate the function of kinship in the socialization and control of members of the social group.

The interview of Jeanette Armstrong (Okanagan) by Dagmar Thorpe (Sac and Fox) explores the concept of traditional Indian education in Okanagan culture as opposed to education in mainstream educational institutions. Before the 1960s "new Indian" movement, Indian young people attending white-run schools and colleges all too often ended up not only poorly trained and educated but also left in deep cultural conflict and psychological confusion. This kind of "education" for Native Americans resulted in marginalized persons who were not accepted or at ease in either the Indian or the non-Indian world. The growing political awareness and cultural revitalization that occurred in the 1960s and 1970s, however, placed a positive emphasis on retaining Indian traditions (including family), religion, and language. Indian individuals who retain a knowledge of their culture and have a positive Indian self-image are more likely to achieve educational success in both Indian and mainstream institutions than are Indian individuals who are not knowledgeable about their culture or who have a poor self-image.

Armstrong particularly takes note of the Okanagan educational tradition of democratic consensus making, in which every community member has a voice and is respectfully listened to. This is known as the *enow'kin* process. A second "educational" principle is what she calls the "Okanagan spirit." This spirit, or reinforcing of social solidarity, takes place not only in religious ceremonies and in secular events such as pow-wows and festivals but also in everyday, routine events. The spiritual leaders say that "any time people can pull together to do something, make or build something, to pool together to make something happen . . . This is what pulls our people together spiritually." Tim Giago, former editor of *Indian Country Today,* further explores this theme in the box titled "Reservation Schools Fail to Assimilate All Students."

In the fourth selection, Mary Brave Bird (Crow Dog), a Lakota Indian, recounts her experience in an old-fashioned, Catholic mission school during the 1960s. The contrast between the love and permissiveness that surround Indian children in the bosom of their family and the sterile, harsh discipline of the boarding school, whether religious or public, is startlingly traumatic. Indian children as young as six years of age were taken from their families and sent hundreds, sometimes thousands, of miles away to boarding schools. Some never saw their families again until they were in their twenties. Steve Talbot recalls an Indian friend whose younger brother, when sent to the same boarding school that Mary Brave Bird attended, was so traumatized that he blanked out for more than a week and had to be dressed, fed, and led around by his older sibling. To this day, the younger brother has no memory of this period. Indian children who were never physically punished at home were often brutalized in these schools, as was the case in Mary Brave Bird's experience.

Brave Bird points out, also, the exploitation of Indian child labor that routinely took place under this system in the name of "saving the Indian" by white do-gooders and the forced acculturation that led Indian youth to become "caricatures of white people . . . neither wanted by whites nor by Indians." The resulting marginality and damaged self-image often contributed to alcoholism among those who attended boarding schools in their youth.

In the fifth selection, Susan Lobo describes an American Indian preschool and after-school program, *Hintil Kuu Ca* (Indian children's house), that was organized in the early 1970s by concerned Indian parents in conjunction with the Oakland Public School System. Later, Hintil expanded to include a kindergarten group, after-school programs for first through sixth grade, and tutoring. Key features of Hintil are the involvement of Indian teachers and the Indian community and an emphasis on Indian values and cultural materials. The Indian children "graduating" from Hintil into the higher grades have had a lower dropout rate and better educational success than their non-Hintil predecessors. Not the least of the preschool's accomplishments has been the education of school authorities and the non-Indian community regarding the presence, cultural traditions, and special needs of Oakland's Indian schoolchildren. Before Hintil, when a teacher, as is commonly done, asked students to tell the national heritage of their parents or grandparents, Indian children were often informed that, no, they could not be American Indian because there are no more Indians left today (or because the children in their classes did not fit their stereotype of what an Indian is supposed to look like). The "invisibility" of Indians as an urban minority has been lessened as a result of Indian-initiated efforts such as Hintil. Another type of Indian-centered school is described in the box titled "Survival Schools."

In the last selection, Jeffrey Wollock, research director of the Solidarity Foundation, traces the historical development of Indian higher education in the United States: the founding in 1879 of the Indian boarding school system under Richard Henry (Colonel) Pratt; the Indian Allotment Act period and the assimilationist (cultural genocide) phase of the first quarter of the twentieth century led by the Society of American Indians and other "friends of the Indian"; the early attempt by Carlos Montezuma to develop an Indian university; the New Deal reforms in Indian education under the 1934 Indian Reorganization Act; the impact of the G.I. Bill after World War II; the new attempts to reform Indian education in the 1950s; the heightened struggle that emerged during the 1960s Great Society and the "new Indian" movement, which included the efforts of the National Indian Youth Council, among others; the Tribally Controlled Community College Assistance Act, passed in 1978; and the many Native American Studies departments and programs found in colleges and universities today. (See the map of Tribal Colleges.)

The tribal community college story is both a hopeful and, at the same time, a tragic one. A major feature of the tribal colleges that distinguishes them from non-Indian institutions of higher learning is the integration of tribal heritage and traditions into the curriculum. The Indian family, kin network, and community are integrated into the program and operations of the college. All of the current tribal colleges have adopted this practice. In contrast, in 1989, the Carnegie Foundation for the Advancement of Teaching investigated the current status of the tribal colleges and, although finding them to be a real success story, concluded that their main problem was the lack of adequate funding.[3] Students range in age from 17 to 70, and over 80 percent live below the poverty line with annual per capita incomes between $1,300 and $5,000. Most are first-generation college students who live on reservations and have to travel great distances under difficult circumstances to attend classes.[4] Although the tribal community colleges are among the most successful community colleges in the nation, they are at the same time shockingly underfunded. Whereas the Tribally Controlled Community College Assistance Act of 1978 authorized Congress to spend $5,820 per student, the actual amount budgeted is now less than $3,000. By contrast, the average community college in the United States gets $4,600 a year in federal and local aid for each student. Non-Indian community colleges enjoy both federal and local financial support, but the tribal colleges are dependent almost entirely on federal dollars. In 1999, with the biggest federal surplus in U.S. history, Congress was still stonewalling in underwriting the tribal community colleges: the Senate approved only $1.5 million of the recommended $6.4 million in extra money for the badly underfunded tribal colleges, and the House voted no extra money at all.

Most of the tribal colleges are located in the Northern Plains states of Montana, North Dakota, and South Dakota. Both Sinte Gleska (Rosebud Reservation) and Oglala Lakota (Pine Ridge Reservation) have four-year programs, and the former now offers a master's degree in education. D-Q University, located near Sacramento, California, is unique in that it is intertribally sponsored rather than tribally sponsored. One positive feature of D-Q University is its close cooperation with the well-established Department of Native American Studies at the nearby University of California–Davis. Two of the community college's key founders, David Risling (Hupa) and Jack D. Forbes (of Powhatan-Renape and Delaware-Lenape background), were also founders of Native American Studies at UC-Davis. The Indian tribal colleges are producing some of Indian country's finest new leadership.

NOTES

1. James R. Walker, *Lakota Society,* ed. Raymond J. DeMallie (Lincoln: University of Nebraska Press, 1982), 3–4.

2. John (Fire) Lame Deer and Richard Erdoes, *Lame Deer, Seeker of Visions* (New York: Pocket Books, Simon & Schuster, 1972), 22.

3. *Tribal Colleges: Shaping the Future of Native America,* with a foreword by Ernest L. Boyer. (New York: Carnegie Foundation for the Advancement of Teaching, 1989).

4. Statistics from a fund appeal letter of the American Indian College Fund, 21 West 68th St., Suite 1F, New York, N.Y. 10023.

ASGAYA-DIHI

Wilma Mankiller and Michael Wallis

Native Americans regard their names not as mere labels, but as essential parts of their personalities. A native person's name is as vital to his or her identity as the eyes or teeth. There is a common belief that when a person is injured, her name is maligned, just as she might be bruised when in an accident.

Throughout Native American history, there was often a need to conceal one's name. This is probably why Powhatan and Pocahontas are known in history under assumed identities, their true names having been hidden from whites so that their names could not be demeaned, defiled, or destroyed.

If prayers and medicine fail to heal a seriously ill person, the spiritual leader sometimes realizes that the patient's name itself may be diseased. The priest then goes to the water and, with the appropriate ceremony, bestows a new name on the sick person. The healer then begins anew, repeating sacred formulas with the patient's new name, in the hope that these measures will bring about restoration and recovery.

Asgaya-dihi. Mankiller. My Cherokee name in English is Mankiller.

Mankiller has survived in my own family as a surname for four generations before my own. It is an old Cherokee name, although it was originally not a name at all, but a rank or title used only after one had earned the right to it. To call someone Mankiller would have been like calling another person Major or Captain.

There were many titles in the early days of the Cherokees. Each Cherokee town, for example, had its own Water-goer (Ama-edohi) and its own Raven (Golana), and each town had its Asgaya-dihi.

My own people came from near Tellico, from the land now known as eastern Tennessee. My great-great-great-grandfather's name was written down as Ah-nee-ska-yah-di-hi. That translates literally into English as "Menkiller." No record exists of the names of his parents, and the only name recorded for his wife is Sally. The son of Ah-nee-ska-yah-di-hi and Sally was listed as Ka-skun-nee Mankiller. The first name, Ka-skun-nee, cannot be translated, but it is with this man, my great-great-grandfather, that the name Mankiller was established in the family line as a surname.

Jacob Mankiller, born in 1853, was a son of Ka-skun-nee Mankiller and Lucy Matoy. Jacob married Susan Teehee-Bearpaw and, in 1889, they had a son they named John. He was the oldest of eight children. John Mankiller was my grandfather. He married

Bettie Bolin Bendabout Canoe. Her Cherokee name was Quatie. Born in 1878, she was nine years older than her husband. My father, Charley Mankiller, was their son.

I know that Lucy Matoy, my great-grandmother and the wife of Ka-skun-nee, came from what we call one of the Old Settler families. Sometime after 1817, these families immigrated of their own free will to what became the Cherokee Nation West, an area west of the Mississippi in the far reaches of Arkansas and beyond, in what would later become Indian Territory. This voluntary immigration occurred two decades before the federal government, anxious to seize native people's land, evicted Cherokees from their homes in Georgia, Tennessee, North Carolina, and Alabama, forcibly removing them on what was known as "the trail where they cried." As far as the name Matoy is concerned, our history tells us that in 1730, a Chief Moytoy was declared "emperor" of the Cherokees by Sir Alexander Cuming, an unofficial envoy representing the English Crown in America. I can't prove it, but I strongly suspect that the surname Matoy is but another form of the name or title Amaedohi, which had been corrupted by the English into Moytoy. As far as I can determine, all of my ancestors on my father's side, other than this Matoy line, moved west later on, in the late 1830s, on the Trail of Tears.

At the turn of the century, there was another attempt to ravage our people through several legislative acts which in effect almost destroyed the Cherokee Nation and its ability to function as a sovereign entity. In 1907, Indian Territory was finally devoured and ceased to exist when Oklahoma became a state. Land held in common by the Cherokee Nation was parceled out in individual allotments of 160 acres per family. The land we now call Mankiller Flats in Adair County was assigned to my paternal grandfather, John Mankiller. I never met my grandfather,

although I often feel the connection between the two of us. I live on my grandfather's allotment. I have built my house several hundred yards from where his home once stood. Each spring, Easter lilies bloom in what used to be his yard. They remind me of him and of our ancestry.

My father, Charley Mankiller, was born in his father's frame house on November 15, 1914, just seven years after Oklahoma statehood. At the time of his birth, much of the land that had been allotted to the Cherokees was being taken away by unscrupulous businessmen with the cooperation of Oklahoma's judicial system. Unspeakably greedy people would arrange to be appointed guardians of Cherokee children, and then take control of their individually allotted Cherokee land. As documented in Angie Debo's impressive book, *And Still the Waters Run,* this was practiced most widely in the early 1900s when oil was discovered in Oklahoma and the boom years started.

My father's mother died in 1916 when her son was only two years old. She died in one of the dreaded influenza epidemics that tore through America during World War I. Jensie Hummingbird, my father's older half sister, helped raised him. I remember Aunt Jensie. She spoke no English at all. She did not own a car or get around very much. She tended to stay close to her home. We visited her quite a bit. She was a very kind woman who was sick most of her life. Aunt Jensie had only one son, Charley Hummingbird, who cared for her until she died in 1990.

My grandfather went off to join the army and took part in the Great War that became known as World War I. In fact, a large number of American Indian people served in World War I. This interests me. As a student of Native American history, I realize that the question of United States citizenship for native people was addressed in the Dawes Act, or the General Allotment Act, of 1887. This was the law that prepared native people for the eventual termination of tribal ownership of land by granting 160-acre allotments to each Indian family, or eighty acres to an individual. All of the allottees were to become United States citizens, subject to the same criminal and civil laws as other American citizens. Even though Theodore Roosevelt called the Dawes Act "a mighty pulverizing engine to break up the tribal mass," the act failed because Native Americans considered land not as a possession but as a physical and spiritual domain shared by all living things. Many of our people were reluctant to turn away from the traditional view of common ownership of land.

Despite these early measures, Native Americans were not considered official citizens of the United States until 1924. That was the year Congress passed the Indian Citizenship Act, bestowing voting rights and citizenship on all Indians "born within the territorial limits of the United States." Native people, however, were still considered to be outside the protection of the Bill of Rights. Among many native people, there is a feeling that citizenship was conferred uniformly in 1924 because so many American Indians, like my grandfather, had volunteered for military service during the war.

In 1936, twelve years after the Indian Citizenship Act became law and nine years before I was born, Grandpa Mankiller died. He was only forty-six years old. The official cause of death was pernicious anemia, but we now believe that his death resulted from kidney failure caused by polycystic kidney disease. Severe anemia is a common side effect of kidney failure. My father, in turn, inherited this disease from my grandfather, and it was passed on to several of his children, including me.

There were only two children to mourn their father's death, my father Charley and his only full sibling, his older sister, Sally.

She was a beautiful girl who liked to wear fine dresses with her black hair piled on her head. People who knew her as a girl say she was very dainty, always carrying a parasol when she walked in the sun. Sally later married a full-blooded Cherokee named Nelson Leach, and they lived near Rocky Mountain on a portion of the Mankiller family allotment.

Like my dad, Aunt Sally was forced to attend Sequoyah Training School near Tahlequah. This was very customary of the period. Sally began classes there in the 1920s when she was a little girl and stopped attending the school in the early 1930s when she became a young woman.

Sequoyah Training School started as an orphan asylum. The Cherokee National Council passed an act establishing the asylum in 1871 to provide housing for children orphaned by the Civil War. The war was fought partly in the Cherokee Nation, and Cherokees served in both the Union and Confederate armies. Later, the orphan facility became an asylum for Indian people who experienced mental or physical problems of such severity that they could not cope without assistance. Finally, it was turned into a boarding school for Indian children.

In 1914, our people authorized Cherokee Chief W. C. Rogers to sell the school and its forty acres to the United States. It then became a federal institution under the control of the secretary of the interior, and was maintained as an industrial school for "the Indian orphans of Oklahoma of the restricted class," meaning native people of one-half degree of Indian blood or more. Congress passed an act in 1925 changing the name of the school to Sequoyah Orphan Training School in honor of Sequoyah, the man credited with developing our Cherokee syllabary.

It is still a school for native people today, but now it is not an orphanage. Known simply as Sequoyah High School, it is one of five Native American educational facilities in

Oklahoma. The school, including its residential program, is funded by the Bureau of Indian Affairs and operated by the Cherokee Nation of Oklahoma. Our people not only maintain Sequoyah School, but also oversee the policies that govern it, and the twelve campus buildings. Most of the students are Cherokee, but as many as sixteen other tribes are also represented, coming to Sequoyah from many Indian nations.

Back in the bad old days, the BIA representatives who maintained boarding schools such as Sequoyah would go hundreds of miles and return with native children. The philosophy, reflecting an errant missionary zeal, was to get native children away from their families, their elders, their tribes, their language, their heritage. They isolated native children so they would forget their culture. The boarding-school concept was simply another way for the federal government to deal with what its officials always called "the Indian problem." After first trying to wipe all of us off the face of the earth with violence, they attempted to isolate us on reservations or, in the case of many people such as the Cherokees, place us in an area that the government called Indian Territory. All the while, they systematically conjured up policies to kill our culture. So the federal government rounded up Indian youngsters and forced them to attend boarding schools whether they wanted to or not. This was true for most tribes, not just the Cherokees.

At Sequoyah School, south of Tahlequah, the capital of the Cherokee Nation, my father and his little sister were forbidden to speak their native language. They could not speak a word of English when they first went there, so they were whipped for speaking Cherokee. The whole idea behind those boarding schools, whether they were government operated like Sequoyah or a religious operation, was to acculturate native people into the mainstream white society and, at the same time,

destroy their sense of self. The boarding-school officials hoped to make the "little Indians" into "ladies and gentlemen." So they cut their hair short and did not allow them to utter one word of their native language. Oftentimes, all visits to family and friends back home were denied. The idea was to "civilize" the children. There was even a popular expression about "killing the Indian and saving the man."

> When I was about seven years old they took me to this damn Indian school of the government's and we had to stand in line and they cut my hair off. They just cut my braids off and threw them into a box with all the other children's braids. My old grandmother went over there and got them and my grandfolks stayed at the winter camp all winter to be near me. . . . It was hard being an Indian in them days. Later I learned to be proud.
>
> Archie Blackowl, a Cheyenne,
> *The Indians in Oklahoma*

All his life, my father had mixed emotions about the school named Sequoyah. He spoke of having been punished for only the slightest infractions, and of the many other problems he experienced there. On the other hand, he could get sentimental about the place. It had an orchard, a big garden, and a lot of farm animals. The students provided all the labor necessary to keep the operation going. One Sequoyah superintendent my father spoke well of was Jack Brown, who was part Cherokee and had a great interest in history and literature. Sequoyah was my father's home for twelve years. It was not a perfect home or even a loving place, but it was there that he developed lasting friendships with other Cherokee children and youths from other tribes. At Sequoyah, he also acquired his love of books, a gift he passed on to his children. Most people have mixed emotions about their home. My dad's feelings were perhaps a little more intense because of the acculturation program and what must have been a lonely life in a barren dormitory.

Still, the fact remains that the primary mission of Sequoyah and the other boarding schools was for the children to leave everything behind that related to their native culture, heritage, history, and language. In short, there was a full-scale attempt at deracination—the uprooting or destruction of a race and its culture. Consequently, many young Cherokees and other native people subjected to the boarding-school experience, including my father, came away from those years of indoctrination more than a little brainwashed.

At many of those schools scattered across this country and Canada, much mental and physical abuse occurred. I have a friend from a Canadian tribe who lived in a traditional community as a girl. It was very isolated. She can recall the young men coming home from religious boarding schools with all sorts of problems. Many of them never married, but stayed to themselves. They turned to alcohol and drank themselves to death before they reached their thirtieth birthdays. My friend and other concerned tribal members were puzzled by this phenomenon. When they examined the problem, they discovered that there had been widespread sexual abuse of the young men in the boarding schools. All of it was documented. And incredibly, some of those problems still exist at some of the boarding schools that remain in operation. In the late 1980s, a Senate select committee investigated sexual-abuse cases at Native American boarding schools. So this is not ancient history.

I am thankful that even though my father was raised in such a boarding-school environment, he did not buy into everything that was being taught. Fortunately, he came from a strong family, and because of his traditional upbringing, the school was not successful in alienating him from his culture. He was a confident man and, to my knowledge, he never felt intimidated in the non-Indian world—a world he came to know even better after he met my mother.

Her name is Clara Irene Sitton. She was born in Adair County on September 18, 1921, to Robert Bailey Sitton and Pearl Halady Sitton. My mother's family was made up primarily of the Sitton and Gillespie families, and their ethnic background was mostly Dutch and Irish. She does not have a drop of Indian blood in her veins, although she sometimes forgets she is white. From the day she married my father, her own life became centered around Cherokee family life.

My mother's ancestry goes back to North Carolina, where her kinfolk from the Sitton side were some of the first iron makers, while the Gillespies were craftsmen who turned out fine long rifles. It is an intriguing possibility that the Sittons were related somehow to Charles Arthur Floyd, the Dust Bowl–era bandit from rural Oklahoma who was better known as "Pretty Boy" Floyd. They came from the same county in northern Georgia as Floyd and his kinfolk. This family legend has never been proved, but it was always exciting for me to consider, because "Pretty Boy" was a Robin Hood-style bandit, the subject of much myth.

My mother's father was born in 1874. I have been told that Grandpa Sitton was tall and distinguished looking. He was a farmer all of his life. He died, like my father's father, at a relatively young age, in 1932, during the Great Depression when my mother was only eleven years old. A few years before his death, my grandfather had skinned some rabbits and then went to the barn to harness his mules to plow. The mules apparently smelled the rabbits' blood on his hands and became frightened. They wanted to get out of the barn and, in the panic, they pushed my grandfather up against the wall. He suffered serious internal injuries which probably shortened his life.

My mother's mother was born in 1884 and lived until 1973. Her mother died when she was very young, so my grandmother went to live with her half sister, Ida Mae Scism Jordan, in Washington County, Arkansas. In 1903, when she was nineteen years old, Grandma Sitton left her home in Arkansas to visit friends. She came to the Wauhillau community in Indian Territory. That's where she caught the eye of my grandfather. At twenty-nine, Robert Sitton was a confirmed bachelor, but the vivacious, diminutive young woman captured his heart. After a brief courtship, they were married that same year and soon started their family. My grandparents set up housekeeping near Wauhillau, where my grandfather's parents, William and Sarah Sitton, lived. Wauhillau was a thriving new settlement made up of Cherokee people and white pioneers, many of whom had come from Georgia about the same time as the Sittons in 1891.

After a few years, my grandparents packed their belongings in a wagon and a two-seated buggy and moved. They settled on a small farm they bought near the eastern Oklahoma town of Titanic, presumably named after the famous British transatlantic liner that had sunk on her maiden voyage in 1912. They cleared the land to make it suitable for farming. Except for their oldest daughter, Sadie, who stayed with her grandparents in Wauhillau, they sent their children to the one-room Titanic schoolhouse. My grandparents had seven children—three sons and four daughters—born between 1904 and 1921. My mother was their youngest child.

After a couple of other moves, including a stop at the town of Foraker, Oklahoma, in the Osage country, where my grandfather worked for the railroad, they located in Adair County. Grandma Sitton was determined to raise her family in the fresh country air, so she was delighted when they found a farm for sale not far from the community of Rocky Mountain. That was where my mother was born.

I have heard it said that there was not a job on the farm my grandmother would not tackle, including plowing the fields. Folks described her as being spunky. Some years after my grandfather died and her children were raised, she sold her farm and moved into the town of Stilwell to run a boardinghouse.

My parents met when they were young. They had been around each other in the same area most of their lives. They would bump into each other at the general store in Rocky Mountain, a tiny settlement that attracted families from miles around. Mother can recall my dad teasing her when she was a girl. One time she even threw a pie at him. Even though he could make her as angry as a hornet, she was attracted by his good looks and quiet charm. They had a whirlwind courtship.

When they married, my mother was only fifteen years old. Dad was twenty-one. Of course, back in those days in the country, many folks married when they were quite young. My father was earning a rather precarious living by subsistence farming. He raised strawberries and peanuts for cash crops, picked berries and green beans for extra money, and traveled all the way to Colorado during the harvesttime to cut broomcorn.

My grandmother was dead set against the marriage. My dad was older and had been raised in an Indian boarding school. He had also worked here and there, and had generally "gotten around." Although her oldest daughter, Sadie, had married a mixed-blood Cherokee, Grandma Sitton did not approve of my father because he was Cherokee. He was different. She objected strenuously to their relationship. But my folks were in love. They simply did not listen. They got married anyway. They went to the Baptist church in the Adair County community of Mulberry, where a Reverend Acorn married them on March 6, 1937. The relationship between my grandmother and parents was strained for the next several years.

By the time I was born in November of 1945, my mother, Irene, had come to learn the culture of the Cherokees. The name Mankiller, which sounds strange to most white people, was not foreign to her because she had lived in Cherokee country all her life and had attended school with many Cherokee people. And even years later, when I grew up, the Cherokee last names were not at all odd sounding to a girl in rural Oklahoma. In fact, Cherokee names in my family were familiar and, quite often, revered. I know family and friends whose surnames are Thirsty, Hummingbird, Wolf, Beaver, Squirrel, Soap, Canoe, Fourkiller, Sixkiller, Walkingstick, and Gourd. Names such as those just are not unusual.

> The name of honor was received after a person had attained some kind of special distinction in the tribe. This would occur through the performance of an act of great character, or it could be given by a secret society. The second name marked a moment of excellence in a person's life and was not a hereditary position. Hereditary names, such as that of an Iroquois chief, were passed down successively to whoever filled the position for as long as there were people to fill it.
>
> Gerald Hausman, *Turtle Island Alphabet*, 1992

As I matured, I learned that *Mankiller* could be spelled different ways and was a coveted war name. One version is the literal *Asgaya*, meaning "man," combined with the personal name suffix *dihi*, or "killer." Another is *Outacity*—an honorary title that also means "Man-killer." Our Cherokee historians and genealogists have always told us that Mankiller was a military title, but we also heard that there was another kind of Mankiller in our past. We know that in the Cherokee medicinal and conjuring style, Mankillers were known to attack other people to avenge wrongs that had been perpetrated against themselves or others they served. This Mankiller could change things,

often for the worse. This Mankiller was capable of changing minds to a different condition. This kind of Mankiller could make an illness more serious, and even shoot an invisible arrow into the body of an enemy.

Most of what I know about my family's heritage I did not learn until I was a young woman. That is when I discovered that many distinguished leaders from the past held the title of Mankiller throughout the various tribal towns. In the eighteenth century, for example, there was the Mankiller of Tellico, the Mankiller of Estatoe, and the Mankiller of Keowee. One prominent warrior and tribal leader, Outacity, or "Man-killer," apparently joined a delegation of Cherokees visiting London in 1762, during the troubled reign of King George III, fourteen years before the Revolutionary War broke out.

Even though our family name has been honored for many centuries, during the years, I have had to endure occasional derision because of my surname. Some people are startled when I am introduced to them as Wilma Mankiller. They think it's a fierce-sounding name. Many find it amusing and make nervous jokes, and there are still those times when people display their ignorance. For example, I was invited in December of 1992 to attend President-elect Bill Clinton's historic economic summit meeting in Little Rock, Arkansas, just about a month prior to his inaugural. *The Wall Street Journal*, one of America's most respected newspapers, made a rather unfortunate remark about my surname that is best described as a cheap shot.

"Our favorite name on the summit list," stated the *Journal* editorial, "we have to admit, is Chief Wilma Mankiller, representing the Cherokee Nation, though we hope not a feminist economic priority."

Tim Giago, publisher of *Indian Country Today*, a Native American newspaper, quickly fired back at the *Journal:* "The fact that this powerful lady has been featured in several major magazines . . . has appeared on countless television shows, and has been given tons of coverage in major, national newspapers, appears to have escaped the closed minds at the *Journal.* One has to ask if they ever get out into the real world."

Fortunately, most people I come across in my travels, especially members of the media, are more sensitive and generally more aware than that editorial writer. When someone unknowingly or out of ignorance makes a snide comment about my name, I often resort to humor. I look the person in the eye and say with a straight face that Mankiller is actually a well-earned nickname. That usually shuts the person up.

There were times in my childhood when I put up with a lot of teasing about my name. I would want to disappear when roll call was taken in school and everyone would laugh when they heard my name. But my parents told me to be proud of my family name. Most people these days generally like my name, many of them saying that it is only appropriate and perhaps a bit ironic that a woman chief should be named Mankiller. The name Mankiller carries with it a lot of history. It is a strong name. I am proud of my name—very proud. And I am proud of the long line of men and women who have also been called Mankiller. I hope to honor my ancestors by keeping the name alive.

But I have started my story far too early. Especially in the context of a tribal people, no individual's life stands apart and alone from the rest. My own story has meaning only as long as it is a part of the overall story of my people. For above all else, I am a Cherokee woman.

"Toka" (Ball Game). © 1994 Leonard Chana, Tohono O'odham artist.

TRAVELING TRADITIONS

Deanna Kingston

Today, after a century of U.S. government policies concerning Alaskan Native people, it is not unusual to find someone like myself who claims a King Island Inupiaq identity without ever having lived on King Island, Alaska. I would like to demonstrate here how I, a native Oregonian, can actively claim this identity even though I currently live in the "Lower 48." My situation is not unique as there are many Native Americans throughout this continent who find themselves in a similar situation, due to various federal government policies that removed Natives from their lands, sent Natives to boarding schools, and strongly encouraged them to move to urban areas. Situations such as mine, which fundamentally change our concepts of identity formation, are common throughout the world. One theorist whose work helps to conceive of these new identities and cultures that are no longer bound by territory is Ulf Hannerz.

Hannerz uses the term *the global ecumene* to mean "the interconnectedness of the world, by way of interactions, exchanges and related developments, affecting not least the organization of culture" (1996:7). Hannerz prefers the term *transnational* over *globalization* because these linkages are not necessarily international as the term *globalization* implies. One aspect of this "transnational global ecumene" is the situation whereby "collectivities" of

people who once resided in and were bounded by a particular territory are no longer limited to this territory. In other words, in the past, people's identities were usually defined by where they live. Now, however, because of the ease with which people travel and relocate to other territories, combined with the ability to communicate instantaneously with kin back home, our concept of "culture" must change. Due to this global ecumene, Hannerz now defines "cultures" as "packages of meanings and meaningful forms." Before, it was our assumption that cultures were distinctive to particular "collectivities" and "territories." But because of the ease with which people travel and communicate today, they can bring their traditions and other meaningful forms with them, showing that "culture" cannot be contained within a territory. Thus, the King Islanders, like other Native American peoples, bring their cultures with them as they move from their original territories.

Here, I intend to show the interconnectedness and transnational nature of the King Island Inupiaq community, which still exists although we live as far away from each other as Florida, Connecticut, Oregon, Arizona, and Alaska. The King Islanders are an Eskimoan peoples who used to live on a tiny island in the Bering Strait, 40 miles from the Alaskan mainland. However, due to various reasons, not the least of which is the BIA's (Bureau of Indian Affairs) decision to close the school in 1959, King Islanders are dispersed

"Traveling Traditions" by Deanna Paniatuq Kingston, King Island Inupiaq. Reprinted by permission.

throughout Alaska and the Lower 48 States. Although the distances are far, we use various technological means to keep in touch with each other. Bear with me as I share an example.

In early fall 1998, on a Thursday evening in my (then) new home in Connecticut, I received an e-mail message from my maternal parallel cousin, Aisana. She told me that her father called her with the news that our mutual cross-cousin, Iilana, had been flown to the Alaska Native Service hospital in Anchorage, where she was in a coma. I was worried because Iilana was only a few years older than I and had always been very supportive of my research. I immediately forwarded Aisana's message to my mother since Iilana was one of my mother's favorite nieces. The next night, my mother called and said that both her brother, Aaluguq, and her step-brother, Aannayak, had called to tell her that Iilana had died. I e-mailed Aisana and then called her to see if she had heard the news, but I was unsuccessful in reaching her. The next day, I received an e-mail message from yet another cross-cousin, Quiruna, who lives in Nome and who is a parallel cousin to Iilana. Quiruna told me that Aisana was on her way to Nome for Iilana's funeral and would be staying with her. (Yes, I have many King Island cousins through my mother). Several days later, I e-mailed the news to yet another cousin, Kukuluk (or as he is known in English, Mark), who is a cross-cousin to me and Aisana and a parallel cousin to both Iilana and Quiruna and who lives in Arizona. He replied that his father had told him about her death over the phone.

Although the situation related here was a sad one, it does show how I, a King Islander in Connecticut, can keep and maintain my connections to my King Island kin, the children of four of my mother's siblings, who live in Oregon, Arizona, and Alaska. Today's telecommunication technology enables these connections and interactions to occur. However, I will note that these connections happened only because of and were facilitated by actual face-to-face interactions. In other words, although technology helps to maintain our connections, it is not a substitute for creating those connections in the first place.

Which brings me to the topic at hand: my interactions with my cross-cousin Mark, who now lives in Arizona. In 1997–1998, we were both living in Corvallis and working at or attending Oregon State University. Mark and I and our siblings were, for the most part, born and raised in Oregon. Thus, we are both King Islanders and Oregonians, which appears to be a contradiction in terms. My cross-cousin Mark and I share a special relationship, one that was traditionally characterized by teasing. The purpose of this "teasing" or "joking" relationship, which is widespread among Eskimoan peoples, is well documented in the ethnographic literature. Specifically, sets of teasing cousins would engage in behavior designed to embarrass one another. Ernest Burch (personal communication) recorded an example from a Kotzebue man: this man and his teasing cousin were hunting for seal on the ice. Just as they spotted a seal near its breathing hole and were crawling quietly toward it, the man farted, startling the seal, who disappeared into the breathing hole. The man's teasing cousin, who was crawling in front, looked back in shock, only to find his teasing cousin laughing at him. Teasing cousins were not to be offended or to get angry at these actions. This is because this relationship served another purpose: if a person misbehaved or acted inappropriately, it was the teasing cousin's job to tell him to change his behavior, an action which is *not* appropriate in any other context. The aspect of this relationship with which I am most familiar has to do with the composition of songs: in the King Island community, there were several sets of teasing cousins who composed humorous songs about each other. Once a teasing cousin song was composed by one person, his or her teasing cousin would "retaliate" with another song and dance (see Kingston 1996).

Mark's father (my uncle) lives in Portland, Oregon. He began teaching me and a few others how to Eskimo dance in 1991 (an aspect of King Island traditions traveling to Oregon). Part of our performance repertoire included several teasing-cousin songs and dances. At the time, I was a master's student at Oregon State, and the experience of this dance group became the basis of my master's thesis (Kingston 1996). In 1997, after a four-year absence, I moved back to Oregon and again became involved in my uncle's dance group. Both of my parents and my brother performed with the group as well as my teasing cousin, Mark. Mark was in his final year of undergraduate study at Oregon State. I was at OSU on a one-year teaching position in anthropology.

Since Mark is my teasing cousin—and since we have several teasing-cousin songs in our repertoire—at our very first performance that year, I teased Mark in order to demonstrate the concept for our mostly non-Native audience. Thus, began the teasing between the two of us. From then on, whenever Mark and I were both able to dance, our performances were characterized by retaliations and counterretaliations, which proved to be as much fun for the audience as they were for us. What follows is a brief description of some of this teasing.

In early November 1997, we performed at a benefit for Indian Art Northwest in Portland, Oregon. To retaliate from the September performance, Mark told a couple of jokes about me. In the first joke, he said that "Dede is so slow! If you want her to laugh at a joke on Monday, you have to tell it to her on Friday!" His second joke was as follows:

> Dede and two friends decided to go to a conference, but instead of driving, they took the train. At the train station, when buying their tickets, they bumped into three other people also going to the same conference. However, these three people bought only *one* ticket. Dede asked why they only got one ticket instead of three and they told her to watch. So, all six got on the train. The other three people crowded into one bathroom and when the conductor yelled for the ticket, one person stuck his arm out holding it. Dede and her friends thought that that was pretty smart, so after the conference was over, they bought only one ticket for the three of them. The other three people did not buy one at all. Dede asked why they didn't and they replied, "Watch and you'll see." So, they all got on the train and the other three crowded into one bathroom and Dede and her two friends crowded into the other. Then, when Dede and her friends weren't looking, one of the other three got out of the bathroom, walked by the door and yelled for the ticket as if he was the conductor. Dede put just her arm out and the other three got their ticket.

I had also planned some teasing for this performance. Several King Island dances involve the use of long gauntlet gloves. They are shoulder-length gloves made of dyed red sealskin with rattles attached to them. Shamans traditionally used them in their dances. I decided that, as a joke, I would make Mark a pair of these gloves. However, sealskin is rather rare in these parts, so I went to a local ladies' boutique and bought a pair of long, tight, white evening gloves that go up to the shoulder. I even bought some brown dye, but since the gloves were polyester, the dye turned the gloves a light lavender in color! Going along with the flow, I then decorated the gloves with bells (in place of rattles) and put some purple felt and fluffy cotton along the opening. I presented these lavender, belled evening gloves to Mark at this particular performance and subsequently made him dance wearing them. I do not know if the audience thought it was funny, but our group laughed so much, I guess the audience had to laugh with us.

Also, in October 1997, Mark was given the Best Undergraduate Oral Presentation award at the national AISES (American Indians in Science and Engineering Society) conference. This award came with laptop, $500, and a trip to Florida to go to the Kennedy Space Center. The OSU AISES chapter asked him to present the same paper at one of their meetings. I asked if I could introduce him, wanting to take advantage of another opportunity for teasing. I was proud of his accomplishments, but I was mindful that the teasing-cousin tradition was also used as a leveling mechanism, designed to keep people from getting too boastful. So, in my introduction, I alluded to one of Mark's bad habits. That year, Mark asked me to teach him a little bit about the Inupiaq language. We made appointments to meet once a week, and Mark was always late. When I introduced him at the AISES meeting, I said "Mark, as smart as he is, is unable to tell time. So, I am giving him this children's book that will specifically tell him how to do it!" Of course, most of the audience knew about Mark's predilection to be late, and they all got a kick out of it.

Mark retaliated the next month. At a performance at the Blazer's Boys and Girls Club in Northeast Portland, Mark gave me a shovel, since I was working on my Ph.D. and would need something to dig out of that which was being "piled higher and deeper," and a toy stethoscope, since I was going to become a "doctor." He made me dance wearing the stethoscope.

In January 1998, we performed at the Corvallis Public Library. To help advertise the event, I made up a flier. Mark's father is a big fan of Elvis and had taken to performing an Eskimo Elvis impersonation during our dances. Using that as a point of departure, I designed a flier in which I cut and pasted Mick Jagger's hair onto a picture of Mark dancing. The idea behind it was that just as Mark is the next generation of King Islanders after his father, so too Mick Jagger was the next generation of

rock-and-rollers after Elvis. The result was a flier that advertised an Eskimo dance, complete with impersonations of Eskimo Elvis and "Kukuluk" Jagger. In retaliation, Mark asked the audience to sing the following words to the tune of the Oscar Meyer bologna song:

My teasing cousin has a first name.
It's D-E-A-N-N-A.
My teasing cousin has a second name.
Its -K-I-N-G-S-T-O-N
(make it fit).
Because Dede Kingston has a way
Of getting teasing by Mark each day.

In February, we had several performances. Mark was still late or not showing up for his Inupiaq lessons. In one performance, I gave him a calendar for the next five months, highlighting his appointments with me that he needed to keep and future dance performances (since he was constantly asking me, "When was that performance again?") and reminding him to show up for his own graduation. He retaliated with a limerick about me, which I unfortunately (or is that fortunately?) do not remember.

During a performance in May, Mark was still late or not showing up for appointments, so I gave him a pad that could be hung on the refrigerator. The pad had seven sheets, and, on each sheet, I put a reminder or a saying that Mark was to repeat for that day. It was designed to be used over and over again each week. Examples of the reminders and sayings are: "I will remember to check my calendar for upcoming appointments"; "I will wear a watch"; "I will not overcommit myself." Mark retaliated with a placard, which I was to hang in my office, that said: "I will get my Ph.D. in 1998 and I will beat Mark to it." At this point, I thought I would be finished, but because of procrastination on my part, it had not quite happened, so this was Mark's dig at me to keep me humble. What's interesting about this poster is that one can tear off the top sheet and the next sheet says "1999" and subsequent sheets say "2000," "2001," and "2002." (I did finish it in 1999.)

Finally, in June 1998, I cannot remember what I did to Mark, but he made me a pair of Eskimo-style boots to dance in. However, these boots consisted of a pair of old blue socks, into which were stuck the soles of an old pair of tennis shoes. He made me wear these makeshift boots just as I had made him wear the makeshift gloves the previous November.

Since we moved to Arizona and Connecticut in the summer of 1998, we have not teased each other as much. But because of what Hannerz calls the global ecumene, or the interconnections that are available to people because of our technological accomplishments, Mark and I have managed to continue. The latest two retaliations have occurred via regular mail and via the Internet. I sent him a poster I created in which I tease him for various silly things he has done throughout his life. He recently (March 2000) e-mailed me and said to check his Web site, where he provides a link to my "puny" Web site (which my institution posted before it was ready). Thus, he has retaliated for my poster of him.

The result of these actions and our dancing is that Mark and I and our families have become closer. We have formed our own King Island enclave in Oregon, thus demonstrating how we can be both King Islanders and Oregonians. Within this enclave, we try to practice some King Island customs: singing, drumming and dancing, and teasing. In other words, we brought some local King Island traditions into a more global context in Oregon. However, this traveling of traditions is not unusual. For instance, Fogel-Chance (1993) showed how North Slope Inupiaq women living in Anchorage established and maintained their sharing networks among themselves and their relatives in Barrow in

order to continue cultural ideals of food and resource distribution. These women also kept up cultural patterns of communal (rather than nuclear) child rearing and extended (rather than nuclear) family households. Fienup-Riordan (1998) also argued that Anchorage ("the largest Alaskan village") was undergoing a "Yupification" in that the Yupiit in Anchorage are building Yup'ik steambaths, practicing and performing Yup'ik songs and dances, and maintaining their sharing networks. She also notes that Athabaskans and Inupiat people living in Anchorage are doing the same thing, showing that global practices are not replacing local ones; rather, these people who are traveling and living elsewhere tend to bring their local practices and identities into a more global setting.

But what has not necessarily been addressed is how the extension of these local practices and identities into a more global context has caused changes in those practices. Of course, folklorists have been aware for some time how different audiences and circumstances give rise to changes in performance, and our dance performances are no different. For instance, in our King Island enclave in Oregon, no matter how true to the local form we have tried to be, this change in context, particularly performing for a non-Native audience, has given rise to changes in the King Island dances we perform. First, we have a narrator or an announcer, usually me, who explains in English what our songs, stories behind the songs, and dances are. I give these long explanations because I find myself unable to appreciate Native American dancing at Pow-wows because I do not know what is going on and because of my earlier experience; when I heard my uncle play tapes of King Island songs in 1985, I found myself bored because I did not know the translation or why my uncle might suddenly laugh. So, I developed a style where I gave in-depth explanations of

the movements, the teasing-cousin relationship, translations of the songs, and a narrative about the song's composition, so that the
audience could appreciate our performances.
However, when the Nome community
dances at King Island hall, such explanations
are never given because they are not needed.
In fact, this sort of behavior on my part may
be seen as an act of hubris. In performances
for an outside or non-Native audience in
Nome, someone may introduce the dance
and give a brief statement about it. I have also
witnessed King Islanders, now living in
Anchorage, giving a dance performance in
New York City, and they also employed
someone to explain the dances to the audience, although not to the extent that I did.

Another change we introduced into our
performances was the very overt teasing that
Mark and I engaged in. In fact, we do this
teasing specifically for the audience's benefit. However, we rarely tease each other outside of the public sphere. In private, we
generally abstain from this behavior, preferring instead an easygoing friendship. However, as we saw in Burch's example from
Kotzebue, teasing between cross-cousins in
local communities happened in both the private and the public spheres. Third, in a more
local context, community and audience
members join in the dances when they feel
like it or if they know a particular song and
dance. This participation, of course, does not
happen with a non-Native audience. Fourth,
our performances last anywhere from fifteen
minutes to an hour. In the local context, these
events often lasted for hours. Fifth, most of
the dances we perform are the masked
dances or the teasing-cousin songs with
humorous stories. However, in the local context in Nome, with just community members
present, an hour or more of bench dancing
usually occurs. We rarely perform bench
dances because non-Native audiences tend
to respond more to the sight of exotic people

dancing dramatic masked dances and to the
humor in the teasing-cousin songs, so we
consciously do these songs in order to entertain our audience. Sixth, we often created different dance motions to the King Island
songs, so that, even though we use the same
songs, our dance motions are different from
those of the King Islanders in Nome or in
Anchorage. Seventh, for each dance performance, my uncle carefully plans the
sequences of songs we perform. In the local
Nome community song sequences are not
planned, although I believe the Anchorage
group did plan their New York City performance. Finally, in recordings of songs from
the 1930s and 1940s, Eskimo singers use a
high-pitched voice, which is frequently commented on in the ethnographic literature. In
contrast, my uncle, who was (and still is)
influenced by Elvis and early rock and
who has some training in Western music,
sings in a voice that is lower-pitched than the
tradition singers' voices, so there has been
some leaking of global styles into the
local form.

Thus, the change in performance context
has caused some changes in King Island
dance forms. Although we use the same
songs as King Islanders in Nome or in
Anchorage, and we share some similarities,
we have created our own style of dance performance. How we relate to an audience,
giving four- to five-minute explanations between dances in a planned sequence, is different from how the Nome community
performs—without explanations and without a plan. Our performances are different
yet again from the Anchorage King Islanders,
who give explanations to their dances but not
to the extent that I do. As Hannerz (1996:8)
noted, and as Fogel-Chance (1993) and
Fienup-Riordan (1998) imply, the general
assumption is that cultures are homogeneously distributed within collectivities.
In other words, since we are all part of the

King Island collectivity, the practices and understandings of teasing-cousin songs and dance performances are thought to be homogeneous. However, Hannerz reminds us (1996:8), this "assumption that [culture] is homogeneously distributed within collectivities becomes problematic, when we see how their members' experiences and biographies differ." I hope I have shown that because our experiences and biographies in Oregon differ from those in Anchorage or in Nome, our performances have also differed. Thus, although local traditions traveled into the global context, when performed in these different settings, they become localized once again. I am reminded of a time when my uncle Aakaagak and his wife, Aapak, visited us from Nome and attended our performance at Oregon State. I asked them later what they thought of our dances, hoping that they enthusiastically approved of our efforts. Instead, they just said they thought they were okay. I was puzzled, but my mom and my uncle both thought that uncle Aakaagak and his wife liked our dance. So, I must assume that our performance really was all right, but they probably were puzzled at the length of my introductions and explanations.

REFERENCES

Fienup-Riordan, Ann. *Yup'ik Community in the 1990s: A Worldwide Web.* Manuscript, 1998.

Fogel-Chance, Nancy. "Living in Both Worlds: 'Modernity' and 'Tradition' among North Slope Inupiaq Women in Anchorage." *Arctic Anthropology*, 1993. 30(1): 94–108.

Hannerz, Ulf. *Transnational Connections: Culture, People, Places.* London: Routledge, 1996.

Kingston, Deanna M. "Illuweet (Teasing Cousin) Songs As an Expression of King Island Inupiaq Identity." *Anthropology Northwest*, no. 9. Corvallis: Oregon State University Department of Anthropology, 1996.

© 1997 H. J. Tsinhnahjinnie.

THE SPIRIT OF THE PEOPLE HAS AWAKENED AND IS ENJOYING CREATION THROUGH US

AN INTERVIEW WITH JEANETTE ARMSTRONG, OKANAGAN

Dagmar Thorpe

I think about education in the way that we have been developing it in the Okanagan community and Okanagan nation. Over the past 100 years there has been a slow internal disintegration of the survival principles developed over thousands of years. There are a number of ways of speaking about education in the Okanagan tradition. These ways have little to do with *schooling* which is not even counted as education in Okanagan.

I grew up in a family that practiced traditional education. In high school I started to question the contemporary situation we found ourselves in. The society that colonized this country and surrounds us dictates to our community a type of education that is destructive to our people and their people as well. One of the things I could see but could not articulate was that this form of education was not oriented toward how human beings need to interact with one another to be healthy—spiritually and emotionally—as people, families, and communities. Studying sociology, psychology, or

political science was like looking through a telescope at something far removed, something external to yourself. Public mass education has to do with that separation from yourself as a human being and as a part of family, of the land, and the community.

When I decided to go to the university I wanted to be able to find my own answers about education. If the answers made sense to me, then they should help make a change happen in my community. I guess the question that always entered my mind was why is it such a hard thing to convince ourselves to be happy? When I completed high school and started college in the early '70s, I could see the breakdown in our community, the factionalism between various groups of people and the breakdown in the family. I could see the abandonment of principles which were central to our being as Okanagan people and as caretakers of the land.

Our conduct displays our change in values and our lack of good education. I could say in my own language what we needed to be educated in as individuals, family and community, and in terms of human interaction with the land. I could not see in the contemporary world how to make that possible without stepping back into history and living in the old way. This is the work that I have been involved in—finding answers to those questions about how it is possible, how it can happen. That has led to the development of a number of things which have become a widespread movement in the Okanagan. I can't say that I am responsible because I did not have the answers or the solutions either. All I had were questions and I thought they were good questions.

I also had some understanding from my own upbringing and family that these principles were solid and could outlast anything and that through them we could interface with the land and overcome whatever challenges there might be as individuals, family, or community. It is how you apply those principles given different circumstances and how you re-interpret and re-integrate them, every time new circumstances happen. The key is in the process of how to re-integrate and how to reinterpret these principles continuously.

When I completed my program at the university I decided that if I wanted to begin my Okanagan education, I had to come home. I had to educate myself with the help of other people, in history, tradition, ceremonial ways, language, social and political structures. I also had to educate myself every time new learning came along, as to what that means in today's world. I spent two years working on an internal dissertation in my mind, looking at beliefs, ceremonies, political movement, in relation to our history and the understanding of our land, ecology and understanding the society itself. How that integrates itself into an everyday process that reveals itself in the kinds of actions, activities and decisions we make every day? My thinking flip-flopped between the externalized form of decisions that can be documented (the political) and the everyday things that we do in order to express that in community (the sociological).

In the 1970s there was a movement across the country of political thought in resistance to colonialism. At the same time, there was a resurgence of awareness about what being Native might be and a revival of ceremony and tradition. In the Okanagan we questioned how these things become expressed in our world, how we work at our jobs, and how we socialize in the community at functions. Those questions fascinated me. That is where change takes place. Change takes place around the table, at your work place, and the places you socialize.

So I started asking, how do we socialize, how do we approach our work, how do we approach each other in our family? What are the things that have changed from the way they were to what we are doing now? Are there things we need to relearn in order to make for a healthy change to happen where disintegration has taken place? Questions like that were occurring to me. That is why I say it was like a dissertation during that period.

Right off I thought, what do I really truly know about the Okanagan traditional lifestyle? What do I really know about family organization, family interface with community, how each individual fits in terms of work, responsibility, roles, and their own freedoms and liberties to express themselves? How did that traditionally happen? How does the land tie in with that?

There were many missing gaps, even for me and I am a traditional person. I was brought up in a family that does ceremony, that goes out every year and brings in the four main foods and we feast on those four main foods, and every winter we have the medicine dance, and we have the sweats ongoing. Yet, I had no understanding of these things.

So I started talking to the elected leaders in the Okanagan. I speak Okanagan fluently and have been an interpreter of

Okanagan. So I could go to any reserve and be welcomed. I would ask a lot of questions and we would get discussions going. In the early '70s, there were discussions from one reserve with the other for about three years. Some people who could not express those issues in words, expressed them in frustration and in feelings and emotions of anger and grief. The issues were not being expressed in words, but in actions and things we do and don't do.

The meetings themselves demonstrated that this was a natural process for our people. We had, I guess you could call it, democratic consensus-making, which people depend on to give them voice and a feeling of strength. Even if we don't know what and how this is going to come together, we are all in it together. It took us a year to realize that the process itself, in how we were gathering and talking with everyone, was putting trust, hope and strength into the movement. The process was the backbone of the movement.

We looked at that process and said we need to recognize and re-institute it in all of our decision making in the Okanagan, wherever we can. We need to articulate it as a way of carrying out one of the main principles of our people—respect. We respect difference and the need for everyone to be included and for no one to be left out, no matter how small a minority. Everyone has the ability to participate and to say, "no, that is something I do not like and here is why," and be listened to and not be argued with.

This is known as the enow'kin process. This process does not presume an agenda, outcome or direction. It presumes we all have minds, that we all have good thinking, that we all have the best intentions but we do not know what everybody else is thinking. If we know what everybody else is thinking, that can help us make the best decisions because we care about each other.

The underlying thing is that we care about how the other person feels. We are in community. We care how we make decisions. If we can make decisions that feel good to everyone, then that is the best that we can do. If we do that together we are more likely to be healthy and stronger in that process. That process is how we learn and reintegrate things into the older principles we have. The underlying principle is respect of each other and caring for one another. That means taking responsibility for listening to the other, hearing the other from their perspective, and understanding why it is important for them and then seeing how it comes up against your perspective. Where those two things come into conflict, you take the responsibility to find a way to make it more comfortable for the other person.

If everybody in a room or everybody in a nation does that, it creates solidarity. It does not mean that everybody gets what they want, but it means that everyone understands clearly why they must make compromises. You can't do that by insisting that your thinking is the only right way. This became one of the underlying principles of the movement. That is why enow'kin to us is the central spirit, the spirituality of our people.

With that we began to look at the traditions of our people. So that began for me the process of finding all those people who were interested in looking at the ceremonies and spiritual practice of our people and how that interprets into an everyday sense.

From all of our research, we know that historically the people were very spiritual. They did not even eat food without it being a spiritual act. The gathering, the blessing and the feasting of the foods were spiritual acts. They did not make any kind of clothing or implements without recognition of where those things came from and how they were gathered. All of those things were incorporated into their ceremonial process, which they recognized in how they treated each other. All of this was incorporated into the social customs that we have and the ceremonies that underlie those customs.

I could see this structure starting to develop in my mind and understanding that what seemed like the non-sacred and non-spiritual is really a spiritual act, if it is tied back to the understanding and to the process itself. If the structure is in synchronization with that process, so that it does not become something extraordinary or out of the ordinary, it becomes something very ordinary. In other words, it is so natural, that it is not even seen as a spiritual act. I was looking at our community in that sense and asking what things have survived that still do that. If you are a community developer, you need to engage the community in looking for that and understand the tradition, how those traditions become reinterpreted, and then understanding how to strengthen those, so that they reintegrate back into people's lives in a natural way.

I found many things. I thought there had been a big loss, and there has, but actually many things have evolved, reinterpreted and displayed themselves in a very different way. I found that we as Okanagans find any excuse to get together. If somebody says that we are going to do something, then all of a sudden everybody will start showing up and participating. That is an Okanagan thing. If somebody said, these people over here need furniture or something built, so we are going to have this flea market or this supper or this rifle shoot, people who do not even engage in those things will show up. If everybody knows that people are raising money and half of the jackpot is going to go for nails or whatever for the longhouse, people will show up who do not even shoot rifles, who are not part of the hunter families. They will show up and they will pay their $5 and get

their three targets and they will hire somebody to shoot or whatever.

Inside of us as Okanagans, we want to help people to do things. We want to do it in a way that is enjoyable to us, so that is not like welfare or something like that. There is an understood principle that those people are putting time and effort into organizing themselves, so we need to assist with that. We will enjoy one another and will commune with one another. We will all take part in that good feeling.

In simple words, it is the good feeling more than the obligation to give that is the underlying motivation. We know that we do not have to say it but we can all feel it together. That is a communing to me, in a real community sense. That is the real strength and a tool that you could think about in reinstituting certain values in the community. It is an underlying functional process for a value that says that I enjoy giving because all these people enjoy giving. It is not so much dwelling on the responsibility which is where the emphasis is placed in some other religions but on the fun, the communal aspect.

We need to look at ways to reintegrate this aspect of our lives into education, not in a regimented, institutionalized sense, but as a way to expand and enrich our community. This does a number of things that politics and formal meetings can't do. It accomplishes things among people who are progressive and positive about community and economics and the material things that we need from each other.

In addition to the enow'kin, a democratic process where everyone is listening and engaging and which gives strength to each person, there is the internal spiritual need we are born with as humans. That is the creative need we have to feel part of others, the community, family, and nation, and the need to have that reinforced by our actions. While that is easily implemented because it is a natural process already there, it needs someone to give more permission and focus to it. So our educational process looked at teaching people about finding ways that families and whole communities can engage in that process. We talked about this with our leaders, the people in our communities, and with our elders especially. They said yes, that is the spirit of our people, that is the spirit of the Okanagan. That is the most important part of us. Otherwise, we could be anything else, and we will be anything else, unless we can as a community recognize how to keep that going.

The spiritual leaders, the medicine people who had done ceremonies during this process told us that we had their permission to go out as spiritual leaders, understanding that the spirituality of our people has to do with the internal spirit of our people. So wherever there is a communing of our people, that is a celebration of our spirit as Okanagan. It does not have to be in the traditional sense, like we used to have big pow wows and festivals. There can be a pow wow once a year but that is only once a year. You can have a festival maybe two or three times a year to feast different kinds of foods but only some of the people get to that. The awakening of the communal spirit is done maybe once or twice a year, where it needs to be awakened all the time. So they said, this may not appear to be spiritual processes or awakening because it is not recognized as ceremony, but any time people can pull together to do something, make or build something, to pool together to make something happen, in other words to be able to work together and give of each other, that is a spiritual practice. This is what pulls our people together spiritually.

RESERVATION SCHOOLS FAIL TO ASSIMILATE ALL STUDENTS

Tim Giago

The attempts to assimilate the Indian people into the great "melting pot" that is the United States through the education process has failed for many reasons.

First of all, in order to convince the young people that an education is beneficial, you must offer a guarantee for the future. When many Indian children discovered that there was no future for them, they reacted by dropping out of school. If getting an education meant being taken from family, friends and home and being isolated in a boarding school under the supervision of strict, often cruel, disciplinarians, then education was a thing to be feared.

Secondly, by isolating the Indian tribes on reservations, far away from the mainstream, the federal government insured solidarity in peer identification.

By including the destruction of a culture into the educational process using a hit-and-run approach, the Indian child became a human guinea pig and, therefore, fair game for every well-intentioned do-gooder and despot willing to give it a try. In order for white educators to create a new kind of Indian, in his own image, he first had to erase the Indian child's culture, religion and identity in order to have a clean blackboard to write his own ideas on.

As each experiment failed, a new one would spring up in its place, and this process was repeated over and over for more than 100 years. Is it any wonder that the Indian people finally said, "Enough is enough!"?

It is as American as apple pie for the average citizen to serve on the PTA or the school board. Do you realize that it wasn't until the 1970s, after the passage of Public Law 93-638, the Indian Education and Self-Determination Act, that Indian parents were allowed the same participation in the education of their children?

One teacher, an Indian woman, became absolutely furious when she was told by a white school administrator that "I'm glad to see that Indian parents are, at last, taking an interest in the education of their children." Her anger was understandable to most Indians. The parents of Indian children were totally excluded, in fact, were discouraged from sharing in the educational processes of their own children. Every aspect of education was in the hands of the BIA or the religious order that ran the mission schools.

The school system was intended to eliminate all ties with the past, not reinforce them.

Entire families were moved to the urban ghettos of this country during the great "relocation" experiment of the 1950s and 1960s. Men and women were encouraged to attend vocational schools and "learn a trade." You will find more unemployed "welders" and "iron workers" on Indian reservations than anywhere else in the United States. After all, what good does it do to teach a person a profession or trade if there are no jobs available in the field when he returns to the reservation?

In discussing the failures of many experiments in the education of Indian children, I am not referring to ancient history. I'm talking about my generation and the generation that followed mine into the reservation school system.

Not long ago I had a reunion with two classmates from an Indian mission school on the Pine Ridge Reservation, and, as usually happens when schoolmates get together, our conversation soon turned to other classmates.

We compared notes on the frequency of tragic incidents that were commonplace among our friends—incidents of tragic death, imprisonment, suicide or alcoholism permeated our conversation. Were these former classmates of ours victims of a misguided experiment in education? To those of us who survived this onslaught on our senses, it was a chilling thought.

Editorial by Tim Giago in *Indian Country Today*, 15, no. 34 (February 15, 1996). Copyright 1996 by Indian Country Today. Reprinted with permission.

CIVILIZE THEM WITH A STICK

Mary Brave Bird (Crow Dog) with Richard Erdoes

. . . Gathered from the cabin, the wickiup, and the tepee,
partly by cajolery and partly by threats;
partly by bribery and partly by force,
they are induced to leave their kindred
to enter these schools and take upon themselves
the outward appearance of civilized life. . . .
—Annual report of the Department
of Interior, 1901

It is almost impossible to explain to a sympathetic white person what a typical old Indian boarding school was like; how it affected the Indian child suddenly dumped into it like a small creature from another world, helpless, defenseless, bewildered, trying desperately and instinctively to survive and sometimes not surviving at all. I think such children were like the victims of Nazi concentration camps trying to tell average, middle-class Americans what their experience had been like. Even now, when these schools are much improved, when the buildings are new, all gleaming steel and glass, the food tolerable, the teachers well trained and well intentioned, even trained in child psychology—unfortunately the psychology of white children, which is different from ours—the shock to the child upon arrival is still tremendous. Some just seem to shrivel

up, don't speak for days on end, and have an empty look in their eyes. I know of an eleven-year-old on another reservation who hanged herself, and in our school, while I was there, a girl jumped out of the window, trying to kill herself to escape an unbearable situation. That first shock is always there.

Although the old tiyospaye has been destroyed, in the traditional Sioux families, especially in those where there is no drinking, the child is never left alone. It is always surrounded by relatives, carried around, enveloped in warmth. It is treated with the respect due to any human being, even a small one. It is seldom forced to do anything against its will, seldom screamed at, and never beaten. That much, at least, is left of the old family group among full-bloods. And then suddenly a bus or car arrives, full of strangers, usually white strangers, who yank the child out of the arms of those who love it, taking it screaming to the boarding school. The only word I can think of for what is done to these children is kidnapping.

Even now, in a good school, there is impersonality instead of close human contact; a sterile, cold atmosphere, an unfamiliar routine, language problems, and above all the maza-skan-skan, that damn clock—white man's time as opposed to Indian time, which is natural time. Like eating when you are hungry and sleeping when you are tired, not when that damn clock says you must. But I was not taken to one of the better, modern schools. I was taken to the old-fashioned mission school at St. Francis, run by the nuns and Catholic fathers, built sometime around the turn of the century and not improved a bit when I arrived, not improved as far as the buildings, the food, the teachers, or their methods were concerned.

In the old days, nature was our people's only school and they needed no other. Girls had their toy tipis and dolls, boys their toy bows and arrows. Both rode and swam and played the rough Indian games together. Kids watched their peers and elders and naturally grew from children into adults. Life in the tipi circle was harmonious—until the whiskey peddlers arrived with their wagons and barrels of "Injun whiskey." I often wished I could have grown up in the old, before-whiskey days.

Oddly enough, we owed our unspeakable boarding schools to the do-gooders, the white Indian-lovers. The schools were intended as an alternative to the outright extermination seriously advocated by generals Sherman and Sheridan, as well as by most settlers and prospectors overrunning our land. "You don't have to kill those poor benighted heathen," the do-gooders said, "in order to solve the Indian Problem. Just give us a chance to turn them into useful farmhands, laborers, and chambermaids who will break their backs for you at low wages." In that way the boarding schools

were born. The kids were taken away from their villages and pueblos, in their blankets and moccasins, kept completely isolated from their families—sometimes for as long as ten years—suddenly coming back, their short hair slick with pomade, their necks raw from stiff, high collars, their thick jackets always short in the sleeves and pinching under the arms, their tight patent leather shoes giving them corns, the girls in starched white blouses and clumsy, high-buttoned boots—caricatures of white people. When they found out—and they found out quickly—that they were neither wanted by whites nor by Indians, they got good and drunk, many of them staying drunk for the rest of their lives. I still have a poster I found among my grandfather's stuff, given to him by the missionaries to tack up on his wall. It reads:

1. Let Jesus save you.
2. Come out of your blanket, cut your hair, and dress like a white man.
3. Have a Christian family with one wife for life only.
4. Live in a house like your white brother. Work hard and wash often.
5. Learn the value of a hard-earned dollar. Do not waste your money on giveaways. Be punctual.
6. Believe that property and wealth are signs of divine approval.
7. Keep away from saloons and strong spirits.
8. Speak the language of your white brother. Send your children to school to do likewise.
9. Go to church often and regularly.
10. Do not go to Indian dances or to the medicine men.

The people who were stuck upon "solving the Indian Problem" by making us into whites retreated from this position only step by step in the wake of Indian protests.

The mission school at St. Francis was a curse for our family for generations. My grandmother went there, then my mother, then my sisters and I. At one time or other every one of us tried to run away. Grandma told me once about the bad times she had experienced at St. Francis. In those days they let students go home only for one week every year. Two days were used up for transportation, which meant spending just five days out of three hundred and sixty-five with her family. And that was an improvement. Before grandma's time, on many reservations they did not let the students go home at all until they had finished school. Anybody who disobeyed the nuns was severely punished. The building in which my grandmother stayed had three floors, for girls only. Way up in the attic were little cells, about five by five by ten feet. One time she was in church and instead of praying she was playing jacks. As punishment they took her to one of those little cubicles where she stayed in darkness because the windows had been boarded up. They left her there for a whole week with only bread and water for nourishment. After she came out she promptly ran away, together with three other girls. They were found and brought back. The nuns stripped them naked and whipped them. They used a horse buggy whip on my grandmother. Then she was put back into the attic—for two weeks.

My mother had much the same experiences but never wanted to talk about them, and then there I was, in the same place. The school is now run by the BIA—the Bureau of Indian Affairs—but only since about fifteen years ago. When I was there, during the 1960s, it was still run by the Church. The Jesuit fathers ran the boys' wing and the Sisters of the Sacred Heart ran us—with the help of the strap. Nothing had changed since my grandmother's days. I have been told

recently that even in the '70s they were still beating children at that school. All I got out of school was being taught how to pray. I learned quickly that I would be beaten if I failed in my devotions or, God forbid, prayed the wrong way, especially prayed in Indian to Wakan Tanka, the Indian Creator.

The girls' wing was built like an F and was run like a penal institution. Every morning at five o'clock the sisters would come into our large dormitory to wake us up, and immediately we had to kneel down at the sides of our beds and recite the prayers. At six o'clock we were herded into the church for more of the same. I did not take kindly to the discipline and to marching by the clock, left-right, left-right. I was never one to like being forced to do something. I do something because I feel like doing it. I felt this way always, as far as I can remember, and my sister Barbara felt the same way. An old medicine man once told me: "Us Lakotas are not like dogs who can be trained, who can be beaten and keep on wagging their tails, licking the hand that whipped them. We are like cats, little cats, big cats, wildcats, bobcats, mountain lions. It doesn't matter what kind, but cats who can't be tamed, who scratch if you step on their tails." But I was only a kitten and my claws were still small.

Barbara was still in the school when I arrived and during my first year or two she could still protect me a little bit. When Barb was a seventh-grader she ran away together with five other girls, early in the morning before sunrise. They brought them back in the evening. The girls had to wait for two hours in front of the mother superior's office. They were hungry and cold, frozen through. It was wintertime and they had been running the whole day without food, trying to make good their escape. The mother superior asked each girl, "Would you do this again?" She told them that as punishment they would not

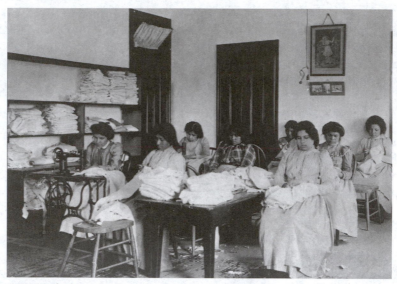

A 1890 clothes-mending class at the Carlisle Indian School in Pennsylvania.

be allowed to visit home for a month and that she'd keep them busy on work details until the skin on their knees and elbows had worn off. At the end of her speech she told each girl, "Get up from this chair and lean over it." She then lifted the girls' skirts and pulled down their underpants. Not little girls either, but teenagers. She had a leather strap about a foot long and four inches wide fastened to a stick, and beat the girls, one after another, until they cried. Barb did not give her that satisfaction but just clenched her teeth. There was one girl, Barb told me, the nun kept on beating and beating until her arm got tired.

I did not escape my share of the strap. Once, when I was thirteen years old, I refused to go to Mass. I did not want to go to church because I did not feel well. A nun grabbed me by the hair, dragged me upstairs, made me stoop over, pulled my dress up (we were not allowed at the time to wear jeans), pulled my panties down, and gave me what they called "swats"—twenty-five swats with a board around which Scotch tape had been wound. She hurt me badly.

My classroom was right next to the principal's office and almost every day I could hear him swatting the boys. Beating was the common punishment for not doing one's homework, or for being late to school. It had such a bad effect upon me that I hated and mistrusted every white person on sight, because I met only one kind. It was not until much later that I met sincere white people I could relate to and be friends with. Racism breeds racism in reverse.

The routine at St. Francis was dreary. Six A.M., kneeling in church for an hour or so; seven o'clock, breakfast; eight o'clock, scrub the floor, peel spuds, make classes. We had to mop the dining room twice every day and scrub the tables. If you were caught taking a rest, doodling on the bench with a fingernail or knife, or just rapping, the nun would come up with a dish towel and just slap it across your face, saying, "You're not supposed to be talking, you're supposed to be working!" Monday mornings we had cornmeal mush, Tuesday oatmeal, Wednesday rice and raisins, Thursday cornflakes, and Friday all the leftovers mixed together or sometimes fish. Frequently the food had bugs or rocks in it. We were eating hot dogs that were weeks old, while the nuns were dining on ham, whipped potatoes, sweet peas, and cranberry sauce. In winter our dorm was icy cold while the nuns' rooms were always warm.

I have seen little girls arrive at the school, first-graders, just fresh from home and totally unprepared for what awaited them, little girls with pretty braids, and the first thing the nuns did was chop their hair off and tie up what was left behind their ears. Next they would dump the children into tubs of alcohol, a sort of rubbing alcohol, "to get the germs off." Many of the nuns were German immigrants, some from Bavaria, so that we sometimes speculated whether Bavaria was some sort of Dracula country inhabited by monsters. For the sake of objectivity I ought to mention that two of the German fathers were great linguists and that the only Lakota-English dictionaries and grammars which are worth anything were put together by them.

At night some of the girls would huddle in bed together for comfort and reassurance. Then the nun in charge of the dorm would come in and say, "What are the two of you doing in bed together? I smell evil in this room. You girls are evil incarnate. You are sinning. You are going to hell and burn forever. You can act that way in the devil's frying pan." She would get them out of bed in the middle of the night, making them kneel and pray until morning. We had not the slightest idea what it was all about. At home we slept two and three in a bed for animal warmth and a feeling of security.

The nuns and the girls in the two top grades were constantly battling it out physically with fists, nails, and hair-pulling. I myself was growing from a kitten into an undersized cat. My claws were getting bigger and were itching for action. About 1969 or 1970 a strange young white girl appeared on the reservation. She looked about eighteen or twenty years old. She was pretty and had long, blond hair down to her waist, patched jeans, boots, and a backpack. She was different from any other white person we had met before. I think her name was Wise. I do not know how she managed to overcome our reluctance and distrust, getting us into a corner, making us listen to her, asking us how we were treated. She told us that she was from New York. She was the first real hippie or Yippie we had come across. She told us of people called the Black Panthers, Young Lords, and Weathermen. She said, "Black people are getting it on. Indians are getting it on in St. Paul and California. How about you?" She also said, "Why don't you put out an underground paper, mimeograph it. It's easy. Tell it like it is. Let it all hang out." She spoke a strange lingo but we caught on fast.

Charlene Left Hand Bull and Gina One Star were two full-blood girls I used to hang out with. We did everything together. They were willing to join me in a Sioux uprising. We put together a newspaper which we called the *Red Panther*. In it we wrote how bad the school was, what kind of slop we had to eat—slimy, rotten, blackened potatoes for two weeks—the way we were beaten. I think I was the one who wrote the worst article about our principal of the moment, Father Keeler. I put all my anger and venom into it. I called him a goddam wasičun son of a bitch. I wrote that he knew nothing about Indians and should go back to where he came from, teaching white children whom he could relate to. I wrote that we knew which priests slept with which nuns and that all they ever could think about was filling their bellies and buying a new car. It was the kind of writing which foamed at the mouth, but which also lifted a great deal of weight from one's soul.

On Saint Patrick's Day, when everybody was at the big powwow, we distributed our newspapers. We put them on windshields and bulletin boards, in desks and pews, in dorms and toilets. But someone saw us and snitched on us. The shit hit the fan. The three of us were taken before a board meeting. Our parents, in my case my mother, had to come. They were told that ours was a most serious matter, the worst thing that had ever happened in the school's long history. One of the nuns told my mother, "Your daughter really needs to be talked to." "What's wrong with my daughter?" my mother asked. She was given one of our *Red Panther* newspapers. The nun pointed out its name to her and then my piece, waiting for mom's reaction. After a while she asked, "Well, what have you got to say to this? What do you think?"

My mother said, "Well, when I went to school here, some years back, I was treated a lot worse than these kids are. I really can't see how they can have any complaints, because we was treated a lot stricter. We could not even wear skirts halfway up our knees. These girls have it made. But you should forgive them because they are young. And it's supposed to be a free country, free speech and all that. I don't believe what they done is wrong." So all I got out of it was scrubbing six flights of stairs on my hands and knees, every day. And no boy-side privileges.

The boys and girls were still pretty much separated. The only time one could meet a member of the opposite sex was during free time, between four and five-thirty, in the study hall or on benches or the volleyball court outside, and that was strictly supervised. One day Charlene and I went over to the boys' side. We were on the ball team and they had to let us practice. We played three extra minutes, only three minutes more than we were supposed to. Here was the nuns' opportunity for revenge. We got twenty-five swats. I told Charlene, "We are getting too old to have our bare asses whipped that way. We are old enough to have babies. Enough of this shit. Next time we fight back." Charlene only said, "Hoka-hay!"

We had to take showers every evening. One little girl did not want to take her panties off and one of the nuns told her, "You take those underpants off—or else!" But the child was ashamed to do it. The nun was getting her swat to threaten the girl. I went up to the sister, pushed her veil off, and knocked her down. I told her that if she wanted to hit a little girl she should pick on me, pick one her own size. She got herself transferred out of the dorm a week later.

In a school like this there is always a lot of favoritism. At St. Francis it was strongly tinged with racism. Girls who were near-white, who came from what the nuns called "nice families," got preferential treatment. They waited on the faculty and got to eat ham or eggs and bacon in the morning. They got the easy jobs while the skins, who did not have the right kind of background—myself among them—always wound up in the laundry room sorting out ten bushel baskets of dirty boys' socks every day. Or we wound up scrubbing the floors and doing all the dishes. The school therefore fostered fights and antagonism between whites and breeds, and between breeds and skins. At one time Charlene and I had to iron all the robes and vestments the priests wore when saying Mass. We had to fold them up and put them into a chest in the back of the church. In a corner, looking over our shoulders, was a statue of the crucified Savior, all bloody and beaten up. Charlene looked up and said, "Look at that poor Indian. The pigs sure worked him over." That was the closest I ever came to seeing Jesus.

I was held up as a bad example and didn't mind. I was old enough to have a boyfriend and promptly got one. At the school we had an hour and a half for ourselves. Between the boys' and the girls' wings were some benches where one could sit. My boyfriend and I used to go there just to hold hands and talk. The nuns were very uptight about any boy-girl stuff. They had an exaggerated fear of anything having even the faintest connection with sex. One day in religion class, an all-girl class, Sister Bernard singled me out for some remarks, pointing me out as a bad example, an example that should be shown. She said that I was too free with my body. That I was holding hands which meant that I was not a good example to follow. She also said that I wore unchaste dresses, skirts which were too short, too suggestive, shorter than regulations permitted, and for that I would be punished. She dressed me down before the whole class, carrying on and on about my unchastity.

I stood up and told her, "You shouldn't say any of those things, miss. You people are a lot worse than us Indians. I know all about you, because my grandmother and my aunt told me about you. Maybe twelve, thirteen years ago you had a water stoppage here in St. Francis. No water could get through the pipes. There are water lines right under the mission, underground tunnels and passages where in my grandmother's time only the nuns and priests could go, which were off-limits to everybody else. When the water backed up they had to go through all the water lines and clean them out. And in those huge pipes they found the bodies of newborn babies. And they were white babies. They weren't Indian babies. At least when our girls have babies, they don't do away with them that way, like flushing them down the toilet, almost.

"And that priest they sent here from Holy Rosary in Pine Ridge because he molested a little girl. You couldn't think of anything better than dump him on us. All he does is watch young women and girls with that funny smile on his face. Why don't you point him out for an example?"

Charlene and I worked on the school newspaper. After all we had some practice. Every day we went down to Publications. One of the priests acted as the photographer, doing the enlarging and developing. He smelled of chemicals which had stained his hands yellow. One day he invited Charlene into the darkroom. He was going to teach her developing. She was developed already. She was a big girl compared to him, taller too. Charlene was nicely built, not fat, just rounded. No sharp edges anywhere. All of a sudden she rushed out of the darkroom, yelling to me, "Let's get out of here! He's trying to feel me up. That priest is nasty." So there was this too to contend with—sexual harassment. We complained to the student body. The nuns said we just had a dirty mind.

We got a new priest in English. During one of his first classes he asked one of the boys a certain question. The boy was shy. He spoke poor English, but he had the right answer. The priest told him, "You did not say it right. Correct yourself. Say it over again." The boy got flustered and stammered. He could hardly get out a word. But the priest kept after him: "Didn't you hear? I told you to do the whole thing over. Get it right this time." He kept on and on.

I stood up and said, "Father, don't be doing that. If you go into an Indian's home and try to talk Indian, they might laugh at you and say, 'Do it over correctly. Get it right this time!'"

He shouted at me, "Mary, you stay after class. Sit down right now!"

I stayed after class, until after the bell. He told me, "Get over here!" He grabbed me by the arm, pushing me against the blackboard, shouting, "Why are you always mocking us? You have no reason to do this."

I said, "Sure I do. You were making fun of him. You embarrassed him. He needs strengthening, not weakening. You hurt him. I did not hurt you."

He twisted my arm and pushed real hard. I turned around and hit him in the face, giving him a bloody nose. After that I ran out of the room, slamming the door behind me. He and I went to Sister Bernard's office. I told her, "Today I quit school. I'm not taking any more of this, none of this shit anymore. None of this treatment. Better give me my diploma. I can't waste any more time on you people."

Sister Bernard looked at me for a long, long time. She said, "All right, Mary Ellen, go home today. Come back in a few days and get your diploma." And that was that. Oddly enough, that priest turned out okay. He taught a class in grammar, orthography, composition, things like that. I think he wanted more respect in class. He was still young and unsure of himself. But I was in there too long. I didn't feel like hearing it. Later he became a good friend of the Indians, a personal friend of myself and my husband. He stood up for us during Wounded Knee and after. He stood up to his superiors, stuck his neck way out, became a real people's priest. He even learned our language. He died prematurely of cancer. It is not only the good Indians who die young, but the good whites, too. It is the timid ones who know how to take care of themselves who grow old. I am still grateful to that priest for what he did for us later and for the quarrel he picked with me—or did I pick it with him?—because it ended a situation which had become unendurable for me. The day of my fight with him was my last day in school.

URBAN AMERICAN INDIAN PRESCHOOL

Susan Lobo

During the past 15 years, American Indians in the San Francisco Bay Area have established and maintained an early childhood education school to meet the community's special needs. The results have been significant

Susan Lobo, "Urban American Indian Preschool," *Cultural Survival Quarterly,* 10, no. 4. Copyright 1986 by Cultural Survival. Reprinted with permission.

and far-reaching. A setting has been created that reinforces a strong and positive sense of self-identity for Indian children, while developing social and academic skills. The extended family has become strengthened while participating in the process of school building, and parents (particularly mothers) have been freed to find employment or to study. In addition, the Indian community, structured as a web of relationships with various spheres of activity, has been fortified over the long term by sustaining the school in the face of many crises.

FOUNDING THE PRESCHOOL

Since the 1940s, the San Francisco Bay Area has acted as a magnet for American Indian people from throughout the United States. They have migrated primarily from rural and reservation areas. Many have come to escape dire living conditions or crisis at home, or to follow the hope of a better life in the city. This migration swelled substantially in the 1950s with the establishment of the Federal Relocation Act. Oakland was designated as one of the national relocation sites, creating there a large, active, and multitribal Indian community. Current estimates based on the 1980 census indicate approximately 40,000 American Indians in the greater Bay Area.

One result of the residential dispersion in the city has been that Indian people come together in ways other than sharing a neighborhood: through sports teams, at the Indian centers in Oakland and San Francisco, in the Indian bars, and at the many Indian agencies and organizations that developed as specialized needs were recognized. The development of the American Indian Pre-School has been a particularly effective response to the educational needs of the children.

In 1971–72 a group of Indian parents with children at Hawthorne Elementary School formed Concerned Parents of Oakland. The need for appropriate and good education for their children was something that touched all families in a very personal way. It touched off the process of learning about the Oakland Public School system, and how to make a change in that system.

Hawthorne School had a high Indian enrollment, and also the only American Indian teacher then in the district. As the group began to meet and draw in more and more parents, they began to articulate their motivations.

> We know that a part of our survival means maintaining ourselves as a people. . . . We have a consciousness that there is an educational history of our values being taken away from us at boarding schools. . . . Here in the city we were seeing the same kinds of things happening. Maintaining our values as Indian people is very important.

The Concerned Parents of Oakland was formed to work with the superintendent and the school district in a collaborative way to address these needs. The superintendent at that time was responsive, particularly when the Concerned Parents pointed out the extremely high dropout rate for American Indian children, even in elementary grades. An American Indian liaison position was established.

At that time federal and state money was becoming available for educational innovations. The American Indian liaison working with the Oakland Public School staff and the Concerned Parents wrote a proposal, and received a three-year Title III ESEA grant for the American Indian Pre-School. Previously established Chicano and Chinese pre-schools affiliated with the Oakland Public School system created a precedent for the concept, and served as a model for structuring the pre-school.

In the fall of 1973, the pre-school was started in the large recreation room of Intertribal Friendship House in Oakland. Intertribal, established in 1955, had long been the focal point of community social services and a meeting spot where many Indian community issues are worked out.

The pre-school started with one morning and one afternoon class with 25 children, one teacher and four parents per class. Since this was a parent participation pre-school, each parent worked one day a week in the classroom and attended a weekly one-day parent workshop. Parents received a stipend of $25 per month, which assisted with transportation and other necessities for their participation and that of their children. The room was painted, toys and games were donated, and shelving was built through parent effort.

One of the strengths of these first years was the weekly workshop in which the parents made materials for the school representing different tribes. There were pottery workshops and cooking workshops, and beading and weaving demonstrations for the children. Parents and grandparents became "cultural consultants," and were eventually paid by the school district. One mother comments:

> One elder tells stories to the kids, and the kids tell us, and it goes into their writing. It is all linked. It all comes back to us in that way.

A teacher says:

> It has helped to have the grandparents involved. They taught the younger teachers to be more patient.

During the Friday parents' workshops there were many discussions on ways of surviving in the city, and how it was different raising children in the city than in the country or on a reservation. A teacher says:

> The workshops particularly became a gathering spot and focus of community action and decision making. It was a structure that allowed people in the community to have a voice and to participate.

The pre-school increasingly played a role in strengthening the fabric of the Indian community. A teacher comments:

> There are different spheres in the community. Then something comes along that cross-cuts those spheres and brings the community

together. For 15 years, that's what the pre-school has done.

While Intertribal Friendship House was an ideal setting for the pre-school in terms of the social support represented, there were also drawbacks, and the program eventually outgrew its quarters. By the end of the first three-year grant period, enrollment had increased to 100 students.

Again there were trips to the school board. In response to wide parent support and effective appeals, it was finally decided that the pre-school could be funded through the Oakland Public Schools Child Centers Program, and that a more permanent site would be located. A mother says,

> Once my daughter (who was 10) went to the school board and spoke. I was really proud of her. It takes care of the families, and then the families take care of the pre-school. It is now a part of our way of life.

The pre-school relocated to the Carl Munck School, at the same time changing its name to Hintil Kuu Ca, a Pomo Indian phrase meaning "Indian children's house."

There were other changes, too. Hintil expanded to full day care from 7 A.M. to 5:30 P.M. Enrollment was limited to 110 and there is a waiting list. In addition to the pre-school group, there is a kindergarten group, and first through sixth graders participate in before- and after-school programs. Tutoring for grade schoolers is also provided. There are six teachers and aides for the pre-school, and four for the before- and after-school program. There is a parent education teacher and an educational resource teacher. Over the years, the school's existence has created a large pool of Indian teachers and aides with classroom experience.

The school district's criterion for accepting children in the school is that parents are working or in school. Some feel there has been a shift away from active parent participation and that this might mean a "professionalization," and a move away from the community-based decision making and control that had characterized the pre-school from the beginning.

Yet in the characteristically strategic style that the parents had carefully honed by years of dealing with the school district, resources and structures were found or shaped to fit their needs. For example, although the Friday parents' workshop no longer exists, a class in parent education functions similarly to the original parents' workshop. This group continues to act as a support group for the school, making classroom materials that reflect tribal values and orientation.

At Hintil, the introduction of a resource teacher furthers the use of educational materials that reinforce the children's cultural identity. The designs from basketry and beadwork are used in matching games. Parents continue to make tribal outfits that children use on special days and at community-wide events. Teachers use stories and legends of the various tribes and often have children use natural materials found outside for their classroom projects.

At the high school level, Indian youth in Oakland who were in elementary school before Hintil have difficulties, some of which are reflected in the extremely high dropout rate. For example, in 1983 there were 41 Indian students in ninth grade in Oakland public schools. By 1986, that class had dwindled to 12 Indian students, and of those, only five graduated. Parents and teachers who have seen children go through the pre-school and the support system offered by Hintil feel they are doing better than their older brothers and sisters who did not have this opportunity. These younger children did generally well at Carl Munck and graduated from the sixth grade in June 1987. They represented one-third of the school's population; they stayed in school; and in many ways their lives reflected the values that were taught during their early pre-school years. Through the 1990s the school continued to be a cornerstone of the Bay Area Indian community.

Since the beginning of the pre-school, an educational philosophy has taken form. This philosophy took shape in an urban intertribal setting, with strong participation by parents and teachers, many of whom had spent their school years in boarding schools far from their homes, their parents and community participation in the educational process.

Teachers and parents at Hintil speak of the school's philosophy of reinforcing the children's sense of self-identity:

> The original idea has been to have a place to strengthen the young child, to give them a good positive image of themselves, an image of Indian people before they had to go into kindergarten in a mixed environment. We are helping support the families in giving the child self-confidence. Fifteen years ago, there wasn't even that option.
>
> The emphasis in public schools is on what can be measured, not how you feel about things, which can't be measured. Self-awareness and self-image are never tested in public schools.
>
> The education in the White world is for different purposes. There one is successful as an individual through competition. In tribal society what's important is finding one's place and relating to a large number of people. This is a very different perception of what a real human being is. Every Indian person is working on reconciling these different philosophies. . . .

Many acknowledge that the federal program of relocation, with the underlying goal of assimilating Indians into the larger society, ironically helped the Oakland Indians create an educational setting in which Indian parents are active participants, and tribal values can be passed down to the children. The school is another victory for Indian survival, and another demonstration of the tenacity and energy that can be directed toward assuring that survival.

SURVIVAL SCHOOLS
THE MOHAWKS IN MONTREAL

Julian Burger

The movement to set up indigenous schools in the United States and Canada spread during the 1960s and 1970s, when indigenous peoples began to recognize that only through the re-education of their children could indigenous nations survive. The Kahnawake School is one of a number of survival schools, established and run by indigenous peoples.

The idea of a school for Montreal's Mohawk children began after a snowball fight between two boys in 1971. Both were guilty, but only one was suspended. The punished boy was Indian and the other was white. As a protest indigenous children at the school occupied the main auditorium for three days. They felt unwelcome in the school, they said. They had no Mohawk history or language lessons, and they faced daily discrimination. In a school of 2700 students only 400 or so were indigenous. The only Mohawk staffmember in the school was the janitor.

The children were backed by their parents. They demanded accredited courses on Mohawk culture and indigenous teachers. Not only were indigenous peoples losing their identity in the national education system, they realized, but they were coming out of it with the lowest grades. A change was necessary. The parents won some concessions from the Quebec government; an Indian counsellor was appointed, some native teachers were recruited, and classes in Mohawk history and language were opened. But the people still felt unhappy. In 1978 they called a referendum to decide whether to create an Indian high school. There was overwhelming support from the community, but a firm "no" from the government. Once again the children and their parents demonstrated, calling for assistance from their community. Teachers volunteered to work for

nothing, while community leaders and local people found equipment and space. On 9 September 1978, after only four days, the Mohawk community had set up its own Indian-run school in Canada; the Kahnawake Survival School. "Educating our own children is the bottom line to our survival, which we hold to be the most important and urgent priority before us." Rokwaho, for the Mohawk Council of Chiefs of Akwesasne.

From Julian Burger, *The Gaia Atlas of First Peoples*. Copyright 1990 by Gaia Books Ltd., London. Reprinted with permission.

PROTAGONISM EMERGENT
INDIANS AND HIGHER EDUCATION

Jeffrey Wollock

No facet of 20th century Native life more dramatically illustrates the adaptive, transformative power of Indian cultures than higher education. At the start of this century, the number of Indian college graduates could be counted on one hand. And to the question of the Indian's future in America, only one answer seemed possible: total assimilation. Today, there are thousands of Native college graduates, and more than 30 reservation communities have their own colleges. . . .

TOTAL ASSIMILATION

In 1887, the General Allotment Act, also known as the Dawes Act after its chief sponsor, was enacted specifically to extinguish tribalism and turn Indians into "useful" citizens. Vast tribal lands, held communally, were to be broken up and allotted in severalty to Indian individuals, and all "surplus" land was to be sold off to non-Indians. Although it was not written into the legislation, the supporters of Allotment, notably Sen. Dawes himself, emphasized that success depended on educating Indians in agriculture, ranching, and industrial skills,

From "Protagonism Emergent: Indians and Higher Education," by Jeffrey Wollock, *Native Americas* (Winter 1997). Reprinted by permission of Akwe:kon Press. Portions of the original article have been omitted.

as well as in English, and the responsibilities of citizenship. When deemed by the government "competent," Indians would become citizens and, hopefully, at some point in the near future, so assimilated as to be indistinguishable from any other Americans.

This mission would be accomplished through a system of federal Indian boarding schools championed by Richard Henry Pratt (1840–1924). It was Pratt's belief that the only way to get Indians into American culture was to separate them at an early age from all Native cultural influences and place them in the midst of mainstream society. This philosophy was embodied in the federal boarding schools, located far from reservations and run with military discipline, and the "outing system," which temporarily placed Indian students in the homes of white families and schools, and sometimes in jobs working with whites. Under this policy, which would reign until 1934, the characteristic form of Indian education was vocational.

The first of the federal Indian boarding schools, Carlisle, had been founded by Pratt in 1879, and by 1900 there were 26 of them. Aside from basic training in "the three Rs," the emphasis was on trades, agriculture and industrial arts, and none of the schools went beyond the eighth grade. Yet the education offered at many of them was solid as far as it went. It should be pointed out that at that time most whites did not have a high-school education either, and an eighth-grade education meant a lot more than it does now. Furthermore, many Indian students started late, sometimes very late, and some were well into their 20s by the time they graduated.

Pratt's goal of breaking up tribes, along with his unshakable belief in the worthlessness of any aspect of Indian culture for future development, might make him appear to be some kind of racist. But in fact, he and his followers were liberals. All his theories were based on the premise that Indians had exactly the same capacities as whites and were absolutely capable of equal achievement—a notion that was by no means universally held at that time. Pratt believed it was only their antiquated tribal culture and their isolation that held Indians back from successfully competing in the white man's world. Conservatives, in contrast, simply believed that Indians had no future and thus, schools for them were a waste of time and money.

Pratt's theory was simple and clear but, like any ideology, it embodied much wishful thinking and many false and simplistic assumptions. Among the biggest fallacies were that Indian culture was a dead end, that Indians did not know what was best for their own good, and that the reformers did. However, while Pratt's theory was monolithic, its effects on the thousands of youngsters who went through this kind of education were anything but. The schools were not exactly alike, and all of them changed over time. In general, it can be said that although along with trauma and cultural loss, the schools also fostered a kind of pride in achievement and—since the students were, after all, entirely Indian and some of the staff as well—an *esprit de corps.* Indeed, rather than

stamping out Indian identity altogether, the federal schools unintentionally created an entirely new phenomenon, one that would have enormous consequences for the 20th century: pan-Indianism.

THE NEW INDIAN ELITE

At the opening of the 20th century, higher education had almost no place in Indian life. Attempts since colonial days to develop university training for Indians had been a complete failure. Long after some tribes had made the transition to European-style agriculture and accepted the value of some kind of education on the European model, no need for higher education was felt by either the tribes or the Indian Bureau. "The need of higher education among the Indians is very, very limited," stated Theodore Roosevelt in his presidential report of 1901. At a time when a college degree was rare even among whites, the barriers to Indians were especially formidable. Although a few private institutions like Bacone College, Armstrong Academy, and the Santee Normal School offered a somewhat more academic program, there was no Indian school in 1900 that could be said to prepare its students for higher education.

Nevertheless, by the early years of the century a tiny core of college-educated Indians already existed and was active on the national level. Most, though not all, were admirers of Pratt and were strongly influenced by his assimilationist philosophy. Thus, the idea of Indian higher education in this century was born in contradiction. The Allotment ideology saw a college education only as an advanced stage in the assimilation process. Yet this first generation of college-educated Indians by no means ceased to be Indians, rather, they saw themselves as the vanguard, the Indian of the future. They gravitated together in 1911 to form the Society of American Indians, the first national pan-Indian organization, in an attempt to assert control over the Indian rights movement, which until then, was dominated by non-Indians.

Not all of this new generation were convinced of the wisdom of total assimilation. Gertrude Bonnin had attended Carlisle and taught there from 1898 to 1902. In autobiographical sketches published in *Harper's* and *Atlantic Monthly* in 1900 and 1901, she expressed criticism of Pratt's suppression of Indian language and culture based on her experiences at Carlisle. Between 1912–1920 Laura Cornelius Kellogg designed a plan for Indian development, the "Lolomi Plan," that would be customized to the circumstances of each tribe. Far from breaking up the reservations, she advocated turning each one into a self-sufficient community based on economic development appropriate to each culture and region, in many ways foreshadowing the ideals of John Collier two decades later.

Some even tried, with considerable success, to influence American society to become more "Indian." Charles Eastman reconciled assimilation into the larger society with his cultural pride as a Sioux, endeavoring through writings and lectures, work with the Boy Scouts, and with Ernest Thompson Seton, to make American youth more appreciative of Indian social and environmental values.

Rather than disappearing, this group found itself increasingly called upon for the first time to think about and articulate an Indian perspective on what it meant to be Indian in the midst of white society, a subject that, at the time, the liberals as well as the conservatives had hoped to render moot. Given their ideological indoctrination and lack of models, it is not surprising that many of this new elite's ideas were self-contradictory, half-formed, or ambiguous.

But they discussed these ideas, commenting and arguing about the benefits of citizenship, whether the Indian Bureau should be abolished, land claims and other legal issues, and of course, what kind of education was best for Indians. While many saw these college-educated Indians as elitists out of touch with their own people, they were, nonetheless, Indians discussing an Indian future. No matter what their views, all of them were concerned with what they called "building up the race," and helping their people. From this standpoint, they were already articulating the importance of higher education to Indians. Some were already thinking about the possibility of an Indian college or university.

AN INDIAN UNIVERSITY

Pratt always opposed the idea of an Indian college or university, seeing it as a segregating device that would tend to undo all his work to get the Indian into the midst of white society. In a letter to Carlos Montezuma [Yavapai, 1866?–1923—M.D., Chicago Medical College, 1889] in 1914, he even criticized the idea of an Indian preparatory school. Yet as early as 1911, August Breuninger, a mixed-blood Menominee, advocated an Indian university with Indian cultural emphasis in a letter to Carlos Montezuma. So did Arthur C. Parker in "The Philosophy of Indian Education," a talk at the First Annual Conference of the Society of American Indians, held in Columbus, Ohio, in 1911. In the November 1912 issue of *The Southern Workman*, the Hampton Institute's monthly magazine, Parker wrote of "The great need of teaching the Indian to appreciate and measure his own culture in the full knowledge of others . . ." and "the necessity of an Indian college or university. Others, both Indian and non-Indian, share in this belief . . . graduates of the higher schools might be trained in the arts, literature, history, ethnology, and the philosophy of their people. Along with such subjects might be taught political and social sciences and such other academic branches as might be found necessary."

To promote interest, the Society of American Indians had solicited essays by pre-college students on the value of higher education to Indians. Some were printed in the first issue of *The Quarterly Journal of the Society of American Indians,* published in the summer of 1913. Parker, the editor, included his own essay, "The Real Value of Higher Education for the Indian." While he favored the idea of an Indian university, he did not expect to see one any time soon. Until then, he recommended a "white man's education" as essential to Indian survival and independence. "Not every Indian ought to go to college," he wrote, "any more than every white . . . but there should be as many Indian college men in proportion to the number of Indians as there are white college graduates in proportion to the number of white Americans."

The number of Indians in four-year institutions, though still very small, was increasing. Much of the problem was college preparation. As mentioned above, the federal Indian schools were not geared towards this, and in the early 1900s there were few institutions of this kind for Indians. Henry Roe Cloud's article "Education of the American Indian" in the July-September 1914 issue of *American Indian Magazine* (reprinted in *Southern Workman,* January 1915), is one of the best discussions from that period. In a speech in 1914, given at the 32nd Lake Mohonk Conference, an influential gathering of Indian rights activists, Cloud [Winnebago, 1884–1950—D.D., Emporia, 1932] criticized the BIA's exclusive concentration on vocational subjects and limit to eight grades, noting that it gave no

opportunity for capable students to get a higher education. While still at Yale, Cloud had unsuccessfully tried to persuade Yale to fund an Indian high school.

Establishing a preparatory school to develop Christian Indian leadership had been the dream of Cloud's mentor, the Rev. Walter C. Roe, a highly respected missionary. While Roe, who died in 1913, did not live to see his dream become a reality, his protege, now an ordained Presbyterian minister, founded a high school for Indian boys. The Roe Indian Institute, later renamed the American Indian Institute, opened at Wichita, Kansas in 1915, with six students. The faculty included three Indians: James Ottipoby (Comanche), Robert Starr (Cheyene-Arapaho), and Roy Ussery (Cherokee). Ottipoby, who taught history, had a bachelor's degree from Hope College; Starr, who taught agriculture, was a graduate of Oklahoma State. Ussery taught science. Religion was also taught. Until 1923, the AII was one of only three Indian high schools in the country. Challenged by Cloud's example, the Bureau that year added the high school grades to six of its boarding schools.

The AII's student body was never large. There were six graduates in 1926 and nine in 1932. Most graduates did enter college, only four ever got degrees: Lyman Priest, 1931; Jay Hunter, 1933; Levi Beaver, 1937, all at Wichita State; and George Martin, at Friends University, Wichita. The main problem seems to have been lack of funding, as John Charles (Navajo), a former student, testified at a congressional hearing in 1931. Cloud left the Institute when he took a position with the BIA in 1931. The school was taken over by the Presbyterian Board of Home Missions, and there were 46 students by 1931–32. In 1933, however, it was decided to terminate the program, mainly because the Bureau now had high schools. The

Institute became a dormitory for Indians to live in while attending public high schools or colleges in Wichita. It closed for good in 1939.

During the 1920s, while the policies of the Indian Bureau impeded development, churches, as they had for more than a half a century, exercised a major influence in Indian higher education. There was, in fact, already one Indian institution of higher learning, Bacone College, a small junior college. Founded by Baptist missionaries in Indian Territory in 1880, it was moved in 1881 to land donated by the Creek Nation at Muskogee. Influential, especially in the arts and education, Bacone prepared many Indians to continue at four-year colleges. Important in the development of Indian art, the college gave birth to a style known as the "Bacone school," which drew on tribal traditions. The art program there dates back to 1935, when it was headed by Acee Blue Eagle (Creek/Pawnee, 1907–1959), then by Woody Crumbo (Potawatomi, 1912–1989), and in 1947, Richard West Sr. (Cheyenne, 1912–1996).

Bacone was also the home of Mary Stone McLendon (Chickasaw-Choctaw, 1895–1967), known as Ataloa, an educator, artist and musician with a bachelor of arts from the University of Redlands and a master of arts from Columbia Teachers College. In the mid-1920s she was at the International Institute at Columbia on an honorary scholarship, the first, and at the time, the only Indian there. She taught English and philosophy at Bacone from 1927 to 1935, and founded an Indian art museum there, even designing the building and interior furnishings herself. . . .

In 1928, students at Haskell, a federal Indian high school in Lawrence, Kansas, wanted to turn it into a junior college. They did not quite achieve this, but a junior college program was set up that year,

graduating its first class of 28 in June 1929. Unfortunately it was abolished in 1932 because the BIA believed it impeded assimilation. One of the most important graduates of the short-lived Haskell junior college program was Robert Benett, later Commissioner of Indian Affairs under President Lyndon Johnson. Haskell would eventually become a junior college in 1970 and a university in 1993.

At the University of Pennsylvania, the anthropologist Frank Speck made a special effort to train Indians in ethnology. Often they came as non-matriculated students. Among them were Louis Shotridge (Chilkat), who was there before World War I and did field work in Alaska; Molly Spotted Elk (Penobscot, 1903–1977); and Gladys Tantaquidgeon (b. 1899), who studied there from 1919–1927, going on to found the Mohegan Museum in 1931, the first museum in the United States founded and run by Indians.

The influential Meriam Report of 1928, which Henry Roe Cloud had helped prepare, came down against the conversion of one of the federal schools into a college, recommending all high schools be retained to prepare students for college. Later, in the 1940s, Archie Phinney tried unsuccessfully to get the BIA to set up an "Indian Service College." It would not be until the 1960s, in a growing wave of pan-Indian nationalism and increasing public concern, when all advisory studies recommended strengthening community control of Indian education, that the idea of an Indian university surfaced once again. In 1961, Dr. Jack D. Forbes (Delaware-Powhatan, b. 1934) wrote a "Proposal to Create an Indian University," to be "Indian-centered and Indian controlled." This time, the idea would become a reality. Forbes' efforts would culminate in the founding of D-Q University at Davis, California, in 1971.

EDUCATION'S NEW DEAL

In 1923, Henry Roe Cloud served on the Committee of One Hundred, a body appointed by Secretary of Interior Hubert Work to report on conditions in Indian country. Also on the Committee were Charles Eastman (Sioux) and the Rev. Philip Gordon (Ojibwa), at that time the only ordained Indian Catholic priest in the country. Though Cloud initially was opposed to government funding, his experience on the committee made him realize that most Indian students simply could not attend college without government help. Thus, the Committee's final report recommended government scholarships for Indians to go to high school and college.

In 1926, Cloud was the only Indian named to the 10-man staff preparing the Meriam report, a successor to the Committee of One Hundred. The section on education was written by W. Carson Ryan, whom Indian Commissioner Charles J. Rhoads would soon appoint head of the Bureau's educational work. The Meriam Report also recommended federal scholarships and loans. Strongly influenced by the Meriam report, Rhoads took a great interest in higher education. He hired Cloud—the youngest of the founding members of the Society of American Indians, now one of the few to make the transition to the post-Meriam BIA—as field representative in September of 1931. In this position, which he would hold for two years, Cloud started his own education program.

Another important appointment was a young Cherokee educator and community development activist named Ruth Muskrat Bronson (1897–1982), a former eighth-grade teacher at Haskell, educated at the University of Oklahoma, the University of Kansas, and Mount Holyoke College in Massachusetts (B.A., 1925). Like Cloud and

Ataloa, Bronson in the 1920s was already campaigning for a kind of education that was not strongly assimilationist, one that would allow the preservation of "what was best" in Native cultures. The Meriam Report had recommended that the Indian Bureau hire a "guidance and placement specialist." In 1930 Bronson took a position with the new Guidance Office in the BIA's Office of Education.

The Meriam Report also emphasized the need for scholarship and loan programs. In 1928, by far the largest share of Indian students in the country (200) were at the University of Oklahoma. In 1930, Congress instituted a loan fund for post-secondary students in nursing, home economics, and forestry, allocating $15,000 annually. In 1932, it authorized $10,000 annually for a tuition fund. In that year, when Bronson took charge of the loan program, there were only 385 American Indian and Alaska Natives in all four-year colleges and only 52 known college graduates. Also in 1932, the University of Michigan inaugurated a scholarship for Indians, becoming one of only five institutions of higher learning to have such a program.

In 1933, President Franklin D. Roosevelt appointed John Collier (1884–1968) commissioner of Indian Affairs. The Collier administration, whatever its shortcomings, represented a momentous change in official Indian policy. Here for the first time was an administration officially committed to the existence and continuity of tribal communities and cultures. The Indian Reorganization Act of 1934 ended Allotment and encouraged tribes to form constitutional governments. Preferential hiring of Indians, a policy inaugurated by the Rhoads administration, was written into law under the IRA. The Indian Bureau now became a magnet for educated Indians who began to transform this notoriously corrupt and ineffective institution and to develop a real Indian intelligentsia and professional corps.

Henry Roe Cloud supported the IRA because he believed in Indian cultural survival and had come to understand the need for federal support of education. The Act set aside $250,000 for post-secondary loans. Between 1935 and 1944, 1,933 students received them, and of these, 743 graduated, 458 from four-year colleges and universities, 159 from postsecondary vocational schools, 126 from nursing schools. Though the loan program would continue until 1952, time would prove that too many recipients were unable to pay back the loans, and it would be essentially replaced by the nonreimbursable scholarship program of 1948 (HEGP), which continues today.

In August 1933, Cloud was named Superintendent of Haskell, the first fullblood to head a federal Indian boarding school. Though he believed Indians needed to modernize, he greatly respected Native culture. Asserting that under his watch, "Haskell is definitely committed to the preservation of Indian race culture," he instituted new courses on Indian history and art. Yet, consistent with the Meriam Report, he did not favor an Indian college or university, believing that all emphasis should go toward preparing Indians to enter existing universities. When urged by A.A. Exendine of the Bureau (letter, Aug. 23, 1933) to convert Haskell into a college, he respectfully declined.

In 1934–35, there were still only 515 American Indian college students, 181 of whom were receiving federal or tribal assistance. Ruth Bronson, who had been working out of Kansas, moved to Washington in 1935. The following year, Cloud became supervisor of Indian Education, remaining in that position until 1939. Collier also added to his staff a number of young college-educated Indians who would play an important role in the development of higher education, especially D'Arcy McNickle (1904–1977) and Archie Phinney (1904–1949).

McNickle (Flathead), studied history and literature at Montana State University (1921–1925), though he did not graduate. He studied privately at Oxford in the fall of 1925 but, finding himself out of his element and dismayed when he learned it would take two years just to earn a bachelor's degree, soon returned to the United States. In 1929, he enrolled in Columbia University, where he took history courses through 1931.

In 1935, McNickle applied for a job with the BIA. His frustration with the application process illustrates the point that the "Indianization" of the BIA was also a professionalization, with all the good and bad points that implies. For McNickle was a brilliant generalist, a superb writer and historian, but had no "official" qualification in a specialty. His study of anthropology, for example, grew mainly out of a correspondence with anthropological linguist William Gates of Johns Hopkins. McNickle's application was finally approved in February 1936, and he became administrative assistant in the Indian Organization division, though he often worked with the Tribal Relations division as well.

Archie Phinney, on the other hand, a Nez Perce anthropologist and scholar, was probably the most "qualified" applicant the BIA had ever seen. The first Indian ever to graduate from the University of Kansas, with a bachelor of arts in sociology in 1926, Phinney was hired as a clerk in the BIA in Washington, and took evening graduate courses in ethnology and philosophy at George Washington University. From 1928 to 1932, he did part-time community social work with New York University's Extension Division while continuing graduate research at Columbia University in historical processes in race and cultural contacts under anthropologist Franz Boas, with special emphasis on Indian reservation life.

In January 1944, Phinney served briefly as superintendent of the Fort Totten reservation, North Dakota, but was promoted in November to superintendent of the Northern Idaho agency, his own reservation of Nez Perce, where he tried to set up a viable IRA government and worked to help the tribe preserve their traditions, including the establishment of museum and a library.

Phinney played a central part in developing support for a national Indian organization. The idea actually went back to 1939, when he was one of several Indian delegates sent by Collier to attend a conference on North American Indians in Toronto. Annoyed by lack of opportunity for participation, the Indian delegates, including McNickle, Parker, Louis Bruce, David Owl and Ruth Bronson, staged a walkout on the last day and held a separate meeting. This group kept in touch to discuss the possibility of a national pan-Indian organization that could lobby on Capitol Hill. A few others were brought in. The origin of the National Congress of American Indians, the most important national Indian lobbying organization, lies in this educated Indian bureaucracy of the 1930s.

Most of the NCAI organizers were the college-educated "Young Turks" of Collier's BIA, including Hoover appointees Ben Dwight and Ruth Bronson, and Collier appointees D'Arcy McNickle, Archie Phinney, Ben Reifel (Brule Sioux, 1906–1990—M.S. in biochemistry, South Dakota State, 1932), and Charlie Heacock (Rosebud Sioux—M.S. in biochemistry, South Dakota State, 1933). Some older career BIA men were also involved, such as Peru Farver (b. 1894) who, like fellow-Choctaw Ben Dwight, was an Armstrong Academy graduate, and had also attended Oklahoma A & M College.

Bronson's retirement from government service in 1943 left her more time for the project.

Actual legwork among tribes began in 1944. Phinney, by this time superintendent at Nez Perce, was one of the most active organizers. He was elected councilman at the organization's constitutional convention in 1944. Ben Dwight played a key role as chairman of that convention, and Ruth Bronson would run the NCAI's legislative review service in the earliest years of its existence. Bronson was executive director between 1946 and 1949, a period which saw the renewal of pressure on Indians to assimilate and to terminate the existence of tribes, and where it would be up to Indian organizations such as NCAI to protect the gains made under Collier.

THE PROTAGONIST EMERGES

After World War II, Indian veterans began attending college under the GI Bill. In 1948, the BIA also replaced the prewar loan program with a new higher education grant program. However, the Eisenhower administration represented a real downturn for Indians. His Indian Commissioner, Dillon S. Myer, fired most of the old Collier staff, replacing them mainly with people who had no direct experience with Indians. McNickle had been acting chief of tribal relations 1949–1950. His classic work, "They Came Here First," probably the first history of Indian-White relations by a Native author, was published in 1949. Though he became chief of tribal relations in 1950, and hung on for another two years as a moderating influence, his position became increasingly difficult, and he finally resigned to pursue Indian affairs outside government.

In 1953, the termination policy, unofficially in place since the end of the war, was made the official "sense of Congress" by House Concurrent Resolution 108. It was a concerted effort to reverse the new philoso-phy and achievements of the Collier years and a return to the philosophy of allotment, dedicated to the elimination of reservations and dispersal of Indians around the country, especially into urban areas.

A few of the Collier appointees sup-ported termination. Ben Reifel, for example, had joined the Bureau in 1933 advising Indian farmers at Pine Ridge, and had been transferred in 1935 to the Organization Division, and was sent to Plains reservations to help implement the IRA. Reifel now said that Native people should not "cling to the past" and should "adjust to new economic realities." After the war he became superin-tendent of the Fort Berthold reservation, helping the Bureau of Reclamation force an agreement on the Three Affiliated Tribes for the building of the infamous Garrison Dam. In 1949, he received a scholarship to the Littauer School of Public Administration at Harvard, receiving a master's degree in 1950 and a doctorate in 1952. He then returned to Fort Berthold before becoming superinten-dent of Pine Ridge in 1954 and area director in 1955. He served in Congress from 1960 to 1971. After his retirement, he would remain active in Indian issues, serving briefly as commissioner under President Gerald Ford.

On the whole, the new NCAI played an extremely important role in the ultimately successful fight against termination. This is not to suggest that college-educated Indians deserve all the credit for this or subsequent advances, but their skills certainly did not hurt and from this point on they would play an increasingly significant leadership role.

Under termination, Indians could not aim for Indian-controlled education. The pri-ority was simply survival. However, termi-nation had effectively mobilized Indians on a national level, and the increased effort would pay off, for of all items on the Indian agenda in the second half of the century, education would make the greatest substan-tial gains. Eventually true Indian control and content would be achieved.

Some of the important Collier people were already gone—Archie Phinney died in 1949, Henry Roe Cloud in 1950, Ben Dwight in 1953—but at this point two survivors, Ruth Bronson and D'Arcy McNickle, became involved in a project that would soon set a new stage in motion. In March 1957, the Fund for the Republic formed a commission to appraise the status of Indians. Its sum-mary report on education, Brophy & Aberle, 1961, condemned previous policies and rec-ommended enlisting "the support of the Indian community, its neighbors, and tribal and local government officials."

In the mid-1950s, Indian college enroll-ment continued to increase, but observers were disturbed to find the dropout rate high and apparently unrelated to academic ability. By 1955 there were about 2,000 Natives in post-secondary education, but the ratio of degree graduates remained small: only 66 natives graduated from four-year institutions in 1961. In that year, Ruth Bronson and representatives of support or-ganizations suggested setting up a summer workshop to investigate the problem and plans were drawn up under the direction of anthropologist Sol Tax (1907–1995). Students would attend these Workshops on American Indian Affairs from 1956 through 1963.

The workshops, most of which were held at the University of Colorado, Boulder, brought to the fore a new figure of the first postwar generation, Cherokee anthropolo-gist Robert K. Thomas (1925–1991). Thomas got his bachelor's and master's (1954) at the University of Arizona and was working toward a doctorate at the University of Chicago under anthropologist Sam Stanley. By the time of the Workshops, he was Professor of Anthropology at Montieth College, Wayne State University, Detroit.

From 1981 until his death he would direct the American Indian Studies Program at the University of Arizona in Tucson.

Thomas was director of the second summer workshop in 1957, assistant director in 1961, and regular lecturer for 1962 and 1963. Though most of the staff was non-Indian, Thomas played the central role. According to McNickle, who observed the development of the workshops from 1960 through 1963, it was Thomas who "most influenced the shaping of the workshop as a center for discovery and understanding. The teaching faculty looked to him for intellectual challenge, while the students responded by improving academic performances . . . [He was] equally capable of reaching students and encouraging them to stretch their intellectual grasp."

The workshops revealed that most of the students suffered from confused identity and loss of cultural moorings, had internalized white stereotypes of Indians, and knew little of their history and culture. The staff tried to give the students a clearer sense of Indian identity by explaining both Native and white cultures objectively. The response was very positive.

The American Indian Chicago Conference was held in June 1961, at the University of Chicago. It was described as the first comprehensive investigation of the state of the American Indian since the Meriam Report. The method, however, was direct participation. Indians representing hundreds of tribes from every part of the country would come together to draw up a declaration of purpose that would express their common goals. The declaration itself would be a truly representative statement, but the discussions that had to take place in order to arrive at it, and the lasting contacts that would, it was hoped, be made, were no less important.

As the organizers intended, this would already have been a historic gathering, not only for its scope, but for the way it was planned, with local Indian participation in a series of preliminary regional meetings. They had not expected it to become the birthplace of the "Red Power" movement, however.

A group of younger people, led by Clyde M. Warrior (1939–1968)—an active student participant in both the 1961 and 1962 Workshops—felt that the Declaration of Indian Purpose, while correct, was too mild and, in any case, needed to be backed up with organization and activism. Thus, the National Indian Youth Council, in many ways the precursor to the more successful American Indian Movement a decade later, was founded at the conference. Warrior himself seems to have been close to Bob Thomas, and in the 1960s Thomas, though by no means a militant himself, would keep in touch with the NIYC, publishing a number of articles in their newsletter "ABC: America Before Columbus." He coined the term "internal colonization" to describe the situation of American Indians and other indigenous peoples in the modern world. His writings were important in the development of the militant pro-sovereignty movement of the 1970s. Ward Churchill has called Thomas "the first to openly and coherently apply the concept of colonization to American Indians."

The National Indian Youth Council was made up almost exclusively of young college students who would inaugurate increasingly confrontational tactics, such as "fish-ins," protesting fishing rights violations, to advance Indian causes. As the decade progressed, Indian college students would become further radicalized by the '60s antiwar movement, Black power, and other anti-establishment influences, so much so that the 1969 Alcatraz occupation, though begun by the local Bay Area community, was soon taken over by Indian college students, bringing this kind of protest culture into the Indian movement for the first time.

McNickle's immediate reaction to the Chicago Conference was disappointment. He felt it had not achieved its goals. Only later would its great importance come into perspective. The baton had been passed. To the young radicals of the 1960s and 1970s, the Young Turks of the Collier Era looked like old fogeys. The NCAI, which had itself germinated from a protest walkout in 1939, and was the first national Indian organization formed entirely by and for Indians, was now "the Establishment."

THE GREAT SOCIETY

In the mid-1960s, the United Scholarship Service was the only national Indian organization involved in Indian education. The Economic Opportunity Act, passed in May 1965, made major non-BIA funding available to Indians for the first time. The Higher Education Act (1965) set aside Title III funds for Indian Colleges. Educational opportunities came especially through the Head Start Program.

By 1965, post-secondary Indian enrollment had increased to 7,000 nationwide, but the ratio of graduates from four-year institutions was no larger: in 1968 there were only 181. Enrollment continued to grow rapidly: by 1970, it had reached approximately 15,000. Several thousand received degrees in the 1960s, but Brophy and Aberle, in their final Fund for the Republic report of 1966, still reported a dropout rate of 60 percent.

The stage was now set for a real turning point for Indian higher education. This came during the Johnson and Nixon administrations under two exceptionally important commissioners: Robert L. Bennett and Louis R. Bruce Jr.

Robert LaFollette Bennett was another veteran of the Collier days. A Wisconsin Oneida, he was a graduate of Haskell's short-lived junior college program in 1931 and joined the BIA two years later, serving at the Ute Agency and in Washington. After receiving a law degree from Southeastern University in 1941, and briefly working with the Navajo, he joined the Marines. After the war he worked at the Veterans' Administration, helping Indian veterans get their benefits under the G.I. Bill.

Interior Secretary Stewart Udall, spurred by the rising expectations of Johnson's "Great Society" program, needed to replace outgoing commissioner Philleo Nash with someone who would be respected by tribes and by Congress alike. Bennett, who as area director of the Juneau Area Office in Alaska (1962–1966) had won the respect of Indian leaders around the country for his efforts to protect Native land claims, was appointed Indian Commissioner on Apr. 27, 1966. He was the first Native of the 20th century to hold this position, and the second in history.

In 1969 came the publication of "Indian Education: A National Tragedy," the report of U.S. Senate Special Subcommittee on Indian Education of the Senate Committee on Labor and Public Welfare. Hank Adams, of the National Indian Youth Council, helped Sen. Robert Kennedy draft the report. Now under pressure, Bennett expanded the Bureau's educational efforts, doubling the funding for higher education. Nevertheless, he was criticized both by the Red Power movement and the NCAI for not moving fast enough. The leasing of Indian natural resources that grew out of his promotion of tribal self-determination would also be targeted by the American Indian Movement in the 1970s and 1980s.

After Nixon took office, Bennett resigned on May 31, 1969, in favor of Louis Rook Bruce Jr. (Oglala Sioux/Mohawk,

1906–1989). Bruce had attended Cazenovia Seminary in the 1920s and got a bachelor's degree from Syracuse University in 1930. In the Depression, he developed a program to send Indian youth to teach Indian lore and crafts at summer camps. While not a veteran of the Collier BIA, he had directed the WPA programs for New York Indians in the 1930s and was a founding member of the NCAI. He later taught part-time at Columbia, Penn State and Cornell.

Bruce began to establish programs for off-reservation Indians who had suffered under the relocation policies of termination and to formalize the self-determination policies begun by Bennett. President Nixon officially ended the hated termination policy in 1970, and in May of that year, the Zuñi tribe was given the right to administer all BIA activities in their pueblo, and the Miccosukees of Florida soon followed.

THE TRIBAL COLLEGE

In July 1968, by special federal legislation, the Navajo Community College in Tsaile, Ariz., became the first college founded and controlled by an Indian tribe. Since 1996 it has been known as Diné College.

Part two of the 1969 Senate subcommittee report "Indian Education: A National Tragedy," on higher education, called for more Indian community colleges, advocated Native American Studies programs, suggested improvements in scholarship granting by BIA, and recommended "special recruiting and orienting programs." It also urged that higher education programs for Indians be included in Title III (Developing Institutions) of the Higher Education Act (1965), which would take some power away from the BIA, and that funds from the vocational Education Act (1963) and Higher Education Act be used to support BIA programs.

In 1971, recently retired Indian Commissioner Bennett and John C. Rainer Sr. (Taos Pueblo), founded American Indian Scholarships, Inc. at Albuquerque, N. Mex., to provide grants to Indian graduate students. Since 1989, the organization has been known as the American Indian Graduate Center. Bennett's original motivation was to help more Indians qualify for important positions in the BIA. Fifteen students were funded the first year; in 1994–1995, it would fund nearly 700. As of 1996, AIGC would be assisting 95 percent of the Indian graduate students in the United States, disbursing about $2 million per annum.

The Indian Education Act (1972) allocated funding for university programs to train Native teachers of tribal students in elementary and high schools. In 1974, by amendment to this act, a special higher education program was set up to provide funds to graduate students, giving priority to the fields of business, education, law, engineering, natural resources, and health. This program was contracted to the American Indian Graduate Center. In 1994, 580 of these grants would be awarded.

At the end of the 1960s, American Indian Studies programs were created at a number of universities. Founded in 1969, the American Indian Studies Program at California State University–Long Beach was the first. Today there are scores of them.[1]

In 1970, on the heels of "Indian Education: A National Tragedy," Will Antell (White Earth Chippewa), Rosemary Christianson and Elgie Raymond founded the National Indian Education Association in Minnesota. In the fall of 1972, Native American Studies programs in a number of universities attempted to form a national organization to secure Title III funding under the Higher Education Act (1965). By this time, however, there were already more than 10 tribally controlled community colleges and one, D-Q

University, not under tribal control. Seeing a threat, the colleges, supported by the National Indian Education Association, moved to found the American Indian Higher Education Consortium in January 1973. Its mission was to (1) help Indian-controlled junior colleges get accreditation, possibly to become an accrediting body itself; (2) help find general funds; (3) help develop curriculum, and (4) coordinate communication and contacts among the colleges.

Largely as a result of pressure from AIHEC, the Tribally Controlled Community College Assistance Act was passed in 1978, authorizing funding for all Indian community colleges either chartered or sanctioned by tribal governments. Colleges sanctioned by a tribal government are not under its control—the only leverage being the threat to withdraw the sanction.

In 1970, Haskell Institute, which had long been a high school and was now one of the few surviving federal boarding schools, became Haskell Indian Junior College. It would finally achieve university accreditation in October 1993, offering a bachelor of science degree in elementary teacher education. Since then, it has been known as Haskell Indian Nations University, and is one of three tribal colleges operated directly by the BIA, the others being Southwestern Indian Polytechnic Institute in Albuquerque, and the Institute of American Indian Arts in Santa Fe.

A descendent of the summer Workshops on Indian Affairs, NAES College was opened in 1975 as Native American Educational Services, originally affiliated with Antioch College. Sol Tax and Robert Thomas were active on its board of directors and one of its founders, Robert V. Duncan, was a participant in the 1960 Workshop. As Duncan stated "we have modelled NAES on this notion—the functional role of tribal knowledge and learning for the student and the community." Accredited since 1984 to grant a bachelor of arts in Community Studies, NAES now has branch campuses at Fort Peck, Mont. (1978), Northern Cheyenne (1980), the Twin Cities, Minn. (1988), and Menominee, Wis. (1989).

The American Indian Science and Engineering Society helps American Indians and Alaska Natives pursue studies in science, engineering, business and other academic arenas. It provides financial, academic and cultural support to Native students from middle school through graduate school. It trains teachers to work with Native students and develops culturally appropriate curricula and publications. Based in Boulder, Colo., AISES was founded in 1977 by a number of American Indian scientists, engineers and educators, among them Hopi-Laguna geneticist Frank C. Dukepoo (b. 1943), who were concerned about the low enrollment and graduation rates, and the high dropout rates of Indian college students compared with other ethnic groups, as well as the great underrepresentation of American Indians in science and engineering. Since 1983, AISES has been directed by Norbert S. Hill Jr. (Oneida, b. 1946).

In 1993, the Packer Foundation inaugurated a Tribal Colleges Science Program to assist American Indian students with their scientific education so as to be better able to manage the vast land and water resources on their reservations. In 1994, tribal colleges were awarded 11 grants of approximately $50,000 each, to support science programs, renewable for up to three years.

The BIA's Higher Education Grant Program still provides grants to undergraduates. In 1972, 12,438 were awarded, and in 1994, more than 14,800.

On Oct. 20, 1994, the tribal colleges gained land-grant status through passage of a rider to the reauthorization of the Elementary and Secondary Education Act,

(108 Stat. 404851), bringing with it a $23 million endowment. As of 1997, there were 30 tribal colleges, 27 of which are two-year institutions. Only Sinte Gleska, D-Q, and Haskell Universities have four-year programs. In 1995–96, these colleges served more than 25,000 students from over 200 tribes. Many entering students are the first in their families ever to attend college.

The American Indian College Fund, in Denver, Colo., raises funds for the member colleges of AIHEC, approximately $800,000 per annum. The Fund contributes an additional $1.5 million to an endowment set up to benefit the tribal colleges. It has a Fund for Cultural Preservation, funded by a National Endowment for the Humanities grant. Its total income in 1994 was $5,238,000.

As indigenous peoples begin to take their rightful place as peoples of the world, the tribal college is better preparing American Indian youth, if need be, for continuing education in universities anywhere in the world. The fact is that Native people with a sheepskin have greater power to defend and better their community. College as an institution, after all, is simply a tool a society uses to better achieve its goals. In the context of the twentieth century, the borrowing of this institution from Euro-American society, at first regarded as impossible or at least inappropriate, gradually became a necessity.

The tribal colleges and the university Indian programs are still modest institutions with quite limited resources. Yet their existence and growth confirm that from here on, Indians, whether they attend tribal or conventional colleges, will relate to the larger society by developing their communities and cultures, not destroying them. This is a tremendous victory when seen from the perspective of the whole century.

Most uniquely, through its goal of integrating and applying all fields of knowledge to the health and balance of the community, and the larger definition of community which sees the Earth as an interlocking community of communities, the tribal college represents a Native adaptation of the ideal of the university, for in Indian cultures, learning means discovering the principles and the relations of everything. Embodied in a new social form, this return to the university ideal can develop into a great contribution not only to the survival of Native society, but also to the survival of the world through the community of learning.

BIBLIOGRAPHICAL NOTES

In the preparation of this article I am indebted to a number of excellent studies by Western Shoshone historian Steven J. Crum:

"Henry Roe Cloud, a Winnebago Indian Reformer: His Quest for American Indian Higher Education," *Kansas History*, 11 (Autumn 1988), 171–184.

"The Idea of an Indian College or University in Twentieth-century America before the Formation of the Navajo Community College in 1968." *Tribal College*, 1.1 (Summer 1989): 20–23.

"Higher Education," *Native America in the Twentieth Century*, ed. Mary B. Davis. (New York & London: Garland, 1994), 237–239.

And by the late Dr. Bobby Wright, Chippewa-Cree educator and historian from Rocky Boy's Reservation, Mont.

"American Indian and Alaska Native Higher Education: Toward a New Century of Academic Achievement and Cultural Integrity." *Indian Nations at Risk Task Force, Commissioned Papers* (1991, 16 pp.). ERIC Document 343771.

"The Broken Covenant: American Indian Missions in the Colonial Colleges," *Tribal College* 7.1 (Summer 1995): 26–33.

Readers may also wish to consult:

John Williams & Howard L. Meredith, *Bacone Indian University: A History. Oklahoma City* (Western Heritage Books, 1980).

[1]See *A Guide to Native American Studies Programs in the United States and Canada*, Robert M. Nelson, editor, published by the Association for the Study of American Indian Literatures, 28 Westhampton Way, Box 112, University of Richmond, Va. 23173.

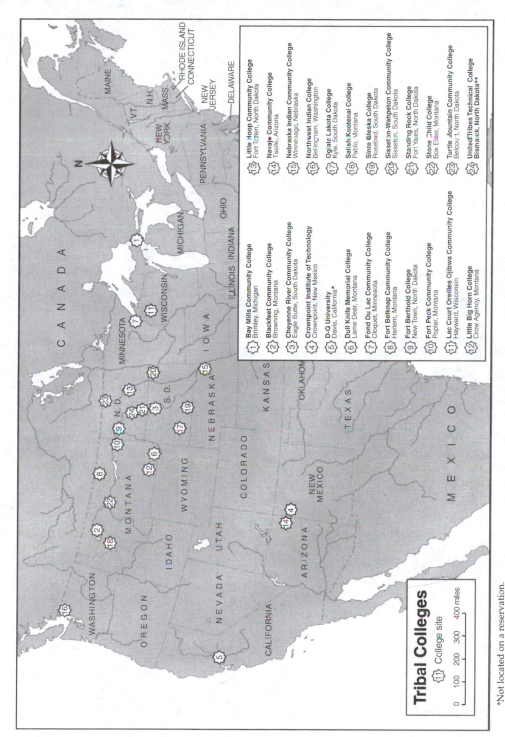

*Not located on a reservation.
**Does not receive funds under the Tribally Controlled Community College Assistance Act; not located on a reservation.
Note: Since this map was drafted, more than half-a-dozen more tribal community colleges have been established.

Part Review

DISCUSSION QUESTIONS

Wilma Mankiller and Michael Wallis,
Asgaya-Dihi
1. What does *Asgaya-dihi* mean, and why is this name important to the author in terms of her family heritage and Cherokee culture?

Deanna Kingston, *Traveling Traditions*
1. Describe the nature of the "teasing" or "joking" relationship that the author has with her cross-cousin Mark.
2. How do song and dance enter into this custom?
3. What does the author mean by "traveling traditions"?

Dagmar Thorpe, *The Spirit of the People Has Awakened and Is Enjoying Creation through Us*
1. What is "traditional education," and how does it differ from education in the mainstream sense of the word?
2. What is the *enow'kin* process? The Okanagan spirit?

Tim Giago, *Reservation Schools Fail to Assimilate All Students*
1. According to the editorial by Tim Giago, why has assimilation through the mainstream educational process failed?

Mary Brave Bird (Crow Dog) with Richard Erdoes, *Civilize Them with a Stick*
1. Give several examples of the abuses suffered by Mary Crow Dog and her fellow

Indian students at St. Francis Mission School. Contrast her school experience to your own.
2. In what ways did Mary Crow Dog rebel?

Susan Lobo, *Urban American Indian Preschool*
1. What were the major concerns that led the Concerned Parents of Oakland to start an American Indian preschool?
2. What were the major accomplishments of Hintil Kuu Ca (Indian children's house) after it expanded?

Julian Burger, *Survival Schools*
1. Why did the Canadian Mohawk set up their own school, and how were they able to do it?

Jeffrey Wollock, *Protagonism Emergent*
1. Describe the Indian educational policy in the United States from the 1887 Indian Allotment Act to the 1930s New Deal.
2. What role did educated Indians play in the New Deal reforms of the 1934 Indian Reorganization Act?
3. Summarize the emergence and the subsequent development of the Tribal Community Colleges and Native American Studies programs in the 1960s.

KEY TERMS

"All my relations"
American Indian Chicago Conference
Asgaya-dihi
assimilation
boarding school
cross-cousin
D-Q University
enow'kin process
gynocentric
Hintil Kuu Ca
Indian Reorganization Act of 1934
Intertribal Friendship House (Oakland)
Inupiaq

Kahnawake Survival School
"Kill the Indian but save the man"
Montezuma, Carlos
National Congress of American Indians (NCAI)
Navajo Community (Diné) College
Pratt, Richard Henry
Roe Cloud, Henry
Society of American Indians
teasing or joking relationship
ti-ospaye
Tribally Controlled Community College
    Assistance Act, (1978)

SUGGESTED READINGS

ALLEN, PAULA GUNN. *The Sacred Hoop: Recovering the Feminine in American Indian Traditions.* Boston: Beacon Press, 1986.

BAYLOR, BYRD. *Yes Is Better Than No.* Illustr. Leonard Chana. Tucson, Ariz.: Treasure Chest Publications, 1991.

ERDRICH, LOUISE. *Love Medicine: A Novel.* New York: Holt, Rinehart, and Winston, 1984.

JAINE, LINDA. "Industrial and Residential School Administration: The Attempt to Undermine Indigenous Self-Determination." *Journal of Indigenous Studies,* 2, no. 2 (Summer 1991): 37–48.

KAWAGLEY, A. OSCAR. *A Yupiaq Worldview: A Pathway to Ecology and the Spirit.* Prospect Heights, IL: Waveland Press, 1995.

LOBO, SUSAN. *A House of My Own: Social Organization in the Squatter Settlements of Lima, Peru.* Tucson: University of Arizona Press, 1982.

MANKILLER, WILMA, and MICHAEL WALLIS. *Mankiller: A Chief and Her People.* New York: St. Martin's Press, 1993.

MEDICINE, BEATRICE. "American Indian Family: Cultural Change and Adaptive Strategies." *Journal of Ethnic Studies,* 8, no. 4 (1982): 14–23.

MOMADAY, N. SCOTT. *The Names: A Memoir.* New York: Harper & Row, 1976.

SARRIS, GREG. *Grand Avenue.* New York: Hyperion, 1994.

SENESE, GUY B. *Self-determination and the Social Education of Native Americans.* New York: Praeger Publishers, 1991.

Tribal College: Journal of American Indian Education. A quarterly publication of the American Indian Higher Education Consortium, P.O. Box 720, Mancos, Colorado 81328.

Where the Spirit Lives. Feature film, filmed in Canada. Beacon Films, 930 Pitner Avenue, Evanston, Ill. 60202.

WILSON, DARRYL BABE. *The Morning the Sun Went Down.* Berkeley, Calif.: Heyday Books, 1998.

VI

SPIRITUALITY

Missionaries

Floyd Red Crow Westerman and Jimmy Curtiss

Spread the word of your religions
Convert the whole world if you can
Kill and slaughter those who oppose you
It's worth it if you save one man
Take the land to build your churches
A sin to tax the house of God
Take the child while he is supple
Spoil the mind and spare the rod
Go and tell the savage nation
That he must be Christianized
Tell him, and his heathen worship
And you will make him civilized
Shove your gospel, force your values
Down his throat until it's raw
And after he is crippled
Turn your back and lock the door

Like an ever circling vulture
You descend upon your prey
Then you pick the soul to pieces
And you watch as it decays
'Cause religion is big business
As your bank accounts will show
And Chirst died to save all mankind
But that was long ago

Missionaries, missionaries, go and leave us all alone
Take your white God to your white man
We've a God of our own.

Although each tribe or peoples has its own unique system of spiritual beliefs and practices, there are some commonly held philosophical ideas that are generally shared by Native American people throughout the Western Hemisphere. The natural world is the focal point of Indian spirituality. From this foundation springs a number of understandings regarding the nature of the world, and the cosmos in general, as well as the appropriate role of human beings in it. Humans are viewed as intimately linked, and morally bound, to the natural world in such a way that one's individual, family, and community pasts are intertwined with the Old Stories that teach how things came to be as they are today and right behavior for ensuring that future generations will continue to rely on a balanced relationship with the natural world. All creatures—the two-legged (humans), four-legged, winged, and green things, creatures that swim in the rivers and seas, even the rocks and things that, from a non-Indian philosophical perspective, are considered inanimate—are part of this spirituality or sacred life force. For many Indians living today, this circle of the sacred to which we human beings are connected, ideally in balance and harmony with nature, also includes the life-giving sun, the many stars of the night sky, and Mother Earth herself. Because this perspective encompasses all time, all places, and all beings, Native Americans generally prefer the term *spirituality* or *the sacred* rather than *religion*.

Indigenous spirituality has continually come under attack throughout the history of Western conquest of the Americas. In Part III we examined the deleterious consequences of the early Christian missionaries. Sometimes the imposition of Christianity also had its humorous side. Inuit journalist Rachel Attituq Qitsualik reports that "Christianity as brought to Inuit required no small amount of tweaking to make it more palatable." And even then, some things make sense. For example, Sunday, *Naattiinguja,* translates into English something like "waiting for the long day to be over." As she observes: " 'Long day, indeed, when I was a child, for on Sunday I was not allowed to pick flowers, play, chew gum, read (except the Bible), sing, or do anything else resembling fun. Instead, I had to memorize Old Testament verses."[1]

Spirituality is really the linchpin of traditional Native American culture; it acts as the axis around which all the other components of culture revolve, such as the institutions of government, economy, defense, education, kinship, and the family. There has not been the separation of church from state; Indian political and military leaders were formerly also the spiritual leaders. The great Lakota (Sioux) fighting chief Crazy Horse, for example, was also a holy person. Spirituality thus integrates Indian society and gives it its collective consciousness and social solidarity. It constitutes the "glue," or social cement, of Indian culture: that is, its basic philosophy and values and what it means to be Indian.

It is worth noting that the early French sociologist Emile Durkheim studied "the elementary forms of the religious life" and concluded that religion embraces more than the anthropomorphized state religions found in the large-scale, class-stratified societies of Europe. Moreover, Durkheim concluded that "the religious life" is universal among all peoples of the world, both Western and non-Western, because the essence of religion is found not in its institutional aspects but, instead, in its sacred community of believers.[2] Religion can therefore be universally defined as *a system of belief and practice relative to sacred things that unite its devotees into a single moral community called a church.* Durkheim's classic definition of religion therefore includes American Indian spirituality in all of its manifestations.

Although "the sacred" underlies everything in the Indian world, some things and places are especially holy. Durkheim was also the first European scholar to understand that all peoples divide the world into two cultural domains, the sacred and the profane, or the secular. How cultures make this division, however, can differ considerably. The sacred can include an object, a place, or a ceremony or rite. But which objects, places, or rites are considered sacred and which are considered secular can vary greatly from culture to culture. Christians are accustomed to viewing the crucifix as a sacred object; among many North American Indian nations an eagle feather holds a similar sacred quality. Also, the Navajo hogan where curing ceremonies are performed is sacred, much as is a Christian church or a Jewish synagogue in Western culture. This difference in the way the sacred and the profane are defined in today's pluralistic world is posing a serious point of conflict between Indians and non-Indians, whether in North, Central, or South America.

In a similar vein, sacred places play a major part in Native American spirituality. Among other things, certain mountains, springs, rivers, lakes, caves, and rock formations can be a part of a sacred landscape that is the basis for spiritual belief and practice. The river Jordan holds a sacred significance for Christians, and the Ganges is sacred to the Hindu. In the same way, the Chewana, or Columbia River, is sacred to the fishing Indians of Oregon and Washington. Native American sacred geography has often become a source of conflict between Native peoples and others. In the mainstream culture of the United States, and throughout the Americas, land is defined as real estate, private property that produces profit for its owners. Tourists or hikers entering into areas they consider recreational, but which are sacred to Native Americans, are also a source of conflict. Land is secularized in Western capitalist society, in contrast to traditional Native American thought, in which land is an expression of the sacred.

Indians and other Native peoples also have sacred ceremonies; a Lakota "sweat" purification and an Apache woman's "coming out," or puberty ceremony, are just as sacred in the traditional Indian world as is the Christian communion or baptism in the Western religious tradition. Until 1934, most Indian religious ceremonies in the United States were banned and punished by fine or imprisonment or both. The First Amendment to the Constitution of the United States begins, "Congress shall make no law respecting an establishment of religion, or prohibiting the free exercise thereof . . ." Yet, since first contact, Native peoples have had to struggle against laws and actions that prohibited and curtailed this human and constitutional right to religious freedom. The legacy of this abridgment of religious freedom is a continuing source of friction in U.S. Indian–white relations.

Finally, among all peoples in the world, the dead are sanctified after death, although the particular practice or custom varies from culture to culture. American Indians hold an ideal of deeply respecting elders and ancestors. From an Indian perspective, the dead are always buried or cremated in a sacred manner, but from a Western perspective these Indian dead lay in unmarked graves and therefore become objects for scientific collection and study. These aspects of Native American spirituality and related issues are examined in this chapter.

The first selection, by Lakota medicine man Lame Deer and his collaborator Richard Erdoes, describes the Indian vision quest, which has been widely practiced among the Indian peoples of the western United States. It is a traditional way for young men to seek spiritual power that will guide them on the "good Red Road" of life. For many years the vision quest and many other spiritual customs were suppressed by the Spanish and later by the United States and Canada, so that they were carried on in secret, if at all. The Indian Act of Canada outlawed participation in ceremonies that were central to many Indians, such as the Plains Sun Dance, or the Northwest Coast potlatch. The vision quest, or "crying for a dream," is now being revived in the United States. Today, the practice includes young women as well as men. Since the 1960s and 1970s there has been a strong revitalization or rebirth of American Indian spiritual belief and practice.

In the box titled "A Maidu Creation Story," Marcus Peters (Anishinabeg), a graduate student in Ethnic Studies, Native American Concentration, at San Francisco State University, narrates a traditional Maidu creation story and follows the narration with an analysis that he terms a "mytho-epistemological critique." All too often, one only hears or reads a beautiful account of how a Native people and their world came to be, but, in this selection, Peters compels us to take a Native American perspective in thinking more critically about the significance and deeper meanings of these creation stories.

Also in this part is a selection on Indian art by Frank LaPena, a Nontipom-Wintu Indian artist and professor of Indian studies. He beautifully describes the holistic nature of the Indian spiritual world and how it permeates every facet of traditional Indian culture. The continuity with the past, the place of oral traditions and the role of elders, and the link between the physical and spiritual worlds all figure prominently in Native American culture.

In the third selection, academician Russell Thornton (Cherokee) examines the issue of repatriating the several hundred thousand Native American human remains that have come to reside in the U.S. government's Smithsonian Institution as well as other "scientific" collections. Among the many critical issues that Indians of the United States face, this, without doubt, is one of the most troubling and one about which they feel most deeply. How is it, they ask, that only indigenous people are the objects for scientific collection and study? Why not white people? The answer, of course, lies in the history of oppression and racism that characterize Indian–white relations. In 1983 Jan Hammil of American Indians Against Desecration gave a scathing address to an annual meeting of the American Anthropological Society in which she challenged the scientific community to stop demeaning Indian people by storing the sacred remains of ancestors in the "bags, boxes, and paper sacks" of museums and anthropological laboratories. Thornton details the history of this issue, the contemporary Native American repatriation movement, and the status of the corrective legislation, which is discussed further in the box titled "Indians Are Not Specimens—Indians Are People."

In the United States, the Native American Graves Protection and Repatriation Act (NAGPRA) was passed by Congress in 1990. NAGPRA requires museums to return human remains and funerary objects to tribes. The law mandated that by November 1993, museums were to summarize sacred funerary objects and cultural items in their collections and mail the summaries to interested tribes. Then, by 1995, museums were to give "culturally affiliated" Indian tribes, Alaska Native villages or corporations, and Native Hawaiian organizations similar data on all human remains and "associated funerary objects." Adequate funding by Congress to carry out NAGPRA has been slow in coming, and the deadlines have been difficult for museums to meet. According to Thornton, however, the once-reticent Smithsonian Institution is now beginning the task of repatriating Indian remains and grave goods. A difficult aspect of the law for many Native groups, however, is how to prove their cultural affiliation to the ancient remains and objects, because they were formerly nonliterate communities relying on oral tradition. They lacked written records that would establish such an affiliation in U.S. courts. Furthermore, hundreds of thousands of other Indian people are currently unrecognized by the federal government and are therefore ineligible under NAGPRA to apply for the repatriation of the remains of their dead relatives and grave goods.

Apart from the repatriation issue itself, another serious issue involving spirituality is the fact that imprisoned Native people are still being denied protection of their cultural and religious rights. Sweat lodges have been torn down by some prison authorities, and Indian religious ceremonies involving the Pipe religion and the Native American Church have been denied. It is unfortunate that an omnibus bill introduced by Senator Daniel K. Inouye of Hawai'i in 1994, the Native American Cultural Protection and Free Exercise of Religion Act, that would have ended this aspect of religious discrimination, failed to pass Congress.

In the fourth selection, Victoria Bomberry, a Muskogee Lenape scholar, examines the issue of the theft of sacred textiles belonging to the Aymara Indians of Bolivia. In this deeply insightful article, she considers the serious ramifications of the removal of the Coroma textiles from this indigenous community and explains both the historical and spiritual nature of the textiles, as well as the linkage they provide in integrating the entire fabric of Aymara culture. The repatriation issue (the return of sacred items to Indian societies) has become a key issue throughout the hemisphere and is now an important item on the international indigenous rights agenda of the United Nations and before the "court" of world opinion. Another example of repatriation is discussed in the box titled "Zuni Repatriation of War Gods."

In the last selection, Hopi/Me-wuk poet and anthropologist Wendy Rose discusses the issue of "whiteshamanism." By this term she is referring to white people who adopt bits and pieces of Native American spirituality and set themselves up (for a fee) as New Age medicine men and women. These contemporary spiritualists and "gurus" are modern missionaries in reverse: instead of suppressing Native American religious beliefs and practices as was done in the past, they seek to appropriate Native spirituality and appoint themselves as the expert practitioners of it. This development is of grave concern to traditional Native peoples on two counts: first, Indians frequently say that their spirituality forms the very core of their Indianness and in some instances it is the only thing they have left; and second, these "whiteshamans" are appropriating Native spirituality in a shreds-and-patches fashion and completely out of context. As we stated above,

Durkheim defined religion as a sacred community of believers. How, then, can one have a Native American religious ceremony if it is not practiced as part of the Indian community and ceremonial calendar, and if only white people are doing it at a for-a-fee weekend seminar or reading about it in a New Age publication? In fact, as Rose points out, the word *shaman* has a Siberian paleo-Asiatic origin and is foreign to most indigenous peoples of the Americas. In North America, Native religious specialists are often termed medicine men, medicine women, or doctors. Rose goes on to explore many other ramifications of the phenomenon of whiteshamanism, which in the final analysis constitutes a current variant of the continuing violation of Native American religious freedom and must be treated as such.

NOTES

1. Rachel Attituq Qitsualik, *Indian Country Today*, 9, no. 37 (March 1, 2000): A5.

2. Emile Durkheim, *The Elementary Forms of Religious Life*, trans. Joseph Ward Wain (London: Allen and Unwin, 1915).

ALONE ON THE HILLTOP

John (Fire) Lame Deer and Richard Erdoes

I was all alone on the hilltop. I sat there in the vision pit, a hole dug into the hill, my arms hugging my knees as I watched old man Chest, the medicine man who had brought me there, disappear far down in the valley. He was just a moving black dot among the pines, and soon he was gone altogether.

Now I was all by myself, left on the hilltop for four days and nights without food or water until he came back for me. You know, we Indians are not like some white folks—a man and a wife, two children, and one baby sitter who watches the TV set while the parents are out visiting somewhere.

Indian children are never alone. They are always surrounded by grandparents, uncles, cousins, relatives of all kinds, who fondle the kids, sing to them, tell them stories. If the parents go someplace, the kids go along.

But here I was, crouched in my vision pit, left alone by myself for the first time in my life. I was sixteen then, still had my boy's name and, let me tell you, I was scared. I was shivering and not only from the cold. The nearest human being was many miles away, and four days and nights is a long, long time. Of course, when it was all over, I would no longer be a boy, but a man. I would have had my vision. I would be given a man's name.

Reprinted with the permission of Simon & Schuster from *Lame Deer, Seeker of Visions,* by John (Fire) Lame Deer and Richard Erdoes. Copyright 1972 by John (Fire) Lame Deer and Richard Erdoes.

Sioux men are not afraid to endure hunger, thirst and loneliness, and I was only ninety-six hours away from being a man. The thought was comforting. Comforting, too, was the warmth of the star blanket which old man Chest had wrapped around me to cover my nakedness. My grandmother had made it especially for this, my first *hanblechia,* my first vision-seeking. It was a beautifully designed quilt, white with a large morning star made of many pieces of brightly colored cloth. That star was so big it covered most of the blanket. If Wakan Tanka, the Great Spirit, would give me the vision and the power, I would become a medicine man and perform many ceremonies wrapped in that quilt. I am an old man now and many times a grandfather, but I still have that star blanket my grandmother made for me. I treasure it; some day I shall be buried in it.

The medicine man had also left a peace pipe with me, together with a bag of *kinnickinnick*—our kind of tobacco made of red willow bark. This pipe was even more of a friend to me than my star blanket. To us the pipe is like an open Bible. White people need a church house, a preacher and a pipe organ to get into a praying mood. There are so many things to distract you: who else is in the church, whether the other people notice that you have come, the pictures on the wall, the sermon, how much money you should give and did you bring it with you. We think you can't have a vision that way.

For us Indians there is just the pipe, the earth we sit on and the open sky. The spirit is everywhere. Sometimes it shows itself through an animal, a bird or some trees and hills. Sometimes it speaks from the Badlands, a stone, or even from the water. That smoke from the peace pipe, it goes straight up to the spirit world. But this is a two-way thing. Power flows down to us through that smoke, through the pipe stem. You feel that power as you hold your pipe; it moves from the pipe right into your body. It makes your hair stand up. That pipe is not just a thing; it is alive. Smoking this pipe would make me feel good and help me to get rid of my fears.

As I ran my fingers along its bowl of smooth red pipestone, red like the blood of my people, I no longer felt scared. That pipe had belonged to my father and to his father before him. It would someday pass to my son and, through him, to my grandchildren. As long as we had the pipe there would be a Sioux nation. As I fingered the pipe, touched it, felt its smoothness that came from long use, I sensed that my forefathers who had once smoked this pipe were with me on the hill, right in the vision pit. I was no longer alone.

Besides the pipe the medicine man had also given me a gourd. In it were forty small squares of flesh which my grandmother had cut from her arm with a razor blade. I had seen her do it. Blood had been streaming down from her shoulder to her elbow as she carefully put down each piece of skin on a handkerchief, anxious not to lose a single one. It would have made those anthropologists mad. Imagine, performing such an ancient ceremony with a razor blade instead of a flint knife! To me it did not matter. Someone dear to me had undergone pain, given me something of herself, part of her body, to help me pray and make me stronghearted. How could I be afraid with so many people—living and dead—helping me?

One thing still worried me. I wanted to become a medicine man, a *yuwipi*, a healer carrying on the ancient ways of the Sioux nation. But you cannot learn to be a medicine man like a white man going to medical school. An old holy man can teach you about herbs and the right ways to perform a ceremony where everything must be in its proper place, where every move, every word has its own, special meaning. These things you can learn—like spelling, like training a horse. But by themselves these things mean nothing. Without the vision and the power this learning will do no good. It would not make me a medicine man.

What if I failed, if I had no vision? Or if I dreamed of the Thunder Beings, or lightning struck the hill? That would make me at once into a *heyoka,* a contrarywise, an upside-down man, a clown. "You'll know it, if you get the power," my Uncle Chest had told me. "If you are not given it, you won't lie about it, you won't pretend. That would kill you, or kill somebody close to you, somebody you love."

Night was coming on. I was still lightheaded and dizzy from my first sweat bath in which I had purified myself before going up the hill. I had never been in a sweat lodge before. I had sat in the little beehive-shaped hut made of bent willow branches and covered with blankets to keep the heat in. Old Chest and three other medicine men had been in the lodge with me. I had my back against the wall, edging as far away as I could from the red-hot stones glowing in the center. As Chest poured water over the rocks, hissing white steam enveloped me and filled my lungs. I thought the heat would kill me, burn the eyelids off my face! But right in the middle of all this swirling steam I heard Chest singing. So it couldn't be all that bad. I did not cry out "All my relatives!"—which would have made him open the flap of the sweat lodge to let in some cool air—and I was proud of this. I heard him praying for me: "Oh, holy rocks, we receive your white breath, the steam. It is the breath of life. Let this young boy inhale it. Make him strong."

The sweat bath had prepared me for my vision-seeking. Even now, an hour later, my skin still tingled. But it seemed to have made my brains empty. Maybe that was good, plenty of room for new insights.

Darkness had fallen upon the hill. I knew that *hanhepiwi* had risen, the night sun, which is what we call the moon. Huddled in my narrow cave, I did not see it. Blackness was wrapped around me like a velvet cloth. It seemed to cut me off from the outside world, even from my own body. It made me listen to the voices within me. I thought of my forefathers who had crouched on this hill before me, because the medicine men in my family had chosen this spot for a place of meditation and vision-seeking ever since the day they had crossed the Missouri to hunt for buffalo in the White River country some two hundred years ago. I thought that I could sense their presence right through the earth I was leaning against. I could feel them entering my body, feel them stirring in my mind and heart.

Sounds came to me through the darkness: the cries of the wind, the whisper of the trees, the voices of nature, animal sounds, the hooting of an owl. Suddenly I felt an overwhelming presence. Down there with me in my cramped hole was a big bird. The pit was only as wide as myself, and I was a skinny boy, but that huge bird was flying around me as if he had the whole sky to himself. I could hear his cries, sometimes near and sometimes far, far away. I felt feathers or a wing touching my back and head. This feeling was so overwhelming that it was just too much for me. I trembled and my bones turned to ice. I grasped the rattle with the forty pieces of my grandmother's flesh. It also had many little stones in it, tiny fossils picked up from an ant heap. Ants collect them. Nobody knows why. These little stones are supposed

to have a power in them. I shook the rattle and it made a soothing sound, like rain falling on rock. It was talking to me, but it did not calm my fears. I took the sacred pipe in my other hand and began to sing and pray: "Tunkashila, grandfather spirit, help me." But this did not help. I don't know what got into me, but I was no longer myself. I started to cry. Crying, even my voice was different. I sounded like an older man, I couldn't even recognize this strange voice. I used long-ago words in my prayer, words no longer used nowadays. I tried to wipe away my tears, but they wouldn't stop. In the end I just pulled that quilt over me, rolled myself up in it. Still I felt the bird wings touching me.

Slowly I perceived that a voice was trying to tell me something. It was a bird cry, but I tell you, I began to understand some of it. That happens sometimes. I know a lady who had a butterfly sitting on her shoulder. That butterfly told her things. This made her become a great medicine woman.

I heard a human voice too, strange and high-pitched, a voice which could not come from an ordinary, living being. All at once I was way up there with the birds. The hill with the vision pit was way above everything. I could look down even on the stars, and the moon was close to my left side. It seemed as though the earth and the stars were moving below me. A voice said, "You are sacrificing yourself here to be a medicine man. In time you will be one. You will teach other medicine men. We are the fowl people, the winged ones, the eagles and the owls. We are a nation and you shall be our brother. You will never kill or harm any one of us. You are going to understand us whenever you come to seek a vision here on this hill. You will learn about herbs and roots, and you will heal people. You will ask them for nothing in return. A man's life is short. Make yours a worthy one."

I felt that these voices were good, and slowly my fear left me. I had lost all sense of time. I did not know whether it was day or night. I was asleep, yet wide awake. Then I saw a shape before me. It rose from the darkness and the swirling fog which penetrated my earth hole. I saw that this was my great-grandfather, Tahca Ushte, Lame Deer, old man chief of the Minneconjou. I could see the blood dripping from my great-grandfather's chest where a white soldier had shot him. I understood that my great-grandfather wished me to take his name. This made me glad beyond words.

We Sioux believe that there is something within us that controls us, something like a second person almost. We call it *nagi*, what other people might call soul, spirit or essence. One can't see it, feel it or taste it, but that time on the hill—and only that once—I knew it was there inside of me. Then I felt the power surge through me like a flood. I cannot describe it, but it filled all of me. Now I knew for sure that I would become a *wicasa wakan*, a medicine man. Again I wept, this time with happiness.

I didn't know how long I had been up there on that hill—one minute or a lifetime. I felt a hand on my shoulder gently shaking me. It was old man Chest, who had come for me. He told me that I had been in the vision pit four days and four nights and that it was time to come down. He would give me something to eat and water to drink and then I was to tell him everything that had happened to me during my *hanblechia*. He would interpret my visions for me. He told me that the vision pit had changed me in a way that I would not be able to understand at that time. He told me also that I was no longer a boy, that I was a man now. I was Lame Deer.

A MAIDU CREATION STORY
MYTHO-EPISTEMOLOGICAL CRITIQUE

Abstract by Marcus Peters

In the beginning, there was nothing but a vast, black sea, with a sky so bleak it was difficult to tell where the water ended and the sky began. Everything was dark, empty, and cold. Floating through this nothingness was a tiny raft with two spirit beings, Pehe-ipe and Anosma. Pehe-ipe (the Watcher) and Anosma (Turtle) didn't know how they got on the raft, where they came from, or where they were going. They were afraid and lonely. Finally, Pehe-ipe said, "We can't just float here forever. There must be somebody who can make a world for us. Let's sing and call to this being, maybe he'll come."

Turtle and the Watcher wailed, cried, and sang for a long time. Suddenly, the sky above them split open and Pokelma (a rope made of feathers) came flowing down. Pehe-ipe and Turtle were brave, but still afraid. They cowered down while looking up, shielding their eyes when a great spiritual being climbed down the rope onto the raft. World Maker's face was covered and never seen, but his body shone like the sun. "You called the World Maker," the great being said, "and I've come. Why do you want me?"

There was a pause while Anosma and Pehe-ipe collected their wits. Then, words tumbled out all at once. World Maker listened until they began to repeat themselves, then he raised one of his hands. "Hush, hush," he said, "I can make a world for you, but I can't make it out of nothing. I need something to start with, so if you can get me a little ball of mud, I can make a world." The Watcher and Turtle looked around the vast ocean of cold, dark water. "Right," one of them said with a touch of sarcasm. "Just a little ball of mud. How are we going to get that in the middle of the ocean?" World Maker was patient and replied, "Oceans have bottoms. There you'll find some mud. All I need is a handful."

Turtle, who was the best swimmer in the world and a good diver, knew what World Maker meant. He stood up, took a deep breath, and prepared to jump from the raft. But World Maker stopped him and said, "Don't be so hasty." World Maker pulled down the rope of feathers from the sky and tied one end to Turtle's ankle. "This is a magical rope," he said. "However far you dive, you'll be safe. When you find the mud, just tug on the rope and we'll pull you up."

Turtle dove into the ocean and swam as deep as he could. Some people say his dive lasted five days, some say five months or five years, while others say only a few hours. Since the sky was so bleak, nobody could tell how much time had passed. Turtle couldn't find the bottom and grew frightened. He was running out of air, far beyond the ocean's surface. Finally, when he knew he could take only one more stroke, he kicked hard and reached out as far as he could. He thought he could feel something, but it slipped away. Out of air, he pulled on the rope and swam up quickly.

Turtle burst from the water and landed on the raft. For a long time, all he could do was gasp for air. Finally, he turned to World Maker and said, "I tried the best I could and I guess we're just going to have to stay here." World Maker replied, "You're being hasty again, Turtle." World Maker took out a stone knife and carefully used it to clean beneath Turtle's fingernails. When he was done, he had a speck of mud the size of a tiny seed. "Turtle," he said, "you tried as hard as you could and that's all anybody ever needs to do. I said I needed a ball of mud, but this is enough."

World Maker placed the tiny seed of mud in the center of the raft and said, "Now, we have to sing our power song. You have to help me. We must sing a song of power to make the world." They began to sing. "We are singing for the mountain of the world. For the mountain of the world, we sing." As they sang over and over, the little ball of mud began to quiver. With a pop, it became as big as a pea. They sang some more and it grew to the size of Pehe-ipe's head. "Hey," Pehe-ipe said, "we really are making a world." They sang louder, stomping their feet and clapping their hands because there weren't any drums in this world that wasn't yet a world. The ball of mud got bigger and bigger until, with a great roar, a cluster of mountains rose from the water.

The mountain that World Maker, Pehe-ipe, and Anosma sang into existence is known as the Middle Mountain. The three of them climbed to its highest peak, where World Maker created the rivers to drain the water from the land. When the land was ready, World Maker went deep into a secret cave in the interior of the Middle Mountain, where he created the first man and first woman and then sent them out into the newly made world.

I. What Is the Essence of the Creation Story?

The nature of this creation story is to explain the genesis of the California Indians known as Maidu. The story reveals the origin of land and human beings, while functioning as a guiding principle for life.

1. From what process did humans result?
   First, a powerful spirit being had to be summoned through song. Then, Turtle had to perform an incredible act to show his commitment to making land. A power song was then sung by all three spirit beings to produce land. Once the land was ready, World Maker created the first humans in secrecy.
2. What are the characteristics of creation?
   Singing was used to call the World Maker, and the first mountain was sung into existence. This Middle Mountain became the origin of land. Within this mountain, a secret cave represents the womb of Mother Earth. It is from this earthen womb that people first emerged. Since World Maker was the only being present in the secret cave, the womb is considered a sacred place, and the process of making humans within the womb is known only to World Maker.
3. What are the qualities and characteristics of the "creator"?
   World Maker, also known as Earth Initiate, is a powerful spirit being who came from the sky. World Maker's face is covered and never seen, while his body shines like the sun or a great, glowing spiritual light. Although I use a masculine pronoun, the creator's sex and gender are unknown and unspoken, so these characteristics are irrelevant. World Maker is receptive when the two spirit beings call upon him, and his response shows accessibility and reachability. The creator displays patience and concern for other spirit beings. World Maker instructs the spirit beings on how to solve their problem and lets them participate in the solution. World Maker creates the first humans in secrecy, giving only him the power to make people.

II. The Mythical Beings

1. What are the features, attributes, and qualities of the mythical beings?

   Pehe-ipe is a spirit being whose name literally means "Father of the Secret Society." He is also called "The Watcher" and tends to be a witness during certain events in Maidu history. He displays humanlike emotions, such as fear, loneliness, courage, respect, sarcasm, and hope.

   Anosma is a spirit being whose name means "Turtle." He is considered the best swimmer in the world and a good diver. He also displays humanlike emotions and characteristics, such as fear, loneliness, courage, weakness, and hope. Turtle is also symbolic of Mother Earth, land, and North America.

   World Maker is a powerful spirit being who comes from the sky. World Maker's body shines like a great light, and the face is covered and never seen. World Maker is accessible, understanding, patient, compassionate, creative, caring, and tolerant.

   Middle Mountain is the origin of land and people. It was sung into existence by World Maker and the two spirit beings. It started as a seed of mud and grew into great proportions. It contains a secret cave from which people first emerged.

2. What are the implied qualities of human beings?

   Since the first people came from World Maker, they possess some of the same qualities. They include understanding, patience, compassion, creativity, caring, and tolerance. Human conception begins in the womb, just as it does in the story, and it's considered sacred and secretive.

III. Mythical Symbols and Signs

1. What images and symbols are found in the myth?

   Black sea, bleak sky, tiny raft, singing, sky split open, a rope of feathers, dark water, a ball of mud, magical rope, stone knife, Turtle's fingernails, a speck of mud the size of a tiny seed, power song, a great roar, a cluster of mountains, Middle Mountain, highest peak, land, rivers, and a secret cave.

2. Can any of these be interpreted as signs?

   Floating in a tiny raft in a vast black sea with a bleak sky overhead can represent isolation and loneliness. Seeing the great spirit being come from the sky is a sign that the Watcher and Turtle were never really alone. A speck of

mud growing to the size of a mountain is a sign that you can create something out of nothing. The secret cave is a sign for the womb.

3. Are there behaviors that are evidence of innate releasing mechanism?

   Fear, cowering down, and being apprehensive when a great spirit being approaches are evidence of innate releasing mechanism. The Turtle knowing innately that World Maker wanted him to dive down to the bottom of the ocean. Maidu people having a special innate bond with Middle Mountain.

IV. Mythical Events

1. What do the events or drama of the myth imply about interactions or relations?

   Even though World Maker is a powerful spirit being, he is always accessible and approachable. Maidu people can speak and relate to this being through song. Turtle tried his best to retrieve the mud and thought he had failed, but his effort was important to World Maker and he was rewarded. Working in unison, these spirit beings were able to create something wonderful.

2. What are the principles that govern conduct?

   Knowing that a great spirit being exists and is responsible for creation leads to respect for all living things in the universe. Although World Maker is unseen, just knowing he is around is enough to lead a productive and ethical life. World Maker is also tolerant and accepting, so our shortcomings and failures are not detrimental. Trying your best is always seen in a favorable light. Working together is very important to realizing our potential.

V. Mythical Places

1. What are the places identified in the myth?

   A tiny raft in the middle of a dark sea. A bleak sky that splits open and reveals the World Maker's origin. The darkness of the bottom of the sea. The Middle Mountain (Sutter Buttes) in the Sacramento Valley.

2. What are the implied relationships between the locations of the mythical places?

   The tiny raft in the middle of the black sea represents nowhere or nothingness. From the bottom of the sea is a speck of mud that will become a mountain. The relationship shows that out of nothing came everything.

VI. What Does the Myth Reveal?

1. Cosmology (origin and structure)

   At one point in time, the world was nothing but water. From this situation, World Maker created the land. Rivers were used to drain the water from the land. Plants and animals were then created. Last, when this new world was ready, people were created and sent forth from a mountain.

2. Ontology (nature of existence)

   All things were created by the same spiritual being, so all things possess similar characteristics and qualities. Turtle and the Watcher wanted land, and World Maker made it for them. However, these two spirit beings said nothing about humans, and World Maker was alone when people were created. The nature of existence is different for animals than for humans. Both exist because of World Maker, but both have a different place within the universe.

3. Axiology (primary characteristics)

   The two spirit beings and World Maker displayed humanlike characteristics and emotions. Understanding, patience, caring, tolerance, and compassion are encompassed in all living beings.

4. World view (the natural order of the universe)

   Without land, there is nothing but ocean. The land is most important because it supports all life. Plants provide food for animals and humans, along with having medicinal purposes. Without land, there would be no plants. Without plants, there would be no animals. Without plants and animals, there would be no humans. Everything is connected and dependent upon each other. The world view reflects this natural order of all living things.

5. Ideology (how things should be)

   All living things should be respected because they all came from the same spirit being. When there is disrespect, the natural order is out of balance and everything is affected. When one thing suffers, everything suffers because they are all connected.

6. Ethos (set of guiding principles)

   Remember where you came from and the process of your genesis. The qualities of World Maker are your qualities. Patience, understanding, and tolerance are important to your existence. There is a balance to all things because all things are related.

"A Maidu Creation Story" by Marcus Peters. Reprinted by permission.

I first heard this story during an internship at Indian Grinding Rock State Historic Park in the early 1990s. The narrator and date of publication are unknown. There are several versions of the Creation Story within the different Maidu communities. In the book *The Way We Lived: California Indian Stories, Songs & Reminiscences,* published in 1981 by Heyday Books, a similar version can be found. The Middle Mountain (Sutter Buttes) from the story is located in the Sacramento Valley, between the Coastal Ranges and the Sierra Nevada.

MY WORLD IS A GIFT OF MY TEACHERS

Frank R. LaPena

When singers and holy people were killed, not only was a human bond broken and lives interrupted, but the way to renew the vital connection between the spiritual and the common world was interrupted drastically.

To understand the meaning of contemporary Indian art, it is necessary to consider the bond between the traditional arts and contemporary art as well as several other factors such as the symbiotic relationship between human beings and nature, the function of traditional ceremony and storytelling, and the relationship of vision and dreams to imagery. In Northern California, as in other Indian areas and regions, certain themes flow through the consciousness of the tribal society and its members. The themes are related through creation myths, stories, and songs. These, in turn, relate to understanding and controlling the philosophical and ethical foundation that helps one make a good and meaningful life.

Maintaining the oral tradition of history and stories as part of one's life establishes a relationship between the physical and spiritual realms. In the story of creation, the world is described. Special places such as Mt. Shasta, Doctor Rock, Bag of Bones, Sutter Buttes, Glass Mountain, and other sacred geological features significant to tribal history are identified along with plants, animals,

Frank R. LaPena, "My World Is a Gift of My Teachers," *The Extension of Tradition.* Copyright 1985 by the Crocker Art Musuem, Sacramento, CA. Reprinted with permission.

and birds. All things in the physical world—including many spiritual entities connected to the world and certain actions, identified as belonging to the spiritual dimension, that affect this world—are noted.

As one hears different stories, one begins to realize that images of nature and life known and related to by the dominant society are estranged from the Native American view of the world. The Native American sees the world as a "different place" from that seen and described by the dominant society. As a Native American, my world is a gift of my teachers. These elders, who were wise and gentle people, were singers and medicine people—practitioners of the sacred traditions, customs, and ceremonies. We are taught to respect the earth, for it is a place of mystery, wonder, and power. The earth and the universe are alive, living entities.

Listening to the stories that talk about the sacredness of the world and how it came to be, we also learn how to maintain balance and harmony by adhering to proper rules and restrictions. The magic, wonder, and "commonness" of traditional stories introduce us to a rich source of ideas and concepts useful for the artist. There are also stories of encounters with spiritual entities. Sometimes these circumstantial or accidental encounters are good, sometimes they are bad, sometimes the stories speak of the two kinds of encounters as watershed events that forever affect individuals and history. One important event remembered in oral tradition relates to the "first" contact with the white people. The first time white men were seen by the Wintu, the white men were named "Red Crane" people. The Sandhill Crane was common and loved by the Wintu people, while the red crane was rare and uncommon. We know the world changes; we hear this in our stories, sometimes we can see it change. In today's society, we see such a rapid change that sometimes we wonder how we will be able to maintain tradition.

Despite a dissonance between the traditional and contemporary ways, we confirm the ancient teachings of the earth to have valid lessons for today. Art helps to create order through the use of symbols. These symbols help to maintain the connection between traditional and contemporary cultures by reminding us of our responsibility for the way we choose to live, the way we relate our lives to the universal connection of the sacred circle.

If a person has not seen the dance ceremonies, or if one has not viewed indigenous traditional Indian art, s/he will not know the significance of contemporary Indian art; nor will that person know that the source is traditional and that it has a symbolic meaning. A non-Indian viewer may look at the art and see only artistic designs, forms, and shapes that validate these expressions as art. But they do not explain what the concepts are, where they come from, why they exist as they do, or that they make reference, as this exhibition does, to Indian tribes indigenous to California.

Indian artists work on several artistic levels: conceptual, realistic, and spiritual.

Furthermore, there is an acceptance of these three levels of meaning by Native Americans. We are told by our elders how the earth and human beings and other living things came to be. This helps us realize and understand how we can develop our own sense about how we fit into the universe, space, and time and how dreams and visions function to help us maintain the quality of life that is beautiful and powerful. Sometimes our art is done through the instruction that we receive in dreams. We may even be given new symbolic forms in our dreams and visions. The elders' information about the world is a way of understanding the philosophical basis of tradition that teaches us about ethics. When we have an opportunity to have traditional feather basketmakers speak of their craft and their art, they tell us that there are certain restrictions, certain kinds of feathers that must be used and why.

California Indians are known the world over for their featherwork. In the "making" of featherwork, each item must be thought of in terms of its eventual use and purpose. Dance headgear and skirts require certain feathers, while feather baskets require another kind. Feathers are not indiscriminately used, but the proper and right kind are used for each object. When the rules are learned and a person has been trained to respect the natural material, then s/he will respect the philosophy that helps the traditional arts to function and be maintained. A fine example of a traditional feather object is the Maidu feather blanket given to John Sutter by the Wilkes expedition in 1841.

In order to connect with other kinds of ideas that help maintain tradition, we need to talk about some of the ideas that are universal to the practice of ceremony. These values and concepts are recognized by other people who wish to maintain a connection to the earth. All things in and of the earth relate one to another and are interrelated in the concept of a sacred circle. This idea, of sacredness, includes all living things; all things in life are living and thus interconnected.

In this relationship, we have the responsibility to maintain and protect all living things, whether flying, crawling, swimming, or human. All of these things are connected, and we recognize the importance of that connection by ceremonies and prayers that speak to that unity. We pray for all things to help maintain harmony and balance in our lives. By uniting spiritual and physical beings in all four directions, with the below and the above, and the spiritual with the natural, we begin each new day as a new beginning.

In renewal ceremonies, such as the Sacred White Deer Dance of the northwestern California people and the Big Head ceremony of the Central Valley, we have an opportunity to think about our place on earth in relationship to the living spirit. The value of maintaining and respecting life is the recognition and importance of helping maintain this ordered symbiotic relationship.

I use the term "art documentation" when a person tries to create a "realistic" presentation of a dance or other subject matter. Whether it is a presentation of the way designs are used specifically or whether it shows overall activity, the art work is primarily to duplicate reality. This art work can be made in a "primitive," naive way or in a super-realistic style. Frank Day, Dal Castro, and Karen Tripp work this way in their paintings. Art done in the spiritual or conceptual way may result in strong design, or it may emphasize certain color connotations, such as intensity in hue—dark or light. The emphasis is on the spiritual in the sense that we have identified the spiritual and the realistic as the duality of life. This is accepted

and dealt with in ceremony and traditional thought, and also affects art.

All of the artists in this exhibition have an understanding of these factors, although Frank Tuttle and Brian Tripp are perhaps most abstract and conceptual in the execution of their work. My artwork is more realistic than abstract. When I work in an abstract style, it is usually because I have participated in the ceremony and have had the actual experience, and I feel more comfortable in approaching the subject matter in a more conceptual fashion.

People marketing Indian art are concerned with promoting art to protect the Indian art market. On the other hand, Indian artists are making expressions from their Indianness or traditional training, if they have been lucky enough to receive it. At the same time they are part of today's society and express their art in a contemporary way. Indian societies are not static or dead; they are dynamic and ever-changing. They are still vital and still concerned about what happens around them. They still participate in helping define and determine what the outcome of their life will be. Harry Fonseca's Coyote, on the other hand, has its own flexibility and irreverence for society that allows Coyote's individualism to cope with whatever life throws at him.

In emphasizing the ceremony, ceremonial activities, and the sacred, we acknowledge the major impact of traditional activities on Native Americans today. A person may dress in a cowboy hat, cowboy boots, or in a suit, but when he comes back to the ceremonial grounds and participates in a ceremony, he must dress in traditional gear and immerse himself in a direct, simple, and non-complex relationship. If a person looks at traditional activities and traditional art, there is no separation between everyday life and the traditional way. George Blake works in both the traditional arts and contemporary art forms, which is an expression of his personality. He also has a marvelous sense of humor and social conscience, which are found in some of his art. This concept of unity helps explain why Indian people, and Indian artists in particular, are able to maintain their creativity and their Indianness in their life and in their art. This contrasts with the dominant society, which fractionalizes life, separates avocation and vocation, and makes compartments and separations of the sacred from everyday life.

To maintain the traditional activities, we must also actively pursue traditional art forms. Many of the artists in this show are dancers, singers, or regalia makers; all are active in their communities in other roles.

The traditional way seeks unity in the unitive vision and holistic approach to living. In tradition, we believe that to make a whole and complete person is more desirable than to create a fractionalized person who would be disjointed and nonconnected in body and spirit. Therefore, we use different techniques and styles and are concerned about many things. We can talk about the sacred, we can talk about the spiritual, we can talk about the realistic—we see in the art work exactly that range and variety. If a person were to try to analyze Indian art, s/he would find that Indian art is done in different styles, and that all styles are accepted as valid by the Indian community. Acceptance and recognition of individual effort allows a complete expression to take place.

When we address the universe, we speak to the four directions and to the earth and sky. We include certain powers from each direction and certain significant symbols that we mention which connect ourselves to all of these things. Not only are there specific forms and symbolic imagery associated with different colors from those directions, but in addressing the universe we receive information about the universe and how to live our lives.

The world is alive and all things on her are physical and spiritual in essence. Song is a reflection of this joy and understanding; it is worth reviving and maintaining, for it connects us to our godliness and the spirit that is the power of the universe. In the singing, in the music, and in the words of songs are many dynamic stories and vital types of connections. Song may speak of the physical earth, or it may speak of the spiritual realm. Songs do this by means of symbolic as well as realistic natural imagery. When I think of song as a source of inspiration and imagery, individual singers, fire songs, handgame songs, cry songs, all the places where song is used and the emotions associated with those places come to mind. One of the most important functions of song is in dance.

In analyzing dance as a source for art, we find many paintings relate directly to the ceremony of dance, and reflect the continuity of dance ceremonies as cultural preservers and revival catalysts in Northern California. In the Native American artist, we find a certain sensitivity and relationship to the traditional idea that life is a learning process. We know that as we live our lives, we can learn through experience and come to an understanding of the meaning of our lives. Frank Tuttle speaks of this process when he conceptualizes his art as starting on a journey, beginning with the first step. As he journeys through, his perception and comprehension define his imagery from what he learns. It is somewhat like moving from room to room with new experiences in each room. He keeps moving through these doors and rooms. When he reaches the end and he has an art piece, he will have gone from one door to another, from one dimension and experience to another. Both his thinking and feeling become integrated, which results in a painting that encompasses the full dimension of his journey. I believe that is true of much of the art of Native Americans: the value of the piece is as much a function of the process, beauty, and meaning that goes into creating it as the end result or finished art piece.

A connection to nature is emphasized in much of Jean LaMarr's work. Jean says she likes to use flowers in her paintings, not only because they are beautiful and their shapes and designs are delicate and good to look at, but because there is also a traditional connection that the old people knew and appreciated in the beauty of flowers. When a girl was ready to be named, she was often given the name of a traditional wildflower. The Wintu gathered flowers in the spring and took time to admire and appreciate their beauty. Sometimes a flower was compared to the beauty, delicacy, and transitory life of a human being.

We live our lives by the turning of the seasons and the passage of the Milky Way. We direct our actions by the fullness of the moon and the need to do ceremonies, to put things to rest in winter and awaken them in spring. With our lives and our works we create a metaphor of the universe; all things are one with us. We arrange things according to tradition and pay attention to detail. The essence of color is its power to heal. It is also a spiritual element and represents the four directions.

We carry the best part of humanity here, sharing our dreams in song, dance, and prayer. Dreams have no limits, a desire is once and again human, with all of the weaknesses and strengths. Those whose responsibilities are dreams give us prophecies or answers on ways we should live and think. These dreams direct our actions, give dimension to our symbols, and extend the metaphor of art. What was true once is still meaningful; although it changes as we change, its essence is always the same.

I believe when I pray for the people, the earth, and the universe I am heard. When we begin a ceremony by praying, we give notice of our intentions and our convictions—it is not a frivolous action but a conscious act of will that makes what we do proper and respectful.

It is said a proper place is a sacred place. Fire makes this so. By its warmth and its flame we dedicate our ceremonies and actions. And mountains can be sacred just as Round-houses and dance pits, sacred rocks or ponds, and caves are connected to the holy.

It is no secret that the act of purification is associated with water. It is elemental and by its purpose of being is the basis of life. I extend myself outward and connect to being. I express myself in images to give you dance and art. These actions are limited, the vastness of thought and meaning endless.

If in my mind, I focus on things near to my eyes, my vision is easy; but if I return my vision to the place of origin, I have seen stars move around with anticipation. This has given me excitement and wonder. The "old ones" used to say we are all bound together because time has no boundary and space is only one continuity. We can go to the stars by thinking ourselves there as fast as we think it. There is no separation in the common sense, though certainly we feel distances are real, just as earth is real. It is a living thing—its breath is the wind, its veins the rivers. And if we listen within ourselves we find similar sounds in all living things.

WHO OWNS OUR PAST?
THE REPATRIATION OF NATIVE AMERICAN HUMAN REMAINS AND CULTURAL OBJECTS

Russell Thornton

On the morning of Friday, October 9, 1993, a small group of Northern Cheyenne arrived at the Smithsonian Institution's National Museum of Natural History. They had come for their dead. Almost 115 years earlier, on January 9, 1879, at least 83 members of a band of 149 Northern Cheyenne led by Dull Knife (a.k.a Morning Star) had been massacred by U.S. government soldiers near Fort Robinson, Nebraska, after a final, desperate attempt at freedom. The Northern Cheyenne had fled toward their homelands in Montana, after having been moved to a reservation in Oklahoma to live with the Southern Cheyenne in 1877. They were captured and held in the stockade at Fort Robinson with little food, water, or even heat. They attempted to escape after two weeks. At least 57 Northern Cheyenne were killed during the attempt. Thirty-two others found a brief freedom, until they were trapped on January 22 at the edge of Antelope Creek, where 26 of them were killed during the resulting massacre. Most Cheyenne killed in the escape attempt

were buried near the fort; those killed at Antelope Creek were buried nearby in a mass grave. The bones of 17 of the Northern Cheyenne were collected after their brutal deaths for scientific study by the U.S. Army Medical Examiner. Nine of these were obtained from the mass grave at Antelope Creek, which was exhumed in 1880. The bones—mostly crania—were later transferred to the Smithsonian's National Museum of Natural History. The bones were from Cheyenne ranging in age from forty-nine to a three-year-old child massacred at Antelope Creek. All were now being returned to their people in a joint repatriation with the Peabody Museum of Archaeology and Ethnology at Harvard, which also had some skeletal remains from the Antelope Creek massacre, collected about a month before those of the Army Medical Museum by a Peabody museum curator.

At the repatriation ceremony the human bones were officially turned over to the Northern Cheyenne delegation. The delegation was impressive. The Northern Cheyenne were represented by the tribal chair, the Crazy Dogs society of warriors, the Elk Horn society, Sun Dance priests, four women who were fourth-generation de-

Russell Thornton, *Studying Native America: Problems and Prospects.* © 1998. Reprinted by permission of The University of Wisconsin Press. Notes have been omitted.

scendants of Dull Knife, and, most important, James Black Wolf, Keeper of the Sacred Buffalo Hat. The remains were carefully arranged on small Pendleton blankets; a pipe ceremony was performed, words and prayers were said, and a drum was played and songs were sung. Each person's bones were then wrapped in a blanket and interred in cedar boxes for the journey home to Montana and final rest. During the ceremony, it was discovered that a shattered lower part of a skull from the Harvard museum matched an upper part of a woman's skull from the Smithsonian. Either at death 115 years earlier or sometime afterward, the woman's head had been broken into two pieces, with each piece ending up at a different location. She was collected as two different people, one part of her going to the Army Medical Museum and eventually the Smithsonian, the other part going to the Peabody. On that day, October 9, 1993, not only was the young Northern Cheyenne woman reunited with her people; her skull itself was reunited.

During the ceremony, a young Native American man from the Smithsonian came up to me and told me about the three-year-old's skull. "The child was a little girl. I saw her. She was dressed in white and had yellow ribbons in her hair. I told the Cheyenne I had seen her, and that she was now happy. They were very pleased. They thanked me for telling them."

After the ceremony in Washington, the remains were taken to Montana for burial. A stop was made on October 12 at Fort Robinson, Nebraska, for ceremonies. The journey then continued to Busby, Montana, where a wake, giveaway, and offerings to the dead took place. A small teddy bear was given to the little girl and placed on the cedar box with her remains. Her remains and those of the other massacred Cheyenne were buried shortly after noon on October 16, 1993, on a hill near Two Moon Monument.

I attended the ceremony in Washington, D.C., as the chair of the Smithsonian Institution's Native American Repatriation Review Committee, which was created by the Congress of the United States to oversee the return of Native American human remains and grave objects held at the Smithsonian Institution. It was an even more meaningful ceremony for me than it would ordinarily have been. My mother had died a few days before; I had stopped in Washington to attend the ceremony while on my way to Vian, Oklahoma, for her funeral the following day. At the ceremony in Washington, I kept thinking that my mother would be laid to rest only a few days after her death, but that these Northern Cheyenne had waited in museums for over a century before they could be buried. My mother had a long, full life and died peacefully. The Northern Cheyenne men, women, and children had short lives, ended by violent, cruel deaths.

REPATRIATION OF HUMAN REMAINS AND CULTURAL OBJECTS

The repatriation of the Native American human remains and also of funerary and other cultural objects is occurring today because of determined efforts by Native Americans to achieve legal changes in American society. It reflects perhaps a new significance for Native Americans in American society, and an important development in the relationship between Native Americans and that society. This legally mandated repatriation is also recognition of tribal sovereignty: remains and objects are repatriated to tribal entities (individuals may make claims if they can prove direct descent), though the transfer is not from U.S. government to tribal government, but from museum to tribal government. Repatriation certainly should be an important contemporary topic within Native American studies. It has additional significance for the ways native peoples and the scholarly community relate to each other, including how their respective ethics, values, conceptions, and even bodies of knowledge come together.

Native American Remains As Objects of Study

It has been estimated that skeletal remains of "tens and tens of thousands," possibly "hundreds of thousands," of Native American individuals are held in various universities, museums, historical societies and even private collections in the United States: one number frequently given is 600,000. (Skeletal remains of Native Americans are also held in other countries.) Whatever the actual figure, these estimates show a sizable problem. How many objects belonging to Native American groups these collections hold is pure speculation. In addition to funerary objects (included in burials, made specifically for burials, or designed to contain human remains), there are "objects of patrimony" owned by the entire people, such as wampum belts, and sacred objects, such as medicine bundles. It is also estimated that the skeletons, or more typically pieces of them, of several hundred Native Americans and the countless objects buried with them are uncovered every year in highway, housing, and other types of construction.

Native American remains and grave goods have been objects of study and fascination to non–Native Americans for centuries. In 1620 Pilgrims searching for caches of Indian corn to rob uncovered a grave containing "the bones and head of a little child . . . strings and bracelets of fine white beads. . . . and some other odd knacks. . . . We brought sundry of the prettiest things away with us," they wrote, "and covered the corpse up again." Reports of

systematic excavation of Native American burial sites and mounds date from the eighteenth century. Thomas Jefferson excavated burial mounds on his property in Virginia, and in so doing became the "father of American archaeology." He wrote of his excavation of a mound, "I first dug superficially in several parts of it, and came to collections of human bones, at different depths, from six inches to three feet below the surface. These were lying in the utmost confusion, some vertical, some oblique, some horizontal, and directed to every point of the compass, entangled, and held together in clusters by the earth. . . . I conjectured that in this barrow might have been a thousand skeletons."

Native American crania became objects of particular scientific interest in the early nineteenth century, and remain so today. Scholars evaluated theories of migration to North America from Asia by comparing Native Americans with Asians. They sought physical evidence to explain physical and cultural differences among native peoples and between them and other peoples; often cultural differences were seen as a result of racial ones. Various scholars actively collected Native American remains, including Albert Gallatin and Samuel G. Morton. In 1839, Morton published *Crania Americana*, reporting that Caucasians had larger brain capacities and therefore higher intelligence than Native Americans. The "science" of phrenology soon developed, and collecting crania became more widespread as scholars attempted to relate intelligence, personality, and character to skull and brain size.

The Smithsonian Institution opened in 1846 and provided further impetus for the development of American archaeology, physical anthropology, and ethnology. Native American remains and cultural objects were, of course, important. The U.S. Army also became very much involved as its mandate to handle the "Indian problem" expanded after the U.S. Civil War.

On May 21, 1862, Surgeon General of the United States William Hammond suggested that an Army Medical Museum be established in Washington, D.C., to "facilitate the study of methods to diminish mortality and suffering among soldiers." This was during the Civil War, and for the first several years most specimens acquired related to "the injuries and diseases that produce death or disability during war."

After the Civil War, as the former Union Army turned its attention westward to confront Native Americans on the plains, the Army Medical Museum sought to update its collections to reflect this new conflict. On April 4, 1867, Surgeon General J. K. Barnes requested that medical officers also collect:

1. Rare pathological specimens from animals, including monstrosities.
2. Typical crania of Indian tribes; specimens of their arms, dress, implements, rare items of their diet, medicines, etc.
3. Specimens of poisonous insects and reptiles, and their effects on animals.

Nine months later, on January 13, 1868, Surgeon General Madison Mills wrote to army medical directors at the Department of Missouri at Fort Leavenworth (Kansas), the Department of the Platte at Omaha (Nebraska), the Department of New Mexico at Santa Fe, and the Department of Dakota at Fort Snelling (Minnesota), urging them to have their medical officers collect "specimens of Indian crania and of Indian weapons and Utensils." "The Surgeon General," he wrote, "is anxious that our collection of Indian Crania, already quite large, should be made as complete as possible."

By September 1868, the museum had a collection of 143 crania, 47 of which were Native American, representing various tribes. A memorandum issued then said that the museum "chiefly desired to procure sufficiently large series of adult crania of the principal Indian tribes to furnish accurate average measurements. In 1870 Dr. G. A. Otis, then the curator of the museum, reported his conclusions to the National Academy of Sciences during a meeting held there: "Judging from the capacity of the cranium, the American Indians must be assigned a lower position in the human scale than has been believed heretofore."

More than four thousand Native American skulls were eventually collected—from burial scaffolds, graves, and ossuaries, and from battlefields and sites of massacres—and then sent to the Army Medical Museum. Many other museums participated in the collecting of Native American skeletal remains, including the Peabody Museum at Harvard University, the American Museum of Natural History in New York, and the Field Museum of Chicago, which obtained some Native American remains originally sent to Chicago for the 1893 World's Columbian Exposition.

Human ancestors began to bury their dead in some fashion more than 200,000 years ago. Native Americans developed a variety of methods of caring for their dead. These ranged from merely leaving them on the ground, sometimes covering them with stone, to placing them in wooden coffins on the surface of the ground or in caves, to placing them on scaffolds or in a tree, to burial underground, even under the floor of their homes, to cremation. Some tribes kept the remains of their dead in special houses or ossuaries. For example, the Inca Garcilaso de la Vega describes a burial temple in the province of Cofachiqui: "Along all four walls the Indians had set wooden chests. . . . Within the chests . . . , the infidels had entombed the bodies of their dead without any more preservatives against decomposition than if they were giving them burial in the earth."

Most Native American peoples attach an important spiritual quality to the remains of their ancestors. Chief Seattle, for example, explained: "To us the ashes of our ancestors are sacred and their final resting place is hallowed ground, while you wander far from the graves of your ancestors and, seemingly, without regret." During battles, rival tribes would sometimes attempt to destroy the ossuaries, knowing how much pain this would inflict on their enemies. Many native people think that treating their ancestral remains as objects of curiosity or scientific study is also disrespectful to them and their ancestors. To the Zuni, the removal of human remains from their ancestral lands so desecrated their ancestors that they cannot be returned to Zuni Pueblo for reburial! Many cultural objects are of spiritual significance, sometimes sacred to Native Americans. That skeletons of ancestors and sacred tribal objects are held by museums, scholarly and other institutions, and even private individuals is painful to most contemporary native peoples.

Collecting Human Remains and Objects

Many human remains and objects subject to legal repatriation were obtained appropriately, with the permission if not actual support of Native Americans at the time. However, many were not; that human remains and objects were obtained by "grave robbing," theft, and fraud adds to Native American discomfort and further legitimizes claims for repatriation, as the four cases briefly described below illustrate.

A major smallpox epidemic among Indian tribes of the central and northwest regions of the United States in the early 1800s killed the great Omaha chief Washinga Sakba ("the Blackbird"). The artist George Catlin, who traveled among Native Americans from the Dakotas to Indian Territory in the 1830s and 1840s, painting the natives he encountered, describes Washinga Sakba's funeral in his journal. Catlin writes that Washinga Sakba was buried on a bluff above the Missouri River, mounted on his favorite white horse, "with his bow in his hand, and his shield and quiver slung—with his pipe and his *medicine-bag*—with his supply of dried meat, and his tobacco-pouch replenished to last him through his journey to the 'beautiful hunting grounds of the shades of his fathers'." When he visited the grave site, Catlin adds, he dug up Washinga Sakba's skull to add it to "others which I have collected on my route."

On December 29, 1890, several hundred Sioux men, women, and children were massacred by troops of the First Squadron of the Seventh Cavalry at Wounded Knee Creek. The Sioux had fled their reservation to practice their new religion—the Ghost Dance. The massacre occurred after the troops had captured them and were attempting to disarm them. The cavalry left with their dead and wounded after the massacre, and sent out a burial detail a few days later. Meanwhile, other Sioux learned of the massacre and collected some of their own dead. When the burial detail arrived on January 1, 1891, a heavy blizzard had covered the remaining bodies with snow. Eighty-four men and boys, 44 women and girls, and 18 children were collected and buried in a mass grave Some Sioux had been wearing sacred Ghost Dance shirts; they were stripped of these shirts before being dumped into the grave.

Six shirts ended up at the National Museum of Natural History; one was displayed in a museum exhibit with the caption stating that it was taken from the Wounded Knee "Battlefield." In the fall of 1986, I was a fellow at the museum. I remember vividly a trip one afternoon with a curator into the building's attic to examine some of the North American Indian collections. He volunteered to show me these shirts. He pulled out a drawer from a large cabinet, and there they were. Almost a hundred years after it occurred, I was a witness to the legacy of the massacre at Wounded Knee. The shirts have bullet holes and are stained with blood; some still have medicine bags attached.

The Smithsonian officially had twenty-nine "objects" taken from those massacred at Wounded Knee. Besides the six Ghost Dance shirts, they include a blanket from "a dead body," a pair of boys' moccasins, and baby jackets and caps. Their return to the descendants of those slain at Wounded Knee occurred in September of 1998. The Cheyenne River Sioux Tribe represented the descendants in negotiating the request.

Ales Hrdlicka, recognized as a father, if not the father, of physical anthropology, visited Kodiak Island off the coast of Alaska in the 1930s. Representing the Smithsonian Institution, he removed the remains of about a thousand people and 144 associated burial items from an archaeological site called Uyak. The people later said that they resented the intrusion and the removal of the remains, but Hrdlicka was a representative of the government, and they did not know what to do. They never gave him permission. But "he had no regard for the people here. And we had no laws. None that we knew about. We just stood by."

A final, well-known example occurred at the American Museum of Natural History. In 1897, Robert Peary brought to New York City from Greenland six Inuit (Eskimo) and the famous Cape York meteorite, a sacred object to the Inuit. Four of the six soon died of tuberculosis; one, Uisaakassak, eventually returned to Greenland. The sole remaining Eskimo was the well-known Minik, who lived until 1918, after returning to Greenland in 1909, and then coming back to the United States in 1916 to live in New Hampshire. The first of the four to die was Qisuk, father of the then-eight-year-old Minik. After his death, in January 1899, his "bones were preserved, boiled and varnished and mounted as a perfect skeleton." The other three Inuit who died were likewise dissected, and their skeletons added to the museum's collections. Hrdlicka published a paper on Qisuk's brain in 1901, complete with pictures (he called him Kishu or Kissuk). A fake burial had been performed for Qisuk. It was noted by a young anthropologist, Alfred Kroeber, who had studied the six Eskimos in New York and wrote a paper on the Eskimo of Smith Sound without leaving the city. Kroeber indicated that Minik was instructed to "visit the (supposed) grave of his father." Later, Minik discovered that his father's bones were actually on display in the museum. "I can never be happy till I can bury my father in a grave," he lamented. "It makes me cry every time I think of his poor bones up there in the museum in a glass case, where everybody can look at them. Just because I am a poor Esquimau boy why can't I bury my father in a grave the way he would want to be buried?"

The answer, in his case as in the other three described here, was that the bones were being kept in the interest of science.

Important Research

Nearly all of the 4,000 crania at the Army Medical Museum were eventually transferred to the Smithsonian's National Museum of Natural History and added to the remains of approximately 14,500 other Native Americans there (along with non–Native American remains). This supposedly represents the largest single collection of Native American remains in the United States, followed by some 13,500 held by the Tennessee Valley Authority. The University of California also has a very large collection. The Hearst (formerly Lowie) Museum at its Berkeley campus has "the third largest number of catalogued skeletal entries in the United States (more than 11,000)." Most of these remains, "representing more than 8,000 individuals," are from California's northern coast and Sacramento Valley. As for artifacts, there are "roughly 1 million or more pieces" at Berkeley. UCLA and other campuses of the University of California system have smaller numbers of Native American human remains and artifacts.

Research on native skeletal remains has generated much important knowledge about such diverse topics as population size and composition, cultural patterns of tooth mutilation, diseases present among Native American populations and treatments for those diseases, life expectancies, growth patterns, population affinities, origins and migrations, and diets, including dates at which corn was introduced among various peoples of North America. We now know from studying these remains that tuberculosis was present in this hemisphere before European contact in 1492, as were some infectious diseases, including treponemal infections, that certain native groups had serious iron deficiencies from a diet heavily dependent on corn, and that among some groups males with more social prestige—as reflected by burial objects—were physically larger than males with less social prestige (perhaps because they had better diets, perhaps because bigger men were simply given more prestige).

Native American skeletal remains have become even more important as objects of study, scholars assert, given recent advances and probable future advances in scientific technology, including the detection of immunoglobulin and DNA sequencing from bone. The study of immunoglobulin could enable scholars to establish explicit disease histories for the skeletons; deciphering their DNA code could enable scholars to establish genetic relationships among historical populations. Moreover, science progresses, and unforeseen and foreseen advances will enable scholars to generate increasingly greater knowledge from the skeletal remains. This is no small issue, and much of the knowledge to be gained could benefit both Native American and other peoples of the world.

Some Views

Native American views that repatriation must occur are typically held despite any scholarly or public good, past or future, derived from the study or display of the remains and objects. Scholars and others assert that the scientific and public value of the remains and cultural objects outweigh any claims Native Americans may have. As scholars attempt to reconstruct histories of Native Americans, they argue that the scientific benefits are important not only to the public at large, but also to native peoples themselves. Some have even sued to be allowed to retain or study remains or objects, as is the case with a recent discovery: Native American remains 9000 years old (or older) and showing some "caucasoid features," an individual dubbed the "Richland" or "Kennewick Man." Other lawsuits have involved the ability to study the remains before actual repatriation.

A related view is that the remains and objects now housed in museums and educational institutions belong not to Native Americans but to all Americans, even to all peoples of the world. They are part of the heritage of all people, not only Native American people. Another view is that the scholars are keeping and studying the remains because Native Americans do not know what they are doing when requesting repatriation. "Someday," they say, "Native Americans will want this knowledge. It is up to us to preserve it for them." (This assertion that scientists are "saving the Indians from themselves" is both patronizing and insulting.)

Native Americans, conversely, assert that other factors outweigh science and education, noting that our society places all sorts of restrictions on research. Obviously, research that physically harms humans (and, to a lesser extent, animals) is prohibited. Under conventional ethical standards, one must get "informed consent" from subjects who are aware of the nature and implications of the research, the research must not harm subjects psychologically, and subjects may not be identified without their permission. Yet studying the human remains of their ancestors, for example, causes great psychological pain, Native Americans argue.

Native Americans also point out that skeletons obtained from battlefields and massacres, as many of those in the Army Medical Museum were, are remains of Native Americans who died defending their homelands: all of the United States of America was once Native American land. American society has given much attention to returning to the United States the remains of Americans killed in World War II, the Korean Conflict, the war in Vietnam, and other wars. Do we owe less to those who defended America against the Europeans and the Euro-Americans who took their land? Are Native American warriors killed in battle less deserving of an honorable burial than American military personnel who died for the United States? (And what about "civilians" killed in battles and massacres?) Most Americans strongly support efforts to repatriate the remains of all fellow Americans who died in Vietnam and elsewhere. What would be the reaction if the Republic of Vietnam refused to return the skeletal remains of American service men and women killed there? What if they said: "We want to keep them and study them. They have much scientific value"?

THE REPATRIATION MOVEMENT

Native Americans have attempted legally to prevent the collection of their human remains and cultural objects for more than a century. During the last few decades, they have increasingly demanded that ancestral remains and sacred objects be returned to them for proper disposal or care. This effort is a social movement: "a concerted and continued effort by a social group aimed at reaching a goal (or goals) common to its members. More specifically, the effort is directed at modifying, maintaining, replacing, or destroying an existing social institution." Thus, social movements are determined and organized group efforts to bring about some objectives, particularly types of social change. Repatriation is an organized effort to return Native American human remains and cultural objects to the communities from which they came.

Social movements are shaped by societies and cultures; goals and objectives are achieved by means available and acceptable at particular times in particular societies and cultures. Social movements in American society today often involve such political processes as obtaining public support and sympathy, lobbying legislators, and getting specific laws passed. This is exactly what occurred in the repatriation movement.

Repatriation is also a pan-Indian movement in two ways: it involves many different Native American peoples, with or without strong tribal affiliations (though, as noted, repatriation is only carried out with tribes or direct descendants); and Native American tribes have joined in it to pursue common, though tribally specific interests. For many Native Americans, with strong tribal ties or otherwise, the repatriation movement ranks in importance with the social movements of other groups in American society—the civil rights movement, the women's movement.

The repatriation movement has given Native Americans a new sense of respect—from American society and also for themselves.

Repatriation might also be considered a revitalization movement, a "deliberate, organized, conscious effort by members of a society to construct a more satisfying culture." My own view is that a revitalization movement is a special type of social movement designed "to create a better social and/or cultural system while reviving or reaffirming selected features." Repatriation is truly revitalizing and breathing new life into Native American communities by seeking to recover what has been taken from them.

During past decades, the pan-Indian repatriation movement became successful through the passage of federal and state laws not only calling for the repatriation of human remains and objects to descendants, if known, or, otherwise, appropriate tribes, but also preventing the further disenfranchisement of remains and objects. (Native peoples in Canada have raised similar issues, but similar changes in Canadian law have not yet occurred.) Not only has the success of the repatriation movement revitalized Native America and provided new self-esteem; the task of actually winning repatriations of human remains and cultural objects has also revitalized communities by bringing members together for this struggle as well as reaffirming important knowledge about many cultural and sacred objects.

It is not always an easy undertaking, although the result may be worth it. "As difficult as implementation of the repatriation policy and laws may be in the non-Native world," Suzan Shown Harjo comments, "the truly complex issues are being examined by Native Peoples, who must arrive at a consensus in matters for which most lack specific historical and ceremonial context. Each detail of repatriation, including whether or not to request repatriation, must be worked out within each family, clan, society or nation."

This process can be very important when it comes to sacred objects, sources of much power or "medicine." How does one handle them? Can one handle them? Much of this knowledge was lost by Native Americans, and they may find it difficult to know exactly what to do. One may compare Native American sacred objects with the Ark of the Covenant containing the ten commandments, a source of great power in some religions. What would people do if the Ark was suddenly discovered? Would they open it? Would they touch the stones on which the ten commandments are carved? The ten commandments are on stone given by a god or creator, and Native American sacred objects also may be of stone, given by a creator.

I attended the 1995 Southeast Alaska Indian Repatriation Conference, sponsored by the Tlingit and Haida Indian Tribes of Alaska in Juneau. During the conference, a TeleVideo hookup with the National Museum of Natural History allowed tribal members to view objects held there. It was gratifying to see a packed room at the University of Alaska Southeast Campus where tribal members ranging from elders to young children had gathered to view important objects. The moderator of the conference, David Katzeek, caretaker (*Hit-s'aati*) of the Shangukeidee clan (Thunderbird of Klukwan, Eagle moiety), and his mother, Anna Katzeek, followed ceremonial protocol and wore regalia as a sign of respect for all involved. Responses by members of other clans also followed the protocol. During the TeleVideo session, elders talked and debated about the masks, hats, and bear knife shown on the video screen, sharing their knowledge with tribal members. It appeared to be a time of real intellectual revitalization for the Tlingit and Haida. One respected participant responded after the conference: "Everything has power, has spirit. The power was strong there this morning, and emotions were strong. . . . One day all the things that have been lost will be returned."

It is important to note, however, that the costs of repatriations, legal or otherwise, may be considerable, straining limited tribal resources.

Much of the early focus of the movement was upon the Smithsonian Institution, since it is the national museum of our country. I was a visiting scholar at the Smithsonian's National Museum of Natural History in 1985–1986. At that time one curator of physical anthropology was Douglas Ubelaker, whose forensic work was popularized in his book *Bones*. Ubelaker has also done extensive scholarly work on the population history of North American Indians, one of my own topics of interest.

At that time, the Smithsonian Institution was being subjected to extreme political pressure from national pan-Indian organizations to return its Native American skeletal collections to Native American tribes. The decision was made by Smithsonian administrators to inform tribes of the skeletal collections and suggest to them that some ancestral tribal members might be among the skeletons of the Smithsonian.

Ubelaker sought my advice. We talked about the draft of a letter informing the tribes of the Smithsonian's holdings along with a computer printout detailing the geographical origin of the Native American skeletons. I made a suggestion or two, and the revised letter was sent by Adrienne L. Kaeppler, then chair of the Department of Anthropology, to 225 federally recognized tribes. I thought from the beginning that the tribes would show little interest. They were generally focused on local issues; repatriation was not yet an issue of concern to them—at least I had not heard much about it from tribal

people. Rather, I told Ubelaker that the demands for repatriation were mainly articulated by "urban" Native Americans. Tribes might very well be supportive of those demands and might eventually become involved, but they had not yet done so to a significant extent. The likely response, I thought, would be no response. My prediction proved correct. Only a handful of responses came in.

National Native American leaders, such as Walter Echo-Hawk of the Native American Rights Fund and Suzan Shown Harjo of the National Congress of American Indians, continued to seek the repatriation of human skeletal remains from the Smithsonian and elsewhere. Native American organizations, such as the American Indians Against Desecration (AIAD), a project of the International Indian Treaty Council, issued a statement calling for repatriation. Native American protests took place at specific museums, such as the Illinois State Museum at Dickson Mounds. Professional associations such as the Council for Museum Anthropology, Society for American Archaeology, American Anthropological Association, and American Association of Museums became involved and issued position papers. A Panel for a National Dialogue on Museum/Native American Relations was established. Various universities also debated the issues, forming committees and panels to develop policies. The University of California system formed a "Joint Academic Senate–Administration Committee on Human Skeletal Remains" in 1990 to develop a policy for the system, and individual campuses formed local committees to implement the policy.

Senator Daniel K. Inouye (Democrat of Hawaii) took up the cause as chair of the Select Committee on Indian Affairs and, as discussed below, linked it to the acquisition of the collection of the Museum of the

American Indian in New York City to form the National Museum of the American Indian. One idea considered but discarded was to establish a national mausoleum where Native American remains "'which are not useful for scientific inquiry' would be buried, 'giving due regard to the religious and ceremonial beliefs and practices of those Indians, Aleuts and Eskimos whose ancestors may be included in the Smithsonian collection.'"

The private sector also became involved in the repatriation movement, just as it did in the civil rights movement. Elizabeth Sackler purchased three Hopi and Navajo ceremonial masks for $39,050 at a Sotheby auction in New York City in May 1991. Her intent was to return them to the tribes. She then established the American Indian Ritual Object Repatriation Foundation to help native groups win the return of important cultural objects in the hands of private individuals and organizations. The foundation continues to be active in repatriation.

State and Federal Laws

Repatriation legislation was enacted on both the state and federal levels.

"All states have laws that address in some manner the disposition of prehistoric aboriginal remains and grave goods," concludes Marcus Price. Although some states "merely apply their criminal laws against grave robbing, trespass, and vandalism, or their general public health and cemetery laws," ever more, he notes, they are establishing "legislation specific to the problem," yet, "there is little consistency in approach." An important example of state legislation was Iowa's reburial statue of the mid-1970s, which protects "prehistoric burial mounds and unmarked cemeteries and presumes ultimate reburial of ancient remains." The landmark state legislation, however, probably was Nebraska's 1989 Unmarked Human Burial Sites and Skeletal Remains Protection Act. In passing the act, Nebraska became the first state with a general repatriation statue. It provides for the protection of unmarked burial sites throughout the state and the repatriation (within one year of a request) to relatives or American Indian tribes of human remains and associated burial goods held in state-sponsored or state-recognized public bodies. In 1991 California, after much effort by Assemblyman Richard Katz, established a new law providing for the repatriation of Native American human remains and funerary objects. The original bill was vetoed by the governor in 1990, but after further amendments was passed again and approved by the governor on September 6, 1991. In large part, Katz's efforts were inspired by the large number of Native American remains held by the University of California system. The University of California had lobbied against the law, preferring instead to develop its own repatriation policy.

The federal government has repeatedly enacted legislation aimed at protecting the rights of Native American groups vis-á-vis ancestral remains and sacred objects. Twentieth-century legislation may be dated from the Antiquities Act of 1906, which granted the federal government jurisdiction over all aboriginal remains and artifacts on federal property. Other important legislation includes the Historical Sites Act of 1935 (supplemented by the Reservoir Salvage Act of 1960), the National Historic Preservation Act of 1966, the Department of Transportation Act of 1966, and the National Environmental Policy Act of 1969.

Recent federal legislation has been sparked by the outspokenness and political sophistication of Native Americans themselves. Native groups have successfully lobbied lawmakers and obtained public support for their repatriation efforts. On August 11, 1978, Senate Joint Resolution 102, the American Indian Religious Freedom Act

(AIRFA), made it "the policy of the United States to protect and preserve for American Indians their inherent right of freedom to believe, express, and exercise the traditional religions of the American Indian, Eskimo, Aleut, and Native Hawaiian." Included in this freedom was "use and possession of sacred objects." The Archaeological Resources Protection Act (ARPA) of 1979 soon followed, specifically mandating that the AIRFA be considered in the disposition of archaeological resources, and that "archaeological resources recovered from Indian land are the property of the tribe."

The next important federal legislation on repatriation was Public Law 101-185, the National Museum of the American Indian Act of November 1989, which established the National Museum of the American Indian (NMAI) as part of the Smithsonian Institution. A component of this law mandates that "if any Indian human remains are identified by a preponderance of the evidence as those of a particular individual or as those of an individual culturally affiliated with a particular Indian tribe, the Secretary [of the Smithsonian], upon the request of the descendants of such individual or of the Indian tribe shall expeditiously return such remains (together with any associated funerary objects) to the descendants or tribe, as the case may be."

In October 1990, Public Law 101-601, the Native American Graves Protection and Repatriation Act (NAGPRA), was established. It specifically considers the disposition of Native American human remains and artifacts in federal agencies (other than the Smithsonian), mandating that "any institution or State or local government agency, including any institution of higher learning, that receives Federal funds and has possession of, or control over, Native American human remains or cultural items must comply with NAGPRA." NAGPRA will, therefore, affect

most of the approximately eight thousand museums in the United States.

The law increases the protection of Native American graves on federal and tribal land, makes illegal the commercial traffic in Native American remains, requires the inventorying and repatriation to culturally affiliated tribes or descendants of all collections of Native American remains and associated funerary objects held by federal agencies and federally funded museums (and universities), and also requires the repatriation of Native American sacred objects and cultural patrimony. Human remains, funerary objects (either associated or unassociated with currently held remains), sacred objects, and objects of cultural patrimony shall all "be expeditiously returned." ("Cultural affiliation" as defined in NAGPRA means "that there is a relationship of shared group identity which can be reasonably traced historically or prehistorically between a present day Indian tribe or Native Hawaiian organization and an identifiable earlier group.") Under the provisions of NAGPRA, a seven-person review committee monitors and reviews repatriation activities. Three of the members are appointed from a pool nominated by Native American groups and religious leaders; at least two of them must be "traditional Indian religious leaders." Three members are appointed from nominees of museum and scientific organizations, and one member is appointed from a list suggested by the other six members.

The Smithsonian Institution decided to follow Public Law 101-601 as well as Public Law 101-185, thereby extending the mandate of repatriation to include not only human remains and funerary objects but also sacred objects and objects of cultural patrimony. In the fall of 1996, an amendment to the NMAI Act was introduced into the U.S. Senate by Senator McCain (Republican of Arizona), and passed a few months later. It amends the act along the lines of the NAGPRA legislation, setting a strict time schedule and legally requiring the repatriation of objects of cultural patrimony and sacred objects. The Smithsonian is committed to completing its inventory of Native American human remains and funerary objects by June 1, 1998; a summary of ethnographic objects was sent to all tribes shortly after the December 31, 1996 deadline.

The NMAI Act of 1989 contains a provision whereby a Repatriation Review Committee is appointed "to monitor and review the inventory, identification, and return of Indian human remains and Indian funerary objects." This committee is composed of five individuals, at least three of whom are to be selected from individuals nominated by Native American groups. The committee was empaneled in March 1990 and four of the five members were selected from those nominated by Native American groups; two of these are American Indians. The 1996 amendment to the act added two members to the committee, both of whom are to be traditional religious leaders.

The collections of the Smithsonian's newly created National Museum of the American Indian, however, are not under the purview of this committee; rather, the museum's repatriation activities are the responsibility of its own board of trustees, as stated in the act. Consequently, NMAI has its own policies and procedures for repatriation, established in 1991. Recently, the NMAI has been criticized by both Native Americans and museologists for its handling of repatriation. In fact, the Smithsonian Institution as a whole has not been immune to criticism in this regard. Some changes are underway.

International Developments

U.S. federal and state laws for repatriation pertain only to claims made by Native American groups in the United States, and only for remains and objects in the United States. For example, human remains of Native Americans from Mexico or Central or South America are not within the purview of the laws, nor are wampum belts from Iroquois in Canada. Similarly, U.S. law does not apply to remains or objects in any other country. Nevertheless, ever more native groups in the United States are attempting to recover their ancestors and histories from elsewhere in the world. For example, the Zuni are recovering war gods from other countries, and the Wounded Knee Survivors' Association is attempting to recover from the Kelvingrove Museum in Glasgow, Scotland, a Ghost Dance shirt "reputedly taken from a body at Wounded Knee." The response of the museum in the latter instance was that "it is a very difficult issue for us. It could be seen as a precedent that could open up our collection to other claims for repatriation."

There are important recent developments concerning international repatriation, however. The Inuit Circumpolar Conference (ICC) is held every four years. This international organization represents around 115,000 Inuit in the Arctic regions of the United States (Alaska), Russia (Chukotka), Canada, and Greenland. Its purposes are to further Inuit unity, rights, and interests, foster policies that safeguard the Arctic environment, and be a full partner in the development of the circumpolar regions. At its 1995 conference, held in Nome, Alaska, the Keepers of the Treasures, Alaska, sponsored a symposium on international repatriation. (The Keepers of the Treasures, a national organization, is dedicated to preserving, affirming, and celebrating Native American cultures.) Speaking at the symposium, I commented that "all repatriation in the United States is international repatriation, given what should be an independent status of native tribes. Unfortunately, it didn't turn out this way. Native groups are forced to negotiate with museums and institutions rather than with the federal government as equal entities."

Only a month before the ICC, a diplomatic conference was held in Rome to discuss the adoption of the draft UNIDROIT Convention on the International Return of Stolen or Illegally Exported Cultural Objects. Delegates from some seventy countries, with observers from eight, voted to approve the text of the convention, derived after "eleventh hour negotiations following weeks of debate between the art-rich 'source countries' and the so-called 'market countries' where most of the trade in cultural objects takes place." It calls for the return of stolen and illegally exported cultural objects under certain specified conditions. The United States eventually approved the act, a small but important step in international repatriation.

In the international repatriation movement, Native Americans join with other exploited peoples of the world to claim the objects of their history, plundered by thieves as well as colonial or war-occupied governments. The objects at stake include art looted during World War II and the Elgin marbles, Greek works currently in London.

Some Repatriations

According to its own established procedures, some 2,500 of the approximately 18,500 skeletal remains in the collections of the National Museum of Natural History have been repatriated by the Smithsonian to Native American groups, including some to Hawaiian Islanders. To date, the largest number of repatriated remains were returned to Larsen Bay, Alaska, in October 1991. These were the remains of about a thousand people from the site on Kodiak Island excavated by the Smithsonian physical

anthropologist Ales Hrdlicka between 1932 and 1936. In January 1992 the associated funerary objects were returned.

The Smithsonian has also returned human remains to the Cheyenne River Sioux (including the brain of Leon Pretty Voice Eagle), Yankton Sioux, Devil's Lake Sioux, Sisseton-Wahpeton Sioux, Oglala Sioux (the remains of Chief Smoke were returned to a descendant), Two Kettles Sioux (the remains of Chief Puffing Eyes were returned to his family), Southern Arapaho, Shoshone-Bannock, Makah, Pawnee, Southern Cheyenne, Yerington Paiute, Ninilchik, Spokane, the Warm Springs Confederated Tribes, and various Alaskan villages. (Some remains were returned before the federal legislation; in 1984 remains including the skull of the well-known Captain Jack were returned to the Modoc; others were restored to the Blackfeet in 1988.) Funerary objects have been returned to Alaskan groups, and to the Pawnee and the Cheyenne River Sioux. Included in the Warm Springs repatriation were 86,085 objects, mostly beads.

Among the remains repatriated to the Southern Cheyenne were those of Native Americans killed at the infamous massacre at Sand Creek, Colorado Territory, on November 29, 1864. The Colorado militia led by Colonel John Chivington had dismembered and decapitated victims on the spot, sending some to the Army Medical Museum. The remains repatriated to the Pawnee included the crania of six Pawnee, believed by some to have been beheaded after being killed by the U.S. Army only one month after their honorable discharge from the U.S. Army as scouts. A repatriation ceremony for these and other Pawnee remains from the Smithsonian, complete with a military escort, was held at Fort McNair in Washington, D.C., on June 6, 1995. The small wooden boxes containing the remains of the six scouts had folded U.S. flags on top, acknowledging their status as veterans. Senator McCain, the chair of the Select Committee on Indian Affairs, spoke and apologized to the Pawnee on behalf of the U.S. government for what had happened and for the fact that it had taken the government so long to return their dead. The following day, the remains were taken under a military escort to former Pawnee lands at Genoa, Nebraska, for burial. At Genoa, the location from which the Pawnee had earlier been removed to Oklahoma, the remains were buried with other Pawnee remains at the cemetery and covered with a slab of concrete to prevent further disturbance. (Pawnee cemeteries in and around Genoa had been looted for a century by scientists and others seeking bones and artifacts.) A week later, as is the custom of the Pawnee, a final feast for the dead was held by the Pawnee tribe in Pawnee, Oklahoma, where they are now centered.

Other museums, institutions, agencies, and collectors have also returned Native American skeletal remains, both before NAGPRA and as a response to it. California Indian remains have been repatriated to appropriate groups by the Catholic church; the state of Nebraska has returned Pawnee and Omaha skeletons; the University of Minnesota returned 150 sets of remains to the Devils Lake Sioux; Stanford University returned remains of some 550 individuals to the Ohlone; and the University of Tennessee returned 190 sets of remains to the Cherokee.

Cultural and sacred objects have also been returned, by the Smithsonian and other museums, institutions, and private individuals. The Smithsonian repatriated a few cultural objects to the Zia Pueblo (in 1982) and Zuni Pueblo (in 1987) before the legislation, and some others

to Native Hawaiians since the legislation. Wampum belts, masks of the False Face Society, a *kano:wa* or ceremonial turtle rattle, and two antler hair combs have been returned to the Iroquois; various ceremonial shields and weapons and altar figurines have been repatriated to the Jemez Pueblo by the NMAI; and medicine bundles and prayer boards have been returned to the Navajo and Hopi. Hopi kachinas have also been repatriated; and several dozen twin War Gods or *Ahayu:da* have been repatriated to the Zuni—nearly all that were missing. Finally, the Omaha's sacred pole was returned to them by the Peabody Museum, as were the skeletal remains and burial offerings of almost one hundred Omaha held by the University of Nebraska.

The NAGPRA legislation of November 16, 1990, gave institutions five years (with a possible extension) to complete inventories of human remains and funerary objects, and three years to provide summaries of unassociated funerary objects, sacred objects, and objects of cultural patrimony. After the inventory, six months are allowed for notifying tribes of affiliated remains and funerary objects. Therefore, only now, at the end of the decade, are full repatriation efforts under NAGPRA commencing, and the Smithsonian is ahead of most other museums and institutions, if not all, in actual repatriations. Nevertheless, many issues remain to be settled in implementing NAGPRA. Two important ones are whether nonfederally recognized tribes are entitled to repatriated remains and objects (as they are by the Smithsonian), and what are institutions to do about remains or objects where cultural affiliation cannot be established? In 1997 an interim rule established penalties for noncompliance with NAGPRA. . . .

INDIANS ARE NOT SPECIMENS—INDIANS ARE PEOPLE

The Smithsonian Institution holds the world's largest collection of Indian skeletal remains. These total more than 18,500, plus an additional 17,000 grave goods. Nationwide, estimates indicate more than 600,000 skeletal remains in universities, research institutions and museums. Indian tribes throughout the United States demand that these skeletal remains and associated grave offerings be returned.

The museums, including the Smithsonian Institution, have been reluctant to release any of their holdings even when the gravesite violations are well documented. But recently there have been exceptions. In 1868, the Army Surgeon General directed medical officers in the west to collect Indian skulls and bones and send them to Washington for study of infection and disease. They collected over 4,000 specimens by plundering Indian gravesites. The Army Medical Museums transferred the "specimens" to the Smithsonian which now owns the looted articles. In 1988, the Smithsonian, when faced with a letter documenting how one army officer in 1892 "collected" the skulls of Blackfeet people, returned the remains of fifteen Blackfeet for proper reburial on the reservation. Last year, Stanford University returned the remains of 550 Indians to the Ohlone-Costanoan Tribe. The University of South Dakota returned 1,200 pounds of remains in August of this year to the Pine Ridge reservation.

As more and more reporters write and broadcast about institutions and their collections of skeletal remains, moral outrage has increased and public sentiment has shifted in favor of the Indians' demands for repatriation. For years, the Smithsonian has taken a hard-line stance that no repatriation will be permitted except when lineal descendants can prove that the museum is holding the skeletons or sacred objects of one of their ancestors. The Smithsonian, however, holds on to the critical documentation. There are some Indian people who feel responsible for all of their ancestors, lineal descendents or not. Consequently, Indian tribes and individuals are calling for the Smithsonian to make available all the skeletal remains taken from certain areas including ancestral and present-day lands. The tribe would decide whether or not to accept the remains.

Faced with mounting pressure from both Indian and non-Indian interests, including members of Congress, the Smithsonian recently agreed to allow the repatriation of skeletal remains to tribes, not just lineal descendants, where "a preponderance of the evidence" indicates that the remains in its collection can be traced to a specific tribe. By limiting the repatriation to cases where it can identify tribal relationship, the Smithsonian has taken a middle of the road stance. A large portion of its collection may ultimately remain in its possession.

The Legislation

At one point, at least six different bills were pending in Congress dealing with the repatriation issue as well as the creation of the new Museum of the American Indian as part of the Smithsonian Institution in Washington, D.C. Disagreement has centered around the Smithsonian's desire to keep its entire collection of Indian bones versus the growing public sentiment calling for the proper respect of the dead. Note: President Bush signed the National Museum of the American Indian Act on November 28. The legislation describes the Smithsonian's policy on repatriation of Indian human remains. If any remains are identified as those of a particular individual or as those of an individual culturally affiliated with a particular Indian tribe, the Smithsonian, upon request of the descendants of the individual or tribe, will return the remains.

BATTLING FOR SOULS
ORGANIZING THE RETURN OF THE SACRED TEXTILES
TO THE COMMUNITY OF COROMA, BOLIVIA

Victoria Bomberry

In 1986 the Aymara community of Coroma issued a statement denouncing the theft of their sacred weavings in *Presencia*, the newspaper of record in La Paz, Bolivia. This unprecedented move by an Indigenous community in Bolivia represented an incursion into a medium dominated by a *criollo* elite. The statement that was signed by the *kurakas*, the local traditional authorities of the community launched a sophisticated, long-term struggle to regain the weavings. The kurakas demanded that U.S. art dealers and collectors return all photographs and negatives taken during All Saints Day, which is the only day during the entire year when the ancient textiles are displayed. The *kurakas* urged the dealers to stop acquiring the textiles. Letters were sent to U.S. dealers imploring them to return the stolen textiles to Coroma. Unfortunately, no one knew which dealers and collectors had possession of the weavings.

The statement issued by the elders of Coroma raised issues of cultural property and Indigenous rights, as well as important questions of how Indigenous culture is viewed in industrial nations. The people of Coroma provoked an examination of how "art is constructed and perceived in the West," while offering a contextualized vision of the multiple roles the sacred weavings play in their own community. In the case of Coroma, religious beliefs became a powerful driving force for regaining the weavings. The weavings are a necessary part of every aspect of life in Coroma. Weaving is done by the women of Coroma who record and interpret the religious life of the community. Because of this important function the weavings can be considered sacred texts. Additionally, the weavings are the repository of the history of the *ayllus* which make up the community of Coroma.

The case of Coroma illustrates how formal and informal international networks can be successfully activated by local indigenous groups. The Coromeños were able to mobilize indigenous groups in Bolivia and the United States, anthropologists, sociologists, archaeologists, communications experts, and attorneys in Bolivia and the United States.

In the following statement (Cruz 1990:1) the Coromeños articulate what the theft of the textiles means to the community.

1. The destruction of the history of the people of Coroma. The textiles are a form of documentation whereby the history of each ethnic group and also the differences between the *ayllus* are written.
2. The dispersion of the different *allyus* that make up the community of Coroma, as the *q'epis* give identity to the member of each one of the groups.
3. The dismantling of the borders between ethnic groups. In Coroma not only are the *q'epis* guardians for the *J'ilaqatas* and *alcaldes cobradores*, but there are also *q'epis* situated in the corners of the *ayllus* of Coroma demarcating the lands of the *ayllus*. The *q'epis* are also used to mark the boundaries between adjacent groups.
4. The disappearance of the textiles breaks the ties with the ancestors. The textiles are the nexus of communication with the ancestors who are the founding souls of the *ayllus*. Each *awayo*, each *ajxu*, each *unku*, each *llaqota* of the *q'epi* of each *ayllu* has a particular name that is the name of a founding person of the *ayllu*.
5. The loss of the supernatural and religious power that the *q'epis* give to the *J'ilaqatas* during their year of care, conservation and ritual practices. The spirits of the ancestors who reside in the *q'epis* teach the *J'ilaqatas* and give them religious insight.
6. The destruction of the social organization. The *J'ilaqata* of each *ayllu* mediates the naming of the new authorities, the new *J'ilaqatas*, *alcaldes cobradores*, *Kurakas*, *watarunas*. This is done through a rite called *K'anchaku* in which the *J'ilaqatas* consult with the souls of the ancestors.
7. The loss of the documentation of different epochs. They are the documentation of the history of weaving. (Bubba nd:5)

Each of these points involves complex social factors. In the first, for instance, the textiles are represented as text which can be read. Andean scholar Veronica Cereceda (1986:149) writes that a "specific message behind which lies a system that explains the message" is contained in Andean weaving. Cereceda argues that the system is similar to the knots of *quipu* which were used by the Inca to keep historical records and accounts in Pre-Columbian times; her work focused on decoding the system. According to the Coromeños, their weaving expertise was recognized and highly regarded by the Inca.

The history represented in the textiles is specific to the Aymara community of Coroma and reinforces the solidarity of the community. The message and history is read by Coromeños who re-enact, record, and add to the narrative contained in the sacred weavings and *q'epis*. The meaning of the textiles operates in a field of complex systems of knowledge that is integrally tied to the sacred. For the Coromeños, the textiles contain the souls of ancestors who are loved and cared for by the community.

Appropriating the textiles as "art" decontextualizes and reinterprets them as a rarefied aesthetic that can be commodified. In 1983, for example, the Smithsonian Institution collaborated on a traveling exhibition with dealers and collectors of Aymara textiles. A glossy, 159 page catalog, filled with brilliantly colored photographs, accompanied the show. In the introduction William J. Conklin (1983:9) suggests an affinity between Western artists and Bolivian weavers:

> Imagine, then a world in which textiles are the most valued and respected products of the culture—where textiles are the art of the culture—they are movies, the painting, the very color of daily life—where textiles carry meaning and identification—where designer

names are your names or perhaps your great-grandmother's.

Conklin equates the sacred weavings of the Aymara with movies and paintings which are accessible and recognizable to Western urbanites. Conklin constructs an individual master artist and links this idea with the world of high fashion and commerce. The reader is invited to see the Aymara equivalent of Calvin Klein come to life on the page.

Conklin's words reveal the enormous gulf between the force of the textiles in their own community and what the words convey to the Western urban dweller. The cultural context of Andean culture falls away. The textiles are not merely the material manifestation of the technical expertise of the individual weavers, but are imbued with a sacred value that is rooted in the creative act. Each thread vibrates between the spiritual realm and everyday lived experience of the community. The threads connect to memory and history in a way that is unrecognizable to the Western audience which voyeuristicly peers at what it imagines to be its own lost past. Conklin (Ibid:9) describes the longing for an unalienated existence that he sees represented by the textiles.

> Something in each of us yearns to see and touch the evidence of time when "things" were not so disposable, when love, and art, and life were conveyed by design—when men, women and children were artists together. The weaving of the aymara, an amazing Bolivian cultural survival from pre-Columbian times, provides just such an opportunity.

In two sentences Conklin evokes a unified past shared by all humanity at some distant time. By juxtaposing the Western artists' affinity to the Indigenous artist with the representation of the Aymara as a survival in anthropological terms, he invites viewers to tour their own unalienated past.

The survival metaphor also signals the rarity of the weavings, which makes them even more attractive in a global marketplace. Aymara culture is commodified and the vehement emphasis on enterprise echoes the project of Columbus, who saw the New World as an exploitative enterprise with gold as the ultimate acquisition. The textiles are the new gold of the Andes that can be excavated in out of the way places, exported and depleted in the space of a generation.

In the same catalog Laurie Adelson (1983:18) remarks on the growing interest in Aymara weaving.

> Not until the late seventies was any serious research directed specifically toward this important textile tradition. The obvious and unfortunate consequence of this lack of interest is that much valuable information has been lost, especially since aymara costume has changed significantly during the last 50–100 years.

Adelson refers to a time period which coincides with the first visits of art dealers into Coroma. This problematizes the relationship of researchers and their institutions and what James Clifford calls "the aesthetic appropriation of non-western others." Incomplete identification of the textiles occurs throughout the catalog. The textiles are identified by the department from which they come, but never by community or *ayllu*. There is no mention of the method of collecting the textiles and most of the "loaned" textiles carry the tag "anonymous lender" which masks the complicated relationships between collectors, dealers and museums.

In another section Laurie Adelson (Ibid.:39) makes a point of accentuating the superior technology of the Aymara before the adoption of European dyes.

> In short the raw materials for making fine high quality fabrics are no longer readily available to the common Aymara. Many of the highly

developed arts, including natural dye technology and fine spinning skills that had developed over thousands of years declined rapidly and along with them went the unique fine quality of aymara cloth.

Reversing the more common notion that Indigenous people had inferior technology mystifies the past while it increases the value of antique textiles in the marketplace. The narrative separates the weaving technology from a whole way of life. The category of weaving is the focal point rather than the unique ongoing culture where weaving is still a part of daily activity. Quality is placed in the past, which implies that Aymara culture is in decline. Denying the ongoing Andean weaving tradition where innovation and improvisation constantly occur is necessary in order to keep the myth of vanishing cultures alive. Vanishing, rare, newly discovered textile arts are appealing to collectors as investments and displays of superior sensibilities and taste.

Although countless Indigenous communities have been victimized by the unrestrained greed of Western art dealers and collectors, the Aymara community of Coroma embarked on a multi-layered campaign to recover the stolen textiles. Because of their persistence and dedication to the project of bringing the ancestors home a series of fortuitous events remarkably unfolded. In early 1988, John Murra, Professor Emeritus of Anthropology at Cornell University, sent a postcard to Coroma announcing an ethnic art show in San Francisco. Murra is considered one of the founders of Andean Studies and has repeatedly expressed his concern about the disappearance of ancient textiles from the Andean region. For at least a year, talk of the theft of ancient textiles from the Andean region and from Coroma in particular had dominated academic circles. Featured on the color postcard was a ceremonial *unku*

(a man's tunic made of one piece of cloth) from Coroma. Murra realized that this sale could be a gateway to locating the missing weavings. When the *kurakas* (elders of the community) received the postcard, they were convinced that it was a message sent by the ancestors who were yearning to come home. They immediately decided to send representatives of the community to the United States to locate and retrieve the weavings.

By February 1988, Pio Cruz and Cristina Bubba arrived in San Francisco to locate the textiles and to find the means of bringing them home. They contacted Susan Lobo, a cultural anthropologist who coordinates the Community History Project at Intertribal Friendship House in Oakland. Lobo would play a key role in informing people about the sacred weavings and activating important North American networks of Native Americans, anthropologists, archaeologists, art historians, and textile experts.

Cruz and Bubba pored over documents trying to find legal means to retrieve the textiles. Fortunately, in a meeting with U.S. Customs officials, they learned that if basic customs laws have been violated, cultural property may be recovered. In the case of smuggling, false declaration or false entry, the country of origin must make a claim of ownership in writing for the property to be returned.

From the Bay Area, Cruz and Bubba went to Washington, D.C., where they advised the U.S. Cultural Property Advisory Committee of the theft of the weavings. Cruz and Bubba then returned to Bolivia to organize support from the Bolivian government. By May 6, 1989, the government of Bolivia submitted a formal request for emergency U.S. import restrictions on antique textiles from the community of Coroma.[1]

Within the year the committee recommended unanimously that the United States impose emergency import restrictions on the antique textiles of Coroma for a period of five years. On March 4, 1989, a notice was published in the *Federal Register* which described the textiles that were denied entry. It was only the second emergency action taken by the United States under the UNESCO Cultural Property Convention and the 1983 Convention on Cultural Property Implementation Act. Previously, emergency import restrictions were imposed on pre-Columbian artifacts from the Cara Sucia region of El Salvador in 1987.

By February 1990, the people of Coroma intensified their efforts to bring the sacred weavings back to the community. They sent a delegation once again to the United States to continue the painstaking process of legal negotiations, identification and documentation of the sacred weavings from Coroma, and a new effort to forge cultural and spiritual alliances with Native American groups in California. Pio Cruz, Salustiana de Torrez, Clemente Perez, Cristina Bubba and Benedicto Flores were entrusted with these tasks. The late Salustiana de Torrez was an accomplished weaver who was intimately familiar with the weaving tradition of Coroma. Doña Salustiana was able to identify the weavings confiscated by U.S. Customs by the weave structure and the patterning unique to Coroma textiles. Other members of the delegation who had participated all their lives in the care and maintenance of the sacred weavings could identify them by style and type as well as by marks left by certain ceremonies conducted by the community. It was a heart wrenching time for the delegates because they could view and touch their sacred weavings but they knew that many more obstacles had to be overcome before the souls of the ancestors could be returned to Coroma.

On this occasion the delegates from Coroma and Native people from California pledged mutual support in Indigenous rights efforts. People from the Central Valley representing Tule River Reservation, and the Fresno area participated in the meetings and spiritual ceremonies that followed. For the past twenty years there has been a movement dedicated to cultural revitalization occurring in the Central Valley, as well as other parts of the state which has resulted in tremendous strides in all areas of native life. The two delegations found common concerns in many aspects of their lives. Joe Carrillo from Tule River remarked during the meeting:

> I have met and discussed this [the Coroma repatriation efforts] with the key spiritual leaders for Central California. Everyone agrees that to be involved to assist in their return would be a spiritual responsibility. A part of this teaching is for some of us to travel and do our share as human beings to allow the spirit to help all Indian people to come together in a spiritual way throughout the world. If in any small way we can contribute to the spiritual process that's happening, then it is good to do. For our people to travel to Bolivia [when the weavings return] is not just a meeting between people, but a coming together of the spirits from our tribes.

During this visit, the delegations forged relationships that were to develop into a strong alliance between diverse groups. Most importantly the meeting created a symbolic space that reenacted the coming together of the people from North and South America. In an exchange of rituals the ancestors from the south were introduced to the ancestors from the north in order that their souls might be comforted during their stay in California. The Coromeños and the representative from California pledged support to one another in their repatriation efforts and religious freedom.

The valiant efforts of the Coromeños to repatriate their sacred weavings back to their community deeply moved diverse sectors of the population. Public sentiment overwhelmingly elevated the Coromeños to the status of the heroic protectors of cultural property. After their first journey North, a Supreme Decree issued by the Bolivian government in May 1988 prohibited exportation of any textile made prior to 1950. The decree, which was signed by Bolivian President Jaime Paz Zamora, also stated that the sacred weavings must be returned to Coroma rather than to a national museum. The victory upheld local customary practice which recognizes the communal ownership of cultural property on the local rather than national level. Clearly, the Coromeños were engaged in multiple negotiations which reaffirmed and at times redefined local and national contracts.

On the local level, the people of Coroma had to deal with the breach of community solidarity that the loss of the textiles engendered. Since the weavings are communally owned, a fact which the Supreme Decree certified, no individual was culturally or legally empowered to sell them. Nevertheless, the men who fell victim to the offers of the dealers felt that they had no choice other than to give up the weavings. One of the men described his anguish over the fact that his family and community were living under conditions of near starvation. In another instance, a man accepted an old tractor in exchange for the textiles. He believed the tractor would make a difference between starvation and survival for the community. It is important to understand the motives of the community members and the unequal power relations between them and the dealers. However, in order to heal the breach within the community the Coromeños chose to see themselves as powerful actors participating in the events leading to the crisis.

The *kurakas* employed traditional methods to determine the factors which were at play throughout the period. The men's failure to protect the *q'epis* from depredation was determined to be a breach in the entire fabric of life of the community. It was paramount for the community to respond appropriately in order to repair the damage. Therefore, one of the immediate responses was to impose jail sentences on those who succumbed to the pressure to give up the textiles. In my view, this is yet another example of how Coromeños began to assert their right to determine the ways in which the community and its ancestors are represented to the outside world. Fortunately, now all but one of the men have been successfully reintegrated into the community. On the other hand none of the art dealers have been imprisoned for the illegal export of the textiles.

Steven Berger, one of the art dealers operating in Bolivia during this time defended his actions in an article appearing in the *San Francisco Chronicle* (Doyle 1992) on September 26, 1992, that reported the return of the textiles: "Believe me, these Indians wanted to sell their textiles. It was the only thing they had of value." His statements revealed his cultural biases, as well as clouded his complicity in destroying the religion and lifeways of the Coromeños. He continued: "This was a tradition in the process of breaking down. A well respected anthropologist told me that if the people show you their sacred objects, the tradition is already broken. So at that point I felt free in what I was doing. . . . I love these textiles." Berger's statement reflects not only paternalism, but a dangerous distortion common in Western audiences who read indigenous cultures as broken and lost. What is left unsaid, but is nevertheless implied, is that loss and destruction is the natural order of things which only reflects deadly defects or lacks in indigenous people.

The Western audience's response to the textiles is to feel what cultural anthropologist Renato Rosaldo calls "imperialist nostalgia," which longs and mourns for what it has destroyed or changed. In the context of the sacred weavings, engaging in "imperialist nostalgia" performs the additional task of erasing the ongoing brutalization of native peoples. Berger relies on a rescue narrative to create the appearance of altruism and innocence; he obstinately obscures the role he plays in continuing a pattern of abuse and denial. The failure on the part of national and international agencies to adequately respond to the extreme economic crisis brought about by years of drought remains unacknowledged and in fact, hidden from view.

The video produced by the community of Coroma (Council of Authorities of Corona 1988), *El Camino de las Almas,* responds to these glaring omissions. Continuing the strategic trajectory of the *Presencia* statement and the jail sentences imposed on the *watarunakuna,* the Coromeños insist on their right to control the representations of their community. The video rigorously exposes the method of "collecting" employed in Coroma[2] by focusing on the events that led to the discovery of the theft. The video ends with the community's elected envoy, Pio Cruz, bicycling across the *altiplano* to begin the search for their sacred textiles. Although the video focuses on the events leading to the pillage of the *q'epis,* it also depicts the daily lives of the people, including ceremonial activities. This courageous act of self-representation straightforwardly asserts their cultural difference from metropolitan audiences that view the video. The video also contradicts the narrative of a defeated people and lost culture. One of the most powerful images of the video is a woman shouting, "Justice!" as she leads people through the street in Coroma. In sharp contrast to the image of pitiful remnants of a lost high culture that Berger most clearly articulates, her presence and attitude mark her and her colleagues as capable social actors who brilliantly delineate the problems facing their community. Against all odds they marshall the resources necessary to get their message to the national and international communities where their struggle to repatriate the textiles will take place.

El Camino de las Almas was awarded the Bolivian Silver Condor for best documentary of 1989. On the international level, the video is used to heighten awareness of the theft of the sacred weavings, as well as to illuminate the problem of international traffic in sacred objects. Its showing in New York in 1990 brought the offer of pro bono legal services by the Center for Constitutional Rights in New York.

Originally, the community envisioned the video as a means to offer testimony in the litigation with the art dealers in the United States. As production began, however, the video emerged as a powerful organizing tool. After each shoot the community gathered to critique the footage which gave them the opportunity to discuss the events and brought more and more Coromeños into the talks and production. A sense of empowerment grew as more people were involved in the project to represent themselves and their point of view to the world.

Young people who had begun to drift away from the community began to show renewed respect and interest in traditional activities and religious rituals since the campaign to regain the weaving began. To some extent the conflicts and tensions between evangelical Christians and traditionalists have been eased through the valorization of Aymara culture by the Bolivian public. On the national level, many urban Aymara and Quechua people re-embraced the common cultural heritage they share with Coromeños. Even though they may reside in the cities of Bolivia, they were summoned by the remembrance and recognition of their own rootedness in indigenous cultural practices.

After years of struggle forty-two sacred weavings were returned to Coroma on September 24, 1992. Intertribal Friendship House, the oldest urban Indian Center in the United States, sponsored the California delegation that has continued its work with the people of Coroma. Joe Carrillo, Sidney Rubio, and Clarence Yager represent the Central Valley, Susan Lobo and I continue our roles as organizers and cultural mediators. New members of the group include Paiute/Pit River artist Jean La Marr and Hopi videographer Victor Masayesva. We are on our way to meet with the people once again to offer thanks for the safe return of the souls of the ancestors. We are eager to develop new strategies for the safe return of the weavings that are still lost and wandering the world.

The following are excerpts from my journal. I offer them here in an attempt to outline my own reactions as a native scholar committed to social change. I was stunned by the intense familiarity the people of the Andes and the *altiplano* landscape evoked in me. I was forced to consider our shared and divergent stories as native subjects living through the post-colonial era, at a time that is described by many Aymara/Quechua political activists in the Andes as *pachacuti,* translated roughly as a time of violent upheaval and reversals. I felt as if we were poised on the verge of a distinct opening that would allow us to see our realities more clearly and passionately. I was forced to confront the reality of native losses in the United States where you can wander though large cities like San Francisco, New York, Dallas, or Chicago without once encountering another native person. When I think of loss, I think of the actual an-

nihilation of native bodies that cannot help but be awakened every time I walk down the street. I found myself experiencing the intense pain of raw grief at the same time that I was exhilarated by the presence of the sheer mass of native people. The desire for wholeness with which the colonial experience has marked me became almost unbearable in those moments of recognition.

Fredy Yepez, the Bolivian office manager and expert driver from the Inter-American Foundation is at the wheel of the Jeep. He points to one of the many stone *tambos* or Inca inns where messengers and Inca officials spent the night on their journeys through *Tawantinsuyu,* Inca Land. Although the roof of the deserted *tambo* has long ago turned to dust the familiar stairstep-like Andean cross stands in sharp relief against the dark blue evening sky. It reminds me of Northern symbols of the four directions that signal the comfort and intimacy of home. The intricate stonework sends a shiver of longing through me.

The paved road from la Paz ends long before Coroma. Little rain has fallen in the canton of Coroma for six years. The land resembles the long stretches of Nevada desert more than the high plains region of Montana and Wyoming that I expected to see. The whole department of Potosi is stricken with drought. Occasionally, the car crosses railroad tracks and then there is no road at all. The wind has swept all traces of tire tracks from the *altiplano,* and I can hear the tires crunch against the dry earth.

We are still several miles from the village. It is a moonless night and the stone markers where the dry river bed is the easiest to cross are hard to see. A short distance away a bonfire sends crackling sparks into the night sky. We can make out the soft outline of a sheepherder warming himself by the fire. When we approach we see that he is a young boy. As soon as he sees the car he runs away. We stop the car; get out and call to him. He timidly makes his way back toward the car. His shyness passes and he points us toward the gently sloping bank of the river bed where we can safely cross.

Although Coroma is hard hit by drought, the people remain on the land. The population is approximately six thousand in the canton. The township is surrounded by outlying homesteads where the Coromeños make their living as farmers and herders. Crops include the staple items: potatoes, quinoa, and maize, while herders raise the Andean camelids—llama and alpaca as well as sheep. In many places we see dark green potato leaves pushing through the recently sown fields. Cristina Bubba explains that during the school year Coroma is a village of children who come from the outlying areas to attend school. Living in their family homes in Coroma, they keep house and care for one another when school is in session. It is a clear December summer now, and the village is quiet because many children are helping their parents farm and herd.

We arrive early the next morning, a few hours before the sun rises. No one is awake yet so we go to the door of our hosts to get the key. We exchange a few sleep laden words before going to the house where we will stay. The next morning Susan, Jean and I are greeted by Serinina Veles and Valentina Mendita Cruz, the sister of Don Pio. We sit together in the garden between the house and the kitchen as Doña Serinina and Doña Valentina spin the lustrous wool of the llama. We talk about life in Coroma. Later we are to take part in ceremonies for the sacred textiles but now we talk about our lives as native women from opposites ends of America. Wool filaments stream through the fingers of the women to their drop spindles. The spindles are smaller than those used by Dineh women in the Southwest and a quick

spin with the fingers sends the spindles whirring in hand carved wooden bowls. Doña Valentina spins the finest thread I have ever seen done by hand. As the thread lengthens she deftly winds it on the spindle. She says in a matter of fact way: "You should have seen us before the gringos [art dealers] came. We were beautiful then." I feel a fierce pride mixed with rage echo through me.

There are many preparations that have to be attended to before we begin the rituals. The head *Kurakas* and the *J'ilaqatas* consult coca leaves several times to find the most auspicious time for the ceremonies. A ritual specialist is called upon to read the coca leaves. We learn that there are some souls that have yet to make the long journey back to Coroma even though the sacred weavings have returned. There is concern for the safety and well-being of these souls as well as the sacred weavings that are still missing. We are told that the best time for the rituals to begin is in the early afternoon. The *q'epis* will be present during the rituals

Serenina Veles is an accomplished weaver and leader from Coroma, Bolivia.

which will be held in the new community building that was recently completed by the community. It is an open, bright building with newly whitewashed walls. There are several colored posters on the walls announcing meetings and offering health information. It looks very similar to Native American community buildings in the United States.

That afternoon we gather in the community building for the rituals. Sacred objects and gifts are exchanged by the people from the North and South. The spiritual leaders of the Central Valley have sent eagle feathers along with instructions on the care and significance of each feather. Libations are offered to the spirits of the ancestors and offerings are burned at the altar. Coca leaves play a central role in all the ceremonial activities. Coca is offered to the spirits of the ancestors and is passed to everyone attending the rituals. Again the coca leaves are consulted and the religious leaders find that we will continue the rituals for another day. There are things that must be prepared for the following day. A pall of anxiety hangs over the group because we have learned that there are souls desperately trying to make their way to the sacred bundles.

The next day we continue the offerings. The ritual specialist goes outside and we hear the rich full sound of a bell. When he reenters the community building, people are talking excitedly of the return of the ancestors who had been making their way back to the community. Relief and joy are visible on all the faces in the room.

Later we join the secular meeting taking place in the building adjoining the government office. In this context we reaffirm our commitment to support each other on repatriation efforts. The precedent setting example of Coroma is a major victory for indigenous people. They have been successful in creating a network of allies and heightening international awareness of cultural property issues. The community is in the process of establishing safeguards to protect themselves from loss and theft of cultural property. The tractor sits idly in an old building as the people discuss whether or not they will use it in their community. They debate the impact it will have on community relations, whether it will build community cooperation or impede it. What effects will the introduction of this technology have on the community where traditional farming practices have assured self-sufficiency? What does it mean to have to maintain the machinery and buy the gas? These are some of the questions the people of Coroma have to answer for themselves.

Currently, there are numerous sacred weavings that have yet to be recovered. Although in May 1993 the U.S. ban on imports of Bolivian textiles was extended for another three years, there is no law on the books that stops the exportation of Bolivian textiles. Some of the Coroma weavings may now be in Europe and Japan, where they may be more difficult to recover. Existing international law does not effectively protect cultural property. Attention also needs to be given to situations in which communities believe (rightly so given current levels of assistance) they have no other alternative than to sell their cultural property. In these cases some people will invariably fall prey to unscrupulous dealers or collectors.

National governments and international organizations must support communities as they seek viable alternatives. There are projects operating in Bolivia to ensure the continuation of the weaving tradition, such as the one administered by the Textile Museum in Sucre. People who are interested in Andean textiles should support these efforts. Weaving is a living tradition and there are appropriate ways to acquire works of art, beauty, and fashion that support Indigenous people rather than continue the old patterns of exploitation and violence.

NOTES

1. The request was made under Article 9 of the UNESCO convention of the Means to Prohibiting and Preventing the illicit Import, Export and Transfer of Ownership of Cultural Property. The convention was adopted by UNESCO in 1970 and ratified by the U.S. Senate in 1972.

2. The video was produced in collaboration with UNITAS (National Union of Social Action Institutions) land video producer Eduardo Lopez, and with the cooperation of Katy Degado, Lucha Costa, Sergio Claros, Julio Quispe, Oscar Palacios, Monica and Juan Claudio Lechin.

WORKS CITED

Adelson, Laurie, and Arthur Tracht. *Aymara Weavings* (Washington, DC: Smithsonian Institution Traveling Exhibition Service, 1983.)

Bubba, Cristina, et al. "El propositio de las culturas: Los Textiles de Coroma." *Unitas.* enero, numero 11.

Cereceda, Veronica, "The Semiology of Andean Textiles: The Talegas of Isluga." Anthropological History of Andean Polities, ed. J.V. Murra, et al. (London: Cambridge University Press, 1986.)

Conklin, William J. *Aymara Weavings* (Washington, DC: Smithsonian Institution Traveling Exhibition Service, 1983.)

Council of Authorities of Coroma, Bolivia. *Paths of the Souls.* Video. (Dramatized version of the disappearance of the sacred weavings), 1988.

Cruz, Pio. Personal interview conducted by Susan Lobo. Kensington, California, April 2, 1990.

Doyle, Jim. "S.F. Dealer Defends Trade in Rare Textiles." *San Francisco Chronicle,* September 26, 1992.

ZUNI REPATRIATION OF WAR GODS

Roger Anyon

Twelve years prior to the passage of the Native American Graves Protection and Repatriation Act (NAGPRA) in 1990, the Pueblo of Zuni repatriated the first of many War Gods. This active but quiet campaign has led to the repatriation of 85 War Gods, from museums and private collectors throughout the United States since 1978. Much of the Zuni effort became integral to the intent of NAGPRA and the definition of cultural patrimony.

Zuni religious leaders and Tribal Councils have always maintained that War Gods are communally owned by the entire Zuni Tribe, and that any War Gods not in their proper shrines on the Zuni Reservation are stolen property. War Gods cannot be sold, given away, or transferred through any means into the possession of others. No one can have title to a War God other than the Zuni Tribe.

War Gods (Ayahu:da in the Zuni language) are wooden images, two of which are created each year and placed in their shrine. They are the spiritual guardians of the Zuni People. When they are removed from their shrines Zuni religious leaders cannot pray to them, and their vast powers cause fires, earthquakes, wars, storms, and wanton destruction in our world. For this reason the Zuni religious leaders have called for the return of all War Gods, wherever they may be.

THE GREAT PRETENDERS
FURTHER REFLECTIONS ON WHITESHAMANISM

Wendy Rose

They came for our land, for what grew or could be grown on it, for the resources in it, and for our clean air and pure water. They stole these things from us, and in the taking they also stole our free ways and the best of our leaders, killed in battle or assassinated. And now, after all that, they've come for the very last of our possessions; now they want our pride, our history, our spiritual traditions. They want to rewrite and remake these things, to claim them for themselves. The lies and thefts just never end.

Margo Thunderbird, 1988

I am that most schizophrenic of creatures, an American Indian who is both poet and anthropologist. I have, in fact, a little row of buttons up and down my ribs that I can press for the appropriate response: *click,* I'm an Indian; *click,* I'm an anthropologist; *click,* I'll just forget the whole thing and write a poem. I have also been a critic of the "whiteshaman movement," to use an expression coined by Geary Hobson, Cherokee critic. The term "whiteshaman," he says, rightly belongs to "the apparently growing number of small-press poets of generally white, Euro-Christian American background, who in their poems assume the persona of the shaman, usually in the guise of an American Indian medicine man. To be a poet is simply not enough; they must claim a power from higher sources." Actually, the presses involved are not always small, as is witnessed by the persona adopted by Gary Snyder in his Pulitzer Prize-winning book of verse, *Turtle Island.* In any event, Hobson is referring to a group of writers, including Louis Simpson, Charles Olson, Jim Cody, John Brandi, Gene Fowler, Norman Moser, Michael McClure, Barry Gifford, Paul Steinmetz, and David Cloutier, all of whom subscribe to—and go decisively beyond the original intent of—Jerome Rothenburg's 1976 assertion that:

> The poet, like the shaman, withdraws to solitude to find his poem or vision, then returns to sound it, give it life. He performs alone— because his presence is considered crucial and no one also has arisen to act in his place. He is also like the shaman in being at once an outsider, and yet a person needed for the validation of a certain type of experience important to the group . . . like the shaman, he will not only be allowed to act mad in public, but he will often be expected to do so. The act of the poet—& his poetry—is like a public act of madness. It is like what the Senecas, in their great dream ceremony, now obsolete, called "turning the mind upside down." . . . It is the primal exercise of human freedom against/& for the tribe.

I would expand upon Hobson's definition by observing that not all whiteshamans are Americans, poets, nor even white. A perfect example is that of Carlos Castaneda, author of the best-selling series of "Don Juan" epics purporting to accurately reveal the "innermost secrets" of a purely invented "Yaqui sorcerer." I would further add that whiteshamans pretending to higher sources may or may not refer to themselves as shamanic. Some of those within the movement have professed more secular intimacies with Native American cultures and traditions. This is well illustrated by Ruth Beebs Hill, who pretended in her book *Hanta Yo* to have utilized her association with a single American Indian man—"Chunksa Yuha," otherwise known as Alonzo Blacksmith—to uncover not only 19th-century social, sexual, and spiritual forms, but an "archaic dialect" of the Lakota language unknown to the Lakota themselves.

Such claims, whether sacred or secular, are uniformly made with none of the community acknowledgment and training essential to the positions in question. Would it not be absurd to aver to be a Rabbi if one were neither Jewish nor even possessed an elementary knowledge of Judaism? Or that one were a jet aircraft pilot without having been inside an airplane? Yet, preposterous as whiteshaman assertions may be on the face of it, there seems to be an unending desire on the part of the American public to absorb such "knowledge" as the charlatans care to produce. Further, the proliferation of such "information" typically occurs to the exclusion of far more accurate and/or genuinely native material, a matter solidly reinforcing the profound ignorance of things Indian afflicting most of society. As the Lakota scholar Vine Deloria, Jr. has put it:

> The realities of Indian belief and existence have become so misunderstood and distorted at this point that when a real Indian stands up and speaks the truth at any given moment, he or she is not only unlikely to be believed, but will probably be contradicted and "corrected" by the citation of some non-Indian and totally inaccurate "expert." More, young Indians in universities are now being trained to see themselves and their cultures in terms prescribed by such experts rather than in the traditional terms of the tribal elders. . . . In this way, the experts are perfecting a system of self-validation in which all semblance of honesty and accuracy is lost. This is not only a travesty of scholarship, but it is absolutely devastating to Indian societies.

Hobson and others have suggested that the assumption of shaman status or its secular counterparts by non-native writers is part of a process of "cultural imperialism" directly related to other claims on Native American land and lives. By appropriating indigenous cultures and distorting them for its own purposes, their reasoning goes, the dominant society can neatly eclipse every aspect of contemporary native reality, from land rights to issues of religious freedom. Pam Colorado, an Oneida scholar working at the University of Calgary in Canada, frames the matter:

> The process is ultimately intended to supplant Indians, even in areas of their own customs and spirituality. In the end, non-Indians will have complete power to define what is and is not Indian, even for Indians. We are talking here about an absolute ideological/conceptual subordination of Indian people in addition to the total physical subordination [we] already experience. When this happens, the last vestiges of real Indian society and Indian rights will disappear. Non-Indians will then "own" our heritage and ideas as thoroughly as they now claim to own our land and resources.

Whiteshamans and their defenders, assuming a rather amazing gullibility on the part of American Indians, usually contend they are "totally apolitical." Some have pointed out that the word "shaman" is itself of Tungus (Siberian) origin and insist that their use of it thus implies nothing specifically

Native American, either in literal content or by impression. They often add the insulting caveat that American Indian writers know less of their ancestral traditions and culture than non-native anthropologists. Finally, most argue that "artistic license" or "freedom of speech" inherently empowers them to do what they do, no matter whether Indians like it (and, ultimately, no matter the cost to native societies). Native American scholars, writers, and activists have heard these polemics over and over again. It is time to separate fact from fantasy in this regard.

ANATOMY OF WHITESHAMANISM

First, it must be noted that the term "shaman" is merely one of convenience, as are the terms "Indian," "American Indian," "Native American," and so on. The Siberian origin of the word is in this sense irrelevant at best and, more often, polemically obfuscatory. Moreover, whiteshamans do not construct their writings or antics after the Siberian model, even when they use the term "shaman" to describe themselves and the processes of their craft. Their works, whether poetic, novelistic, or theoretical, are uniformly designed and intended to convey conceptions of "Indian-ness" to their readers. This remains true regardless of the literal content of the material at issue, as is readily evident in "Blackfoot/Cherokee" author Jamake Highwater's (aka: Jay Marks, a non-Indian) extended repackaging of Greek mythology and pop psychology in the garb of supposed "primal Native American legends."

Further, during performances, whiteshamans typically don a bastardized composite of psuedo-Indian "style" buckskins, beadwork, headbands, moccasins, and sometimes paper masks intended to portray native spiritual beings such as Coyote or Raven. They often appear carrying gourd rattles, eagle feathers, "peace pipes," medicine bags, and other items reflective of native caremonial life. Their readings are frequently accompanied by the burning of sage, "pipe ceremonies," the conducting of chants and beating of drums of vaguely native type, and the like. One may be hardpressed to identify a particular indigenous culture being portrayed, but the obviously intended effect is American Indian. The point is that the whiteshaman reader/performer aspires to "embody the Indian," in effect "becoming" *the* "real" Indian even when actual native people are present. Native reality is thereby subsumed and negated by imposition of a "greater" or "more universal" contrivance.

This leads to a second major point. Whiteshamanism functions as a subset of a much broader assumption within the matrix of contemporary Eurocentric domination holding that non-Indians always (inherently) know more about Indians than do Indians themselves. It is from this larger whole that whiteshamanism draws its emotional and theoretical sustenance and finds the sense of empowerment from which it presumes to extend itself as "spokesperson" for Indians, and ultimately to substitute itself for Indians altogether. Illustrations of this abound, especially within anthropology, linguistics, and the various social sciences. Allow me to recall, by way of example, a few of my own experiences as an employee of a large, university connected anthropology museum during the mid-to-late 1970s.

- One famous anthropologist whose specialty is northern California insisted that northwestern California Indians were no longer familiar with their ancient form of money, long shells called "dentalia" or tooth-shells. The comment was stimulated by the fact that I was wearing some of these very same shells—which had been given to me by a Yurok woman as payment for a painting—around my neck.

- A basket specialist assured me that basket-hats are no longer worn by California Indian women. Yet, nearly every weekend such women attended the same social functions as I, wearing basket-hats that had been passed down through their families and, more importantly, were still being made.

- A woman who was both an anthropologist and an art collector told me that pottery was no longer produced at Laguna Pueblo. She continued to insist on this, even after I told her the names of the women who produce it there.

- A famous ethnohistorian informed me that I'd never see a California Indian woman with chin tattoos. I have in fact seen them, albeit rarely.

- A very well-known linguist asked me to escort a group of Yuki elders around the museum, and then confided to me that it was a shame no one spoke Yuki anymore. The elders spoke to one another in Yuki the entire time they were there.

- The "expert" on Laguna Pueblo pottery said to me, face to face, that Indians only *think* they know more about themselves than anthropologists. She wanted to impress upon me how "pathetic" my own people really were, and how much more enlightened and superior were her own.

Taken singly, these episodes are not important. But taken together, and added to the enormous pile of similar events and conversations Indians might collectively recount, it is apparent that a pattern exists: taken as a group, Euroamericans consider themselves to be uniquely qualified to explain the rest of humanity, not only to Euroamerica, but to everyone else as well. Coupled to this bizarre notion, whiteshamanism is simply the acting out of a much greater dynamic of cultural usurpation, employing a peculiarly "ritualistic" format.

THE "PIONEER SPIRIT"

What are the implications of this? Consider that a working (if often sublimated) definition of "universality" is very much involved. It is reflected perfectly in the presumed structure of knowledge and in the real structure of "universities" through which this knowledge is imparted in contemporary society. The "core" of information constituting the essential canon of every discipline in academe—from philosophy to literature, from history to physical science, from art to mathematics—is explicitly derived from thought embodied in the European tradition. This is construed as encapsulating all that is fundamentally meaningful within the "universal attainment of human intellect." The achievements and contributions of all other cultures are considered, when they are considered at all, only in terms of appendage (filtered through the lens of Eurocentric interpretation), adornment (to prove the superiority of the Euro-derived tradition), esoteric specialization (to prove that other traditions, unlike those derived from Europe, are narrow and provincial rather than broad and universal).

Always and everywhere, the inclusion of non-European intellectual content in the academy is absolutely predicated upon its conformity to sets of "standards" conceived and administered by those adhering to the basic precepts of Euro-derivation. The basic "qualification" demanded by academe of those who would teach non-European content is that they first receive "advanced training" and "socialization" in doctoral programs steeped in the supposed universality of Euro-derivation. Non-European subject matters are thus intrinsically subordinated to the demands of Eurocentrism at every level within U.S. institutions of higher learning. There are no exceptions: the intended function of such inclusion is to fit non-European traditions into positions assigned them by those of the Eurocentric persuasion. The purpose is to occupy and consume other cultures just as surely as their land and resources have been occupied and consumed.

Such circumstances are quite informative in terms of the more generalized sociocultural situation. In the construction at hand, those who embrace the Euro-derivation of "universal knowledge" are considered by definition to be the normative expression of intellectual advancement among all humanity. They are "citizens of the world," holders of "the big picture," having inherent rights to impose themselves and their "insights" everywhere and at all times, with military force if need be. The rest of us are consigned by the same definition to our "parochialism" and "provinciality," perceived as "barriers to progress" in many instances, "helped" by our intellectual "betters" to overcome our "conceptual deficiencies" in others. The phenomenon is integral to Euroamerican culture, transcending all ideological boundaries demarcating conservatism and progressivism; a poster popular among science fiction readers of both political persuasions shows a 15th-century European ship sailing a star-map and asks: "What would have happened if Ferdinand and Isabella had said no?"

If, as the academics would have it, Indians "no longer really know" or at least lack access to their traditions and spirituality (not to mention land tenure), then it follows that they are no longer "truly" Indian. If culture, tradition, spirituality, oral literature, and land are not theirs to protect, then such things are free for the taking. An anthropologist or folklorist hears a story or a song and electronically reproduces it, eventually catalogues it and perhaps publishes it. According to the culture of the scholar, it is then *owned* by "science" in exactly the same fashion as native land, once "settled" by colonizers, is said to be owned by them. Stories, songs, ceremonies, and other cultural ingredients can be—and often are—stolen as surely as if they were tangible objects removed by force. There is a stereotype about the "savage" who is afraid a camera will steal his soul. It will indeed, and much more, as will the tape recorder, the typewriter, and the video cassette. The process is as capable, and as purposeful, in first displacing and then replacing native people within their own cultural contexts as were earlier processes of "discovery" and "settlement" in displacing us from and replacing us upon our land. What is at issue is the extension across intellectual terrain of the more physically oriented 19th-century premise of "Manifest Destiny."

Anthropologists often contend they do not have any appreciable effect upon their own societies, but the fact is that the public does swallow and regurgitate anthropological concepts, usually after about twenty years. At that point, one generally finds efforts undertaken to put to popular use the cultural territory that anthropology has discovered, claimed, and tentatively expropriated in behalf of the dominant society. The subsequent popular endeavors serve to settle and "put to good use" this new cultural territory. This is the role of the white-shamans. Theirs is a fully sanctioned, even socially mandated activity within the overall imperial process of Eurocentrism. It should thus come as no surprise to serious students of American culture that editors, publishers, reviewers, and most readers greatly prefer the nonsense of whiteshamanism to the genuine literature of American Indians. The situation is simply a continuation of the "Pioneer Spirit" in American life.

APPROPRIATION AND DENIAL

The anthropologist of me is always a little embarrassed. When I am called upon to speak anthropologically, I find myself apologizing or stammering that I'm not *that* kind of anthropologist. I feel like the housewife-prostitute who must go home to clean house for her unknowing husband. She must lie or she must admit her guilt. Native Americans expect me to reflect the behavior they have come to anticipate from non-native anthropologists. If I live in *their* camp, the native reasoning goes, it follows that I must have joined ranks with them; it is therefore expected that I will attempt to insinuate myself into tribal politics where I have no business. Non-native anthropologists expect me either to be what Delmos Jones has called a "superinformant" or a spy for the American Indian Movement, watching their every action with the intent of "causing trouble."

The irony of all this is that I'm really NOT that kind of anthropologist. My dissertation involves a cultural-historical perspective on published literature by American Indians. Such a degree should be, perhaps, granted by the English or literature departments, but such is not the case. At the university where I worked toward my doctorate in anthropology, the English department refused to acknowledge two qualified American Indian applicants for a position during the '80s, with the statement—made to the Coordinator of Native American Studies—that "Native American literature is not part of American Literature." In the same English department, a non-Indian graduate student was also awarded a degree on the basis of a dissertation on "Native American Literature."

The student focused upon the work of four authors, *none* of whom was an Indian. The four writers are all known whiteshamans.

Native American literature is considered (by Euroamericans) to be "owned" by anthropology, as American Indians themselves are seen as "owned" by anthropologists. Our literature is merely ethnographic, along with our material culture and kinship systems. This is not, of course, restricted to Native American societies; Fourth World peoples everywhere are considered copyrightable in the same way. Maori, Native Hawaiian, Papuan, Cuna, Thai, and other people around the globe have been literarily colonized just as they have been economically, politically, and militarily colonized. Not so the literature of the Euro-derived (with certain exceptions, such as homosexuals, prisoners, etc.—all groups not "normal"). My position is that all literature must be viewed ethnographically. All literatures provide information about the culture of both writer and subject. All literatures are potential tools for the anthropologist—but not one "type" of literature more than any other. What literature is not ethnic? What person has no ethnicity? American Indians are not "more ethnic" than Polish-Americans or Anglo-Americans; they are simply called upon more frequently and intensively to deal with their ethnicity.

I do not believe the work of N. Scott Momaday, Leslie Marmon Silko, and Simon J. Ortiz is "ethnic" more so than the work of Robert Creeley, Studs Terkel, or Charles Bukowski. But you will not usually find Momaday, Silko, and Ortiz in bookstores or libraries according to their genre (fiction or poetry). Their work will most often be shelved as "anthropology," "Native Americana," "Indians," "Western," or even "Juvenile" (Indians being "kid stuff"). One plays Indian, one dresses up and pretends. Bookstore managers have told me that neither Leslie

Silko's novel *Ceremony* nor her later volume of prose and poems, *Storyteller,* could be classified or sold as "regular fiction" because no one would buy them unless they were specifically interested in Indians. Hence, the work is shelved under "Indian" Period. A book by Silko thereby becomes a mere artifact, a curio. It is presumed to be unimportant that hers also happens to be some of the finest prose and poetry available from any author, of either gender or any ethnic background. The same can be said of the writing of others—Maurice Kenny, Joy Harjo, James Welch, Linda Hogan, Barnie Bush, and Mary TallMountain among them— forced into the same "quaint" pigeonhole of classification.

But, if a Native American writer happens to gain international prominence, as in the case of Scott Momaday–his novel *A House Made of Dawn* won the 1969 Pulitzer Prize for Literature—the critics and ethnographers exclaim that the author and his or her work is "not really Indian." Rather, it suddenly falls within the "mainstream of American letters." On the other hand, the stereotypical and grossly distortive work of Hyemeyohsts Storm, a man only marginally Indian, and whose material earned him the wrath of the Northern Cheyenne people with whom he claimed affiliation, was considered by a specialist in "minority American literature" to be more "genuinely Indian" than the writing of Momaday, whose genetic and cultural heritage cannot be questioned (his father is a well-known Kiowa artist, his mother an equally well-known Cherokee educator). A great many comparable examples of this phenomenon might be cited. . . .

DISPLACEMENT

Aside from the psychological and spiritual impact of whiteshamans on American Indian writers, there are practical effects as well.

Indian writers are struggling like others in an age of budget cuts and lack of respect for literature. Most Indians write in English and use literary forms that are European and Asian in origin. These forms are generally combined with images, subject matter, and philosophy drawn from the native heritage. Few of us consciously think about what part of a particular poem came from what heritage, but the combinations are there to be studied. Not only have we adopted aspects of form and style that are non-native, but many of us have adopted the concept of what it *means* to be a writer. Even while this concept is in conflict with native sensibilities, we understand that, as professional writers, we are entitled to earn a living if we work hard enough and well enough, that we may profit from earning degrees in college, that if we give a reading and do a good job we will receive applause and people will say nice things about us in public.

Still, behind all this is the native idea that, if we succeed as writers, we are making a valuable contribution to our communities. We become role models for younger people, we speak at community gatherings (and may be asked to do so by those who respect our special skills with words), and the like. When we are in our communities, we are artists, or storytellers, or historians, in the native tradition. We are accepted, found worthy and useful. We fit in, and are thereby fulfilled. And yet, being of peoples who are now physically colonized, we must also sustain ourselves in other ways. So, when we go out to the lecture halls of fancy universities, we must become artists in a much more Euro-derived sense (though not all the way, because we never actually believe in it). To do this, we want and need our work to be read by both natives and non-natives, to be respected, to be reviewed, and to sell. Ours is always the balancing act between selling and selling out; the market for sell-outs is invariably a good one.

As a poet, I am continually frustrated by the restrictions placed on my work by the same people who insist that poets should not be restricted. It is expected—indeed, *demanded*—that I do a little "Indian-dance," a shuffle and scrape to please the tourists (as well as the anthropologists). Organizers of readings continually ask me to wear beadwork and turquois, to dress in buckskin (my people don't wear much buckskin; we've cultivated cotton for thousands of years), and to read poems conveying pastoral or "natural" images. I am often asked to "tell a story" and "place things in a spiritual framework." Simply *being* Indian—a real, live, breathing, up-to-date Indian person—is not enough. In fact, other than my genetics, this is the precise opposite of what is desired. The expectation is that I adopt, and thereby validate, the "persona" of some mythic "Indian being" who never was. The requirement is that I act to negate the reality of my—and my people's—existence in favor of a script developed within the fantasies of our oppressors.

I can and do refuse. Sometimes, I am invited to read anyway. More often, I am told that there are other poets "out there" who will prove to be more compliant with the needs of the organizers and, frequently, of their audiences. Invariably, by this it is meant that there are non-Indian poets ready and willing to assume the role of what "real Indians" are "supposed" to be like. As an Indian, I am rendered "unreal." By the same token, the non-Indians displace me as "Indian reality." On more than one occasion when I ended up sharing a podium with whiteshamans, I have been told pointblank that I am only a prop to make them look more "authentic." Even in the best of settings, when I read poetry about a political issue or anything else that is not a part of native culture (as perceived by non-natives), people frequently express disappointment, even outrage. Every other American Indian poet I know has undergone exactly the same sorts of experiences.

A logical consequence of these circumstances is that when "Indian content" is sought in a literary event, non-Indians are far more likely than Indians to be solicited to participate in the representation of "Indianness." Whiteshamans attract far more invitations to read their "Indian poetry" than do actual Indian poets. Correspondingly, because of their relative celebrity, they tend to accrue larger fees and honoraria for readings than do Indian poets, even when appearing in the same programs. A further consequence is that they are placed in positions from which to publish their "Indian" material, in larger press runs, often at higher prices and at higher royalty rates, than are most Indian writers. The "Indian biz" has proven quite lucrative for a number of whiteshamans. Not so the careers of all but a scant handful of Native American writers. The result has been a marked stilling of the genuine voice of Native America and its replacement by the utterances of an assortment of hucksters and carnival barkers.

CULTS OF THE CULTURE VULTURES

One thing Indians are spectacularly ill-equipped to do that whiteshamans appear to do quite effortlessly is build a cult around themselves. The whiteshamans become self-proclaimed "gurus," dispensing not only poetry but "healing" and "medicine," "blessing" people. In this area, they have no competition at all. I do not know of a single Native American poet who would make such a claim, although you will find a scattering of non-poets, such as the notorious "Sun Bear" (Vincent LaDuke) involved in these goings on. You will find whiteshamans at bogus "medicine wheel" gatherings, er-satz sweat-lodge ceremonies, and other fad events using vaguely Indian motifs. You will not usually find them around Indians at gen-uine Indian events. Even Sun Bear, who is a Chippewa by "blood," admitted to members of Colorado AIM that he never participated in or attended bona fide native activities. Given the nature of his own transgressions against the cultural integrity of his people, he felt—undoubtedly accurately—that he'd be "unwelcome."

When you deal with cultists, you are in deep waters. A while ago, in Alaska, I spoke to a university audience and made some mention that I believed the information in books by Carlos Castaneda to be fabricated. A non-Indian woman stood up and angrily shouted that I was anti-semitic and proba-bly didn't believe in the Holocaust either. At a more recent event at a small university in upstate New York, I was confronted by a non-native man who took it upon himself to "explain" to me how Jamake Highwater's transparently bogus ramblings had "done more for Indians than the work of any other writer." When I and several Indian col-leagues sharply disagreed, the man in-formed us we were "hopelessly deluded." I know of no legitimate Indian writer with such a fanatical following, for Indians are taught, above all, to value truth. The sancti-ty of language must not, within our tra-ditions, be used to abuse this value. The last thing a Don Juan cultist wants is to meet a *real* Yaqui holy person.

This is standard fare in whiteshaman cir-cles, and it knows no ideological boundaries. A truly amazing example involves a sector of Euroamerican feminism devoted to "re-discovering the lost power of women through the ages." Not unnaturally, native women—who have traditionally experi-enced a full measure of social, economic, political, and spiritual empowerment with-in their own cultures—have become the focus of considerable attention from this quarter. But, given their interest in Indian women, have these feminists turned to their native sisters for insight, inspiration, and guidance? No. Instead, they flock to the books and lectures of Lynn Andrews, a white woman from Beverly Hills who has grown rich claiming to have been taught by two tra-ditional Cree women (with Lakota names) in Canada about the eternal struggle be-tween the righteousness of native women's "spirit power" against malignantly evil male spirits.

Andrews, of course, maintains she has been "sent back as a spiritual messenger" by her invented teachers to spread the word of these utterly un-Indian "revelations." And, inevitably, any time a native woman—even a Cree such as Sharon Venne—attempts to refute the author's false assertions, she is shouted down by her white "sisters," often for not knowing the "inner meaning" of na-tive culture as well as Andrews, and usual-ly for having internalized the "sexism" by which "Indian men prevent the truth from being known" by women. Typically, sub-scribers to the Andrews cult describe the *Indian* women who confront their guru as being "arrogant and insensitive," a truly in-credible projection of their own psychologi-cal and behavioral characteristics upon the primary victims of their actions. Small wonder, under the circumstances, that Na-tive American women have always been conspicuously absent from "the women's movement."

When I discussed my view of Andrews' *Medicine Woman* with a well-known white male scholar of Indian literature, I was star-tled when he stated his belief that such lu-dicrous fiction could be true—as it was and is promoted to be true—because if a person *were* to serve as a "bridge" between Indians and whites, it would *have* to be a white person. He could never really articulate why he thought this to be so necessarily true. Such unidirectional presumption lies at the very core of all Eurocentric cultural imperialism and offers lucid illustration as to the crux of what has served to impair intercultural understanding and communication in this society for so long. In the end, he is as much a part of the Andrews cult as any of the near-giggling groupies lining up to obtain autographed copies of her "literary works."

FEAR AND LOATHING AMONG THE LITERATI

Before closing, I would like to talk about certain misunderstandings regarding criticism by Native Americans of the whiteshamans and their followers. The fear exists among non-native writers that we are somehow trying to bar them from writing about Indians at all, that Indian people might be "staking a claim" as the sole interpreters of Indian cultures, most especially of that which is sacred, and asserting that only Indians can make valid observations on themselves. Such fears are not based in fact; I know of no Indian who has ever said this. Nor do I know of any who secretly think it. We accept as given that whites have as much prerogative to write and speak about us and our cultures as we have to write and speak about them and theirs. The question is how this is done and, to some extent, why it is done.

The problem with whiteshamans is one of integrity and intent, not topic, style, interest, or experimentation. Many non-Indian people have—from the stated perspective of the non-native viewing things native— written honestly and eloquently about any number of Indian topics, including those we hold sacred. We readily acknowledge the beauty of some poetry by non-natives dealing with Indian people, values, legends, or the relationship between human beings and the American environment. A non-native poet is obviously as capable of writing about Coyote and Hawk as an Indian poet. The difference is in the promotion, so to speak. A non-native poet cannot produce an *Indian* perspective on Coyote or Hawk, cannot see Coyote or Hawk in an Indian way, and cannot produce a poem expressing Indian spirituality. What can be produced is another perspective, another view, another spiritual expression. The issue, as I said, is one of integrity and intent.

The principle works in both directions. As an Indian person who was deeply impressed with the oral literature of the Catholic Church during my childhood, I might compose verse based in this poetic form. I might go on to publish the poems. I might also perform them, with proper intonation, as in Mass. All of this is appropriate and permissible. But I would not and *could* not claim to be a priest. I could not tell the audience they were actually experiencing the transmutation that occurs during Mass. At the point I did endeavor to do such things, a discernible line of integrity—both personal and artistic—would have been crossed. Artistic freedom and emotional identification would not make me a priest, nor would the "uplifting" of my audience—no matter how gratifying to them, and to me—make them participants in Mass. To evoke my impression of the feel of the Mass and its liturgy does not necessitate my lying about it.

There is a world of difference between a non-Indian man like Frank Waters writing about Indians and a non-Indian man like Jamake Highwater claiming through his writing that he has in fact *become* "an Indian." Similar differences exist between a non-Indian woman like Marla N. Powers who expresses her feelings about native spirituality honestly, stating that they are her perceptions, and white women like Lynn Andrews and "Mary Summer Rain" perpetrating the fraud of having been appointed "mediums" of Indian culture. And, of course, the differences between non-Indians like John Neihardt who rely for their information upon actual native sources, and those like Andrews and Castaneda who simply invent them, should speak for themselves. As an Indian, as a poet, and as an anthropologist, I can wholeheartedly and without inconsistency accept the prerogatives claimed by the former in each case while rejecting the latter without hesitancy or equivocation. And I know of no American Indian aligned with his or her own heritage and traditions who would react otherwise.

CONCLUSION

So what is to be done about all this? For starters, readers of this essay should take the point that whiteshamanism is neither "okay," "harmless," nor "irrelevant," no more than any other form of racist, colonialist behavior. Correspondingly, they must understand that there is nothing "unreasonable" or "unfair" about the Indian position on the matter. As concerns the literary arena, we demand only informational and artistic integrity and mutual respect. It is incumbent upon Euroamerica, first and foremost, to make the whiteshamans and their followers understand that their "right" to use material from other cultures stems from those cultures, not from themselves. It must be impressed on them in no uncertain terms that there is nothing innately superior separating them from the rest of humanity, entitling them to trample upon the rights of others, or enabling them to absorb and "perfect" unfamiliar material better than the originators of that material. The only *right* they

have when dealing with native-derived subject matters is to present them honestly, accurately, and—if the material is sensitive or belongs to another group or specific person—with permission. If their response to what they've seen, heard, or otherwise experienced is subjective and interpretive, we insist only that they make this known from the outset, so as not to confuse their impressions with the real article.

Application of a bit of common sense by the public would prove helpful. Those who have a genuine desire to learn about American Indians should go out of their way to avoid being *misled* into thinking they are reading, seeing, or hearing a native work. Most whiteshamans have demonstrated a profound ignorance of the very traditions they are trying to imitate or subsume, and so they have mostly imitated each other. Many of them claim to deploy an authentically Native American model, but speak rhetoric about "inventing their own myths," a literal impossibility within *real* indigenous traditions. Any mythology stemming from experiences in a university or along city streets is unlikely to include any recognizable coyotes, and confusion in this area precludes genuine intercultural communication faster and more thoroughly than any other single factor. Until such communication is realized, we are all going to remain very much mired in the same mess in which we now collectively find ourselves, interculturally speaking.

Adoption of a pro-active attitude in this regard on the part of avowed progressives would likely prove effective. If they are truly progressive, they will demand—loudly and clearly—that not only authors, but publishers and organizers of events make it plain when "the facts" are being interpreted by a representative of a non-native culture. The extension of misinformation along these lines should be treated as seriously as any other sort of propaganda, and transgressors discredited—branded as liars, or perhaps sued for fraud—when revealed. It follows that bookstores—especially alleged "alternative" outlets—need to hear, with emphasis, that their progressive clientele objects to both their stocking of whiteshaman trash *and* to the absence of real Native American material on their shelves. Those who queue up to participate in, defend, or apologize for whiteshamanism must at last be viewed and treated as what they are. An unequivocally negative response to this sort of cultural imperialism on the part of large numbers of non-Indians would undoubtedly go far toward ending at least the worst of the practices at issue.

Native people, on the other hand, must come to understand that whiteshamans did not just pop up out of the blue and decide to offend Indians. They are responding, at least to some extent, to a genuinely felt emotional need within the dominant society. The fact that they are concomitantly exploiting other people for profit according to the sanctions and procedures of their own culture does not alter this circumstance. In spite of itself, whiteshamanism has touched upon something very real. An entire population is crying out for help, for alternatives to the spiritual barrenness they experience, for a way out of the painful trap in which their own worldview and way of life have ensnared them. They know, perhaps intuitively, that the answers—or part of the answers—to the questions producing their agony may be found within the codes of knowledge belonging to the native peoples of this land. Despite what they have done to us during the past 500 years, it would be far less than Indian of us were we not to endeavor to help them. Such are our Ways, and have always been our Ways.

Perhaps we can treaty now. Perhaps we can regain a balance that once was here, but now seems lost. If poets and artists are the prophets and expressers of history—as thinkers of both the American Indian and Euro-derived traditions have suggested in different ways—then it may well be that our task is simply to take back our heritage from the whiteshamans, shake it clean and bring it home. In doing so, we not only save ourselves from much that is happening to us, but empower ourselves to aid those who have stolen and would continue to steal so much from us, to help them locate their *own* power, their *own* traditions as human beings among human beings, as relatives among relatives not only of the human kind. Perhaps then they can come into themselves as they might be, rather than as they have been, or as they are. Perhaps then we can at last clasp hands, not as people on this land, but of this land, and go forward together. As Seattle, leader of the Suquamish people, once put it. "Perhaps we will be brothers after all. . . . We shall see."

PART REVIEW

DISCUSSION QUESTIONS

Floyd Red Crow Westerman and Jimmy Curtis, *Missionaries*
1. What is the Native American view of Christian missionaries in this poem?

John (Fire) Lame Deer and Richard Erdoes, *Alone on the Hilltop*
1. What is a vision pit, and what is its significance to traditional Lakota?
2. What does Lame Deer mean by "the spirit is everywhere"?
3. What is the significance of the sweat lodge?

Marcus Peters, *A Maidu Creation Story*
1. What is the main purpose of this creation story? Why is it so important in Maidu oral hisotry?
2. What does the creation story reveal about Maidu world view and ideology?

Frank R. LaPena, *My World Is a Gift of My Teachers*
1. How do Native Americans see the world "as a different place from that seen and described by the dominant society"?
2. In what way are songs, dances, and ceremonies an inspiration for Indian art?
3. What does the author mean by the statement "the world is a gift of my teachers"?

Russell Thornton, *Who Owns Our Past?*
1. What does the author mean by the article's title, "Who Owns Our Past"?

2. Explain how so many Native American human remains came to reside in universities, museums, historical societies, and private collections.
3. What two key laws mandate the protection and repatriation of Native American human remains and sacred objects? What two problems remain?

Indians Are Not Specimens—Indians Are People
1. The U.S. government's Smithsonian Institution holds the largest collection of Indian human remains and associated grave offerings in the nation. How did it come to have such a large collection, and how do Indian people feel about this collection?

Victoria Bomberry, *Battling for Souls*
1. The sacred weavings of the Aymara Indians of Bolivia record and interpret the religious life of the community. What is the cultural and spiritual significance of the theft of these textiles to Indian culture and life?

Wendy Rose, *The Great Pretenders*
1. What is meant by the term *whiteshamanism,* and what is wrong with it from an Indian viewpoint?
2. What is the author's criticism of anthropologists? Of writers and poets?

KEY TERMS

American Indian Religious Freedom Act of 1978
Coroma textiles
Durkheim, Emile
elders
First Amendment rights
hanblechia
Indian crania
National Museum of the American Indian (NMAI) Act of 1989

Native American Graves Protection and Repatriation Act (NAGPRA) of 1990
repatriation
revitalization movement
the sacred
Smithsonian Institution
whiteshamanism
World Maker
Zuni War Gods

SUGGESTED READINGS

American Indian Studies Center. "Special Edition: Repatriation of American Indian Remains." *American Indian Culture and Research Journal,* 6, no. 2 (1992).

ANYON, ROGER, "Zuni Protection of Cultural Resources and Religious Freedom." *Cultural Survival Quarterly* (Winter 1990): 46–49.

BARSH, RUSSEL LAWRENCE. "The Illusion of Religious Freedom for Indigenous Americans." *Oregon Law Review,* 65 (1986): 363–412.

BECK, PEGGY V., and ANNA L. WALTERS. *The Sacred: Ways of Knowledge, Sources of Life.* Tsaile [Navajo Nation], Ariz.: Navajo Community College Press, 1977.

CHAMPAGNE, DUANE, ed. "Religion." In *The Native North American Almanac.* (Detroit: Gale Research, 1994.)

DELORIA, VINE, JR. *God Is Red.* New York: Grosset and Dunlap, 1973.

DELORIA, VINE, JR. "A Simple Question of Humanity: The Moral Dimensions of the Reburial Issue." *NARF Legal Review,* 14, no. 4 (Fall 1989): 1–12.

DEMALLIE, RAYMOND J. *The Sixth Grandfather: Black Elk's Teachings Given to John Neihardt.* Lincoln, Nebraska: University of Nebraska Press, 1984.

ECHO-HAWK, WALTER. "Native American Religious Liberty: Five Hundred Years after Columbus." *American Indian Culture and Research Journal,* 17, no. 3 (1993): 33–52.

ERDOES, RICHARD. *Crying for a Dream: The World through Native American Eyes.* Santa Fe: Bear and Co., 1989.

GREEN, RAYNA, et al. *American Indian Sacred Objects. Skeletal Remains, Repatriation and Reburial: A Resource Guide.* Washington, D.C.: The American Indian Program, National Museum of American History, Smithsonian Institution, 1994.

HORSE CAPTURE, GEORGE, ed., *The Seven Visions of Bull Lodge.* Ann Arbor, Mich.: Bear Claw Press, 1980.

HULTKRANTZ, AKE. *The Religions of the American Indians.* Trans. Monica Setterwall. Berkeley: University of California Press, 1979.

LIMMERICK, PATRICIA NELSON. "The Repression of Indian Religious Freedom." *NARF Legal Review,* 18, no. 2 (Summer 1993): 9–13.

LOFTIN, JOHN D. "Anglo-American Jurisprudence and the Native American Tribal Quest for Religious Freedom." *American Indian Culture and Research Journal,* 13, no. 3 (1989): 1–52.

MARTIN, KALLEN M. "The Beginning of Respect: The U.S. Repatriation Law." *Native Americas,* 14, no. 3 (Fall 1997): 24–29.

TALBOT, STEVE. "Desecration and American Indian Religious Freedom." *Journal of Ethnic Studies,* 12, no. 1 (1984): 1–18.

TROPE, JACK F. "Existing Federal Law and the Protection of Sacred Sites: Possibilities and Limitations." *Cultural Survival Quarterly* (Winter 1996): 30–39.

VII
SUSTAINABLE DEVELOPMENT: ECONOMY AND THE ENVIRONMENT

It Was That Indian

Simon J. Ortiz

Martinez
from over by Bluewater
was the one who discovered uranium
west of Grants.
That's what they said.
He brought that green stone
into town one afternoon in 1953,
said he found it by the railroad tracks
over by Haystack Butte.
Tourist magazines did a couple spreads
on him, photographed him in kodak color,
and the Chamber of Commerce celebrated
that Navajo man,
forgot for the time being
that the brothers
from Aacqu east of Grants
had killed that state patrolman,
and never mind also
that the city had a jail full of Indians.
The city fathers named
a city park after him
and some even wanted to put up a statue
of Martinez but others said
that was going too far for just an Indian
even if he was the one who started that area
into a boom.
Well, later on,
when some folks began to complain
about chemical poisons flowing into the streams
from the processing mills, carwrecks on Highway 53,
lack of housing in Grants,
cave-ins at Section 33,
non-union support,
high cost of living,
and uranium radiation causing cancer,
they—the Chamber of Commerce—pointed out
that it was Martinez
that Navajo Indian from over by Bluewater
who discovered uranium,
it says so in this here brochure,
he found that green stone over by Haystack
out behind his hogan;
it was that Indian who started that boom.

There are three issues around which Native peoples are waging a resistance today, as in past centuries, to the neocolonialism and exploitation by the dominant states of the Western Hemisphere: they are land, self-government, and indigenous rights. Of these, land is viewed as primary, not only for its economic value but also because of its deep spiritual significance to Native peoples. Land conflict (and by extension, the exploitation of plants, animals, water, and other natural resources and the expropriation of the labor of the resident indigenous populations on the land) has always been at the base of Indian and non-Indian relations. Dispossession of the aboriginal land base and its environmental destruction stand next to genocide in order of tragic consequences for Native peoples in their historical relations with European-derived populations of the Americas. The great Lakota leader Red Cloud is said to have observed: "They made us many promises, more than I can remember, but they never kept but one: they promised to take our land and they took it."

Native Americans hold a deep emotional and spiritual attachment to the land. This relationship has been described as stewardship rather than ownership, where "the earth is our mother." Land is seen as a homeland, a tribal heritage, a sacred place. One writer described the Indian land ethic in the following manner:

> Land is the basis of all things Indian. . . . The relationship of a tribe to its land defines that tribe: its identity, its culture, its way of life, its fundamental rights, its methods of adaptation, its pattern of survival. Land also defines the Indians' enemies—those who covet the land and desire to expropriate it for their own use. Because Indian land is, or may be, of value, it has been, and remains, the source of almost every major conflict and every ongoing controversy between the Indian and the white man.[1]

There are three major perspectives concerning land and its resources, and by extension, the environment. The first is the constitutional-legal perspective, which is found chiefly in the treaty relationship in the United States and Canada concerning Native peoples. In Latin America the concept of treaties and treaty making is rarely found. From the European legal perspective at the time of first contact, large tracts of land were "given" by the Spanish and Portuguese Crowns to their citizens without recognizing any legal entitlement of Native peoples. In the United States, a multicultural nation built on immigration, only the Indians are a truly territorial minority, and their quest for equity and justice stands alone in being founded on a recognized body of treaties and laws. The aboriginal "right to the soil" (land) is recognized under the U.S. Constitution, 371 treaties, and various laws and Supreme Court decisions. In 1823, however, a Supreme Court decision, *Johnson v. McIntosh*, ruled that the European "right to discovery" took precedence over the Native American "right to the soil" or aboriginal rights. The doctrine was codified into law in a later, 1955, Supreme Court decision, *Tee-Hit-Ton v. United States,* that ruled that Indian occupancy is not a property right; it can be terminated without compensation at any time by the United States. Despite the fact that the plenary power of Congress now takes precedence over aboriginal rights, leading to land alienation and resource depletion at the whims of Congress, aboriginal rights are nevertheless recognized under international law, and this fact gives U.S. Indian nations more political clout in their quest for justice than is the case for many other Indian peoples of the Americas.

The economic perspective refers to land and its resources as necessary to build viable economies for Indian communities. Land was formerly the basis for aboriginal economy under the natural-mode production, which was for use, not profit. Land and its resources constitute the foundation on which the larger nations, such as the Mayas in southern Mexico and Guatemala, are able to carry out their basic human right to self-determination and sovereignty now and in the future. Utilization of a viable land base is also a way for the smaller nations to achieve a measure of economic self-sufficiency and political autonomy. It is ironic that the astronomical rates of unemployment and poverty found on U.S. Indian reservations do not reflect the existence of ample resources which, for most of the larger tribes, would allow them to become self-supporting. Unfortunately, non-Indian operators and corporations are the chief beneficiaries of these resources. The 1975 American Indian Policy Review Commission found that Native Americans received less than one-third of the total value of range and farm products grown on Indian lands. Estimates vary as to the amount of energy resources found on Native American lands in the United States, but Indian coal reserves alone may be worth more than $1 trillion, and, according to a 1975 Federal Trade Commission report, Indian lands hold two-thirds of the uranium under federal jurisdiction. Yet, Indians in the United States realize only a small fraction of the worth of these resources and are left with the negative impact of strip mining and other destructive technologies, which threaten to leave their reservations and historical lands as "national sacrifice areas."

In Central and South America there remain immense resources (oil, gas, coal, copper, uranium) in Indian lands that are currently under "development" by the energy multinationals and the venture capitalists at the expense of indigenous peoples. The current, ongoing destruction of the great rain forests in Amazonian South America, which have been described as the "lungs" of the Western Hemisphere, is the chief example, but the assault on the forests is occurring in Central America as well. When the environment is destroyed or irreparably damaged, the term *ecocide* is used, and when it takes place on the traditional lands of Native peoples then it becomes part of the general ethnocide. One can only speculate as to the ancient knowledge of herbs and medicinal cures that are being lost to humanity as a whole, since most of the flora has never been studied and cataloged by modern science. Perhaps the cure for cancer is there, or for AIDS. Some Western pharmaceutical companies are beginning to appropriate and patent traditional medicine plants. This "biopiracy" brings into question the ethical issue of the intellectual property rights of indigenous peoples (see "Amazonian Confrontation" by Benjamin Craig in the Suggested Readings).

Frequently overlooked in discussions of the land, economy, and environment is the third perspective of the question, the ideological linkage or spiritual attachment to the land by Native peoples. William Brandon reports that during the removal period of the nineteenth century by the expansionist United States, "Whites could not comprehend the Indians' fanatical attachment to a particular part of the earth" and that "some watching Whites were moved and some amused when departing Indians went about touching leaves, trees, rocks and streams in farewell."[2] Christopher Vecsey, in an article on American Indian religions and the environment, contends that "environmental concerns constitute a foremost dimension of American Indian religions, regardless of specific ecosystem."[3] There is a sacred quality to the relationship between Native peoples and the land with its resources. Fishing, for example, "is more than a job, more than a right, more than a way to make a living in a money economy. It is a way of life, a relation with the source of life, a means of identity as an Indian."[4] For example, living today, during the first years of the twenty-first century, when most of us spend our evenings and nights in the enclosure of a house, most often in an urban setting, and frequently surrounded by pollutants in the air and the artificial lights of cities, all of which obscure the night sky, it is easy to become unmindful of the stars and other celestial phenomena that permeated the lives of those living in a more natural environment as well as the integral role that an awareness of the sky has played in explaining and guiding life.

Today, throughout the Americas, Native people's right to their land and environment is under attack by the energy multinationals in what environmentalist Al Gedicks terms "the new resource wars" (see Suggested Readings). The Yanomami Indians of Brazil face extinction, dying from diseases to which they have no natural immunity, brought in by miners looking for the rich deposits of tungsten, titanium, gold, uranium, bauxite, and tin found on the Indians' lands. In Colombia, the exploitation of one of the world's richest undeveloped coal fields is under way. The development project is a joint venture of the Colombian government and a subsidiary of the oil giant Exxon. In Colombia, also, the U'wa Indians have threatened mass suicide unless Occidental Petroleum ceases its encroachment on and despoilment of their traditional lands. In Canada, the Inuit (Eskimo) and Cree Indians are fighting Hydra-Quebec, a multibillion-dollar utility owned by the Quebec government, which intends, in a project known as James Bay II, to flood thousands of square miles of natural habitat where the Native peoples sustain themselves by hunting and trapping its river systems. (James Bay I, begun in the 1970s and completed in 1984 as a series of dams along the Le Grande River in central Quebec, had already destroyed Native habitat for hunting and trapping.) In the southwestern United States, huge, coal-fired electric generating plants rise from the high desert plateaus of the Eastern Pueblo, Hopi, and Dineh Indians like surrealistic cities out of a science fiction scenario. These plants use coal from strip mines on Indian lands and precious ancient water aquifers to slurry the coal hundreds of miles to the plants, all in the name of supplying electrical power to non-Indian industries and cities. The Indian peoples are left with the resultant pollution in the form of airborne particulate matter and dangerous residues going into streams and soil as a result of the mining. In an arid environment like the Southwest, the scars from strip mining can never be healed. Furthermore, there is a very real danger that the meager supply of groundwater available to Pueblo and other Indian farmers will disappear because of the even deeper pumping of the ancient water aquifers.

A newly recognized, insidious threat that is quietly poisoning Native communities and disrupting the web of tribal life is POPs, persistent organic pollutants.

POPs are a class of long-lasting toxic chemicals, which includes PCBs, DDT, and dioxins, that build up in the food chain and slowly poison the environment, animals, and humans. They are invisible, tasteless, and odorless (see *Drumbeat for Mother Earth* in the Suggested Readings).

It is therefore not surprising that Native Americans increasingly recognize the danger to their sacred environment, economic livelihood, and sense of place caused by Western industrialism and the expanding global economy.

From a Native American perspective, the solution is sustainable development, which is defined as "development that meets the needs of the present without compromising the ability of future generations to meet their own needs." Gedicks, in his work *The New Resource Wars,* states that the concept was first used in a report by the 1987 United Nations World Commission on Environment and Development and it later "received a great deal of attention in the discussions leading up to the U.N. Conference on the Environment and Development, or the Earth Summit, held in Rio de Janeiro, Brazil, in June 1992."[5] This environmental concept parallels that of "planning for seven generations," used by many Native peoples of the Americas. The Seven Generations concept is that human societies should plan for the future generations in terms of the economy and the environment and not for the immediate gratification of those living today.

The poem by Acoma poet and storyteller Simon Ortiz, which begins this part, comments in bitter irony how "that Indian," Martinez, was first lauded for the uranium boom in New Mexico and then blamed for the environmental costs of uranium development when they began to become apparent to the non-Indian community. Today, there are dozens of uranium mines in the Grants Mineral Belt and the San Juan basin. Radioactive pollution is rampant, so much so that many of the small Indian nationalities, such as the Pueblo Indian communities, are in danger of eventual extinction from cancer death and related illnesses. This phenomenon is termed *radioactive colonialism* by Ward Churchill (Creek/Cherokee/Métis) and Winona LaDuke (Anishinabeg). Ortiz's poem is therefore a fitting introduction to the comprehensive article by Winona LaDuke.

LaDuke is a recognized international expert on the environment and a spokesperson for American Indian environmental concerns. In the 1996 presidential election she was a vice presidential candidate on the Ralph Nader for president, Green party ticket and is again running in the same position in the 2000 national election campaign. Deep ecology and bioregionalism are key concepts of the Greens, which make them potential allies of American Indian traditionalists. Deep ecology is defined as going beyond science and ethics to a sense of spiritual oneness with the cosmos; a bioregion is simply an identifiable geographic area whose life systems are self-contained, self-sustaining, and self-renewing. As both an Indian traditionalist and an environmentalist, in the broader sense of the word, LaDuke contrasts the indigenous view of harmony with nature and respect for Mother Earth with that of the exploitative one of colonialism and capitalist development. She briefly discusses the concept of sustainable development (which is close to the Greens' notion of bioregionalism): that is, non-exploitative economic uses of the environment, the land, water, air, and sky. The bulk of her article documents in graphic detail the extreme harm that unrestrained capitalist development is causing Native American peoples throughout North America.

The second article in this part takes up a somewhat different topic, one that is usually overlooked by specialists on the U.S. Indian question: the expropriation of Native American labor by capitalist development. Anthropologist Alice Littlefield argues that the vicissitudes caused by U.S. Indian policy were not the result of mistaken or uninformed framers of these policies, but, instead, were a reflection of the marketplace in capitalist political economy and its changing needs for Native American labor. She reexamines the assimilationist period in U.S. Indian relations, 1880 to 1930, and explains that the goal was actually proletarianization. The 1887 Indian Allotment Act coincided with a transition from competitive to monopolistic capitalism. The Indian tribes lost over half of their land base during this period. She writes: "Both Mexico and Guatemala also enacted policies during this period aimed at facilitating expropriation of indigenous people's lands and the utilization of their labor in cash-crop production." Similarly, she documents the labor needs of the dominant economy for two other major policy periods in U.S. Indian history: the 1930s Indian New Deal, under the 1934 Indian Reorganization Act, and the post–World War II period, with its policies of reservation termination and population relocation to industrial cities.

The biggest economic boom in Indian country in the United States today is Indian gaming, a subject taken up by Tim Johnson (Mohawk) in the third selection. Nationwide, Indian gambling is a multibillion-dollar industry. California tribes alone generated $1.5 billion in gaming revenue in 1997. But is it a curse or a blessing? Does gaming result in a "one-crop," distorted Indian economy, and will it have a negative impact on traditional culture? Most Indian tribes believe that the positive aspects greatly outweigh any negative consequences. With state lotteries and gambling fever sweeping the country, Congress passed the Indian Gaming Regulatory Act in 1988. Its aim was to stimulate the tribal economies that did not have adequate resources to support development. Today, several hundred tribes nationwide are conducting some form of gaming, and many are operating casino games such as slot machines, blackjack, and roulette. In Connecticut, the 383 members of the Mashantucket Pequot tribe share profits from a casino that clears more than $1 million a day from slot machines alone and employs 10,000 people. Many tribes, even with larger memberships, do not clear that kind of money, however, and a number have yet to see a profit. Most tribes see gaming as a short-term possibility to raise the capital to underwrite other forms of economic enterprises. In the meantime, for those tribes that have benefited from gaming, welfare roles, unemployment, and poverty rates have dropped precipitously. Indian gaming has created full employment for tribal members, and most of the surplus revenues go for education, social services, and environmental and health programs.

Gaming has not been without controversy, however. Trouble has flared at Michigan's Keweenaw Bay Indian Community, for example, where dissidents contend that the tribe has strayed from its cultural roots and that tribal leaders and outside management corporations have lined their pockets with casino profits while stripping the voting rights of those in the tribe who challenge them. Perhaps even more seriously, the Indian gaming law requires that the tribes negotiate with the respective states. This aspect of the law is viewed with concern by some authorities as evidence of further ceding Indian sovereignty over to state governments. The U.S. Constitution (Article I, section 8) gives the U.S. Congress, not the states, the power to regulate commerce with Indian tribes. Some state politicians want to tax tribal government gaming enterprises, or, as is the case in California, require the "casino tribes" to share their profits with other Indian groups. Profit sharing would force gaming tribes to pick up the tab for state services in the areas of education, health, and welfare.

Salmon is to the Indian peoples of Pacific Coast North America what the buffalo were to the Plains Indians of the past century. Unlike coal mining and other fossil fuel expropriation, fishing involves a renewable resource; if managed properly, the salmon will return forever. That has not been the case, however, because of the profit-oriented and consumer-generated demands of the wider society whose commercial interests led them to overfish salmon runs and dam and pollute the coastal rivers, streams, and estuaries. The reading by the Native American Rights Fund (NARF), a legal service and advocacy firm run by Indian people, examines the question of the Indian's right to fish. The legal case documented is that of Katie John (Athabascan), the elder matriarch of Mentasta Village in south-central Alaska. As the article points out, a majority of the fish taken by Alaska Natives is for subsistence, to feed families. But unlike the situation in the Lower 48, there are no treaty rights in Alaska to protect hunting, fishing, and gathering rights. The NARF article traces the long and convoluted legal battle to force the state of Alaska to conform to Title VIII of the 1983 Alaska National Interest Lands Conservation Act (ANILCA) and to reopen a traditional fishery in Batzulnetas. It was not until 1995, in a legal ruling made by the courts, that Native subsistence rights were validated. Without the assistance of the NARF, this decision would have not been possible. The state of Alaska, however, immediately challenged this legal decision. For more than a decade, the Alaska Federation of Natives (AFN), representing 13 Native regional for-profit corporations, 12 regional nonprofit corporations, and more than 196 Native villages across Alaska, patiently negotiated with the state to resolve the Native hunting and fishing rights issue. By February 1999, the AFN vowed it would no longer support efforts to return subsistence management to the state of Alaska until the state acknowledges the real needs of Alaska Natives.

Farther to the south, in Colombia, the U'wa Indians are threatening mass suicide if Occidental Petroleum expands its operations into indigenous territory (see the box titled "Peace, Not Oil: The U'wa and International Petroleum.") Oil drilling has already contaminated the ground water and compromised the ecosystem on which the U'wa rely for their subsistence. In addition, U'wa land has a spiritual dimension that is subject to desecration.

In 1999, an international delegation that included Ingrid Washinawatok-El Issa (Menominee) was assassinated by leftist guerillas while attempting to assist the U'wa (see Part IX, introduction).

In the fifth selection, Haunani-Kay Trask (Native Hawaiian), former director of the Center for Hawaiian Studies at the University of Hawai'i and a leader in the Native Hawaiian sovereignty struggle, documents the commodification of Hawaiian culture and introduces the concept of "cultural prostitution" to underscore the harm that is being done to Native Hawaiian traditions and people. She examines the negative impact on four key areas of culture: homeland, which includes the idea of stewardship of the land, seas, and heavens; language and dance; familial relationships; and Hawaiian women. Since World War II, tourism has transformed the Hawaiian Islands and, today, has taken the place of the once-mighty sugar industry. Millions of tourists flood the islands annually, many times outnumbering the local residents and bringing millions of dollars in revenues to the tourist industry. Yet this development has not transferred benefits to Native Hawaiians and most other local residents: tourist industry jobs are dead-end, low-paying, and humiliating jobs; land dispossession caused by the development of hotels, resorts, tourist beaches, and golf courses has increased the numbers of homeless or near-homeless island residents; and the cost of living is now the highest of any place in the United States. Not the least of the negative impacts caused by tourism is the destruction of the once-pristine island environment.

In the last selection, anthropologist Mac Chapin sketches the historical background of the current "assault on the forests" and the resident indigenous populations of Central America. This small region, he reminds us, is extremely diverse, with forty-three distinct indigenous groups comprising five million people. Yet, today, the impact of outside economic forces on the Indian peoples constitute, in his words, "a Second Conquest." While detailing the environmentally damaging operations of multinational companies, he nevertheless ends on the hopeful note of Native resistance. A plethora of indigenous confederations and support groups have arisen to do battle. One is reminded of the growing worldwide coalition of forces, including indigenous organizations, that have been protesting the policies and operations of the World Trade Organization, the World Bank, and the International Monetary Fund. Chapin lists five of the reasons that "it would be advantageous to all to place the indigenous inhabitants in charge of management of the forests in which they live."

NOTES

1. Edgar S. Cahn, *Our Brother's Keeper* (Washington, D.C.: New Community Press, 1969), 68.

2. William Brandon, *The American Heritage Book of Indians* (New York: Dell, 1961), 223.

3. Christopher Vecsey and Robert W. Venables, eds., *American Indian Environments: Ecological Issues in*

Native American History (Syracuse: Syracuse University Press, 1980), xviii.

4. Ibid., 26.

5. Al Gedicks, *The New Resource Wars: Native and Environmental Struggles against Multinational* Corporations (Boston: South End Press, 1993), 198.

INDIGENOUS ENVIRONMENTAL PERSPECTIVES

A NORTH AMERICAN PRIMER

Winona LaDuke

INDIGENOUS NATIONS TODAY

At the outset, it is useful to note that there are over 5,000 nations in the world today, and just over 170 states. "Nations" are defined under international law as those in possession of a common language, landbase, history, culture and territory. North America is similarly comprised of a series of nations, known as "First Nations" in Canada, and, with few exceptions, denigrated in the United States with the term "tribes." Demographically, Indigenous nations represent the majority population north of the 55th parallel in Canada (the 50th parallel in the eastern provinces), and occupy approximately two-thirds of the Canadian landmass.

Although the United States has ten times the population, Indian people do not represent the majority, except in few cases, particularly the "four corners" region of the United States, or the intersection of Arizona, Utah, New Mexico, and Colorado, where Ute, Apache, Navajo, and Pueblo people reside. Inside our reservations however (approximately four percent of our original land base

in the United States), Indian people remain the majority population.

In our territories and our communities, a mix of old and new co-exist, sometimes in relative harmony, and at other times, in a violent disruption of the way of life. In terms of economic and land tenure systems (the material basis for relating to the ecosystem), most Indigenous communities are a melange of colonial and traditional structures and systems. While American or Canadian laws may restrict and allocate resources and land on reservations (or aboriginal territory), Indigenous practice of "usufruct rights" is still maintained, and with it traditional economic and regulatory institutions like the trapline, "rice boss," and family hunting, grazing (for those peoples who have livestock), or harvesting territories.

These subsistence lifestyles continue to provide a significant source of wealth for domestic economies on the reservation—whether for nutritional consumption or for household use, as in the case of firewood. They also, in many cases, provide the essential ingredients of foreign exchange—wild rice, furs, or woven rugs and silverwork. These economic and land tenure systems (specific to each region) are largely "invisible" to American and Canadian government agencies, economic analysts who consistently point to Native "unemployment," with no recognition of the traditional economy.

In many northern communities, over seventy-five percent of local food, and a significant amount of income, is garnered from this traditional economic system. In other cases, for instance, on the Northern Cheyenne reservation in Montana, over ninety percent of the land is held by Cheyenne, and is utilized primarily for ranching. Although not formal "wage work" in the industrial system, these land-based economies are essential to our communities. The lack of recognition for Indigenous economic systems, though long entrenched in the North American colonial view of Native peoples, is particularly frustrating in terms of the present debate over development options.

Resource extraction plans or energy mega-projects proposed for Indigenous lands do not consider the significance of these economic systems, nor their value for the future. A direct consequence is that environmentally destructive development programs ensue, many times foreclosing the opportunity to continue the lower scale, intergenerational economic practices which had been underway in the Native community. For many Indigenous peoples, the reality is that, as sociologist Ivan Illich has noted, "the practice of development is in fact a war on subsistence."

The following segment of this paper includes an overview of North American Indigenous environmental issues, in the format of generalized discussions and case studies. The paper is far from exhaustive, but is presented with the intention of providing information on the environmental crises pending or present in our communities. It is the belief of many Native people that due to our historic and present relations with the United States and Canadian governments,

we may be "the miner's canary," or a microcosm of the larger environmental crisis facing the continent. In a final segment of this paper, we return to the discussion of sustainable development, and offer, once again, some present documentation of the practice of "pimaatisiiwin," interpreted as good life or continuous birth, within the context of our Indigenous economic and value systems.

URANIUM MINING

> . . . Uranium mining and milling are the most significant sources of radiation exposure to the public of the entire nuclear fuel cycle far surpassing nuclear reactors and nuclear waste disposal. . . .
>
> Victor Gillinsky,
> U.S. Nuclear Regulatory Commission, 1978

> . . . Perhaps the solution to the radon emission problem is to zone the land into uranium mining and milling districts so as to forbid human habitation. . . .
>
> Los Alamos Scientific Laboratory,
> February 1978

The production of uranium or yellowcake from uranium ore usually requires the discharge of significant amounts of water and the disposal of significant portions of radioactive material. Uranium mill tailings, the solid wastes from the uranium milling stage of the cycle, contain eighty-five percent of the original radioactivity in the uranium ore. One of these products, Radium 226, remains radioactive for at least 16,000 years.

In 1975, 100% of all federally produced uranium came from Indian reservations. That same year there were 380 uranium leases on Indian lands, as compared to four on public and acquired lands. In 1979, there were 368 operating uranium mines in the United States. Worldwide, it is estimated that seventy percent of uranium resources are contained on Indigenous lands.

NAVAJO NATION

Spurred by the advice of the Bureau of Indian Affairs and promises of jobs and royalties, the Navajo Tribal Council approved a mineral agreement with the Kerr McGee Corporation. In return for access to uranium deposits and a means to fulfill risk-free contracts with the U.S. Atomic Energy Commission, Kerr McGee employed 100 Navajo men as uranium miners in the underground mines.

Wages for the non-union miners were low—$1.60 per hour, or approximately two thirds of off-reservation wages. In addition, regulation and worker safety enforcement were exceedingly lax. In 1952, the mine inspector found that ventilation units were not in operation. In 1954, the inspector found that the fan was operating only during the first half of the shift. When he returned in 1955, the blower ran out of gas during an inspection. One report from 1959 noted that radiation levels at the operations were ninety times above tolerable levels.

Seventeen years later most of the readily retrievable ore had been exhausted, and the company began to phase out the mines. By 1975, eighteen of the miners who had worked in the Kerr McGee mines had died of lung cancer and twenty-one more were feared to be dying. By 1980, thirty-eight had died and ninety-five more had contracted respiratory ailments and cancers. The incidence of skin and bladder cancer, birth defects, leukemia and other diseases associated with uranium mining also accelerated.

In its departure from the Shiprock area of Navajo, Kerr McGee abandoned approximately seventy-one acres worth of uranium mill tailings on the banks of the San Juan River, the only major waterway in the arid region. As a result, radioactive contamination spread downstream. Southeast of the facility, the Churchrock uranium mine discharged 80,000 gallons of radioactive water from the mine shaft (in "dewatering") annually into the local water supply.

In July of 1979, the largest radioactive spill in United States history occurred at the United Nuclear uranium mill near Churchrock on the Navajo reservation. The uranium mill tailings dam at the site broke under pressure and 100 million gallons of sludge flooded the Rio Puerco River. Although the company had known of the cracks in the dam for two months prior to the incident, no repairs had been made. The water supply of 1,700 Navajo people was irretrievably contaminated, and subsequently over 1,000 sheep and cattle ingested radioactive water.

By 1980, forty-two operating uranium mines, ten uranium mills, five coal fired power plants and four coal stripmines (spanning 20–40,000 acres each) were in the vicinity of the Navajo reservation. Approximately fifteen new uranium mining operations were under construction on the reservation itself. Although eighty-five percent of Navajo households had no electricity, each year, the Navajo nation exported enough energy resources to fuel the needs of the state of New Mexico for thirty-two years.

The birth defect rate in the Shiprock Indian Health Service area is two to eight times higher than the national average, according to a study supported by the March of Dimes Research Support Grant #15-8, and undertaken by Lora Magnum Shields, a professor at Navajo Community College in Shiprock and Alan B. Goodman, Arizona Department of Health.

LAGUNA PUEBLO

Approximately fifty miles to the east of the Navajo reservation lies Laguna Pueblo, until 1982 the site of the largest uranium strip mine in the world. The Anaconda Jackpile mine comprised 7,000 acres of the reservation, operating from 1952 to 1971, when the economically retrievable ore was exhausted. An "Indian preference" clause in hiring ensured the employment of Laguna workers, and by 1979, 650 persons were employed at the mine, with this reservation reflecting some of the highest per capita income in the region. The significance of this employment, as indicated in other health and economic statistics, had a mixed impact on the local community.

Prior to 1952, the Rio Paguate coursed through an agricultural and ranching valley that provided food for the Pueblo. Rio Paguate now runs through the remnants of the stripmine, emerging on the other side a fluorescent green in color. In 1973, the Environmental Protection Agency discovered that Anaconda had contaminated the Laguna water with radiation.

In 1975, the EPA returned to find widespread groundwater contamination in the Grants Mineral Belt. And in 1978, the EPA came back again, this time to inform Laguna that the water was contaminated and to inform the people that the Tribal Council building, the Paguate Community Center, and the newly constructed housing were all radioactive. In addition, Anaconda was reprimanded for having used low-grade uranium ore to repair the road system on the reservation.

PINE RIDGE RESERVATION

On June 11, 1962, 200 tons of uranium mill tailings from the uranium mill in Edgemont, South Dakota, washed into the Cheyenne River and traveled into the Angostora Reservoir. The Cheyenne River flows from this reservoir down through the hills and across the reservation. The Cheyenne passes within several hundred feet of the Red Shirt Table. These tailings are a part of an estimated seven and a half million tons of radioactive material, abandoned from the uranium mill at the Edgemont mine.

Water samples taken from the Cheyenne River and from a subsurface well on the Redshirt Table revealed a gross alpha radioactivity level of nineteen and fifteen picocuries per liter respectively. Federal safety regulations state that a reading greater than five picocuries per liter is considered dangerous to life. In June of 1980, the Indian Health Service revealed water test results for the Pine Ridge reservation community of Slim Buttes (adjacent to the same area) to indicate gross alpha radiation levels at three times the federal safety maximum. A June 10, 1980 report of the Office of Environmental Health, Bureau of Indian Affairs, Aberdeen indicated that the gross alpha radiation reading for the Slim Buttes water sample was fifty picocuries per liter. A water sample taken from Cherry Creek, on the Cheyenne River Reservation to the north acted as a control sample. It contained 1.9 picocuries per liter, one tenth of that on the Red Shirt Table.

A preliminary study of 1979 reported that fourteen women, or thirty-eight percent of the pregnant women on the Pine Ridge reservation, miscarried, according to records at the Public Health Service Hospital in Pine Ridge. Most miscarriages were before the fifth month of pregnancy, and in many cases there was excessive hemorrhaging. Of the children who were born, some sixty to seventy percent suffered from breathing complications as a result of undeveloped lungs and/or jaundice. Some were born with such birth defects as cleft palate and club foot. Subsequent information secured under Freedom of Information Act requests from the Indian Health Service verified the data. Between 1971 and 1979, 314 babies had been born with birth defects, in a total Indian population of under 20,000.

CANADIAN URANIUM MINING

We have always been here, and we will stay here. The mines will come and go, they won't have to live with their consequences. We will. . . .

Dine Elder, Wollaston Lake

Previous uranium mining in the north of Canada including Port Hope, has left over 222,000 cubic meters of radioactive waste. Other dumps, including those in the villages of Port Granby and Welcome, contain a further 573,000 cubic meters of toxic radioactive waste. By 1985, over 120 million tons of low level radioactive waste was abandoned near now defunct uranium mines. This amount represents enough material to cover the Trans-Canada Highway two meters deep from Halifax to Vancouver. Present production of uranium waste from the province of Saskatchewan alone occurs at the rate of over one million tons annually.

Uranium mining began at Elliot Lake, Ontario, in 1958, adjacent to and upstream from the Serpent River reserve of Anishinabeg. The uranium mining has continued until recently, but now most of the mine shafts are being closed, as uranium mining investment has shifted to the open pit mines of northern Saskatchewan.

During the mine operations at Elliot Lake, a significant number of miners were exposed to high levels of radiation. According to a report commissioned by Member of Parliament Steven Lewis (and former Ambassador to the United Nations), "in no individual year between 1959 and 1974 inclusive . . . did the average underground dust counts for the uranium mines of Elliot Lake fall below the recommended limits. In another instance, workers at the thorium separation plant operated by Rio Algom (in Serpent River) until the 1970s were exposed to up to forty times the radiation level

recommended by the International Commission for Radiological Protection."

Between 1955 and 1977, eighty-one of the 956 deaths of Ontario uranium miners were from lung cancers. This figure is almost twice that anticipated. Another inquiry into the health of uranium miners revealed that there are ninety-three persons suffering from silicosis, ascribed to the Elliot Lake operations by the end of 1974. By early 1975, nearly 500 miners had lung disabilities, wholly or partly ascribed to dust exposure in the mines and mills. Over the next five years, more than 500 new cases had developed.

The Elliot Lake uranium mines produced over 100 million tons of uranium wastes. Most of these were left abandoned by the roadsides and mine sites, where, according to one observer ". . . local residents continue to pick blueberries within a forty foot high wall of uranium tailings. . . ."

In 1978, the Elliot Lake uranium operations continued to spew out 14,000 tons of solid and liquid effluent daily. Most of that effluent was discharged, untreated, into the Serpent River basin. By 1980, dumping of tailings was so extensive that liquid wastes from the mines comprised between one half and two thirds of the total flow. In 1976, the International Joint Commission on the Great Lakes identified the outflow of the Serpent River into Lake Huron as the greatest single source of Radium 226 and thorium isotopes into the freshwater. Perhaps more significant was a 1976 report by the Ontario Ministry of the Environment, which concluded that eighteen lakes in the Serpent River system had been contaminated as a result of uranium mining to the extent that they were unfit for human use and all fish life had been destroyed.

The most significant longterm impact of the Elliot Lake operations will be borne by the Serpent River and other Anishinabeg bands downstream from the operation. A study carried out by the Toronto Jesuit Center for the Environmental Impact Protection Program between 1982–4 documented the following:

- Twice as many young adults (people under the age of thirty-six) reported chronic disease at Serpent River than at two adjacent reserves. The other two reserves had no direct uranium impacts.
- The Serpent River band reported the largest proportion of participants of all ages with chronic disease.
- Pregnancies ending prematurely with fetal death were more prevalent at Serpent River.

In males over 45, "ill health" is reported by more men with exposure to the plant or uranium mine (seventy-five percent) as compared to forty-three percent in men who did not work at the facilities. Additional birth defects were reported in children of men who worked in the uranium related facilities.

By 1986, uranium production in Saskatchewan had doubled, up to over $923 million in exports annually to American utilities. From previous exposure to radiation (resulting from uranium mining over the past twenty years in the north of Saskatchewan), it is estimated that Native people already have eighty times as much radiation in their bodies as residents of the south. The contamination of the north will only become worse with increased uranium mining.

Uranium mining is projected to expand 100% in Canada in the next few years. Five proposed projects are now awaiting environmental impact assessment. (Three of them will be using existing EIS, with two new programs.) The mines include Dominique-Janine Extension (AMOK-a French Company), South McMahon Lake Project (Midwest Joint Venture), McClean Lake Project (Minatco Ltd.), MacArthur River and Cigar Lake mines. Two of the existing three uranium mines, Cluff Lake and Rabbit Lake/Collins Bay are currently expanding, after exhausting original ore bodies. Most of the exploration and test mine work is occurring just west of Wollaston Lake. The Canadian Crown Corporation, Cameco remains the key owner in most of the mining ventures with 20% ownership of Cluff Lake, 66.6% ownership of Key Lake and Rabbit Lake and 48.75% ownership of Cigar Lake.

In November of 1989, a two million liter spill of radioactive water occurred at Rabbit Lake uranium mine. The spill was not reported by the company to the community, but was seen by the community people, who requested to be informed on the contents of the spill from the facility. Almost half of the spill ended up in Wollaston Lake adjacent to a Dene community. The following spring, Cameco pleaded guilty to negligence in the spill, and paid a $50,000 fine.

Evidence of the possible impact on future generations from longterm exposure to low levels of radiation was recently released by a British scientific study. This evidence may have some bearing on uranium mining communities, where longterm health studies have not been undertaken. The study found that exposure of male workers to consistent levels of radiation may cause a mutation in sperm resulting in higher rates of leukemia in their offspring. According to a study by the Medical Research Council of Southampton University (Great Britain), workers exposed to radiation may father children with an increased risk of leukemia. After examining a host of variables, the study team found that children of fathers who worked at the Sellafield Nuclear power plant had a two and one-half times higher risk of contracting leukemia. Fathers who had received the highest dosages over their working life stood six to eight times as high a chance of producing a child with leukemia. Overall, the study found fifty-two cases of childhood leukemia in the health district, with the town of Sellafield exhibiting a ten-fold excess over average figures.

KERR MCGEE SEQUOYAH FUELS FACILITY: CHEROKEE NATION, OKLAHOMA

> In 1968, when Kerr McGee began building a uranium processing plant in our community, the people were happy at the thought of employment. Kerr McGee assured the safety of the plant, and now seventeen years later, we have a situation that the majority of us would have never imagined. Most of the waste has been stored in plastic lined ponds, one of which has been leaking since 1974. . . ."
>
> Jessie Deer in Water, Vian, Oklahoma

Sequoyah Fuels Corporation (Kerr McGee) operates a uranium fuels processing plant in Gore, Oklahoma. The plant is within the borders of the Cherokee nation, home to a resident population of over 100,000 Cherokees. The plant converts yellowcake (U 308) into uranium hexaflouride using a "wet process." The products of the plant are trucked onto nearby Interstate 40 for delivery to more than fifty customers, including twenty-five nuclear power plants, seven nations, and the Department of Energy.

The process generates two main streams of liquid wastes, the fluoride stream and the nitrate stream. The fluoride stream is treated, and then discharged into the Illinois River under a National Pollutant Discharge Elimination System permit issued by the state. The nitrate stream is processed and discharged into a series of sludge ponds, most of which are at their capacity.

Some of the wastes are processed into a "byproduct" known as raffinate. Essentially a toxic sludge, the material contains radioactive elements like radium 26, thorium 230, and uranium as well as a host of other toxic and heavy metals. According to Kerr McGee's own data, the raffinate it sprayed in 1982 contained 178,000 percent more molybdenum than the maximum allowable concentration for irrigation water. Each year, the liquid (now in the form of raffinate) is used as a fertilizer on various portions of the site and other lands owned by the corporation. In total, over 10,000 acres of land are further exposed to radiation by the use of raffinate fertilizer. Over 11.8 million gallons of the fertilizer were used in 1986 alone. One of these sites is the Rabbit Hill Farms, where in 1987, 11,000 bales of hay from the farm were donated to Navajo sheepherders during a hard winter. "Although it hasn't been a banner year for the company, Kerr McGee decided to help because of our longstanding relationship with the Navajos because of mining and oil and gas leases in the area," the company explained.

There have been a number of spills at the site including an overflow of a settling basin in the spring of 1972, 1,450 pounds of uranium hexaflouride spilled into a surface stream in December of 1978, a major spill in December of 1980, and ongoing leaks at the bottom of raffinate pond number two, which has been leaching continuously into the groundwater for ten years. Dr. Richard Hayes Phillips, of the University of Oregon, conducted some research into the effluent discharge of the facility. His findings included the above statistics, and documentation of concentrations of uranium, radium, and thorium in the surface effluent stream which have been measured at 21.3, 2,387 and 5.15 times higher (respectively) than permissible levels.

Within a ten mile radius of the plant, over 200 cancers and birth defects have been recorded. In the town of Vian, population 1,500, 124 persons, or eight percent of the population, had cancer.

COAL STRIPMINING

In 1976, four out of the ten largest coal strip-mines in the country were on Indian lands. Today, the circumstances are very much the same, with over one-third of all western low-sulfur strippable coal reserves underlying Indian lands. The majority of the remaining resources are adjacent to the reservations. These statistics are particularly stark in light of a present move to develop low-sulfur coal resources as an alternative to more polluting coal supplies. The North Cheyenne reservation has been at the center of this conflict for almost two decades.

NORTH CHEYENNE COAL

The North Cheyenne reservation lies at the very center of the country's largest deposit of coal. The reservation itself has billions of tons of strippable coal, but the Cheyenne have vigorously opposed this exploitation for over thirty years. Multinational energy corporations working with the approval of the federal and state governments are surrounding the Cheyenne reservation with coal strip-mines, railroads, electric generating plants, and transmission lines. Indeed, the largest coal stripmine in the United States is fifteen miles from the reservation, and the four coal generating plants at Colstrip loom just off the reservation border.

The 500,000 acre reservation now sits adjacent to the Powder River coal lease. In 1982, the Secretary of the Interior sold federal public coal for pennies a ton along the entire eastern boundary of the reservation. This was the largest federal coal sale in the history of the United States. It stretches from the Wyoming border, running along the major water source, the Tongue River. Five to seven new coal stripmines are planned proximate to the reservation.

The environmental and social impacts of the coal stripmining are devastating. First of all, the present mining area is included in a vast region known for meager rainfall and limited reclamation potential. According to a 1973 study by the National Academy of Sciences, [in] "those areas receiving less than seven inches of rainfall, reclamation should not be attempted at all, and instead those lands should be designated as a National Sacrifice Area." The stripmining process divests the land of much of the aquifer system, disrupts groundwater systems, and contaminates a good portion of the remaining groundwater.

Centralized electrical generation causes relatively pristine regions, like the North Cheyenne and the adjacent Crow reservation, to bear the burden of reduced air quality, while the end user of electricity is relatively free from the pollution of production. The North Cheyenne, for a number of years, have sought to keep their air quality at a premium by designating their airspace as a "Class One" air quality standard, as recognized by the Environmental Protection Agency. Unfortunately, airborne contaminants from both the mining and the power plant process cause adverse health conditions for the Cheyenne people, including higher incidence of respiratory disease, and lower birth weights.

NAVAJO NATION: BIG MOUNTAIN

> My Mother Earth has been totally hurt. The Peabody Coal mine is going on and also uranium has been mined. We have been badly hurt and she has been hurt. Our ancestor told us that the land has guts just like a human. Heart, liver, lung. All of these things she has inside of her. And now all of these things are in critical condition. . . .
>
> Roberta Blackgoat, Diné Elder—
> Big Mountain

Similar circumstances occur in the region of the Navajo nation, where at least five coal-fired power plants are located on or adjacent to the reservation. One of those plants, the Four Corners Power Plant was the only man-made object seen by Gemini Two astronauts from outer space. These power plants are fueled by coal from mines such as Black Mesa, where after two decades of stripmining by Peabody Coal and General Electric, the groundwater is contaminated and the water table lowered. This has caused severe hardship to Navajo and Hopi people who live in the area. Perhaps the most significant impact, however, is the forced relocation of over ten thousand Navajo people (an estimated 2,553 families) from the area over the Black Mesa Coal Field. The field contains over twenty-two billion tons of coal, and is presently being mined, with new power plants and a new coal slurry pipeline proposed.

The relocation is legislated under federal law—the Navajo-Hopi Indian Relocation Act, which partitions into two equal parts 1.8 million acres of land formerly held in common by the two peoples. The removal of people from the area makes mining possible, causing their imminent cultural and psychological destruction. There is no word for relocation in Navajo, to move away simply means to disappear.

GWICHIN NATION

Gwichin territory spans the United States-Canadian border in what is known as the Yukon and Alaska. They have continuously inhabited that region for perhaps 30,000 years and retain a way of life based on the land, primarily the porcupine caribou herd, which numbers around 170,000. The health of the herd is essential to Gwichin survival since every year they may harvest up to 10,000 animals just for domestic consumption.

In light of the Persian Gulf war and insatiable demands for oil, pressure has been building to open up the Arctic National Wildlife Refuge to oil exploitation. The Refuge, presently referred to as America's Serengetti is huge and contains vast concentrations of wildlife. The nineteen million acre refuge hosts perhaps the largest complex Arctic ecosystem, as yet unaltered by industrialization. It is also the only coastline in Alaska still off limits to oil leasing, but it makes up only about 105 miles out of 1,200 miles of coastline.

Prudoe Bay and the Beaufort Sea lie just north of the Refuge, and through the Trans Alaska Pipeline system to Valdez, Alaska, presently supply around two and two tenths million barrels a day. This represents about a quarter of the United States' domestically produced crude oil, and one eighth of total daily consumption. It is estimated that by the year 2000, this oil will be depleted to the point where the pipeline will be operating at twenty-five percent capacity.

Oil in the Gwichin territory of the ANWR represents possibly less than 200 days of American oil needs. If the oil is exploited it will devastate the calving grounds of the porcupine caribou herd, and cause widespread desolation in the animals and the Gwichin. In the fall of 1991, legislation to open the refuge, pending in the American Congress was narrowly defeated.

HOBBEMA: THE IMPACT OF OIL EXPLOITATION

The Cree people near Hobbema, Alberta, have come under great stress as a direct result of oil exploitation in their territory. Four bands live adjacent to Hobbema—the Samson, Ermineskin, Louis Bull, and Montana bands—with a total population of around 6,500. Oil was discovered in their territory in the 1940s, but it was not until the 1970s that oil royalties began to flood into their coffers. By 1983, at the peak of the oil boom, the four bands were receiving

185 million dollars annually in royalties. Oil royalties gave the average Hobbema family 3,000 or more in monthly payments.

Social upheaval was a direct result of the rapid transition from a land based economy into a cash economy. A century ago, French sociologist Emil Durkheim found a strong connection between suicide and collective crisis. In an 1897 study of suicides in Italy, he charted the relationship between large-scale industrial growth, economic prosperity, and suicides. Incomes skyrocketed by thirty five percent between 1873 and 1889, suicides jumped thirty-six percent between 1871 and 1877 and another eight percent between 1877 and 1889. Similar statistics were reported in other countries undergoing rapid industrialism.

A study of the oil-rich bands of Alberta was commissioned by the Department of Indigenous Affairs in 1984. The study confirmed a similar syndrome—sudden wealth was causing profound social disruption in the bands. The unexpected influx of money led to alcoholism, drug addiction, and suicides. "When we had no money, we had a lot of family unity," recalls Theresa Bull, vice chairman of the Hobbema Health board. "Then we had all this money and people could buy anything they wanted. It replaced the old values. . . . It doesn't bring happiness. It put more value on materialistic possessions. The family and the value of spirituality got lost. . . ."

The town of Hobbema had one of the highest suicide rates in North America from 1980 to 1987. From 1985 to 1987, there was a violent death almost every week in Hobbema, and the suicide rate for young men was eighty-three times the national average. There are as many as three hundred suicide attempts by Hobbema Indians every year. The oil money "stripped them of self respect and dignity," said a social worker. Researchers believe that the true rate for Indian suicides nationally (in Canada) is twelve times the national average.

MERCURY CONTAMINATION AT GRASSY NARROWS

In 1956, the first massive outbreak of mercury poisoning occurred in Minimata Japan. By 1968, the Minimata disaster and the nature of mercury poisoning were well documented. No less than 183 medical papers have been published on the subject. By that year, the number of deaths from the poisoning in Japan had approached 100, with several thousand maimed.

In 1960, four years after the Minimata disaster, Dryden Pulp and Paper began to contaminate the Wabigoon River with suspended solids. In March of 1962, Reed Paper opened its Dryden chlor alkali plant which used mercury to bleach paper products, and then released it into the river to form toxic methyl mercury. An estimated twenty pounds of mercury per day were released into the river. On September 8, 1975, the Ontario Minister of Health publicly admitted that twenty to thirty of the Native people living on the Grassy Narrows reserve had shown symptoms of Minimata disease. He also publicly admitted that they may have underestimated the severity of the problem. Tests were reported where Native people had as high as 358 parts per billion mercury in their blood, but at that time did not show signs of mercury poisoning. Mercury poisoning, however, accumulates in the body over time.

Commercial fishing was closed down, causing a total disruption in the economy. An attempt at getting unpolluted fish from a lake near the White Dog reserve failed when non-Indian lodge owners in the vicinity successfully appropriated the lakes' fish for tourism. With commercial fishing banned since 1970, unemployment on the reserves rose over eighty percent. Between 1969 and 1974 welfare tripled on the White Dog Reserve. At Grassy Narrows, it nearly quadrupled from 29,000 dollars to 122,000 dollars. During that same period of time (between January 1970 and June 1972), 200 Native people in the Kenora area died violent deaths. Since in its early stages mercury poisoning can lead to highly destructive behavior, sometimes falsely associated with alcoholism, this report should have been enough to initiate a fullscale study of mercury poisoning among the Native people.

Mercury discharge continued, virtually unabated until 1970, when more than 20,000 pounds of mercury had been dumped into the English-Wabigoon River system (with 30,000 pounds more unaccounted for). Mercury is in the English River system, and unlike Minimata Japan, which has the advantage of ocean currents, it will take an estimated sixty to one hundred years to clean itself out. There is no evidence that Dryden is even going to clean up the mercury pool below the plant, which is still being flushed into the river system.

ALBERTA TIMBER SALES

The province of Alberta has dealt away timberlands almost the size of Great Britain. This new land rush was completed in December of 1988, with the primary beneficiary being the Japanese multinational Diashowa. Diashowa just completed construction of a pulp mill ten kilometers north of the village of Peace River, and has plans for building two more.

The Alberta government granted Diashowa a twenty year lease to 25,000 square kilometers adjacent to the Peace River, and an additional 15,000 square kilometers plus money for roads, rail lines and a bridge. The company also purchased the rights to log the Wood Buffalo National Park, the last great stand of old-growth spruce in Alberta. The lease expires in 2002, and the mill will pump 5,000 tons of chlorinated organic compounds into the Peace River annually. The land leased to Diashowa overlaps with the traditional lands of the Lubicon Lake First Nation.

The Lubicon Cree have been opposing any development in their territory since they were invaded by oil companies in the late 1970s. By 1982, there were over 400 oil wells in their territory, and traditional hunting and trapping trails were turned into company roads. The ability of the people to sustain themselves from the land decreased significantly. Trapping incomes were devastated, and welfare soared from ten percent in 1980 to ninety-five percent in 1983. While the people suffered, an estimated one million dollars worth of oil was extracted daily from the land.

EMISSIONS DISCHARGE

Formaldehyde is a water soluble gas that is known to irritate the eyes, respiratory tract, and skin. It is also a suspected carcinogen, and has been linked to cancer of the skin, lungs, and nasal passages. Airborne formaldehyde can cause ocular damage and allergic dermatitis. Young children and the elderly are especially vulnerable to the effects of this toxin.

At the rate of between twenty-two and thirty-two pounds per hour, the Potlatch Timber Corporation near Cook, Minnesota is emitting formaldehyde into the air over the Nett Lake reservation. At the conservative rate of twenty-two pounds per hour, this figure represents 164,208 pounds annually of emissions.

HYDRO-ELECTRIC EXPLORATION

James Bay, at the base of Hudson Bay, is the largest drainage system on the North American continent. Virtually every major river in the heartland ends up there. This makes the bay a rich ecosystem teeming with wildlife, the staging ground for migratory birds, and a feeding area for the largest migratory herd of mammals on the continent—the George's River Caribou herd. Approximately 35,000 Cree, Innu, Inuit, and Ojibway people live within the region and are dependent upon the ecosystem. The way of life is landbased subsistence—hunting, harvesting, and tourism economy in which at least fifty percent of the food and income for the region originates.

The James Bay I project, introduced in 1972, was intended to produce 10,000 megawatts of electricity by putting eleven and one-half square kilometers of land under water and behind dams. The project concentrated along the East Main and Rupert Rivers and ruined the ecology of some 176,000 square kilometers, an area about two-thirds the size of West Germany. The Native people of the area did not hear of the project until planning was well underway.

Following years of futile litigation, 400 kilometers of paved road, three power stations, and five reservoirs were built. Four major rivers were destroyed and five 735 KV powerlines cut a swath through the wilderness. The environmental impact is enormous. Mercury levels at the reservoirs are six times safe levels, and some two-thirds of the people downstream from the reservoirs have mercury contamination in their bodies, some at thirty times the allowable level. Vast amounts of hunting and trapping territory have been devastated, causing economic and social dislocation from loss of food and cultural activities.

If the project continues, Phase Two will be even more devastating. The area to be impacted is the size of New England, or 356,000 square miles. These projects, according to Jan Bayea of the National Audubon Society will mean that ". . . in fifty years, this entire ecosystem will be lost."

TOXIC WASTE DUMPS

> When Waste Tech wanted to build an incinerator and dump on our land, they said they would give us thousands of dollars and a nice two-story house. But I thought about the land and how we rely on it—this dump would poison the water and the land. It's not just temporary, my children and grandchildren will have to live on this land forever. Don't listen to these thieves that want our land—we need to protect Mother Earth. . . .
>
> Jane Yazzie, one of the organizers of Citizens Against Ruining Our Environment, which helped defeat a toxic waste dump proposal at Dilcon on the Navajo reservation

Most insidious is the recent set of proposals to dispose of toxic wastes in Native communities. Largely a result of stiff and successful opposition in urban areas, toxic waste operators have increasingly looked to reservations and so-called third world countries as possible disposal sites. The "labor pool" and "underdeveloped economies" of many reservations provide an apparent mandate for development. Additionally, the sovereign status of Indian nations, exempt from state and local laws, in which there is minimal federal regulation of waste dumping, has provided an additional incentive.

In the past few years, over forty-five Indian communities have been approached by waste companies offering multi-million dollar contracts in exchange for the right to dump or incinerate on Indian lands. East of San Diego alone, over eighteen rancherias (small Indian communities) have been approached as possible dumping grounds for garbage and toxic wastes. One community that has already been impacted by a toxic waste dump is the Akwesasne Mohawk reservation.

AKWESASNE

The Akwesasne Mohawk reservation spans the United States/Canadian border, and is home to approximately 8,000 Mohawk people. Through the center of their territory is the St. Lawrence River, the waterway of their people. For generations, the Mohawk have relied upon the river for fish, food, and transportation. Today, the river is full of poison.

In Canada, the Akwesasne reserve has been singled out from sixty-three Native communities located in the Great Lakes basin as the most contaminated. On the American side in 1983, the Environmental Protection Agency designated the area as one of the top "Superfund sites" in the United States.

The General Motors Massena Central Foundry is possibly the most significant PCB dump site in North America. The chemical is known to cause brain, nerve, liver and skin disorders in humans and cancer and reproductive disorders in laboratory animals. Five PCB saturated lagoons, and a number of sludge pits dot GM's 258 acre property, a site adjacent to the reservation. Contaminant Cove, at the conflux of the Grasse and St. Lawrence Rivers, is perhaps the worst. According to the Environmental Protection Agency, fifty parts per million PCBs is classified as hazardous waste. Sludge and vegetation at the bottom of Contaminant Cove have been documented at 3,000 parts per million. A male snapping turtle was located with 3,067 parts per million of PCBs in its body.

At present, a project known as the Akwesasne Mothers Milk Project is undertaking a study of breastmilk, fetal cord, and urine samples of Mohawk mothers on the reservation. A total of 168 women are participating in the study. The primary organizer of the project, Katsi Cook Barreiro, is a practicing midwife who has delivered many children on the reservation. "I've got myself four one hundredths parts per million of mirex (a flame retardant) and eighty-four one-thousandths parts per million PCBs in my body," she explains. "This means that there may be a potential exposure of our future generations. The analysis of Mohawk mother's milk shows that our bodies are, in fact, a part of the landfill."

NUCLEAR WASTE CONTAMINATION

The Hanford nuclear reservation is well within the treaty area of the Yakima Indian Nation on the Columbia River. The nuclear site contains 570 square miles of land, and a significant portion of it is contaminated with radiation. In August of 1973, over 115,000 gallons of liquid high-level radioactive waste seeped into the ground from a leaking storage tank. The waste contained cesium 137, strontium 90, and plutonium. Other leaks from August of 1958 to June two decades later included over 422,000 gallons reported on the site.

Soil at the site is so contaminated that much has been removed as high-level radioactive waste. The Department of Energy changed concentrations from ten nanocuries per gram of soil permitting a rise to 100 nanocuries per gram of soil allowing for plutonium contamination to rise indefinitely at the site by changing the definition of high-level waste.

Hanford produces a dry fallout of small respirable dust particles that are contaminated with plutonium. This airborne dust is released from smokestacks at the site, and is not contained by the site boundaries.

A significant portion of these wastes are contaminating the air and water in the region of the Hanford reservation, an area in which approximately twenty different Indigenous peoples live.

INUIT BREASTMILK

Studies of Inuit breastmilk in the Hudson Bay region of northern Canada indicate that Inuit women have levels of PCB contamination higher than those recorded anywhere else in the world. The maximum PCB concentration considered "safe" by the Canadian government is one and five tenths parts per million. A Laval University Study, conducted by Dr. Eric Dewailly, in 1988, discovered much higher levels in Inuit women. Dewailly's study of twenty-four samples (one third of all nursing mothers in that year), recorded an average concentration of three and fifty-nine hundredths parts per million of PCBs in breastmilk. Some samples were recorded at fourteen and seven tenths parts per million. The average concentration of PCBs in breastmilk in Quebec is five tenths parts per million.

According to an Inuit spokesperson, Mary Kaye May of the Kativik Regional Health Council, the findings brought "fear and great sadness" to the village. It is assumed that the higher levels are attributed to the Inuit diet of fish and marine mammals (at least nine meals per month) which are known to be concentrating PCBs in the food chain. The PCBs have appeared in the Arctic food chain in recent years, largely attributed to atmospheric distribution of heavy metals, and toxins from southern industries, and from abandoned military, radar, and communications installations utilizing PCBs.

While the toxic contamination of infants is of great concern to the Inuit, there are, for all major purposes, no alternatives. "If the women stop breastfeeding," Mary Kaye May continues, "and with the cost of baby formula at seventeen dollars a can, we will face a frightening number of cases of infant malnutrition."

Related contamination includes radioactive cesium, DDT, toxophene, and other pesticides. Many of them have been banned in North America, but are still used in many developing countries. Dr. Lyle Lockhart (Canadian government Fisheries and Oceans Department, Winnipeg, Manitoba) indicates that "toxins will distill off the warm land and plant surfaces in many of these countries and circulate in the air possibly for years, and gradually condense and accumulate in colder regions like the Arctic and Antarctic, which are becoming the world's dump for these things." As an example, toxophene, a pesticide most commonly used in cotton fields was discovered in a study by Lockhart to be located in the livers of two freshwater fish taken in the Mackenzie River of the Northwest Territories. The severity of the problem is indicated in another study of the polar bear which, because of its high level on the food chain, could be forced into extinction by the year 2006 due to sterility caused by PCB contamination.

ACID RAIN CONTAMINATION

The Anishinabeg treaty areas of northern Michigan, Wisconsin, and Minnesota are impacted by airborne contamination from acid rain at an alarming level. The traditional Anishinabeg diet consists, to a great extent of wild rice, fish, deer, waterfowl, fruits, and herbs. The major protein sources comprising the traditional diet are foods most impacted by acid rain.

Acid pollution is accumulating in the northern lakes, and during spring run-off causes toxic shock to the northern ecosystem, eliminating millions of fish eggs, young fry, molting crayfish, and other animals on the food chain. The secondary impact is the leaching of heavy metals, including mercury into the food system as a result of the acidification process. Presently a number of lakes in the northern area have fish consumption advisories due to mercury contamination. Since 1970, Minnesota has documented a five percent per year increase of mercury in fish tissue. This contamination is attributed to atmospheric deposits originating from coal fired power plants and garbage incinerators. At the present rate of increase, by the year 2015 mercury concentrations in fish tissue will be dangerously high.

MILITARY OCCUPATION

"The militarization, that's what you have to fight," explains Francesca Snow, an Innu woman who has been working actively to stop the siting of a NATO base in her homeland. "They will destroy the land. They will destroy the animals, and they will destroy our life." Father Alexis Jouveneau, a priest who has lived with the Innu for many years, issued a warning to the Canadian government about the NATO base, "You are destroying not only their lifestyle, you are destroying their whole life so that you may proceed with military exercises. At that point, you might as well build a psychiatric clinic right here, and it will soon be over-filled." "If the military goes ahead," says Innu elder Antoine Malec, "You will not see us cry. We will not cry, but our hearts will bleed. . . ."

THE WESTERN SHOSHONE NATION

All nuclear weapon states explode their bombs on unconsenting nations. No nuclear state tests bombs on its own lands and people. The United States doesn't set off nuclear weapons in Santa Barbara or Washington D.C. It bombs the Western Shoshone Nation.

Since 1963, the United States has exploded 651 nuclear weapons and "devices" on Newe Sogobia, the Western Shoshone nation. Because they cause destruction, the 670 nuclear explosions in Newe Sogobia have been classified by the Western Shoshone National Council as bombs rather than tests.

In 1863, the representatives of the United States and Western Shoshone nation signed the Treaty of Ruby Valley. The United States proposed the treaty in order to end Shoshone armed defense of Sogobia, acquire gold from the territory, and establish safe routes to California. The United States Senate ratified the treaty in 1866 and President Grant confirmed it in 1869. The treaty is still in effect.

The nation of Newe Sogobia has an area of 43,000 square miles, about the size of Honduras, and is bounded by western Nevada, southern Idaho and southeastern California. To maintain control over the area, the United States has usurped almost ninety percent of Shoshone land and resources and placed them under the Departments of Interior, Energy, Defense, Transportation, and other agencies. The Western Shoshone, however continue their occupancy of their traditional lands. They have maintained this, and resisted government efforts to terminate their title through the Court of Claims, by continuing their opposition to a twenty-six million dollar proposal to "settle" their claims and compensate them for their land.

In a recent effort to secure occupancy of the land, the Bureau of Land Management has been attempting to remove the livestock of the Dann family, one of the leading families in challenging the occupation.

HAWAII

Hawaii was the last frontier in an era of United States expansion. It was designated as a state in 1959, eighteen years after Pearl Harbor. Over 180,000 Native Hawaiian people have traditional rights to most of the Islands, and today maintain a precarious land-based existence in the face of increasing tourism and military occupation.

Hawaii is the most militarized state in the country, serving as the center for the Pentagon's Pacific Command. It serves as the headquarters for military activities which purport to control more than half the earth's surface—from the west coast of North America to the east coast of Africa, from the Antarctic to the Arctic.

There are more than 100 military installations in the Hawaiian islands and fully ten percent of the state and twenty-five percent of Oahu are under direct federal control. Hawaii is the loading and reloading base for the Pacific fleet. In 1972, Oahu alone was the storage site for some 32,000 nuclear weapons. One island of the Hawaiian archipelago, Kaho'olawe was a bombing site for almost five decades for Pacific rim countries. . . .

PULLING DOWN THE CLOUDS

Ofeliá Zepeda

Ñ-ku'ibadkaj 'ant 'an ols g cewagĭ.
With my harvesting stick I will hook the clouds.
'Ant o'i-waññ'io k o 'i-hudiñ g cewagĭ.
With my harvesting stick I will pull down the clouds.
Ñ-ku'ibadkaj 'ant o 'i-siho g cewagĭ.
With my harvesting stick I will stir the clouds.

With dreams of distant noise disturbing his sleep.
the smell of dirt, wet, for the first time in what seems like months.
The change in the molecules is sudden, they enter the nasal cavity.

He contemplates that smell.
What is that smell?
It is rain.

Rain somewhere out in the desert.
Comforted in this knowledge he turns over and continues his sleep,
dreams of women with harvesting sticks raised toward the sky.

"Pulling Down the Clouds" from *Ocean Power* by Ofeliá Zepeda. © 1995 Ofeliá Zepeda. Reprinted with the permission of the University of Arizona Press.

NATIVE AMERICAN LABOR AND PUBLIC POLICY IN THE UNITED STATES

Alice Littlefield

United States policy toward the indigenous peoples within its borders has experienced a series of shifts, usually described as swings back and forth between a policy of assimilation and a policy of self-determination. Major swings of this nature occurred during the 1880s (with the General Allotment Act and the expansion of the off-reservation boarding school system), the 1930s (with the reversal of allotment, recognition of tribal rights of self-government, and the curtailment of the boarding school system) and the 1945–55 decade (with accelerated resolution of land claims, termination of reservations, and urban relocation). Studies and critiques of these major policy shifts have frequently noted that the assimilation policies often failed to assimilate, and that the self-determination policies often failed to provide for meaningful self-determination. Looking beyond the discourse of the reformers who claimed credit for these policy shifts, it can be observed that the material interests of various sectors of American capital

Alice Littlefield, "Native American Labor and Public Policy in the United States," *Marxist Approaches in Economic Anthropology,* Monographs in Economic Anthropology, No. 9. Copyright 1991 by Society for Economic Anthropology. University Press of America. Reprinted with permission. References that appeared in the original have been omitted.

were often well-served by the workings of particular policies.

Scholars of federal Indian policy have described how the demands of settlers, land speculators, railroads, mining companies, and other large corporations for access to Indian-owned land, timber, and mineral resources affected the policy-making process. Although these interests were certainly of great importance, I argue that changing labor needs dictated by the larger economy were also important in decisions to expand or retrench particular programs. In doing so, I challenge a tendency toward "American exceptionalism" in the analyses of U.S. policy toward the indigenous peoples within its borders.

Over the past twenty years, analyses of colonialism and dependency in Latin America, South Africa, and elsewhere have pointed to the frequency with which the separation of indigenous peoples from their means of production forced them into the wage labor market. Such policies provided dual advantages to national and transnational capital: the capitalists not only gained access to valuable resources (often at below-market cost); they simultaneously acquired a cheap labor force to work the lands, timber reserves, or mines. At the same time, these agricultural and extractive enterprises often experienced seasonal variations in labor needs, or fluctuations in world markets which affected the demand for their products. It was thus convenient for employers that indigenous workers retain enough resources to eke out their own subsistence during periods of unemployment, thereby reducing the cost to the employer of shelving labor during periods of low demand. Indeed, some Marxists, dating back to Rosa Luxemburg, argue that the existence of such subordinate modes of production is necessary to the reproduction of the dominant capitalist mode of production.

Analyses of the United States, on the other hand, have tended to regard the labor of the indigenous people as irrelevant to capitalist development. It has been argued that indigenous labor was quantitatively insignificant compared with the role played by European, Asian, and Mexican immigration in meeting the demands of an expanding economy for cheap labor. In recent decades, the significant role of indigenous labor has been obscured by high reservation unemployment rates.

In this paper, I hope not only to situate the issue of labor in the analysis, but to argue that major shifts in federal policy were more than responses to swings in the business cycle. Rather, periods of policy reform coincided with periods of major restructuring of the national and international economies, and consequently with restructuring in the deployment of labor.

In what follows, I attempt to sketch out the lines of such an analysis, without filling in all the supportive details—a task which would require a far more lengthy work. In attempting to deal with national and international trends, I necessarily generalize at a level which excludes much of the complexity and variation in the specific trajectories

experienced by particular indigenous groups. Some tribes, such as the Navajo, entered the wage labor force in significant numbers rather later than did others, and were less affected by the allotment policy than were the peoples further east.

1880–1930: ASSIMILATION OR PROLETARIANIZATION?

In the latter half of the nineteenth century, the frontier regions of the United States filled rapidly with Euro-American settlers, the railroads penetrated the most remote areas, and the shift from subsistence to commercial agriculture accelerated throughout the continent.

As in other developing capitalist countries, all pre-capitalist economic relations in the United States, such as the slave-based economy of the Southern states, came under attack and were either destroyed or modified to meet the needs of capital. With regard to the indigenous peoples, their communal economies were undermined, and their land and labor transformed into commodities, through the twin policies of allotment and education.

The earlier policy of treating with the tribes as sovereign nations and persuading them to relocate beyond the frontier of settlement became obsolete as the frontier itself disappeared. A variety of interests clamored for changes in federal policy. The most vocal reformers of the period consistently raised two demands: (1) the allotment in severalty of reservation lands; and (2) the expansion of federal efforts to educate Indians in the practical activities which characterized the rural economy of the dominant society.

These demands led to the General Allotment Act (often called the Dawes Act) of 1887. It provided for the allotment of reservation lands to individual natives, usually in 160-acre plots, with "surplus" lands opened up to Euro-American settlers. Once a tribe's land had been allotted, the allottees were to become full U.S. citizens, with full civil rights and obligations, including the payment of taxes.

This period also brought a major expansion of the off-reservation boarding school system operated by the Bureau of Indian Affairs. Nineteen off-reservation schools were established between 1878 and 1893, beginning with the Carlisle School in Pennsylvania. All emphasized the teaching of English and vocational skills, and the eradication of Indian customs.

The effects of these policies were quite different from those anticipated by the "Friends of the Indian" who pushed for them. Allotment was supposed to encourage the development of Native American farming; in practice, it brought a decline in indigenous farming. Many allotments were lost through sale, debt, or fraud as soon as they became alienable, and many others were leased to Euro-American farmers rather than worked by their owners. Only a small proportion of allottees became moderately prosperous independent farmers.

Numerous studies have attested to the effects of the allotment programs in separating the indigenes from their means of production. Between 1887 and 1934, when the policy was finally repealed, the Native American land base was reduced from 139 million acres to 48 million acres. Two-thirds of the land lost during this period disappeared during the first decade of allotment, through sales of "surplus" lands to settlers.

The off-reservation boarding schools were designed to assist the process of allotment by teaching indigenous youth the skills of the Euro-American settlers. In addition to reading and writing in English, boys were taught carpentry, smithing, harness-making, and agricultural skills; girls learned Euro-American styles of cleaning, sewing, cooking, and food preservation.

In practice, however, the skills learned were often found to have little application in the reservation setting. Over time, the schools tended to become employment agencies, channelling indigenous youth into rural wage labor. After a few years' instruction, boys were sent to work on farms, ranches and railroads; girls became domestic servants. In balance, the effect of the schools was more one of proletarianization than assimilation.

The vocal reformers who lobbied for these policies appear to have envisioned a future in which Native Americans would be assimilated into the class of small-scale independent farmers. During the period under consideration, however, American society was already changing. Enterprises, both industrial and agricultural, were increasing in size, and ever-larger masses of cheap labor were needed to feed economic expansion. Grain cultivation in the Great Plains was already becoming highly commercialized and increasingly mechanized. The labor needs of agriculture were shifting away from the permanent hired hand to the use of large numbers of seasonal workers. Further West, railroad expansion facilitated the rapid growth of commercial livestock production and, somewhat later, the introduction of specialized, labor-intensive crops such as cotton, citrus, and sugar beets.

The railroads were among the most powerful business interests lobbying to break up the reservations and turn the "surplus" lands over to settlers. By 1880, the capital stock of railroads amounted to $5.4 billion, rivalling the combined value of industrial capital ($2.7 billion) and commercial bank assets ($3.4 billion). The rail companies were often able to negotiate rights of way through treaty lands, but then found that, to be profitable, they required vastly expanded commercial production in the areas through which their roads passed.

The allotment policies greatly facilitated the growth of commercial agriculture throughout the Plains and Far West, as well as providing greater opportunities for mining operations. All of these activities, and the building of the roads themselves, required an abundant supply of cheap labor.

Before the indigenous peoples could be drawn into the rural wage labor force, however, several obstacles had to be overcome. They had to be separated from their means of production, and during the period under consideration this was largely accomplished through the allotment policy. Rations and annuities, which allowed Indians to survive without working for others, were phased out. Finally, education was necessary to teach the natives English and disciplined work habits. It was reasoned that the boarding schools could accomplish this best by separating the children from their parents and communities.

In Congress, support for these reforms, including the boarding school system, came most consistently from Northeastern Republicans. Rapid development of the West was actively supported by dominant business interests based in the Northeast, including the railroad companies. Western expansion also provided ready access to supplies of raw materials and markets for growing Northeastern industries.

Western politicians were less supportive of these initiatives in federal Indian policy. Some favored taking over all of the reservation lands, and opposed wasting money trying to educate savages. Support gradually grew, however, when it was seen that allotment would place large amounts of Indian

land on the market, and that the boarding schools injected federal dollars into local economies and provided cheap child labor to local employers.

The reforms coincided with the onset of a national and international transition from competitive to monopoly capital. The railroads and large-scale commercial agriculture were expanding throughout the hemisphere, often financed by international capital. Both Mexico and Guatemala also enacted policies during this period aimed at facilitating expropriation of indigenous peoples' lands and the utilization of their labor in cash-crop production.

By 1930, the wage labor force in the United States had absorbed a significant proportion of the indigenous population. Almost half of indigenous men reported as employed in agriculture were employed as farm laborers (25,124) rather than as farmers (26,521). Others were employed in rural non-agricultural activities, such as lumbering, especially in the Great Lakes region and the Northwest. Census figures indicate that only 9.9 percent of the indigenous population lived in cities in 1930. The concentration of Native Americans in rural areas may have led researchers to overlook their heavy dependence on wage labor in the early part of this century.

THE 1930s: NEW DEAL; SAME GAME

During the 1920s, debate over federal Indian policy grew. The shortcomings of the allotment policy and the boarding school system were increasingly criticized. With the advent of the Great Depression, Congress was receptive to new initiatives in Indian affairs, as in other matters.

Among the voices which had been clamoring for reform during the 1920s was John

Collier. A Democrat with close ties to Harold Ickes (Roosevelt's Secretary of Interior), Collier was placed in charge of the Bureau of Indian Affairs in 1933 and was largely responsible for steering the Indian Reorganization Act through Congress in 1934.

In its original version, the IRA represented a far-reaching attempt to reconstitute tribal economies and polities by consolidating dispersed allotments under the control of tribal governments. Collier had a strong faith in the ability of communities to deal with their problems through collective action. During the Congressional hearings on the IRA, he cited Mexico's system of rural collectives or *ejidos* as an example which he hoped to emulate among U.S. Indians.

The original version of the IRA was opposed by Western Congressmen, and the law that was eventually passed simply provided that no further allotments of remaining tribal lands would be undertaken. Some provision was made for voluntary consolidation and government purchase of lands, and about two million acres of land was added to the indigenous land base during the New Deal period. About half of this came from the public domain.

The IRA also provided for the formation of tribal governments with specified rights of self-determination. The Bureau, however, continued to exercise significant control over the economic affairs of the tribes, including the leasing of agricultural lands and mineral rights.

Collier's BIA also moved to close some of the Bureau's boarding schools, to create more community day schools, and to place indigenous children in state-funded public schools wherever possible. These changes had been advocated for some time, and earlier steps in this direction had been taken under the Hoover Administration. In 1934, the Johnson-O'Malley Act was passed to facilitate the transfer of educational responsibilities to the states. The remaining boarding schools were restructured to emphasize secondary education and vocational training more suitable to the changing economy.

Collier conceived of the reservation day schools as community institutions which would support community economic development, and toward this end a number of innovations were made in the curriculum and operations of the schools. Aspects of traditional culture, especially arts and crafts, were given recognition in the curriculum, and some bilingual materials were developed.

In retrospect, Collier's reforms have usually been seen as positive for the indigenous peoples, with the exception of such frequently cited disasters as the Navajo livestock reduction program. Obviously, reforms which sought to strengthen tribal institutions were accepted in part because of the unusual political context of the early 1930s, when innovative reforms occurred in many aspects of public policy. Nonetheless, it seems relevant to examine more closely the economic context which shaped these policies, and the interests which were ultimately served by their implementation.

Although we think of the Great Depression as occurring on the heels of the stock market cash of 1929, American agriculture had been suffering from depressed conditions since the recession of 1921. The late 1920s brought a wave of farm bankruptcies and continued low prices for agricultural products. In some parts of the country, drought and other natural disasters exacerbated farmers' problems. For many Indian allottees, income from both farming and leasing declined or disappeared. Rural unemployment rates were high.

The allotment policy had responded to conditions of growing demand for land by both settlers and speculators. As the rural depression set in, land prices fell. Consequently, a policy which put an end to allotment was acceptable to both indigenous and non-indigenous farming interests during this period. For corporate agribusiness and mining enterprises, the end of allotment could even be seen as advantageous. It was often easier and cheaper to acquire leases to large areas when these were consolidated under tribal ownership or BIA control rather than dispersed among hundreds or thousands of allottees. Federal policies which vastly expanded public lands during the Depression also served in part to shore up land prices.

The market for rural labor was likewise declining during the same period. Indians who had been encouraged to seek jobs in mining, lumbering, and commercial agriculture found less and less demand for their labor as the crisis deepened.

The New Deal economic programs for Indians had two thrusts. One was to encourage subsistence farming through tribal development projects and tribal loan funds. The other was to employ large numbers of natives in work programs, especially the Indian Emergency Conservation Works, the Indian version of the Civilian Conservation Corps. During the course of its existence, about 85,000 indigenous youth were employed by the IECW, and most of them sent money home to their families. Given a total indigenous population of about 400,000 in the U.S. during the 1930s, it can be estimated that a significant proportion of all Native American families derived some income from this program. The IECW projects also made significant improvements on tribal lands in terms of soil conservation, reforestation, pasture improvement and the like. Ironically, many of these improvements

benefitted Euro-American lessees when the demand for land again increased during the 1940s.

Collier was frequently accused of launching programs that were romantic or even communistic because of their emphasis on community self-sufficiency. Congress systematically underfunded certain aspects of the program, especially land acquisition. Viewed from another angle, however, the New Deal programs served the interests of corporate capital. As with other federal programs of the period, they served to maintain a large reserve of labor during a period of low labor demand. Just as immigrant Mexican laborers were sent back across the border until needed again in the 1940s, Indian laborers were sent back to the reservations to support themselves through subsistence agriculture.

As for the changes in education policy, these supported the shifts in land and employment policies. An interesting continuity with the earlier period was the ideology that BIA schools could teach natives to be better small-scale farmers. This continuity in theory, however, masks an important shift in practice. The off-reservation boarding school system, whatever its stated aims, was more successful at channelling young people into the wage labor force than in making small farmers out of them. This was even the stated aim of Indian education for some policymakers of the earlier era, including Francis Leupp, Commissioner of Indian Affairs from 1905 to 1909.

By the 1930s, however, rural unemployment had assumed enormous and troubling proportions. Educational policy had to become congruent with economic policy. Hence the innovations in community schools to support community-level economic development projects. As the demand for rural wage labor dried up, the BIA turned toward reconstituting the indigenous polities, economies, and cultures it had once tried so hard to destroy.

THE POST-WAR PERIOD:
RETURN TO ASSIMILATION?

The preoccupation of the federal government with World War II brought an end to much of the Indian New Deal by the early 1940s. In the decade after the War, prevailing opinion among those making Indian policy held that it was time to end the wardship status of the tribes and to dismantle special government programs for indigenous people. Several new policy initiatives reflected these goals.

The Indian Claims Commission was established in 1946 to expedite the process of resolving Indian land claims. The legislation specifically precluded land restoration as a remedy for tribes or individuals, allowing only monetary compensation for the value of the lands lost at the time they were taken. Some Congressmen saw Indian land claims as obstacles to the withdrawal of federal responsibility from the tribes. Expediting the resolution of such claims, though costly, would in the long run facilitate government withdrawal of services, and the monies awarded would allow for Indian integration into the general population. The Claims Commission legislation also coincided with renewed capitalist demand for indigenous lands for agriculture, lumbering and mineral extraction.

Several bills to terminate federal recognition of the tribes and the trust status of their lands were introduced in Congress in the 1945–53 period. Most were phrased in terms of civil rights—that is, freeing Indians from the restrictions imposed on them by existing laws and policies.

Dillon S. Myer, appointed Commissioner by President Truman in March 1950, was an advocate of immediate termination and dissolution of the BIA. He pushed leftover Collier appointees out of the BIA and replaced them with people who shared his views.

House Concurrent Resolution 108, better known as the termination resolution, passed Congress without serious debate in July 1953. HCR 108 enunciated the aim of Congress to make Indians subject to the same privileges and responsibilities as other citizens as rapidly as possible, thus ending their status as wards of the government. Senator Arthur Watkins of Utah compared it to the Emancipation Proclamation.

HCR 108 singled out thirteen tribes for withdrawal of trust status. By 1960, the government had processed 109 cases of termination affecting 1.3 million acres of Indian land and about 12,000 Indians. Most of these terminations, however, were carried out in the short period from 1954 to 1956. By 1958, Interior Secretary Fred Seaton announced that the administration would no longer support legislation to terminate tribes without their consent. This semi-reversal was in part a response to mounting opposition from the tribes, as well as from states which did not want to assume the cost of providing services to Indians. It is worth noting, however, that the loss of termination momentum also coincided with a period of economic recession.

HCR 108 was accompanied by Public Law 280, passed in August 1953. PL 280 transferred civil and criminal jurisdiction over reservations to the state governments in five states: California, Minnesota, Nebraska, Oregon and Wisconsin. It was envisioned by its supporters as a first step toward complete transfer of Indian affairs to the states.

World War II had interrupted federal economic development programs for reservations, and they were not revived in the post-war period. In December, 1951, Myer announced a basic program of training and placement for those Indians who wanted to seek jobs off the reservations. Thus began the urban relocation program, the latest in a long history of relocation programs for indigenous peoples. What was different about this one was its emphasis on moving Native Americans into the heart of the large industrial cities. Further, they were to move as individuals or families, not as tribes or communities. Myer had accumulated experience with relocation through his direction of wartime relocation for Japanese Americans.

The relocation program included provisions for adult vocational education in construction, auto mechanics, cosmetology and other skills expected to be useful in seeking urban employment. From the end of World War II through 1957, an estimated 100,000 Indians left reservations, most to seek jobs in urban areas. Three-quarters of these, however, made the transition without federal assistance. Clearly, the urban relocation program simply facilitated a trend that was occurring anyway, as urban industry expanded and agriculture became ever more mechanized. People moved to the cities because that's where the jobs were, and because federal support for reservation economic development had been curtailed. In the context of an expanding post-war economy, the movement of native labor from the countryside to urban areas was supported and subsidized by government policy.

By 1970, 45 percent of Indians responding to the Census lived in urban areas, and about half of these lived in large metropolitan areas. The period from 1950 to 1970 was also marked by sharp declines in farm-related employment, and increases in both non-farm employment and unemployment. Even on reservations, income from agriculture fell to an estimated 12 percent of family income. By 1970, only 2.3 percent of Indian males were classified as farmers and 5.7 percent as farm laborers, compared to 46.7 percent and 21.7 percent respectively in 1940.

The post-war reforms, with their emphasis on abolishing the reservations and incorporating rural natives into the urban labor force, reflected the period of economic expansion which followed World War II. Industrial production in the U.S. was stimulated by pent-up domestic demand and by the rebuilding of Europe. Most importantly, it was during this period that overseas markets and U.S. foreign investment vastly expanded in the regions now referred to as the Third World. The U.S. had become the major global economic power.

In the context of this post-war economic expansion, there was a strong demand for labor in the U.S., and the labor unions had achieved unprecedented strength. Policies which could increase the labor supply while holding down its cost, including those policies described here, were in line with employers' needs.

CONCLUSIONS

Existing analyses of Indian policy in the United States have tended to focus on the ideas and efforts of individual reformers and politicians, and to view the results of their efforts in terms of good intentions gone awry. Few attempts have been made to situate these events in the context of major shifts taking place in the larger political economy.

In this paper, I have pointed out that major changes in federal Indian policy coincided with periods of significant restructuring of the national and international economies, and I have argued that the policies that were adopted at each of these major turning points served the interests of the dominant sectors of capital emerging in each period.

I have also argued that the policies adopted were based not only on the needs of an expanding economy for land and other natural resources, but also on the need for ready supplies of cheap labor. Although immigration from Europe, Asia, and Mexico supplied a large part of this need through the late nineteenth and early twentieth centuries, Native Americans were also channelled into the rural and later urban wage labor force as a result of the policies pursued by the federal government. This process has been overlooked in earlier analyses, perhaps because of the high reservation unemployment rates of recent decades.

If the assumptions informing this analysis are valid, significant changes in federal indigenous policy can be expected in the next decade. The current restructuring of the global economy is changing the old equations in several important ways. Among other things, the demand for unskilled and semi-skilled labor is being reduced through the deployment of radically new technology, while there is increasing pressure to exploit natural resources on tribal and public lands.

Current controversies over treaty rights, Indian gaming, and corruption in tribal government suggest that an intense struggle over indigenous policy is underway, a struggle in which powerful economic interests, as usual, are at stake. Proposals emanating from Congress and the executive branch in the last decade, encouraging private enterprise on reservations and seeking to reduce the federal role in tribal affairs, can be analyzed in this light.

THE DEALER'S EDGE
GAMING IN THE PATH OF NATIVE AMERICA

Tim Johnson

Enclosed behind the glass walls of a private dining room in the Radisson Inn's upscale

Tim Johnson, "The Dealer's Edge: Gaming in the Path of Native America," *Native Americas,* 12, nos. 1 & 2 (Spring–Summer 1995). Copyright 1995 by Akwe:kon Press. Reprinted with permission.

Shenandoah Restaurant, Oneida Nation Territory, Wisconsin, sat a circle of Indian leaders. Passers-by, en route to their tables or the salad bar would occasionally glance inside, perhaps not suspecting that the women and men seated there, some dressed in jeans and

T-shirts, others in dark business suits, were the managers of one of Native America's most successful business operations—the Oneida Nation of Wisconsin.

Twenty-six years ago, before the returns on Oneida's economic development strategy accelerated like a rocket, there were but nine employees of the nation—four planners, two teachers, a Head Start director, a cook, and a custodian. Today 3,391 people are employed by the Oneida Nation. Of these, 1,613 are tribal members, 357 are from other Indian nations, and 1,421 are non-Indians from surrounding Wisconsin communities including Ashwaubenon, Green Bay, De Pere, Howard, Allquez, and Bellevue. The Oneida Nation's annual budget climbed from less than $50,000 in 1969, when virtually all funding came from the federal government, to $158 million for fiscal year 1995, of which 90 percent is now generated from the nation's own profits. Oneida unemployment went from over seventy-five percent to under five percent. In addition, Oneida Nation businesses stimulate over $1 billion worth of economic activity in the surrounding area.

The vehicle that rocketed the Oneidas to such dramatic economic growth was Indian gaming. Looking at the ways they have steered that vehicle within the principles of Oneida traditions, and past obstacles that have disrupted other Indian communities, provides insight into a successful economic development planning model that has merged Indian culture with corporate practices and left the Oneidas in a position to protect, preserve, strengthen, and project their identity far into the future—toward the Seventh Generation.

Along the gaming path they and other Indian nations are shattering stereotypes of Indians that are rooted historically in the fabric of American society. Notions that Indians are incapable of managing resources and market opportunities are vanishing amid a strong record of success in cases where resources are not stolen and access to markets is not prevented. The Oneida story is significant beyond the obvious economic ramifications—and not only for Indians.

Within the Oneida community there is a common generosity in distributing credit for the economic success. Elma Webster and Sandy Ninham are identified as the "mothers" who first brought gaming to the reservation. Some point to Ernie Stevens Sr., an elder who one tribal member said "embodies Oneida oral tradition." Others mention with pride his son Ernie Stevens Jr., who has astutely carried the family mantle. Debby Doxtator, Oneida Nation chair, is perceived as a base of stability. Loretta Metoxen, vice-chair, is identified as a brilliant endowment investment specialist. Bob Brown is largely credited with leading the resurgence of the traditional longhouse culture. All around the community, people talk like team members who are used to passing the ball liberally before scoring the winning goal. Noticeably absent from the discourse are the heated blasts of outward discontent that often plague dysfunctional communities.

Nation general manager Artley Skenandore Jr. is the recipient of substantial praise. Skenandore has the qualities of an affable, yet highly intelligent and articulate lineman, a man whose presence is matched by boundless energy. Highly respected for his efficient vision and organizational skills, Skenandore has driven forward the capitalistic machine of economic growth and progress while remaining true to his Native values. That his fellow community members apparently do not see this as a contradiction is proof that the Oneidas have infused their development strategies with educational values and communication processes. Skenandore is equally at ease whether negotiating with state officials, explaining traditional longhouse principles, or lifting weights with the casino security guards in the nation's health facility.

"As a manager of a nation, organizationally, I consider it very important that we are about results," said Skenandore. "And those results must be based on principles and sound theory, and at looking at our own indigenous theory, for example, as the benchmark.

"I've studied organizational development all across the world and it comes down to some real fundamental things no matter which model you use. One, that you communicate and really tell your story. Two, that you listen to see if people are hearing your story. Three, that you be effective with your resources and your commitment—in other words, that you do the very best for yourself (the nation) which will then impact others. The fourth one is efficiency—that you use your resources in an efficient way and that you have a foundation to build from, the resources [needed] for that Seventh Generation."

The management approaches that Skenandore talks about flow from his mind and off his tongue as easily as the dollars that slip between the fingers of the estimated six million (and growing) day-trippers who attend the Oneida gaming operations each year. The ever-increasing market includes gamblers from a 200-mile radius. By the carloads and busloads they come to bet on a chance to win $250,000 at high stakes bingo, drop coins into over 5,000 slot machines where a lucky return could reach $1 million, or sit at any of the 90 black jack tables where limits range from $2 to $200.

Most of them will lose money and have a great time doing it. Such is the quixotic lure of gambling, the siren's call that, while perplexing to some and morally repulsive to others, is wildly entertaining to masses of American consumers. But most importantly to managers like Skenandore, gaming is simply a profitable business upon which economically dormant Indian nations can regain long lost territory, cultural prerogatives, and community structures built upon respect.

In lieu of tax revenues collected by non-Indian local, state, and federal governments to support their public programs, the Oneidas generate their national budget from gaming profits. The process by which these funds are accounted for and allocated is a case study in "transparency," open and honest, fair and equitable distribution of resources to community priorities. This is not to say that serious disagreements don't arise over budget issues as disparate interest groups clamor for funds, but rather that the managerial processes are able to sustain credibility at a functional and highly proactive level. Communication is seen as a key ingredient.

"We've utilized state of the art technology and state of the art processes to provide as much information as possible for our membership to make good decisions," said Skenandore. "And our cornerstone . . . as a learning organization is to commit to continuous improvement."

Skenandore refers in part to the biannual printed and bound reports that are sent to every member of the Oneida Nation of Wisconsin, whether living on or off the reservation. These include reports from the divisions of gaming/casino, enterprise, development, governmental services, from the committees of business, legislative operating and other numerous boards and commissions that oversee everything from health to housing, as well as a review of each year's projected fiscal budget. Virtually every decision-making process is available for scrutiny and input by community members within the guidelines of structural processes designed to be highly efficient and productive. The net result is an improvement in the membership's informed participation and a reduction in causes for protest by community obstructionists.

What appears to hold it all together, however, are the shared values that have been crystallized in the form of an Oneida Nation Mission Statement, a Seventh Generation Vision Policy, and a list of ten National Priorities. Through its communications strategies, the entire community regularly works its way through strategic and financial management planning exercises.

The first point of the mission statement reads. "The mission of the Oneida is to sustain a strong Oneida Nation by preserving our heritage through the Seventh Generation." Point one of the list of ten National Priorities also stands out, particularly given the political acrimony that often blocks Indian community leadership from reconciling disputed issues. It reads, "Oneida leadership will encourage each other to honor Oneida cultural values of peace, respect, and friendship, in our use of time, our public conduct, and our personal behavior."

The success of their gaming operations, communications, and management structures has had its share of problems. But what separates the Wisconsin Oneida from some historically-linked Iroquois Confederate nations in New York State—where conflicts over gaming have led to two deaths at

Akwesasne and more recent beatings and killings within the Seneca Nation of Indians at the Cattaraugus and Allegany Reservations—is their ability to negotiate through problems by using constructive dialogue within a process that allows for volatile human dynamics. According to Oneida tradition, no one is above the interests of the community and leadership is more successful when it recognizes that it must accommodate diverse viewpoints. The Wisconsin Oneidas have emerged from a painful history by addressing the need not just to retain culture, but to strengthen it in the midst of sweeping economic change.

The Oneidas, split over the centuries by various institutional incursions in religion, education and government, found common ground by identifying and moving forward on shared values—values that did not diminish under the whip of the boarding school proctors. Education, social services, environmental and health programs account for 62.5 percent of the total budget for fiscal year 1995. This represents a formidable commitment to children, elders, and the land on which they live. Separate line items include specific additional funding for an elderly program at 2.1 percent, a nursing home at 5.7 percent, an arts program at 1.2 percent, a conservation program at 2.7 percent, and a museum at 3.5 percent.

Not far from the Oneida Nation Museum, in the reservation's southern valley of Duck Creek, is the three-year-old ranch house of Carol Cornelius, an enrolled Oneida who is director of American Indian Studies at the University of Wisconsin at Green Bay. A cultural specialist who has researched the consequences of United States Indian policy, Cornelius spoke openly about the precipitous historical ledge from which the Oneidas have extricated themselves. Looking out her back door windows, she surveyed the surrounding lands while referring to the historical sequence of events that, until recent times, led to the loss of territory.

"We are now empowered to undo the U.S. government policies that took away our land, our language, our culture and our ceremonies," said Cornelius. "This is all checkerboard here. The piece of land that I'm on was owned by non-Indians. The one right next to me is owned by non-Indians. But on my right side there's an Oneida family and the house beyond this one is an Oneida family."

Prior to the American Revolution, Oneida Nation territory extended to at least 5.3 million acres in central New York State. Following the war and before the development of the U.S. Constitution, villages were destroyed and Oneida lands were yielded through two treaties in 1785 and 1788. These treaties were largely contrived by the state of New York and various land companies.

In 1821 the Oneida purchased fertile land from the Menomince and Winnebago nations in what is now the state of Wisconsin. At least three significant migrations of Oneidas from eastern areas are recognized. "The First Christian Party" relocated 448 Oneidas. "The Second Christian Party" was composed of 206 Oneidas, and in 1841, the "Pagan Party" of 44 Oneidas—the only group that had not converted to Christianity—arrived. These groups settled respectively around the Grand Chute and Kaukauna area, along Duck Creek, and in a place dubbed Chicago Corners.

The "checkerboard effect"—as Cornelius referred to the division of reservation land between Indians and non-Indians—was the result of the Dawes Act, or more specifically the 1887 Indian Allotment Act. By allocating land to individual owners, the Dawes Act effectively removed territory from collective national Oneida domain. As a result, destitute Indians were often forced to sell their land to predatory land companies and speculators. The Oneidas' more than 5.3 million acres of land was reduced to a few hundred acres in about seven generations, or 150 years. This harsh reality, along with the subsequent history of social problems and self-directed and self-defeating hostilities, set the framework for Oneida consciousness today, and established the challenges for their new management.

"We have not had viable economies until the last five years," said Cornelius. "So when I walk into that casino, I'm overwhelmed. I think, 'my people did all this.' We've had five years to acquire all this business sense.

"Twenty-five years ago when I graduated from high school there were no jobs. As young folks we went to Milwaukee and found out we couldn't handle city life. There just wasn't a future. Now I see all of these young people working and I think, 'all of these people now have job skills.'

"Now we have leaders in our government who have been able to say that our traditional ways must be a part of our government. I think what Artley (Skenandore) has done is take a community that moved out here in 1822 . . . and built it back up. Of the 65,400 acres we originally had here in this part of Wisconsin, it is estimated in 1970 we only had 4 to 5 percent of it and maybe now we're back up to 12 percent. Now, we're buying our land back daily.

"We founded our new high school on the principle of a two hundred percent student—one hundred percent able to speak his or her language, know his or her ceremonies, to know how our government works and to function within our community and one hundred percent able to work (off of the reservation) if he or she wants to. That's our twenty-year goal. We've got an income coming in now and the first thing we have done is to provide for the children and the elders."

The ability to address those challenges adequately emerged with the October 17, 1988 passage of Public Law 100-497, the Indian Gaming Regulatory Act (IGRA). As defined under its declaration of policy the purpose of the act is:

1. to provide a statutory basis for the operation of gaming by Indian tribes as a means of promoting tribal economic development, self-sufficiency, and strong tribal governments;
2. to provide a statutory basis for the regulation of gaming by an Indian tribe adequate to shield it from organized crime and other corrupting influences, to ensure that the Indian tribe is the primary beneficiary of the gaming operation, and to assure that gaming is conducted fairly and honestly by both the operator and players, and
3. to declare that the establishment of independent Federal regulatory authority for gaming on Indian lands, the establishment of Federal standards for gaming on Indian lands, and the establishment of a National Indian Gaming Commission are necessary to meet congressional concerns regarding gaming and to protect such gaming as a means of generating tribal revenue.

The basis for IGRA's passage was rooted in the desire to provide an economic stimulus for the many Indian nations that did not have adequate resources to support development. The lack of vibrant economies on reservations has led to Native Americans being among the poorest people in the United States. In addition, most reservations were dependent on federal aid.

The IGRA legislation was prompted by, among other cases, a 1987 federal court decision in *California v. Cabazon* that ruled tribes could operate forms of gambling that were not prohibited by the state. This U.S. Supreme Court decision established the distinction between criminal/prohibitory and civil/regulatory jurisdiction of the states and the tribes. Essentially, if a state regulates gaming in any form then it cannot prosecute Indian nations and is obligated to enter into negotiations with them.

IGRA directs that net revenues from tribal gaming are not to be used for purposes "other than to fund tribal government operations or programs, to provide for the general welfare of the Indian tribe and its members, to promote tribal economic development or to help fund operations of local government agencies."

But the passage of the bill and the subsequent negotiations conducted between the tribes and states who have negotiated gaming compacts came at a cost to Indian sovereignty—IGRA added another layer of legislation over Native right to self-government. Some bemoan the loss while others suggest that IGRA represents a trade-off that places the interests of badly-needed community economic development ahead of the state's marginal criminal and taxation jurisdictional advances that had already been de facto realities for many tribes.

To leave no doubt, however, IGRA has contributed to limiting the sovereignty of American Indian nations. A tribe must now request the state in which its territory resides to enter into gaming compact negotiations prior to development of gaming facilities. IGRA was designed to balance the rights of Indian nations to conduct gaming with the states' public interests. From the Native American perspective the act was anything but perfect, yet it allowed Indian nations to proceed with gaming developments free from state intervention. In fact, IGRA stipulates that the states must enter into good faith negotiations with the tribes.

On a whole, IGRA cements the idea that while Indian sovereignty is still a perception and holds true in some areas, it has been obscured under the weight of federal and state legislation. IGRA Section 21 states, "The United States shall have exclusive jurisdiction over criminal prosecutions of violations of State gambling laws that are made applicable under this section to Indian country unless an Indian tribe pursuant to a Tribal-State compact . . . has consented to the transfer to the State of criminal jurisdiction with respect to gambling on the lands of the Indian tribe." The legislative shift toward state jurisdiction over Indian affairs combined with the need for tribes to renew temporary gaming compacts with the state raises an important question: Is Indian gaming sustainable?

Part of the answer may rest in the new capital clout of Indian managers and lobbyists armed with resources never before imagined and objective economic studies detailing the benefits to local and state economies. The other part lies with the capacity of individual tribes to diversify their business activities by converting gaming profits into investments in other non-gaming enterprises and endowments.

For example, when ranked by employment, seven of the top ten largest minority-owned businesses in Wisconsin are owned by Indian nations. The Oneida Nation ranks number one, followed by the Wisconsin Winnebago Business Committee (2), the Menominee Indian Tribe (3), the St. Croix Wisconsin Chippewa (4), the Lac du Flambeau Band of Lake Superior Chippewa (7), the Forest County Potawatomi Community (8), and the Lac Courte Oreilles Band of Lake Superior Chippewa (9).

American Indian nations own fifteen Class III gaming facilities in the state of Wisconsin. According to a 1993 Deloitte & Touche study, these facilities saved the state of Wisconsin an estimated $51.7 million in 1992, itemized as follows: $2.2 million from welfare savings, $14.2 million from gas taxes, $17.3 million from sales taxes and $18 million from income taxes. The study estimates that about 30,000 jobs are either directly or indirectly supported by Indian gaming, and, "crime rates were lower in those communities with gaming facilities."

Skenandore and other Oneida Nation managers are aware of the need to press forward with a diplomatic agenda, particularly since their gaming compact with the state runs out in December of 1997. As part of this agenda, Skenandore believes that the nation must recognize its status as an economic contributor and partner in the state economy, commit to "diminishing the learning curve" around issues of impact, and develop a protocol of sovereign-to-sovereign relations emerging out of respect and recognition.

To remain sustainable, the Oneidas need adequate resources derived from their business and endowment investments to carry their community's operating budget. "The basic operating principle of our budget process is to look at what it costs for our operation," said Skenandore. "Then we look at how we support our enhancement

strategies and how we will continue to facilitate good measures of planning into the
future. We've scheduled endowment funds
to coincide with the end of the [gaming]
compact. If we are unsuccessful at negotiating another compact with the state, we will
have a measure of economic stability. We
will continue to be able to move forward as
a nation."

According to Skenandore, the Oneida
Nation's endowment strategy is driven by
social responsibility and managed by an internal investment committee. The committee's policy combines low-risk investment
with an aggressive pool of high-risk investments that allow a greater return. "We've
managed our funds since 1985 ourselves,
and these have grown over time," said
Skenandore.

Perhaps nowhere is this emerging economic power more evident or more strategically applied than by the Mashantucket
Pequots of Connecticut, an indigenous nation of 350 members located on 2,000 acres
of trust land. At the Foxwoods Resort Casino
in Ledyard—where visitors can gamble,
shop, pamper themselves at "The Salon in
the Woods" or "The Spa," visit the Pequot
museum, or see performances by the likes of
Frank Sinatra, Bill Cosby, and Ray Charles—
the sheer magnitude of IGRA-facilitated economic empowerment for Indian nations is
on display. With about 190,000 square feet
devoted to gaming, the Foxwoods Resort
Casino is the largest in the country. It now
features 3,900 slot machines and 15 restaurants and food courts. Among the top 10 employers in Connecticut, the Mashantucket
Pequot employ some 10,000 people.

"Capital from gaming provides the opportunity for Indians to be a player in the
national scene, to actually lobby to protect
their rights," said Bruce Kirshner, senior vice
president of Foxwoods. "Indians are merely
taking advantage of the law. People in this
society use the law to their best advantage.
This is what is done in the American system.
The law in this case benefits Indians, so it is
smart to use it."

In Connecticut, the Mashantucket
Pequot operation is now the second largest
contributor to the state treasury, behind only
the federal government. Their compact-
negotiated $150 million contribution to the
state treasury has had a discernible impact
on Connecticut's budget. And in a show of
generosity in 1993, the Pequots made it possible to balance the state budget with an
extra $15 million contribution. Federal sup-
port of the Pequot community is now only
2.5 percent and, within a few years, will
be nothing. In 1994, they awarded the
Smithsonian Institution's National Museum
of the American Indian a $10 million contri-
bution, providing American Indians with a
substantial stakeholding in that organization. They have also established a lobbying
office in Washington, DC.

"The gaming revenues have taken a
community that was poor and marginalized and allowed it to empower itself," said
Kirshner. "Even to research and practice our
culture, we have more time now. We have
more resources. So, if a nation member
wants to research our history, wants to study
our traditional culture, the council now can
back that individual so the family can be
sustained and yet the person can take the
time. This is possible now and it was not
before."

Much like the Wisconsin Oneidas, the
Pequots are building a museum to tell their
own history, buying back their land, and investing in other businesses including a pharmaceutical company and a sand and gravel
company. Gaming revenues provide for all
community services.

"Gaming is a viable business for the
foreseeable future, certainly five years down
the road," said Kirshner. "It is important to

continue to capitalize and to diversify as you go, as long as you can."

But gaming was not a quick or easy development for the Pequots. Their first tribal referendum on gaming failed in 1985 due to unsubstantiated rumors about organized crime and social decay. The council then suggested that members operate a small bingo to see how it runs. "Let us prove ourselves—we believe we can handle it," Kirshner says the council told its members. Ten years later, the Pequots handle the most substantial gaming operation in the country and have helped Connecticut through a difficult economic transition during a time when thousands of jobs in the defense industry were lost.

Sixty-eight percent of Americans polled in a national survey conducted in all states excluding Nevada and New Jersey, support casino gambling on Indian reservations for reasons including job creation, state revenue, welfare reduction. "In addition," states the Glen M. Feldman Survey of Public Opinion Regarding Indian Gaming, "the American people support Indian gaming because they view it as a legitimate exercise of tribal self-government and a means of achieving economic self-sufficiency for Native Americans." Public support is further evident by the tens of millions of customers drawn to Indian casinos each year.

Such rapid development has not come without its share of problems for Indian communities. Beyond the name calling, fist fights, burnings, beatings, and shootings that have preceded several communities' entrances into the realm of gaming, other subtle and unforeseen problems have emerged from the rapid burst of business development with which managers must now contend.

At Oneida Wisconsin, for example, wages paid to casino workers often exceed wages paid to other professional positions that require greater training, education, and work experience. Cornelius calls this "internal brain drain." She said, "Young folks who have gone off to school and acquired skills are not using them because they can make more money working at the casino." To solve this problem, the nation has just completed an analysis of wage structures which indicates that employees outside of gaming are grossly underpaid. Skenandore says this process will result in the implementation of a more equitable national wage structure.

Another major concern is the manner in which casino resources are made available to tribal members. While IGRA stipulates that resources be directed to tribal governmental programming, there is a provision in section eleven for per capita distribution provided that the Indian tribe meets certain specific requirements.

"We've been challenged like other communities with per capita," said Skenandore, "and we've asked our membership to look toward the future. We've adopted a planning approach called 'Seven Generations' for the explicit purpose of ensuring that our plans go beyond ourselves, and actually beyond our children as well."

For the 250-member Shakopee Mdewakanton Dakota community in Minnesota that owns three casinos—Mystic Lake, Dakota Country, and Little Six—the gaming path followed a different ridge. Known for their distribution of high annual per capita payments—reportedly in the hundreds of thousands of dollars—they and other such Indian nations have been placed under the looking glass of both community managers researching models for their own revenue disbursement structures and opponents of Indian gaming.

Don Crofut, principal and vice-president of Dream Catcher Gaming Group, a casino management and development company, says that the Shakopee experience has evolved from a natural progression of events. "Generally I think the per caps were looked at initially as a mechanism for a Christmas fund," he said. "And from a policy issue, it is my belief that it was a mechanism to support the tribal membership in some of their endeavors. I also look at it as more of a mechanism, from a tribal government standpoint, to support the membership with resources to be able to start entrepreneurial activities."

Crofut does not claim that Indian gaming or per capita payments of gaming profits are a "panacea for all tribes." Simple math supports his argument. For example, a tribe of 15,000 members that generates $100 million in net profits would only provide $6,666 to each community member if dispersed on a per capita basis—not nearly enough to provide a living. Such tribes would be far better off developing public services such as housing, health care, and college funds that could be accessed by all members. In addition, many tribes are not located in marketable areas to attract customers to casinos.

Crofut also stresses that dramatic improvements have been made to his community. "Twenty years ago it was a dirt road with basically faulty health—septic and water system problems," he said. "There was an outbreak of hepatitis 15 years ago. The houses were generally federal housing, HUD (Housing and Urban Development) houses. Now we have paved streets with curbs . . . a water and sewer treatment plant, businesses, a strip mall, government center, convenience stores, schools, credit union and housing that's more middle class," he said.

Raymond "Sonny" Crooks, the chairman of the board of directors of tribal corporations at Shakopee, confirms Crofut's observations while stressing that accountability must be a priority for tribes establishing gaming operations. "The tribe has its own business organization and we are the gaming enterprise corporation," said Crooks. "We are directly answerable to the tribe. All of the monies that we make from gaming are directly transferred to the tribe for disposition into the various programs and businesses that have been developed. Not only do we have three casinos on site, we have a major government center with a day care center that's been in place for at least six years. And just recently we have been able to open up a three-story unit called Playworld that can house up to 500 kids at one time."

Perhaps more than in any other state, Minnesota Indians are armed with information from studies that chart the economic and social impact of Indian gaming. There are 17 Indian casinos in Minnesota that generate more than $300 million after prizes and provide more than 10,300 jobs. The ten Minnesota counties with Indian casinos show better economic performance than counties with no casinos. Casino counties experienced $182 million more in economic activity in 1990 and 1991 than they would had they grown at the same rate as the rest of the state. The volume of bar and restaurant business is higher in casino counties, there is no evidence that crime has increased, and lawful gaming has contributed $79 million to charitable purposes.

The Indian Gaming Regulatory Act seems to serve its intended purpose of building active Native American economies and strong, well-managed tribal governments. The Wisconsin Oneida experience and others like it are examples that when access to resources and markets is not prevented, Indians have a tremendous capacity to build nations in accordance with their cultural values. IGRA is a trade-off—gaming profits are exchanged for federal and state taxation collection and gaming-related state criminal jurisdiction over tribes. But few of the financial beneficiaries of IGRA statutes are complaining.

"The thing about this community (Oneida Wisconsin) is that we had a chance to get out of being perpetual victims and we took it," said Cornelius. "We're empowered now. There's no way they are going to reduce us to being victims again. Being defeated is a mindset. Even when you're confronted with ten facts to the contrary, it's what you know."

And while riding a conservative wave in American political seas, the Oneida story highlights one of the most traditional approaches to community development in America. Precise and highly-monitored financial controls and strategies serve to inform and empower citizens. Seventy percent of the population has been taken off the unemployment and welfare doles and put to work. And when it comes to family values, no community is more steadfast than the Oneidas, where the interests of stable and healthy family development are expressed in national budgets that place children, elders, nutrition, and health care at the top of their national agenda.

Paul Fell, courtesy Lincoln (NE) Journal Star.

ALL WE EVER WANTED WAS TO CATCH FISH

NARF Legal Review

On April 20, 1995, the Ninth Circuit Court of Appeals ruled in favor of two Athabaskan elders who are long time Native American Rights Fund (NARF) clients, who were denied their right to subsistence fishing by the State of Alaska and the federal government. The Ninth Circuit held that the federal government has the obligation to provide subsistence fishing priority on all navigable waters in Alaska in which the United States has a federally reserved water right. The Court instructed the Departments of Interior and Agriculture to identify those waters for the purpose of implementing federal, rather than state regulation of subsistence activities.

Katie John, more than any other subsistence case currently pending before State or Federal court in Alaska, exemplifies the contentious battle being waged between federal, tribal and state interests over jurisdiction of Native fishing rights. For a decade now, NARF has been at the forefront of this battle.

In 1984, NARF attorneys Lawrence Aschenbrenner and Robert Anderson were sent to Alaska to open a new office. Their work for the most part would be consumed by advocating for and protecting the tribal sovereignty and subsistence rights of Alaska Natives. "The word 'subsistence' reminds

most Americans of dirt-poor farmers, scratching a hard living from marginal land. In Alaska, however, subsistence means hunting, fishing, and gathering. More than that, it means a way of life that—far from being marginal—fulfills spiritual as well as economic needs."

The subsistence way of life is essential for the physical and cultural survival of Alaska Natives. Most of the two hundred small Native villages in Alaska are located on or near the shores of a river or a lake, or located on the coast of the North Pacific or Arctic Ocean. The proximity to water is no accident and reflects the dependence of Natives on the harvest of fish stocks for sustenance and the basis of their traditional way of life. "In many Native villages fresh meat, fish and produce are unavailable except through the subsistence harvest." Consequently, rural residents harvest 34–40 million pounds of food annually for subsistence uses and most of that harvest is fish— approximately 60% according to Alaska Department of Fish and Game statistics.

As important as Native hunting and fishing rights are to Alaska Natives' physical, economic, traditional, and cultural existence, the State of Alaska has been and continues to be reluctant to recognize the importance of the subsistence way of life. The State views subsistence as nothing more than a taking of a natural resource, and as something that all citizens of the state should be entitled to engage in on an equal opportunity basis with little distinction between sport and trophy hunting and subsistence needs.

Unlike tribes in the contiguous 48 states, Native hunting and fishing rights in Alaska were never recognized through treaty. The treaty making period ended in 1871 and thus had long since passed by the time Congress finally got around to dealing with the aboriginal claims of Alaska Natives. It wasn't until 1971 that Congress extinguished aboriginal claims to lands in Alaska through the Alaska Native Land Claims Settlement Act (ANCSA). ANCSA set aside 44 million acres of land to be deeded in fee title to newly created Native corporations, and provided for a cash settlement of nearly $1 billion dollars. ANCSA also extinguished aboriginal hunting and fishing rights. Section 4(b) provided: "All aboriginal titles, if any, and claims of aboriginal title in Alaska based on use and occupancy, . . . including any aboriginal hunting and fishing rights that may exist, are hereby extinguished." Despite this extinguishment, Congress made clear its intent to continue federal protection of Native hunting and fishing rights. The ANCSA Conference Report states: "The Conference Committee expects both the Secretary and the State to take any action necessary to protect the subsistence needs of the Natives."

By the late 1970s, however, it was clear that the State and Secretary were not living up to the expectations of Congress. "At least until 1983, it was a fact of Alaska political life that the State's Department of Fish and Game was dominated by non-Native urban, sports and commercial hunting [and] fishing interests." Work thus began on a subsistence title for inclusion in what became the Alaska National Interest Lands Conservation Act (ANILCA). Title VIII of ANILCA granted rural subsistence users a priority to harvest fish and game on public lands whenever the resource was insufficient to accommodate all other consumptive users. An agreement was struck with the State, allowing the State to regulate fish and game on public lands as long as the State likewise adopted a preference for subsistence users analogous to ANILCA. In anticipation of ANILCA's passage, Alaska enacted its first subsistence law in 1978. At the State's insistence, Congress elected to adopt a rural, rather than purely Native, priority. Congress was advised and believed that "because of restrictions imposed on State action by the Alaska Constitution . . . it would have been impossible for the State of Alaska to have developed a subsistence management program which provided a priority for Alaska Natives."

Four years after ANILCA was signed into law, the State Board of Fisheries refused the request of two Ahtna elders, Katie John and Doris Charles, to re-open a historic subsistence fishery at Batzulnetas. NARF heard about the plight of the two women and filed suit on their behalf. Katie John is a seventy-nine year old Ahtna Athabaskan Indian and the daughter of the last chief of Batzulnetas. Doris Charles is a ninety-three year old upper Ahtna Athabaskan Indian who was born in Batzulnetas in 1902 and continued to live there on a permanent basis until the early 1930s.

Batzulnetas, which means "Roasted Salmon Place," is a historic upper Ahtna village and fish camp and is located at the confluence of Tanada Creek and Copper River within the Wrangell-St. Elias Park. Both Katie John and Doris Charles own Native allotments at Batzulnetas.

Batzulnetas is a revered spot among the upper Ahtna who have fiercely protected this site for generations. Oral history and early written accounts tell of a massacre of Russians by the upper Ahtna at Batzulnetas around 1794, provoked by the abduction of women and driving out the men in the winter without adequate clothing. In 1885, nearly one hundred years later, Lt. Henry T. Allen arrived in Batzulnetas. With the Ahtna's help, he became the first non-Native explorer to cross one of the passes from the Copper River to the Tanana River in Alaska's interior.

Batzulnetas was occupied by the upper Ahtna on a year-round basis until the mid-1940s when the villagers were relocated to Mentasta so that their children could attend school. Batzulnetas continued to remain an important summer fish camp.

Alaska achieved Statehood in 1958 and assumed management of fish and game in 1960. In 1964, the State used its authority to close down the subsistence fishery at Batzulnetas and nearly all the other traditional fishing sites in the upper Copper River and its tributaries. Closure of Batzulnetas to subsistence fishing ended its regular use as a fish camp. Nevertheless, Katie John, Doris Charles, other residents of Mentasta village and former residents of Batzulnetas returned regularly to visit grave sites and to experience the spiritual and cultural satisfaction derived from being present at the place where they grew up.

In 1984, Katie John and Doris Charles submitted a proposal requesting the Alaska State Board of Fisheries to open Batzulnetas to subsistence fishing. Their request was denied, despite the fact that downstream users were permitted to take hundreds of thousands of salmon for sport and commercial uses. NARF filed suit against the State in late 1985 pursuant to Title VIII of ANILCA to compel the State to re-open the historic Batzulnetas fishery. The State subsequently adopted regulations providing for a limited fishery. In 1990, the district court set aside this state regulation as too restrictive and remanded the case to the Board of Fisheries for further proceedings consistent with

applicable state and federal law. Before further action could be taken by the Alaska Board of Fisheries, the Alaska Supreme Court's decision in *McDowell v. Alaska*, 785 P.2d 1 (Alaska 1989), struck down the "rural" definition from the State's subsistence preference law as unconstitutional, and the Board of Fisheries refused to act on any new regulatory proposals. The effect of *McDowell* was to divide subsistence management into two distinct legal regimes—one governed by state law and the other by federal law.

In the hope that the State would amend its Constitution, or otherwise bring its program into compliance with ANILCA, the *McDowell* decision was stayed until July 1, 1990. After the Legislature failed to take action, the Secretaries of Interior and Agriculture announced their intent to take over the management of subsistence uses on public lands effective July 1, 1990.

From the outset of the federal takeover, the federal agencies adopted a "minimal intrusion rationale" to "minimize disruption to traditional state regulation and management of fish and wildlife." Pursuant to this policy, the Secretaries adopted a regulation providing for a subsistence fishery at Batzulnetas which was identical to the state regulation the federal court ruled invalid in *John, et al. v. Alaska*, No. A85-698 (HRH) (D. Alaska). Since that regulation infringed on Katie John and Doris Charles' traditional fishing practices, NARF petitioned for reconsideration of the Secretaries' regulation. Instead of ruling on the merits of this request, the federal agencies responded that Tanada Creek and the Copper River were navigable waters and that navigable waters did not constitute "public lands" subject to Title VIII's subsistence priority for rural residents. The federal government's explanation was that although ANILCA expressly encompasses *interests in waters* within the definition of "public lands," its temporary regulations excluded navigable waters from the "public lands" definition because "[t]he United States generally does not hold title to navigable water."

NARF filed suit against the Secretaries claiming that their construction of the "public lands" definition was unlawfully narrow. Section 102 of ANILCA defines "public lands" as "federal lands." Federal lands "means lands, the title to which is in the United States after Dec. 2, 1980." Finally, "the term 'land' means lands, waters and interests therein." The United States Supreme Court has melded this tripartite definition, concluding that Congress defined "'public lands' as 'lands, waters and interests therein' 'the title to which is in the United States.'" In construing the definition of "public lands" in *Village of Gambell,* the Supreme Court rejected the notion that "title" to an interest refers to fee title, or some other technical record or deed title; rather, it is simply the right to control or dispose of an interest. Accordingly, NARF argued that fee title was unnecessary for ANILCA's priority to attach to navigable waters because such waters are "public lands" by virtue of the federal government's "interest" in navigable waters under the navigational servitude and the reserved rights doctrine.

The question of whether navigable waters and federally reserved waters constitute "public lands" was first argued in December 1991. Before the issue was decided on the merits, however, the *Katie John* case was consolidated with *State v. Babbitt,* a case filed by the State to challenge the Secretaries' day-to-day management authority to regulate fish and game on public lands when state law has been found to be out of compliance with ANILCA.

The question of whether navigable waters and federally reserved waters constitute "public lands" was argued again on March 18, 1994. The federal government changed its position on the reserved waters issue, now agreeing with Katie John and Doris Charles that all waters in Alaska subject to federally reserved water rights constitute "public lands" as defined by ANILCA. However, the federal government continued to assert that the navigational servitude is not a sufficient interest to allow navigable waters to be encompassed within the definition of "public lands."

On March 30, 1994, the district court issued a 42-page decision in these consolidated cases. First, the court concluded that the federal government, and not the State, has the authority to regulate the taking of fish and wildlife for subsistence purposes on the public lands. The court then ruled that, "for purposes of Title VIII of ANILCA, the United States holds title to an interest in navigable waters in Alaska." The court did not reject the notion that the reserved water rights doctrine could have some application, rather, it concluded that "the geographic scope of Title VIII is better determined by use of the navigational servitude, as being compatible with the findings and policies of Title VIII of ANILCA." The order was stayed, allowing the parties sixty days to file an interlocutory appeal to the Ninth Circuit.

After the November 1994 elections, Alaska's new Democratic Governor filed a stipulation to withdraw the State's appeal of the District Court's finding in *State v. Babbitt.* The Republican dominated Alaska Legislature and the Alaska Outdoor Council (AOC), a state-wide umbrella organization composed of forty-five member organizations representing sport hunting interests, unsuccessfully attempted to intervene to continue the appeal. The Legislature and AOC currently have petitions pending before the

United States Supreme Court on *writs of certiorari* over their denial of intervention. Oral argument on *Katie John* was heard before the Ninth Circuit Court of Appeals on February 7, 1995.

On April 20, 1995, the Ninth Circuit issued its opinion rejecting the district court's "highly expansive definition of public lands, holding that the subsistence priority applies to all Alaskan waters subject to the federal navigational servitude." Instead, the Court ruled in Katie's favor on the narrower theory that the subsistence priority applies to navigable waters in which the United States has reserved water rights. The federal agencies must now determine the geographic scope of reserved waters in Alaska.

PEACE, NOT OIL:
THE U'WA AND INTERNATIONAL PETROLEUM

The U'wa People of Colombia in South America have waged a struggle to maintain their homeland since 1992, when Occidental Petroleum was granted exploration rights in much of the traditional U'wa territory. Luis Caballero, vice president of the Traditional U'wa Authority explains, "Oil is the blood of Mother Earth. It belongs in the ground, where it sustains the world below. Up here, it only causes violence and death." Based on a spiritual resolve to maintain and sustain their homeland and way of life, the U'wa are caught between a complex series of often contradictory forces: the Colombian government seeking to "modernize" while at the same time destabilized internally due to various political entities' vying for power, a flourishing international drug economy, international monetary institutions exerting pressures on Colombia and many other South American countries to pay off tremendous debts, and the multinational petroleum industry including Occidental, Shell, and Ecopetrol that are driven by strategies for resource exploitation and financial gain. The presence of these highly charged forces has created an environment of militarization and violence that the U'wa are forced to live with daily. Berito KuwarU'wa, President of the Traditional U'wa Authority has said, "We would rather die, protecting everything that we hold sacred, than lose everything that makes us U'wa."

Edited portion from Project Underground, *Blood of Our Mother: The U'wa People, Occidental Petroleum and the Colombian Oil Industry* (Berkeley, Calif.: Project Underground, 1998).

LOVELY HULA HANDS

CORPORATE TOURISM AND THE PROSTITUTION

OF HAWAIIAN CULTURE

Haunani-Kay Trask

This paper was first delivered at a Law and Society conference in Berkeley. The response was astounding since most Americans are simply shocked to learn that even one Native thinks of tourism as a colonial imposition on Hawaiians. Of course, it could be that part of the shock was that this message was delivered by a Hawaiian intellectual, something most American racists consider a contradiction in terms.

I am certain that most, if not all, Americans have heard of Hawai'i and have wished, at some time in their lives, to visit my Native land. But I doubt that the history of how Hawai'i came to be territorially incorporated, and economically, politically, and culturally subordinated to the United States is known to most Americans. Nor is it common knowledge that Hawaiians have been struggling for over twenty years to achieve a land base and some form of political sovereignty on the same level as American Indians. Finally, I would imagine that most Americans could not place Hawai'i or any other Pacific island on a map of the Pacific. But despite all this appalling ignorance, five million Americans will vacation in my homeland this year *and* the next, and so on into the foreseeable capitalist future. Such are the intended privileges of the so-called American standard of living: ignorance of, and yet power over, one's relations to Native peoples.

Thanks to post-war American imperialism, the ideology that the United States has no overseas colonies and is, in fact, the champion of self-determination the world over holds no greater sway than in the United States itself. To most Americans, then, Hawai'i is *theirs*: to use, to take, and, above all, to fantasize about long after the experience.

Just five hours away by plane from California, Hawai'i is a thousand light years away in fantasy. Mostly a state of mind, Hawai'i is the image of escape from the rawness and violence of daily American life. Hawai'i—the word, the vision, the sound in the mind—is the fragrance and feel of soft kindness. Above all, Hawai'i is "she," the Western image of the Native "female" in her magical allure. And if luck prevails, some of "her" will rub off on you, the visitor.

This fictional Hawai'i comes out of the depths of Western sexual sickness which demands a dark, sin-free Native for instant gratification between imperialist wars.

Haunani-Kay Trask, From *A Native Daughter*. Copyright 1993 by Haunani-Kay Trask. Published by Common Courage Press, Monroe, Maine. Reprinted with permission. The present version is slightly revised.

The attraction of Hawai'i is stimulated by slick Hollywood movies, saccharine Andy Williams music, and the constant psychological deprivations of maniacal American life. Tourists flock to my Native land for escape, but they are escaping into a state of mind while participating in the destruction of a host people in a Native place.

To Hawaiians, daily life is neither soft nor kind. In fact, the political, economic, and cultural reality for most Hawaiians is hard, ugly, and cruel.

In Hawai'i, the destruction of our land and the prostitution of our culture are planned and executed by multinational corporations (both foreign-based and Hawai'i-based), by huge landowners (like the missionary-descended Castle and Cook—of Dole Pineapple fame—and others) and by collaborationist state and county governments. The ideological gloss that claims tourism to be our economic savior and the "natural" result of Hawaiian culture is manufactured by ad agencies (like the state supported Hawai'i Visitors' Bureau) and tour companies (many of which are owned by the airlines), and spewed out to the public through complicitous cultural engines like film, television and radio, and the daily newspapers. As for the local labor unions, both rank and file and management clamor for more tourists while the construction industry lobbies incessantly for larger resorts.

The major public educational institution, the University of Hawai'i, funnels millions of taxpayer dollars into a School of Travel Industry Management and a Business School replete with a Real Estate Center and a Chair of Free Enterprise (renamed the Walker Chair to hide the crude reality of capitalism). As the propaganda arm of the tourist industry in Hawai'i, both schools churn out studies that purport to show why Hawai'i needs more golf courses, hotels, and tourist infrastructure and how Hawaiian culture is "naturally" one of giving and entertaining.

Of course, state-encouraged commodification and prostitution of Native cultures through tourism are not unique to Hawai'i. They are suffered by peoples in places as disparate as Goa, Australia, Tahiti, and the Southwestern United States. Indeed, the problem is so commonplace that international organizations—e.g., the Ecumenical Coalition on Third World Tourism out of Bangkok, the Center for Responsible Tourism in California, and the Third World European Network—have banded together to help give voice to Native peoples in daily resistance against corporate tourism. My focus on Hawai'i, although specific to my own culture, would likely transfer well when applied to other Native peoples.[1]

Despite our similarities with other major tourist destinations, the statistical picture of the effects of corporate tourism in Hawai'i is shocking:

Fact: Over thirty years ago, at statehood, Hawai'i residents outnumbered tourists by more than 2 to 1. Today, tourists outnumber residents by 6 to 1; they outnumber Native Hawaiians by 30 to 1.[2]

Fact: According to independent economists and criminologists, "tourism has been the single most powerful factor in O'ahu's crime rate," including crimes against people and property.[3]

Fact: Independent demographers have been pointing out for years that "tourism is the major source of population growth in Hawai'i" and that "rapid growth of the tourist industry ensures the trend toward a rapidly expanded population that receives lower per capita income."[4]

Fact: The Bank of Hawai'i has reported that the average real incomes of Hawai'i residents grew only *one* percent during the period from the early seventies through the early eighties, when tourism was booming. The Census Bureau reports that personal income growth in Hawai'i during the same time was the lowest by far of any of the 50 American states.[5]

Fact: Ground water supplies on O'ahu will be insufficient to meet the needs of residents and tourists by the year 2000.[6]

Fact: According to the *Honolulu Advertiser,* "Japanese investors have spent more than $7.1 billion on their acquisitions" since 1986 in Hawai'i. This kind of volume translates into huge alienations of land and properties. For example, nearly 2,000 acres of land on the Big Island of Hawai'i was purchased for $18.5 million while over 7,000 acres on Moloka'i went for $33 million. In 1989, over $1 billion was spent by the Japanese on land alone.[7]

Fact: More plants and animals from Hawai'i are now extinct or on the endangered species list than in the rest of the United States.[8]

Fact: More than 20,500 families are on the Hawaiian trust lands' list, waiting for housing or pastoral lots.[9]

Fact: The median cost of a home on the most populated island of O'ahu is $450,000.[10]

Fact: Hawai'i has by far the worst ratio of average family income to average housing costs in the country. This explains why families spend nearly 52 percent of their gross income for housing costs.[11]

Fact: Nearly one-fifth of Hawai'i's resident population is classified as *near-homeless,* that is, those for whom any mishap results in immediate on-the-street homelessness.[12]

These kinds of random statistics render a very bleak picture, not at all what the posters and jingoistic tourist promoters would have you believe about Hawai'i.

My use of the word "tourism" in the Hawai'i context refers to a mass-based, corporately controlled industry that is both vertically and horizontally integrated such that one multi-national corporation owns an airline, the tour buses that transport tourists to the corporation-owned hotel where they eat in a corporation-owned restaurant, play golf and "experience" Hawai'i on corporation-owned recreation areas, and eventually consider buying a second home built on corporation land. Profits, in this case, are mostly repatriated back to the home country. In Hawai'i, these "home" countries are Japan, Taiwan, Hong Kong, Canada, Australia, and the United States. In this sense, Hawai'i is very much like a Third World colony where the local elite—the Democratic Party in our state—collaborates in the rape of Native land and people.[13]

The mass nature of this kind of tourism results in mega-resort complexes on thousands of acres with demands for water and services that far surpass the needs of Hawai'i residents. These complexes may boast several hotels, golf courses, restaurants, and other "necessaries" to complete the total tourist experience. Infrastructure is usually built by the developer in exchange for county approval of more hotel units. In Hawai'i, counties bid against each other to attract larger and larger complexes. "Rich" counties, then, are those with more resorts since they will pay more of the tax base of the county. The richest of these is the County of Honolulu which encompasses the entire island of O'ahu. This island is the site of four major tourist destinations, a major international airport, and 80 percent of the resident population of Hawai'i. The military also controls nearly 30 percent of the island with bases and airports of their own. As you might imagine, the density of certain parts of Honolulu (e.g., Waikīkī) is among the highest in the world. At the present annual visitor count, more than 5 million tourists pour through O'ahu, an island of only 607 square miles. According to a statistician I met at an international tourism conference in Germany in 1986, Hawai'i suffers the greatest number of tourists per square mile of any place on earth.

With this as a background on tourism, I want to move now into the area of cultural prostitution. "Prostitution" in this context refers to the entire institution which defines a woman (and by extension the "female") as an object of degraded and victimized sexual value for use and exchange through the medium of money. The "prostitute" is then a woman who sells her sexual capacities and is seen, thereby, to possess and reproduce them at will, that is, by her very "nature." The prostitute and the institution which creates and maintains her are, of course, of patriarchal origin. The pimp is the conduit of exchange, managing the commodity that is the prostitute while acting as the guard at the entry and exit gates, making sure the prostitute behaves as a prostitute by fulfilling her sexual-economic functions. The victims participate in their victimization with enormous ranges of feeling, including resistance and complicity, but the force and continuity of the institution are shaped by men.

There is much more to prostitution than my sketch reveals but this must suffice for I am interested in using the largest sense of this term as a metaphor in understanding what has happened to Hawaiian culture. My purpose is not to exact detail or fashion a model but to convey the utter degradation of our culture and our people under corporate tourism by employing "prostitution" as an analytic category.

Finally, I have chosen four areas of Hawaiian culture to examine: our homeland, or *one hānau* that is Hawai'i, our lands and fisheries, the outlying seas and the heavens; our language and dance; our familial relationships; and our women.

NĀ MEA HAWAI'I—THINGS HAWAIIAN

The *mo'ōlelo*, or history of Hawaiians, is to be found in our genealogies. From our great cosmogonic genealogy, the *Kumulipo,* derives the Hawaiian identity. The "essential lesson" of this genealogy is "the interrelatedness of the Hawaiian world, and the inseparability of its constituent parts." Thus, "the genealogy of the land, the gods, chiefs, and people intertwine one with the other, and with all aspects of the universe."[14]

In the *mo'ōlelo* of Papa and Wākea, earth-mother and sky-father, our islands are born: Hawai'i, Maui, O'ahu, Kaua'i, and Ni'ihau. From their human offspring came the *taro* plant and from the taro came the Hawaiian people. The lessons of our genealogy are that human beings have a familial relationship to land and to the *taro,* our elder siblings or *kua'ana.*

In Hawai'i, as in all of Polynesia, younger siblings must serve and honor elder siblings who, in turn, must feed and care for their younger siblings. Therefore, Hawaiians must cultivate and husband the land which will feed and provide for the Hawaiian people. This relationship of people to land is called *mālama 'āina* or *aloha 'āina,* care and love of the land.

When people and land work together harmoniously, the balance that results is called *pono.* In Hawaiian society, the *ali'i* or chiefs were required to maintain order, abundance of food, and good government.

The *maka'āinana* or common people worked the land and fed the chiefs; the *ali'i* organized production and appeased the gods.

Today, *mālama 'āina* is called stewardship by some, although that word does not convey spiritual and genealogical connections. Nevertheless, to love and make the land flourish is a Hawaiian value. *'Āina*, one of the words for land, means *that which feeds*. *Kama'āina*, a term for Native-born people, means *child of the land*. Thus is the Hawaiian relationship to land both familial and reciprocal.

Our deities are also of the land: Pele is our volcano, Kāne and Lono our fertile valleys and plains, Kanaloa our ocean and all that lives within it, and so on with the 40,000 and 400,000 gods of Hawai'i. Our whole universe, physical and metaphysical, is divine.

Within this world, the older people or *kūpuna* are to cherish those who are younger, the *mo'opuna*. Unstinting generosity is a value and of high status. Social connections between our people are through *aloha*, simply translated as love but carrying with it a profoundly Hawaiian sense that is, again, familial and genealogical. Hawaiians feel *aloha* for Hawai'i whence they come and for their Hawaiian kin upon whom they depend. It is nearly impossible to feel or practice *aloha* for something that is not familial. This is why we extend familial relations to those few non-Natives whom we feel understand and can reciprocate our *aloha*. But *aloha* is freely given and freely returned, it is not and cannot be demanded, or commanded. Above all, *aloha* is a cultural feeling and practice that works among the people and between the people and their land.

The significance and meaning of *aloha* underscores the centrality of the Hawaiian language or *'ōlelo* to the culture. *'Ōlelo* means both language and tongue; *mo'ōlelo*, or history, is that which comes from the tongue, i.e., a story. *Haole* or white people say we have oral history, but what we have are stories passed on through the generations. These are different from the *haole* sense of history. To Hawaiians in traditional society, language had tremendous power, thus the phrase, *i ka 'ōlelo ke ola; i ka 'ōlelo ka make*—in language is life, in language is death.

After nearly 2,000 years of speaking Hawaiian, our people suffered the near extinction of our language through its banning by the American-imposed government in 1896. In 1900, Hawai'i became a territory of the United States. All schools, government operations and official transactions were thereafter conducted in English, despite the fact that most people, including non-Natives, still spoke Hawaiian at the turn of the century.

Since 1970, *'ōlelo Hawai'i,* or the Hawaiian language, has undergone a tremendous revival, including the rise of language immersion schools. The State of Hawai'i now has two official languages, Hawaiian and English, and the call for Hawaiian language speakers and teachers grows louder by the day.[15]

Along with the flowering of Hawaiian language has come a flowering of Hawaiian dance, especially in its ancient form, called *hula kahiko*. Dance academies, known as *hālau*, have proliferated throughout Hawai'i as have *kumu hula*, or dance masters, and formal competitions where all-night presentations continue for three or four days to throngs of appreciative listeners. Indeed, among Pacific Islanders, Hawaiian dance is considered one of the finest Polynesian art forms today.

Of course, the cultural revitalization that Hawaiians are now experiencing and transmitting to their children is as much a *repudiation* of colonization by so-called Western civilization in its American form as it is a *reclamation* of our own past and our own ways of life. This is why cultural revitalization is often resisted and disparaged by anthropologists and others: they see very clearly that its political effect is decolonization of the mind. Thus our rejection of the nuclear family as the basic unit of society and of individualism as the best form of human expression infuriates social workers, the churches, the legal system, and educators. Hawaiians continue to have allegedly "illegitimate" children, to *hānai* or adopt both children and adults outside of sanctioned Western legal concepts, to hold and use land and water in a collective form rather than a private property form, and to proscribe the notion and the value that one person should strive to surpass and therefore outshine all others.

All these Hawaiian values can be grouped under the idea of *'ohana,* loosely translated as family, but more accurately imagined as a group of both closely and distantly related people who share nearly everything, from land and food to children and status. Sharing is central to this value since it prevents individual decline. Of course, poverty is not thereby avoided, it is only shared with everyone in the unit. The *'ohana* works effectively when the *kua'ana* relationship (elder sibling/younger sibling reciprocity) is practiced.

Finally, within the *'ohana,* our women are considered the lifegivers of the nation, and are accorded the respect and honor this status conveys. Our young women, like our young people in general, are the *pua,* or flower of our *lāhui,* or our nation. The renowned beauty of our women, especially their sexual beauty, is not considered a commodity to be hoarded by fathers and brothers but an attribute of our people. Culturally, Hawaiians are very open and free about sexual relationships, although Christianity and organized religion have done much to damage these traditional sexual values.

With this understanding of what it means to be Hawaiian, I want to move now to the prostitution of our culture by tourism.

Hawai'i itself is the female object of degraded and victimized sexual value. Our *'āina,* or lands, are not any longer the source of food and shelter, but the source of money. Land is now called real estate; rather than our mother, *Papa.* The American relationship of people to land is that of exploiter to exploited. Beautiful areas, once sacred to my people, are now expensive resorts; shorelines where net fishing, seaweed gathering and crabbing occurred are more and more the exclusive domain of recreational activities: sunbathing, windsurfing, jet skiing. Now, even access to beaches near hotels is strictly regulated or denied to the local public altogether.

The phrase *mālama 'āina*—to care for the land—is used by government officials to sell new projects and to convince the locals that hotels can be built with a concern for "ecology." Hotel historians, like hotel doctors, are stationed in-house to soothe the visitors' stay with the pablum of invented myths and tales of the "primitive."

High schools and hotels adopt each other and funnel teenagers through major resorts for guided tours from kitchens to gardens to honeymoon suites in preparation for post-secondary jobs in the lowest-paid industry in the State. In the meantime, tourist appreciation kits and movies are distributed through the State Department of Education to all elementary schools. One film, unashamedly titled "What's in it for Me?," was devised to convince locals that tourism is, as the newspapers never tire of saying, "the only game in town."

Of course, all this hype is necessary to hide the truth about tourism, the awful exploitative truth that the industry is the major cause of environmental degradation, low wages, land dispossession, and the highest cost of living in the United States.

The above caricature of Polynesian people is a typical example of how corporate tourism in Hawaii commodifies Native culture for the global tourism market.

While this propaganda is churned out to local residents, the commercialization of Hawaiian culture proceeds with calls for more sensitive marketing of our Native values and practices. After all, a prostitute is only as good as her income-producing talents. These talents, in Hawaiian terms, are the *hula;* the generosity, or *aloha,* of our people; the *u'i* or youthful beauty of our women and men; and the continuing allure of our lands and waters, that is, of our place, Hawai'i.

The selling of these talents must produce income. And the function of tourism and the State of Hawai'i is to convert these attributes into profit.

The first requirement is the transformation of the product, or the cultural attribute, much as a woman must be transformed to look like a prostitute, i.e., someone who is complicitous in her own commodification. Thus *hula* dancers wear clown-like make-up, don costumes from a mix of Polynesian cultures, and behave in a manner that is smutty and salacious rather than powerfully erotic. The distance between the smutty and the erotic is precisely the distance between Western culture and Hawaiian culture. In the hotel version of the *hula,* the sacredness of the dance has completely evaporated while the athleticism and sexual expression have been packaged like ornaments. The purpose is entertainment for profit rather than a joyful and truly Hawaiian celebration of human and divine nature.

The point, of course, is that everything in Hawai'i can be yours, that is, you the tourist, the non-Native, the visitor. The place, the people, the culture, even our identity as a "Native" people is for sale.

Thus, Hawai'i, like a lovely woman, is there for the taking. Those with only a little money get a brief encounter, those with a lot of money, like the Japanese, get more. The State and counties will give tax breaks, build infrastructure, and have the governor personally welcome tourists to ensure they keep coming. Just as the pimp regulates prices and guards the commodity of the prostitute, so the State bargains with developers for access to Hawaiian land and culture. Who builds the biggest resorts to attract the most affluent tourists gets the best deal: more hotel rooms, golf courses, and restaurants approved. Permits are fast-tracked, height and density limits are suspended, new ground water sources are miraculously found.

Hawaiians, meanwhile, have little choice in all this. We can fill up the unemployment lines, enter the military, work in the tourist industry, or leave Hawai'i. Increasingly, Hawaiians are leaving, not by choice but out of economic necessity.

Our people who work in the industry—dancers, waiters, singers, valets, gardeners, housekeepers, bartenders, and even a few managers—make between $10,000 and $25,000 a year, an impossible salary for a family in Hawai'i. Psychologically, our young people have begun to think of tourism as the only employment opportunity, trapped as they are by the lack of alternatives. For our young women, modeling is a "cleaner" job when compared to waiting on tables, or dancing in a weekly revue, but modeling feeds on tourism and the commodification of Hawaiian women. In the end, the entire employment scene is shaped by tourism.

Despite their exploitation, Hawaiians' participation in tourism raises the problem of complicity. Because wages are so low and advancement so rare, whatever complicity exists is secondary to the economic hopelessness that drives Hawaiians into the industry.

Refusing to contribute to the commercialization of one's culture becomes a peripheral concern when unemployment looms.

Of course, many Hawaiians do not see tourism as part of their colonization. Thus tourism is viewed as providing jobs, not as a form of cultural prostitution. Even those who have some glimmer of critical consciousness don't generally agree that the tourist industry prostitutes Hawaiian culture. To me, this is a measure of the depth of our mental oppression: we can't understand our own cultural degradation because we are living it. As colonized people, we are colonized to the extent that we are unaware of our oppression. When awareness begins, then so too does de-colonization. Judging by the growing resistance to new hotels, to geothermal energy and manganese nodule mining which would supplement the tourist industry, and to increases in the sheer number of tourists, I would say that de-colonization has begun, but we have many more stages to negotiate on our path to sovereignty.

My brief excursion into the prostitution of Hawaiian culture has done no more than give an overview. Now that you have heard a Native view, let me just leave this thought behind. If you are thinking of visiting my homeland, please don't. We don't want or need any more tourists, and we certainly don't like them. If you want to help our cause, pass this message on to your friends.

NOTES

Author's note: *Lovely Hula Hands* is the title of a famous and very saccharine song written by a *haole* who fell in love with Hawaii in the pre-Statehood era. It embodies the worst romanticized views of *hula* dancers and Hawaiian culture in general.

1. The Center for Responsible Tourism and the Third World European Network were created out of the activism and organizing of the Ecumenical Coalition on Third World Tourism (ECTWT). This

umbrella organization is composed of the following member bodies: All Africa Conference of Churches, Caribbean Conference of Churches, Christian Conference of Asia, Consejo Latinoamericano de Iglesias, Federation of Asian Bishops Conference/Office of Human Development, Middle East Council of Churches, Pacific Conference of Churches. In addition, sister organizations, like the Hawai'i Ecumenical Coalition on Tourism, extend the network world-wide. The ECTWT publishes a quarterly magazine with articles on Third World tourism and its destructive effects from child prostitution to dispossession of Native peoples. The address for ECTWT is P.O. Box 24 Chorakhebua, Bangkok 10230, Thailand.

2. Eleanor C. Nordyke, *The Peopling of Hawai'i* (Honolulu: University of Hawai'i Press, 2 ed., 1989), pp. 134–172.

3. Meda Chesney-Lind, "Salient Factors in Hawai'i's Crime Rate," University of Hawai'i School of Social Work (n.d.).

4. Nordyke, *ibid.*

5. Bank of Hawai'i Annual Economic Report, 1984.

6. Estimate of independent hydrologist Kate Vandemoer to community organizing group, *Kupa'a He'eia*, February 1990. Water quality and ground water depletion are two problems much discussed by State and county officials in Hawai'i but ignored when resort permits are considered.

7. *Honolulu Advertiser*, April 8, 1990.

8. David Stannard, Testimony against West Beach Estates. Land Use Commission, State of Hawai'i, January 10, 1985.

9. Department of Hawaiian Homelands, Annual Report, 1989.

10. *Honolulu Star-Bulletin,* May 8, 1990.

11. Bank of Hawai'i Annual Economic Report, 1984. This figure is outdated. My guess is that now, in 1992, families spend closer to 60% of their gross income for housing costs. Billion-dollar Japanese investments and other speculation since 1984 have caused rental and purchase prices to skyrocket.

12. This is the estimate of a State-contracted firm that surveyed the islands for homeless and near-homeless families. Testimony was delivered to the State legislature, 1990 session.

13. For an analysis of post-statehood Hawai'i and its turn to mass-based corporate tourism, see Noel Kent, *Hawai'i: Islands Under the Influence*, op. cit. For an analysis of foreign investment in Hawai'i, see *A Study of Foreign Investment and Its Impact on the State*, Hawai'i Real Estate Center, University of Hawai'i, 1989.

14. Lilikalā Kame'eleihiwa, *Native Land and Foreign Desires* (Honolulu: Bishop Museum, Press, 1992), p. 2.

15. See Larry Kimura, "Native Hawaiian Culture," in *Native Hawaiians Study Commission Report*, Vol. 1, op. cit., pp. 173–197.

THE STRUGGLE OVER LAND ON CENTRAL AMERICA'S LAST FRONTIER

Mac Chapin

INTRODUCTION

Central America is a land bridge connecting North and South America, the two largest terrestrial ecosystems of the Western Hemi-

Revised and translated from Spanish by the author. © 2000 Mac Chapin. Abridged and reprinted by permission.

sphere. Its total land area of approximately 530,000 km^2 runs diagonally northwest to southeast in a thin strip separating the Pacific Ocean from the Caribbean Sea. It is an extremely heterogeneous mosaic of climate, landforms, soils, vegetation, and animal life. Species from both North and South America intermingle along this isthmus, making it one of the richest zones of biological diversity in the world. More than 850 species of birds, for example, have been recorded for Costa Rica and Panama alone, and some 225 types of birds use Central America as a seasonal migratory corridor.

Central America is also a region of considerable cultural diversity, with 43 distinct indigenous/linguistic groups making up a population of more than five million people, which is somewhere between 15 and 20 percent of the total population of the region. These cultures have managed to survive, some more successfully than others as they have been modified and shaped by the flow of history. The measure of success has been, to an extent that cannot be exaggerated, their ability to hold onto their land and their natural resources.

The largest concentration of indigenous peoples is found in Guatemala, where as much as 50 percent of the total nine million population belongs to one of 23 different ethnic/linguistic groups. Virtually all of the remaining indigenous peoples of Central America live in the lowland forests of the Caribbean slope, stretching from Belize down the length of the isthmus as far as the Panamanian border with Colombia. Until recently, these groups had lived in isolation, cut off from the mainstream national cultures by the lack of roads and alternative means of transportation into their homelands. With the exception of the Miskito in Honduras and Nicaragua and the Kuna in Panama, both of which have never been conquered or otherwise subjugated and have kept a relatively high national profile, many of the Caribbean coastal groups are unknown and essentially invisible to the non-indigenous majority within their countries.

Today, however, this isolation and the protection it brought are threatened by what has become a many-pronged assault. As the forests are being overrun by a variety of forces—landless peasants from the over-populated and environmentally degraded interior provinces, logging operations, cattle ranchers, and multinational companies in search of cheap natural resources—the indigenous peoples who make them their home are facing what amounts to a Second Conquest.

PREHISTORY AND HISTORY

. . . Nomadic Paleo-Indian hunters and gatherers were well represented along the Central American isthmus by the ninth millennium B.C. Their numbers were still small; they had not yet developed agriculture and adopted sedentary settlement patterns; and their modification of the natural environment, which was primarily tropical rain forest, was minimal.

At some point during the next two millennia clusters of the new resident Central American population began domesticating plants and establishing small permanent villages. Maize cultivation had taken hold, having spread from its origin in Mexico as far to the south as Panama, by the year 5,000 B.C.; squash and beans, together with a variety of other cultigens, were added over time to the farming repertoire. The population increased gradually and permanent settlements proliferated; through time they expanded their range of occupation, laying claim to the Pacific coastal slope, the central highlands, and the humid forests and savannahs of the Caribbean watershed.

When Spanish boats began appearing off the Caribbean coast on the eve of the 16th century, Central America's indigenous population had reached an estimated five to six million people. The areas of densest settlement were found along the Pacific watershed, where the climate was more agreeable and the soils better for agriculture. It is romantic folly to believe that the region was largely covered with pristine forests at that time. Agriculture had evolved from its humble beginnings some nine thousand years earlier into a sophisticated and widespread subsistence strategy. Pre-Hispanic farmers had domesticated an ample variety of plants and large areas of the region had been cleared of vegetation by their slash-and-burn technology: the Peten of Guatemala was, by the first millennium A.D., reduced to stubble and savannah; and when the Spaniards arrived in Panama, they walked over extensive grasslands on their march from the Darien across to what are today the interior provinces of the Azuero Peninsula. They felt right at home; it reminded them of the cattle ranches of their native Spain.

In the years that followed European contact, however, disease, enforced slavery, and warfare joined together to decimate the native inhabitants, whose numbers dropped as drastically as 80 percent in some regions. Most of those who survived the decimation escaped or were driven into the most inaccessible and difficult corners of the isthmus—what the Mexican anthropologist Gonzalo Aguirre Beltrán has referred to as "regions of refuge." In Central America, the two major regions of refuge were the rugged volcanic highlands of Guatemala and the lowland forests of the Caribbean Coastal slope, stretching in a largely unbroken strip from Belize to the north down through Panama (see map).

During the next three centuries, the natural environment of the suddenly depopulated isthmus recovered. Although the Amerindians in pre-Hispanic times had deforested extensive areas for agriculture, they always left intact large tracts of natural vegetation about the landscape near their settlements for gathering food and materials, as well as for hunting. These remnants served as "genetic banks" from which the forests throughout Central America made a rapid comeback after Conquest and began to reclaim a good portion of the territory they had formerly occupied. In this way, the man-made savannahs of the Darien were transformed into the dense tropical forests that characterize this region today. In similar fashion, the Peten was overgrown with a thick mantle of rain forest.

As the forests recovered, so did Central America's population, slowly but steadily. By 1900 there were approximately 3,750,000 people in the region, most of them concentrated along the Pacific slope, where the original indigenous peoples had made their home. The Indians who had not been absorbed by the expanding mestizo population, and had survived conquest and colonization with their cultures intact, were found largely in the outlying regions, in the Guatemalan highlands and the Caribbean rain forests. In these regions, they remained largely isolated from the political and economic life of the new republics.

The demographic pace gradually picked up during the first decades of the century, and by 1940 Central America's population had nearly doubled, growing to an estimated 7,200,000. Over the next 50 years, the population literally exploded, approaching 30 million by the early 1990s, with more than 80 percent of the population concentrated in the central highlands or along the Pacific slope. Fueled by this sudden population growth, which was intertwined with the steadily increasing concentration of the best farmland in the hands of wealthy farmers, the spread of cattle ranching and multinational monocrop agriculture, and the concomitant degradation of ecosystems, Central America entered a period of accelerated change. Until this time, the region's tropical forests along the Caribbean watershed and the indigenous groups living within them had been largely protected from the outside

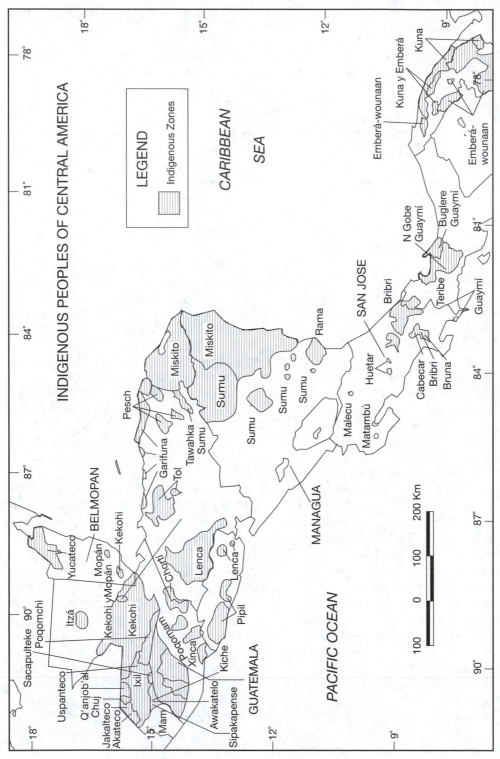

INDIGENOUS PEOPLES OF CENTRAL AMERICA

LEGEND

Indigenous Zones

CARIBBEAN SEA

PACIFIC OCEAN

BELMOPAN

GUATEMALA

MANAGUA

SAN JOSE

Yucateco
Mopán
Kekohi
Pesch
Garifuna
Tol
Tawahka
Sumu
Miskito
Sumu
Sumu
Sumu
Rama
Sacapulteke
Itzá
Poqomchi
Kekohi y Mopán
Kekohi
Poqomam
Chortí
Lenca
Lenca
Uspanteco
Q'anjob'al
Chuj
Jakalteco
Akateco
Ixil
Mam
Xinca
Kiche
Pipil
Awakatelo
Sipakapense
Huetar
Malecu
Matambú
Cabecar
Bribri
Bruna
Teribe
Guaymí
N Gobe Guaymí
Buglere Guaymí
Bribri
Emberá-wounaan
Kuna y Emberá
Kuna
Emberá-wounaan

200 Km
100   0   100

Source: "The Coexistence of Indigenous Peoples and the Natural Environment in
Central America," *National Geographic*. A special map supplement to *Research and
Exploration*, a scholarly publication of National Geographical Society, Spring 1992.
© 1992 Mac Chapin.

404

world. Within the space of a few decades, however, the earlier trend in the direction of forest regeneration and the replenishment of natural ecosystems in general was dramatically reversed.

THE ASSAULT ON THE FORESTS

In the 1940s and 1950s, new technologies appeared, and the invasion of the region's remaining tropical rain forests and related ecosystems began in earnest. Chain saws, tractors, bulldozers, heavy-duty trucks, and other motorized machines facilitated the construction of roads and the clearing of land at an unprecedented rate. Advances in public health controlled malaria and other endemic diseases, making settlement in the humid lowlands not only possible but, for the first time, attractive. In succeeding decades, cattle ranching, working in tandem with logging operations, spread into the forests to meet the growing demand of foreign markets. Governments throughout the region, faced with burgeoning populations in the increasingly overcrowded interior provinces, launched frontier settlement programs. Behind such rallying cries as "the conquest of the Atlantic Coast" and "the expansion of the agricultural frontier," both organized and spontaneous colonization began along the newly built penetration roads into the remaining forests of the Caribbean coastal plains.

Multinational operations in the form of the large banana companies first began penetrating the Caribbean coastal region at the turn of the twentieth century. This penetration continues today and has even expanded, with many corporations carving out more extensive plantations and diversifying their crops to include pineapple and citrus, as well as more "exotic" fruits such as papaya and passion fruit, for consistently expanding international markets. During the last decade, seafood has become yet another target for foreign buyers. This has prompted the destruction of mangrove forests along the Pacific coast for the construction of shrimp farms and the virtual extinction of lobsters over large stretches of the Caribbean coast.

Companies such as the Stone Container Corporation, a Chicago-based paper bag and cardboard box manufacturer, and Equipe Nicaragua. S.A., a Nicaraguan-Taiwanese venture, attempted in 1991 to gain lumber concessions in the Mosquitia region of Honduras and Nicaragua, in Miskito and Sumu territory; and in 1992 Texaco made a strong bid for drilling concessions in the Bocas del Toro area of Panama, where the Ngöbe have lived for centuries. After fierce campaigning by alliances of conservation and indigenous groups, these projects were rejected; but the threat is constantly on the verge of resurfacing. Still another threat has appeared in recent years from mining companies, primarily Canadian firms, as well as small-scale illegal operations throughout remote river systems in the region. The Canadian firms have gained concessions to exploit indigenous lands in Panama in Kuna, Emberá, and Ngöbe territory; illegal mining has been infiltrating the Kuna Comarca near the Colombian border, the Talamanca region in Costa Rica, the Atlantic Coast region of Nicaragua, and the upper reaches of the Patuca River in Honduras.

THE INDIGENOUS RESPONSE

With all of these forces converging, the indigenous inhabitants of the last remaining forests in Central America find themselves hemmed in. No longer can they retreat before the advances of the colonization front and redraw their territories beyond the periphery of the modern world. They have, quite simply, run out of space. With their backs to the sea, as it were, and the chain saws moving ever closer, many of the indigenous groups have begun to organize themselves and stand firm. Throughout the 1980s, and gaining considerable steam as they crossed over into the 1990s, indigenous federations have been appearing and demanding recognition from their national governments. Virtually all of this activity has been focused on the issue of land, and the tactics have changed. Whereas in the past armed resistance and violence were common strategies (which generally failed), today Indians are relying more and more on legal structures and negotiation.

The Kuna of Panama have been actively involved in land legalization and protection issues since the early years of this century. They have used a combination of legal tactics, diplomacy and insurrection, and they have been successful; in 1938 they managed to secure legal title to their autonomous territory, the Comarca de Kuna Yala (San Blas), from the Panamanian government. But holding onto what is legally their land is another matter, one that has only recently begun to heat up. In response, the Study Project for the Management of Wildlife Areas of Kuna Yala (PEMASKY) was created in 1983 by a team of Kuna professionals with the main objective of protecting the Comarca from the incursion of non-Indian colonists. Since that time, the Kuna have moved forward with demarcation of their territorial limits, the penetration of colonists has been stemmed, and Kuna political leaders have launched an aggressive campaign to recover lands they have lost at the western end of their territory.

Also in Panama, the Kuna residing on the Pacific slope of the isthmus in the region of Madungandi had their Comarca ratified by the Panamanian government in 1997; farther to the southeast in the Province of Darien, the Kuna of the region of Wargandi are proposing a similar designation with the government, and the Emberá, Wounaan, and the Kuna of the communities of Púcuru and Paya (near the Colombian border) are pushing for land claims. In western Panama, the Ngöbe recently were partially successful in securing a pared-down version of their Comarca; but their attempts to stave off Canadian mining companies in the area of Cerro Colorado have been less than satisfactory.

Costa Rica has eight distinct indigenous peoples with a total population of approximately 30,000 people, which represents less than 1 percent of the total population. The Bribri and the Cabécar, the two largest groups in the country, inhabit the largest remaining tract of natural vegetation in Costa Rica, in the Valle de Estrella-Talamanca region, running south from the Caribbean coastal plain across the Talamanca Mountain range and down the Pacific slope into the municipality of Buenos Aires. Much of this area is covered by La Amistad Biosphere Reserve, a bi-national park spilling over into Panama's Bocas del Toro Province. In recent years a number of groups, such as SOSWAK and CODEBRIWAK, have formed in Bribri territory with the joint objectives of recovering cultural traditions and defending territorial rights.

The Miskito of the northeast coastal region of Nicaragua have begun to organize around the creation of the Miskito Coast Protected Area. This is a response to the illegal and semi-legal activities of a variety of outsiders to exploit their marine resources. The University of the Autonomous Regions of the Caribbean Coast (URACCAN) has been leading in the fight to preserve Miskito and Sumu lands and resources, and other organizations, such as the Council of Elders, have become active in national-level protest campaigns, demarcation, and mapping projects among the communities of the coast. Inland and to the south of the Coco River, the Bosawas region, one of the largest intact areas of tropical forest in Central America, and its Miskito and Sumu communities are simultaneously under siege; the Sumu organization SUKAWALA has initiated demarcation of their territorial limits in the face of considerable violence and what is perhaps best described as anarchy.

Honduras has witnessed a flurry of organizational activity on the part of the indigenous groups throughout the '90s. Most recently, the Honduran Confederation of Autochthonous Peoples (CONPAH), which brings together the Pech, Miskito, Lenca, Tawahka, Chortí, Tol (Xicaque), and Garifuna peoples, has focused much of its attention on legal battles over land. Another support group working with land issues is MOPAWI, which concentrates on the Mosquitia. Moskitia Pawisa (MOPAWI—"Development of the Mosquitia") collaborated with the Miskito group Moskitia Asla Takanka (MASTA—"Unity of the Mosquitia") in 1992 on a land use mapping project that has become the basis for recent campaigns for the protection and legalization of indigenous land claims. Among other developments, the mapping has stimulated the formation of seven indigenous federations in the Mosquitia, all of which came together to confront the land issue. The Tawahka nation has formed the Indigenous Tawahka Federation of Honduras (FITH) in the upper reaches of the Patuca River. In recent years, the Tawahka have successfully lobbied to have their territory declared an indigenous reserve. Now they are faced with their biggest challenge: protection of what is legally theirs.

In the Department of Yoro, the Tol (Xicaque) have been involved in land disputes with neighboring large landholders for decades. They are now working through the Federation of Indigenous Xicaque Tribes of Yoro (FETRIXY) on legal strategies to resolve their claims. The Garifuna, who live along the north coast of Honduras, have been working through several different organizations on land claims; and in 1994, the Lenca of the Department of Intibucá organized a march to protest abuses of their territorial rights; as a result, the Honduran government proclaimed the departmental capital, La Esperanza, an "Indigenous Municipality." And the Chortí, long dormant, have emerged to take on the government in a push, amid violence, to gain title to a portion of their ancestral territory in the southwest corner of the country, in the Provinces of Ocotepeque and Copán.

In southern Belize, the Mopan and Kekchi Mayan groups have formed the Toledo Maya Cultural Council (TMCC) and the Toledo Alcaldes Association to seek recognition of a Maya Homeland. In 1996, they worked with the GeoMap Group out of Berkeley, California, and the Indian Law Resource Center to map their lands and produce the *Maya Atlas: The Struggle to Preserve Maya Land in Southern Belize*. All of this activity has stimulated the Garifuna to take a more active approach to their lands. Through the National Garifuna Council, and working through the recently organized Belize National Indigenous Council (BENIC), they have been working with the indigenous affairs office of the International Labor Organization (ILO), located in San José, Costa Rica. This effort is serving to have the Belizean government ratify ILO Convention 169, which deals with the protection of the rights of indigenous peoples; a key piece of this convention deals with land rights.

El Salvador's Indians are a tragic case that stands apart from many of the neighboring groups. They had no regions of refuge into which they might retreat, and with the abolition of their communal lands in the 1800s their fate was sealed. Although they have survived physically and presently number more than 500,000, they have lost their lands, their autonomy, their language, and a large part of their culture. At the same time, less than 2 percent of El Salvador's original forest cover remains.

The Petén region of Guatemala presents a somewhat anomalous case. This was the core area of Classic Maya civilization up until the middle of the 9th century A.D.; and up until the time of the Spanish conquest it was heavily populated. Through the colonial period, however, the indigenous population declined; and by the middle of the twentieth century the only surviving native group was a handful of Itzá Maya living in the vicinity of Lago Petén Itzá. Since the 1960s, the invasion of colonists has been extreme—with the population of the region escalating from approximately 20,000 in 1960 to close to 600,000 today. While the flow of people has been fueled by corruption and government ineptitude in every shape and form, it is notable that many of the colonists are Q'eqchi' Maya from the overcrowded highlands of Alta Verapaz.

THE CASE FOR INDIGENOUS PARTICIPATION IN CONSERVATION PROGRAMS

A cursory look at the National Geographic map "The Coexistence of Indigenous Peoples and the Natural Environment in Central America," published in 1992, shows that virtually all of the surviving forest is inhabited by indigenous peoples. Beyond this, where indigenous groups have lost their forests and ownership rights to their lands, they have also lost their languages, much of their aboriginal culture, and their autonomy. Examples are the Pipil of El Salvador, the Lenca and the Chortí of Honduras, and the Xinca of southeastern Guatemala. For whatever reasons, it is clear that cultural and biological diversity correspond to a remarkable degree.

What role can indigenous peoples play in the fight to preserve the few—and rapidly disappearing—tropical rain forests in Central America? According to the authors of "The Kuna Indians and Conservation" [Ventocilla et al. 1996], there are at least five reasons it would be advantageous to all to place the indigenous inhabitants in charge of management of the forests in which they live.

First, they have the commitment, as no other group does, to the sustainable use of their natural resources; this is not merely an economic matter, "but something that affects their way of life, for it affects the foundations of their culture." Second, it is a general rule that participation of the local population is essential to any successful attempt at community development, and the same is true for conservation. Unfortunately, they add, "it has been the tradition of conservationists to ignore the opinion and active participation of communities in their attempts to manage the natural resources that these communities depend on for their livelihood." This is a major reason for the failure of so many conservation schemes throughout the world.

Third, indigenous peoples have knowledge of their ecosystems that outsiders do not, and they have an ethic that is oriented toward protecting their resources rather than merely exploiting them. Yes, they utilize the products of the forest—they kill or sell quetzal birds and macaws, for example, and they cut down trees for a variety of purposes. They may not be perfect, in the sense that they do not hold to the strict standards of most conservation biologists; but they are the best conservationists around. The authors add, in the context of the Bayano and Darien region of Panama, which over the last three decades has been invaded by a relentless army of intruders:

Indigenous people understand the need to protect their forests far better than peasant farmers and cattle ranchers. These people are recent colonists with no sense of how to manage the lush tropical forest, and in any case they are much more interested in clearing the forest to make as much money as they can in the shortest time possible.

Fourth, although there is a tendency among some Indians to misrepresent themselves with an overly romanticized image of the innate conservationist, the fact remains that indigenous belief systems still contain strong elements of the conservationist ethic. These form the basis for the collective behavior of the majority of indigenous peoples. The problem is—and a very real problem it is—that there is occurring a serious erosion of traditional belief systems as Western capitalism extends its seductive reach into indigenous communities.

And fifth, indigenous peoples tend to think and act as collective personalities, through their tribal congresses or whatever, and it is relatively easy for outside agencies to negotiate with them. National governments, for example, and conservationist groups, can deal directly with these collective organizations. By contrast, peasants or large landholders are highly individualistic.

CONCLUDING REMARKS

The fate of the indigenous peoples of Central America is intimately bound up with the fate of the region's forests. The future prospects of both are dismal if we follow along the path being taken by the combined chaotic forces of capitalist expansion, government corruption, demographic overflow, and lack of coherent planning. Above all, there has been a blatant lack of political will on the part of those in power, both in the private and public sectors. The reality of widespread poverty has tipped the scales for many politicians in favor of economic growth models at the expense of environmental protection. But this is an example of short-term thinking. The rapid erosion of the natural resource base in Central America is undermining the economy of the region and simultaneously allowing for the destruction of the unique cultures residing inside the few remaining wilderness areas.

Any long-term, viable solution to the economic and political problems besieging Central America must begin with restoration and protection of its ecosystems, and this will necessarily include the participation of indigenous peoples. It will also have to be carried out collaboratively, with working relationships formed among indigenous peoples, conservationists, and national governments. Creating alliances of this sort has been difficult thus far. But for the health of all of us, indigenous and non-indigenous peoples combined, efforts must be made to create them and make them work.

RECOMMENDED READING

"The Coexistence of Indigenous Peoples and the Natural Environment in Central America," by Mac Chapin. Map supplement to *Research & Exploration*. National Geographic Society, Washington, D.C., 1992.

"The Kuna Indians and Conservation," by Jorge Ventocilla, Valerio Núñez, Heraclio Herrera, Francisco Herrera, and Mac Chapin, pages 33–56 in *Traditional Peoples and Biodiversity Conservation in Large Tropical Landscapes*, ed. Kent H. Redford and Jane A. Mansour. The Nature Conservancy, Arlington, V. 1996.

La Lucha por la Tierra en la Ultima Frontera de Centroamérica, ed. Mac Chapin. Special issue of *Mesoamérica*. Centro de Investigaciones Regionales de Mesoamérica (CIRMA), Antigua, Guatemala, June 1995.

Plants and Animals in the Life of the Kuna, by Jorge Ventocilla, Heraclio Herrera, and Valerio Núñez. University of Texas Press, Austin, 1995.

Regiones de Refugio: el desarrollo de la comunidad y el proceso dominical en mestizo América. Instituto Indigenista Interamericano, Mexico, 1967.

PART REVIEW

DISCUSSION QUESTIONS

Simon Ortiz, *It Was That Indian*
1. The poet is speaking satirically in this poem. What is the underlying message?

Winona LaDuke, *Indigenous Environmental Perspectives*
1. What is the relationship between colonialism and indigenous underdevelopment?
2. What have been the environmental consequences of uranium mining on Native American tribes and nations of the United States and Canada?
3. What other environmental problems does the author document in terms of the impact of resource expropriation on North American Indian lands?

Alice Littlefield, *Native American Labor and Public Policy in the United States*
1. What is the author's thesis with respect to the role of Indian labor in the development of capitalism in the United States?
2. How did the termination and relocation policies in post–World War II United States respond to national labor needs?

Tim Johnson, *The Dealer's Edge*
1. What are the benefits of gaming to the Indian community?
2. Are Indian gaming or per capita gaming profits a panacea for all tribes? Explain.

NARF Legal Review, *All We Ever Wanted Was to Catch Fish*
1. Why are subsistence hunting and fishing important to Alaska Natives?
2. What legal action did NARF attorneys file in 1985 on behalf of Alaska Native subsistence rights, and what was the outcome of this suit?

Project Underground, *Peace, Not Oil*
1. Why have the U'wa threatened mass suicide?

Haunani-Kay Trask, *Lovely Hula Hands*
1. Discuss the impact of tourism on Native Hawaiian employment opportunities, housing, cost of living, and the environment.
2. How has "cultural prostitution" harmed the Native Hawaiian people in four important areas of traditional Hawaiian culture?

Mac Chapin, *The Struggle Over Land on Central America's Last Frontier*
1. Describe the ecology and environment of Central America before 1900.
2. What has been the indigenous response to the "assault on the forests" that began in the 1940s and 1950s and continues to the present?
3. Why should indigenous peoples manage the forests of Central America?

KEY TERMS

Alaska Native Claims Settlement Act (ANCSA) of 1971
allotment policy
aloha
bioregionalism
casino
cultural prostitution
deep ecology
ecocide
Indian Gaming Regulatory Act (IGRA) (1988)

Kuna
Miskito (Mosquitia)
Native American Rights Fund (NARF)
'ohana
proletarianization
radioactive colonialism
Seven Generations
subsistence hunting and fishing
sustainable development

SUGGESTED READINGS

ANDERSON, TERRY L. *Sovereign Nations or Reservations: An Economic History of American Indians.* San Francisco: Pacific Research Institute for Public Policy, 1995.

BASSO, KEITH H. *Wisdom Sits in Places.* Albuquerque: University of New Mexico Press, 1996.

BENJAMIN, CRAIG. "The Self-Destructing Seed: Genetic Engineering Threatens Food Sovereignty." *Native Americas* (Spring 1999): 29–35.

BENJAMIN, CRAIG. "Amazonian Confrontation: Native Nations Challenge the Patenting of Sacred Plants," *Native Americas* (Winter 1998): 24–33.

BROWN, DENISE FAY. "Mayas and Tourists in the Maya World." *Human Organization,* 58, no. 3 (1999): 295–304.

CHURCHILL, WARD. *Struggle for the Land: Indigenous Resistance to Genocide, Ecocide and Expropriation in Contemporary North America.* Monroe, Maine: Common Courage Press, 1993.

CHURCHILL, WARD. "A Breach of Trust: The Radioactive Colonialization of Native North America." *American Indian Culture and Research Journal,* 23, no. 4 (1999): 13–69.

Drumbeat for Mother Earth. Film produced by the Indigenous Environmental Network and Greenpeace.

GEDICKS, AL. *The New Resource Wars: Native and Environmental Struggles against Multinational Corporations.* Boston: South End Press, 1993.

GRINDE, DONALD A., JR., and BRUC E. JOHANSEN. *Ecocide of Native America: Environmental Destruction of Indian Lands and Peoples.* Santa Fe: Clear Light Press, 1998.

LADUKE, WINONA. *All Our Relations: Native Struggles for Land and Life.* Cambridge, Mass.: South End Press, 1999.

MURPHY, KIM. "Alaska Struggles to Recover 10 Years after Exxon *Valdez.*" *Los Angeles Times,* March 20, 1999: A1, A12–13.

Project Underground. *Blood of Our Mother: The U'Wa People, Occidental Petroleum and the Colombian Oil Industry.* Project Underground, 1847 Berkeley Way, Berkeley, Calif. 94703, 1998.

SUTTON, IMRE. "The Continuing Saga of Indian Land Claims," *American Indian Culture and Research Journal,* 24, no. 1 (2000): 129–162.

TALBOT, STEVE. "Native Americans and the Working Class." Pages 65–95 in *Ethnicity and the Workforce.* Vol. 4, Ethnicity and Public Policy Series. Ed. Winston A. Van Horne. Milwaukee University of Wisconsin System American Ethnic Studies Coordinating Committee/Urban Corridor Consortium, 1985.

ULRICH, ROBERTA. *Empty Nets: Indians, Dams and the Columbia River.* Corvallis: Oregon State University Press, 1999.

VECSEY, CHRISTOPHER, and ROBERT W. VENABLES, eds. *American Indian Environments: Ecological Issues in Native American History.* Syracuse, N.Y.: Syracuse University Press, 1980.

WEISS, LAWRENCE. *The Development of Capitalism in the Navajo Nation.* Minneapolis: MEP Publications, 1984.

VIII
COMMUNITY WELL-BEING: HEALTH, WELFARE, JUSTICE

Ruby's Welfare

Esther Belin

Standing in line
after being told
Indians don't stand in line
'cause a Kiowa woman at window #6
helps the skins

Time passes me
still in line

Man at window #1
tells me welfare is a luxury
and how come I don't have a job
check the time
I smile
place my forms in the box marked
LEAVE FORMS HERE
black black and bold
welfare is a luxury
place your form in our box
play by our rules

I laugh
sit
smoke a Virginia Slim
and talk to the spirits

People talk about luxury
but what they mean is obligation
to remain lower class
for food
$5.15 an hour
doesn't feed three

Again
I check the time
light another Virginia Slim
not finished with the spirits

Luxury
the U.S. forgot the definition
forgetting who allowed them to create the U.S.
obligation of treaty
honored through
IHS and a truckload of commods
luxury overextended
obligation 500 years behind

Ready to light Virginia Slim #3
I'm called by window #6

Reprinted by permission of the author.

Because everything in the indigenous world is interrelated, the integrity of the Native American community and an individual's sense of well-being are based on balance and holism. All forces, both animate and inanimate, must be taken into account in order for the whole person, and by extension, the entire community, to remain in good health—physically, emotionally, socially, and spiritually. This perspective stands in contrast to the highly individualistic, technology-driven, science-for-profit orientation of Western society. In terms of general health and welfare, the indigenous perspective places value on community as well as individual rights, and it values social capital over productive capital. Western individualistic society, on the other hand, measures a nation's greatness through its industrial productivity (gross domestic product) by counting only those things that can be monetarized. This part examines some of the implications surrounding these and related issues.

Today, the Native peoples of the Americas have possibly the worst health problems of any other ethnic or minority group. Native Americans in the United States, the most affluent country in the world, have a statistical health profile more in keeping with Third World populations than a modern, industrialized nation. A glance at the health statistics contained in the box entitled "Native American Statistics—United States, 1990," in Part I tells part of the story. Trachoma and tuberculosis are all too common, as are dysentery and gastroenteritis. The rates of heart disease, cancer, and stroke, which used to be lower than in the general population, are increasing significantly. Diabetes is now rampant in Indian country in the United States. Among some Southwestern tribes, as many as 60 percent of their members have diabetes. Toxic wastes from uranium mining and other harmful activities, which we examined in Part VII, are having extremely negative health consequences for indigenous populations throughout the Western Hemisphere. For example, stillbirths and spontaneous abortions have increased on the Lakota Sioux reservations where uranium and other mining have left toxic residues in the soil and groundwater. Allergies and chemical sensitivities are becoming commonplace for many reservation or rural Indian populations in the United States, whereas those conditions were unheard of in the past.

A major cause of poor health is the modern diet that has replaced the former natural diets of U.S. Indian people. For example, for that third of the Indian population that resides on reservations, there are the negative effects of government commodities. "Commods," as they are termed on U.S. reservations, are government surplus food items such as fatty cheese, white flour, and powdered milk (indigestible for most Indian people, who lack the enzyme to digest it), which are distributed to the poor. These modern foods are starchy, are high in fats and sugar, and lack the proper vitamins and nutrients for a healthy diet. With the abandonment of aboriginal diets and reliance on modern junk food, American Indians have gone from a basically healthy population to one of very sick people, as evidenced by a twenty-year-shorter life span than the general U.S. population.

The health situation in Latin America has become increasingly grave as diets deteriorate because of current economic forces associated with "free trade" and global capitalism. In some Latin America countries, Indian communities are growing coca (cocaine) in order to meet their current cash needs. Their formerly self-sufficient economies have become subverted by neocolonialism and the neoliberal policies promulgated by the World Bank and the International Monetary Fund. The rebellion by the Zapatistas in Chiapas, Mexico, was fueled in part by passage of the North American Free Trade Agreement (NAFTA), which allowed the U.S. corporate grain industry to dominate the Mexican corn market and thereby deprive Mayan Indians and other peasant farmers of their traditional livelihood.

One of the tragic contradictions in considering these depressing circumstances is the fact that early European observers were nearly unanimous in proclaiming the relative good health of those Indians who had not been in contact with Europeans. From early documents and letters we learn that "it is verie rare to see a sicke body amongst them . . . They are never troubled with Scurvey, Dropsy, nor Stone. The Phthisick, Asthma, and Diabetes, they are Wholly Strangers to. Neither do I remember I ever saw one Paralytick amongst them."[1] Much of Native American good health was due to their customs of sanitation—clean bodies, clean clothing, and clean homes, to which early Europeans were often unaccustomed—and to diet and exercise.

The original medical contribution of Native America to the world are incalculable. More than 200 medicines used by American Indians have been listed in the *Pharmacopoeia* of the United States since its first edition in 1820, and in the *National Formulary,* first published in 1888. They include well-known drugs such as belladonna (used in eye examinations), cascara sagrada (the most widely used cathartic in the world), wintergreen (a precursor of aspirin), cocaine from coca leaves (used for altitude sickness and as a pain reliever), curare (a muscle relaxant), digitalis (for heart disease), quinine (for malaria), and vitamin C from pine bark (to prevent scurvy and as a vitamin supplement).

The original peoples of the Americas are also well acquainted with what contemporary medicine calls psychotherapy. Curing ceremonies and practices by medicine people and Indian doctors are still widely carried out, often with good results. The mind–body (or spiritual) connection that Western medicine is only now beginning to recognize has been part of the curing practices in the Americas for thousands of years.

Ironically, two medicines used by Native Americans for centuries in their generic or natural state without any ill effects now account for millions of injuries and deaths from their overuse: these are cocaine and tobacco. Cocaine is a bitter crystalline alkaloid derived from coca. Although useful as a local anesthetic, if taken in large doses, it leads to intoxication and drug dependency. The custom of chewing coca leaves, on the other hand, has been used by some Andean indigenous peoples for centuries to allay thirst and hunger without harmful side effects. Those Native Americans using tobacco before European contact used it only in ceremonies, where it was (and still is) considered sacred. Most often, Native peoples mixed tobacco with other herbs to form a milder substance, such as *kinnikinnik,* which was smoked ceremonially. European colonists, on the other hand, commercialized and exported tobacco for profit, leading to its overuse and addictive consequences. Today, in the United States, with the rediffusion of commercial tobacco back into the Native American community, Indians have the highest rate of secular use of tobacco of any population segment; the line between ceremonial and secular use has become blurred.

Social well-being and criminal justice have a story similar to that of community health. Originally, Native Americans lived in self-governing communities, and they managed their justice systems on the basis of norms and mores that were learned through the Indian extended family or clan and from elders in the community. Culture, customary law, and collective sanctions kept the society integrated and deviance in check. There were no police or jails. Under the impact of Western colonialism and oppression, however, the collective rights of Indian tribes and nations became subordinated to, if not completely replaced by, the larger nation-states, which were controlled by a governing class of non-Native people.

Land alienation, especially, has had a serious effect on indigenous health and community well-being because of the destruction of native foods, such as the near extinction of the North American Plains buffalo. Agents of the land dispossession include the 1887 Indian Allotment Act in the United States, under which half of the then-remaining tribal land base was lost; the post–World War II "development" of the Amazon basin that has caused the displacement and deaths of thousands of Indians; the 1971 Alaska Native Claims Settlement Act, which abridged aboriginal hunting and fishing rights; and the recent Mexican law privatizing the *ejido* land tenure system of peasant and Indian communal lands. In the absence of an effective resistance movement to those external pressures, Native American values and customs break down, the fabric of communal life is torn, and many individuals become alienated, psychologically depressed, and even self-destructive. Alcohol addiction (alcoholism) and alcohol abuse must be viewed within this context of historically based physical and emotional pain that is perpetuated across many generations.

The deleterious effect that the boarding school system had on Indian individuals and their families was discussed in Part V. Equally harmful was the practice of "out-adoption," which allowed non-Indians to adopt or foster care Indian children. Most of these children were removed against their parents' will and came from families that were judged by state entities as "unfit." Tens of thousands of Indian children in the United States were lost to their families and tribal communities through this harmful policy.

In 1958 the Bureau of Indian Affairs and the Child Welfare League of America made it official policy to promote the adoption of Indian children by white families as a solution to the "Indian problem." Rather than addressing the underlying structural problems of neocolonialism and resource and labor exploitation that plague Indian tribes, these agencies saw the Indian family and community as the causes of the general social disorganization of tribal life. Other public and private agencies also began promoting the policy of out-adoption. Between 1954 and 1976 alone, the Indian Student Placement Program of the Church of Jesus Christ of Latter-Day Saints placed 38,260 Indian children in

Mormon homes. Many of those adopted became marginalized, feeling neither Indian nor white, and suffered severe mental and emotional problems.

Current "welfare reform," signed into law by President Clinton as the Personal Responsibility and Work Opportunity Reconciliation Act of 1996, could have a significant and possibly tragic impact on U.S. Indian tribes that typically have large numbers of their populations on Aid for Dependent Children (AFDC) and at the same time experience astronomical rates of unemployment, with little or no reservation economic activity. The new law replaced the Aid for Dependent Children program with the Temporary Assistance for Needy Families (TANF) program. The law's title implies that work is available for those willing to work; but with 31 percent of American Indians living below the poverty line, and reservation and rural unemployment running well over 50 percent, it is doubtful that most of the former Indian welfare clients will be able to find jobs. The Navajo Nation estimated it would have to create 2,500 new jobs just to meet the first year work participation requirements of the welfare-to-work law. Training programs are essential in order for the law to work, yet funds for training are so far inadequate. Furthermore, as James Shanley points out (see Suggested Readings), if a tribe chooses to administer TANF itself, it will lose from 30 to 50 percent of the welfare benefits currently being received by eligible families on AFDC, unless the federal or state government agrees to provide the missing state matching funds and administrative costs. This welfare "reform" may also have a negative effect on those seeking to graduate from Indian tribal colleges. The law as it now stands does not support those who wish to attain higher degrees; instead, the former welfare clients must enroll in pre-employment classes rather than transfer courses. Without the creation of jobs and adequate funding for training programs, the projected reform is doomed to fail in Indian country and can only lead to the further pauperization of reservation and rural Indian communities.

In the United States, Indian arrest rates are among the highest of any ethnic group, and the incarceration rate exceeds that of the general population. The high Indian arrest rates, the frequency of alcohol-related crimes, and the higher than average imprisonment ratios in Indian country are most often explained by mainstream theorists as the result of individual deviance or as being due to Indian "culture conflict," "living between two worlds," or a "pathological reservation subculture" rather than as a result of the structural conditions of racism and ethnic oppression. Contemporary theories that seek to explain Indian criminality in terms of individual pathology and social disorganization are engaging in what more discerning social scientists term "victim-blaming theory": blaming the victim instead of the victimizer.

In the first selection in this part, Byrd Baylor describes a typical day in the life of an urban Indian woman, Maria Vasquez, who is coping with the Anglo health establishment in Tucson, Arizona. The many, and often meaningless, rules, regulations, and surveys of mainstream bureaucratic institutions, such as health and welfare agencies that target the oppressed minorities, have been termed "urban imperialism" by their critics. Urban imperialism toward the poor, in this case, a woman and her five children, is a daily reality for many Indian families. How ironic it is, then, that rather than improving the health and sanitation of urban Indians, the dysfunctional application of Health Department regulations may actually force some Indian families into homelessness. Baylor also points out that, when an Indian individual is questioned by Anglo officials, it is best to give answers that the questioners want. Read the selection to find out why yes is better than no.

Many of the health problems plaguing Native Americans today, such as diabetes, cancer, hypertension, and alcoholism are new and increasing in most indigenous communities. As a result, there is renewed interest among many tribes in North America to improve nutrition and health through traditional food gathering and preparation and through exercise and spiritual ceremonies. In the second selection, Gary Paul Nabhan examines the question of the increasing incidence of diabetes, gallbladder disease, hypertension, and heart trouble, which are ravaging the contemporary O'odham peoples (Pima and Papago) of the southwestern United States. These are nutrition-related diseases. He believes that the answer lies in the Native metabolism, which is well adapted to the seasonality of traditional foods, native to the desert, but which cannot adapt to the modern American diet. To understand the magnitude of the change in diet that appears to have led to the current disease crisis, he examines the traditional gathering practices of these Desert People. He concludes that a preventive approach that integrates traditional desert foods into the modern Indian diet is the answer.

In the box titled "Delfina Cuero: Her Autobiography," a California Indian elder describes how a young woman learned to give birth and to care for her babies "in the real old days." It is through the traditional process of passing knowledge of health practices from generation to generation that family and community well-being are maintained. When this process is disrupted, the overall health of a people declines.

Misconceptions held by non-Indian and Indian alike surround the subject of Indian drinking and alcoholism. Many people believe that Native Americans are genetically predisposed to alcoholism. This stereotypic view is also held by the ladino class of non-Indians in Latin America about Native peoples and provides one of the rationales for the structured inequality found in countries such as Bolivia. In the third selection, Philip May, a professor of sociology and psychiatry at the University of New Mexico, sets out to debunk these and related misconceptions. Epidemiology is the branch of medicine that deals with the incidence, distribution, and control of disease in a given population. The first step in any scientific procedure is to define the research problem. The author therefore carefully distinguishes between Indian deaths that are associated with alcohol dependency, or chronic alcoholic drinking, which is only part of the problem, and alcohol-abusive drinking patterns (sporadic, binge drinking). He also examines demographic factors, such as geographic, political, and cultural variables, that seem to explain the high rates of alcohol-related problems among the Native American populations of the United States. Ironically, more non-Indians consume alcohol as a percentage of their total population (60 percent) than do Indians (40 percent). But among Indians who do drink alcohol, alcoholism and alcohol abuse are extremely serious problems.

"They picked the five of us with the best report cards. And our parents couldn't stop them because they had guns." In the fourth selection, Joan Smith recounts the personal biographies of several Indians who were virtually kidnapped from their families and deprived of their Indian identity through the federal Indian boarding schools and the policy of out-adoption. Until the passage of the Indian Child Welfare Act in 1978 (passed only after an intense lobbying effort by Indian organizations), these two institutions, the boarding school and out-adoption, separated one in three Indian babies from their families and tribal cultures. Dakota poet Tom LaBlanc, whose poem introduces Part IX of this book, was one of these. The purpose of the 1978 law was to reverse the socially destructive consequences of wholesale displacement of Indian children from their families and tribal communities. The passage of the Indian Child Welfare Act, however, has not been fully successful. The California Department of Social Services, for example, broke the law in 80 percent of Indian baby placements, failing to notify either the child's tribe or the Secretary of the Interior. Recent court decisions that have effectively weakened the 1978 law even further may well lead to many more tragic stories such as the ones that the author of this selection documents.

Tharon Weighill (Chumash) is an anthropologist who has studied the traditional use of tobacco among Indians. The box titled "Traditional Tobacco Use Amongst the Indians of Southern California" is an excerpt from a longer, more fully developed article. In this selection, Weighill makes the important distinction between tobacco as it was used in traditional or original Southern California Indian cultures, seemingly without harmful consequences, and the commercial use of tobacco today, with its associated lung cancer and other serious diseases.

In the final selection, sociologist Luana Ross (Salish) employs an in-depth interview methodology to obtain a better understanding of the causes for the high rate of incarceration of Indian women in the United States. In 1994, for example, Native Americans constituted 2.9 percent of both federal and state prison populations although Native people were only 0.6 percent of the total U.S. population; in Alaska and the northern Plains States, the incarceration ratio was even higher. Ross contends that these findings can be explained by the history of violence, both personal and institutional, that has marked the lives of Indian women. She cites one study that found that 88 percent of imprisoned women had been violently victimized before their incarceration. In fact, "the contextualizing of the criminalization process is central to the understanding of female deviance." Furthermore, the violence is institutionalized not only through agencies such as the Indian boarding school and foster home placement but also by the system of incarceration itself. The life history of Catherine (Cedar Woman), fits the typical profile of Indian women prisoners and supports Ross's theory that Indian criminalization is both racialized and genderized.

NOTE

1. Quoted in Virgil J. Vogel, *American Indian Medicine* (University of Oklahoma Press, 1970), 151. (Original source: John Lawson, *History of North Carolina* [1714, reprint; Garren and Massie, 1692, 237–238.])

YES IS BETTER THAN NO

Byrd Baylor

MARIA VASQUEZ

Down the street from the B-29 bar is the shrine of St. Jude. Stiff armed and staring into space, St. Jude. Dry bougainvillea leaves in his plaster hair today, but fewer candles than usual. Yesterday a drunk vomited on him, poor man, pouring out his excuses, his grief, his thirty-nine-cent Thunderbird wine. They had to take away the candles.

Today Maria passes by on her way to the B-29 bar but she only glances. Not so much as the sign of the cross. Not really even a nod.

From *Yes Is Better Than No*, by Byrd Baylor. Copyright © 1991 by Byrd Baylor. Courtesy, Treasure Chest Publications, Inc. Illustration "Maria Vasquez" by Leonard Chana, Tohono O'odham artist. © Leonard Chana.

Jude, I'll be back. Don't worry. Maybe I'll spend the night. We'll watch the moon rise together yet.

How would it be to spend the night with a saint anyway?

Her mother had once said, "Remember, nothing is impossible to this saint. For myself, I ask St. Martin first, but then second I go to St. Jude for impossible needs . . . for impossible situations. Situations like this life." And she had smiled as she said it.

That was before Maria left the reservation. So long ago that nothing had ever been impossible enough to force her to seek out St. Jude. And now, dear God, she knows him well enough to dispense with formality. Just half a nod. . . .

Maria walks down the dusty sidewalk slowly, slowly, evenly as Indian women walk. Though she is still young, her hips don't swing; she doesn't dance along the way Mexican girls do. Instead, she moves her feet on the city sidewalk as though she were moving barefoot across the desert. As though that journey might take all night, all week, a lifetime. The foot falls solidly to meet the earth, feels the pull of the earth. A heavy walk, but easy and animal-like. No man who watches women walk here mistakes the black-eyed, black-haired Indian girls for Mexicans. You can tell that walk a block away.

She comes to the B-29 bar. Going into its darkness means passing from the harsh reality of the town into the safety of a mystical home. A sacrament, crossing that doorway. Believe me, Jude, there are more sacraments than those the priest mentions.

Outside, the light of the hot desert sun; inside, the dimness of a cave. Well, ceremonial wine houses on the reservation are dim too.

Outside, Tucson street noises; inside, the easy sounds of Papago language. Papago and Spanish too, not much English. And the English that is spoken by Indians sounds like Indian, anyway, resting in the hollows of the throat, each word coming out soft as a baby rabbit.

Papago language has the right sound for people of the desert. It holds the quiet of the mesas; it rolls words into the natural shapes of breathing so they come from the mouth still soft around the edges, small winds that might blow across a hill of summer weeds. That kind of sound.

Papago is a language much too quiet for anger. Let them have English for anger and authority and commands and papers to sign. Even a social worker would not sound so important, perhaps, if she made Papago sounds instead of words that come flying out of the mouth stiff as boards. You feel their sharp splinters in the air. . . .

Maria slides across the beer-sticky wooden bench and sinks back against the crumbling pink plaster which clings to the adobe walls. Breathes in . . . breathes out . . . believes it is the only breath she has drawn all day.

The mood here is slow and quiet in spite of the deafening jukebox music. Purifying in its terrible intensity. Time never moves here. Noon, midnight, three A.M.; it's all the same at the B-29.

Maria's friend, Rose, comes to sit beside her, just sits, doesn't ask anything.

Maria unties a handkerchief, puts fifteen cents on the wooden table. Rose adds thirty-five cents more.

The bartender, Anglo, burly, with levis and boots and red cowboy shirt beneath his dirty white apron, comes over and puts down a pitcher of beer and four glasses. There will be others at the table later.

It isn't for a long time yet, maybe half an hour, that Maria says, "I don't have the house anymore."

"You didn't pay?"

"I paid. I'm paid for another week still."

She finishes a glass of beer, pours another and sits looking into its depth. "The man that brought all the papers—he came and nailed it up today because it's not fit to live in. That one."

Rose shrugs.

They both accept the fact that the invisible rules by which their lives are governed are completely, desperately, insanely senseless. There is no use trying to understand them. Haven't they all been told a thousand times: "But those are our regulations, Mrs. Garcia. There is nothing we can do about it. . . ." "Sorry, Mr. Escalante, but we all have to abide by certain rules. . . ." "No, Mrs. Gonzales, if we let *you*, they'd all be asking. . . ."

So Maria had not said to the man from the health department that, yes, she knew it was bad with all those holes in the walls but still it was all she could afford and where would she and the five children sleep tonight if he went ahead and nailed that board across the door?

Now she only says to Rose, "Since I'm paid up for almost a week, we'll sleep in the yard. Maybe it won't rain."

"Maybe."

"At least he didn't say the yard wasn't fit to live in. Just the house."

"You sure?"

She isn't sure, of course.

On the reservation you know certain rules that haven't changed since the people came up from the underworld. But here in town they change the rules every day. Out there when the fine balance of the world is upset there are still things that can be done. But there's no ceremony or song or blessing or magic in a medicine man's bag that will help you against the white people who come to nail boards across your door.

Your stomach twists and doubles and knots when you talk to those people—the ones who make rules which no one could ever guess beforehand. It takes darkness and Indian voices and sometimes a pitcher of beer to let your insides settle again. It takes music and a man to come over and sit close enough so you can feel his leg against you and see the dark hairs on his wrists and breathe the man smell of him. Sometimes it takes the closeness of a man in bed all night and even then, God knows, you can still wake up afraid.

"Lucky it's so hot now," Rose says. "Everybody sleeps out anyway."

"Sure."

The bar is filling, and through the open door you can see that the sky is purple against the mountains, almost dark. It is a good time of day. All those who have been working at the rich houses on the east side of town are home again, the men who have been doing yard work, the women who have been doing housework. There are more women than men, of course, because it is easier to find housework than yard work.

The bus stops at the corner and through the open door you can see them getting off, going home. They're slow, tired. A few come into the B-29, pushing back their wide-brimmed straw hats, peering into the dimness.

One of the men is Lopez. Rose has been waiting for him, so she moves across the table from Maria and Lopez slides into the booth and puts his arm around Rose, touching her breasts. He speaks to her first in Papago even though it is only a greeting. Hi. They pour another glass of beer.

Lopez has been working. Now he brings out five dollars and says, "Okay, you can buy his goddamn fly tonight."

Rose holds tightly to her glass and nods.

Lopez waves across the room to an old man, a Mexican, wearing somebody's give-away white tennis shoes with his levis and work shirt. No laces. The shoes would fall off if he picked his feet up from the floor, but he glides carefully along.

"You got the money tonight? You want the cure?

Lopez holds up the five dollars.

Rose says, "I want the cure."

"All right then," the old man says. "I got the fly."

He takes a small package from his levi pocket—a fly in a small wax paper bag. Shakes it.

"Wait a minute now," Lopez says. "If it doesn't work do you give us back our money?"

The old man looks at him sideways, offended. "It works, man."

Maria is only glad that no one is trying to cure her of the pleasure of a glass of beer. But Rose . . . she goes to jail so often for it.

"We should start with a full pitcher," the old man says, standing over them. A medicine man almost.

"Then you buy," Lopez says. "You got the money now."

But as they motion to the bartender, they notice that someone who doesn't belong there is standing in the doorway. The regulars always feel uneasy when a white stranger comes to the door and looks them over. This place should be a sanctuary from Anglos. Of course, you expect the police now and then; you just try not to look up at them even though you feel your hands tighten, your stomach flip.

This man is young and wears levis and a blue work shirt and a fine big Navajo silver and turquoise belt buckle. He looks all right, maybe even friendly, but everyone sees immediately that he is carrying a clipboard and papers. That's bad. . . .

He stands at the door looking around the dim room and then strides in long certain steps over to the bartender and holds out his hand.

"Henry Cunningham." He smiles seriously.

The bartender puts down a bottle of tequila and slowly extends his hand.

"Listen," the young man says, "maybe you'd do me a little favor." You can tell he is used to favors. "We're doing a study at the university on motivational backgrounds among off-reservation Indians, and . . ."

Motor vehicle something or other is what it sounds like to those close enough to hear. The bartender wipes his hands and squints. He's still waiting to hear what the favor is. So is everybody else. The young man goes on talking about how he tried to set up a meeting for this afternoon over at the Southside Hall—notices on the bulletin board, letters to the Indian Center, everything—"But no one showed up to be interviewed."

"Yeah," says the bartender.

"And before that, home interviews. But of course nobody ever came to the door. You know how it is."

"Yeah," says the bartender.

"And there's a deadline for this study. So I was wondering . . . could I ask some of your customers a question or two?"

Maria turns her face toward the peeling plaster, doesn't look back. But she can hear

the bartender say, "Aw, you won't do no good here."

At least he is that loyal to his customers. He *tries*, but the man with the papers in his hand says, "Listen, it's painless. Anyway, I only need to talk to the Indians."

Not an Indian looks up now, though the Mexicans relax and watch the young man pay for his beer and select a ballpoint pen from among the three in his shirt pocket.

Maria's table is near the back of the room. She can hear his voice at the next booth even though she tries not to.

The thing is that you don't know which Anglos are the ones you *have* to answer. You don't know which ones can really board up a house or take away a welfare check or even put you in jail or take your children to foster homes. You don't know which are the papers you *have* to sign. Almost all white people speak in a way that sounds so important, how can you tell?

For instance, there was that social worker who had told Maria not to have any more babies. So when the last one was born what could she do but hide her when anyone from welfare came around. Hide her or say, "Look, I'm keeping my cousin's baby." Even now Maria isn't certain whether that woman could come and take Carmen away.

Now the young man with the papers is standing at their table. The two women look down but Lopez and the old man standing over the pitcher say hello.

"You people *are* Indian, aren't you? Papago?"

They nod.

"Mind if I sit down a minute?"

Maria moves closer to the wall and he sits beside her, puts his glass of beer on the table. The jukebox is quiet for a moment and the fly moves helplessly within its wax paper bag in the center of the table.

The young man starts to say something, notices the fly, and stops. No one answers his questioning look, however, and he turns back to the clipboard.

"Now then, just let me chat with you a few minutes. This won't take long." He offers a pack of cigarettes and they all smoke silently, waiting.

The paper on top of the clipboard is titled *Motivational Background and Current Achievement Levels Among Off-Reservation Papago Indians.*

"We just want to find out whether you were encouraged as youngsters to prepare yourselves for good jobs. Encouraged or discouraged. . . ."

Lopez moves his hands from Rose's unbuttoned shirt front to some less noticeable spot under the table. The old man remains standing, watching the occasional movements of the captured fly.

"Let's put it this way: Have you achieved your own personal employment goals? Were you able to become whatever it was you dreamed of being, and if not—"

They look at his face to see whether an answer is expected.

The music starts again, this time a wildly plaintive song in Spanish. Lost love and tears. The fly which had been quiet for a long time now begins to move, frantically dancing. Maria, Rose and Lopez all notice this and laugh gently.

The young man laughs too. "I agree with you. They're crazy sounding questions, all right. Every one of them."

The three want to laugh again because he has misunderstood but they stop themselves and look back at him, stiff, polite and serious.

"Who was the most important motivating figure for you between the ages of six to twelve, twelve to fourteen, fourteen to eighteen. That is . . . who made you *want* to succeed?"

They give this some thought.

"Your parents? Tribal leaders? Classmates? Anybody who encouraged you to go ahead and make it in the world. Anybody who gave you confidence in yourself."

They look at each other.

"That could be your teachers, of course."

Yes, they all agree. Certainly. Teachers.

"Do you believe there is any correlation between your earning power today and your educational opportunities?"

"By all means," Lopez answers for them.

The three Indians at the table, like all the others in the B-29 this evening, have been interviewed by similar young Anglos on similar topics. They have each learned long ago to try to give answers which will most please the questioner. At times this is hard to figure out, but they try. Everyone knows, for instance, that white people are very pleased when Indian girls say they wish to become nurses or teachers. So most of them give those answers.

Another thing. If a yes or no answer is required, they try to say yes. In most of their dealings with white people Indians find that it is easier and more polite to say yes than no. This saves arguing and has, of course, nothing at all to do with one's actions. It simply puts off any ill feeling, makes the moment happier.

Maria speaks so softly that the young man has to lean forward to hear her answers. He has jotted down the facts so far: Papago. Age 29. Five children. Husband's occupation: laborer (unemployed). Husband's boyhood ambition: priest.

Maria had been undecided whether to say priest or doctor since white people like both answers. But thinking how long it had been since she had seen Joe Vasquez and how funny he would look out there in the Yuma melon fields dressed in a priest's robes, she made her choice. "Yes, he always wished to be a priest."

Wife's occupation: housework. Girlhood ambition: nurse.

"And your children. Have they expressed vocational preferences yet? Told you what they wish to become?"

"Nurses."

"All of them?"

"All the girls. Yes."

"And their ages?"

She pauses, can't remember, guesses. "Two . . . five . . . seven, no, eight . . . nine. The girls."

"And even those very young ones have expressed an opinion?"

"Oh, yes. They all want to be nurses. And the boy, a doctor."

"A doctor. He's certain of that?"

She nods. "If not that, then a priest."

There is a pause but the young man finally fills in his questionnaire. His eyes keep returning to the fly.

He has to ask. "Whose . . . fly?"

The old man says, "It's mine. But it's for her." He nods his head toward Rose.

"It's to put in my beer," she says. "It's a cure. You know."

"Oh, yes. In your beer."

The old man pours four glasses of beer—for himself, Maria, Rose and Lopez. "You want some more?" he asks the young man with the clipboard.

"Oh, no thanks. No." He gathers up his papers and stands watching the old man shake the fly from the bag into his hand and close his stiff fingers over it. From time to time he shakes his hand and holds it up to his ear like a great earth-brown seashell.

"Now, you can just tell me to mind my own business if you like . . . but did I understand that this lady is going to put the fly in her beer?"

"No," the fly's owner explains patiently. "No, I have to put it in when she's not looking. Otherwise no cure."

"And if you don't mind my asking, what is it that a fly in beer cures?"

They all look at him, but they wait for the old man to answer. After all, it's his fly.

At last the old man tells him. "It cures beer drinking."

And the young man goes away.

As soon as he is out of sight, the B-29 relaxes again. There is a different sound to the arguments, to the laughter, to the singing, to the curses, even a different shape to people's motions. Time stretches out again, flat as it should be on a hot summer night.

People come and go at the booth where Maria sits but she does not tell anyone else about the house being boarded up. She doesn't want to think of it herself either. After all, that's the reason she is here, to put it off for a moment more. She laughs now and then, taps her foot to the music, wishes the B-29 were a place for dancing. It would be good to dance all night. When you're dancing it doesn't really matter whether there is a board nailed across the front door or not.

A tug at her arm. "Mama. Hey, mama." It is one of her girls, Anna, the oldest, ten. She is holding the baby heavily on her hip, her bare feet sidestepping the cigarette butts glowing on the cement floor.

"They're fussing because they can't get in the house. They want somebody to take the board off the door."

Maria takes the baby and gets up. Rose reaches for the baby, cuddles her a minute, hands her back to Anna.

"Okay, we'll go." One last sip of beer and they leave, Maria carrying the baby now, rocking her as she moves. One last glance back at Rose, at the old man whose left hand is still cupped around the fly.

It's dark and they walk home slowly. Past the Chinese grocery store, past the Friendship Rescue Mission, past the shrine of St. Jude (tomorrow, Jude) and around the corner to the dusty alley where they stop in front of the boarded-up shack with the CONDEMNED sign in the center of the front door. Under it, the picture of the Virgin of Guadalupe and the notice: *Welcome to this house where our Lady of Guadalupe is Queen. This is a Catholic house. Propaganda of other religions will not be admitted.* It is written in both Spanish and English.

"We could get in," Anna says, "with a rock or with a knife. Either one."

"We better not. It's against the law."

There are three mattresses, all thin, on the ground. One is a double-bed size and the other two are singles. There are several cardboard boxes, some of them for dirty clothes and some for clean, one for pots and pans and dishes.

The girls have already organized things. Anna has a single mattress to herself. Amelia and Jane, both tiny, share the other single. The baby, Carmen, and the boy, Errol Flynn, will sleep with Maria. Some of them are almost asleep now, their heads on the mattresses, their feet and legs dangling in the dirt. Maria looks in the boxes, finds sheets and scraps of blankets to put over them.

"Didn't you leave me a tortilla?"

"Beans too, a little."

The wood stove is under a mesquite tree. Maria finds a cold tortilla in the pan and folds it around a small mound of frijoles and a piece of green chile. Then she walks back across the yard and sits down on the bed, takes off her shoes, moves her toes in the dirt.

While she is eating, the girls sit up and begin to ask her, "Did you dance, Mama? Did you drink beer?"

"Go to sleep."

"Did you have to pay, Mama? A man bought you beer, no?"

She can barely see their faces around her. "Go to sleep." And then she says it in Papago too.

But no one sleeps yet. Finally Maria says into the darkness, "Who wants to be a nurse? Anna, you want to be a nurse someday?"

"Not me."

"Amelia? A nurse?"

"I hate nurses. Nobody's going to make me be a nurse."

"I hate nurses too," says Jane.

Maria smiles to herself. "Okay," she says. "Sleep."

There is Mexican music from somebody's radio. A car that won't start tries and dies again and again. The stars are very bright now, clear wide patterns to follow across the sky. Maria knows only a few of the Papago names for stars, none in English. She lies looking up, searching for the five stars which mark the touch of *I'itoi's* fingers, for once during the creation of the world the sky began to fall and *I'itoi* thrust up his great arm to hold the sky in place. . . .

Carmen sleeps next to Maria. On the other side, Errol Flynn, the only boy. He is looking up too.

"Errol Flynn, a doctor? You want to be a doctor?"

"Not me," he says, sleepy.

They are all quiet now, only a stray puppy wandering from bed to bed, sniffing each child. And that car still trying to start.

Even though the bed is so crowded that Maria is lying on the edge with her hand resting in the warm sand, she feels that she is sleeping alone. In any bed without a man, you lie alone.

Every night Maria goes to sleep thinking of a man unless she is too tired to think at all. Different men for different reasons. Sad reasons that lead you down the street to St. Jude. But others too—reasons that keep you wanting to live.

She thinks most often of her husband, Joe Vasquez. Jose. It's true she may forget him all day when things are bad, but this time of night she remembers how he used to lie in the darkness and tell her stories of movies. Any movie. One he had seen that day or the day before or one from years ago.

Everybody used to know Joe Vasquez as the man who liked movies. It was true. His hunger for movies was almost as great as his thirst for wine, and if he had those two pleasures there was nothing else that really mattered to him—maybe two pints of wine a day and a movie once or twice a week. If he'd been rich, then a movie every day.

So whenever they could find the money Joe used to spend the afternoon at the cheapest theater in town. He always walked to the bus with Maria when she went to do housework, and he would stay watching the story over and over until time to go to the bus to meet her in the evening. They would walk home together then but he never told her the story until they were in bed.

Poor Joe Vasquez, sick from years of too little food and too much wine. Pains in his stomach. The Anglo doctor at the clinic had said it was from his own drinking, but the *maka:ii* had found that it was rattlesnake sickness and, another time, whirlwind sickness, and Joe seemed better for a while. But he couldn't work a full day anymore. Sometimes two or three hours, but he would be shaking at the end of that time.

Whenever he was in jail, of course he had to stay the full ten days. Maria never had enough money to bail him out, but she would save what she could so that there would be a bottle of tokay waiting for him and movie money hidden behind the picture of St. Francis Xavier.

It was nice, hearing those stories. Joe always told them slowly as though he were one of the old Papago storytellers measuring out his stories through the winter nights.

How many nights—surely a hundred— had Joe described the strange green jungle where Tarzan and Jane escaped from tigers and lions and gorillas. Maria had never seen it herself but she almost knew the sound of the bird cries there and the way the water closed over the round eyes of hidden hungry crocodiles. That was the land Joe liked most of all, and theirs was the way of living he most admired. Free and wild as animals. They often talked of how much easier it was for Tarzan and Jane to survive than for their own ancestors, those Indians who had gone as bare but who had toiled so hard to stay alive, had walked such rocky land, had eaten roots and mesquite beans and cactus fruit while Tarzan only reached overhead for a banana.

"What language did they speak?" she once asked him, filled with wonder.

"Mostly sign language," he said. "But a little English too. Not good English though. Not school English."

And Maria had felt she knew those two. It was in honor of that beautiful dark-haired Jane who could swing so gracefully from the branch of a jungle tree that they had called their own child Jane. Actually, Jane Ann because you need one saint's name too, of course.

And the boy, Errol Flynn. He too was named for someone Maria had never seen, but Joe had described his wavy hair, his small mustache, his marvelous flashing sword, the way he leapt over chairs and tables and fought up and down long flights of stairs in dark ugly castles.

By now Maria has forgotten the names of the countries but she remembers that this man laughed aloud as he fought. Joe often said he was the bravest of all men in the movies. In battles he was the one to volunteer for the dangerous ride over the white hills by moonlight. He was the one to fight on alone while the others made it safely over the drawbridge. He was the one who carried the wounded to safety before they found that he too had been shot. . . .

Maria thinks of that Errol Flynn now as she sees that her own small son Errol Flynn has rolled off the mattress and is lying on his back in the dirt, asleep, his thumb in his mouth.

Tarzan and Jane were without a house too. At least Joe never spoke of one. They probably lay down on a mat woven of soft green grasses, not a smelly mattress from the Salvation Army store. They probably had a pillow stuffed with flower petals.

And then Jane had a man, a strong naked man with a leopard skin wrapped around him. But Maria sleeps alone in the back yard. Well, after all, this is no movie.

GATHERING

Gary Paul Nabhan

We always kept gruel in our house. It was in a big clay pot that my mother had made. She ground up seeds into flour. Not wheat flour—we had no wheat. But all the wild seeds, the good pigweed and the wild grasses. . . . Oh, good that gruel was! I have never tasted anything like it. Wheat flour makes me sick. I think it has no strength. But when I am weak, when I am tired, my grandchildren make me a gruel out of the wild seeds. That is food.

Chona, *in Autobiography of a Papago Woman*

Today, all is not well among the Papago. Nutrition-related diseases virtually unknown in *Pimería Alta* a half century ago are taking their toll within the Papago and River Pima population. Nearly non-existent among Indians prior to 1940, diabetes and gall bladder disease have been affecting these Northern Pimans at an alarming rate since the mid-1950s. Today, more than half of all adult Papago suffer from these diseases. The prevalence of adult onset diabetes among Northern Pimans is possibly the highest on the planet. More recently, the incidence of hypertension and heart disease has begun to rise. Both of these problems are known to have been *extremely* infrequent among the Papago before the 1950s. Since the 1940s, nurses routinely examining the skin, gums, tongues, lips, and eyes of Papago children have noted the physical effects of certain vitamin and mineral deficiencies. A Papago nurse grieved, "My people are just being wasted away by these diseases."

As I talked with Lusiano Dolores over a meal, the discussion turned to diabetes.

"Gathering," from *The Desert Smells Like Rain*, by Gary Paul Nabhan. Reprinted with permission of the author.

What bothered him about the prevalence of this disease today is that it seemed to have come from nowhere.

"Maybe it was the foods they ate, but the Old People never had sugar diabetes. Those people got to be real old too, some over a hundred, and they just kept on working. They didn't need any insulin or to have their legs cut off because the blood stopped reaching them. But now we wonder where this sickness came from all of a sudden, and can't figure it out. One man told me once that maybe they let some germs out during the World War that just floated through the air, and finally settled here, way down low in the desert where we live. I have thought about that, and other things, and I just don't know."

Doctors have yet to offer a clear explanation of why these nutrition-related diseases increased so suddenly. They note in passing that the Indian diet has changed for the worse, but what does that mean? Papago have readily accepted foreign foodstuffs such as beef, lard, melons, sugar, white flour, and coffee since the 1600s. It is simplistic to assume that any one of these foods is the cause of the problem, because all of them were introduced decades before the sharp rise in disease. Nor is it true that many Papago and Pima are obese and diabetes-prone because they consume inordinately more calories than the rest of us. An overweight, diabetic *O'odham* adult can ingest a comparatively modest number of calories every day, yet maintain a weight of 200 to 300 pounds. Diet studies in the villages have indicated that the average *O'odham* today consumes about the same number of calories, and the same amounts of carbohydrates and fat, as the average U.S. citizen.

The real problem may just be that the Papago *do* eat like the average European-American. Their metabolism may be adapted to an altogether different diet. To understand the extent to which the modern American diet deviates from the traditional diet of the Papago, we must get a sense of the ecology of their native food resources.

"Oh, this little wild onion, *I'itoi siwol*, is that what you mean?" Lean old Casimiro Juan squinted at me, then off at the mountains. "Don't you know? You can't find those ones now, sometimes you can't even see them until it gets cold. They're still sleeping underground."

"Are they hard to find at the right time?" I asked.

"No, not if you know where to look," he laughed. "That's why I'll come with you and show you, but you gotta wait until it is the right time—You know, my brother who's not here anymore was the one who took me over there to *Waw Kiwulik* the first time to pick them. I had been hearing about those onions there, and he knew it, so he said, 'Well, get your horse and we'll go over there.'

"We were riding and I was looking up into the mountains wondering where those onions were hiding. We were in a big sandy wash just below the first rocks when my brother said, 'Look down around the horse.' Then I looked around on the ground and it was all covered with the *siwol* coming up.

"I got down off my horse and started to dig them out of the sand and put them into a big gunny sack. My brother went off to hunt for a while but pretty soon he came back. He started laughing. I said, 'Why you laughing so hard?' He said, 'Who gonna carry that gunny sack back home?' Then I looked at it and it was too full and heavy to even get on my little horse.

"That's when I knew I picked too many. So I just opened the bag and saved a bunch of big ones. Then I sat down and planted most of those onions I picked back in the sand so that they could grow again. When you take me there, I'll show you. They still keep coming up there."

Papago country consists of well over two and a half million acres in the heart of the Sonoran Desert. For at least 8,000 years it has supported people, first by food they gained from hunting and gathering, and later by domesticated as well as wild resources. Even in the driest pocket of North America—the Pinacate—Papago historically subsisted on legumes from hardy trees, lizards, bighorn, and a root parasite called sandfood. Occasionally, runoff from volcanic slopes was enough to produce a cultivated crop.

While the desert appears unproductive to most visitors from tropic or temperate zones, it served the Desert People well, given their population levels. There is reason to believe that during most years, the desert produced more food than could be harvested by local Papago villages. This includes greater quantities of favored foodstuffs than could be gathered even if the Desert People had the time: mesquite pods, palo verde and ironwood beans, saguaro seed and pulp, cholla cactus buds, prickly pear pads and fruit, greens, chia and tansy mustard seeds, rabbits, game birds, and underground stems, roots, and bulbs.

Some of these wild masts can fail with drought, or in years of late frost, but it is unlikely that all major food sources could be laid waste within the same year. Movement to other wild stands and barter with other villages also buffered Desert People from the effects of local fruit failure.

From recent analyses of desert food composition and yield in the wild, it appears that neither harvestable calories nor protein are limited in Papago country. Energy-rich carbohydrates were available in mesquite pod flour, seeds of winter ephemerals, saguaro and wolfberry fruit, and other locally abundant desert plants. In adjacent mountain ranges within a day's distance from some Papago villages, acorns, roots, and piñon nuts can be found. Add to that the variety of cultivated beans, squash, and grains grown by the Papago, and it is clear that their diet could also have been high in protein *quality*—there was enough overlap between the amino acids of various plant food sources to provide a complete protein when they were eaten together in the customary pattern.

Then what of vitamins and minerals? These are more inequitably distributed through the edible products of the plant kingdom. Yet the Sonoran Desert has such a diversity of lifeforms that fortunately a full range of nutrients can be found among its many productive species.

Nutritionist Ruth Greenhouse has recently discovered good to excellent sources of iron and calcium in many of the wild greens the O'odham gather. She also confirmed an earlier finding that the flower buds of cholla cactus, relished by Papago, contain more calcium in a four-ounce serving than there is in a glass of milk. Wolfberries and chiltepines, the wild perennial chile of the desert, are sources of considerable amounts of vitamins A, B_2, and C. Saguaro, gourd, and devil's claw seeds are rich in edible oils that generally carry with them certain B vitamins. At particular times of the year, it appears that certain required nutrients were available in abundance.

This is not to say that historic Papago never exhibited the deficiency symptoms such as bleeding gums or loose teeth that nurses noted in the 1940s. In the old days, to be sure, there was much more variation than there is now in the availability of nutrients, both from season to season and from year to year.

Yet it is difficult to imagine a Papago with a vitamin C deficiency while living in a saguaro-harvesting camp, or lacking calcium for the weeks following a cholla bud pit roast. The same person, however, may show deficiency symptoms during the "lean months" of late winter before desert fruits reappear.

This seasonal flux in nutrient availability may be what best characterizes the traditional Papago diet. Except for a few easily stored mainstays such as mesquite pod flour, roasted corn, dried beans, and chiles, most foods were available only for brief periods each year.

There are historic accounts of the *O'odham* gorging themselves on saguaro fruit for weeks, gaining weight rapidly during that time. They then went back to their fields and sometimes lived on bloodroot amaranth greens until the crops ripened.

Over an annual cycle, as many as six discrete pulses of wild foods can occur, each with its own complex of plant species that reach harvesting stage simultaneously. Because some of these wild foods do not lend themselves to long-term storage, the Desert People take advantage of them while available. They have relied on their own bodies to store this energy.

As another harvesting period rolled around, the people looked upon it as a blessing. As we were gathering greens one spring, an *O'odham* woman told me that "*Jewed Makai*, the Earth Maker, gave us different green things for each time of the year."

A harvest is also a welcome change of pace. "Oh, that was such a good time," Maggie laughed, recalling the acorn harvest up in the mountains near *Ali Wak*. "I guess it was like our vacation, getting away from our houses to go where it is cool. We went up to *Waik Wiyo:di* and all us ladies would just sit and talk and gather those *wiyo:di* all day long. It wasn't even like work. First we put the tarp on the ground and made one of the kids go up and shake the tree to get those acorns to fall. Then it rained hard and swept most of them away. So we just rolled up our pants to the knee and waded across the stream until we found a tree with some left hanging. We stayed in the shade all day, picking them one by one, like they were berries. . . . I don't even know how many we came home with, because we cracked them open as we picked them, and ate a lot right while we were there, before the bugs got into them."

The major change in the Papago diet over the last half century may be the demise of seasonality. Papago men who joined the Civilian Conservation Corps or military service in the thirties became accustomed to a "regular diet" of highly processed foods with long storage life. By the forties, government rations were introduced to the reservation as well. At the same time, many Papago abandoned their own farming and gathering activities to work for wages in irrigated cotton fields. The stores where they spent their wages for food had a limited number of foodstuffs, mostly white flour, pinto beans, coffee, salt, sugar, and other "staples." These became the cotton picker's diet *day after day*. In 1959, surplus commodity food distribution was a notable part of government aid to Indians. By 1968, the commodities distributed through the EFMS (Emergency Food and Medical Services) program had become the predominant food source for some Papago families, further reinforcing redundancy.

While some would argue that the program did bring enriched flour and fruit (canned) to people who desperately needed the nutrients that those foods contained, it is crucial nevertheless to know what these foods replaced. Dr. Doris Calloway and associates have shown that nearly all the commodity foods are lower in mineral and protein content than the counterpart foodstuffs that the Papago, Pima, and Hopi traditionally gathered or grew in their fields. It has also been speculated that these government-introduced foods have higher sodium chloride (salt) content than food previously available to Papago, a possible factor in the increase in hypertension. Historically, mineral salt was available only after pilgrimages to the Gulf of California, although consumption of plant ash, halophytic greens, and clay provided trace minerals at other times. It is also probable that the government-subsidized foods are lower in fiber and favor sucrose over fructose, compared to traditional foods.

But the change in *kinds* of food was not all; equally important was the change from a seasonally responsive diet to one of year-round uniformity. The Papago metabolism may not be adapted to such uniformity, if National Institutes of Health epidemiologists are right. They feel that the diabetes-prone metabolism of the Papago and Pima worked positively in the time when there were wide seasonal and annual variations in the availability of foods. Although food availability is said to have varied according to "a feast and famine pattern," implying complete food failure at times, it may have simply been that the Papago diet was relatively richer in energy foods in certain seasons, and poorer in calories during other seasons.

Dr. Peter Bennett has suggested that certain genetic traits of Papago and Pima may now be maladaptive:

> It has been suggested that this population has been subjected to alternating periods of feast and famine. Could it be that those who were genetically predisposed to develop diabetes survived because of their ability to store as much food as possible when the food was plentiful, enabling them to avoid starvation when serious periods of famine take place?

Those predisposed to diabetes did likely gain weight quickly, but when sugars or fats were out of season, rapid weight loss improved insulin secretion, and diabetic symptoms would vanish. But as the regularity of availability of such foods increased, diabetes has become more persistent. In Papago diabetics today, insulin is not being produced in the right amounts at the right time.

Bennett's associate, Dr. Roger Unger, likens this desert-adapted human metabolism to that of desert rodents. When rains produce an abundance of energy-rich seeds, desert rats eat until they become obese. The energy stored in body fat is used until the next rainy season.

"But if you put the desert rat in a cage," Dr. Unger says, "and give him plenty of food, he gets so fat he can barely move." And that, he thinks, is what the modern diet has done to the Papago.

It's hard to point to any one factor that can altogether reduce the vulnerability of Papago to the problems of diabetes. There has been some success in combining exercise and gradual diet change into weight control programs for obese *O'odham*, reducing the day-to-day risks of this disease. While some medical practitioners recommend that patients come into clinics for "starvation diets" to drastically reduce weight, others point out that the weight is frequently gained back as soon as the person returns to village life. Some Papago and Pima diabetics turn not to modern medicine for help, but to traditional curing. Papago women now buy medicinal plant packages reputed to cure diabetes from Mexican herbalists at the Magdalena fiesta each October.

On the other hand, what about more emphasis on *gathering*, seasonally responding to locally available fresh foods? These native foods have proved to be nutritious, and the outdoor exercise involved in collecting them would certainly be beneficial. In another vein, one study has shown that eating prickly pear pads, a traditional Papago food, can beneficially control blood sugar levels of diabetic Indians. While no one expects the Papago to return entirely to a hunting and gathering mode of existence, there is plenty of room for a resurgence of part-time native food collecting. And who would want to see the *O'odham* go any farther the *other* way, accepting a dull diet that makes them like the unhealthy, hopeless desert rats stuck in a medical researcher's cage?

"Chicken Scratch" (Tohono-O'odham style polka). © 1988 Leonard F. Chana, Tohono O'odham artist.

DELFINA CUERO:
HER AUTOBIOGRAPHY
Florence Connolly Shipek

Many stories were told us all the time. The stories used to tell how people are and what to expect from other people in the way of behavior. I only remember a few of the stories now; it is so long since I have heard them.

In the beginning of time lots of wild animals were like people and could talk. There was a coyote and he was a bad man. He was always trying to deceive people and do things that he shouldn't. Then there were these two beautiful girls who were crows and who lived in a tree. An old woman was taking care of the girls and guarding them. But she went to sleep because she was too old. The coyote sneaked up and tried to climb the tree but he couldn't. Then he jumped and jumped but he couldn't reach the girls. The girls couldn't go to sleep because coyote made so much noise jumping. So the girls flew up into the sky and coyote was chasing them and crying and begging them to take him along. The younger girl asked, "Why can't we take him with us?" The older one said, "No, he can't fly." The younger replied, "Why can't we throw something down and pull him up so he can go with us?" But the older one said, "He's too bad; he would eat us." The younger girl must have been falling in love with him because she felt sorry for him. She finally threw down the end of a rope and coyote began climbing up into the sky toward the crow girls. As coyote climbed, he began talking about how he wanted to grab that girl. The older sister got upset and then mad as she heard him talking. She said, "Let's get rid of him. He'll hurt us. He's too different." The older sister cut the rope so that coyote fell and died.

This story explains how we have to watch men—there are some good and some bad men. We knew that these stories were told to teach us how to behave and what to expect. The old people did not have to tell us what the story explained at the end of the story, but I am saying what it meant to us.

Things like that I was told by my grandmother. I still live by the old rules and I've never been sick. I stay away from my daughters when they are pregnant too. When a lady is pregnant, she must not look at anything that is bad, or even see a fox or a snake. You must not look at anything like that or it will mark the baby. You try not to see anything when you are pregnant. The oldtimers would not let a pregnant woman or a menstruating woman go into a garden. She had to stay by herself and not bother anything. She could not gather wild greens, or wash and do things like that. She could not go near sick persons or garden plants without hurting them.

Grandmothers taught the girls that when they were pregnant they must not eat too much or the baby will be born big or have some kind of trouble. They can eat anything they want unless it makes them sick, except they must stay away from salt. Women are weak nowadays. Long time ago, they just kept on doing regular work, they went out and gathered food and whatever was needed, even heavy things, and it didn't hurt them. They just had to be careful not to see bad things.

In the real old days, grandmothers taught these things about life at the time of a girl's initiation ceremony, when she was about to become a woman. Nobody just talked about these things ever. It was all in the songs and myths that belonged to the ceremony. All that a girl needed to know to be a good wife, and how to have babies and to take care of them was learned at the ceremony, at the time when a girl became a woman. We were taught about food and herbs and how to make things by our mothers and grandmothers all the time. But only at the ceremony for girls was the proper time to teach the special things women had to know. Nobody just talked about those things, it was all in the songs.

But I'm not that old, they had already stopped having the ceremonies before I became a woman, so I didn't know these things until later. Some of the other girls had the same trouble I did after I was married. No one told me anything. I knew something was wrong with me but I didn't know what. Food was becoming hard to find then and we had to go a long way to find enough greens. My husband was away hunting meat. Sometimes the men were gone for several days before they found anything. One day I was a long way from Ha-a looking for greens. I had a terrible pain. I started walking back home but I had to stop and rest when the pain was too much. Then the baby came, I couldn't walk any more, and I didn't know what to do. Finally an uncle came out looking for me when I didn't return. My grandmother had not realized my time was so close or she would not have let me go so far alone. They carried me back but I lost the baby. My grandmother took care of me so I recovered. Then she taught me all these things about what to do and how to take care of babies.

After that, I had my babies by myself. I didn't have any help from anybody. My grandmother lived near us but she knew that now I knew what to do, so she never helped me. I did what I had been taught. I used xa'a· nayul [*Trichostema parishii* Vasey, mint family] or kᵂa·s [*Rhus laurina* Nutt., sumac] to bathe in and I drank a little kᵂa·s tea also.

I dug a little place and built a hot fire and got hot ashes. I put something, bark or cloth, over the ashes and put the baby in it to keep the baby warm.

So that the navel will heal quickly and come off in three days, I took two rounds of cord and tied it, and then put a clean rag on it. I burned a hot fire outside our hut to get hot dirt to wrap in a cloth. I put this on the navel and changed it all night and day to keep it warm till the navel healed. To keep the navel from getting infected, I burned cow hide, or any kind of skin, till crisp, then ground it. I put this powder on the navel. I did this and no infection started in my babies. Some women didn't know this and if infection started, I would help them to stop it this way.

When each baby was new born, I bathed it in elderberry blossom or willow bark tea. Then after I had washed the baby's face with elderberry blossom tea, I burned some honey real brown, then put water with it and cleaned the baby's face all over. This takes any stuff [scale?] off the baby's face. The afterbirth is buried in the floor of the house.

Some people are not careful and they eat right away and then the mother nurses the baby and it gets infected. The mother must wait a while to eat, then first eat atole. Next, the mother eats lots of vegetables and drinks lots of herb or mint teas. Never drink water! Never eat beans when nursing a baby, it will ruin the baby.

I did all this myself. When my children were older, if they got sick, I used herbs. That is all I used and my children got well again. There are herbs for stomach pains, colds, tooth aches, and everything that the Indians knew. There is a real good one to stop bleeding right away from a bad cut. There is another good one for bad burns and to stop infection. If a woman drinks lots and lots of xa'a· nayul she can keep from having babies, but there is another herb, even better, that the Indians used to use to keep from having babies every year. They are hard to find now because we can't go everywhere to look for them any more.

I named all of my children myself. I didn't know anything about baptizing them then; I just went ahead like the Indians did and gave them names. When my oldest child was a year or two old, they had a party to welcome him to the group. Everybody got together and they built a big ramada for me and they brought their food together. We had a big fire. I had an uncle that lead the singing and dancing. He led a big xa·tu·p i·mac [fire dance]. They circled around the fire hand in hand and following each other, and jumping with both feet and singing. They were glad because they would have more Indians, another baby added to the group. All the people brought presents for the baby—baskets, ollas, food, mud dolls, or bow and arrows and different things, whatever was right to start the child. Sometimes they also brought tiny things like the real ones, tiny ollas and baskets and bow and arrows. The child was given its name at the party.

By the time my second child who lived was old enough, we didn't have parties for the new children any more. I don't know why, maybe it was too hard to get enough to eat. I'm just telling what happened to me, what I know.

From *Delfina Cuero: Her Autobiography. An Account of Her Last Years and Her Ethnobotanic Contributions,* by Florence Connolly Shipek. Reprinted by permission of the author.

THE EPIDEMIOLOGY OF ALCOHOL ABUSE AMONG AMERICAN INDIANS
THE MYTHICAL AND REAL PROPERTIES

Philip A. May

Because of the drunken Indian stereotype and other myths often associated with American Indians, it is important to critically examine the detailed evidence that best defines the epidemiology of alcohol abuse among Indians and particular tribal communities. Public health understandings and programs must be based not on myth but on fact. In this paper, twelve major myths, statements, and questions about the nature of the alcohol abuse problem are reviewed. An analysis of current mortality data and an understanding of the extant literature will reveal that many current myths are either false or, at best, half-truths. . . .

IS ALCOHOLISM THE NUMBER ONE HEALTH PROBLEM AMONG AMERICAN INDIANS?

That alcoholism is the leading health problem among Indians is probably the most popular and common statement about alcohol and Indians that one hears from laymen

and health professionals alike. It is accepted as gospel by many and is seldom questioned or elaborated on in the planning and implementing of alcohol abuse prevention programs. Yet it is a half-truth at best.

In table 1, an analysis of the most recent Indian Health Service data from 1986 to 1988 indicates that 17.0 percent to 19.0 percent of all Indian deaths are probably alcohol-related. Similar patterns and data are common in other years as well. These data are quite complete in scope, for they include an estimate of the percentage of alcohol-related deaths from motor vehicle and other accidents, suicide, homicide, and alcoholism/alcohol dependence. Therefore, it is true that alcohol is involved in a very high percentage of Indian deaths—substantially greater than the general U.S. average of 4.7 percent. But the term *alcoholism* can be very misleading. Alcoholism generally denotes only alcohol-dependent or chronic drinking behaviors, which are only part of the problem. In table 1 the data are broken down to compare deaths from behaviors that are generally the result of alcohol-abusive drinking patterns (sporadic, binge drinking) with those that result from alcohol-specific/alcohol-dependent drinking styles (chronic, "alcoholic" drinking). In 1986–88, 2,213, or

TABLE 1: Estimated Alcohol-Involved Deaths of American Indians in Reservation States, 1986–1988, and the U.S. General Population, 1987

Cause of Death	Total Indian Deaths (N) ×	Estimated % Alcohol Involved =	Indian Alcohol-Involved (N)	Alcohol-Involved U.S. (N)	Alcohol-Involved from Nine IHS Areas* (N)
Alcohol Abusive					
Accidents					
Motor Vehicle	1,687	(.65)	1,097	31,389	847
Other	1,278	(.25)	320	11,683	250
Suicide	534	(.75)	401	23,099	302
Homicide	494	(.85)	395	16,962	279
Subtotal	(3,993)		(2,213)	(83,133)	(1,678)
Alcoholic/Alcohol-Specific**	(742)	(1.00)	(742)	(15,909)	(580)
TOTAL	4,735		2,955	99,042	2,258
Deaths as a percent of total deaths	27.2%		17.0%	4.7%	19.0%

SOURCE: Computed from U.S. Indian Health Service, *Trends in Health and Regional Differences in Indian Health.*

* IHS states that data are more complete in nine of their service areas (Aberdeen, Alaska, Alburquerque, Bermidji, Billings, Nashville, Navajo, Phoenix, and Tucson). The far right column only includes these nine areas.

** Alcoholic-specific deaths include the following causes: alcohol dependence syndrome, alcoholic psychoses, and chronic liver disease and cirrhosis specified as alcoholic.

74.9 percent, of all alcohol-related deaths were from alcohol-abusive causes, while 742, or 25.1 percent, were from alcohol-specific/alcohol-dependent causes (alcohol dependence syndrome, alcoholic psychosis, and chronic liver disease specified as alcoholic). Therefore, one would be more accurate in stating that alcoholism per se is not the leading cause of death among Indians. More accurately, alcohol abuse and alcoholism combine to be the leading cause of mortality.

Alcohol-induced morbidity (sickness) is also a great problem among Indians. Again, though, alcohol abuse and alcoholism combine to cause the illness. In fact, alcohol-abuse produces more sickness and injury than do alcohol-specific or alcoholic behaviors. This is also true in mainstream U.S. society.

The importance of these distinctions is great. If public health officials and citizens focus solely on chronic alcoholic behaviors and problems in their planning of intervention and prevention, they will miss the majority (three-fourths) of the problem. Complete alcohol abuse prevention and intervention programs must address the full range of alcohol-abusive and chronic alcoholic behaviors.

DO INDIANS METABOLIZE ALCOHOL DIFFERENTLY OR MORE SLOWLY THAN DO PEOPLE OF OTHER ETHNIC GROUPS?

The most persistent myth about Indians is that they have particular biophysiological reasons for "not being able to hold their alcohol." In fact, not only do non-Indians believe this, but many Indians also believe that their ethnic group has a biological deficit in metabolizing alcohol. One survey among the Navajo asked if Indians have a biological weakness to alcohol that non-Indians do not, and 63 percent of the respondents said yes.

This myth has virtually no basis in fact. Only one study ever reported that Indians metabolize alcohol more slowly than non-Indians, but it was criticized as highly flawed in its use of controls and other methods. All of the remaining studies of alcohol metabolism among Indians have found Indians to metabolize alcohol as rapidly as, or more rapidly than, matched controls who were non-Indian. Furthermore, liver biopsies have shown no discernible difference in liver phenotype between Indians and non-Indians.

Therefore, no basis at all for this myth is found in the scientific literature, and it should not be a consideration in current prevention and intervention programs. Major reviews of alcohol metabolism among all ethnic groups usually conclude that alcohol metabolism and alcohol genetics are traits of individuals and that there is more variation within an ethnic group than there is between ethnic groups. Further, when biophysiologic investigators attempt to explain major alcohol-related behaviors, they generally point to sociocultural variables as the major factors.

ARE INDIAN ALCOHOL-RELATED PROBLEMS UNIQUELY INDIAN?

Certainly some alcohol-related behaviors in which Indians participate seem to be unique in their manifestations. Indeed, this was a major theme of the early literature. But what is often overlooked in practical explanations of Indian drinking behavior is that there are many similarities between Indians and other groups. Further, there may also be common explanations for both Indian drinking and that practiced by other groups.

First, the fact that Indians have high rates of alcohol-related death is influenced by demographic traits. The American Indian population is very young in almost every community. The median age of Indians is in the low twenties overall and is commonly much lower on some reservations. In 1988,

the U.S. median age was 32.3. Young populations tend to have much higher rates of death from a number of alcohol-related causes (e.g., motor vehicle and other accidents, suicide, and homicide) than do populations that are elderly or middle aged. Because of the demography of many Indian communities, one would expect to find higher rates of these problems than in the more middle-aged U.S. mainstream. Conversely, one would also expect lower rates of death from chronic diseases such as heart disease, stroke, and cancer among Indians.

Second, geography plays a role in alcohol-related statistics. Because the majority of Indians still live in rural western states, higher death rates are to be expected due to factors such as higher-risk environments, distance from care, time lag to care, and reduced availability of services. Alcohol-related injuries may be more common in rural western environments. Also, serious injuries (from events such as motor vehicle crashes) often become deaths because of the distance to, and timing of, care.

Third, social, political, legal, and local policies may create conditions that exacerbate alcohol-related problems and rates. The low socioeconomic status of many Indians shapes their behavioral patterns. Also, because most reservations are still under prohibition, drinking styles and patterns are such that higher rates of alcohol-related arrest, injury, and mortality are more likely to occur. Changes in policy similar to those enacted in other groups and societies might eventually produce very different alcohol consumption characteristics and patterns of alcohol-related problems. In addition, upward changes in social class and education in the future would change drinking and alcohol-related behavior patterns.

Finally, tribal culture or social practices may contain some of the seeds of both problems and solutions. Elevated rates of alcohol-related death from automobile accidents may arise from dangerous cultural practices such as not wearing seat belts and not being licensed and well educated in safety and/or defensive driving. The same can be said of many other subgroups of the U.S. population. Even if a person is driving while intoxicated, he might not become an alcohol-related statistic if he is strapped in by a seat belt. Unpublished data from New Mexico surveys show a lower use of seat belts among the youth of some tribes as compared with non-Indian youth in the same schools. But some tribes have higher rates of belt use than others.

In summary, the explanations of high rates of alcohol-related problems and their solutions may well be found in demographic, geographic, political, and cultural variables that are not necessarily uniquely Indian. Researchers, planners, and others must not overlook these relatively simple and conventional explanations in either their studies of etiology or their designs of solutions.

IS THERE A HIGHER PREVALENCE OF DRINKING AMONG INDIANS?

It is often said or implied that a vast majority of Indians drink. Frequently, I have asked audiences at a number of reservations, "What percentage of your adult population drinks?" The response for most sites was frequently "90 percent" or greater. Similar responses about Indians are also common within the mainstream population of the U.S.

The evidence in the published literature is quite different from what most people believe. In fact, there is extreme variation in prevalence of drinking from one tribal group to another. Unfortunately, however, only a handful of extant adult prevalence studies have been published. Nevertheless, from these studies one can conclude that adult prevalence is lower in some tribes than the U.S. general averages; in others, it is about the same as or higher than U.S. averages. Furthermore, drinking prevalence may vary over time in many tribal communities.

Two prevalence studies among the Navajo in 1969 and 1984 indicate that, in both periods, fewer Navajo adults drank at all (31 percent and 52 percent) than adults in the general population of the U.S. (67 percent). But these same studies indicate that Navajo drinking prevalence is increasing.

Two similar studies among the Standing Rock Sioux showed that prevalence was decreasing (69 percent to 58 percent). In 1960, overall drinking prevalence was about the same as in the general population; twenty years later, it was lower than U.S. averages (67 percent).

Studies were also carried out among two other tribes. The Southern Ute and the Brokenhead Ojibway of Canada demonstrated drinking prevalence rates (80 percent and 84 percent) higher than U.S. averages. The prevalence of adult drinking among Indians, therefore, varies widely from tribe to tribe and over time. Variation over time is also found with Indian youths.

These prevalence studies provided other significant findings as well. Among those who do drink in these tribes, there is a substantially higher prevalence (two to three times) of problem and excessive drinking indicators than among the general U.S. population. Consumption of more than five drinks per situation, as well as experience with delirium tremens (DTs) and blackouts, are much higher in these studies. Therefore, among those Indians who drink, there is a substantial number of problem drinkers who produce a high frequency and variety of problems such as arrests, morbidity, and mortality.

More positive findings are also found in these studies. For example, among Indian males who are in their middle age and older, more have completely quit drinking than among most other groups of U.S. males. Also, in virtually every tribe, a lower proportion of the women drink.

Therefore, the overall prevalence of drinking among Indians is not the most important variable in the epidemiology of drinking. What is more important are the drinking styles, some of which emphasize very problematic behaviors.

DO ALL INDIANS DRINK IN THE SAME MANNER OR STYLE?

Tribal and urban studies have reported various styles of drinking. Most researchers describe two patterns that cause either no or few alcohol-related problems: abstinence and moderated social drinking. But at least two problem drinking patterns are common among subgroups or "peer clusters" in many tribal communities. One is a chronic alcoholic drinking pattern that Frances Ferguson has called "anxiety" drinking. The other is the "recreational" pattern defined by Ferguson and others.

Recreational drinkers are predominantly young (age 15–35) males who are students or relatively new participants in the work world; they drink sporadically for special occasions, at night and on weekends, away from home, and in a celebration or party manner. Some young females also participate in this pattern, but they are less involved and generally for a shorter period of time. This drinking style is not unlike college fraternity drinkers. Indian recreational drinkers are at very high risk for alcohol-related injury, arrest, and death because of the emphasis on high blood alcohol levels for a "blitzed" experience. Many people mature out of this pattern, but a disproportionate number of Indians die young from recreational drinking.

Anxiety drinkers, on the other hand, are more typical of the chronic alcoholic. They are downwardly mobile, unemployed, and socially marginal to both Indian and non-Indian society. They are predominantly male, but some females fit this pattern. They tend to drink chronically, whether alone or with other drinking buddies. Anxiety drinkers are commonly found spending long periods of time in border towns or in skid row areas of many western cities.

These two types of problem drinkers produce the alcohol-abusive and alcohol-specific problems described earlier. The recreational drinkers produce many of the accident and suicide deaths, while the anxiety drinkers produce the alcoholism deaths (e.g., cirrhosis of the liver) and a preponderance of the pedestrian-vehicle collision deaths.

In summary, there are a number of drinking styles among Indians that affect the epidemiological patterns and create a challenge for prevention and treatment. There is no one Indian drinking pattern.

WHY ARE INDIAN RATES OF DEATH FROM ALCOHOL-RELATED CAUSES SO HIGH?

Many of the answers to this question have already been presented in previous sections. However, the common, stereotypical answer to this question is that "Indians are like that." Just as it is said that the "Irish drink because they are Irish," it is said that "Indians drink because they are Indian." The simple, logical extension of this, then, is that high rates of drinking produce high rates of alcohol-related death and other problems. But we have seen that the prevalence of drinking alone does not explain the high rates of alcohol-related death among Indians.

Recent IHS data (see table 2) indicate that Indians die more frequently than the

TABLE 2: Age-Adjusted Mortality (rates per 100,000) from Alcohol-Abusive and Alcohol-Specific, Causes for American Indians, 1986–1988, and the U.S. General Population, 1987

Cause of Death	Estimated Alcohol-Involved	All IHS Area	All U.S.	Ratio IHS/U.S.	Nine IHS Areas*	Ratio Nine Areas/ U.S.
Alcohol-Abusive						
Accidents						
Motor Vehicle	.65	57.5	19.5	2.95	75.2	3.89
Other	.25	45.5	15.2	2.99	61.5	4.05
Suicide	.75	17.9	11.7	1.53	22.8	1.95
Homocide	.80	16.9	8.6	1.97	20.1	2.34
Subtotal		(137.8)	(55.0)	(2.51)	(179.6)	(3.26)
Alcoholic/Alcohol-Specific**	1.00	(32.7)	(6.0)	(5.45)	(45.8)	(7.63)
TOTAL		170.5	61.0	2.79	225.4	3.69

SOURCE: Computed from U.S. Indian Health Service, *Trends in Indian Health and Regional Differences in Indian Health.*

* IHS states that data are more complete in nine of their service areas (Aberdeen, Alaska, Albuquerque, Bermidji, Billings, Nashville, Navajo, Phoenix, and Tucson). The far right column only includes these nine areas.
** Alcoholic-specific deaths include the following causes: alcohol dependence syndrome, alcoholic psychoses, and chronic liver disease and cirrhosis specified as alcoholic.

U.S. averages from motor vehicle accidents (2.95 to 3.89 times higher); other accidents (2.99 to 4.05 times higher); suicide (1.53 to 1.95 times higher); homicide (1.97 to 2.34 times higher); and alcoholism (5.45 to 7.63 times higher). These ratios of Indian to U.S. averages reflect rates, not the actual numbers of deaths. There are three elements of explanation for this different experience. One element can be found in the previous sections, which deal with demographic, social, and political considerations discussed in the literature. The second element of explanation is centered on drinking style. The flamboyant drinking styles that are very common in a number of Indian peer clusters (recreational and anxiety drinkers) emphasize abusive drinking and high blood alcohol levels. Further, heavy drinking peer groups among many tribes encourage, or do not discourage, the frequent mixing of alcohol impairment, risky behavior, and risky environments. Driving while intoxicated, sleeping outside in the winter, aggression, and other unsafe practices are examples of this element.

The mixing of (1) high-risk environments, (2) flamboyant drinking styles, and (3) risky post-drinking behavior combine to elevate Indian rates of alcohol-related death far above those of the general U.S. population. This is true as well with arrest, injury, and other problems for which statistics are recorded.

HOW IS THE DRUNKEN INDIAN STEREOTYPE PERPETUATED BY A NAÏVE AND UNCRITICAL USE OF STATISTICS?

Many authors and speakers on the topic of Indian drinking and alcohol-related problems often cite statistics that do not capture an unduplicated count of the individuals involved in abusive drinking. For example, if one looks at alcohol-related arrest rates, there generally is little opportunity for knowing if the data reflect the experience of a few or a large number of individuals. In Gallup, New Mexico, Ferguson found that 115 alcohol-dependent Navajo males accounted for almost twelve hundred arrests in 1.5 years. A careless or uncritical researcher could report this as twelve hundred Navajo with a problem, rather than one hundred with a chronic drinking problem and repeated arrests.

When working on my doctoral dissertation in Montana, I stumbled across a situation and calculated an overall arrest rate that further emphasizes this point. On one small Northern Plains reservation (<3,000 people) the arrest rate was 100,103 per 100,000 from 1970 to 1974. In other words, a literal and naive interpretation would be that every man, woman, and child had been arrested at least once during the five-year period. My, what a criminal place one could imagine with these data! Further, 75 percent of these arrests were for alcohol-specific crimes on a dry reservation. Could this mean that three-quarters of all the men, women, and children are such problem drinkers that they are arrested? Certainly not. It was a situation where a small proportion of the population (mainly males) spent time in a "revolving door" situation. They drank excessively in nearby border towns and on the reservation and were in and out of jail, time and time again. How absurd the uncritical use of aggregate and duplicative data such as these arrest statistics can be! But such data frequently are presented uncritically in newspapers, lectures, and even academic and agency program papers.

The same can be said of morbidity data. One person with a drinking problem can generate literally dozens of visits to a clinic, inpatient admissions, and emergency incidents. IHS data showing a large number of patient encounters should not be taken to indicate the prevalence of the problem. Counts of individuals, not visits, should be used for epidemiological purposes, and, even then, one is dealing only with treated prevalence. For example, in a chart review study of IHS records in the Southwest covering ten years, 21.4 percent of the individuals who visited six IHS general clinic facilities were seen at least once for a mental health or alcohol abuse problem. This is not a substantially high percentage based on U.S. estimates. The vast majority of inpatient episodes (83 percent) by these individuals, however, were for alcohol and substance abuse, as were 53 percent of outpatient visits. On average, each episode of mental health and alcohol-related illness presented by these individuals accounted for 3.9 outpatient and inpatient visits before the problem was fully dealt with or was cured. Therefore, just from looking at visits, one might conclude that the problems were much more extensive. Thus, morbidity data, like arrest data, can be highly duplicative in counting or estimating problems, even when estimating treated prevalence.

One should always ask, then, "Are the prevalence data that are being presented representative of true prevalence or treated/clinic prevalence?" Or, more importantly, "Are they nothing more than workload data?" Too often, arrest, morbidity, social welfare caseload, and other statistics are merely workload, contact, or activity counts. Unduplicated data, such as random surveys of individuals in the population to document adult drinking, are best for estimating prevalence. Further, school-based youth surveys tell us little or nothing about adults. Mortality data are much better for estimating prevalence, because people die only once. Indian epidemiological information has suffered greatly over the years, because data used have not often enough been unduplicated counts that provide valid measures of prevalence. In populations with a substantial concentration of high-risk, heavy drinkers, this has led to inaccuracy and distortion of the true extent of the problem. Measuring the repetitive, high-risk, and problematic behavior of a subculture of problem drinkers within a tribe, and using it uncritically, can stigmatize the whole tribe.

WHAT IS THE LEVEL OF SEVERITY OF DRINKING AMONG THE ALCOHOL-ABUSING POPULATION?

Within the drinking populations of most Indian communities, a substantial number of people drink very heavily. These people are found in both the recreational and anxiety drinker populations.

More than 70 percent of Indians who die in traffic accidents in New Mexico have been drinking. A University of New Mexico study of all ethnic groups in the state found that American Indian decedents from crashes had very high blood alcohol concentrations (BAC). The average BACs of those who had been drinking and were killed in vehicular crashes in New Mexico were Indian .191, Hispanic .189, and Anglo .128. All ethnic groups, therefore, were averaging levels well above the legal intoxication level (.10). Indians killed in alcohol-related crashes had BACs significantly higher than those of the Anglos but not much higher than those of the Hispanics. A full 85.7 percent of the Indian and 82.5 percent of the Hispanic victims who had been drinking were above the legal limit. This compared with 55.4 percent of the Anglos. Thus, the level of drinking among the Indians and Hispanics who drink is very high, probably indicating similar sociocultural patterns of drinking by certain peer clusters among the two groups.

A comparable pattern of blood alcohol levels exists for Indian decedents from suicide. Among those Indians who die from suicide in New Mexico, 69 percent to 74 percent (depending on the year studied) are alcohol-involved, with the alcohol level being quite bimodal. In other words, one-fourth of the victims tend to be completely sober, while three-fourths have very high BACs, as above (work in progress).

Research indicates, then, that those who are members of alcohol-abusing peer clusters in many tribes drink in a manner that produces very high blood alcohol levels. Both suicide and motor vehicle accidents are alcohol-related in a majority of cases. These results also support the notion that there is a connection between heavy drinking and risky behavior.

WHAT IS THE RELATIONSHIP BETWEEN CHILD ABUSE, CHILD NEGLECT, AND ALCOHOL?

The one major study that has examined, in detail, the relationship between child abuse and neglect and alcohol use demonstrates clearly that alcohol often is involved. In northern New Mexico, 85 percent to 93 percent of the Indian child neglect cases and 63 percent of the child abuse cases involve alcohol. Neglect, abuse, and alcohol problems were found to be part of a complex found in a number of multiproblem families where intergenerational transmission of pathology was present.

A subsequent paper from the above study compares the abuse/neglect sample to a matched group of Indian control families. Alcohol use and abuse was found to have been present in 58 percent of the control homes at one time or another, as compared to 88 percent in the abuse/neglect target groups. This control study concluded that alcohol seems to be a necessary, but not sufficient, condition for child abuse. This is not unlike the relationship with suicide.

IS ALCOHOL ABUSE ONLY A MALE PROBLEM?

Alcohol abuse, in the form of both alcohol-related and alcohol-specific/dependent behavior, takes its greatest toll among Indian males. IHS data from 1986 to 1988 (see table 3) indicate that the number of Indian male deaths from alcohol-related and

TABLE 3: Estimated Alcohol-Involved Causes of Death for U.S. Indians and Alaska Natives, 1986–1988, and the U.S. General Population, 1987, by Age, Sex. Rates per 100,000, and Number.

					Rates							
Cause of Death	15–24		Ratio	25–34		Ratio	35–44		Ratio	45–54		Ratio
	Ind.	U.S.		Ind.	U.S.		Ind.	U.S.		Ind.	U.S.	
Male												
MV accident	97.0	55.5	1.7	104.7	36.8	2.8	86.2	25.6	3.4	65.7	21.8	3.0
Other accdt	42.5	18.6	2.3	63.5	23.6	2.7	77.1	23.8	3.2	59.9	23.4	2.6
Suicide	40.7	21.3	1.9	49.6	24.8	2.0	30.3	22.9	1.3	21.7	23.8	0.9
Homicide	32.1	21.9	1.5	44.7	23.3	1.9	38.6	17.1	2.3	19.4	12.1	1.6
Alcoholism*	0.8	0.1	8.0	21.8	3.2	6.8	65.5	12.9	5.1	98.6	24.4	4.0

Total deaths for above causes	4307 2705
% of all Indian deaths	19.6% 12.3%
% of all male Indian deaths	42.1% 26.5%

Cause of Death	Ind.	U.S.	Ratio	Ind.	U.S.	Ratio	Ind.	U.S.	Ratio	Ind.	U.S.	Ratio
Female												
MV accident	30.7	19.7	1.6	39.5	11.5	3.4	32.2	9.3	3.5	27.8	9.2	3.0
Other accdt	8.2	3.5	2.3	13.1	4.8	2.7	16.9	5.2	3.3	13.3	6.4	2.1
Suicide	6.5	4.3	1.5	8.3	5.9	1.4	9.3	7.2	1.3	5.0	8.5	0.6
Homicide	10.2	6.0	1.7	10.4	6.9	1.5	9.3	4.8	1.9	4.4	3.6	1.2
Alcoholism*	1.2	0.1	12.0	16.8	1.4	12.0	25.1	4.2	8.4	57.3	7.6	7.5

Total deaths for above causes	1474 951
% of all Indian deaths	6.7% 4.3%
% of all male Indian deaths	20.5% 13.2%

SOURCE: Computed from U.S. Indian Health Service, *Trends in Indian Health*.

* Alcoholism deaths include the following causes: alcohol dependence syndrome, alcoholic psychoses, and chronic liver disease and cirrhosis specified as alcoholic.
** Includes all Indian and Alaska Natives in all parts of the 32 reservation states served by IHS (total deaths in reservation states 1986–1988 = 21,943).

alcohol-specific causes is much higher (N = 2,705) than for Indian females (N = 951). This is true in every category. Twenty-six percent of male deaths are alcohol involved, whereas 13 percent of female deaths are. Stated another way, in a typical three-year period, 12.3 percent of all Indian deaths are related to alcohol use by males, and 4.3 percent are related to alcohol use by females.

Further, according to the rates in table 3, male Indians fare far worse than U.S. males in general. For example, in a comparison of Indian and U.S. males ages 25–34, the rate for motor vehicle accident deaths among Indians is 2.8 times higher, for other accidents

2.7 times higher, for suicide 1.9 times higher, and for homicide 1.5 times higher; the alcoholism rate is 6.8 times higher.

Indian females, however, do not fare much better in comparison with U.S. female rates. In the same age category (25–34 years), Indian female rates are 3.4, 2.7, 1.4, 1.5, and 12.0 times higher than U.S. females. Thus, Indian females have higher rates of alcohol-involved death than U.S. females in general, and this is true in most age categories and alcohol-involved causes.

Therefore, although the numbers indicate that alcohol-abusive mortality and alcohol abuse are mainly (in numbers) an Indian male problem, Indian females are also

Rates						Number		
55–64		Ratio	65–74		Ratio	Total Deaths (all ages)	× Est. % alcohol-involved	Total alcohol-involved (all ages)
Ind.	U.S.		Ind.	U.S.				
52.2	21.7	2.4	65.6	24.6	2.7	1452	(65%)	944
82.3	30.3	2.7	113.0	42.6	2.7	1139	(25%)	285
12.2	26.6	0.5	16.7	34.8	0.5	546	(75%)	410
13.0	8.8	1.5	12.6	6.2	2.0	521	(80%)	417
95.4	33.1	2.9	79.5	27.0	2.9	649	(100%)	649
18.3	10.2	1.8	17.7	13.7	1.3	577	(65%)	375
22.8	10.6	2.2	43.7	21.1	2.1	358	(25%)	90
4.6	7.7	0.6	2.4	7.2	0.3	107	(75%)	80
4.6	2.5	1.8	1.2	2.8	0.4	132	(80%)	106
50.2	9.4	5.3	20.1	7.3	2.8	300	(100%)	300

at high risk compared to other U.S. women. This should be kept in mind for alcohol treatment and prevention in Indian Country. Indian women who are in the alcohol abusing categories also have a strong need for attention, especially regarding alcohol-specific causes. The number of female deaths from cirrhosis of the liver (w/alcohol), alcohol dependence, and alcoholic psychosis is one-half the number (46.2 percent) of Indian male deaths from these causes. Chronic alcohol dependence problems are, therefore, more equally shared among Indian females and males than the other alcohol-related causes of death.

IS FETAL ALCOHOL SYNDROME (FAS) A MAJOR PROBLEM FOR INDIANS?

Like many of the problems mentioned above, FAS rates vary greatly from one reservation to the next. Two studies have been carried out on Canadian Indian communities with widespread alcohol abuse, and high rates of FAS have been found. Another study found higher rates of FAS recorded on Indian birth certificates in the U.S. than among any other ethnic group. One other study found both high- and low-risk communities in the same region, with variance based on differing sociocultural and drinking patterns found in the communities. The range of FAS rates in these studies is from a high of 190 per 1,000 children to a low of 1.3 per 1,000 children. However, studies that were based on the largest populations of Indians who were living in relatively stable reservation communities documented rates only slightly higher than the U.S. estimated rate in the 1980s. The overall Southwestern Indian rate in 1978–82 was 4.2 per 1,000, compared to 2.2 for the U.S. overall. Further, the U.S. rate for all races may well be underreported.

Bray and Anderson and Chavez et al. suggest that, among Indians, better surveillance and more complete reporting of FAS occurs. This may be true both in the disrupted Indian communities that were highly alcohol-abusive and therefore were studied by researchers, and also in general birth certificate recording.

Much of the newspaper, popular media, and conference coverage of FAS has been highly dramatic and quite distorted. The figures quoted of "one in three" or "one in four" Indian babies being FAS have no support at all in screening, epidemiologic or scientific studies. This is even true for the small, most highly alcoholic communities such as the one studied by Robinson et al. Furthermore, the more disrupted communities studied are not representative of Indian communities in general. In the studies done among Indian populations where culture and society are more intact, FAS rates are much lower. It is no more accurate to project an FAS rate from one or two disrupted, alcohol-abusing communities onto all Indians than it would be to project the rate from an urban, skid row census tract to all of the U.S. population.

In general, the scientific literature points out that FAS is an "equal opportunity" birth defect and can affect any ethnic group where there are sufficient levels of maternal drinking. FAS, to a great degree, depends on the quantity, frequency, and timing of maternal drinking. In many tribes, there are more alcohol-abstaining women than in the general U.S. population. This obviously protects a substantial portion of Indian children from FAS and lowers levels of prenatal alcohol damage. In almost every population ever studied, a very small number of women produce all of the FAS children. This is very true in Indian epidemiologic studies of other problems as well.

FAS prevention, however, has been cited as an extremely promising area for American Indians. In fact, it is apparent that Indians today are very aware of FAS as a problem, and a large number of established FAS initiatives and prevention programs are underway in Indian communities.

CAN PREVENTION PROGRAMS DESIGNED FOR ONE TRIBE BE ADJUSTED AND APPLIED TO OTHERS?

In spite of the unique social and cultural nature of each tribe, prevention and intervention programs designed for one tribe can be used in others. It has often been implied that each tribal community is so distinctive that programs have limited or no applicability across tribal settings. But a detailed knowledge of the particular history, culture, and current epidemiological features of alcohol abuse in a community will allow for fine tuning and adaptation to other, somewhat similar tribes and communities.

Knowing the demographic and epidemiologic features (age; sex ratio; cultural, social, and economic indicators; mortality; morbidity; fertility; and gender-specific drinking patterns) of a community will facilitate the design and implementation of successful programs of prevention and treatment. The problem with some efforts in the past was that local data were not utilized or available, and relevant studies were not always done. Further, when epidemiological understandings are very general or poor and programs are based on myth, failure is more likely. Facts such as those presented in this paper are the building blocks of prevention and intervention. Improvement in the alcohol-abuse dilemma of Indian communities will require a detailed and specific understanding of the characteristics and epidemiology of the population. Indian health professionals have a responsibility to seek out such data and apply them carefully and sensitively.

CONCLUSION

Many of the myths and common understandings about alcohol use among American Indians are gross oversimplifications. As Benjamin Franklin once stated, "Half the truth is often a great lie." If they are to succeed, programs of prevention and intervention must not be built on common mythical understandings but on empirical fact. Unfortunately, facts and detailed truths are not sought or believed frequently enough.

"The truth is sometimes a poor competitor in the market place of ideas—complicated, unsatisfying, full of dilemmas, [and] always vulnerable to misinterpretation and abuse." As this paper has demonstrated, the truth about Indian drinking is indeed complicated and quite different from the myths. But the insights and explanations that emerge from seeking the facts are those that will help create meaningful improvement.

INDIAN FOREVER

Joan Smith

The truck came early one August morning the summer Stella Runnels was 10. There was nothing remarkable about it, another cattle truck on the Colville Indian reservation in Tonasket, Washington. But visitors were rare at the Runnels ranch, and the dozen children playing around the house ran up the dusty road to meet it.

It was only when the men with guns got out that Stella understood, in a horrified instant, what was about to happen.

"Everybody knew about the Indian boarding schools," she says, now 70 and living with her husband on a chicken ranch in Sonoma, incredulous now as then that her family could be destroyed in a day.

"Everybody had aunties and uncles and older brothers and sisters who had been taken. I just always thought because my father was a chief in every sense of the word—he was the only person on the reservation to have 5,000 people at his funeral—I always thought because of who he was he'd be able to keep them from taking me."

But Stella's father could not protect her from the Bureau of Indian Affairs. "The men just pointed and said, 'You, you, you, you and you,'" she says. "They picked the five of us with the best report cards. And our parents couldn't stop them because they had guns."

Stella's big brothers George and Louis sneaked out the back door and fled on horseback. But Stella, her older sister Juanita and her little sister Josephine were ordered into the back of the truck.

Stella's mother told her she had 45 minutes to say goodbye to her grandmothers, parents, cousins and nine remaining brothers and sisters. Each child was allowed to take only a paper bag with a comb, toothbrush and change of underwear. So Stella gathered her dolls.

"I had the rag dolls my grandmothers had made for me. And I had one beautiful German porcelain bisque doll with blond hair and blue eyes. I took them and buried them in my mother's rose garden. It was like I was burying my childhood."

The men picked up more children on the way to the Tonasket train station. Stella tried not to think, kept herself busy looking after Josephine, who was only 8. For two-and-a-half days the children slept in their seats and ate peanut butter sandwiches. The train kept stopping. By the time it arrived at the school in Chemawa, Oregon, it was carrying 1,000 crying children. Because they hadn't been permitted to bring toys or games, there was nothing to do "but look out the window and die."

More men with guns met the train in Oregon. The children were taken to the school, lined up and strip-searched. It was the first time Stella was naked in front of white people. She hid herself behind Josephine, then was ashamed that she couldn't protect her baby sister from the humiliating scrutiny. The white people walked up and down the rows of Indian children and, without even undoing their long braids, cut them off.

The children were separated from their cousins and siblings and forced to speak English—lapsing into native tongues meant hours locked in a dark closet. Stella and the other little girls whispered their languages secretly at night, when the white people put them in their cots and turned out the lights.

Stella survived. She learned to play tennis, excelled in school, took care of the younger children and worked in the infirmary. The summer she was 15, Stella went home again. She hadn't seen her family in five years.

It wasn't the homecoming she'd fantasized about all that lonely time at school. No one cried, no one ran to meet her, no one wrapped her in their arms. Her parents stared, awkward, silent. Only her grandmother, who at birth had named her Chu Chu An Alax, Red Bird Dancing, walked up and touched her hair, whispering sadly, "My little bird has had her feathers pulled."

Finally her mother spoke: "I don't know where I'm going to put you."

Stella grabbed a rope, jumped on a horse and fled. Her grandmother, having witnessed many such homecomings, sent Stella's uncle after her. He reached her just as she flung the rope over the branch of a pine tree.

Later, Stella dug up her dolls, found them rotting and mildewed and reburied them. The next day she went with her two aunts to live in British Columbia. She didn't learn until she was 35 that her mother had been thrilled to see her, had only meant there were so many relatives visiting she didn't have an extra bed.

Among Indians, Stella's story is remarkably unremarkable. Like the internment of Japanese Americans during World War II, stories of Indian children being removed from their families come as a shock only to white people. But virtually all of the 1 million Indians left in the United States have grown up in families scattered to the four winds. As

Ronald Reagan made dramatically clear during his recent trip to the Soviet Union, where he told an audience we had "humored" the Indians by "giving" them reservations, white people have always thought the best thing for Indians was assimilation. What has finally become apparent to nearly everyone is the impossible pain of attempted assimilation. The American Indian Lawyer Training Program in Oakland has a book on Indian child welfare called *They Are Young Once, But Indian Forever*. Indians even have an expression for it: "adopted out"—out of the family, out of the tribe. And it happens to one in three Indian babies. Unlike the Japanese internment, the removal of Indian children is still happening.

Tom LaBlanc was one of those babies. His earliest memory is of being tied to a chair by one of many foster parents, a balding white man, who stood over him, shouting and beating him. He still has the scars, including the marks from rope burns on his back and shoulders. Until he was 4 he never lived anywhere more than a month. By the time he left Boys Town in Nebraska at 17, he had been in and out of more than 105 institutions.

Now 41, a poet and Indian activist in San Francisco, he tries to make sense of his turbulent, violent childhood—the years of not knowing that his Dakota Sioux family in Minneapolis wanted him, the years of not knowing what or who he was.

Only when he was 15, after a year badgering the social worker at Boys Town, did he learn his mother was Sioux and his father was presumed Japanese.

Only when he returned from a tour in Vietnam and tracked down his Indian family did he learn he had been taken from them for the same reason so many Indian babies are taken away. They were poor.

His mother, Germaine LaBlanc, was 18 and sick when he was born. She named him Tomas Francois and cried inconsolably when he was taken away. Her sister promised to take the boy, but she and her husband had too many children and too little space to be considered a suitable placement by white social workers. Instead, Tom was moved around constantly until he was 4 and went to live with 14 other children in a foster home run by two kindly white French Canadians.

People were always asking him what he was. It was painful not knowing. He was raised Catholic and always figured he was one of the pagan babies advertised for adoption in ads in *Catholic Digest* or the Maryknoll missionary magazine. One day, a lady he always saw watering her flowers on his way to school stopped him and asked about his background. At home that night he begged his foster mother to tell him. He was reading "Little Black Sambo" in school, so she advised him to tell the lady that's who he was. "I did. I never saw her out watering her flowers again."

It was also at the French Canadians' house that he met his first Indian friends, two older boys named Stan and Paul Rock. The Rocks were from Minnesota and they took him home on visits to their reservation. It was bleak and poor, but he fell in love with their grandmother. "Whose baby is that?" he remembers her asking, and she told him he was Indian. He didn't know whether to believe her, but he was infatuated. The Rocks became his first family and she named him Little Lost Deer.

It was the Rocks who were with him the day he remembered the white man hitting him, remembered what the man had been saying. He was 7 and they were walking to school together and he exchanged greetings with an older boy. Tom considered the big boy a friend because he passed him every day and the boy said hi and made up nicknames for him. But the Rocks looked at him in shock: "How come you let that boy call you those bad names?" So they told Tom what it meant when someone called you Slant-eyes, Chink, Fishhead and Nip.

"All day my brain was exploding. I saw that old man when he was beating me up—'You goddamn Nip.' *Pow*. It was like a Fellini movie in my head, real distorted and grotesque. The bell rang and I just took off running. I only came up to that kid's waist, but I tore into him. Always after that I had kind of a chip on my shoulder."

For Indians, keeping the children is a matter of both tribal and individual survival. For Tom LaBlanc and others like him, the cost of being taken is more than not being able to dance your dances or speak your language. It's a spiritual and emotional void so unbearable that drugs and alcohol seem at times the only palliative. It's not knowing how to be a parent because you've never experienced parenting.

Tom talks about his five sons, living with three different mothers on three different reservations. He is proud they have their tribes and their traditions, but sorry they don't have him. Finally having a family can be unbearable when it only teaches you that you don't know how.

Ironically, Indians have been charged with racism for trying to keep their babies. Congress is considering strengthening the Indian Child Welfare Act, a law passed in 1978 to stop the breakup of Indian families. The law requires state courts, adoption agencies and anyone else placing Indian children to first notify the child's tribe or tribes. In most cases it gives tribal courts jurisdiction over the child's placement and requires those courts to give priority to members of the family, members of the tribe and other Indians who want to adopt the child. But proposals to tighten the law have incurred the wrath of the Reagan administration. Interior Secretary Donald Hodel circulated a memo in his department calling it "pure racism" that ignores "all other aspects of a child's status as a human being."

The Supreme Court jumped in at the end of May, agreeing to review a Mississippi state Supreme Court decision denying the Choctaw Indian Nation's right under the Indian Child Welfare Act to intervene in the adoption of twin Choctaw babies by a non-Indian couple. The lower court said the twins' natural parents had a right to place the babies through the state courts without consulting the tribe.

The law is also the key to the Baby Keetso case—the recent nationally publicized custody dispute between the Navajos and a white San Jose couple that touched a painfully raw place in the psyches of many Indians. Indians resented the media's saga of white parents desperate to keep the Indian child they had raised from birth. What they saw was another Indian baby displaced, another Indian mother—discouraged by poverty and brainwashed by a white culture that values material wealth over family ties—giving her baby away.

The Indian Child Welfare Act was passed the same year as a law guaranteeing Indians religious freedom, an issue that is not unrelated. When President Ulysses S. Grant decided after the Civil War to pacify the Indians by taking their children and putting them in federal boarding schools where they would learn English and other features of the dominant Anglo-Saxon culture, he often used missionaries to do it. Children were locked in closets or beaten, not only for speaking their languages, but for practicing their religions.

More recently, Indian children have been taken from their homes to participate in church-run "educational" placement programs. The Mormons, who believe converting Indian children will bring them closer to the Lord, run the largest such program. The kids spend the school year with Mormon families and the summers at home.

During recent congressional hearings on the proposals to tighten the Indian Child Welfare Act, Mormons told the Senate Select Committee on Indian Affairs that the law has virtually gutted their program. In 1978, they were placing 5,000 Indian children a year in Mormon homes. The children were mostly from non-Mormon families and their ages were 8 to 18. The Mormons told the committee they now place only 700 children a year, all from Mormon families and all at least 15.

Many children are also taken from their families by well-meaning social workers. They have been taken when social workers found them living in traditional one-room hogans without running water or electricity. Social workers once tried to place a Rosebud Sioux baby with a white family while the child was visiting California with her aunt because they said an Indian reservation was not a fit place to raise a child and the white foster parents who wanted to raise her were financially better off. Many children have been taken because social workers discover them living with relatives. Non-Indian caseworkers often fail to appreciate the importance of extended families in Indian tribes.

Her mother was horrified when Carol Weins told her she planned to become a social worker. It was a social worker who had placed Carol, as a 6-month-old baby and against her mother's wishes, with a white Methodist family in Mitchell, South Dakota. It was a social worker, too, who had threatened to take all of Jeanette EagleShield's children from her while she was at the Mayo Clinic caring for a son dying of leukemia. Jeanette had temporarily farmed her other children out to relatives, a situation that does not carry the stigma or sense of deprivation among Indians that it does among whites. Navajos, for instance, often call their grandmothers "mother" and their aunts "little mother." The social worker, never bothering to find out why Jeanette

was at the Mayo Clinic, sent her a letter there threatening to remove her children because she had "abandoned" them.

"When I told her my plans the look on her face was awful," says Carol, who is now 30 and handles most of San Francisco's Indian child welfare cases. "But I told her that if I could prevent what happened to her from happening to one other family it would definitely be worth it."

No one knows exactly what difference a decade of the Indian Child Welfare Act has made. What is clear is that the act is widely ignored, one reason its supporters want Congress to tighten it up. A 1984 survey by the California Department of Social Services showed that county social workers and adoption agencies broke the law in 80 percent of Indian baby placements, failing to notify either the child's tribe or the Secretary of the Interior.

Some of the city's most experienced adoption attorneys, all aware of the act, believe it simply obligates them to fill out an extra form for Indian babies. They complain that the form—which, if the baby's tribe is unknown, goes to a half-time worker in Sacramento, who sends it to the Department of the Interior, which sends it to the Bureau of Indian Affairs, which sends it to the tribe or tribes in question—prolongs the normal six-month adoption process by a year or more.

But the law actually requires caseworkers and adoption attorneys to notify the tribe directly when an Indian child comes up for placement, says attorney Patrick Romero Guillory, who represents Indian children in all of San Francisco's Indian Child Welfare Act cases. "There is so little understanding of this legislation," he says.

Most Indian babies up for placement have been abused or neglected by their parents. In one case, Weins and Guillory persuaded Juvenile Court Judge Daniel Weinstein to return a baby born in the Tenderloin with fetal alcohol syndrome to her great-grandmother on the Northern Cheyenne Reservation in Montana.

San Francisco is unusual among California counties in that it uses experts like Weins and Guillory to handle Indian child welfare cases. There are an estimated 60,000 Indians in the Bay Area, but they are a minority even among minorities, and few attorneys and social workers are willing to specialize in laws affecting them. In what was probably the first-ever home visit to a reservation by an out-of-state presiding superior court judge, Weinstein traveled with Weins and Guillory to the Northern Cheyenne Reservation in March to find out first-hand where he is sending Indian children. "At $8\frac{1}{2}$ months that little girl we sent back there couldn't hold her head up straight," Weins said. "Now she's 3 years old and doing all of the normal things for her stage of development. She's fine, she's normal, she's healthy. The great-grandmother is so happy. That child is going to grow up knowing the history of her tribe, her language, everything about the land and the sacred places. This is such an important law for Indian children. Without it, that baby would have ended up in foster care in San Francisco."

It isn't easy for people to talk about their childhood dislocations. Betty Parent, chair of the American Indian Studies program at San Francisco State, is an Athabascan Indian from Central Alaska who managed to escape being adopted out but lost her baby brother to a white family from Portland. Because their father died when she was an infant and their mother was sick with tuberculosis, 3-year-old Betty and her sisters went to live with Aunt Alice. Betty believes she was never taken because their home near Bethel was so isolated. It was an Indian-style adoption—a familial arrangement frowned

on by white authorities—and Aunt Alice never tried to formalize it because she was afraid she would lose the children.

Betty's mother recovered briefly, had a baby boy named Tony and ended up in another TB hospital. Tony was placed in an orphanage outside Anchorage where white people shopped for babies. Betty often wondered about him. Was he healthy? Happy? Did he go to Vietnam? Did he survive? She didn't find him again until he was 36 years old.

But Betty prefers to discuss the situation in more general terms. She cites the statistics: Indian children in some states are 10 times as likely as non-Indians to be placed outside their homes. Nationally they are six times as likely and in California two-and-a-half times as likely to be taken.

"It's a universal experience for us—so painful we don't talk about it."

It's so painful, Sacheen Littlefeather agrees to talk only because she doesn't want it to happen to anyone else ever again. With the talk come violent tears, screaming anger, a hurt so deep and obvious it's nearly unbearable to witness.

The former Indian activist, now a nutrition counselor who specializes in traditional healing, became famous in 1973 when she turned down an Academy Award on behalf of Marlon Brando. She's been interviewed countless times, but never about this. The first day, while photographer Fran Ortiz shoots pictures, she talks around it, afraid if she tells the story she'll cry and her eyes will swell up and she'll ruin the shoot. A day and a half later, she calls in tears. She's been crying off and on for 36 hours, thinking about what she hasn't ever really talked about. She wants to get it over with.

"I was a child, an innocent child. It wasn't my fault. You meant well. You always meant so well. But you, the dominant society, were hurt by seeing the examples of racism and repeating them. In oppressing others you want everyone to be exactly like you. You are the ones who need to change, and I won't own your sickness. It isn't mine."

As with Stella, who lost her braids at the white boarding school, and Tom, who had his hair cut every week at the French Canadian foster home, the first thing Sacheen Cruz lost when she went to live with her white maternal grandparents was her knee-length black hair.

"My grandmother gave me a perm. She wanted me to be white. I cried and cried because she wouldn't let me have my braids."

Sacheen's father, an Apache/Yaqui who grew up in an alcoholic, abusive family and a series of non-Indian foster homes, beat her so severely when she was a baby that she has developed glaucoma and cataracts that recently required painful eye surgery.

Sacheen's parents lived next door to the house where she and her sisters lived with her grandparents. The strict older couple never liked her father, never wanted her mother to marry him. But Sacheen looked Indian like her father—even with the perm, even trying so hard to please her grandparents, to look and to be as white as they wanted her to be.

"When they were angry they'd say 'You may look like him but you don't want to be like him. He's a worthless good-for-nothing.' And I was always afraid of my father. He'd hurt me, so in many ways I bought into it."

Sacheen's parents were attacked several times walking down the street hand-in-hand in California and Arizona. She remembers stopping at a restaurant once and her mother, sisters and grandparents going inside, everyone except her father. "He sat in the car alone. I remember feeling very funny about it. My mother brought him a sandwich, sort of the way you would the family dog." In high school, her grandparents allowed Sacheen to date only white boys, so there

were no dates. Once a white girl refused to play with her younger sister because she was Indian. "It made what my grandparents were trying to do to us a lie. But it just made them more determined to make us Anglo."

She remembers being deeply depressed as a child, keeping everything inside, suffering migraine headaches so severe she had to stay in bed. She tried to kill herself the first time when she was 9 years old by throwing herself in front of a car, but someone pulled her back at the last minute.

Her father died of cancer soon after she graduated from high school. Her mother seemed to turn on her, blaming her, accusing her of not loving him enough. She felt ugly, unwanted, unloved. She was seeing a school psychologist who visited her family and asked them to lay off. Her family was furious, told her never again to tell anyone outside about her troubles at home. She began to fall apart. The last straw was when she was 19 and her grandparents paid for her and her two sisters to have nose jobs. "It didn't do it. It didn't Anglicize me. God, did it hurt."

She tried to kill herself, mutilate herself, ended up in the hospital with a nervous breakdown. She was catatonic, didn't eat, didn't talk. "I didn't appear to have any feelings, but I had the worst migraine headache of my life."

The suicide attempt touched something in her grandmother and her mother. They started talking to her. They apologized. "There was this realization that all of my life I was put down for who I was and if at that point I wanted to explore being an Indian they would allow me to do this with pride.

"For more than 40 years I never really worked on this issue of being raised by white people. I think I couldn't because it hurts so much. I'm only doing it now because there are other children out there being raised by white people, and I know they are being hurt the way I was hurting, but I was silent and said nothing."

TOBACCO USE AMONGST THE INDIANS OF SOUTHERN CALIFORNIA

Tharon P. Weighill Sr.

. . . A basic understanding from which we can start our dialogue is that tobacco can both give life and take life. It is a very powerful, potent, and magical being whose physical properties can cause great harm when abused. The flip side to that coin is that tobacco can also provide great healing when not abused. . . .

Of all the contributions Native Americans have given the world, tobacco is probably the best known. However, when most people think of tobacco today, they don't consider the depths of its story, or the unique role this powerful plant has had throughout our story—not just history since 1542, but a time before Juan Cabrillo, before America, before today. The story of tobacco is as old as time and grows older with every passing moment under the sun. In other words, the story is endless because it is our story.

I think it is safe to say all our nations understand and use tobacco in our various traditional ways. I also think it is safe to say that a great many of our people have become habituated to the nicotine contained in the plant. This should be of great concern to us all, because we are connected to each other; what affects one affects us all. I don't think it is irrelevant or out of place to say that as an Indian man, I have concerns about the future health of my community, having personally experienced the tragedy of lung cancer in my family, caused by chronic nicotine use. . . .

A discussion of traditional tobacco use is a discussion of the principles our ancestors exercised in the use of this mighty plant person, based on their sense of sacred and complex balance in the universe; our ancestors have handed down principles to guide us in our interactions with certain spirits, so that our walk within creation is healthy for creation. In this modern world, it is easy to lose our connection with the world of our ancestors, to forget that all life is sacred. We Indian people must not ever allow this to happen. The life and spirit of tobacco are sacred. Walk with tobacco in a personal and respectful relationship and it will walk in one with you. It will bring you great things or harmful things depending on which relationship you choose.

I believe that in order to establish a sanctified relationship with the spirit of tobacco we must know how and why it came into being. Creator designed our way of life; our uses for the plants allow us to interact with the rest of our environment with delicacy and reciprocity. . . .

As a young man I was taught by my grandfather that before harvesting or hunting, I should gently give tobacco to Hutash and give thanks for all the things our people receive throughout our time here. My grandfather said the spirit of Axshpa takes our message to our creators and then we are able to harvest and hunt according to our needs. This act of offering tobacco, he said, "would help keep balance in the 'Itiyashup, the middle world of the Quabajai, and maintain our place within the creator's design". . . .

Tobacco is a divine gift from the creator, and our traditional relationship with it is an expression of divinity. Thus, when we talk about the principles of traditional tobacco use, what we are really talking about is the relationship we have with the expression of a divine ideology, maintained by our relationship with the tobacco nations. Therefore, we must realize a traditional or divine consciousness when we interact with its divine spirit. . . .

From "Tobacco Use amongst the Indians of Southern California," by Tharon P. Weighill Sr., *News from Native California* 12, no. 3 (Spring 1999).

PUNISHING INSTITUTIONS
THE STORY OF CATHERINE (CEDAR WOMAN)

Luana Ross

Our family was large, but it was seldom that you ever got a hug. If you did, you were grateful for it.—Catherine

INTRODUCTION

I met Catherine in 1990, at the Women's Correctional Center in Montana. She is currently serving a forty year sentence and is housed at the women's prison in Billings. When Catherine was first arrested, the local media used a simplistic Adam and Eve theory and presented her as a controlling woman and the driving force behind the crime. In reality, Catherine's "crime" was that she was present when the horrendous murder of a young white man was committed. A plea bargain was arranged and she was charged with a lesser crime, not kidnapping and homicide, with the stipulation that she provide testimony against her male co-defendants, who are members of her tribe.

At her sentencing, the judge asked her if she realized why she was sentenced to prison. A bewildered Catherine replied, "No." According to Catherine, the judge responded: "Because you were aware of a crime in progress and did nothing to stop it; therefore, you are just as guilty because you allowed this to happen." Although Catherine did not commit the murder, she lives everyday with the guilt of not halting the crime, as though she could have possibly had the authority to stop two powerfully violent men from killing a young man. To date, Catherine has been in prison for nine years and has been continually denied parole. Because of the seriousness of the crime, in conjunction with the dynamics of racism in the state of Montana, Catherine believes that she is singled out by prison staff and the parole board, and subsequently issued racialized harassment.

Catherine wants her story to be heard because she is committed to breaking the silence of violence and exposing its psychological toll, especially on children. Nevertheless, her identity is disguised in an effort to protect members of her family. Catherine's narrative, only a glimpse into a life filled with turbulence, is based on interviews conducted from 1991 to 1994 and data from legal papers, prison records, newspapers, and personal correspondence.

EURO-AMERICAN CRIMINAL JUSTICE

Native women face overwhelming odds at every stage of the criminal justice system. Rafter (1990) suggests that race and gender influence incarceration rates. Concurring with Dobash, Dobash, and Gutteridge (1986), it is imperative to research the notion of "criminality" by examining the socio-economic conditions in which crimes occur. Some women, Native and non-Native, are imprisoned at the Women's Correctional Center for such "crimes" as killing abusive family members, being at the crime scene, writing "bad checks" to adequately care for their children, and yet others maintain their innocence (Ross 1996, 1997).

Chesney-Lind (1991, 64) submits that the personal lives of imprisoned women and crime-type must be perceived within "the gendered nature of these women's lives, options, and crimes." The contextualizing of the criminalization process is central to the understanding of female "deviance." Personal experiences of imprisoned women reflect the structure of Euro-American society; a structure in which certain subgroups are not only penalized because of their race/ethnicity, gender, and class but controlled as well. This is particularly clear when the violence experienced in prisoners' lives prior to incarceration and their subsequent criminalization is examined. For many imprisoned women the violence began early in their lives, while for others it was not present until they were older (Ross 1997). Chesney-Lind (1991) suggests that 88 percent of imprisoned women in the United States were violently victimized prior to their incarceration. The lives of prisoners in Montana are comparable to the national data. Their histories are characterized by violence of every form: physical, emotional, poverty, racism, sexism, and classism. Moreover, the violence is institutionalized. These women were violated by family members, boyfriends, jail, reform school, Indian boarding schools, and foster and adoptive care. The oppression, thus, is as complex as it is relentless. Catherine's narrative is typical of the cruelty that many women endured prior to their incarceration and while imprisoned (see Ross 1994, 1997).

One cruelty, and a form of violence, is the fact that Native Americans are overrepresented in Euro-America's criminal justice system. In 1994, Native people comprised 2.9 percent of both federal and state prisons, although they were only 0.6 percent of the total U.S. population (Camp and Camp 1995). This disparity is more clearly seen at the state level where Natives are 33.2 percent of the total prisoner population in Alaska, 23.6 percent in South Dakota, 16.9 percent in North Dakota, and 17.3 percent in Montana (Camp and Camp 1995). Native Americans in Montana are approximately 6 percent of the total state population. While Native men comprise approximately 20 percent of the total male prisoner population, approximately 25 percent of the total female prisoner population are Native women (Ross 1997). A study on Native women (Ross 1997) suggests that Native women are more likely to be imprisoned than white women or Native and white men, indicating racism and sexism in Montana's criminal justice system.

Catherine fits the typical profile of an incarcerated Native woman (Ross 1993, 1994, 1997): She was thirty-one when she was initially incarcerated, has six children, was beaten by supposed loved ones, and sexually abused as a child and later as an adult. She has a sporadic employment history, quit high school, and was convicted of a violent crime (her first felony). The influence of violence on one's life is readily depicted by Catherine's story and illuminates how personal biography is tied to the larger societal structure.

CEDAR WOMAN

Catherine, Cedar Woman (her Indian name), was born in a log house and grew up on one of Montana's seven Indian reservations. She was raised in a traditional Native American family by members of her extended family. Catherine fluently speaks both her Native language and English, although she is more comfortable conversing in her Native tongue. Of her early life and the wisdom of elders, Catherine comments:

> I grew up on the reservation and lived with extended family members, and attended a Catholic boarding school. My grandmother often shared with me that our Mother Earth is the caretaker for [God]. Also, when other Indian elders talked about visions, I had doubts and wondered if their visions and predictions were true just like any other child would question and wonder. My grandmother, and other elders of neighboring reservations, made predictions during my youth that are now coming true. They raised me to believe in the Native American Church and I learned to maintain my focus on [God] through any situation. We have learned to have faith in [God] through living life and learning to survive. This journey in life helps us to learn; and at some point we have a spiritual awakening that helps us identify that the freedom we are all seeking is within.

Catherine has four sisters and four brothers; one sister and two brothers are deceased. Another brother was adopted by a white family, and the two have never met. She attended a Catholic Indian boarding school, married at a young age, and began having children.

On the surface, it appears that Catherine was raised in a traditional and functional family; however, this is not the case. Catherine never mentions her father and has many negative memories of her mother. Often Catherine's mother was drinking when she would visit her, which greatly displeased other family members. As a child, Catherine rarely saw her mother. What she remembers most about her mother, aside from her drinking, was that she did not appear to like Catherine. She said: "It seemed like she didn't like me. There was no physical contact—like you give your kids a hug and stuff. She never did do that. She would just sit and look at me. She just kind of floated in and out. And the times that she did show up, she was always with white guys. I didn't even know she was my mom. I thought my aunt was my mom."

As Catherine matured she witnessed her uncle physically abuse other family members, including her aunt and her grandmother. She became increasingly angry with her biological mother and, furthermore, reasoned that brutality was an acceptable behavior:

> I was angry at my real mom because she was my mom and she drank all the time. I just didn't want anything from her. And then I just kind of continued in my little life with that and feeling angry. When I would see my mother, I would let this anger show. Then I started treating her like how I seen my uncle treating my aunt. You know, when my aunt and uncle would go drinking, well when they came back home my uncle would beat her up all the time. There were so many times. I don't know if my brother remembers it, but I always do. We would be the only ones awake and we would watch my uncle. He beat her so many times that sometimes you wouldn't recognize her the next day. And they walked around like nothing happened. . . . I felt funny. I don't know how the other kids felt but I remember feeling real funny. And, I just put my head down and started eating. Then I looked at my grandma and I looked at my aunt. Then my uncle came in and he sat down and started talking. They were all visiting with one another like nothing was going on. You know, like nothing had happened! So then I started thinking that nothing was wrong.

The upheaval and family secrets continued as Catherine grew. She witnessed not only the brutality between her aunt and uncle, she also saw her uncle and biological mother beat her grandmother. Remembering a family thoroughly and painfully immersed in violence, she said: "And he [her uncle] said, 'I'm going to kill your daughter.' And he was just hollering at my grandmother. And they talk about respect for the elders now. And then they wonder why this generation and the ones to come don't have respect for the elders. You learn what you see. I watched my real mother break my grandmother's arm." Despite the turmoil, Catherine's grandmother encouraged her to pray for strength and to leave the reservation. According to Catherine, her grandmother said: "Go somewhere else and learn what's going on out there. Don't be like the rest of them and don't stay around here—it's no good now." To this elder Native woman, the good old days were gone and the reservation grew increasingly violent.

Catherine was eight years old when her uncle began sexually abusing her. Her aunt, rather than stopping the transgression, allowed it to continue. Catherine remembers: "My aunt came and laid down with me one night and she was stroking my hair. I was just a little girl—about eight. She was laying there with me and she was stroking my hair. Then my uncle climbed in bed on the other side and I remember her saying, 'Just lay still and it won't hurt—it'll be OK.' These are the people that loved me; these are the ones I trusted [crying]." Because Catherine's aunt did little to stop the rapes—when her aunt intervened she was abused by her tyrannical husband—she soon became angry with her. As an adult, Catherine discovered that her aunt was taking "sleeping pills" to cope with her own oppression and, subsequently, had little initiative and clearly no power to stop her husband from terrorizing the household.

According to Catherine, her extended family took care of her and her brother, not because of love, but out of a twisted sense of responsibility and family obligation. Catherine watched her family's collapse, which left her feeling insignificant and frustrated:

You know how you watch the wind blowing? It slowly keeps blowing something apart? Maybe you watch it loosening the dirt and it just keeps blowing away a little bit at a time. That's how I seen our family. My grandmother started drinking. I was just slowly watching everything go and when you're a small child growing up watching all of this, it's scary. I can't think of no other word to make it sound easier, softer. It's just plain scary. And nobody to ever talk to. You see, these adults are people that you come to depend on. They're suppose to know what they're doing; they're the smart ones, you know.

During Catherine's childhood, she was shuffled between various relatives and Indian boarding school. One proposed alternative was to live with her mother, who was drinking heavily and frequently physically abused Catherine and her brother. Catherine's stays with her mother were always short-lived. She preferred to live with her grandmother, but ill health and old age prevented a long-term placement. The family secrets and the silence were unbearable to Catherine, and at age twelve she began skipping school and drinking as a way to numb her pain: "I just felt like I was better off being in my own little drunk world and then I didn't have to think about these things anymore. I knew sooner or later that I would pass out and then I'd forget about it—until I sobered up again."

Witnessing men abuse women provoked a pattern in Catherine's life. Not unexpectedly, Catherine was involved in remarkably abusive relationships with men:

That's the only thing I knew. Someone would beat me up and I thought they loved me. And this man did both; he beat me up and he used me in a bad way—in a sexual way. And he was telling me he loved me, and I'd listen to him. The way I was raised, I watched my aunts and no matter how bad they got beat up, they still listened to their husbands. You know, this is what I learned. Then all of a sudden my aunt's saying, "Why do you do that? Why do you let these men beat you up and you always go right back to him?" That's what I'm talking about. They're giving that advice away but they're doing it themselves.

One of the men Catherine was involved with was the man who committed the murder that landed her in prison. Not surprisingly, their relationship was extremely abusive and she lived in continual fear of this man: "I started living with him just about a couple of months before we got in trouble [arrested for the murder]. My kids were scared of him and I was really scared of this man. He beat my ex-husband up really bad. . . . He was going to shoot my ex-husband . . . and I begged and pleaded with him and I promised him, 'I'll do anything you ask—just don't do that.'" Describing a remarkably controlling person, she continues: "I couldn't go anywhere by myself—he'd always come with me, even when I went to the bathroom."

Catherine's co-defendants, as well as some tribal members, viewed her testimony against them as "snitching." To Catherine, however, she was merely telling the truth. Remembering prior beatings and intimidation, she was intensely afraid of her boyfriend (her co-defendant) and consequently unable to make a decision regarding her testimony. Family members prayed with her in jail and instructed her on honesty, a virtue in her tribe. According to Catherine, they told her: "We always taught you never to lie; we taught you to be honest. This is how you were raised. You were raised in the Indian way and that's one of the things is when you are Indian, you should not lie. We told you that. If you know something, you'd better say something."

Catherine was still confused about the role of her testimony and the label "snitch."

That night she had a dream that aided in her decision to tell the truth:

I went to bed and I was sleeping. All of a sudden, I felt really cold. And I was in that cell—that little tiny cell. All of a sudden, I just felt like someone was with me. Pretty soon, it got warm. And then I was sitting on a small couch and my grandmother was sitting there. My mother was there and she was holding my hand, but she wasn't saying anything. When I looked over, my other grandmother was sitting kitty-corner from us. Then my two grandfathers were there. One of my grandfathers lost part of his toes due to frost-bite, so he used a cane. When I looked at him, he was doing like I always saw him at home. He was bouncing his cane off the floor and he was singing real low. My other grandfather was sitting behind him. He seemed like he was listening to my other grandfather. Out of my whole family, my grandmother was the one that always did the talking. I mean, when you heard her voice you knew to be quiet. She was talking and leaning over this way. She said, "When we raised you, we told you when times get really hard to pray. This is how we raised you. We told you that but somewhere along the way, I think you forgot. I always talk to you." Then she turned around and said, "Here, you take this—you're going to need this." And she gave me a piece of cloth. Then she said, "Where you're going, you're going to need this. This is going to help you." Then she turned back around and she said, "We raised you kids right and we always told you to tell the truth. You were raised the hard way, but that was for a reason." She was talking in [Native language]. She said, "We always tell you, don't be crying." I was listening and she turned around and gave me a sandwich. She said, "We told you to pray. Sometimes you have a hard walk. When you get hungry, this is for you." And I turned around and saw my sister [who is deceased]. She was laughing and she said, "Remember we'll always love you." I turned around and put the stuff on a little table behind me. When I turned back around, I was all alone. There was no one there and all of a sudden that warm feeling just started going away and I got really cold again. Then I woke up. I sat there and thought and thought. So that's what helped me make my decision.

Divinely inspired, Catherine made the decision to tell the truth about the crime. That her instructions to do so came in the form of a dream/vision, renders the notion of "snitching" sacrilegious.

MORE PRISONS, MORE VIOLENCE

Because Catherine has been incarcerated for such a lengthy time, she has a keen idea regarding control and punishment. As well, she is cognizant of the racism working within institutional structures. For instance, Catherine was sent to a Catholic Indian boarding school and experienced what she terms a transformation from Indian to Catholic:

> I became aware of disparate treatment years ago when I experienced incarceration after being convicted of an alcohol-related crime, and my experiences in Catholic boarding school. Although some acts of discrimination did not point to race, it suggested indifference toward Indians due to beliefs, traditions, and religions. Addressing issues of discrimination partially refers to Catholic priests and nuns who dictated the attempted conversion of Indians to Christians.

Intensely spiritual, Catherine relies on her Native religion to aid in her survival of the violence in her life prior to her incarceration and the violence of prisonization. She recalls the words of the aunt who raised her: "No matter what they have done, there is always a reason why people do the things they do but there is a solution at the end of every situation and we will all grow from it. And remember to pray before you begin any project because what you put into that project is what you will give to the people."

Similar to many other Native people, Catherine suggests that Native American culture, specifically prayer, gives Native people the strength to endure seemingly insurmountable events. In an effort to analyze discrimination, she questions specifically why Native Americans were subjected to genocidal practices. In an essay she wrote:

> Are Indians targeted in boarding schools and prisons simply because they have their own culture and religion? Does the fact that Indians have strong beliefs, traditions and upbringing make them a challenge for those obsessed to convert them? Perhaps trying to gain control by diverting the Indians attention to a man on the cross and attempting to convince them that their belief in the eagle and Great Grandfather is false or voodoo. Skillfully and manipulatively, authority figures use Indian beliefs in reverse psychology. In this way they gain a false trust, therefore, enabling a slow elimination of Native traditions forcing them to convert to their rules and non-Indian ways.

Catherine recognizes that early efforts to "civilize" and "educate" Native Americans were controlling and punishing. She said: "My memories of Catholic boarding school is one of strict discipline. Military style methods doled out to little Indian children once we were out-of-sight of our parents and grandparents. Little Indian children who could no longer speak Indian nor practice Indian ways were being punished for living their heritage and not allowed to discuss any of the school's disciplinary practices when they went home for visits." Catherine describes the strict regime they encountered as children:

> Disciplinary methods imposed on Indian children by nuns and priests consisted of sitting in the walk-in freezer an hour or more, hitting a brick wall twenty to thirty times with your fists (depending upon the infraction), or kneeling for hours and praying after they made us attend confession. Once four of us little girls would not say the Hail Mary and the Sister Superior marched us into a room and spanked us with a thick wide leather strap until our behinds bled. Then we had to memorize the Hail Mary as part of the sanction, which included attending confession for our disobedience to God. Another occurrence was when some Indian boys stepped out of line and were taken

outside to hit the brick building with their fists. They were brought back into class after hitting the brick wall. They were crying and the tops of their hands were cut open and bleeding profusely. They wore bandages on their hands for awhile.

Of course, many Native people resisted such deplorable treatment. It is well known that many escaped by running away from boarding school. Catherine relays just such an experience and the harsh penalties doled out by supposed servants of the Lord:

A haunting memory of my cousin and her friend who escaped the boarding school left scars that have helped to develop certain fears which strongly influenced future behaviors. The school, with assistance from the police, organized a manhunt and upon finding them returned them to school for disciplinary action with no notification to the parents. Their sanction, without a hearing, consisted of time-out in a walk-in freezer in the cafeteria and for everyone to view them while we eat our meal. Their sanction lasted approximately two and a half hours. After they were released from the freezer, my friend and I helped them to warm up. My cousin shared with me, while I was rubbing her hands and legs, that they attempted to bring back chokecherries for us. But the cherries were taken away and they were told that this was a bad thing and they would have to be punished because they needed to eat healthier foods. The time-out in the freezer depended upon the infraction, and I witnessed some children held in the freezer longer than two hours.

One of the connections Catherine has made is the incredible similarities in Indian boarding schools and the penal system. An introspective journey enabled Catherine to link her past experiences of abuse to her present experiences in the criminal justice system. As a woman who has been incarcerated for many years, Catherine conclusively understands the prison system as biased against Native people. Additionally, she is well aware of the punishing efforts that exist in a system specifically designed as punitive,

although operating under the guise of "rehabilitation."

Regarding the prison's dehumanizing classification process, Catherine said: "The prison system will process individuals by taking all their clothing, jewelry, and any personal items and by conducting a thorough strip search checking all cavity areas for any contraband. Usually the cavity searches are at the discretion of the officers. After the search, they delouse the person with lice shampoo and you are showered and issued your prison attire of a white gown with slippers for your feet. They lock the individual into an intake room for two weeks to a month, depending upon the classification and the conviction. After the classification process, a number is issued and the person is taken to their proper classification unit or allowed in the prison population."

According to Catherine, Indian boarding school had a similar degrading entrance process:

I recall how we had to line up to be deloused. The awful smells of lice shampoo and the haircuts. Little white T-shirts and cotton panties and later cotton pajamas. Everything was white or dark blue and we marched around like little soldiers. For awhile, we wore dark blue uniforms—blue skirts with vests and white shirts. I do not recall what took place when they allowed us to wear our own clothing, although this came probably after I entered the fourth grade. Standing at attention like little soldiers—very still—not daring to flinch or even blink.

The dehumanizing ritual—whether it was Indian boarding school or prison—started with stripping, delousing, and the wearing of uniforms. The regime in prison, similar to boarding school, is militaristically fashioned. Catherine said that today in the women's prison one stands for the prison count "at 6 A.M., 11 A.M., and 3:30 P.M. and if anyone misses count or is considered disruptive, a disciplinary is issued. I remember in the boarding school days how we had to stand at the foot of our beds for morning and night count."

The oppression of the prison system, particularly for Native women, has been noted (Ross 1993, 1994, 1996, 1997; Sugar and Fox 1990). Prisoners are often left to the discretion of the guards and jailers. Catherine reminisces about being in jail with a relative and the frightful exercise of authority:

> I sat in my cell one night visiting with an uncle who was in the next cell and talking between the wall when we heard keys jingling and doors open. I heard the officers' voices on the other side of the cell block talking to someone—asking questions. The individual said he had nothing to say. Suddenly an officer began raising his voice saying he was going to teach him to do as they told him and never to disagree. Then I heard the sounds of loud slaps—the sounds of someone hitting a person. I heard sounds like someone hitting the wall and then crying. The man asked them to stop— that he had had enough. The slaps didn't stop until only a moan and then dead silence. The only sound was the hum of the air and space in the cell block. The beating lasted for approximately twenty minutes. Sitting quietly, my uncle whispers to me the words of advice from someone more experienced about incarceration. "You act like you never heard nothing and you say nothing. When they [the jailers] come and ask you anything, you smile and tell them it's good to see them and you are doing good."

They relocated Catherine's uncle to another jail. Now she was alone and exceedingly vulnerable as she awaited her trial. Sleepless over the loss of freedom and her family, in addition to the maliciousness of the crime, it was during this time that she was raped by a jailer. And not raped just once, but seven times over a period of three and a half months. In an effort to spare herself emotionally, Catherine methodically reports one rape:

> He [the jailer] took me into the office and told me to be quiet. He told me to lay down on the floor. He said he had something he wanted to

> try. He had a red condom. He put this on himself and pulled my shorts off. He raped me. When he finished, he stood there laughing at me. Then he went and got a towel and cleaned himself off. He told me to get dressed and then he sat down and told me to do oral sex on him. He told me to get on my knees and then he grabbed me by the face and started pushing his penis into my mouth until he ejaculated. Then he let go of me. He again laughed at me. He took me back to my cell, locked it, and left.

In an intimidating manner, the jailer told Catherine she better not say anything because he had much to lose and no one would believe her anyway. She was, after all, a Native woman and he was a white male with much power and authority. As the rapes continued, Catherine thought she might be pregnant but was afraid to tell anyone. Fortunately, she was not carrying a child. Although Catherine eventually raised the issue of her rape by the jailer to various authorities, nothing was done. In fact, similar to countless other women who are raped while incarcerated, no one believed her.

Because of the brutality in Catherine's life, she is repulsed by violence. She continues to have nightmares about the rapes, beatings, and crime of which she was eventually convicted. She is unable to watch violent movies on television or read about violence because it nauseates her. The sexual intimidation that presently exists in prison (see Ross 1994, 1997), particularly because of her history, repels her. Recognizing the hypocrisy of the criminal justice system, Catherine said: "The part that really bothers me is when I look around the prison. All these workers, you know, we're under their care. We're under their custody. They're the ones that have the lock and key. . . . And they have the nerve to talk about law and order; and they have the audacity to talk about discipline."

Women are particularly vulnerable in the criminal justice system and another issue that is gender specific is the hysterectomies that occurred while Catherine was incarcerated at the Women's Correctional Center (see Ross 1997). Of this form of violence, Catherine said:

Recalling a personal situation, and as witness to other women experiencing the same, between 1988–1992 there were a great number of hysterectomies within the women's prison. They were referring women for hysterectomies regularly. Without any information presented and the only solutions for the medical problems pertaining to women's monthly cycle or cervical complications, which could have had a simple remedy other than major surgery. The process of my own surgery developed into a debate with the nurse, which eventually resulted into threats of a disciplinary and strong rebuttal to my Indian upbringing. No other remedy or alternative was ever presented except the surgery. It was discovered later that the uterus was in healthy condition with no scarring or spots when inspected, according to my medical reports.

Before the surgery, Catherine argued with a prison nurse and guard, who escorted her to a room and tried to convince her of the "needed" operation. Additionally, they instructed her to "let go" of her Native beliefs because they would not help her. Catherine reasoned that she needed to see an Indian doctor for severe menstrual cramps and heavy bleeding. According to Catherine, the nurse screamed at her and said: "To hell with your traditions and beliefs. This is a medical issue."

The issue of denial of culture is noteworthy. Although the American Indian Religious Freedom Act was passed in 1978 to ensure that Native cultures could be freely practiced (including while one is incarcerated), there is little or no compliance at the Women's Correctional Center (Ross 1994, 1996, 1997). Catherine sent a memo to the chemical dependency counselor regarding her denial of religion. Because sweetgrass and sage were believed by some prison staff to be drugs, she asked the counselor to please offer a cultural-awareness workshop for the staff. White prisoners, as well as prison staff (who are all white), are ignorant of Native culture and frequently refer to Native religion as "voo-doo" (for a thorough analysis see Ross 1996, 1997). In the memo to prison staff it was reported by Catherine that, "One inmate stated to me she has been told by another inmate that Native Americans are fooling staff by telling them we call this sweetgrass when what we have is really opium." Catherine finds much solace in her Native culture, although the full practice is denied by prison staff. Evidently, within the prison Native culture is viewed as a liability, not a strength.

CONCLUSION

Catherine's narrative is reflective: By examining personal experiences we gain perspective into societal arrangements. Interrelated systems of oppression render Native women vulnerable to many types of violence found in social institutions. Critical to the understanding of female "deviance" is the contextualizing of the criminalization process. Catherine directly connects her involvement in an inhuman crime to a childhood devoid of love and filled with violence.

The predominant theme in Catherine's narrative is the reality of violence, whether it is individual or institutional. Moreover, Catherine has been imprisoned her entire life. Her prisons—all based on control—took the form of family, boarding school, abusive relationships with men, jail, and the Women's Correctional Center. As such, Catherine's experiences are gendered and racialized. We need to recognize the various ways in which Native women are imprisoned and raped, not only by individuals, but by institutions.

REFERENCES

Camp, Camille, and George Camp. 1995. *The Corrections Yearbook.* South Salem, NY: Criminal Justice Institute.

Chesney-Lind, Meda. 1991. Patriarchy, Prisons, and Jails: A Critical Look at Trends in Women's Incarceration. *The Prison Journal* 71(1):51–67.

Dobash, Russell P., R. Emerson Dobash, and Sue Gutteridge. 1986. *The Imprisonment of Women.* New York: Blackwell.

Rafter, Nicole Hahn. 1990. *Partial Justice: Women, Prisons, and Social Control* (2nd edition). New Brunswick, NJ: Transaction Publishers.

Ross, Luana. 1993. "Major Concerns of Imprisoned American Indian and White Mothers." In *Gender:*

Multi-Cultural Perspectives, Judith T. Gonzalez-Calvo (ed.). Dubuque, IA: Kendall-Hunt.

———. 1994. "Race, Gender, and Social Control: Voices of Imprisoned Native American and White Women." *Wicazo Sa Review* 10(2):17–39.

———. 1996. Resistance and Survivance: Cultural Genocide and Imprisoned Native American Women." *Race, Gender, and Class* 3(2):125–41.

———. 1998. *Inventing the Savage: The Social Construction of Native American Criminality.* Austin: University of Texas Press.

Sugar, Fran, and Lana Fox. 1990. "Nistum Peyako Seht'wawin Iskwewak: Breaking Chains." *Canadian Journal of Women and Law* 3:465–83.

PART REVIEW

DISCUSSION QUESTIONS

Byrd Baylor, *Yes Is Better Than No*
1. Why is Maria Vasquez about to become homeless even though she has paid the rent? What does she plan to do about it?
2. Describe the scene where Maria Vasquez is interviewed by a university researcher. Why is yes better than no when responding to non-Indian questioners?

Gary Paul Nabhan, *Gathering*
1. What does the author mean by nutritionally related diseases?
2. In what ways did the traditional diet of the Desert People change after the 1950s, and what historical events led to the changes in diet?
3. What does the author mean by "seasonality," and what role did it play in the traditional diet that helped keep the population healthy?

Florence Connolly Shipek, *Delfina Cuero*
1. According to Delfina Cuero's autobiography, "in the real old days," how did a young woman learn to be a good wife and about childbirth and caring for babies?
2. What things did her grandmother teach her about how to take care of babies?

Philip May, *The Epidemiology of Alcohol Abuse among American Indians*
1. Are Native Americans genetically predisposed to alcoholism? Do they metabolize alcohol

differently or more slowly than do members of other ethnic groups?
2. What is the difference between "anxiety drinkers" and "recreational drinkers?"
3. How does the uncritical use of statistics perpetuate the drunken Indian stereotype?

Joan Smith, *Indian Forever*
1. What problem did the 1978 Indian Child Welfare Act attempt to address? Was it completely successful?
2. What are some of the problems faced by children who are adopted out?

Luana Ross, *Punishing Institutions*
1. Catherine (Cedar Woman) grew up in a violent and abusive household. What effect did this fact have on her involvement in the homicide for which she was later convicted and sent to prison?
2. Explain what the author means by the statement that one form of violence which Native American women face is the system of incarceration itself. How is the system of incarceration for Indian women prisoners both racialized and genderized?

KEY TERMS

alcohol abuse vs. alcoholism (addiction)
commods
contextualizing of Indian criminalization
epidemiology
fetal alcohol syndrome (FAS)
incarceration rate
Indian Child Welfare Act of 1978
Indian Health Service (IHS)

Mormons
Personal Responsibility and Work Opportunity
Reconciliation Act of 1996
punishing institutions
seasonality (of foods)
social capital
urban imperialism
victim-blaming theory

SUGGESTED READINGS

DILLINGHAM, BRINT. "Indian Women and IHS Sterilization Practices." *American Indian Journal*, 3, no. 1 (January 1977): 27–28.

ECHO-HAWK, WALTER. "Native Worship in American Prisons." *Cultural Survival Quarterly* (Winter 1996): 58–62.

FLOWERS, RONALD BARRI. "Native American Criminality." In *Minorities and Criminality. Contributions in Criminology and Penology*, No. 21. New York: Greenwood Press, 1988.

JACKSON, MICHAEL. "Locking Up Natives in Canada." *University of British Columbia Law Review*, 23, no. 2: 281–298.

JOE, JENNIE R. "Health: Traditional Indian Health Practices and Cultural Views." Pages 525–547 in *Native America: Portrait of the Peoples*. Ed. Duane Champagne. Detroit: Visible Ink Press, 1995.

LLEWELLYN, K., and E. ADAMSON HOEBEL. *The Cheyenne Way: Conflict and Case Law in Primitive Jurisprudence*. Norman: University of Oklahoma Press, 1941.

Native American Rights Fund. "Alaska Tribes Sue for Equal State Law Enforcement Services." *NARF Legal Review*, 25, no. 1 (Winter/Spring 2000): 1–6.

PEGO, CHRISTINA M., ROBERT F. HILL, GLENN W. SOLOMON, ROBERT M. CHISHOLM, and SUZANNE E. IVEY. "Tobacco, Culture and Health among American Indians: A Historical Review." *American Indian Culture and Research Journal*, 19, no. 2 (1995): 143–164.

ROSS, LUANA. "Resistance and Survivance: Cultural Genocide and Imprisoned Native American Women." *Race, Gender, and Class*, 3, no. 2 (1996): 125–141.

ROSS, LUANA. *Inventing the Savage: The Social Construction of Native American Criminality*. Austin: University of Texas Press, 1998.

SHANLEY, JAMES. "Welfare Reform Will Create More Misery." *Tribal College*, 9, no. 3 (1998): 19–21.

TRAFZER, CLIFFORD E., and DIANE WEINER, editors. "Special Issue: Disease, Health, and Survival Among Native Americans," *American Indian Culture and Research Journal*, vol. 23, no. 3 (1999).

VOGEL, VIRGIL J. *American Indian Medicine*. Norman: University of Oklahoma Press, 1970.

WEATHERFORD, JACK. *Indian Givers: How the Indians of the Americas Transformed the World*. New York: Fawcett Columbine, 1988.

IX

NATIVE AMERICAN RIGHTS, STRUGGLE, AND REVITALIZATION

Indianismo!

Tom LaBlanc (Sisseton Dakota)

Listen! Can you hear the warm southern air flowing
through the bamboo and reeds? Making music out of
this confusing noise. Can you hear the silent heartbeat
of all those massacred? Reach down and touch the
tortured bodies! Touch the tortured bodies hidden
deep within the Peruvian dungeons. Dungeons. . . .
The sacred hoop is whole once again! We are all
related! . . .
We will liberate the natural world. Indianismo! . . .
But now, we will reunite the family of life! We who
love life, as a way of living, now we live. . . .
We will come alive dancing to the same song. We
will liberate the natural world. We who live, as a
way of living, now, we live.

¡Escuchen! ¿Pueden oir el aire tibio del sur, pasando a
través de los junquillos y los bambúes, transformando
este ruido confuso en música? ¿Pueden oir el silencioso
palpitar del corazón de todos los masacrados? ¡Estiren
sus manos y toquen los cuerpos torturados! ¡Toquen
los cuerpos torturados escondidos en los profundos
socavones peruanos, tan profundos! Socavones. . . .
¡El círculo sagrado es completa de nuevo! Somos una
misma familia. . . .
Liberaremos la Madre Tierra. ¡Indianismo! . . .
Pero reuniremos la familia de la vida. Nosotros los
que amamos la vida como manera de vivir. ¡Ahora
vivimos! . . .
Renaceremos danzando la misma música. Liberaremos a la Madre Tierra. Nosotros los que vivimos
como manera de vivir. Ahora vivimos.

(Translation: Lobo/Padilla)

A number of issues of critical importance to Native American peoples as oppressed
minorities in North America, and as oppressed majorities in most Latin American
countries, have been addressed in this book: the hidden heritage, the distortion of
history, genocide, racism and stereotyping, religious oppression, the destruction of
the environment, health and education problems, and structural conditions leading
to high incarceration rates, among others.

To a great extent, the long resistance by Native peoples throughout the Americas
against oppression has been, and continues to be, that of reclaiming self-governing
status in order to freely determine what the relationship should be between Native nations and the larger nation-states that currently dominate them. This ability

is termed self-determination, and, according to the United Nations, is a basic right of sovereign nations under international law. Sovereignty, as Indian activist Hank Adams (Assiniboine/Sioux) once defined it, is the collective authority of a people or nation to govern itself. It is the collective force that binds a national community together and gives it the right to define its membership, choose its form of government, conduct foreign relations, make its own laws, and regulate its property and resources.

What is being debated in the international arena today is whether indigenous peoples, including those of the Americas, have the necessary attributes to govern themselves as sovereign states. If they do, then they should be accorded the right of self-determination. More than that, it is a political question: the larger nation-states have so far been reluctant to relinquish privileges and power over indigenous peoples, their territories, and resources. It is frequently argued that Native peoples cannot exercise sovereignty as independent nations for a variety of reasons. In *Behind the Trail of Broken Treaties,* in a chapter titled "The Size and Status of Nations," the Lakota scholar Vine Deloria Jr. critiqued the five most common arguments against Native American tribes of the United States attaining self-determination.[1] The standard objections are: (1) Indian land areas are too small for nationhood status; (2) Indian reservations are surrounded by the larger U.S. nation (can there be nations within a nation?); (3) the tribal populations are too small; (4) they lack an independent economic base; and (5) they lack sufficient education and technical competence to run their own affairs. He counters each objection by documenting examples of fully recognized, independent states, including those represented at the United Nations, such as Liechtenstein, San Marino, Monaco, or Vatican City, that have one or more of these same characteristics. Then why can't the Native peoples of the Americas have the same right to self-determination and take their place in the international community of nation-states? This right would seem especially obvious for those larger, even majority Indian peoples of Latin America.

In *The Road: Indian Tribes and Political Liberty* (see Suggested Readings), Russel Barsh and James Youngblood Henderson suggest that treaty federalism is a realistic option for Native American tribes in the United States. By this they mean that the federal government would reinstitute the treaty process (which was unilaterally ended by Congress in 1871) to govern the Indian tribes. Another option is statehood, at least for the larger tribes like the Navajo Nation. Currently the U.S. Congress is considering bringing Native Hawaiians into the same federal recognitive status under the 1934 Indian Reorganization Act that governs Indian tribes. All of these options and developments confer a limited status of sovereignty on the indigenous peoples of the United States and provide a model for other native peoples of the Western Hemisphere to follow in their quest for self-determination.

Originally, the federal government of the United States negotiated with the Indian peoples as sovereign nations in nation-to-nation agreements, and this sovereign status was legitimated in more than 300 treaties. Treaties, together with the Constitution and Supreme Court decisions, are the highest law of the land under the U.S. form of government. The problem, of course, arises in the facts that the treaties have all been badly compromised or broken by the United States and Indian sovereignty has been steadily diminished over the decades by the unilateral actions of Congress. This history has been particularly galling to the U.S. Indian peoples who are supposedly protected by the treaty process. As the Native American Rights Fund wrote in a recent fund appeal letter:

> Suppose the government of the United States took your land, lost or stole your money, and broke virtually every promise it ever made to you. Suppose your rights, *your constitutionally guaranteed rights* [emphasis added], were being violated every day . . . and you were a member of the poorest, most undeserved, most discriminated against population in the country. In other words, suppose you were a Native American . . . what would you do to get justice?

What was the original legal justification for the breaking of Indian treaties in the United States, and can the process be reversed? The turning point in the history of United States–Indian relations, according to Indian legal scholars such as Deloria, was the 1823 *Johnson v. McIntosh* court decision, which gave the Right of Discovery by European (Christian) nations and by the United States precedence over the Aboriginal (land-owning) Rights of Native peoples. *Johnson v. McIntosh* was followed by the 1831 Supreme Court decision *Cherokee Nation v. Georgia,* in which Chief Justice John Marshall ruled that rather than completely independent nations, Indian tribes are "domestic dependent nations." This decision paved the way for the plenary power doctrine of Congress, which means that the U.S. Congress can break any treaty or make any law with regard to Indians when it is in the interests of the larger nation to do so. In 1871, for example, Congress unilaterally ended treaty making with the Indian nations.

The 1960s and 1970s saw an upsurge in the Native American struggle in the United States for land, cultural and religious rights, social justice, and *sovereignty.* Some of the events of the "new Indian" movement, as it has been termed, are described in this section and throughout the book. The highlights, however, include the following: the founding in the United States in 1961 of the National Indian Youth Council by militant Indian college students; a series of Indian "fish-ins" in Washington State in support of the treaty right of Northwestern tribes to fish, beginning in 1964; the founding of the Alaska Federation of Natives in 1966 as a response to threatened lands and resources under the Alaskan Statehood Act and the Prudhoe Bay oil discovery; the blockade of the international bridge on the Canadian-U.S. border by the Mohawks at St. Regis in 1968 in support of their 1794 Jay Treaty; the founding of the American Indian Movement (AIM) in Minnesota, also in 1968, initially to combat urban racism but later leading Indian people across the nation in a range of protests. There was also the occupation of Alcatraz Island in San Francisco Bay in 1969; the 1972 Trail of Broken Treaties caravan to Washington, D.C.; and the Indian rights protest at Wounded Knee on the Pine Ridge Reservation in 1973. After the Wounded Knee protest, the year 1975 saw a firefight on the Pine Ridge Reservation between aggressive federal authorities and the

AIM warriors in which two FBI agents and a young Indian man were killed. This event led to the unjust conviction of Leonard Peltier (see "Free Leonard Peltier" in Part IV). The International Indian Treaty Council was founded in 1974 to unite Native Americans throughout Canada, the United States, and Latin America. Indigenous groups throughout the Americas and in Australia, New Zealand, and Scandinavia were organizing and began taking their grievances to the United Nations and other international bodies.

By the late 1970s, both the U.S.-based International Indian Treaty Council in the United States and the Canadian-based World Council of Indigenous Peoples had received nongovernmental status with the United Nations in order to place the case of Native American rights before the court of world opinion. In 1977, the first world gathering of Native American peoples convened at the United Nations headquarters in Geneva, Switzerland; this was the international Conference on Discrimination Against the Indigenous Populations in the Americas. The struggle had become internationalized. Other important events have taken place since then, but the developments cited above were among the forerunners of the contemporary revitalization movement at home and in the international arena, a movement that deepened spiritually and broadened politically in the 1980s and 1990s to include the rights of all indigenous peoples the world over.

At the same time, Native American groups throughout the Americas continued their struggle against oppression at home. The Cree Indians of Canada unsuccessfully fought the flooding of their lands in Quebec by the James Bay hydroelectric project, termed James Bay I, Native villages in Alaska lobbied the U.S. Congress to safeguard their land and monetary rights by passing the 1991 amendments to the Alaska Native Claims Settlement Act. In the Pacific Northwest, treaty tribes were waging an intense struggle to protect their treaty rights "to fish in their accustomed places." Indian groups in the Amazon basin were organizing to oppose the genocidal actions of mining corporations and land developers who were intent on destroying the rain forest and the lands and livelihood of the indigenous peoples. In fact, indigenous groups throughout Latin America were organizing into ethnic associations and political coalitions.

By the 1980s it was clear that a revitalization movement was taking place. The term *revitalization* here means that Native American culture and traditions were having a rebirth; there was a cultural renaissance in Indian country. Academic books and publications noting this development include *The Return of the Native,* by Stephen Cornell; *American Indian Activism,* edited by Troy Johnson, Joane Nagel, and Duane Champagne; *American Indian Ethnic Renewal,* by Joane Nagel; *Return of the Indian,* by Phillip Wearne; and the journal *Native Americas,* published by the American Indian Program of Cornell University (see Suggested Readings). In Canada and the United States, many Native people who had become alienated by the reservation system, Christian missionization, the boarding school system, and termination and relocation policies were returning to their spiritual and cultural roots. Actually, urbanization and relocation resulted in the growth of vibrant and active urban Indian communities, which became the "seed bed" of much of the new leadership for the growing resistance and revitalization movement in the

United States. Resistance and community building go hand in hand. In Latin America, Native peoples were resisting the oligarchical governments of their respective nation-states, the impact of global capitalism and free trade neoliberalism, U.S. interventionist policies in support of corrupt governments and multinational corporations (all in the name of fighting communism or the drug trade), and even some of the policies and actions of rebel groups that often exclude indigenous peoples from their reform agenda.

In the countryside and urban squatter settlements of Latin America, but especially in the cities and metropolitan areas of the United States, a new sense of Indianness and "place" was developing in the Native American community. The Intertribal Friendship House in Oakland, California, and the American Indian Community House in New York City are examples. Since the 1980s there has been a reaching out to the elders and spiritual leaders, many of whom still live "back on the rez." Many "urban Indians" have returned to the reservations, some to stay but others to relearn or strengthen their knowledge of their Native American language, culture, and spiritual traditions. Some have reasserted their Indian identity by returning to their original Indian family names. There has also been a revival throughout Indian country of spiritual practices and traditions: the Sun Dance, the sweat lodge, and tribally specific dances and ceremonies.

At the same time, Native peoples from North, Central, and South America increased contacts and began organizing politically to oppose their common oppression. The United Nations–sponsored Earth Summit, which took place in Rio de Janeiro in June 1992, was attended by Native American representatives from throughout the Americas in the common struggle to protect the environment. Following the North American example, Native peoples in Central and South America formed new political organizations and coalitions to press for recognition and their rights as indigenous peoples before their respective national governments and at the United Nations. Since 1982, FENAMAD, the Federation of Native Communities of the Madre de Diós region of Peru, has represented Indian groups on the issues of land titles, health, and education. FENAMAD is also represented in AIDESEP, a Peruvian Amazon organization. In 1989, after decades of struggle over land rights in Chile, the Mapuche Indians formed their own political party. In Ecuador, where Indians number more than one-third of the country's 12.5 million people, the Confederation of Indigenous Nations of Ecuador, or CONAIE, was formed. Many of these new political organizations eventually received consultative status as nongovernmental organizations (NGOs) with the United Nations and its various internal bodies. AIDESEP and the Coordinating Body of Indigenous Peoples' Organization in the Amazon Basin, or COICA, regularly attend the U.N. Working Group on Indigenous Populations.

The 1990s and the beginning of the new millennium have seen an even further expansion, or "explosion," of activism, including indigenous coalitions and Indian-based political parties in response to continued depredations and oppression. The First Nations in Quebec, Canada, are challenging the Quebec separatists, who want to split off from the larger nation. They are asking, if Canada can be split, why can't the Cree and the Inuit, who are the only permanent residents of the

175,000-square-mile sub-Arctic region of northern Quebec, have their own independent province?

In Hawai'i, following the regressive decision by the U.S. Supreme Court to invalidate Hawaiians-only voting in Office of Hawaiian Affairs elections, one of several Native rights organizations, Ka Lahui Hawai'i, issued a new call for Native unity. Ka Lahui Hawai'i advocates a nation-within-a-nation relationship to the United States as a way for Hawaiians to govern their own affairs. The organization's eventual goal, however, is total independence.

In Latin America, an Aymara Indian leader, Victor Hugo Cardenas, was elected Vice President of Bolivia, and, in Ecuador, the indigenous-led political party Pachakutik (New Dawn in Quechua oral tradition) mounted massive street demonstrations that led to the ouster of a corrupt president and a change in government. Meanwhile, the Colombian army, which the Clinton administration proposes to give $1 billion in aid, including military assistance, continues to maintain close ties to right-wing paramilitary groups responsible for extensive human rights abuses and escalating involvement in drug trafficking. Caught between a corrupt government, violent right-wing paramilitaries, and left-wing revolutionaries, Indian peoples such as the U'wa courageously continue to struggle in defense of traditional lands and culture. In Chile, a thousand members of the Pehuenche people are resisting "resettlement" to make way for the construction of a hydroelectric project financed by the International Finance Corporation, a member of the World Bank Group. The Indians of the interior rain forest and Caribbean coastal plains of Nicaragua, a region collectively known as Mosquitia are opposing the attempts by the current government to overturn the autonomy they had won in the 1980s. Meanwhile, in Mexico, the Zapatista rebellion of Mayan Indians continues to stand off the Mexican army, and in the Sierra Madre del Sur, Mexico's other Indian war, in the states of Guerrero and Oaxaca, continues to press for indigenous autonomy.

The first selection in this final part represents the voices of indigenous people at the United Nations on the eve of the 1993 United Nations–mandated International Year of the World's Indigenous People. On December 10, 1992, Human Rights Day, twenty leaders of indigenous nations from around the world addressed the General Assembly of the United Nations for the first time in history. A few days earlier, under the sponsorship of the Native American Council of New York City, more than 250 representatives of indigenous peoples had met for three days in a grand council to prepare for the meeting at the United Nations. Among the many international indigenous representatives were the Mapuche of Chile and the Haudenosaunee (Iroquois), Lakota (Sioux), Diné (Navajo), and Cree delegates from North America. Presented in this selection are the statement by Oren Lyons, a traditional chief of the Onondaga Nation (Iroquois) and professor of American Studies at the State University of New York–Buffalo, and two regional reports on the current state of Native American peoples. The late Ingrid Washinawatok-El Issa (Menominee), who was assassinated in 1999 while assisting the U'wa Indians of Colombia, reports for North America. (See the box titled "Peace, Not Oil" in Part VII and the box titled "Ingrid Washinawatok" in this part.) José Barreiro, editor of Awe:kon Press, which publishes *Native Americas,* reports on the situation in Central and South America. (José Barreiro also wrote the foreword to this book.)

Indicative of the continuing struggle, however, is the fact that the General Assembly session that the Native American and other indigenous representatives addressed was poorly attended by the member states of the United Nations, and, as Chief Lyons points out, two massacres of South American Indians and other human rights abuses took place during the United Nations 1993 International Year of the World's Indigenous People. Furthermore, some member states at the United Nations were still preventing the adoption of the United Nations Declaration of Indigenous Peoples Rights, which could curb these very abuses. The government of Spain, for example, was at the time bent on commemorating the Columbian Quincentennial and therefore sought to downplay any recognition of Native American rights.

At the Second United Nations open-ended Intersessional Working Group on the Draft Declaration of Indigenous Peoples Rights, held on October 21, 1996, little further progress was made. The indigenous representatives concluded that the participating nation-states continue to exhibit few or no intentions to address the rights of indigenous peoples seriously, and the autonomous American Indian Movement delegation and the Maori delegation from Atearora (New Zealand) walked out. Since then, the indigenous representatives, refusing to become discouraged, have continued to rework the language of the draft declaration and fine-tune its principles, while, at the same time, to negotiate and strategize the means by which it will eventually be adopted by the United Nations.

In the second selection, Joane Nagel, Associate Professor of Sociology at Stanford University, and C. Matthew Snipp, Professor of Sociology at the University of Wisconsin–Madison, present an analysis and classification of the ethnic reorganization now taking place in the Americas. Nagel and Snipp define ethnic reorganization as occurring "when an ethnic minority undergoes a reorganization of its social structure, redefinition of ethnic group boundaries, or some other change in response to pressures or demands imposed by the dominant culture." It comes into play as a mechanism to facilitate ethnic group survival. Nagel and Snipp discuss four types of ethnic reorganization—social, economic, political, and cultural—and they document these processes among the Indian peoples of the United States when faced with demographic and cultural extinction. Social reorganization, for example, includes the reorganization of community or tribal boundaries, the reorganization of marriage rules, the reorganization of tribal membership rules, and the reorganization of the larger American Indian ethnic identity. A related concept, cultural revitalization, on the other hand, involves the rebirth of traditional identity and customs. The founding and development of Hawaiian language schools (discussed in the fourth selection) are a case in point.

The box titled "Aboriginal Peoples and Quebec," by Russel Barsh, Associate Professor of Native American Studies at the University of Lethbridge (Alberta), updates the current situation for the Native peoples of Canada and Quebec. Canadian government Indian policy regarding the aboriginal rights of First Nations peoples (Indian, Métis, and Inuit) have a somewhat different legal history than government policies in the United States. For one thing, the Canadian government made far fewer treaties than did the United States, and, in British Columbia, except for Vancouver Island, virtually no treaties with coastal Indians were made. Furthermore, Native Americans in the United States who are federally recognized are technically under the jurisdiction of the federal government, not the states, but in Canada they are considered provincial citizens, a status that subjects them to all provincially enacted laws. Finally, although the 1982 Constitution Act of Canada affirms "the existing aboriginal and treaty rights of the aboriginal peoples," the federal government, except in the Yukon Territory and the Northwest Territories, has control over very little land in Canada. So in British Columbia, despite current treaty negotiations, the question of Indian aboriginal rights to prevent clear-cutting by logging companies is primarily a legal struggle between Indian nations such as the Nuxalk and the province of British Columbia.

On the other hand, the Canadian government has recently agreed to create a new political province to be called Nunavut out of a 770,000 square mile portion of the Northwest Territories for the 17,500 Inuit people who live there. This new indigenous domain, however, leaves out some of the richest oil and gas deposits of the region. Among the resident Inuit, there are skyrocketing population growth, no employment, and high alcoholism and suicide rates. At the same time, by agreeing to the terms of the agreement to create Nunavut, the Inuit gave up the principle of inherent self-government, which other Native groups are pressing the Canadian government to accept under the new constitution.

Lanada Boyer (Bannock-Shoshone), the author of the selection on Alcatraz, was one of the many young people caught up in the Indian relocation policy of the U.S. government. In 1968 she left the streets of San Francisco to enter the University of California–Berkeley as a student. Against incredible odds she graduated with honors, even while taking a leading role in the nineteen-month occupation of Alcatraz Island and the student strike that created the Native American Studies program on the Berkeley campus. At the same time, she was in those years a single mother rearing two small children. She has recently completed a Ph.D. in political science from Idaho State University and is an example of the enormous strength of character exhibited by Indian women who participated in the Indian movement.

Alcatraz was the first, and in many ways, the most important of the land occupations that took place during the Indian movement of the 1960s and 1970s. Most of the liberation themes of the developing movement were laid out in the proposals and documents of the Indians of All Tribes (as the occupiers called themselves). These themes include self-determination, cultural revitalization, human ecology, rebuilding the Indian land base, economic self-sufficiency, and spiritual revitalization.

A key demand of the Indians of All Tribes on Alcatraz was to either abolish or radically transform the Bureau of Indian Affairs, the federal agency that is responsible for the trust status of Native American tribes and their lands and assets. The existence and performance of the Bureau of Indian Affairs remain controversial subjects, as witnessed in the current Tribal Trust Fund debacle. A lawsuit filed on June 10, 1996, by the Native American Rights Fund charges that the Department of the Interior and its Bureau of Indian Affairs have lost or cannot account for $2.4 billion in Individual Indian Money accounts. More than 300,000 accounts, managed by the Bureau of Indian Affairs, are involved in this class action suit.

The box titled "Roots of Contemporary Native American Activism" traces the roots of the "new Indian" movement in the United States to Alcatraz. In *American Indian Activism*, Johnson and co-editors Joane Nagel and Duane Champagne more fully document the Alcatraz story (see Suggested Readings).

In the box titled "Rigoberta Menchú Tum" is a photo of Rigoberta Menchú Tum, an Indian woman leader of the Guatemalan struggle and a recipient of the 1992 Nobel Peace Prize. Traditional Indians of the United States and Canada have a deep affinity for the Native peoples of Mexico and Guatemala. The governments of Canada and the United States have failed to acknowledge these spiritual and cultural connections. However, Native peoples of both the north and the south have been exchanging visits for hundreds of years and have found enormous commonalties in their traditions and struggles.

In the fourth selection, Leanne Hinton, a professor of linguistics at the University of California–Berkeley and director of the Survey of California and Other Indian Languages, provides a fascinating description of the innovative language schools that are reinvigorating the Native Hawaiian culture. For many years the Hawaiian language was officially discouraged if not suppressed following the loss of Hawaiian independence in the 1898 takeover by the United States. The establishment in 1983 of the Pūnana Leo preschools and the Kula Kaiapuni Hawai'i elementary and high schools have begun to reverse this particular aspect of ethnocide. The ethnogenesis of the Hawaiian people is told in chants and dance, so knowledge of the Hawaiian language is instrumental in preserving Hawaiian identity and culture. Hinton finds that this experiment in Hawaiian language revitalization is very successful, providing a model for the revitalization of other Native American languages. As an aside, the Hawaiian language schools do not exclude non-Native Hawaiian students from attending, but parents and their children must make a commitment to learning the Native language and culture.

The box titled "Maya Indian Rebellion" illustrates what Nagel and Snipp term political reorganization. It details a chronology of the Zapatista Indian movement among the Mayan Indian groups of Chiapas, Mexico.

In the fifth selection, Russel Barsh details the difficult political struggle of Native American and other indigenous peoples' organizations at the United Nations to secure an international covenant. He traces the origin of the international question of indigenous rights to the two precedent-setting conferences in 1977 and 1981 at the European headquarters of the United Nations in Geneva, Switzerland. It is noteworthy that the conference in 1977, which was well attended by Native American and other representatives of indigenous peoples (including Steve Talbot), received front-page coverage in Europe but scarcely a mention in the U.S. media. Barsh documents other important developments in the international arena that led to the International Year of the World's Indigenous People in 1993 and the problems encountered in drafting the historic Declaration on the Rights of Indigenous Peoples.

In a sense, Native Americans are this continent's most valuable human resource, because they give the society a sense of place, a relationship of stewardship to the environment, and a spiritual dimension. Reflecting this role, Native people participated in the December 1999 protest of the World Trade Organization (WTO). Altogether, 50,000 protesters, representing environmentalist, labor, consumer, health and food safety, human rights, and indigenous groups gathered in Seattle, Washington, to protest the closed-door meetings of the World Trade Organization, which had convened to set a global trade agenda for the next two decades. Native American elders, students, and activists were at the forefront of the protest that braved police violence and mass arrests in order to shut down the opening session of the WTO's four-day ministerial conference. The last selection in this part is the Indigenous Peoples' Seattle Declaration, which was developed by the Indigenous Peoples' Caucus during the Seattle protest. It is a comprehensive document that clearly details the many grievances that Native people have with the WTO, and it urgently calls for environmental and social justice, including that the WTO endorse the adoption by the United Nations General Assembly of the Declaration on the Rights of Indigenous Peoples and the ratification of International Labor Organization Convention 169. (The list of Native American signers is a partial list compiled at the time of the immediate protest.)

The WTO is an unelected body that represents corporations and international trade organizations. Yet, it has the power to overturn the laws of sovereign states that, in the opinion of its officers, constitute "unfair competition" for the private interests it represents. Thus, laws and regulations legislated by a nation, state, or province to protect labor, the environment, or the health of its citizens, including the welfare of indigenous people, can be challenged, and there is no appeal process. The WTO routinely rules against health and environmental laws. Even local regulations restricting the cutting of forests or fishing for an endangered species can be stopped by a foreign corporation, which puts profits before people, through the WTO. The Indigenous Peoples' Seattle statement declares that "the World Trade Organization is destroying Mother Earth and the cultural and biological diversity of which we are a part."

It is appropriate to end this part, and the book itself, with the closing statements by two outstanding Native Americans, the late Phillip Deere (Creek) and John Mohawk (Seneca), at the 1980 Fourth Russell Tribunal. The Russell Tribunal on the Rights of the Indians of the Americas, held in Rotterdam, November 1980, provided an international forum for Native Peoples to present their cases before an independent panel of jurists, officials, and prominent citizens. Their messages are for all the peoples of the earth, not just for the indigenous peoples of the Americas. In the final analysis, we share the planet and, ultimately, the same fate.

The People shall continue!

NOTE

1. Vine Deloria Jr., *Behind the Trail of Broken Treaties: An Indian Declaration of Independence* (Austin: University of Texas, 1985), 48–51.

VOICES OF INDIGENOUS PEOPLES
EPILOGUE

Oren Lyons (Joagquisho, Onondaga Nation)

December 10, 1992, was historic for indigenous peoples of the world. Twenty indigenous leaders addressed the General Assembly from the podium for the first time in the history of the United Nations, initiating the International Year of the World's Indigenous People. It was a victory of great consequence. This day vindicated and consecrated the work, perseverance, and spirit of all those indigenous delegates, international lawyers, and nongovernmental organizations (NGOs) who attended the United Nations Geneva conferences on racial discrimination, the protection of minorities, and the human rights of indigenous peoples in Geneva beginning in 1977.

Secretary General Boutros Boutros-Ghali delivered a serious and supportive address that gave hope and raised expectations for the coming International Year. At that time he announced the appointment of 1992 Nobel Peace Prize Laureate Rigoberta Menchú Tum as goodwill ambassador for the International Year of the World's Indigenous People.

The decision to designate this International Year and the support of the Secretary

Oren Lyons, "Epilogue"; Ingrid Washinawatok-El Issa, "North America"; and José Barriero, "Central and South America," in *Voice of Indigenous Peoples*. Copyright © 1994 by Native American Council of New York City. Clear Light Publishers, Santa Fe, N.M. Reprinted with permission.

General were a marked contrast to our first conference in Geneva in 1977. That first visit elicited all the stereotypical reactions of an uninformed world public towards indigenous peoples—Native American delegates were referred to as "Red Indians," for example. Those who did not participate in those formative years may say there has been little or no movement for the advancement of indigenous peoples, but in fact there have been extraordinary advances, especially within the United Nations.

I remember in 1973 we "Red Indians" were not allowed to cross First Avenue across from the United Nations in the cause of supporting the Lakota people who were suffering United States military oppression at Wounded Knee, South Dakota. Twenty years later, it was a Lakota spiritual leader, Arvol Looking Horse, who gave the opening prayer and stood with Apache representative Ola Cassadore as I delivered the opening address of indigenous representatives to the General Assembly.

Then again, one could say there has been no change, and that would also be true. Attitudes of racism still prevail around the world. Certainly the amount raised by the Voluntary Fund for the 1993 International Year of the World's Indigenous People reflected, at the least, disrespect, lack of interest, and neglect on the part of the member-states. Two weeks before the opening day (December 10, 1992) there was only $40,000 in the fund. This was an insult to indigenous peoples and an embarrassment to member-states of the United Nations. Intense lobbying produced an additional $300,000 by opening day. That figure contrasts with the $33 million worth of "indigenous project" proposals submitted to the Secretariat established for the International Year of the World's Indigenous People.

Indigenous people have brought into the United Nations forum an honesty and directness that have been both refreshing and challenging to the subtle diplomacy of United Nations politics. We have confronted, affronted, and offended powerful member-states, sometimes with serious consequences to our delegates, including death.

One could say that the United Nations did not escape some warning and retribution, when the last speaker of that historic December day, Hopi elder Thomas Banyacya, invoked the powers of the natural forces, and New York City experienced the worst storm of this century, with great winds and floods that covered the roofs of cars on East River Drive, flooded the subway systems for the first time, and joined the East River with the Hudson River in Lower Manhattan. Coincidence or invocation, no one can deny that the experience of these powerful forces reminded us that we do not control nature—dramatically amplifying the messages delivered by the indigenous peoples to the United Nations General Assembly.

The June 1993 World Conference on Human Rights in Vienna produced several initiatives regarding indigenous peoples. The conference adopted a resolution to extend the 1993 International Year of the World's Indigenous People to the Decade of Indigenous Peoples and recommended that Secretary General Boutros Boutros-Ghali "consider establishing as soon as possible a permanent forum for indigenous peoples in the United Nations system." We add to this the need for

special accreditation for indigenous peoples to the United Nations.

The efforts to complete the international standards on the rights of indigenous peoples commenced with meetings in Geneva beginning in July by the Working Group on Indigenous Populations. These historic meetings came out of the vision and work of Augusto Williamson-Diaz, who initially shepherded the process and idea through the bureaucratic maze of the United Nations in the early seventies.

Indigenous peoples reached their second plateau when the Working Group on Indigenous Populations was officially instituted within its parent body, the Subcommission on Prevention of Discrimination and Protection of Minorities within the Commission on Human Rights in 1982.

In 1985 Erica-Irene A. Daes became chair of the Working Group and has held that position ever since. Her leadership has been at times passionate, dictatorial, artful, shrewd, manipulative, sagacious, and tough. She has always exhibited her great experience and brilliance in dealing with the often hostile member-states and the inexperience of indigenous nations and peoples new to the intricacies of the United Nations. The diplomatic and political language and protocol of the United Nations is a law unto itself, and it is essential that we understand and learn it. We demand full recognition as peoples and nations—we expect nothing less.

In 1977 Robert "Tim" Coulter (who became director of the Indian Law Resource Center) and the International Indian Treaty Council collaborated to bring indigenous delegations to Geneva. Ann Maytag of the Maytag Foundation was instrumental in furnishing financial support for this event. Her assistance ensured the attendance and leadership of traditional indigenous nations and peoples, including the Haudenosaunee delegation of 26 representatives, with 18 chiefs and clan mothers. There were about 148 delegates at this initial meeting.

Credit and recognition should be given to those inspired and dedicated lawyers (native and non-native) and to the many other individuals who have contributed so greatly through the years of political and diplomatic battles within the United Nations structure as we forged a process of recognition and policy for indigenous peoples.

The Working Group on Indigenous Populations' meeting of July 1993 drew 124 indigenous delegations from around the world, 24 observers from United Nations member-states, and 74 NGOs—totaling over 500 participants.

There were large delegations from Australia and New Zealand representing aboriginal and Maori peoples. The Haudenosaunee delegation, combined with the Lakota, Teton Sioux, and Cree nations, maintained the continuum of the traditional indigenous leadership that inspired the first meeting in 1977. An informal show of hands provided the information that only five individual delegates from that first meeting were attending this eleventh session of the Working Group, two from North America and three from South America. The eleventh session produced this final draft, and it is a strong draft that includes group rights and self-determination but unfortunately no reference to sovereignty. The draft declaration addresses issues of lands, territories, coastal waters, and the environment. There are strong references to spiritual and intellectual property and the recognition of treaties as international instruments.

The most dramatic event of the United Nations meetings was the finalized draft version of the United Nations Declaration of Indigenous Peoples Rights. The group rights issue is particularly important to indigenous peoples, who live in strong family communities. Probably the most contentious issue discussed was the right to self-determination, which brought a strong reaction from the United States delegation, which felt that it was a threat to current United States law.

It is my opinion that most of this reaction comes from misunderstanding and ignorance concerning lifestyles and governance systems of indigenous nations and peoples. Despite strong opposition on this issue, the draft declaration was completed and stands as a great achievement, representing seventeen years of work by indigenous peoples in the fields of international law.

The Subcommission on Human Rights was next on the agenda and convened throughout the month of August. It was decided that the draft declaration would be presented during the next session of the Subcommission (1994). This gives indigenous delegations time to lobby the member-states that they reside in to support the declaration as it stands without change. A highlight of the session of the Subcommission on Human Rights was the adoption of a resolution addressing the broad question of human rights in Guatemala regarding the Mayan peoples.

Unfortunately, the massacre of Yanomamis during the week of August 16 by gold prospectors in the Amazonian state of Roraima and the August 18 massacre in the Peruvian Amazon of 64 Ashaninka Indians by the Maoist guerilla group "the Shining Path" overshadowed all other events concerning indigenous peoples in 1993. The irony of these massacres occurring during the International Year illustrates how little progress has been made in the human rights of indigenous peoples since the landing of Christopher Columbus.

It has been five hundred years of genocide for the same reason: GOLD! These latest atrocities committed against indigenous peoples bring a hard twist to the realities of our times. The gold prospectors responsible for the murders of these innocent people make clear that the savagery of "civilized" peoples in quest for riches at the expense of moral law continues and is expanding with the world market.

Indigenous peoples will continue to be victims of this greed as long as we have lands and territories with natural resources, or until the values of civilization change. These tragedies only strengthen our resolve and will to survive.

There is a race between "profits now" and the survival of our grandchildren.

There is a race between common sense and the world market.

The race is in progress; this generation and the next will determine the outcome.

Who will write that epilogue?

NORTH AMERICA

Ingrid Washinawatok-El Issa

A broad look at the North American continent five hundred years ago would provide some remarkable observations about the indigenous cultures that flourished then. It was a continent that in many respects was a model of diversity. In central Mexico were the grand city-state empires of the Aztecs, the Tarascans, and the Mayas, who built some of the largest pyramids in the world and had sophisticated sciences, technology, and agriculture. In the eastern part of what is now the United States were the large confederacies such as the Iroquois, the Creek, and the Cherokee, with matrilineal governments that were among the most democratic and egalitarian the world has ever known. Along the northwest coast lived the wealthy seafaring fishermen, who communed deeply with the spirits of animals and fish. The frozen north held Inuit people who could live and thrive under conditions that daunt modern technology. In the endless sea of buffalo that made up the Great Plains, the Sioux, Crow, and Comanche lived a free, loose life that continues to capture the imagination to this very day. Indeed, every region was remarkably different, very similar to the

enormous biological diversity that existed at that time.

While it is difficult to estimate the number of Indians living on the continent in 1492, it is known that Tenochtitlan, the Aztec capital, was then among the largest cities in the world, and there was little of this continent that was not settled. The great ability of the native people to work with the environment, rather than against it, gave this continent the appearance of a vast wilderness, though most of it was managed in one way or another. Dispensing with the myth of an empty continent, an estimate of 30 million Indians in 1492 is a conservative figure.

This great continental richness, biological and cultural, was not appreciated by the European settler and conquistador. The great Indian nations were broken up and dispersed and the vast, managed wilderness destroyed. Yet the Indians of North America still hold to their many traditions, cultures, and religions. The continuing diversity of native people is reflected not only in their arts and religion, but also in their struggles.

In the United States, where 90 percent of the native land base has been taken over the past 250 years, one-quarter of the Indians live on over 300 reservations that are autonomous governments under American law, subject only to federal authority. While this autonomy is continually challenged and sometimes chipped slightly, it has allowed for, among other things, an explosive growth in casinos and gaming on Indian reservations, an industry that is illegal in most of the United States. This autonomy has also been seen by producers of toxic nuclear and other wastes as a way to circumvent environmental regulations and public opposition to waste dumps and storage sites. At least two reservations in the United States, those of the Mescalero Apaches and the Skull Valley Goshutes, have entered into negotiations with the federal government to become repositories for high-level nuclear waste.

These industries have been accepted by some Indian reservations largely because of the historic poverty of Indians in the United States. While the Indian nations negotiated hundreds of treaties with the United States government, all were broken, and the former owners of the land were robbed of everything. Even today, Indians in the United States suffer from the highest unemployment rate, the highest rate of poverty, the highest infant mortality rate, the highest rate of teenage suicide, the highest rate of diabetes, the greatest incidence of malnutrition, the highest susceptibility to disease, the lowest per capita income, the shortest life expectancy, the poorest education, the highest federal imprisonment rate, and the lowest standard of living.

Most tribes have not renounced their strong ethic of living in harmony with the environment in return for Western-style development. Most Indian lands are still well cared for, and many support animal and plant species that have disappeared from the rest of the United States. However, the traditions of American Indians are under constant threat of erosion from a continuing lack of religious freedom and the destruction of sacred sites, the continuing racism that pervades American society, or the tremendous dominance and influence of American cultural institutions, such as television. Urban Indians now number more than reservation Indians, and their efforts to pass on their traditions to their children in the environment of the American city face overwhelming odds.

Virtually every Indian community has a struggle of some kind or another, yet some of the most pressing issues involve defending the earth. In the 1980s thousands of Navajos were relocated, and are still being removed, from their lands in the southwestern United States, ostensibly at the demand of the neighboring Hopi tribe, but in reality to pave the way for energy development. In the state of Nevada there is a continuing battle between the Western Shoshone and the Bureau of Land Management, an agency with a poor reputation for environmental protection, in which the bureau is trying to seize Indian lands in defiance of a hundred-year-old treaty. The Lummi of the northwest coast are trying to stop the clear-cutting of forests next to their lands by an insurance company, an act that would destroy salmon runs and disturb the nesting sites of a host of endangered bird species. In the East, the Mohawks of Akwesasne have been fighting smelters and other heavy industries that have virtually destroyed the St. Lawrence Seaway and surrounding regions with toxic wastes and heavy metals, poisoning the reservation's water supply and lands.

While it might at first glance appear that the autonomous nature of Indian reservations might be an aid in combatting struggles such as these, the nature of Indian governments often only exacerbates problems. With the notable exception of the Iroquois Confederacy, almost all Indian governments in the United States were set up by the United States government in the 1930s, without taking into account the traditional Indian process of governance. Many of these new governments were simply puppets of the United States, and its notoriously corrupt Bureau of Indian Affairs, and became agents for further defrauding Indian people. In Alaska, the indigenous communities were turned into corporations, with the native people becoming shareholders by legislation in the 1970s. This arrangement has led to a host of new problems. Leadership conflicts continue in many areas, often dividing Indian reservations into opposing factions. While the Indians of the United States may possess a certain amount of sovereignty that Indians in other countries still strive to achieve, American Indian governments are often still beholden to the United States.

In Mexico, the Indian people hold no such rights. With by far and away the largest population of Indians in the Western Hemisphere today, over 20 million as compared to only 2 million in the United States and 1 million in Canada, Indians are the lowest and poorest class in a Mexican society that is still highly stratified. Over 6 million Mexican Indians still speak one of the 220 Indian languages, more languages than in the United States and Canada combined. Most of the Indians in Mexico, however, have lost their native religions and are largely Roman Catholic.

Unlike Dutch and British policies, which largely practiced the removal of Indians and the segregation of peoples, Spanish doctrine preached the incorporation of Mexican Indians into Spanish society. In practice, Indians became serfs under the *encommienda* system, and the cruelty of Spanish rule helped put Indians at the forefront of the Mexican revolutions that would overthrow European dominance.

Today, Indian governments are not recognized by the Mexican government, and Indians do not have reservations. Their lands, like most lands in Mexico, are the common property of all Mexicans, and arbitrary expropriations, relocations, and destructive development are quite common. Unlike Native American groups in the United States, Mexican Indians have directed much of their political activity toward mainstream politics. Since its inception, Mexico has had three Indian presidents, and Indian votes continue to be crucial in the electoral process. Mexico has also incorporated its Indian heritage into its mainstream culture to a far greater extent than have the United States or Canada.

Yet violations of Indian rights are quite common throughout the country. In the Yucatán and Chiapas rain forest, Mayan Indians are subject to increasing threats from massive forestry projects and encroachment by poor pioneers. Lack of title to their lands means northern Mexican Indians, such as the Yaqui, Apache, and Tohono O'odham, have been forced off their lands by Mexican officials who deed their ancestral lands to settlers and speculators. The poverty of Mexican Indians is widespread and much worse than just about anything experienced in the United States.

The largest threat to Mexican Indians, however, comes from the North American Free Trade Agreement (NAFTA) and other such initiatives. Most Indians live at a subsistence level by cultivating corn or maize, the ancient grain developed in Mexico. Free trade agreements would likely unleash a wave of American corn, grown through modern agribusiness techniques, and force Mexican growers to do the same—probably forcing most of the Indian farmers off their land and into the overpopulated Mexican cities.

Modern free trade also poses a serious threat to Canadian Indians and Inuit peoples, who continue to hold title to the largest natural land areas in the Western Hemisphere. The British, French, and Canadian governments signed few treaties with the indigenous people of Canada. The isolation and harsh climate of the Canadian north have delayed the exploitation of the vast wilderness, but modern technology and the dwindling supply of natural resources are likely to make Canada the new battleground for native rights in the near future.

The Canadian government, like the American, bases its claims to land within its boundaries on a legal philosophy known as the "Doctrine of Discovery." Under this doctrine, the "discovery" of Canada by a European explorer, who then claimed all of it for his Crown, granted to Canada all title to the land. Despite having lived on this continent for thousands of years, if Indians wish to have any rights to their own lands, they must negotiate with Canada for them. The obvious fiction of such a legal doctrine means that in reality many of the Indians have still not given up title to their land, since they neither negotiated nor have signed treaties. Canada has embarked on a pursuit of new treaties and agreements with Indians in an attempt to forestall future challenges to the "Doctrine of Discovery." Among these new treaties is the creation of the territory of Nunavit, carved out from the Northwest Territories. While providing the Inuit with some of their original land base and a significant monetary compensation, the Inuit still cede control over mineral and other development in the region and may be unable to stop the negative environmental and cultural consequences that such projects bring.

Canada needs clear title to Indian lands and resources because it has embarked on projects designed to exploit what is the largest pristine wilderness in the hemisphere. From the lands of the Algonquin Indians in Quebec to those of the Lil'wat in British Columbia, native forests are being clear-cut at a rate much higher even than in the Amazon. Canada, the largest diverter of rivers on the continent, is planning some of the most massive hydroelectric and water transfer projects in the world. Virtually no river in its territories is safe. One project alone, the James Bay II project in northern

Quebec, is the largest industrial project in the history of North America; when completed, it would badly degrade a pristine area the size of France. The Cree and Inuit of Quebec have fought this project to a standstill; however, other Indians are doing less well. The Piegan attempts to stop the Old Man river dam in Alberta and Inuit attempts to fight the Lower Churchill Falls hydroelectric project in Labrador and Moise River diversion in Quebec together with a widely based movement to stop massive water transfers from northern rivers to the southwest and western United States are all ongoing.

Indian governments in Canada are largely modeled after those in the United States, with many of the same problems. However, they have far less power than their American counterparts, and there are frequent attempts by the Canadian government to reduce their influence further. Canada does provide native people with more comprehensive health, educational, and employment benefits than Mexico, where these are nonexistent, or the United States, where they are woefully mismanaged. In addition, a large portion of the Indian and Inuit population is still very traditional, maintaining ancient lifestyles, language, and religion and becoming more active in seeking out their rightful place in Canadian society.

The Indians of North America face many threats, including the inexorable homogenizing effect of modern culture that is transforming and changing native cultures and sometimes extinguishing them. Yet the great wilderness areas that continue to exist are largely in native hands, and native concepts and philosophies regarding how humans should interact with the rest of the world are finding more and more acceptance in the modern world. This is a tribute to the native people of this hemisphere, who have survived many worlds, including the modern one, and may yet survive to see another.

CENTRAL AND SOUTH AMERICA

José Barreiro

In the vast region that includes Central America, South America, and the Caribbean islands, there are today over 500 Indian nationalities, speaking hundreds of native languages, and living in terrain, climate, and under social conditions that are equally distinct. The 40 million indigenous people who live in this region include those with the earliest recorded contact with Europeans, the Tainos, who met Columbus's first voyage; and those with the latest contact, the Yanomami of the remote upper Amazon basin, who were only "discovered" in the late twentieth century.

While their cultures are diverse and often strikingly different—and continually changing—there is a unity that bonds these many nations: they share a common history. They had a distinctly non-Western philosophy and way of thought, and they are today largely dispossessed of their rights as nations of people.

Since the invasion of explorers and conquistadors such as Columbus, who subjugated much of the Caribbean; Pizzaro, who conquered the Inca Empire; and Cabral, who invaded Brazil; whole Indian nations have disappeared through warfare, cruelty, and disease. For five hundred years, Indians have endured the theft of their lands and natural resources, the enslavement of most of their people, and the domination by a new cultural and philosophical system completely alien to them. Indian beliefs were persecuted, their books destroyed, their languages repressed, and they and their children humiliated at every turn, through the introduction of racism.

Yet, today Indians are still unconquered, resisting domination, retaking ancestral lands, demanding a voice in their own affairs, and rebuilding cultures and nations. They struggle and endure despite living in countries that are among the most brutal in the world, despite the tremendous poverty of the region, and despite the enormous national and international pressure to destroy and exploit every natural region and resource. The voice of these people is being heard by more and more of the non-Indian world, and that voice is no longer heard so much for its heresies as for the answers it may offer to the problems of the modern world.

Few periods in history, certainly in the past century, have been as terrifying for a people as the repression of indigenous people in Guatemala. Of its 9 million inhabitants, over 5 million are Mayan Indians, and most of the rest of the population is of mixed blood. Between 1981 and 1983, under the "pacification" programs of the Guatemalan dictator General Efrain Rios Montt, almost 1 million Mayas were forcibly displaced, many of them into "model villages" that more resembled concentration camps. Over 20,000 Indians were killed and more than 250 villages destroyed.

The use of a scorched earth policy as well as torture continued throughout the 1980s. Despite attempts to reform the government, today the military continues to operate independently and is still a force of terror to the native populations. The awarding of the Nobel Peace Prize to Rigoberta Menchú, a Mayan woman who lost most of her family to army massacres and was forced to flee to Mexico, is only a small step in recognizing the terrible plight of many native peoples in Latin America.

A different outcome, through a different set of circumstances, has brought the Miskito Indians of Nicaragua an autonomy that is largely unknown to the rest of the region. Largely isolated on the country's Atlantic coast, they were generally ignored under the repressive regime of General Anastasio Somoza Debayle. His overthrow by Sandinista rebels, who then attempted to consolidate the country, led to conflict between the Miskitos and the Sandinistas. The conflict was made more complex by the larger struggle between the Sandinistas and the United States. Fighting the Sandinistas to a standstill, the Miskitos, through strong village leadership, have now carved out a strong role in Nicaraguan politics. Working to become more self-sufficient, while maintaining their agricultural and fishing lifestyle, they recently rebuffed an attempt by Nicaragua and international interests to log their forests.

As I write this, a massacre has just occurred in Brazil, where 70 Yanomami Indians, men, women, and children, were brutally slain by gold miners who refuse to recognize Yanomami land rights. During the past twenty years the government, at an ever-accelerating rate, colonized and destroyed the great Amazon rain forest, the richest, most biologically diverse region on the planet. This rush to development, which included gold mining, ranching, lumber projects, and road building, was done without any regard for native rights to the land. Like similar land rushes in the past, disease and violence devastated dozens of Indian tribes, including Waimiri and Atroari people, whose population dropped by more than two-thirds in this period. While recently lands have been set aside by the Brazilian government for the Indians of the Amazon, they are still beset by illegal trespassers, who are becoming increasingly violent. Under tremendous international pressure, President Fernando Collor de Mello set aside a natural park for the Yanomami in 1991 and began evicting the miners. His recent removal from office, however, has encouraged the Brazilian Parliament to try to do away with Indian lands altogether.

In Paraguay, only recently people were still hunting Indians like game. Less than twenty years ago, the Ayoreo and Ache people were regularly captured and sold as slaves. Relocations, such as the removal of the Toba-Maskoy people to the barren Chaco Desert, were common. Missionary organizations, which operate in most of Latin America, have largely completed the genocidal process in that country, by descending on a broken people and destroying what was left of their culture.

In Peru, the $9\frac{1}{2}$ million Indians suffer, not only from the usual expropriation of their lands by multinational corporations, exploitation as cheap labor or serfdom, denial of religious freedom, and brutality from an oppressive government, but they are also victimized by Maoist rebels, "the Shining Path." In a violent and terrifying world, especially for Indians, "the Shining Path" is virtually unmatched for its merciless and arbitrary killing sprees. It terrorizes the Quechuas and Aymaras, only this past month massacring a village of 200, simply for the sake of causing terror. Add to that the power and violence of drug lords who preside over billions of dollars of ill-gotten gains, and one must admire and appreciate the great courage of a gentle people who survive as one of the oldest known cultures in the world.

These situations are, of course, only a small sample of the issues affecting the region. Indians in Columbia, Chile, Venezuela, and Bolivia all suffer from governments that do not respect their rights to land, or even existence. Yet vast local and regional movements, such as the Indigenous Confederation of

Ecuador (CONAIE), have become major political forces in their countries.

I would close with the work that is going on, beneath the acts of violence, the destruction of the earth, and noise of Western culture. Even the devastation of Columbus and his successors, who decimated the islands of the Caribbean, could not wipe out the Indian roots of those islands. Today, many descendants of the people of the Caribbean are turning over the layers of progress, like turning over soil, and finding those roots. Nations such as the Taino and Carib are rising from the past, and indeed the work of rebuilding the earth may have just begun.

INGRID WASHINAWATOK

In the spring of 1999 Ingrid Washinawatok, along with Lahe'ena'e Gay and Terence Freitas, made a trip to Colombia to assist the U'wa people in establishing a cultural education system for their children and in support of their continuation of their traditional way of life. Within the continuing violent atmosphere that exists in that part of Colombia, they were kidnapped, and, on March 5th, their families were notified that they had been brutally killed. In the following months, some of those who were friends and worked with Ingrid remembered her with these words.

> We the members of the Indigenous Women's Network [Ingrid was co-chair] address our comments to the world. Ingrid and her companions gave the ultimate sacrifice—their lives—in the struggle for the attainment of human rights for Indigenous Peoples. As Women, we are the Mothers of our Nations. We share the responsibility of being life-givers, nurturers and sustainers of life—as Mother Earth is a life-giver. The Indigenous Women's Network is committed to nurturing our children and planting seeds of truth for generations to come. We do not want to repeat past mistakes. We will continue our work to eliminate the oppression of colonization, and to end the Indian wars. We who work for social justice must ensure that further repercussions do not fall on the U'wa community simply because they sought and received international solidarity and support. . . .
>
> March 8, 1999, statement by the Indigenous Women's Network

The Indigenous Environmental Network, consisting of an affiliation of over 200 Native communities, organizations, traditional societies and tribal nations, expresses our condolences to the families and Friends of Ingrid Washinawatok, Terence Frietas and Lahe'ena'e Gay. Their deaths will not be forgotten. Our mind, heart and spirit will stand with you in solidarity. Already their passing has brought attention to the U'wa tribe of Colombia, who are defending their ancestral lands from oil exploration by Occidental Petroleum as well as violence and human rights violations in Colombia. Their deaths have reconfirmed our commitment to stand fast in defense of our rights as Indigenous People to protect our traditional lands and all lands against unsustainable development and exploitation of natural resources that have sustained us for time immemorial.

> March 8, 1999, IEN Message to the Family and Friends of Ingrid Washinawatok, Terence Freitas, and Lahe'ena'e Gay, who were taken hostage and murdered in Colombia, South America

Ingrid's involvement in the "movement" began early, in the way that it should. She learned about the plight of her people from her parents and grandparents. Her nation, the Menominee, was terminated in the 1950s, and her parents were active in the struggle to regain their recognition and to preserve their traditional territory from abuse and development. . . . Ingrid was probably one of the most radical people I knew in international advocacy, uncompromisingly defending the rights of indigenous peoples to language, land, culture, history, government or any other expression of sovereignty. She never hesitated to lash out at racism or imperialism or commercialism. Yet she never discriminated. Each individual was judged on his or her merits. . . . The issues that she lived in her life are all of great importance and pertain to ancient spiritual truths. But from what I knew of Ingrid, life was rarely solemn. She enjoyed her work and enjoyed those around her. She never floated through the daily events in her life, but

anchored herself firmly in the people and issues with which she worked. She was strong enough to do this work on many fronts and still maintain the loudest, best laugh of anyone I ever met. . . .

Kent Lebsock (Lakota), "She Was So Much: Remembering Ingrid," *Native Americas,* 16, no. 2 (Summer 1999). This is an edited version of a longer article. Reprinted by permission of Akwe:kon Press.

ETHNIC REORGANIZATION:
AMERICAN INDIAN SOCIAL, ECONOMIC, POLITICAL, AND CULTURAL STRATEGIES FOR SURVIVAL

Joane Nagel and C. Matthew Snipp

INTRODUCTION

The way in which indigenous societies, particularly American Indians, have coped with social changes arising from the encroachment of European settlers has been the subject of several recent studies (Thornton 1981, 1986a, 1987a; Champagne 1983, 1992; Hall 1986, 1989; Snipp 1986a). In a much larger body of literature, research on ethnic relations has identified four basic processes

"Ethnic Reorganization: American Social, Economic, Political, and Cultural Strategies for Survival," *Ethnic and Racial Studies,* 16, no. 2 (1993): 203–235. Copyright © 1993. Reproduced by permission of Taylor & Francis, Inc./Routledge, Inc. This is an abridged version of an article that included explanatory end notes and complete references.

arising from contact between minority and majority populations: annihilation, assimilation, amalgamation, accommodation (Linton 1963; Gordon 1964; Enloe 1982; Olzak 1983; Parillo 1985). *Annihilation* refers to the destruction of one group by the other, resulting in the demographic or cultural disappearance of the target population. *Assimilation* refers to the absorption of an ethnic minority group into the dominant culture, where the dominant culture remains essentially unchanged, the result being the elimination of ethnic differences in the population. *Amalgamation* refers to the mutual adaptation and mixing of ethnic populations, resulting in a combined or hybrid population, often described as a "melting pot." *Accommodation* refers to the maintenance of ethnic distinctiveness among different groups, resulting in cultural pluralism.

All these processes have characterized Indian-white relations at various points in American history. Yet none completely captures the reality of contemporary Native American ethnicity in the United States. There is no question of the persistence of American Indians as a distinctive American minority group. According to the 1990 Census nearly two million Americans reported their race to be American Indian with a much larger number indicating some American Indian ancestry (U.S. Bureau of the Census 1991). These figures have been increasing throughout the twentieth century, and along with the continued presence of several hundred distinct American Indian communities, they bear testimony to the failure of programmes of annihilation and assimilation to eliminate American Indian ethnicity. Nevertheless, although American Indians have not been annihilated or assimilated, neither do amalgamation nor accommodation processes paint an entirely accurate picture of the Native American's place in American society. American Indians have had limited influence on American culture, and occupy a disadvantaged and subordinated position in many sectors of American economic, social, and political life. Thus, neither the notion of a melting pot nor cultural pluralism provides a satisfactory depiction of American Indians in the United States.

In this article, we shall argue that there is yet a fifth process characterizing majority-minority relations not entirely captured by the four above processes. We call this process "ethnic reorganization." We argue that ethnic reorganization is characteristic of all minority groups, but it is particularly important in understanding the ethnic survival of indigenous peoples in colonized societies. In this vein, ethnic reorganization is especially useful in accounting for both the persistence and the transformation of American Indian ethnicity in the United States.

Ethnic reorganization occurs when an ethnic minority undergoes a reorganization of its social structure, redefinition of ethnic group boundaries, or some other change in response to pressures or demands imposed by the dominant culture. From this viewpoint, ethnic reorganization is a mechanism that facilitates ethnic group survival, albeit in a modified form. To illustrate the workings of this process, we shall focus on how the ethnic boundaries of the American Indian population have changed over time in the wake of large-scale population losses and the emergence of the United States as a political sovereign. Specifically, we shall argue and present evidence that this process has had a major role, first, in the continuing existence of American Indians as a distinctive ethnic minority, secondly, in accounting for changes in the content and organization of American Indian ethnicity. . . .

. . . In the sections that follow, we specify several types of ethnic reorganization. These include: social reorganization, economic reorganization, political reorganization, and cultural reorganization. We document these reorganization processes among many different American Indian societies faced with demographic and cultural extinction.

FORMS OF ETHNIC REORGANIZATION

Estimates of the number of American Indians living in North America at the time of European contact range from 900,000 (Kroeber 1939) to 18 million (Dobyns 1983, p. 298). Most estimates of the North American Indian population fall between 2 and 5 million (Snipp 1989). In the four centuries following contact, the U.S. Indian population was decimated, numbering fewer than 250,000 by 1890 (Thornton and Marsh-Thornton 1981). The number of American Indians was so small and so tenuously situated at the turn of the century that contemporary American reformers and policymakers predicted the end of the race (U.S. House of Representatives 1934, p. 3315; Vogt 1957, p. 139; Linton 1963, p. vii; Dobyns 1983, pp. 8, 343). Scholars identify a number of factors leading to the dramatic decline in the number of American Indians following the arrival of Europeans. These include disease (Essin 1975; Dobyns 1983; Thornton 1987a), war (Mooney 1928; Driver 1961; Thornton 1987a), forced migration (Prucha 1962; McNickle 1975; Thornton 1984a), and genocidal practices including slavery (Utley 1976, 1984; Thornton 1987a).

In the face of population losses and social disorganization caused by the European and American expansion, Native Americans struggled to survive socially, economically, politically, and culturally. The practices and policies of the colonial and independent American governments comprised something akin to a set of environmental constraints with which Indian communities had to contend. Ethnic reorganization in its various forms, represented a set of strategies for survival. In the sections that follow we describe in detail social, economic, political, and cultural reorganization strategies undertaken by various Native American communities as they faced the challenges confronting them from the time of European contact to the present.

SOCIAL REORGANIZATION

Social reorganization involves the modification, addition, or elimination of social structural norms and arrangements governing group membership, kinship, family organization, social relations, and the like. Several forms of social reorganization have been undertaken by Native American communities in response to various threats to and constraints on their survival. These include reorganization of community or tribal boundaries, reorganization of the rules regulating marriage, reorganization of group or tribal membership rules, and reorganization of the larger American Indian ethnic identity.

Reorganization of Community Boundaries

Population declines due to disease, war, slavery, forced migration, and genocidal practices presented a tremendous challenge to the survival of Native American communities. Such fundamental demographic threats were responded to by survivors in several ways, many of which involved some form of social reorganization. One such response was the reorganization of the boundaries of the band or tribe. Dobyns (1983) reports that groups whose populations were so reduced by disease as to no longer provide an adequate (sometimes culturally defined) community base, often combined forces with other communities. These combined communities were not always ethnographically similar. Thus, the reduction of the Indian population contributed to ethnic change: the disappearance of some groups, the growth of other groups, and the creation of multitribal composite communities. Numerous accounts of Indian societies driven to near extinction are recounted in Swanton (1952), and they vividly depict the blending and amalgamation of people from different bands following a war or an epidemic. Some of these originally linguistically or culturally diverse groups survive as present-day communities both on and off reservations, for example, the non-reservation community of Lumbees of North Carolina (Blu 1980), or the Chippewa-Cree Tribe of the Rocky Boy's Reservation in Montana (U.S. Department of Interior 1978a).

Much social reorganization among American Indians since contact has tended towards an increase rather than a decrease in the scale of organization. Hannan (1979) argues that the expansion of ethnic boundaries serves as a competitive advantage to minority groups contending in modern economic and political arenas. While Hannan focuses on industrial societies, larger-scale organization can serve as an advantage to any group faced with a larger or better organized political or economic competitor. Driver (1961, p. 309) notes that American Indian resistance to European expansion and aggression led to increases in the scale of Indian political units, as villages and bands united to form tribes and ultimately confederations to face the better armed Europeans. Trigger (1978) reports that early confederations of Indian tribes were formed in order to compete more successfully with European and American hunters and trappers.

Ironically, the decline in the number of Native Americans sometimes provided opportunities for larger-scale social reorganization by Indian leaders. Laitin (1985) argues that there is an impetus towards enlarged ethnic boundaries as ethnic entrepreneurs seek to enhance their groups, and hence their own, political fortunes. Phillips' (1975, pp. 45–7) discussion of the consolidation of social divisions among Californian Indians in the early days of American rule provides an example of this entrepreneurial process. While many California Indian lineages ceased to exist as a result of war, removal and disease, many others were reorganized "under the personal control of powerful, self-made [rather than lineage-based] leaders" such as the Cahuilla leader Juan Antonio (Phillips 1975, p. 47).

The creation of the reservation system, implemented by the U.S. government in the 1800s, provided pressures and incentives for social reorganization into larger-scale ethnic units. On many reservations, diverse Native American bands, communities, and tribes were enclosed on the same land, under the jurisdiction of a single Indian Bureau officer. In many instances these groups blended into single social and political units. While some Indian groups remained separate and distinct within the boundaries of a single reservation (e.g., the Arapahoe and Shoshone Tribes of the Wind River Reservation in Wyoming or to a lesser extent, the Assiniboine and Sioux Tribes of the Fort Peck Reservation in Montana), in other cases, reservations served as boundaries around which new, larger identities formed, identities that coexisted with and sometimes superseded the band or tribal components of the reservation population.

For instance, Trosper (1976, p. 267) reports that the Flathead Reservation in Montana is "a source of identity," despite the fact that there are more individuals of Pend D'Orielle and Kootenai ancestry than of Flathead ancestry on the reservation. Cornell (1988a, p. 41) notes a "decline of older subtribal identities in favor of more comprehensive self-concepts," citing several examples of reservation-level identities: the San Carlos Apaches in Arizona, the Santee Sioux in Nebraska, the Warm Springs of Oregon, and the Yakima of Washington (1988a, pp. 34–5). Similarly, Thornton (1986b, p. 123) reports the decline of Yuki tribal identity in favour of the larger, blended identity of the Covelo Indian Community of the Round Valley Reservation in California.

Indeed, a number of researchers credit reservation boundaries with providing a unifying base for tribes whose memberships stem from diverse origins or whose cultural bases have been severely impaired. Bean (1978) and Shipek (1988) cite the reservation as the locus of identification and commonality for members of the Morongo Tribe of California, a group comprised of "several bands of different ethnic nationalities," but which unites as the "entity that owns a reservation" (Shipek 1988, p. 9). Similarly, Budy (1983) finds the reservation is a unifying factor for the ethnographically diverse Pit River Indian Tribe of California. Despite the loss of much of Hupa traditional culture, Bushnell (1972, p. 559) argues that the Hoopa Reservation in California has been central to the survival of the Hupa as a group.

In many cases, reservation-level patterns of identification complement rather than replace prior tribal-level affiliations to produce a layering of ethnic identities commonly observed by ethnic researchers (Horowitz 1985; Bentley 1987; McBeth 1989). For example, the Gros Ventre and Assiniboine members of the Fort Belknap Indian Community of the Fort Belknap Reservation in Montana equally divide representation in the joint Tribal Council, thus maintaining the political tribal boundary between them, although there is much social and economic activity across tribal lines (U.S. Department of Interior 1978a).

In other cases, reservation boundaries represent weaker challenges to internal ethnic divisions among enclosed Indian populations. For example, members of the Duwamish Tribe have long been a part of the Tulalip Tribes of the Tulalip Reservation of Washington. Nevertheless, in 1977, the Duwamish petitioned the federal government for official and separate recognition by the Department of Interior (U.S. Department of Interior 1992). In other cases, such as the Flathead or Pit River Tribes of California, cited above, tribal-level identification seems to be less salient as a basis for social and political organization than the reservation-level ethnic boundary. And in some cases, discussed below, the increase in scale of identification and organization has shifted upward beyond the tribe or reservation, to both regional and national levels: "Mission" Indians in California (Bean 1978, p. 194),

"Oklahoma Indians" (McBeth 1989), "Alaska Natives" (Darnell 1990), as well as "pan-Indian" (Hertzberg 1971; Josephy 1982, p. 216), "supratribal" (Chaudhiri 1985, p. 31; Cornell 1988b), or "Indian nationalist" (Thomas 1968, p. 82; Hertzberg 1971, p. 292).

Reorganization of Norms Regulating Marriage

Another form of social reorganization involves changes in marriage patterns and/or the use of norms governing marriage practices to enhance tribal survival. Hoxie (1987) discusses changes in Crow marriage rules as an adjustment to reservation life. He reports that Crow preferences for clan exogamy and band endogamy were maintained by residential mixing of clans and bands in each district of the reservation. A resulting district endogamy rule operated so that "children of the reservation's first families did not have to leave home to find a spouse" (Hoxie 1987, p. 17). Thornton (1984b, 1986b) examines the role of polygeny in demographic survival. Comparing the Tolowa with the Yuki, both of California, Thornton argues that Tolowa social organization, which permitted exogamous polygyny, allowed the Tolowa to recover from depopulation and to persist as a distinct group. In contrast, he notes, matrilineally organized Yuki social organization did not permit multiple outmarriages, and thus tribal size declined to the point where viability was lost (Thornton 1984b, 1986b).

Reorganization of Norms Regulating Membership

A third form of social reorganization centres on the rules of tribal membership. The U.S. federal government extends formal recognition to more than 300 "Indian Tribal Entities" (Federal Register 1988) in the lower forty-eight states who are eligible to receive services from the Bureau of Indian Affairs. This recognition is extremely valuable to many

Indian communities in that it provides for tax exemptions, limited self-rule, and the provision of a variety of services, including health care, education, housing, roads, economic development funding, and grants to tribal governments.

A major issue in the debate over the cost and legitimacy of federally provided services to Indian communities is the question of who qualifies for tribal services. Qualification generally requires official standing in a recognized tribe. Federally recognized American Indian tribes must keep lists of "enrolled members"; the tribally set rules of enrolment vary considerably from tribe to tribe, but usually involve some designated degree of tribal or Indian ancestry ("blood quantum"), parentage (mother's or father's tribal membership), and/or residency requirements. Changes in the inclusiveness or exclusiveness of enrolment rules which loosen or tighten tribal membership boundaries serve as another mechanism of social reorganization by Indian communities.

Trosper (1976) cites the adoption of tighter, more *exclusionary* enrolment rules by the Flathead Tribe of Montana as a response to pressures to "terminate" (i.e., dissolve the federal trust relationship) the tribe in the 1950s. Federal officials charged that Flathead members were acculturated and no longer needed federal services and protection. This prompted a move by tribal leaders to adopt a stricter set of blood quantum rules to designate members (Trosper 1976). A similar termination threat to the Utes on the Unitah and Ouray Reservation in Utah resulted in a division of the reservation population into "full-bloods" (those with more than half Ute ancestry) and "mixed-bloods" (those with less than half Ute ancestry) (Hagan 1985, p. 322).

Thornton (1987b) catalogues differences in the enrolment rules established by various Native American communities, noting the tendency towards looser, or *inclusionary*

rules on the part of non-reservation based groups, mainly in Oklahoma. The more inclusionary membership rules of Oklahoma tribes may stem from the fact that these mainly non-reservation communities face less competition among members for shares of tribally held or land-based resources, since such resources are limited or non-existent. A more political explanation for inclusionary rules is electoral, since a relatively large percentage of the Oklahoma population is Indian [12.9 per cent in 1990 (U.S. Bureau of the Census 1991)].

Reorganization of American Indian Ethnic Boundary

The final form of social reorganization to be discussed here involves what Thomas (1968, p. 84) terms "a new identity, a new ethnic group, . . . a new 'nationality,'" namely the rise of larger-than tribal identification and organization among Native Americans. Just as the scale of social organization and ethnic identification boundaries for many American Indian groups has shifted upwards, from kin or band boundaries to larger tribal or reservation boundaries, so there has also been a shift in identification on the part of many Native Americans to supratribal, or "pan-Indian," identities and organizational memberships. Supratribal identification, which can be regional or national, adds yet another layer in the multi-tiered American Indian ethnic mosaic.

The upward trend in Native American ethnic identification can be seen in census data. During this century, the percentage of American Indian respondents (those designating their race to be Indian) who fail to specify a tribal affiliation has been increasing. Masumura and Berman (1987, pp. 17–18) report that in 1910 only 8 per cent of American Indians failed to report a tribal affiliation, compared to 11 per cent in 1930, 21 per cent in 1970, and 22.4 per cent in 1980.

That nearly one-quarter of Americans report their race to be "Indian," yet fail to designate a tribe, suggests forces of supratribal social reorganization are at work. Lieberson (1985) notes a similar upward shift in the non-Indian population in the 1980 Census. He reports that 16 per cent of the non-black population with at least four generations of residence in the United States were "'unhyphenated whites' (those unable to name any ancestral country or choosing 'American')" (Lieberson 1985, p. 175). Both the "Indian" and "American" cases represent instances of upward shifts in ethnic identification.

Researchers cite a number of reasons for the emergence of supratribal identification. One factor, no doubt, is the force of external ascription, namely the common Euro-American designation of "Indian" to culturally varied Native American groups (Cornell 1990, p. 16). This uniform label served as the basis for similar treatment of all Indian communities by federal policy-makers, sometimes with unintended consequences. For instance, Witt (1968) reports that the bringing together of tribal leaders for instruction in federal policy changes in the 1930s inadvertently promoted awareness of common problems and common interests among members of different tribes. Trosper (1981, p. 247) suggests that sharing a common treaty background has also helped "American Indians . . . transform . . . themselves from a diverse people with little common identity into an ethnic group." Trottier (1981) argues that the 1969 take-over of Alcatraz Island by a group of mixed-background, mainly urban American Indians provided a "pan-ethnic 'charter'" or symbol around which supratribal identity could emerge. Finally, both the rise of supratribal organizations (e.g., the American Indian Movement) and the growth of Red Power activism of the late 1960s and 1970s have

been linked by numerous researchers to the civil rights movement and the context of social change and ethnic pride characterizing the period (Bushnell 1972, p. 559; McNickle 1973, p. 122; Budy 1983, p. 64; Cornell 1984, p. 46, 1988b; Hoxie 1984, p. 12; Hagan 1985, p. 317; Ziontz 1985, p. 308).

The urbanization of the American Indian population, which occurred mainly during the second half of this century, also provided a basis and rationale for social reorganization along supratribal lines. The role of ethnic organizations (community centres, churches, clubs, voluntary associations, newspapers, neighbourhoods) in aiding immigrant ethnic groups to adapt to city life is well documented in the ethnic relations literature (Cohen 1974; Margon 1977; Portes and Manning 1986). In 1980, 49 per cent of American Indians resided in urban areas (Snipp 1989, p. 83). The urbanization of the American Indian population during and following World War II provided a mixed-ancestry population base for supratribal social reorganization (Nash 1985; Bernstein 1986). Inter-tribal clubs, Indian centres, Indian churches and social organizations of all sorts [e.g., bowling leagues and softball teams (Steele 1975, p. 168; Liebow 1991; Weibel-Orlando 1991)] emerged in cities with significant Native American populations. These organizations provided a basic infrastructure for supratribal identification and social reorganization.

Interestingly, the emergence of supratribal identification and activism has complemented tribal identification and activism. A number of researchers report that the supratribal, Indian nationalist activism of the Red Power movement in the 1970s promoted tribal-level mobilization, and produced a renascence of tribal ethnic identification and pride among such groups as the Pit River (Budy 1983, pp. 64, 115), the Susanville Indians (Budy 1983, pp. 132–34), the Morongo

(Bean 1978, pp. 195–96), the Sioux (White et al. 1974, pp. 284–86), the Northern Utes (Collins 1975, pp. 66–7), the Hupa (Bushnell 1972, p. 559), and the Siletz (U.S. Department of Interior 1978b).

ECONOMIC REORGANIZATION

Economic reorganization involves the modification, addition or elimination of economic norms, activities, and organization. Several forms of economic reorganization have been undertaken by Native American communities in response to various threats to and constraints on group survival. These include the reorganization of the community economic base and the reorganization of economic activity.

Reorganization of Community, Economic Base

The introduction into North America of European goods, technologies and markets motivated large-scale and widespread economic reorganization in many Native American communities. Among the most influential of these external stimuli for change were: the use by American Indians of the Spanish-introduced horse, the voluntary and involuntary incorporation of American Indian communities into the Spanish mission system, the participation of Native American traders in the pan-European fur trade, the voluntary and sometimes involuntary participation in labour markets for waged and slave labour, and the shifting of raiding and pillage from tribal targets to Euro-American targets. These changes in economic opportunities and constraints all provided incentives for or dictated the necessity of American Indian economic reorganization. Often the reorganization of economic activity was undertaken by entire communities.

Economic reorganization is often a route to other forms of ethnic reorganization, and is thus sometimes an example and sometimes

a mechanism of social, political, or cultural ethnic reorganization. For instance, the adoption of the horse as a tool by hunting societies such as the Cheyenne, Shoshones, and Blackfeet is discussed by a number of researchers (see especially Holder 1970). Driver (1961) argues that this new technology improved traditional hunting methods, increased the wealth of some tribes and of some members of tribes, thus introducing stratification among and within a number of tribes (Driver 1961, p. 521). The demand for horses is cited as an impetus to increased raiding against Native American groups as well as against whites, thus increasing levels of inter-Indian and Indian-white conflict (Driver 1961, p. 215; Washburn 1975, p. 76; Hall 1989, pp. 86, 94). Washburn (1975, p. 80) also notes that the increased power horses brought to many Plains tribes permitted them to resist white competition and encroachment.

A number of American Indian communities faced with the conversion and extraction activities of the Spanish mission system in Florida and California adapted their traditional economic activities in a manner that best exploited the economic productive capacity of both mission agricultural and indigenous hunting and gathering niches. Deagan (1985, p. 302) reports a continuation of hunting by sixteenth-century Florida Indian groups in addition to horticultural activity undertaken at the direction of the mission friars. Coombs and Plog (1977) find that the variations in the number of baptisms in southern California missions correspond to the years of drought (more baptisms) and the years of plenty (fewer baptisms). They provide evidence of varied economic activity by Indian mission neophytes, who combined traditional fishing. hunting, and gathering to supplement mission-produced foods, particularly during lean years. Coombs and Plog pose the question: "Why should they [the Chumash Indians] have been willing participants in a [mission] system of cultural extinction?" (1977, p. 316). Their answer is that "the mission system provided them with an additional range of goods that were denied to those remaining out of it" (1977, p. 316). Thus, conversion to Catholicism permitted the Chumash to add new mission-produced agricultural products to their traditional diet.

Reorganization of Economic Activity

Hall (1989) notes the importance of understanding the transformation of American Indian societies from an international perspective. Forces pushing many Native American communities to reorganize their economies are imbedded in (1) the world economic system, (2) the U.S. economic system, and (3) the web of U.S. political policies regulating tribal economies. The view of American Indian reservations as internal colonies (Jorgensen 1978; Snipp 1986a) reflects this awareness, as does Champagne's (1992) analysis of the role of the international markets (e.g., cotton) in the economic and political reorganization of the Five Civilized Tribes (Choctaw, Cherokee, Creek, Chickasaw, Seminole) in the American southeast.

International and domestic trade have played an important role in American Indian ethnic reorganization, particularly the fur trade. Researchers report that the fur trade exerted "profound effects on Indian life" (Washburn 1975, p. 73), leading to more permanent settlements along rivers (for purposes of transportation and trade), a decline in seacoast settlements, increased hunting and demand for better (European) weapons, the establishment of family, clan, and tribal hunting territories and hence the emergence of land ownership, notions of trespassing, sales, inheritance, and private property, as well as the development of social classes on some reservations, and the breakdown of

traditional authority as wealthy fur trading members of the community became independent from tribal economies (Driver 1969; Washburn 1975; Axtell 1985; Thomas 1985; Alter 1987).

The involvement in various wage labour markets had similar consequences. American Indians are reported to have worked in a wide array of paid occupations: as agricultural workers in California (Phillips 1980; Hurtado 1988), in commercial fishing and canning (Axtell 1988; Champagne 1990), in mines (Hurtado 1988), in industry (Voget 1982; Nash 1985), as domestic servants (Phillips 1980; Hurtado 1988), as soldiers (Franco 1990), in lumbering (Voget 1982), and in livestock (Miner 1976), among others. American Indian involvement in labour markets was sometimes forced (Phillips 1980), and sometimes federal policy. For instance, in the 1960s, the U.S. federal government launched a programme designed to relocate and find employment for reservation Indians in urban areas as part of its programme of assimilation and termination of tribal recognition (Fixico 1986).

Many of these changes in economic activity were not themselves significant as forms of ethnic reorganization, but they had important consequences for social, political, or cultural reorganization. For instance, the entry of American Indians into urban wage labour markets resulted in the formation of urban Indian communities which, though not likely to take the shape of Indian enclaves or neighbourhoods, nevertheless contributed to the emergence of pan-Indian or supratribal organizations and identity (Hertzberg 1971; Weibel-Orlando 1991). The participation of American Indians in the armed services during World War II also had social and political consequences beyond those directly involving military service itself. Researchers report that military service acted as a catalyst to increased political activism on and off reservations by returning veterans whose wartime experience revealed to them the inequalities and injustices in federal Indian policy and the need for political organization to improve the situation facing the Indian population (Nash 1985; Bernstein 1986).

Perhaps the most profound impetus to economic reorganization and thus to subsequent social, political, and cultural change in Indian societies was political in origin: the reservation system. This political policy dramatically disrupted the traditional economic practices of many tribes and had wide-ranging consequences for all areas of American Indian life. Not all analyses condemn reservations. Given the alternatives of annihilation or landless assimilation, many researchers credit the reservation system with the survival of Indian tribes as we know them today (Bushnell 1972, p. 559; Trosper 1976, p. 267; Tiller 1983, p. 228; Cornell 1988b, pp. 80–4).

Nevertheless, enclosure on reservations and restrictions by Indian Office officials necessitated community adaptations. For instance, Champagne (1990) describes how the Tlingits shifted from traditional to commercial fishing in the face of official restrictions. Bean (1978) reports that when land allotments disrupted established patterns of farming on the Morongo reservation, residents responded by merging family allotments and forming a cooperative. Swan (1987) found that during the nineteenth century, the Osages of Oklahoma adjusted to a shift from buffalo hunting by combining row agriculture on the reservation with periodic hunting off reservation. Both hunters and farmers participated in traditional patterns of redistribution, which, Swan argued, functioned "to increase the number of subsistence strategies employed and maximize the probability of obtaining an adequate supply of critical resources" (1987, p. 18).

The reservation system and its federal administration have provided the rationale for a more modern form of economic reorganization by most tribes—strategies for obtaining federal resources and enforcing treaty rights. The federal government is responsible for providing a wide array of resources and services to reservation communities (health care, education, roads, housing, economic development assistance, legal assistance, administration of trust lands). Historically, these services were obtained directly from the Bureau of Indian Affairs [BIA] (and other agencies providing services, such as the Indian Health Service). However, the 1975 Indian Self-Determination and Education Assistance Act permitted Indian tribes to contract directly with service providers for many of these services. Knowledge of available services and how to obtain them from the BIA as well as from other public and private providers necessitated the development of an entire class of technical experts on reservations. Some of these workers were members of the tribe, some were not. Tensions developed on many reservations between this technocracy and other segments of the community (Jarvenpa 1985; Champagne 1989).

Another outcome of the reservation system is economic reorganization in the form of economic development programmes. American Indian tribes have implemented a wide variety of development projects during the decades since the 1975 Indian Self-Determination Act which also encouraged tribal self-sufficiency and economic development. These have included light manufacturing, aquaculture, tourism, and gaming (White 1990); Cornell and Kalt 1992). Reservation development has been a self-conscious form of economic reorganization intended to reshape reservation social systems by increasing reservation standards of living, providing employment for residents, and strengthening community viability. The proceeds from these projects have been used to expand and improve reservation health and education systems and to promote cultural renewal programmes, such as instruction in tribal languages and customs (Oppelt 1984; White 1990).

POLITICAL REORGANIZATION

Political reorganization involves the modification, addition, or elimination of political structure, forms of organization, and patterns of participation. Several forms of political organization have been undertaken by Native American communities in response to various threats to and constraints on group survival. These include the reorganization of political structure, tribal political mobilization, and supratribal political mobilization.

Reorganization of Political Structure

Historically the political boundaries of Native American communities have shown much flexibility, expanding to form federations and contracting to divide former communities. While the reorganization of political boundaries and institutions has both internal and external origins, intertribal and Indian-white relations have exerted enormous pressures for political change, both within and among tribes. For instance, Bradley (1987) argues that the sixteenth-century resurgence of the five-nation Iroquois Confederacy was spurred by an internal ideological interpretation of the meaning of European contact and the utility of intertribal peace and cooperation in acquiring European goods. Interaction with Europeans and Americans did not always result in intertribal coalitions. The positions taken by Indian societies in various wars (e.g., the French and Indian war, the U.S. revolutionary war, the war of 1812, the civil war, the

Spanish-American war) resulted in divisions among many Indian tribes (Washburn 1975; Anderson 1978; Champagne 1983, 1989), some of which produced permanent political rifts (e.g., among members of the Iroquois Confederacy). Internal tribal political reorganization was also a response of Euro-American contact. Champagne (1987) discusses the Cherokee shift "from tribal society to democratic state" as Cherokees strove to confront American pressures for land cessions; he outlines the political reorganization of the Cherokee, Chickasaw, Chocktaw, and Creek nations into constitutional governments in order to better contend with U.S. political policies and institutions.

U.S. Indian policies, many of which had explicit political reorganization goals, have been extremely powerful forces for political change in American Indian communities. Nineteenth-century removal and reservation policies decimated and divided tribes, creating multiple homelands for some groups (e.g., the Kickapoos of Kansas and the Kickapoos of Oklahoma or the several recognized Cherokee groups), and consolidating different Native American communities on single reservations (e.g., on the Pine Ridge reservation in South Dakota or the Fort Belknap reservation in Montana). In some cases, Native American resistance to removal policies resulted in tribal political reorganization, as among the Seminoles, some of whom refused to relocate from Florida to Oklahoma, resulting in a permanent division of the tribe between the two states.

The most explicit and powerful twentieth-century federal policy impetus to political reorganization was the 1934 Indian Reorganization Act [IRA]. A part of the "Indian New Deal," the IRA was designed to reverse decades of assimilationist policies and tribal land loss and to revitalize tribal political, economic, and social institutions.

IRA constitutions were adopted by half of all American Indian communities (O'Brien 1989, p. 83), and many who did not adopt IRA forms of government developed constitutional governments according to the guidelines of the IRA. The result for both was large-scale political reorganization most often involving written constitutions, provisions for electing tribal chairpersons and tribal councils, and various tribal business arrangements.

The IRA was reported to have intratribal as well as intertribal unifying consequences. Hicks (1975, p. 89) reported that the IRA produced a "renewal of organizational enthusiasm" among both the Catawba (South Carolina) and Monhegan communities (New England): Boissevain (1959) found that Narragansett reorganization under the IRA charter revitalized the community; and Collier (1963), the author of the Indian Reorganization Act, reported that tribal-level consciousness emerged among the Navajos for the first time in debates over whether to adopt an IRA constitution. The IRA debates also resulted in contact among different tribes as federal officials arranged intertribal meetings to disseminate and market the policy. Witt (1968) reported that the IRA "brought about external pressures for tribal and intertribal communication unknown to that degree in previous history. . . . [which] resulted, in many cases, in the first face-to-face interaction of tribes culturally and geographically remote" (pp. 59–60).

Not all scholars embrace the view that political reorganization resulting from the IRA was a positive development. Deloria and Lytle (1984, p. 13) comment that the policy was imposed by whites on Indian communities even if it was depicted as "self government," and Deloria (1969) refers to IRA tribal councils as "puppet governments." Indeed, while the IRA was a positive force in that it re-established tribal sovereignty and revitalized many Native American communities, it also created long-term divisions on many reservations where the decision to adopt IRA governments was not universally supported. In other cases, the IRA institutionalized tribal divisions, and even generated new recognized tribes. For instance, the United Keetoowah Cherokees became an organized band under the IRA in 1950, permanently separating it from the Cherokee Nation of Oklahoma. Furthermore, on many reservations, IRA-organized governments represent sources of community tension when non-IRA supporters see elected (often with limited voter participation) governments as agents of the BIA, pursuing policies of self- or bureaucratic-interest rather than tribal welfare (Schlesier 1974; DeMallie 1978; Cornell 1988b; Champagne 1989).

Tribal Political Mobilization

Political reorganization can also involve changes in patterns of political participation, for instance the universal suffrage provisions of the IRA resulted in campaigning, running for and holding elective offices, and voting. Political activism is another area of participation that has been reorganized over time. Tilly (1986) notes historical changes in "repertoires of contention," or forms of activism, in all political mobilization. Native American activism is no exception. Surveys of American Indian protest activity show a dramatic increase during the 1960s and 1970s (Bonney 1977; Cornell 1988b; Nagel 1993). This shift towards Native American political activism is mainly attributed to the "cycle of protest" (Tarrow 1989) begun by the civil rights movement in the early 1960s, ending in the late 1970s (Lurie 1968, p. 196; Josephy 1982, p. 228; Cornell 1988b, p. 172).

Some forms of American Indian activism were tribally organized and focused on exclusively tribal matters. Perhaps the best known tribal protest activism was the "fish-in" movement of the 1960s, where tribal members fished in opposition to court orders or to exercise treaty rights (Josephy 1982; Institute for Natural Progress 1992). While tribally organized protest actions occurred throughout the 1970s, much of what is known as the Red Power movement reveals a more fundamental form of political reorganization: the emergence of larger-than-tribal or supratribal American Indian identification and organization.

Supratribal Political Reorganization

The first modern intertribal political organization, the National Congress of American Indians [NCAI] was formed in 1944, partly as a result of IRA intertribal networking, and partly as a result of the return to reservations of American Indian World War II veteran progressives (Nash 1985; Bernstein 1986). While the NCAI focused mainly on matters of concern to Indian tribes, it was an indication of larger-than-tribal reorganization processes at work. The NCAI was followed in the 1960s by the emergence of more youthful, activist supratribal organizations whose membership was mainly urban, of varying tribal backgrounds, and whose orientation was "Indian" rather than tribal. Steiner (1967) referred to this cohort as the "new Indians"; they formed the activist core of the Red Power movement. The National Indian Youth Council [NIYC] and the American Indian Movement [AIM] were the most well-known and visible activist organizations of the Red Power period, particularly AIM whose 1972 week-long occupation of the BIA in Washington, D.C., was followed in 1973 by a siege lasting several weeks on the Pine Ridge Reservation in South Dakota, better known as "Wounded Knee II."

Supratribal identification and activism fed back into reservation politics and spurred tribal-level changes in political participation. Fowler (1987a) describes divisions among Gros Ventre youth groups on the Fort Belknap reservation stemming from their differential exposure to urban supratribal influences. A number of researchers report that the Indian pride and rights movement of the 1960s and 1970s led to renewed interest in tribal history and sparked tribal activism that was often led by reservation-returnees from urban activist experiences (Bushnell 1972; White et al. 1974; Collins 1975; Bean 1978; Budy 1983; Hoxie 1984; Hagan 1985).

CULTURAL REORGANIZATION

Cultural reorganization involves the modification, addition, or elimination of the content, practice, or transmission of material or ideational culture. Several forms of cultural reorganization have been undertaken by American Indian communities in response to various assaults on, and threats to, group and cultural survival. These have included the revision of cultural practices, the blending of Indian and non-Indian cultural practices, and various forms of cultural revitalization.

Cultural Revision

All transformations in Native American societies are the result of both structure and agency (Giddens 1983), where Indian communities, confronting powerful external forces, responded in a variety of ways by sometimes resisting, sometimes participating, sometimes adapting. The reorganization of Native American cultures in response to external pressures reflects this interplay between the external and the internal, but is more controversial than the other forms of reorganization discussed here. Part of the reason for this stems from a "primordialist" view of ethnicity as sacred and rooted in the past (Geertz 1963; Isaacs 1975a, 1975b; see also Scott 1990). Cultural reorganization stresses cultural change and thus raises questions about thc extent to which Native American cultures are simply the artifacts of some earlier era. Cultural reorganization stresses the dynamic, constantly evolving character of cultural systems. An important question about American Indian ethnicity centres on the relationship between ethnic group survival and cultural change. Does cultural change undermine ethnicity or is cultural change the mechanism of ethnic persistence?

Boissevain's (1959) study of the Narragansetts of Rhode Island comes down strongly in favour of the latter argument. She reports that the Narragansetts are "deeply acculturated and integrated into the community at large" (p. 347), without a living native language, and indistinguishable from the larger community "by racial type, distinct traits of culture, or even concentrated residence" (p. 349). By what means, she asks, have the Narragansetts "been able to maintain unity and group identity?" (p. 349). Boissevain's answer rests on three non-traditional Narragansett institutions: tribal (IRA parliamentary) government, an annual pow-wow, and the Indian (Protestant) church. All three institutions are described as quite remote, if not distinct, from their precontact form. None the less, they afford the group several important things: a sense of community and shared undertaking, an opportunity to assert Indian ancestry (judged a status advantage over non-Indian or African ancestry), and a tribal membership that connects Narragansetts to other Indian communities.

The revision of Native American cultural institutions in response to Euro-American "encapsulation" (Fowler 1987a) and coercion is reported by many researchers. Champagne (1990) describes modifications to their traditional potlatch made by Alaskan Tlingits at the turn of the century in order to conceal white-banned rituals, and to spread expenses. The banned family potlatch was opened to the larger community and the banned rituals were either modified or incorporated into Russian Orthodox or Christian ceremonies (Champagne 1989, p. 117). Fowler (1987a) describes nineteenth-century Arapahoe efforts to disguise their ceremonial activities on the Wind River Reservation in Wyoming so that Indian agents "interpreted them as civilized" (p. 250). Similarly, Driver (1969) reports nineteenth-century Apaches of the southwest rescheduled girls' puberty ceremonies to 1–4 July, which was the only time they were permitted to assemble on the reservation. The new schedule was retained even after the ban on assembly was lifted.

Cultural revision is sometimes voluntarily undertaken as a means to preserve practices or institutions. Prucha (1984) links the federal government's assault on the use of peyote by members of many tribes to the origins of the Native American Church, a pan-Indian religion established after World War I. The rationale for establishing the Church rested on the United States constitution. Various legislative efforts at banning peyote "frighten[ed] the peyotists, who organized formally as the Native American Church in order to fall clearly under the protective umbrella of the First Amendment" (Prucha 1984, p. 788).

Bean (1978) describes another instance of cultural revision in response to the decline of the Big Houses on the Morongo reservation in California. These important social and political institutions were clan and lineage-based as recently as 1900. However, the loss of knowledge and rituals and declining resources threatened their functioning. The solution, beginning in the 1960s, was to create a single consolidated Big House whose use (e.g., for funerals) was extended to all Cahuillas on and off the reservation regardless of clan or lineage, and which was headed (not according to tradition) by a woman (Bean 1978, pp. 179–81). The result was the transformation, but survival, of the Big House institution.

Cultural Blending

The blending of various Indian and non-Indian cultural practices represents a second form of cultural reorganization most closely resembling ethnic amalgamation or mixing. Cultural blending can range from cultural "borrowing" where non-indigenous celebrations (e.g., holidays) or practices (e.g., circumcision) are adopted into a culture, to a more equal mixing of two cultural streams. Fowler (1987a) reports the extensive use of the status of U.S. military veterans by Assiniboines and Gros Ventres on the Fort Belknap reservation in celebrations and rituals. For instance, during the reservation's Milk River pow-wow, veterans raise and accompany the American flag, while a drum group sings the Assiniboine Flag Song (Fowler 1987a, p. 163), and veterans hand round free food and gifts at memorial gatherings (p. 185). Similarly, the integration of military veterans into pow-wow opening ceremonies by many Indian communities is reported by Whitehorse (1988, pp. 50–2).

Larger-than-tribal cultural amalgamation resulting from the blending of cultural practices from many tribes also occurs. A number of researchers have reported the emergence of Plains Indian cultural amalgams in the form of dances, costuming, music, food, most notable at pow-wows (Thomas 1968; Hertzberg 1971; Young 1981; Whitehorse 1988). McBeth (1989) discusses the advent of an ethnic amalgam of non-reservation Indian groups in western Oklahoma. She reports the use of the label "Oklahoma Indians" by such non-Oklahoma groups as the Pueblos and Navajos, to refer to members of varied Oklahoma tribes,

such as the Kiowas, Comanches, Kiowa-Apaches, Wichitas, Caddos, and Delawares (McBeth 1989, p. 13). Along parallel lines, Bean (1978) describes the emergence of a Mission Indian subculture in California partly the result of BIA personnel policies that placed "Indians hired to work in bureau-funded jobs on reservations other than their own" (p. 194).

Cultural blending is most evident in the area of religious practices. Syncretism or the mixing of two or more religions is widespread in Indian communities and Indian churches, regardless of denomination. The blending of Christian symbolism, practices, and beliefs with traditional Indian religions has been described among the Mashpees (Clifford 1988), Assiniboines and Gros Ventres (Fowler 1987b), Yaquis (Spicer 1972), Chippewa-Crees (Fowler 1987a), Morongos (Bean 1978), Narragansetts (Boissevain 1959); Cherokees of Oklahoma (Young 1987), and Tlingits (Champagne 1990), among others. The Christian denominations involved in such cultural blends are equally diverse, including the Mennonites (Thompson 1973), Shakers (Young 1987), Orthodox and Roman Catholics (Coombs and Plog 1977; Fowler 1987a; Champagne 1989), Mormons (Collier 1963), and various Protestant sects.

Some researchers identify religious cultural blending as a strategy for protecting native religions from Christian and assimilationist assault, as well as for strengthening Indian communities. For instance, Herring (1988) describes the Kansas Kickapoos' programme of religious and social adaptation, under the leadership of the prophet, Kenekuk, as a "cultural blend [which] provided the Indians with a strong defense against white assaults" (p. 10). Clifford (1988, p. 303) refers to Mashpee conversion to Christianity as "wishful evangelism" on the part of the missionaries, arguing instead that

Mashpee Christian churches became loci of anti-white struggles.

Cultural Revitalization

Cultural revitalization can be built on the back of prior institutions and practices that have slipped into disuse, or can involve the creation of entirely new cultural forms. Whether created or recreated, this form of cultural reorganization falls well into what Hobsbawm and Ranger (1982) refer to as "the invention of tradition." For instance, the Ghost Dance, practised by many American Indian communities, mainly during the 1890s, is an example of a new cultural form. This widespread revitalization movement posited the disappearance of Euro-Americans and the return of precontact economic and cultural traditions. While researchers have put forward various explanations for the spread of the Ghost Dance movement, its rise and spread are uniformly characterized as a form of cultural revitalization (see Voget 1956; Wallace 1956; Thornton 1981, 1986a; Champagne 1983).

Many twentieth-century American Indian communities have undertaken programmes of cultural revitalization that involve the rebirth or birth of traditional practices. In some cases, old ceremonial practices (e.g., giveaways, dances, ceremonies) are redirected in the service of more modern events like school promotions and graduations, scholastic honours, elections to tribal office, sports activities (Voget 1982, p. 183). In other cases, modern institutions and events become the vehicles for cultural revitalization. The ethnographic or historical authenticity of revitalized cultural practices is often less important than the community-building purpose they serve. Fowler (1987a) documents numerous instances of generational disputes over the purpose and propriety of particular Gros Ventre cultural practices, in which elders question the motives, accuracy, and comprehension of younger members' cultural enactments.

The 1960s and 1970s were a period of much cultural revitalization in American Indian communities. This occurred for several reasons, one being the indirect result of Indian claims litigation. Researchers report that litigation of tribal recognition, restoration, or land claims often prompted revitalization efforts (Miner 1976; Trosper 1976; Hagan 1985; Ziontz 1985). For instance, Brodeur (1985, pp. 38–9) describes the relearning of traditional skills by the Mashpees of Massachusetts as they erected frames for wigwams and a longhouse in preparation of a petition for federal tribal recognition. Similar meetings held to pursue tribal restoration resulted in a resurgence of tribal identity on the Siletz reservation in Oregon in the 1970s (U.S. Department of Interior 1978b). Blu (1980) reports that the evolution of Lumbee tribal self-awareness during the 1970s was also the result of community efforts at organizational formation and collective action orientated towards achieving federal tribal recognition. Paredes (1974, 1975) reports a similar identity formation and transformation resulting from land-claims litigation among the Poarch Creeks of Alabama.

Existing reservation institutions also serve as vehicles of cultural revitalization. Perhaps the best example is the role of educational institutions and programmes in recreating American Indian culture, particularly in the area of native languages. White (1990) quotes from a tribal newspaper, *Keq Leyu*, the following Passamaquoddy language instruction advertisement:

> If this is the year you've decided to . . . learn your language, please let us know. . . . No, . . . you adults are not too old to learn to read what you speak; young folks . . . if we don't use it we'll lose it. . . . Come and be a part of the renaissance of our language (White 1990, p. 138).

The role of reservation schools in similar cultural revitalization programmes is reported by many researchers, as Indian languages, history, and culture are incorporated into the curriculum (Bushnell 1972; White et al. 1974; Oppelt 1984).

CONCLUSION

The American Indian case provides a variety of examples of the different facets of ethnic reorganization. Social, economic, political, and cultural reorganization are the mechanisms of ethnic survival, reconstruction, and creation. These processes are not limited to American Indians or to indigenous tribal communities, but can be observed in urban and rural ethnic groups around the world. In all these cases, however, the historical existence of ethnic groups tends to obscure the dynamic, emergent aspects of ethnicity. Most ethnically divided populations can trace the roots of their differentness and sometimes their animosities back through generations and even centuries. However, the organization of contemporary ethnicity and the nature of current ethnic relations reflect contemporary adaptations and continually evolving identities and institutions. . . .

ABORIGINAL PEOPLES AND QUEBEC: COMPETING FOR LEGITIMACY AS EMERGENT NATIONS

Russel Lawrence Barsh

Despite the reprieve offered by a narrow "No" vote in the October 30,1995 referendum on Quebec sovereignty, the political geography of Canada, and indeed the idea of Canada as a nation-state, are still far from settled. Scholars and politicians have forecast everything from Yugoslav-style chaos, to the birth of a uniquely decentralized society which other multiethnic states might do well to emulate. It seems to many bewildered and frustrated Canadians that their country is falling prey to competing ethnonationalisms.

The Parti Québécois remains committed to negotiating independence from Canada. Aboriginal peoples, who comprise a majority in half the territory claimed by Quebec, have stressed publicly that they will not leave Canada willingly. The Acadians of Canada's Maritimes region are debating whether to seek their own independence, attach themselves to Quebec, or remain part of Canada. In Arctic Canada, two new Provinces may soon be created, one in the central Arctic where Inuit are a large majority (Nunavut), and the other in the west, where Inuit and Indians comprise just under one-third of the population. In British Columbia, Indian claims to land and local autonomy are in negotiation under the auspices of a provincial Treaty Commission, and a national-level Royal Commission has tabled a report describing Aboriginal peoples as "partners in confederation."

Canada is being reimagined by a rush of high-level negotiations, which are attempting to reconcile the country's ethnic and linguistic fissures through some new association made up of equally sovereign but dissimilar pieces. This uniquely Canadian political geometry has thus far assumed that the products of elite negotiations will enjoy popular support—an assumption called into doubt by the broad rejection of the Charlottetown Accord in the 1992 constitutional referendum, and by the growing strength of the Reform Party, which

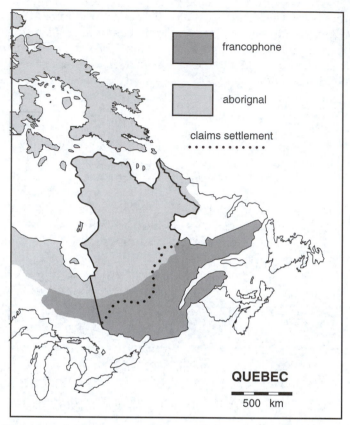

Ethnic and linguistic geography of Quebec and neighboring Canadian provinces in 1991; the dotted line marks the boundary of the territory covered by the James Bay–Northern Quebec Agreement.

From "Ethnic and Linguistic Geography of Quebec and Neighboring Provinces in 1991," *American Indian Culture and Research Journal*, 21:1 (1997) p. 7.

opposes any erosion of the power of existing provinces. While it has been said that Canada works better in practice than in theory, moreover, there are reasons to fear that the transformation of Arctic Canada into new provinces will fail, over the next generation, to satisfy Aboriginal demands for meaningful self-determination. There are also reasons to suspect that a peaceful disengagement of Quebec from Canada is impossible, also because of the unsatisfactory resolution of indigenous peoples' status.

In this paper I will focus on competing linguistic and indigenous claims in Quebec, both in relation to developments in northern Canada, and

the current international environment for the recognition of such claims.

Canada's Northern Frontier

Unlike the contiguous United States, where indigenous people live in relatively small enclaves surrounded by non-indigenous majorities, Canada is characterized by a sharp ethnic and linguistic frontier. Although most indigenous and non-indigenous Canadians make their homes within 200 miles of Canada's southern border with the United States, the northern half of Canada has an

indigenous majority. Only in the MacKenzie valley (developed since the 1920s for its oil), the
Yukon (settled during the 1898 gold rush), and
Schefferville in Quebec (the site of Quebec's iron-
mining industry) are there large, non-indigenous
settlements. The north therefore easily meets the
basic conditions of a claim to self-determination: a
contiguous territory that is distinct geographically
and ethnically from the society administering it.

Canada has long appreciated the tenuousness
of its national claim to Arctic sovereignty, historically based on Elizabethans' "discovery" of Baffin
Island and Hudson's Bay, Stuart grants of "Rupert's
Land" to the Hudson's Bay Company, the Company's 1868 surrender of its title to the Empire, and
subsequent Victorian imperial legislation allowing
the young Canadian dominion to organize a local
government in the region. Inuit played no role in
these early transactions, and it is doubtful that they
were aware of them. Canada's actual presence in
the region continued to be mainly symbolic—the
occasional dispatch of a research ship to show the
flag—despite competing Norwegian and Soviet
claims.

The Cold War and U.S.-Canadian military cooperation on the "polar frontier" with Moscow
brought an end to this laissez-faire approach. Royal
Canadian Mounted Police (RCMP) posts were established near Inuit campsites, and the Inuit were
organized into militia companies, rather patheti-
cally armed with World War I vintage Enfield rifles.
Americans meanwhile constructed a string of
manned radar-stations and airfields, the DEW-Line.
Concern for the welfare of Inuit, whose way of life
was increasingly threatened, as well as interest in
strengthening Canadians' physical presence in the
Arctic led to measures in the 1950s and 1960s to
relocate and consolidate Inuit settlements. Only
then did Canada began to co-opt Inuit leadership
into the formal administration of the territory.

In June 1969, Jean Chrétien, then Minister of
Indian and Northern Affairs in the Liberal Government of Pierre Elliott Trudeau, tabled a White
Paper on Indian policy that called for the legal
evaluation and settlement of claims based on non-
fulfillment of treaties, followed by the dismantling of his Department and equal citizenship for
Aboriginal peoples. Indian leaders nationwide
responded with a "Red Paper," in which they demanded self-government and full respect for the
treaties. Although the White Paper was consequently shelved, Ottawa hastened to settle Northern
land claims after a 1973 Supreme Court ruling in
which the Justices divided equally and (in the minds

of federal bureaucrats) ominously over whether
Indians in British Columbia had residual rights to
their unsurrendered territories. Then a Quebec
judge blocked the James Bay hydroelectric project
on the grounds that Cree hunters might still retain
land rights. Although hastily overturned on appeal,
this ruling nonetheless led to a "comprehensive" settlement of Cree rights, the James Bay and
Northern Quebec Agreement.

Since 1975, similar agreements have been made
covering the entire northern half of Canada. Despite differences in detail they share six elements:

- In exchange for their original, unceded rights to
  the territory as a whole, the Aboriginal peoples
  concerned received statutory title to smaller,
  scattered parcels totalling roughly one-fifth of
  the land area.
- Aboriginal peoples retain hunting, fishing, and
  trapping rights over some of the lands which
  are no longer exclusively theirs. In northern
  Quebec, these harvesting rights cover a much
  larger area than lands remaining in exclusive
  Aboriginal ownership.
- Aboriginal peoples retain mineral rights in certain designated areas only.
- Cash compensation equivalent to between
  $15,000 and $28,000 per capita (CDN) was
  paid to Aboriginal peoples for the settlement.
- Aboriginal peoples are guaranteed a distinct
  role in governing the territory. This ranges from
  co-management of wildlife and purely internal
  self-government in northern Quebec, to regional
  administration of the entire territory in the central Arctic.
- Claims agreements are deemed to be treaties
  under section 35 of the Constitution Act, 1982,
  and thus cannot be modified without Aboriginal
  consent, or a constitutional amendment.

In terms of the structure of Canadian confederation, these recent agreements create three politically distinct regions. Northern Quebec is the first.
The agreements made with the Cree, Naskapi and
Inuit of this territory acknowledge the jurisdiction
of the province of Quebec, although they also create tripartite (federal, provincial, indigenous) institutions to co-manage northern ecosystems, and
local or municipal governments for each indigenous people. The central Arctic, which has never
been included in the boundaries of any province,
and where Inuit are a large majority, has been
promised entry into Confederation as an eleventh
province, Nunavut, in 1999. The western Arctic,

including the Yukon Territory and parts of the Northwest Territories, is a mixed demographic situation with at least eight distinct indigenous peoples, and non-indigenous people are a majority. A constitutional convention began in January 1995 to design a new government for the western half of the Northwest Territories, and it appears that the result will be a highly decentralized regime based on linguistic and ethnic regions.

Although it has already been recommended by Ottawa, the entry of Nunavut into Confederation still requires a constitutional amendment, with the consent of "at least two-thirds of the provinces that have, in the aggregate, . . . at least fifty per cent of the population of all the provinces. In practical terms this means that Ontario, Quebec, or a coalition of the western provinces can block the emergence of any new northern provinces, or demand political concessions from Ottawa as their price for accepting an increase in the number of provinces. The neo-conservative Reform Party, which emerged from western disaffection with Ottawa, has already complained that new northern provinces would be too costly to govern. Newfoundland has particular reasons to fear a larger Aboriginal voice in governing Canada because it could lead to pressure for land claims settlements and self-government in Labrador, the mineral- and hydroelectric power-rich last hope for Newfoundland's fished-out, logged-out economy. Unless Canadians are preoccupied with Quebec (or post-secession chaos) in 1999, it is likely that Inuit will face stiff resistance.

Assuming that Nunavat is proclaimed as a new province in 1999, it will debut as a de facto ethnic politie; however, the Inuit majority will lack constitutional authority to block immigration from southern Canada. Article 6 of the Charter of Rights and Freedoms expressly guarantees the "mobility rights" of all Canadians. Thus if the new Nunavut government succeeds in raising living standards and promoting industrialization, its Inuit majority will erode, and the ability of Inuit to perpetuate their distinctiveness legislatively will diminish.

Inuit leaders seem confident that they can maintain control over Nunavut. Inuit prosperity will nevertheless depend on extracting the region's hydroelectric potential, and its reserves of gold, diamonds, uranium, petroleum, tungsten, copper, lead and zinc. Arctic mining is already dominated by U.S., European and Japanese multinationals, and Nunavut may rapidly become a captive of foreign capital. Québécois nationalism originally emerged as a response to growing domination of the province's industry by anglophones. Young Inuit may launch a new wave of Arctic nationalism some day in response to the same forces.

Developments in the north are certain to influence the course of events in Quebec, in any case. If Inuit in the central Arctic achieve provincial status, why not Inuit in northern Quebec? If Dene secure a distinct political role in the new northwestern province, why not the Crees in northern Quebec? Whether or not Quebec remains a constituent part of Canada's federation, it will confront with expectations raised by the restructuring of government in the north. . . .

"Aboriginal Peoples and Quebec: Competing for Legitimacy As Emergent Nations," by Russel Lawrence Barsh, *American Indian Culture and Research Journal,* 21, no. 1 (1997): 1–29. By permission of the American Indian Studies Center, U.C.L.A. © Regents of the University of California. A portion of the original and the notes have been omitted.

REFLECTIONS OF ALCATRAZ

Lanada Boyer

It was 5 January 1965 when I left on the Greyhound bus from my home reservation of the Shoshone and Bannock tribes to go to San Francisco. I was a participant in the Bureau of Indian Affairs Relocation Program, which sent tribal members from their reservations into the major cities of the nation to get work or learn a trade.

There were no jobs on the reservation, and the "No Indians or Dogs Allowed" signs had barely been taken down in my home town of Blackfoot, Idaho. Poverty, hardship, and despair had grown to be the way of life on the reservation. As a result of governmental rule, our reservation and people were suffering.

I was raised from childhood in an environment of tribal politics. My father was the tribal chairman for a number of years. His resistance to the government's attempts to steal our water and lands through the Shoshone Nation Land Claims put our whole family in jeopardy. I would help my father write letters to officials to get assistance for our reservation, and it was in this way that I began to understand about the continuing war against our people.

Lanada Boyer, "Reflections of Alcatraz," *American Indian Culture and Research Journal*, 18, no. 4 (1994): 75–92. Copyright © 1994 by The Regents of the University of California. American Indian Studies Center, UCLA. Reprinted with permission. The endnotes have been omitted.

It was a very hard time for us all; the 1960s did not bring change. When the BIA offered relocation to the city, I took the opportunity, along with many others who left their reservations. We were not aware that the federal government's plan to "drop us off" in the cities was another insidious method of depriving us of our reservation lands and membership in our tribes. Some of us knew that non-Indians were exerting intense political pressures to gain more of our lands for their economic benefit.

We began our new lives in the cities, socializing primarily with our own people. On the reservations, it was easy to divide Indians against Indians; but in a major city, we are so glad to see other Indians, we don't care what tribe they are. They are natives, and that's all that counts.

The San Francisco Indian Center became a focal point of social life for many relocated tribal members in the Bay Area. The center sponsored both powwows and non-Indian dances. It published a newsletter that many Bay Area Indian residents received. Other Indian organizations, such as the Oakland Friendship House and the San Jose Indian Center, grew out of the Bay Area where Indians were living. Our organizations eventually became a part of the city, and we were acknowledged along with other city minority organizations. Whenever Mayor Alioto went to the Mission District where many of us lived, he would meet with the Latino and

Spanish groups, the Mission Rebels (Blacks), and the Indians. We were recognized as a political unit, and gradually we became politicized.

I cofounded United Native Americans with Lehman Brightman, who actively led our political efforts in the Bay Area. Lee was a former University of Oklahoma football star whose intelligence, wit, and concern led him to become a strong Native American advocate. We networked with other organizations and the California Indian Education Association. One of our first efforts was to seek reform of Bureau of Indian Affairs policies to allow relocated Indians more than a one-way ticket to the city. We wanted to attend the universities in the Bay Area, but, since a college education was beyond our means, we requested assistance from the BIA, which had put us there. Instead, the BIA ended the relocation program in 1966.

With the support of the San Francisco Mission District organizations, I was accepted by the University of California, Berkeley. In January 1968, I was the very first Native American student to be accepted through special admissions into the Economic Opportunity Program, on probationary status. I kept up my grades and went off probation. At first, it was lonely being a native on a campus of fifty thousand students; then I met Patty Silvas, who was a Blackfeet from Salinas, California. She was the only other native on campus and had entered through regular admissions. We worked together to develop good university support.

It was not long before other native students were admitted; my program allowed me to recruit for UC Berkeley. After a while, we had enough students to form our own native student organization, which I chaired. The campus was still simmering from the free speech movement, the civil rights and antiwar protests, and it was natural for us to get caught up in the heat of campus unrest with the Third World Strike.

The Third World Strike at Berkeley in 1969 was the most expensive of the Berkeley campus protests, because the university assembled the largest force of Berkeley police and National Guard ever. They marched in with their bayonets unsheathed and fogged the campus with pepper gas. Every class was interrupted and stopped. All of the Third World Strike leaders were arrested on various charges. After the gas cleared away, I became one of the coalition leaders on the four-person negotiation team for our Third World College. We were victorious in establishing our own Department of Ethnic Studies, consisting of Black, Chicano, Asian, and Native American studies programs within the university. Ours was the very first such department in the nation.

It was during this time that the issue of Alcatraz Island became a target of interest for us. In 1964, after the prison had been abandoned, a group of Lakota, consisting of Russell Means, Hank Means, Belva Cottier, Richard McKenzie, and others, had tried to reclaim the island as federal surplus property. Their efforts had been treated as a joke by the media.

Now the island was being considered for purchase by a wealthy developer who wanted to build a casino there. We were concerned that the developer would be allowed to build his casino and the earlier claim would be ignored. This would mean that the federal government had no intention of honoring either the federal surplus laws giving lands back to native peoples or the 1868 treaty that was the basis of the Lakota claim in 1964. This failure to uphold another treaty was enough to push our buttons.

The students at UC Berkeley and San Francisco State had already formed a native student alliance, so when Richard Oakes, chairman of the San Francisco State student organization, contacted me at Berkeley about having the students symbolically take Alcatraz Island for the Indians, I said, "Sounds great. Let's do it." He informed me that Adam Nordwall, a local Bay Area Indian businessman, was going to rent a boat to sail around the island to publicize the Indians' claim. We made arrangements to get the students together on a Sunday afternoon to sail around the island. Four of our students jumped off the boat and attempted to swim to the island. We got very little publicity, but it was a nice boat ride on a Sunday afternoon, compliments of Adam Nordwall.

During this time, the San Francisco Indian Center burned to the ground. The community was devastated. The students got together and decided to take over the island as our new center for Indians in the Bay Area. On 14 November 1969, we met on the San Francisco docks and looked for a boat to rent. Finally, we spotted some fishermen just pulling in, and I approached the first man off the boat, asking him to take us to the island one way. Since the island was closed to the public, I had to convince him that we wanted to go for a special purpose. I told him we wanted to go to the island for a ceremony, which might take us awhile. He asked where our food was, and I told him we were fasting. He agreed to take us and charged us three dollars per person. Earl Livermore paid for those of us who did not have any money.

As we waited for the rest of our group, it began to grow dark. The fishermen were getting impatient, and I was afraid they would back out, so we pulled away from the dock. As we were leaving, I could see outlines of figures and legs running, so I asked the fisherman to go back and pick up our friends. It was Richard Oakes and a few of the San Francisco State students. This gave us a total of fourteen Indian students. The fisherman took us out to the island and dropped us off.

We were on the island and it was beautiful. The view was a "knockout," with lights all over the Bay Area. Earl Livermore was on the mainland and would contact the press to let them know we were on the island. We split into groups and agreed that, if some of us were found, the others would continue to hide out and hold the island. It felt like a game of hide-and-seek, and we were not afraid. At times, a search party would be very close to us, and it was hard to keep from giggling or laughing. All that night, the coast guard looked for us with searchlights in the old buildings, but we eluded them.

In the morning, we got together and decided to splinter off into smaller groups. A few hours later, Rick Evening, Kay Many Horses, and I were hiding out when we heard our names being called. I said to Rick, "I thought we were going to hold out and not give ourselves up." He said he would go see what was going on. A few minutes later, he came back and said Richard Oakes had identified himself when the press arrived and had made a deal with the coast guard that none of us would be arrested if we all gave ourselves up. I did not want to say anything to Richard in front of everybody for the sake of unity, so, reluctantly, I got into the boat.

When we got back to the mainland, the rest of the students were upset with us for coming back. They had begun mobilizing a statewide effort to get other native students to join us on the island. They were upset with Richard for making a deal to come back. We decided to continue the mobilization effort and go back to the island.

On 20 November 1969, Native American students from the major California colleges and universities arrived with their families to take the island. My sister, Claudene Boyer, and my son, Deynon Means, arrived with this landing party. My oldest son, Devon, was not with me when we went to Alcatraz.

When we arrived on the island and made our way up to the second level, I sensed a wonderful, forbidden excitement among our group. The weather was good and the view spectacular as we set up our lookout points on top of the prison. We camped out in sleeping bags all over the island. It felt great to be there and to direct our energies into a stand for Indian people everywhere.

We took the island because we wanted the federal government to honor our treaties and its own laws. The previous claim had been made back in 1964, so we were the follow-up. We also wanted to focus attention on Indian reservations and communities throughout the nation where our people were living in poverty and suffering great injustice.

The next day, the press and all kinds of people arrived on the island. The international media focus embarrassed the federal government. The United States is always the first to point out human rights violations in other countries, without regard to its own treatment of Native Americans, Blacks, Chicanos, Asians, and poor people. We hoped to expose the atrocities that the federal government has perpetrated and continues to perpetrate against our people. Every day, as news of the island takeover traveled throughout the country, our people kept arriving. We were in full view of the entire world, and the government made no move to take us off the island.

Many people, diverse tribal groups and nonnatives alike, came to visit the island. Some were just now re-identifying as Indians and "wannabe's." We were the tattered remnants of a proud and cultured people— what was left of our once strong and healthy nation. We did not all look or behave like our ancestors, because we were the products of our times. We were finally "civilized Indians," from liars and thieves to genuine Indian chiefs. The government's racist efforts to deny us our heritage and to assimilate us into the American mainstream had backfired with the Alcatraz takeover.

In the weeks to follow, the residents quickly set out to organize the island. Everybody wanted to claim fame and to be included in the formation. I sat back and watched everyone scramble for leadership and for recognition by the media.

We had good leadership. As long as everybody wanted to be involved in the hard work of organization and island logistics, that was great. We had a big job ahead, and everybody was doing what needed to be done. Because I did not intend to drop out of school, I needed to attend to my classes, so I did not want to take on any extra responsibilities unless I had to.

The media identified Richard Oakes as the leader on the island, and he wanted the responsibility, so that was agreeable with us. Richard was smart and aggressive—a handsome Mohawk who always knew what to say. We were proud of Richard. We maintained our student autonomy on the island, recognizing the separate campus organizations and community organizations. The students and their families stayed on the island as long as they could but eventually left to continue their studies.

I continued my residence on the island but kept my apartment on the mainland and commuted to the university to maintain my studies. My sister did not leave the island during most of the occupation. Deynon and I would hitchhike off the docks at Alcatraz and would occasionally catch a sailboat or speedboat to the marina on Sunday afternoon, clean up, and check into my classes.

When the government blocked our water barge and boats from docking on the island, Richard successfully brought in food and provisions on the opposite side of the island, where it was impossible to dock because of the high cliffs. When the government took the water barge away, we brought water over in a boat that Creedence Clearwater Revival bought for us. They bought the boat from "Captain Cliff," whom we hired to take us back and forth from the mainland to the island. We named our boat the *Clearwater*.

Initially, we took up residence in the prison block. It was winter in the Bay Area, and it rained most of the time, but we were able to survive under those conditions, because life was not very different from the poverty on the reservations or in the urban ghettos. It was inconvenient to live on the island without water, electricity, or heat, but most of us became conditioned to the elements. People who were not conditioned to the elements got sick when they stayed.

We formed an island organization called Indians of All Tribes. A lot of rivalry and competition always existed on the island. I sensed that the Indian men did not want to recognize the authority of the women, because they had been assimilated into white society and its male chauvinism.

Everyone had a job on the island—to help on the boats, with the school, or anywhere else they were willing to work. Stella Leach, a registered Indian nurse, and Dr. Tepper had moved out to the island right after the invasion. They operated the first aid unit and provided medical support. Dr. Tepper finally went back to his medical practice in Oakland, but Stella stayed on the island.

Grace Thorpe kept up public relations with the mainland. Sometime later, she bumped heads with the island council and left, but not until after she had helped the Pit River Indians to hold their land in Northern California, which was threatened by Pacific Gas and Electric (PG&E) Company. A group of Alcatraz Indians joined the Pit River Indians to protect their sacred site; in a confrontation with the police, it took nearly

a dozen officers to carry Grace Thorpe off the property.

Richard Oakes was hurt on the mainland during a fight in a bar; he was hit over the head numerous times with a pool stick. He made a miraculous recovery in the hospital, thanks to Thomas Banyacya and an attending group of medicine men (including Mad Bear Anderson) from the Iroquois Confederation, only to face great sadness later. Richard and his family left the island when his daughter Yvonne died after falling four stories in an apartment building in the guards' quarters.

During the occupation, a number of Alcatraz Indians left for Washington State to support the Nisqually Indians, who were fighting for fishing rights at Franks Landing. President Nixon signed a bill that returned the sacred Blue Lake to Taos Pueblo. More funding was appropriated by Congress for programs on the reservations. Indians from Alcatraz supported the Pyramid Lake Paiute people in their efforts to keep their sacred lake. Alcatraz provided help to Indian efforts to establish D-Q University in Davis, California. Alcatraz was a "rock" that hit the water and sent out a thousand ripples: Nearly a thousand documented events resulted from the occupation of Alcatraz.

SPIRITUAL REBIRTH

I took up residence on the second level of a house. My house, which I had painted red, had a beautiful view of the bay, and my room had enough space for my two double beds, like a hotel room. The other bed was for my guests, such as medicine man Pete Mitten and his wife, from New York, who stayed with me during their visit to the island, and Thomas Banyacya and his wife, Fermina.

Thomas Banyacya told me that he had traveled internationally since being appointed as a translator by the chiefs in 1945. After the bombing of Hiroshima, the Hopi had become alarmed at the destructive direction of the United States. According to their rock writings and prophecies, the bomb marked the beginning of a harmful era and had to be stopped somehow by warning as many people as possible of what was to come.

Thomas told me that he and his wife had come to Alcatraz to see for themselves what was happening. In accordance with the Hopi prophecies, the "tree of Indian life" was cut off at the base, but, through the nourishment of the ancient roots, sprouts were growing out of the base of the tree. It was encircled with a design that matched the Bay Area, and the tree growing new sprouts was located where Alcatraz lay in the bay. He said that the young people are the new sprouts growing out of the Indian tree of life. The takeover of Alcatraz symbolized this rebirth.

Thomas told me about the Hopi prophecy. To my understanding, the world had ended three times before this world. It was always the result of misusing modern inventions for destructive purposes instead of for peace. This time, it was not supposed to happen. All people would have the choice of continuing in the destructive direction or coming back to the sacred circle of life and perpetuating the spiritual ways of our forefathers. We need to clean up the earth and the environment now, before the three purifiers come from the east. If the people do not change their ways, the earth will shake to wake up the people. Our ancestors will help us survive through the purification if we maintain our beliefs, practices, and spiritual ways.

My personal experience happened one night while I was asleep in my room. I woke up to see a fire in the curtains. Because I was still half asleep, I did not think; I followed my first instinct, which was to protect my son. I threw myself at the fire and put it out with my hands. There had been two other fires that same night, and the men had just finished battling another blaze on the island. I lived over the dining hall, and the men were downstairs having coffee when I emerged from my room carrying my son, with smoke following behind me.

I handed Deynon over to someone and then fell over. My hands were badly burned, and I had gone into shock. Shock felt good to me, because I felt no pain and it was good to see everyone working together. Several people ran upstairs to see if the fire was out; others rushed to put my hands into cold milk and to carry me to a bed they had assembled in the kitchen. They put my hands into milk because we had no water. There was no boat scheduled until the next day, so they could not take me to the mainland.

They must have suspected arson, because they put me on a cot in the kitchen and guarded me all night. My *eyes* were closed, but my spirit could see everything all around me. It was an experience I'll never forget. I saw Stella sitting by me all night, and I knew when she fell asleep. I knew who looked into the window at me during the night while on guard duty. I remember the first rays of dawn coming over the horizon, and I remember our one rooster crowing. Stella covered me with the Pendleton blanket that my parents had given me. I remembered my mother telling me how to receive spiritual strength from saying her prayers at sunrise. I gathered my blanket around me, slipped out of the kitchen into the yard and over to the edge of the island. I lifted my hands to the sun and prayed as it rose over the Bay Bridge in the east. I experienced a deep knowledge inside me that I would be all right.

Stella Leach, who worked as a nurse on Alcatraz during the occupation, stands in front of the island ten years later, November 1979.

The boat arrived in a few hours, and Stella took me over to Dr. Tepper's office in Oakland. My hands were charred black, and my fingers were huge and swollen like boiled wieners. I had from first- to third-degree burns on both hands. The doctor said they were burned down to the tendons. His medical diagnosis was that I would never be able to use my fingers again.

I refused Dr. Tepper's advice to go to the hospital. He peeled the charred skin off my hands to reveal raw, pink fingers. Then he applied a burn ointment and covered it with bandage dressing. He said it would take six months to a year before I could use my hands. I went back to the island, and, miraculously, my hands healed within six weeks with hardly any trace of scarring. I recovered full use of all my fingers. This was my very first spiritual experience. I had learned what to say by repeating everything my father taught me; I knew what to do by remembering my mother's words of caution and guidance.

The federal government sent Bob Robertson to negotiate with us on the island.

We looked forward to this occasion and were as friendly as possible in order to encourage a good relationship. We did not have much, but we offered him coffee and brownies for this occasion. We did not use sugar, because it attracted insects; instead, we used saccharin in small tablets, which was much more efficient for our living conditions. We asked him if he wanted sugar in his coffee and he said "yes," so we put in saccharin. His report to Washington said that we had put LSD in his coffee and he had refused to drink it. Actually, I never noticed whether he drank his coffee. How paranoid he must have been!

This experience gave me keen insight into how the game of "divide and conquer" is played. Robertson told us he would not work with a "bunch of young militant Indians" who did not have the support of the responsible adult Indian community. We told him we were not militant Indians because we were unarmed.

To further our negotiations to obtain the island for our people, we formed the Bay Area Native American Council (BANAC), composed of all the Bay Area Indian organizations as a support group for Alcatraz. Robertson's first ploy was to fund BANAC, hoping that the Alcatraz residents would resent the government's funding of the off-island organization while the island organization was dependent on contributions. However, this did not cause anyone to blink an eye, because no one knew what it was to be funded in the first place. The money gave BANAC a larger voice in Indian affairs and a more vivid profile.

Next, Allen Miller, a San Francisco State student, and I went to Washington, D.C. to gather more support from the National Congress of American Indians (NCAI). This organization was composed of tribes throughout the country, and we needed their formal support. John Belindo, the NCAI director, was

Oohosis, Cree from Canada, and a friend on the mainland dock on the day of their forced removal from Alcatraz Island, June 11, 1971.

not very receptive. Perhaps Robertson had gotten to him before we did. We were told that it would be up to the delegation. Their national convention was in Alaska, so we had to go to Alaska to seek support.

Bob Robertson was way ahead of us in lobbying against Alcatraz. He knew we had formed BANAC to quash his claim that Alcatraz did not have the support of the responsible adult community. Robertson's propaganda to the tribes was not only that we were young militants but also that we were "urban" Indians. He told the tribes that the urban Indians were after a slice of the "federal economic pie." The reservations were already receiving very little federal funding, and the pie would be sliced even smaller if the tribes supported the militant urban Indians. We could not even get on the agenda, and we were barred from the NCAI convention.

Robertson found adversaries to our cause among various tribal chairmen and established the National Tribal Chairman's Association (NTCA). Thus he created an effective tool to divide Indians against Indians. Tribes fell into the trap. Negotiations on the island disintegrated. The government position was to let us stay, hoping that we eventually would lose support and disappear. To speed the process, they would send out "plants" to observe us and to stir up infighting among the island residents.

The island council appointed me as the island's public relations representative. I started by talking with press people about the island, about our people, and about the reservations. Then I was invited to the mainland to appear on news programs to discuss the island situation.

Several times, the local media reported that the coast guard had seen weapons being loaded on the island. I knew that the federal government was trying to set us up to get killed. When it began to look dangerous for us, I called a press conference on the island to dispel any rumors that we had guns. I had the children line up with their toy guns and throw them away. I said if the coast guard had seen guns, it must have been the children's toys, and now there were none.

I was dead set against guns on the island. My experiences at Berkeley had shown me what happened to the Black Panthers after they were reported to be armed and militant. They were all killed. My mother never allowed guns in our home while I was growing up. She always said that my brothers were too young and hot-headed, so I never had any use for guns. Thomas Banyacya told me that the word *Hopi* meant peace and that our people were the true people of peace. I would not allow the symbolism of Alcatraz to be defiled by violence. Besides, I am a mother, and I would not let anyone endanger my son or the other children on the island.

A San Francisco leftist magazine by the name of *Ramparts* had paid my fine during the Third World Strike at Berkeley. Peter Collier of *Ramparts* asked me if he could take some pictures and do a story about the problems on my reservation. When the story came out, I posed for the cover with a red paintbrush in my hand and the words "Better Red Than Dead." To me, it meant we should be proud of being Native Americans and we should not assimilate and let our culture die. I did not realize I was pushing buttons from the McCarthy era. Since *Ramparts* was not a mainstream magazine, I did not think it would receive wide circulation. I thought speaking out would help create a better understanding, but my words were twisted in the press.

Jane Fonda saw the article and came out to the island. She said she wanted to go to Fort Hall, so I took her to my reservation to meet my parents. After she visited with them and some of my father's friends, she went back to California, inviting me to appear on several local television shows in Los Angeles. My son Deynon and I went to Los Angeles, and then I went to New York for the Dick Cavett Show. Deynon stayed at Henry Fonda's house in California with Jane's husband, Roger Vadim, who remained with their daughter Vanessa and Deynon while Jane and I were in New York.

I had never been on a television show, and it made me feel extremely uncomfortable. During the first commercial break on the Cavett show, I got up and walked off, because I thought I was supposed to leave. I felt awkward, wondering if I was supposed to be witty and funny about the injustices perpetrated against our people.

During this time, after Richard Oakes had left Alcatraz, Stella Leach got fed up with the politics and the constant attacks on her and her family, and she left also. As a member of the Alcatraz council, I had to become more involved, since many of the other members had left.

John Trudell, who ran "Radio Free Alcatraz," became the spokesperson for the island. John had strong leadership qualities and a good speaking voice and always had something meaningful to say. John became the new leader for Alcatraz, and we worked well as a team. I welcomed the opportunity to have John in the spotlight, making the presentations to the media, while I, in the background, prepared the press releases.

It was about this time that I wrote the planning grant proposal for Thunderbird University and Cultural Center, named for a group of Indians in the Bay Area called the

"Thunderbirds." The island chose the architectural firm of McDonald and Associates of San Francisco to develop the design and model. We unveiled our plans on our first anniversary on the island, 20 November 1970.

As the executive secretary of the Bay Area Native American Council (BANAC), I was asked to go to Washington, D.C. with the other officers. Before I left the island, we held a meeting, at which John Trudell became very angry with me and made some rude accusations. I did not want to throw more fuel on the fire by having a confrontation; instead, I rushed down to the docks to catch my boat for the mainland. All of the island residents were aware of the rift.

Ethel Kennedy set up an appointment for me to discuss the Alcatraz situation with Edward Bennett Williams. On 21 January 1971, I wrote a letter to the island, with copies to the island attorneys and BANAC, requesting approval to secure Edward Bennett Williams as legal counsel to pursue the litigative end for Alcatraz.

While in D.C., I stayed with Edgar Cahn, author of *My Brother's Keeper,* and his wife, Jean, who were responsible for many of the poverty and advocacy programs for Native Americans and poor people throughout the country. President Nixon had been elected and was now taking office. Edgar's contact in the White House, Bobby Kilberg, was writing Nixon's inauguration address, which was to be titled the "President's White House Address on American Indians." This message set the tone for programs directed to benefit Indians on reservations throughout President Nixon's administration. The very first and last help we ever received was too short-lived.

When I received no response from the island, I went back to see what was going on. John Trudell told me that the island attorneys had advised him and the other residents not to give approval to litigate.

I wanted to hear what an Indian attorney would recommend and recruited John Echohawk, director of the Native American Rights Fund. Echohawk went to the island and gave his legal opinion that it would greatly benefit the island and the cause if we initiated litigation.

By this time, Trudell's wife, Lou, had given birth to their son Wovoka on the island. The baby was the only Native American born on liberated territory in five hundred years. John had the respect and awe of both the island residents and the non-Indian public. Under the Alcatraz attorneys' advice, the occupiers voted down the litigation. John Trudell could have changed their minds if he had wanted to, but no one could change John's mind about seeking litigation.

I did not give up the litigation issue and went back to the student organizations to seek their support. Richard Oakes had left San Francisco State by then and was living in Northern California with his wife's family and tribe. He was eventually shot to death by white racists. Allen Miller and several of the original Native American students were still attending San Francisco State.

The students at UC Berkeley and San Francisco State were still very concerned about Alcatraz. I told them that the island population was under the influence of the attorneys who had advised against litigation. The island people were down-to-earth, good people who had sacrificed the modern conveniences of the mainland and sometimes went without food in order to "hold the rock." I felt helpless to try to reach them; the divisive gap was just too wide.

The students were very supportive. They decided to take back the island, outnumbering the antilitigation population and putting the movement back on track. I was greatly encouraged by this unselfish gesture. We set the date and met with our groups to arrange for boats to go out to the island. All of the students would take their families to live on the island. It would soon be summer, school would be out, and our academic survival would not be immediately threatened.

The day before we planned to go, the federal government took the remaining people off the island without a confrontation. We were devastated. We suspected that we had had an informer among us.

After the government took Alcatraz back, we all went our separate ways. I guess that is how a tree grows; it splits into many branches. We were always afraid that, if the government had given us Alcatraz, they would have said, "We gave you Alcatraz; you got what you wanted!" They would have expected us to be satisfied with that. No, we want much more.

We want to live as free people in our own country. We want the government to pass laws to respect our Mother Earth, with real enforcement to protect the land, the water, the environment, and the people. We want freedom of religion—the right to be human. We want our ancestors' remains to be returned to our homelands. We want the federal government to stop contributing to the destruction around the world and to set a good example so we can all be proud to be Americans.

The Alcatraz occupation could have gone much more smoothly. People could have cooperated and supported us more. We could have had all the answers and no arguments. We have a long way to go before we can live in a balanced world and be the best people that we can be. We made many mistakes, but this is how we learn and grow.

We can see today that the tree of Indian life is growing stronger, more mature and complex. Our ancient roots continue to give our spirits strength and guidance. We did not get the island, but we aroused the consciousness of all people, including ourselves, to our plight. Every individual and every nation still has a story to be told. Within these stories are our guidelines for the future.

The island is a reminder of our ongoing relationship with the federal government. It is an infamous prison that carries the burden of the wicked deeds of others, the bondage and captivity of our people, the painful stories of human misery and suffering. The federal government has never recognized our claim and has failed to enforce many treaties and federal laws protecting our rights and those of many others.

Under the Department of the Interior, the Bureau of Indian Affairs manages our lives in the same way that Golden Gate Parks and Recreation manages Alcatraz Island. The island is surrounded by the water of the bay, just as we are surrounded by the ignorant and selfish interests of capitalistic industrialized societies. The structures on the island grow old and weatherbeaten, treated with dishonor and disrespect, as are our culture and religion, and the sacred laws of our mother earth.

Today, our people continue to live in poverty—the victims of genocide and injustice. We are political prisoners in our own homelands. We have no individual constitutional protections, because we are considered "political entities." If truth and justice were truly practiced by the federal government, our traditional governments, our religious leaders, and our people would be recognized today. Our hardships have made our spirits grow stronger. We give thanks for our many blessings and pray that the sacred circle of life continues forever.

ROOTS OF CONTEMPORARY NATIVE AMERICAN ACTIVISM

Troy R. Johnson

On 11 June 1971, twenty-five years ago, U.S. government forces reoccupied Alcatraz Island in the San Francisco Bay, ending the Indian occupation of the island that had begun on 20 November 1969. The removal force consisted of ten FBI agents, along with United States marshals from the San Francisco, Sacramento, and San Diego offices, armed with handguns, M-1 thirty-caliber carbines, and shotguns. Supporting the marshals were the federal protective officers, a group that had been formed in April 1971 as a security arm of the General Services Administration (GSA). These officers were equipped with radio transceivers, thirty-eight-caliber revolvers and ammunition, helmets, batons, and flashlights. Only fifteen Indians remained on the island to face this formidable force: six men, four women, and five children. The nineteen-month occupation came to an end.

* * *

Despite its influence, the occupation of Alcatraz Island has largely been overlooked by those who write or speak today of American Indian activism. Much has been written about the battles fought by Indian people for their rights regarding access to hunting and fishing areas reserved by treaties in the states of Washington and Oregon, the continuing struggles for those same rights in Wisconsin and Minnesota, and the efforts of the Six Nations to secure guaranteed treaty rights in the northeastern United States. The 1972 takeover of the Bureau of Indian Affairs (BIA) headquarters in Washington, D.C., and the 1973 occupation of Wounded Knee are well known as well, as is the killing of an Indian man, Joseph Stuntz, and

two FBI agents on the Pine Ridge Reservation in 1975. Yet it is to the occupation of Alcatraz Island twenty-five years ago that one must look to find the genesis of modern-day American Indian activism. The movement began in 1969 and continues to this day.

* * *

In his 1995 autobiography, *Where White Men Fear to Tread,* former AIM leader Russell Means states that "about every admirable quality that remains in today's Indian people is the result of the American Indian Movement's flint striking the white man's steel. In the 1970s and 1980s, we lit a fire across Indian country. We fought for changes in school curricula to eliminate racist lies, and we are winning. We fought for community control of police, and on a few reservations it's now a reality. We fought to instill pride in our songs and in our language, in our cultural wisdom, inspiring a small renaissance in the teaching of our languages. . . . Thanks to AIM, for the first time in this century, Indian people stand at the threshold of freedom and responsibility." It was on Alcatraz, however, that the flint first met the steel and young Indian college students stood toe to toe with the federal government for nineteen months and did not bend.

Troy R. Johnson, excerpts from "Roots of Contemporary Native American Activism," *American Indian Culture and Research Journal,* 20, no. 2 (1996): 128, 129. Copyright © 1994 by the Regents of the University of California. American Indian Studies Center, U.C.L.A. Reprinted with permission.

RIGOBERTA MENCHÚ TUM

"Today, throughout the Americas, people are reflecting deeply about the identity of the indigenous peoples and are starting to take seriously the arguments in favor of pluri-ethnic and multicultural societies. From our diversity will come the true wealth of the Americas.

Even though another millennium is coming to an end without an end to the grave and systematic violations of the rights of indigenous peoples, we have not given up hope on our struggle to establish a new basis for social relations, based on justice, equality, and mutual respect between our peoples and cultures....

After so many years of struggle, this period seems to be the end of five hundred years of injustice, five hundred years of night. We are moving into the light of a new era for our peoples. After so many years of waiting for a new dawn, we believe that our voices will make themselves heard, that you will listen to us, and support our legitimate aspirations."

From the Foreword by Rigoberta Menchú Tum in *Return of the Indian,* by Phillip Wearne (Temple University Press, 1996). (See *I, Rigoberta Menchú,* edited by Burgos-Dubray, in the Suggested Readings.)

Rigoberta Menchú Tum, recipient of the 1992 Nobel Peace Prize. She is a leader of the Guatemalan Indian struggle.

HAWAIIAN LANGUAGE SCHOOLS

Leanne Hinton

. . . Last fall I made my first-ever trip to Hawai'i, and spent three fascinating days touring the Hawaiian Pūnana Leo (preschools) and Kula Kaiapuni Hawai'i (the elementary and high schools), where the Hawaiian language is the language of instruction in all grades. This program, creating a new generation of fluent speakers and thus saving the Hawaiian language from extinction, is by far the most ambitious and advanced language revitalization program in the United States, and has much to teach the rest of us.

HISTORY OF HAWAIIAN LANGUAGE LOSS

Hawai'i, our newest state, was an independent monarchy until the end of the 19th century. The loss of Hawaiian independence began in 1887, when a group of businessmen with ties to the United States and the support of American troops established the "Bayonette Constitution." In 1893, Queen Liliuokalani was deposed, again with the support of American marines. In 1898 the "Republic" of Hawai'i was set up, and soon after that it was annexed to the United States. The Hawaiian people thus lost their power and autonomy.

"Hawaiian Language Schools," by Leanne Hinton, *News from Native California*, 10:4 (Summer 1997). Reprinted with permission of the author. Portions of the original and notes have been omitted.

As for the language, until the political events that led to annexation, Hawaiian was not only the primary language of the islands, but also the main language of the schools. Hawai'i created the first high school west of the Rockies (taught in Hawaiian), and the literacy rate (in Hawaiian) was among the highest in the world. The Hawaiian people had long been aware of the advantages that knowing English could give, and strong efforts had been made by the royal family to give Hawaiians the opportunity to learn English. In fact, in the late 19th century, the Hawaiian princess Pauahi founded the Kamehameha schools, prestigious private schools that can only be attended by children of Hawaiian ancestry. The schools were initiated with English as the language of instruction, so that Hawaiian children would learn to speak that language of such economic importance.

But once the control of Hawai'i was lost to its people, a problem not foreseen by the royal family occurred: it was now the Hawaiian language that children had no opportunity to learn. The story is a variation on a theme well known to Native Californians. The Bayonette Constitution cut out funds for Hawaiian-language education, and finally, English-only legislation in 1896 closed down the Hawaiian-language schools completely. Teachers visited homes to tell the parents not to speak Hawaiian to their children, one of the many factors that soon led to the loss of

Hawaiian even as the language of the home. Out of a population of 200,000 people of Hawaiian heritage, the 1990 census lists less than 9,000 speakers, almost all elderly. (There is one exception to this trend: on the tiny island of Ni'ihau, privately owned and closed to the public, Hawaiian is still spoken natively by all age groups and used as the language of daily communication among the two hundred people there.)

LANGUAGE IMMERSION SCHOOLS

The 'Aha Pūnana Leo was established in 1983 by a small group of educators determined to have their own children and those of other interested families educated in the Hawaiian language. A few of these families had also made the decision to use Hawaiian as the language of their home (even though they themselves knew Hawaiian only as a second language). They developed a series of preschools inspired by the Maori "Language Nest" model, where no English would be used in the classroom, and all education would take place in the Hawaiian language. Once the lead-group was old enough, Hawaiian-language classrooms were established in the public schools. The Pūnana Leo actually began while it was still illegal to use Hawaiian in the schools. It took a three-year campaign at the state legislature by parents and community members to change the laws, thus ending eighty years of outlaw status for the language. From the small beginning of a single preschool, 'Aha Pūnana Leo has grown to have nine preschools scattered among the islands; there are also a public laboratory high school outside of Hilo, thirteen public elementary schools that have Hawaiian-language tracks, and even one K-12 public school that has all-Hawaiian instruction (Ānuenue School near Honolulu).

I had the opportunity to visit several schools on O'ahu and Hawai'i in November 1996. I will try to write about my experiences here more or less in the order that I experienced them.

THE ADVENTURE BEGINS

Hawai'i—my first visit to this state that doesn't seem like part of the United States at all, because it's too far away, too exotic, too fragrant with tropical flowers. It's November, close to Thanksgiving. I have spent a couple of days with my family visiting old friends in Kawaihae, where they have a bamboo farm, and I have become happily accustomed to the pleasant tropical breezes wafting through their beautiful indoor-outdoor house. I have not previously been able to make contact with any of the schools I want to visit, but after speaking with a long chain of friends and friends of friends, the right person is contacted at last. Nāmaka Rawlins, director of the 'Aha Pūnana Leo, gives me permission to visit the schools, and a wonderful adventure begins. I leave my family exploring the beaches and volcanoes of Hawai'i without me, and head off.

WAIMEA PUBLIC SCHOOL

My first visit is to the combined kindergarten/first grade class at Waimea Public School. I come into the spacious, comfortable classroom during lunch break and introduce myself to Kumu Iakona, the head teacher (*Kumu* is a title of address meaning teacher), who makes me feel welcome. The room has a set of low tables with several children's chairs around each. There is also a big rug at the front of the schoolroom, where the class spends most of their time when they are not doing individual projects. Around the walls are numbers, the alphabet, and captioned pictures, all in Hawaiian. Even the screen on the computer shows all Hawaiian words; when I glance at it, it is showing a Hawaiian-language home page on the Internet.

There are many books around the classroom. The one that captures my attention is out on a table for teacher use: the 1995 edition of *Puke Hua'Ōlelo' Mānaka Kaiao—New Words*. This bilingual dictionary, with a new edition put out every couple of years, is the most important language reference work for teachers in the schools. In order to teach all the subjects that must be taught, thousands of new words have to be developed that were never uttered in Hawaiian before. A quick look through the dictionary shows new Hawaiian words for such concepts as electric current, bank account, jet stream, interactive (computer), fax, and pogo stick. Kumu Iakona explains to me that there is a Lexicon Committee that gets together every month in Hilo to make up new words or accept new words sent in by teachers from all over the islands. It is important for all of the schools to use the same new words, rather than making up their own, because the new words will be in books and curriculum materials developed centrally in Hilo and sent out to all the schools. Still, sometimes different islands have their own words—for example, a type of edible sea urchin is *hā'uke'uke* on the island of Hawai'i, *hā'ue'ue* on Maui, and *hā'kue'kue* on Ni'ihau. Ni'ihau, the one place where Hawaiian is the medium of communication for all topics, has coined many of the words that are now in the new words dictionary.

Kula Kaiapuni Hawai'i, the name of the Hawaiian language immersion schools, is a new phrase—*Kula* is from English "school" and has been a part of the language since the early 19th century, but *Kaiapuni* is a new word meaning environment.

In a few minutes the kids come in—about fifteen of them—accompanied by another teacher, who turns out to be a parent helper named Pualani Colburn. All the schools I will visit have parent volunteers helping actively; family involvement is one of the keys to success in the Hawaiian language program. The children sit down on the rug at the front of the schoolroom. They talk quietly until everyone has settled in, and then the teachers begin the session with a Hawaiian song accompanied by percussion on an *ipu* (a gourd instrument), and the children get up and dance to it. Hawaiian music and dance are a very important part of the curriculum at all grade levels. The dances often tell stories, with the beautiful hand and arm movements being a kind of sign language.

The song and dance focus the attention of the class and unite them. When the song is over, one girl comes up with objects and coupons in an envelope. From the back of the room, and with no English being spoken, I can't tell what they are—but I know it is show-and-tell time. The teacher describes the objects and starts a discussion. The whole discussion takes place in Hawaiian, even though not all the children are fluent yet. While some of them have a couple of years of Hawaiian language education at preschool, others started learning Hawaiian only about two months ago when the school year began. Some of the kids seem to be thinking about how to say what they want to say, and the teachers encourage them, saying, "And then what?" (in Hawaiian, of course), or providing a word or phrase. At one point, the children get to talking about Rudolf the Red-Nosed Reindeer. Between Rudolf and the subsequent discussion of Thanksgiving, I know I must still be in the United States after all.

The discussion turns to the coming holiday: the English word "Thanksgiving" is uttered by a few students. The teachers tell the class the Hawaiian way to say it: *La Ho'omaika'i*. Later, No'eau Warner, one of the founders of the movement, tells me that when first starting to set policy, they discussed whether to reprimand children for speaking English, as their grandparents had been reprimanded for speaking Hawaiian. The psychological damage inflicted by that old policy was obvious, and they decided that when a child spoke English, the teachers would just answer in Hawaiian, possibly repeating in Hawaiian what the child had said, for the child's benefit. This policy works well—there are a lot of happy, talkative children here, speaking fluent Hawaiian or on their way to it.

One teacher sets up a table while the other continues the class discussion. A student comes to the teacher who is setting up the table and describes how sore her loose tooth is making her mouth, all in Hawaiian. Pretty soon I understand what the teacher is setting up—she is putting dabs of toothpaste on paper towels for the students to use. Two by two, the students get their toothbrushes and come to brush their teeth while the others watch a Hawaiian-language video about traditional food preparation.

A FEW ABBREVIATIONS IN HAWAIIAN

kk	for *kuaka* "quart"
klk	for *Kelekia* "Celsius"
klkal	for *kilokalame* "kilogram"
kp	for *kapua'i* "foot"

During the video and toothbrushing, Kumu Iakona tells me about how they help parents learn the Hawaiian language, sending them a sheet every week with words and phrases they can use with their kids at home. This week's sheet is based on the word *'ōlelo* "to speak":

'ōlelo hou
to repeat

e 'ōlelo Hawai'i kākou!
Let's all speak Hawaiian! (us inclusive, three or more)

he aha kāna 'olelo?
What did he/she say?

hiki iā 'oe ke 'ōlelo hou?
Can you say it again?

The feeling in this room—like all the schools I visit—is warm, nurturing, and relaxed. I would love to stay all day, but all too soon it is time to leave, for I have another stop to make—the Waimea Preschool, about eight miles outside of town.

WAIMEA PRESCHOOL

At the preschool, the children are napping—a disappointment to me! But it gives me a chance to look around and talk with the teachers and parent helpers. This preschool opened in 1995. The preschools are private, not part of the public school system; and it is the parents and local educators who must have the vision and do most of the work to begin a preschool, finding the site and the funding themselves. Once all the local arrangements are made, the 'Aha Pūnana Leo, centered in Hilo, will train the teachers and provide the curriculum. The vision for this school started in 1990. It took five years of hard work and planning before it could open.

The teachers and parent volunteers here—as in all the schools I visited—are warmly enthusiastic about their work and deeply dedicated to the survival of Hawaiian language and culture. They admit to being what they tell me are called "university speakers," having learned their language in the college classroom. And it is here that I first hear of some of the inevitable conflict that comes with language revitalization: lots of the *kūpuna*—the Hawaiian word for elders—really don't like to hear the language spoken that way, the teachers tell me.

Later I will learn more about this conflict: there are two ways in which university speech differs most obviously from the speech of the kūpuna—one is in intonation, and the other is vocabulary. I see that dictionary of new words in a prominent place in every classroom I visit. There is a much larger dictionary in existence of traditional vocabulary, but it is the new words that the teachers need most in the classroom. If so much of the vocabulary learned by the children consists of new words made up in the last ten years, the kūpuna must sometimes feel that they are hearing a foreign language!

The teachers tell me about a few activities that take place in a typical day in the Pūnana Leo. They open and close the day with a traditional song and prayer, and the same before lunch. Singing, the teachers tell me, is the most important activity in the school; the children pick up more Hawaiian language through singing than through any other activity, and once you start singing you have their complete attention.

Many different things can happen at the Pūnana Leo—sometimes the kūpuna will come in to talk or show the kids how to make things. Sometimes special activities are planned. But always, in the morning after the prayer, there is work with the calendar and the weather. A child is asked each day to go look out the door and then come tell the class what the weather is like. Is it sunny? Raining? Foggy? (Weather changes so quickly in Hawai'i that it may have changed since the children got to school.) I can see around the walls the evidence of other activities the children engage in: there are pictures colored by the children, with Hawaiian labels printed laboriously by three- and four-year-old hands just learning to write; photographic posters with small colored circles and squares stuck to them (this looks like language practice, where children are told "put the orange circle on the milk"); Hawaiian-language books, including some old favorites such as *The Little Engine That Could*, with the Hawaiian version printed on labels and past-ed over the English text; and of course a giant collection of musical instruments—sticks, rattles, gourd drums, and clapper sticks of all shapes and sizes.

The family base is the most important feature of the Pūnana Leo. Those books are made up by the parents, who receive the labels bearing the Hawaiian versions from Hilo and then paste them into the books. A very beautiful, large set of brightly colored building blocks is in one corner—one of the fathers made it. Parents must volunteer eight hours a month in the classroom; they clean and disinfect toys, help the teachers during classes, and make learning materials and toys. They also attend a once-a-week, two-hour evening class in Hawaiian, where they learn things they can say to their kids, in school or at home. They have all been taught the meaning of the Hawaiian-language signs around the classroom. A teacher translated one of them for me:

> *E'olu'olu*
> *E wehe i nā kāma'a*
> *Mahalo!*
> Please remove your shoes—thank you!

Finally it is time for the children to wake up. The teachers wander about the room among the mats that the children are sleeping on, calling out gently, *"E ala mai"* (wake up). While this is going on, one teacher puts on a tape of a group singing a Hawaiian song with *"E ala mai"* in the chorus. The children sleepily put away their bedding and then come to the rug and sit down, yawning. A story book is read to them as they wake up. Much as I wish I could stay longer, I must leave: two of the teachers are giving me a ride to Hilo.

Throughout my trip in Hawai'i I hear English and what the Hawaiians call Pidgin—an English-based creole—everywhere except in these special schools. Most of the time, teachers and the more dedicated parents who have sent their children to the Pūnana Leo speak to each other only in Hawaiian. This is important for people trying to save endangered languages: people who know the language have to make a commitment to speak it to each other, and not be tempted back to English by the presence of English speakers in the conversation. Thus, on the drive to Hilo, my hosts speak to me in English but to each other always in Hawaiian. Through such discipline, the language begins to make its way back into public again.

UNIVERSITY OF HAWAI'I AT HILO

Bill (Pila) Wilson, one of the leaders of the Hawaiian language program at the University of Hawai'i at Hilo, meets me in Hilo. He puts me under the charge of one of the students, Ola, who shows me the workroom for the Hawaiian language program. She shows me the program ClarisWorks, all in Hawaiian—they have an agreement with the company that if they buy a copy of the English version, they get the Hawaiian version with it for free. Ola runs the Hawaiian language newspaper on campus, named *Nā Maka O Kana,* The Eyes of Kana (Kana is a demigod who can stretch his body to reach all the islands). It was founded for the immersion schools, and goes to students, parents, and teachers from preschool to college level. Four thousand copies per month are printed, with one of the immersion schools featured each month. This month's issue also includes information on making Christmas decorations and a serialized portion of the story of Kana.

The workroom and nearby storerooms also house some important archives—Hawaiian-language newspapers from the 19th and early 20th century, used for developing materials for history classes; and fifteen years' worth of a weekly radio show ("Ka Leo Hawai'i," hosted by Larry Kimura,

another leader of the Hawaiian language movement and a professor at Hilo) that aired from 1972 to 1989 and consisted of interviews of Hawaiian native speakers. This is the largest collection of native Hawaiian in existence, and is used a great deal in advanced Hawaiian classes. There is also a collection of videos on Hawaiian culture, all in the Hawaiian language, and copies of the books being produced or translated at a feverish rate for the schools. I see translated copies of *Charlotte's Web, Island of the Blue Dolphins,* and other popular children's books that are state-required reading in the public elementary schools. Other books are traditional Hawaiian literature collected and produced for Hawaiian language arts classes.

The University of Hawai'i (at Hilo and at Mānoa) trains all the teachers who teach in the immersion schools; most of them did not know the Hawaiian language until college age. At the University you can take beginners' through advanced Hawaiian language classes, Hawaiian linguistics, Hawaiian history, and Hawaiian cultural studies such as fish net making, hula, and chant (*oli*). Here you learn vocal styles (high, low, and vibrating), composition, different Hawaiian song types, and *kaona*—metaphor and indirectness—two of the most important literary devices in Hawaiian song. A new master's program in Hawaiian studies, due to begin in fall 1997, will be taught entirely in the Hawaiian language. Teacher certification, which used to be done only in English, will now be done in the Hawaiian language as well.

A HAWAIIAN-SPEAKING HOME

In the evening, Pila and his children Hulilau (tenth grader) and Keli'i (eighth grader) take me out to dinner. At my request we go to a cafe that serves poi (even though it is mainly a Chinese restaurant), so that I can try that traditional Hawaiian food. (I love it!) Hulilau and Keli'i are fine young people, responsible and articulate, with a strong social awareness. They both go to the Hawaiian-language high school in Hilo, Nāwahīokalani'ōpu'u, named after a famous Hawaiian, Joseph K. Nawahī. After supper we go to their home, where I have been invited to spend the night. We arrive about the same time as Pila's wife, Kauanoe Kamanā, who is the senior teacher at the high school. This is one of the first families to decide to run an entirely Hawaiian-speaking household. In the same pattern I have found in the schools and on my car trips, they speak only Hawaiian to each other at all times. To me, they will speak English, but they do not accommodate to my presence when speaking to each other. Nevertheless, I never feel excluded. During family conversations, one of the children will turn to me from time to time to translate; and in the morning when the family sits in a circle to read from the Hawaiian-language Bible, I am invited to sit with them and try reading a paragraph myself.

This consistency in speaking only Hawaiian to each other is one of the most important habits to form for language revitalization. Endangered languages often lose out to English (or other dominant languages) when, because someone in the household does not speak the endangered language, the rest of the household switches to English. The threatened language loses its final stronghold, and the children growing up there will not learn to speak it.

NĀWAHĪOKALANI'ŌPU'U HIGH SCHOOL

The next morning we all head out to the high school after a breakfast of Hawaiian pancakes. The school has 48 teenagers attending, with fifteen teachers (seven full-time). My poor daughter is in a California high school with a much different teacher-student ratio, and I am jealous! A sizable number of the children went to the same Pūnana Leo preschool and have known each other throughout their education. The tenth-graders are the "lead class," the group from the very first year of the founding of the Pūnana Leo. Right now, of course, because the program is still young, the tenth-graders are the oldest children in the school. The school is preparing for them to become eleventh-graders, and then twelfth—the curriculum is being prepared right now at Hilo. And the school is growing—each year it will have more students.

At 7:40 A.M., one of the seventh graders blows the conch shell. The traditional Hawaiian instrument for the call to assembly is used at the school instead of a buzzer. The students enter the assembly room and sit on wooden benches, while Pila escorts me to a bench on the side. After the morning chant, Pila introduces me, and then a student sings for me, as a guest of the school, a welcoming chant and presents me with a lei. (This is the third time that I have been "lei-ed" this trip; I find myself completely charmed. At Pila and Kauanoe's home, I saw dried leis hanging over baby pictures of their children. I saved my leis too, and they hang now in a place of honor at home in Berkeley.) After that, the students go to their classes, and I am invited to wander about and watch. The most memorable period is spent observing Kauanoe herself give a lesson in traditional chant to the seventh graders. She tells me that chanting almost disappeared in Hawai'i under the hostility of missionaries and the government; but she learned it later in life as it was preserved by some teachers of hula, and now through her classes (as well as classes elsewhere), traditional chant is coming back alive. She teaches the students how to chant in a very strong, full voice. Today she is teaching a chant from the old traditional literature, the voice of a goddess singing, "I am standing here on the bank on one side. I've been waiting a long time, I want to cross over. I have great longing to cross. It's cold, it's cold here, it's cold and damp."

At the high school, some classes are taught in English—including, ironically, the Japanese foreign language class, whose teacher does not speak Hawaiian. 'Aha Pūnana Leo recognizes the need for having some education in English. Despite the new Hawaiian-language master's program in Hawaiian studies at the university, it is understood that most of these children will receive much or all of their university education in English. It is not the goal of the parents and teachers to see all their children major in Hawaiian studies. As Pila says, they want these children to become doctors, or lawyers, or storekeepers, or carpenters—they want the Hawaiian language to spread into all walks of life in Hawai'i, so that doctors, nurses, and their patients, storekeepers and their customers, will talk to each other in Hawaiian.

I also get to see the main office, located at the high school, where Hawaiian-language materials and books are produced. Books of all kinds are in boxes ready to ship out to the schools. This is also where the labels for converting books to Hawaiian are produced. In another room there is state-of-the-art computer and video equipment for the production of educational videos.

PŪNANA LEO O HILO

My last visit on the island of Hawai'i is to one more preschool, Pūnana Leo o Hilo, the first Pūnana Leo school on the island. Here I feel like I already know many of the staff, for they are all on a video about the Hawaiian language program that I show regularly to my classes in Berkeley. I meet Nāmaka Rawlins, the director of the whole wonderful Pūnana Leo program, who first gave me permission to begin this odyssey. Nā'ilima Gaison, the head teacher, is telling a story to the children, full of songs and dance-like hand motions which the children do along with him. His expressiveness and the raptness of his students mark him as a master storyteller. Later he explains the curriculum to me. The daily routine goes like this:

7:15	Snack
8:30	Exercise
9:00	First circle
9:15	Class
10:00	Second circle
10:30	Playtime and structured activities
11:30	Lunch
12:30	Nap
2:30	Art
3:00	Story
3:15	Snack
3:30–5:00	Play and structured activities, while parents start coming to take the children home

Nā'ilima also explains the curriculum, which progresses from the self in ever-widening circles: self, family, school, community, the island, Hawai'i, the world.

I can't help but notice that "the United States" is not one of the levels mentioned. Hawai'i is culturally and ecologically distinct from the other states. More tourists visit Hawai'i from Asia than from the U.S. mainland. The Nāwahi High School kids have to take a foreign language, and the one that is taught at the high school is Japanese. And we must remember that it was just about a century ago that political power was wrested from the hands of the Hawaiian queen, and Hawaiians are justifiably bitter about the loss of their independence.

Nā'ilima explains some of the different circles: for the "self," the children learn body parts, hygiene, basic needs, and concepts of independence. "Family" includes the whole extended family, and cultural values such as helping, respect, and giving thanks. "Community" is about different places, safety, transportation, and community helpers. For "the island," they learn about the land and sea, plants, animals, and weather. For Hawai'i, they learn about famous people, the history of the state, multi-ethnic culture, and current events. For "the world," they learn about world history, culture and events, and about how Hawai'i fits into the world as a whole.

It is here at the Pūnana Leo o Hilo that the California connection comes into focus. First of all, I ask Nā'ilima if he knows Cody Pata, a young Nomlaki man who came to Hawai'i as a teenager and spent several years learning the language and teaching in the Pūnana Leo. "Oh, Pueo!" says Nā'ilima, revealing Cody's Hawaiian name. "Yes, he worked with us. How's he doing?" Also, here and at the high school, I meet again the wonderful ladies who came to California a few years ago for a language conference: Ululani Morales, 'Ekelela Aiona, Ō'pūlani Alkino, Leilani Camara, Wailana Purdy Ka'ai, Kaleihōkū Kala'i, and lastly, Lolena Nicholas, a native speaker from Ni'ihau.

Hilo is not the only place on the islands where language action is going on; there are Pūnana Leo and elementary schools on several other islands as well. On O'ahu, there is even a Hawaiian immersion public school that goes from kindergarten through the twelfth grade (well, tenth grade right now, and heading to twelfth as the lead group matures). I fly from the island of Hawai'i back to O'ahu after visiting Pūnana Leo o Hilo, and have supper in Honolulu that night with several of the faculty of the University of Hawai'i at Mānoa, who are also key in the Hawaiian language movement—No'eau Warner, Laiana Wang and his family, and

Kathy Davis, a colleague of theirs in the ESL department. Laiana tells me about a grant they have received recently from the Administration for Native Americans to bring the language beyond the schools into daily community life. They are planning recreational activities like cookouts and a volleyball series, where the Hawaiian language will be used while having fun.

ĀNUENUE PUBLIC SCHOOL

Through No'eau's help, I am able to go the next day to Ānuenue School, the K-12 public school where Hawaiian is spoken in all the classrooms. *Ānuenue* means rainbow, and appropriately, there is a beautiful rainbow over the school as I drive up. I am just in time for the morning chant, which the children sing in the schoolyard. After checking in at the office, I visit a first-grade class. Roll is called, and as their names are called the children come, one by one, to sit on the floor at the front of the room. One child seems to be the teacher of the moment: he points to the calendar and asks what day of the week it is, and then points to each day of the month and the children count the days all the way to today: November 27th. This kid is a good teacher. He asks all kinds of questions I can't follow, but the other children know exactly what is being asked and answer clearly in chorus. Then the grownup teacher, who has been observing from the back of the room, comes to the front and starts asking more questions. She has the children count the number of boys and the number of girls in the room (six of each), and then has them add the two to find out how many students there are altogether. She has them count by fives. Once the math session is over, the class launches into a discussion of the *Mayflower,* the pilgrims, and the origin of Thanksgiving. And again, all of this, throughout the morning, is in Hawaiian.

After a while the teacher sends the children off to get pencils and clipboards, and gives them pictures of the *Mayflower* and other Thanksgiving themes to color. She writes some sentences on the board for the children to copy under their pictures.

I wander off to the kindergarten room, where the children are in their circle, discussing different kinds of fruits. Then they go to their desks—each child has his own desk, but they are linked in groups of six. They get their crayons from their cubbyholes and start coloring pictures of fruits that their teacher has handed out. Some children finish their pictures, and the teacher gives them folders of another project they have already started—the familiar Thanksgiving turkey with cutouts of the children's own hands for tails. One child starts humming "Jingle Bells" (the spirit of Christmas season seems to be just as strong here as elsewhere), and pretty soon he starts singing it softly, using Hawaiian words. Other children join in as they color, and after a while there are at least six children singing "Jingle Bells" in Hawaiian. As they color, I look around to see what is on the walls. Two things catch my attention: one is a poster with the numbers written like this:

Numbers	Nāhelu
1	ʻekahi
2	ʻelua
3	ʻekolu
4	ʻehā
5	ʻelima
6	ʻeono
7	ʻehiku
8	ʻewalu
9	ʻeiwa
10	ʻumi

Another is a "weather circle," a large cutout circle on the wall in four quadrants: rain, sun, clouds, and wind. Each day at circle time, they put a dot-sticker on the appropriate weather, and at the end of the month they can see how many days were rainy, how many were sunny, and so on.

Next I go to the seventh-grade room, where the children are studying Native Americans. There are world maps with pointers to the Aztec, Maya, and Inca taped on. Another map focuses on the Pacific and has arrows pointing from the South Pacific islands to Hawaiʻi along the path of migration.

I make quick stops at other rooms, and tarry longest in the science classroom, where Mahakoa Lujan teaches science. He is obviously a talented and charismatic teacher, and the students love him. He talks with me at some length about the science curriculum, and shows me a fine set of Hawaiian-language books showing general science centered around the Hawaiian Islands— meteorology, marine and terrestrial wildlife, oceanography. Once again the issue of new words comes up. Mahakoa tells me his ideas about how new words ought to be designed, citing "explanatory value" as the most important principle. He points out a poorly designed word: the word for carbon dioxide, which was merely given a Hawaiianized pronunciation: *karabona diokesaside*, or its even more Hawaiianized variant *kalapona kiokekakike*. The original word in English (based on Latin roots) clearly shows that there are two (di-) oxygen molecules to one carbon, and Mahakoa thinks the Hawaiian word ought to be similarly explanatory.

Mahakoa's viewpoint is part of an ongoing debate in the Lexicon Committee about scientific terminology in general. One school of thought is to invent individual Hawaiian terms based generally on Hawaiian morphemes, as is done with other words. The other school of thought asserts that this is a unique set of international terms that scientists use in all languages, with the speakers of each language modifying them slightly to meet their pronunciation and writing traditions. Proponents of the second school of thought also argue that there are so many of these terms, and they are being invented at such a rapid pace, that Hawai'i cannot keep up with inventing new words for them. It would also be a major problem for science teachers to have to commit all these new words to memory, whereas simply committing the international terms to Hawaiianized pronunciation can be done readily and even spontaneously.

At lunch I talk with a number of ninth and tenth graders, including 'Ānela Lopez, tenth grader and student council president. When I ask this outgoing, intelligent deep thinker about her college plans, she replies "University of Hawai'i" without hesitation. "Why would I ever want to leave my beautiful Hawai'i?"

I talk with her, as I have with other tenth graders, about their thoughts on the Hawaiian language. I have heard children, especially those of high-school age, talking a great deal of English (or sometimes Pidgin) to each other. There are at least two theories given to me about why the children do this—probably both of them correct. One is that the kids who went to public schools, even if they were in Hawaiian language classrooms, got into the habit of using English with their non-Hawaiian-speaking friends on the playground, and this habit then transferred over to the Hawaiian-speaking kids as well. The other theory is that the teens talk English to each other as a kind of teen rebellion, to point out their growing independence from the older generation of people who have been running their schools and lives. In either case the question is, what does this usage of English portend for the future of Hawaiian? Despite this practice of speaking English to each other frequently, everyone said "Hawaiian, of course" when I asked what language they thought they would speak when they married and had children.

One of my colleagues is fond of saying that the future of a language lies in whether the teenagers are using it with each other; whatever they speak to each other will become the language of their future homes. But I realized after talking with these teenagers that it is not that simple. One might wonder how many of these children will really end up speaking Hawaiian in the home—certainly many obstacles will be in the way. But in case of doubt, it is important to remember that some of these children have grown up in households where their parents committed to using Hawaiian as the language of the home, even when they didn't learn it until they were college age. Thus these children have a model of conscious decision making about the home language, and will probably use this model themselves. But the decision will be theirs: each generation will have to make its own decision, and each generation is sure to view the situation differently from the preceding one. Some of the high school students I spoke with fear that their knowledge of English is inadequate for good college-level writing. Perhaps they will find that it is not a problem after all when they attend college; but if it is, it may well be that they will want their children to have a better education in English. Perhaps, once Hawaiian is well established in the home, the next generation will experiment with a model that is closer to bilingual education, aimed at a thorough education in both languages. It is impossible to tell now what these children will decide, but I am looking forward to finding out!

FINAL REMARKS

The Hawaiian language immersion program is by far the most successful language revitalization program I have seen in the United

States—indeed, it is one of the three or four major success stories in the world. Like anything else that involves a group of people, it has problems: in this case, factionalization, controversy over language modernization, and constant battles with state agencies.

Right now, one big problem is determining who gets to attend the Hawaiian-language classrooms in the public schools. Many families want their children in this program, not only because of the Hawaiian language and culture, but because of positive academic and social aspects of the program. The state wants a lottery system to decide who gets to attend the Hawaiian immersion classes. This would mean that children who attend the Pūnana Leo preschools could find themselves displaced by English-speaking children when they get to public school. Leaders in the Hawaiian language movement take the view that everyone is welcome, but that children who enter school already speaking Hawaiian and using it at home should have the first priority, with others included if there is room. They argue that Hawaiian-speaking children today are just as likely to lose the language when put into English-speaking classrooms as their elders were. They also note that families who have not already begun to support Hawaiian language use in the home before kindergarten are much less likely to support full use of the language in the home, community, and even the school.

The tough, brave people I met will fight this one through, and will then come up against other problems. But their persistence has created a great program, and it has created a fine future for their language. As Pila said to me, "If we hesitated every time something became controversial, we wouldn't get anywhere."

MAYA INDIAN REBELLION:
CHRONOLOGY OF IMPORTANT EVENTS

1524—Spanish conquistadors sent by Hernando Cortez invade the Mayan lands of present-day Chiapas, Guatemala, and Honduras. The Spanish set up their colonial government. Mayan uprisings continued periodically in the 1600s, 1700s, and the 1850s with the "Caste Wars."

1910–1920—The Mexican Revolution sweeps Mexico, bringing profound changes. However, it largely misses the states of Chiapas and the Yucatan Peninsula. The 1917 Constitution, Article 27, guarantees the rights of "campesinos" (who are mostly Indigenous) to their communal lands. It forbids their division and sale, particularly to foreign interests.

1992—President Carlos Salinas, in order to satisfy United States demands to "open up Mexico" for North American Free Trade Agreement, pushes through a "reform" to the Mexican Constitution which essentially eliminates Article 27. A land rush by corrupt officials and corporations begins a wave of violence in the Mexican countryside. Indigenous lands are stolen to be sold to U.S. corporations.

Jan. 1, 1994—NAFTA goes into effect. The EZLN (Zapatista Army of National Liberation) stages an uprising of Mayan people in the state of Chiapas. Violence continues for 12 days before a cease fire is agreed upon.

February 1994—Peace talks begin between the EZLN and the Mexican government in Christobal de las Casas, Chiapas.

February 1995—Under orders from President Ernesto Zedillo, the Mexican Army breaks the cease fire while still negotiating and stages a surprise attack on Zapatista communities. After several days of creating havoc with Indigenous people, but failing to defeat the EZLN, the offensive stops and the government agrees to return to the negotiating table. However, the offensive has allowed the Federal Army to set up military bases around many indigenous communities.

February 1996—The Federal government, the EZLN, and representatives of many Indigenous peoples throughout Mexico sign the San Andres Accords on Indigenous Rights and Culture. This accord grants many rights to Indigenous people regarding their land, language and culture. Peace looks possible at this point.

September 1996—After President Ernesto Zedillo declares that he will not honor the San Andres Accords, but will offer his own "initiative on Indigenous rights," the Zapatistas break off negotiations citing the bad faith of the government.

December 1996—Zapatistas begin their own campaign to implement the San Andres Accords by setting up Autonomous Municipalities throughout the highlands and Lacandon regions of Chiapas.

Spring 1997—Paramilitary groups, working with the military and State Security Police begin their counterinsurgency campaign. They attack Indigenous villages, assassinating numerous people.

Dec. 22, 1997—The paramilitary campaign culminates in the Acteal Massacre of 45 Tzotzil people, mostly women and children. Mexico is condemned internationally. While some of the assassins are jailed, the military uses the incident to justify further militarization.

January 1998—More communities are invaded by the Mexican Army. A confrontation in Ocosingo results in a Tzeltal woman being killed by the Army.

During the rest of 1998 the incursions by the military continue. More military bases are constructed. Mediators from the Catholic Church declare the peace process is dead due to the bad-faith actions of the Mexican government.

August 1999—The paramilitaries and the Army begin openly cooperating again. The government increases its military pressure on the EZLN by attempting to build a road through the heart of the Lacandon jungle.

Aug. 12–17, 1999—The military occupies the village of Amador Hernandez where EZLN sympathizers oppose the road. The village remains surrounded.

Aug. 25, 1999—The federal army attacks the village of San Jose La Esperanza wounding two villagers. The people of the region are expecting an assault by the Mexican military against Indigenous communities that support the EZLN.

From "Chronology of Maya Indian Rebellion in Chiapas, Mexico," *Indian Country Today* (September 13–20, 1999). Reprinted by permission of Indian Country Today.

A "NEW PARTNERSHIP" FOR INDIGENOUS PEOPLES
CAN THE UNITED NATIONS MAKE A DIFFERENCE?

Russel Lawrence Barsh

In December 1991, the United Nations General Assembly unanimously agreed that the International Year for the World's Indigenous People should begin in autumn 1992, with the official theme, "A New Partnership." After the vote, a spokesman for the Caribbean countries expressed his regret that the General Assembly had avoided an explicit condemnation of "the 500-year history of the collision between explorers and indigenous peoples" and his hope that the indigenous peoples of Amazonia and the Arctic would "exercise increasing controls over their vast ancestral homelands." What does the United Nations mean by a "new partnership," and what can the United Nations do concretely to improve the conditions in which most of the world's indigenous peoples currently live?

THE UNITED NATIONS AND INDIGENOUS PEOPLES

The issue of indigenous peoples has been with the United Nations since 1948, when

Russel Lawrence Barsh, "A 'New Partnership' for Indigenous Peoples: Can the United Nations Make a Difference?" *American Indian Culture and Research Journal*, 17, no. 1 (1993): 197–227. Copyright © 1993 by Regents of the University of California, UCLA American Indian Studies Center. Reprinted with permission. Portions of the original and notes have been omitted.

the Soviet Union unsuccessfully called for a study of indigenous conditions in the Americas. Barely ten years later, such a study was in fact prepared by the International Labour Organisation (ILO) at the request of a number of Andean countries that expressed concern at the growing numbers of unemployed Indians in that region's cities. Latin America was facing a land problem, not a labor problem, the ILO concluded. In 1959, with Latin American leadership, the ILO adopted a "Convention on Indigenous and Tribal Populations" (no. 107) which was eventually ratified by twenty-seven governments. In keeping with the prejudices of its time, convention no. 107 aimed at the "integration" of indigenous peoples but emphasized that this must be voluntary. In the meantime, the convention recognized indigenous peoples' rights to land ownership and to equality of access to education and services.

ILO action in this field spurred the United Nations Centre for Human Rights to reexamine the problem of indigenous rights, and in 1971 yet another study was launched, this time entrusted to Ecuadoran diplomat José R. Martinez Cobo. The Martinez Cobo report, a broad survey of conditions in the Americas and Australasia, took a decade to complete and helped keep the idea of "indigenous populations" on the agenda of United Nations human rights bodies. At the same time, an international indigenous movement was evolving at the grassroots and linking through the World Council of Indigenous Peoples, the International Indian Treaty Council, and a growing number of regional organizations. A 1977 conference that brought indigenous organizations together at the United Nations office in Geneva for the first time added great impetus to this mobilization; at a second conference there in 1981 the director of the Centre for Human Rights, Dr. Theo van Boven, announced plans to create an official United Nations Working Group on Indigenous Populations.

The Working Group was formally approved by the United Nations Economic and Social Council in May 1982 and held its first annual session in July of the same year. It was given two tasks: "review of developments," i.e., data-gathering; and making recommendations for standard-setting. In 1985, the Economic and Social Council endorsed the Working Group's plan to emphasize its standard-setting role, with a view to drafting a "declaration on indigenous rights" for eventual consideration by the General Assembly. This, in turn, helped spark renewed interest within the ILO in the field of indigenous rights. In 1986, the ILO began work on a revision of its convention no. 107. Following two years of intense negotiations, in which indigenous representatives played a major part, the ILO adopted an entirely new "Convention on Indigenous and Tribal Peoples, 1989" (no. 169), which went into force last year. The theme of the new ILO convention is autonomy, not integration, as can be seen in article 7:

> The peoples concerned shall have the right to decide their own priorities for the process of

development as it affects their lives, beliefs, institutions and spiritual well-being and the lands they occupy or otherwise use, and to exercise control, to the extent possible, over their own economic, social and cultural development.

Meanwhile, the Working Group has prepared a nearly complete first draft of its declaration of indigenous peoples' rights and launched an ambitious research program in cooperation with other United Nations agencies, which includes a study of the potential significance of treaties with indigenous peoples, an annual report on the impacts of transnational corporations' operations and investments on indigenous peoples' lands and resources, and a study of strengthening international measures to protect the cultural property of indigenous peoples. Related studies and meetings are planned by UNESCO, UNICEF, and the United Nations Development Programme (UNDP).

CLARIFYING THE "INDIGENOUS PROBLEM"

As this very brief summary suggests, international involvement in the field of indigenous rights is accelerating. Most United Nations system work thus far has been devoted to the drafting of legal principles and to studies of indigenous conditions and legal rights. What more can United Nations agencies do to support indigenous struggles? The answer to this question depends on our assessment of the nature of indigenous peoples' powerlessness in the countries in which they live, and of the resources and political capacity of the United Nations system to take corrective action.

Although, historically, indigenous groups have suffered similar forms of oppression and dispossession, today they differ greatly

International Indian Treaty Council delegation at the 1984 United Nations Commission on Human Rights, Geneva, Switzerland. Left to right: Nilak Butler, Sharon Venne, Bill Means, Antonio Gonzales, Agnes Williams, and Bill Wahpepah.

in their potential power. At one end of the spectrum are the relatively industrialized countries like the United States and Australia, where indigenous people comprise about 1 percent of the population and are found mostly in urban areas and small rural enclaves. At the other end are several Andean and Central American countries, where indigenous peoples form a national majority and inhabit more than half of the national territory. In the middle are Canada, Brazil, and the Russian Republic, where the indigenous population is relatively small (5–10 percent) but concentrated in one large, undeveloped region—"frontier"

situations—and the countries of south and southeast Asia, where 90 percent of the world's indigenous or tribal people live in marginal regions such as mountains and forests, forming large minorities (10–30 percent). To a limited extent, public funds give small populations in North America, the Nordic countries, and Australasia a compensating advantage. In the majority of cases, however, indigenous movements are actively opposed by settlers and extractive industries, if not also by the state.

For the sake of argument, we may distinguish two kinds of cases: those in which indigenous peoples have legal recognition and access to the national political process but lack sufficient numbers to protect themselves through democratic representation; and those in which they have the numbers but lack the rights, opportunities, physical security, or resources to use their numbers. Most indigenous people fall into the second category. Moreover, most indigenous movements in the world are focused on gaining a role in national-level decision-making, while in countries like the United States and Australia, the focus is on local autonomy. Large indigenous movements seek a share of national power; small ones tend to be isolationist. Large movements can be checked, I maintain, only by regimes that are not only discriminatory but undemocratic generally. Small movements can be co-opted or allowed to die of benign neglect. A United Nations program for indigenous rights must recognize these differences and must acknowledge the fact that most indigenous struggles ultimately are about the democratization of countries with minority-rule regimes, not about walling indigenous enclaves off from otherwise unjust societies. . . .

1992–1993: A CONVERGENCE OF UNITED NATIONS ACTIVITIES

This kind of shift in human rights thinking, from legal standards to programs, has already begun within the United Nations, and indigenous peoples have become the "test case." Between June 1992 and December 1993, several important United Nations initiatives on indigenous rights are converging, leading to the establishment of a new kind of global development program—one that is run largely by and for indigenous peoples themselves. In June 1992,

the Earth Summit at Rio adopted the broad framework of this program as part of a comprehensive United Nations plan of action on environment and development. In December, the United Nations General Assembly was scheduled to approve plans for grassroots demonstration projects marking the International Year for the World's Indigenous People, as a first step in building the program adopted at Rio. Indigenous issues will be on the agenda of the United Nations World Conference on Human Rights, in June 1993. Before the Year ends, the WGIP will have completed its draft declaration on indigenous rights, and it could be adopted by the General Assembly in December 1993. If the Year is successful, an institutionally distinct United Nations program for indigenous people will be firmly established.

TAKEOFF: THE INTERNATIONAL YEAR (1993)

The launching pad for this new program will be the International Year for the World's Indigenous People—officially 1993, but with its official opening ceremonies held on 10 December 1992. From the start, the Year has been conceived as a practical, rather than a promotional exercise, "with a view to strengthening international cooperation for the solution of problems faced by indigenous communities in such areas as human rights, the environment, development, education and health." Unlike most previous United Nations "anniversaries," which produced a flurry of posters, postage stamps, and high-level conferences, this Year is not aimed at publicity but at grassroots development. Its focus is projects at the community level, planned and executed cooperatively. At their 1991 annual meetings, the United Nations' largest development-aid agencies, the United Nations Development Programme (UNDP) and UNICEF, with combined budgets of over $1.4 billion, made commitments to meet with indigenous organizations to plan joint projects for the Year. The total effort devoted to projects will depend in part on attracting additional funds from governments and in part on repackaging existing United Nations programs in the countries concerned. Since funding will be limited, in any event, United Nations agencies will focus on a small number of demonstration projects within their ongoing mandates; for example, UNICEF might arrange that some of the many primary schools it helps support in the Andes become Indian-controlled, bilingual-bicultural demonstration schools, or it might try to adapt its Andean infant-feeding programs to special Indian dietary sensitivities.

The administrative machinery for the Year will form a nucleus for building a permanent United Nations agency for indigenous peoples. It will be a troika including the Centre for Human Rights and the ILO in Geneva, as well as the Department of Economic and Social Development (DESD) in New York, chaired by the undersecretary-general for human rights. The DESD houses the United Nations' Administrative Committee for Coordination, basically a clearinghouse for all development-assistance programs and agencies, and the ILO has begun convening semiannual interagency workshops on indigenous peoples. The Australian, Danish, and Norwegian governments lent indigenous professionals to the Centre for Human Rights to serve as a temporary secretariat.

Meanwhile, the General Assembly adopted a number of suggestions for the Year's activities. It also has directed the coordinating team to convene a planning meeting, with organizations of indigenous peoples and United Nations agencies, to agree on the financial arrangements for 1993 and

(i) To identify programme areas or capabilities that are of particular relevance and priority to indigenous people;

(ii) To agree on specific objectives for special projects to be implemented in 1993 as part of the International Year and to ensure their consonance with the theme and objectives of the Year;

(iii) To consider existing project guidelines and recommend effective means for including indigenous people in the initiation, the design and implementation of the special projects to be undertaken in 1993;

(iv) To suggest appropriate procedures and criteria for the evaluation of projects involving indigenous people, in 1993 *and thereafter.*

The concluding phrase, *and thereafter,* is extremely important, since it reflects a commitment to continuing activities for indigenous peoples after 1993. Through their participation in planning the Year, indigenous peoples are building the policy framework for a long-term United Nations program investing in indigenous development and empowerment.

A first planning meeting, held in March 1992, conflicted with the preparatory process for the Earth Summit, and indigenous attendance was poor. Nevertheless, attendees adopted a shopping list of program ideas and agreed to reconvene in August, immediately after the 1992 WGIP session in Geneva. At this reconvened planning meeting, attended by dozens of indigenous organizations and many governments, some more basic aims emerged and attracted broad support. It was agreed that 1993 projects "should directly benefit indigenous peoples and communities" and that the United Nations should launch public information activities "aimed at raising worldwide understanding of the cultures and situations of indigenous peoples." More critically, participants recommended

> that the United Nations system, as one of the objectives of the Year, examine ways and means of establishing a permanent representative body of indigenous peoples to consider the situation of these peoples on a continuing basis.
>
> that each inter-agency organization find ways to involve indigenous peoples in a permanent dialogue, and that they accord status to indigenous representatives to enable them to do so.

Perhaps the greatest achievement of the planning process thus far has been a symbolic one. At the August meeting, indigenous organizations asked that the chair, Professor Ligia Galves, a representative of the Colombian government, be joined by two indigenous vice chairs selected on a regional basis by the indigenous participants. The vice chairs chosen were Rigoberta Menchu of Guatemala (who was awarded the Nobel Peace Prize two months later) and Mick Dodson of Australia. For the first time in United Nations history, an official policy meeting was cochaired by indigenous people.

LONG-TERM PLANNING:
THE EARTH SUMMIT (JUNE 1992)

Negotiations on a long-term program began, significantly, as part of the preparations for the United Nations Conference on Environment and Development (UNCED), popularly called the Earth Summit, which took place at Rio de Janeiro in June 1992. When UNCED was planned two years ago, the United Nations General Assembly was not thinking about indigenous peoples. The industrialized countries proposed the conference, as a way of coordinating and accelerating the drafting of new environmental standards on urgent problems such as global warming and deforestation. Developing countries acknowledged the need for setting environmental quality targets but argued that poor nations could not possibly meet those targets and still feed and clothe themselves, without a massive redistribution of the world's wealth and technology. Having developed their nonsustainable lifestyles at the expense, historically, of most of the resources and ecosystems of the planet, the richer countries of the North should assume financial responsibility for global cleanup efforts—and for helping poor countries develop more environmentally sound industries. In the end, the theme of the conference was widened to include "sustainable development."

How did indigenous peoples become a part of this? There are many reasons, both philosophical and practical. Indigenous peoples live in some of the world's most fragile and threatened ecosystems. Since the 1970s, this has been used symbolically and tactically by environmental groups, particularly in movements for the protection of rainforests in Amazonia and Southeast Asia. Anthropologists and biotechnology firms have recently drawn attention to the tremendous potential value of the genetic resources in these ecosystems, which can be tapped only through indigenous peoples' traditional knowledge of medicine, botany, and zoology. Indigenous peoples themselves equate the struggle for self-determination with the defense of land rights and argue that superior stewardship justifies their land claims. It is not surprising, then, that many indigenous organizations gave

UNCED top diplomatic priority over the past year or that the other participants in the preparatory negotiations, including government representatives (chiefly from environment ministries) and environmentalists, were so willing to give indigenous delegations special status. Indeed, the UNCED negotiations may have been far more successful than work done over the past decade in the United Nations Commission on Human Rights. The "human rights" label is always a red flag to governments, and they are reflexively defensive. Raising "land rights" or self-determination at a United Nations human rights meeting triggers immediate resistance from some governments, while referring to indigenous "management" of land is relatively noncontroversial in the context of UNCED.

At its third bargaining session, the UNCED Preparatory Committee unanimously agreed on the need to consider the "traditional knowledge and practices of indigenous people and other local communities for the sustainable use, conservation, management and development of natural resources and their special relationship to the environment." At its next session, the Preparatory Committee agreed on seven principles:

A. Recognizing the traditional knowledge and resource management practices of indigenous people and local communities as contributions to environmentally sound and sustainable development;
B. Recognizing that traditional and direct dependence on renewable resources and ecosystems, including sustainable subsistence harvesting, continues to be essential to the cultural, social, economic and physical well-being of indigenous people and local communities;

C. Recognizing the need to protect the habitats of indigenous people and local communities from environmentally unsound development projects and from inappropriate integration processes;
D. Strengthening the viability and sustainability of traditional management practices in the context of environmentally sound development, including by means of collaboration between government and the people and communities concerned;
E. Supporting capacity building for indigenous people and local communities based on the adaptation and exchange of traditional experience, knowledge and resources management practices within and between regions;
F. Supporting their development of alternative, environmentally sound means of production, to ensure the improvement of their quality of life so that they can participate in sustainable development;
G. Mobilizing international technical and financial cooperation for the self-development of these people and communities, as a first step by means of the opportunity provided by the International Year for the World's Indigenous People[.]

This reserved a special chapter on "the role of indigenous people and their communities" in *Agenda 21,* the United Nations global program of action on the environment that was ultimately adopted at the Earth Summit in June 1992. In addition to rephrasing the seven principles, with a few significant modifications, *Agenda 21* calls for activities to "empower" indigenous peoples "in full partnership" with the peoples themselves, including "greater control over their lands, self-management of their resources, [and] participation in development decisions affecting them." Three specific measures are to be taken by the United Nations itself. Every United Nations development-aid agency must designate someone as a "focal point," or person responsible for indigenous peoples' concerns. Agencies must also develop procedures to ensure that indigenous people are "informed and consulted and allowed to participate" in decisions at the national level, including the use of United Nations aid, and implementing *Agenda 21.* Finally, United Nations agencies will create new programs to provide financial and technical support for "capacity-building" in indigenous communities, focused on the application of traditional knowledge to contemporary resource management challenges.

The new spirit of partnership affirmed at UNCED is best reflected in the "Rio Declaration," a summary of basic principles intended as a new charter of international environmental law. Principle 22 states,

> Indigenous people and their communities, and other local communities, have a vital role in environmental management and development because of their knowledge and traditional practices. States should recognize and duly support their identity, culture and interests and enable their effective participation in the achievement of sustainable development.

Thus formulated, principle 22 implies that indigenous peoples have the right to manage their own resources in their own way, because they can do a better job. It also suggests that liberating indigenous peoples to pursue their own kind of development can strengthen the economies of nation-states. This new characterization of indigenous economies as stimulating rather than dragging national development can also be found in the charter of the Fund for the Development of the Indigenous Peoples of Latin America and the Caribbean, established a month after Rio. Even more significantly, the governance of

the fund implements "partnership": Half of the board of directors are indigenous people.

A POLICY CHARTER:
THE WGIP DECLARATION (LATE 1993)

When it is finally adopted by the General Assembly, the United Nations Declaration on the Rights of Indigenous Peoples will serve as an even more detailed charter for the evolving United Nations program on indigenous peoples. Approval of the draft declaration in its current form is by no means certain, however, because many governments still think it is too strong. Ordinarily, such documents must be approved by the Commission on Human Rights before being considered by the General Assembly, but a special opportunity for rapid action has been provided by the Year. A major effort by indigenous organizations to link the declaration with the Year will be needed to generate publicity and visibility, and to put pressure on the 48th session of the General Assembly to adopt the declaration without revisions when it meets in 1993.

What is so dangerous about the current draft? Most concerns have been directed at draft paragraph 1:

> Indigenous peoples have the right to self-determination, in accordance with international law. By virtue of this right, they freely determine their relationship with the States in which they live, in a spirit of coexistence with other citizens, and freely pursue their economic, social, cultural and spiritual development in conditions of freedom and dignity.

This promotes the kind of process that has been pursued over the past decade in Canada, in which indigenous peoples negotiate their constitutional status within the state. It presumes that autonomy is preferable to independence, but it does not necessarily rule out secession—hence the concerns expressed by governments. Governments also express concern over draft paragraph 16:

Indigenous peoples have the collective and individual right to own, control and use the lands and territories they have traditionally occupied or otherwise used. This includes the right to the full recognition of their own laws and customs, land-tenure systems and institutions for the management of resources, and the right to effective State measures to prevent any interference with or encroachment upon these rights.

Part of the controversy here is over the use of the past tense in the phrase *occupied or otherwise used,* which implies a right to recover lands that were confiscated or settled upon by outsiders in the past without indigenous consent. Concerns are directed at the "territorial control" element, which some governments regard as an unwarranted assumption that these regions of the country will remain administratively separate forever.

Government reluctance to accept these implications of the current draft has not only threatened its completion and adoption but has helped perpetuate a superficially trivial terminological dispute: whether to use the term *peoples* or *populations* in official texts. The United Nations Charter and its human rights treaties refer to self-determination as a right of *peoples* giving this term symbolic power and possible legal implications. Although convention no. 169 uses *peoples* throughout, it also contains a clause disavowing any "implications" of this choice of words. By the time negotiations were underway in UNCED and on the International Year, a further compromise had been reached on *people,* in the singular, although many United Nations technical reports have been using *peoples* freely for years. An interesting test of the evolution of international consciousness

and government sensitivities on this point will be the promotional documentation distributed by the United Nations for the Year. Thus far, it has stuck safely with *people* or (in Spanish and French) *populations,* drawing sharp criticism from several indigenous leaders.

In any event, the declaration on indigenous peoples' rights must be given a "second reading" at the WGIP's 1993 session in Geneva, then be submitted to higher-level "political" United Nations bodies for adoption. In its final form, it will reflect, more than any other United Nations document, the true nature of the political climate for change.

"A NEW PARTNERSHIP"—
WHAT DOES IT MEAN?

Does all this represent a genuine change of thinking or shift of power? It could be argued that the "new partnership" envisaged by the International Year accepts the practical necessity of working together in the future but does not acknowledge wrongdoing in the past. This, in turn, reflects the political basis of recent developments in the United Nations, which have more to do with the growing strength of indigenous peoples in the Americas than with a change in the philosophy of nationalism among Euro-American societies.

It is illustrated by the long struggle waged by Spain to prevent the General Assembly from proclaiming 1992 as the International Year. Indigenous organizations originally proposed the 1992 date at meetings of the WGIP in 1987, basing it on a recommendation made years earlier in the Martinez Cobo report. At the insistence of Spain, the date was deleted from a Commission on Human Rights resolution acknowledging the idea and asking the WGIP to give it further consideration. A bargain was then struck diplomatically, with Spain to settle for 1993, with a separate understanding that the opening ceremonies might take place in 1992. Meanwhile, the European community backed the Spanish objection, while most of the Latin American countries took sides with indigenous representatives. Spain made substantial grants to UNESCO (which has a Spanish director-general) and to the Organization of American States (OAS) to organize "Encounter of Two Worlds" programs in 1992, without any genuine indigenous participation in the planning. Spain also urged the Europeans to withdraw support for the United Nations Year on the grounds that it would be a waste of money. In the end, it was growing Latin American support and Canada's defection from the European position that made the Year possible.

The Canadian defection was understandable as a short-term measure to deflect international criticism of the Mulroney government's heavy-handed treatment of Mohawk protests that summer (1990) at Oka, Quebec. But it also indicated appreciation, shared with Latin delegations, of the growing power of national indigenous movements and of the need to demonstrate, for domestic purposes, a commitment to indigenous rights. Latin American governments have an added incentive to support a strong United Nations program. Impoverished and fragile, the region's new democracies are unable to build social programs for Indians without external aid. Without something like a major United Nations initiative for Indian development, countries such as Colombia, Peru, and Chile have no means of bringing Indians into existing national democratic coalitions—hardening their civilian regimes against the military and depriving the extreme left of support from alienated Indians. They saw the Year

as a vehicle for justifying added resources and pursued it vigorously as a development exercise, without necessarily admitting their past sins.

When the draft resolution was brought up in the plenary meeting of the General Assembly, four Caribbean countries called for a vote, on the grounds that the draft expressly should have condemned the colonization of the Americas. In the words of the representative of Antigua and Barbuda,

> The draft resolution should have referred to the 500-year history of the collision between explorers and indigenous peoples; and should have been explicit in taking into account the concerns and perils faced by indigenous victims today. More than 200,000 indigenous peoples [*sic*], world wide, perished by violent means in 1989. And the carnage of indigenous peoples in the Caribbean and the Americas after 1492 has been well-documented. The draft resolution does not convey a yearning to correct historical and current injustices.

As it has evolved diplomatically, then, the Year looks ahead rather than backwards. It merely implies, in the word *new*, the fact that political partnership and collaboration have been rare or absent in the past or that what is "new" is the recognition that indigenous peoples have a right, like all other peoples, to a voice in their own destinies. The next five centuries should not repeat the patterns of the last five centuries. Indigenous peoples should interpret the New Partnership as an acknowledgment of their right to share power in the future— not because they were mistreated in the past, but because they still exist as distinct peoples.

If implemented conscientiously, this forward-looking policy would be far more significant than a more explicit European apology. Direct participation in national and international decision-making bodies give indigenous peoples a way of exercising their latent political power, and independent financial and technical resources will enable them to exercise this latent power more effectively. Then, in the not-too-distant future, history can be rewritten truthfully—if anyone still cares to assign blame. Blame, however, is an excuse for powerlessness. Those who blame generally lack the power to act.

"Completing the Circle," by Leonard F. Chana, Tohono O'odham artist. © 1995 Leonard F. Chana.

INDIGENOUS PEOPLES' SEATTLE DECLARATION ON THE OCCASION OF THE THIRD MINISTERIAL MEETING OF THE WORLD TRADE ORGANIZATION, NOVEMBER 30–DECEMBER 3, 1999

We, the Indigenous Peoples from various regions of the world, have come to Seattle to express our great concern over how the World Trade Organization is destroying Mother Earth and the cultural and biological diversity of which we are a part.

Trade liberalization and export-oriented development, which are the overriding principles and policies pushed by the WTO, are creating the most adverse impacts on the lives of Indigenous Peoples. Our inherent right to self-determination, our sovereignty as nations, and treaties and other constructive agreements which Indigenous nations and Peoples have negotiated with other nation-states are undermined by most of the WTO Agreements. The disproportionate impact of these Agreements on our communities, whether through environmental degradation or the militarization and violence that often accompanies development projects, is serious and therefore should be addressed immediately.

Declaration by the Indigenous Peoples' Caucus convened and sponsored by the Indigenous Environmental Network, Seventh Generation Fund in alliance with the Tebtebba (Indigenous Peoples' Network for Policy Research and Education), International Indian Treaty Council, Indigenous Peoples Council on Biocolonialism and the Abya Yala Fund.

The WTO Agreement on Agriculture (AOA), which promotes export competition and import liberalization, has allowed the entry of cheap agricultural products into our communities. It is causing the destruction of ecologically rational and sustainable agricultural practices of Indigenous Peoples.

Food security and the production of traditional food crops have been seriously compromised. Incidents of diabetes, cancers, and hypertension have significantly increased among Indigenous Peoples because of the scarcity of traditional foods and the dumping of junk food into our communities.

Small-scale farm production is giving way to commercial cash-crop plantations, further concentrating ancestral lands into the hands of a few agri-corporations and landlords. This has led to the dislocation of scores of people from our communities who then migrate to nearby cities and become the urban homeless and jobless.

The WTO Forests Products Agreement promotes free trade in forest products. By eliminating developed country tariffs on wood products by the year 2000, and developing country tariffs by 2003, the Agreement will result in the deforestation of many of the world's ecosystems in which Indigenous Peoples live.

Mining laws in many countries are being changed to allow free entry of foreign mining corporations, to enable them to buy and own mineral lands, and to freely displace Indigenous Peoples from their ancestral territories. These large-scale commercial mining and oil extraction activities continue to degrade our lands and fragile ecosystems, and pollute the soil, water, and air in our communities.

The appropriation of our lands and resources and the aggressive promotion of consumerist and individualistic Western culture continue to destroy traditional lifestyles and cultures. The result is not only environmental degradation but also ill health, alienation, and high levels of stress manifested in high rates of alcoholism and suicides.

The theft and patenting of our biogenetic resources are facilitated by the TRIPs (Trade-Related Aspects of Intellectual Property Rights) of the WTO. Some plants which Indigenous Peoples have discovered, cultivated, and used for food, medicine, and for sacred rituals are already patented in the United States, Japan, and Europe. A few examples of these are ayahuasca, quinoa, and sangre de drago in forests of South America; kava in the Pacific; turmeric and bitter melon in Asia. Our access and control over our biological diversity and control over our traditional knowledge and intellectual heritage are threatened by the TRIPs Agreement.

Article 27.3b of the TRIPs Agreement allows the patenting of life-forms and makes an artificial distinction between plants, animals, and micro-organisms. The distinction between "essentially biological" and "non-biological" and "microbiological" processes is also erroneous. As far as we are concerned all these are life-forms and life-creating processes which are sacred and which should not become the subject of private property ownership.

Finally, the liberalization of investments and the service sectors, which is pushed by the General Agreement of Services, reinforces the domination and monopoly control of foreign corporations over strategic parts of the economy. The World Bank and the International Monetary Fund impose conditionalities of liberalization, deregulation, and privatization on countries caught in the debt trap. These conditionalities are reinforced further by the WTO.

In light of the adverse impacts and consequences of the WTO Agreements identified above, we, Indigenous Peoples, present the following demands:

We urgently call for a social and environmental justice analysis which will look into the Agreements' cumulative effects on Indigenous Peoples.

Indigenous Peoples should be equal participants in establishing the criteria and indicators for these analyses so that they take into consideration spiritual as well as cultural aspects.

A review of the Agreements should be done to address all of the inequities and imbalances which adversely affect Indigenous Peoples. The proposals to address some of these are as follows;

1. For the Agreement on Agriculture
   a. It should not include in its coverage small-scale farmers who are mainly engaged in production for domestic use and sale in the local markets.
   b. It should ensure the recognition and protection of rights of Indigenous Peoples to their territories and their resources, as well as their rights to continue practicing their indigenous sustainable agriculture and resource management practices and traditional livelihoods.

c. It should ensure the food security and the capacity of Indigenous Peoples to produce, consume, and trade their traditional foods.

2. With regard to the liberalization of services and investments we recommend the following:

   a. It must stop unsustainable mining, commercial planting of monocrops, dam construction, oil exploration, land conversion to golf clubs, logging, and other activities which destroy Indigenous Peoples' lands and violate the rights of Indigenous Peoples' to their territories and resources.

   b. The right of Indigenous Peoples to their traditional lifestyles, cultural norms and values should likewise be recognized and protected.

   c. The liberalization of services, especially in the areas of health, should not be allowed if it will prevent Indigenous Peoples from having access to free, culturally appropriate as well as quality health services.

   d. The liberalization of finance services, which makes the world a global casino, should be regulated.

3. On the TRIPs Agreement, the proposals are as follows:

   a. Article 27.3b should be amended to categorically disallow the patenting of life-forms. It should clearly prohibit the patenting of micro-organisms, plants, and animals, including all their parts, whether they are genes, gene sequences, cells, cell lines, proteins, or seeds.

   b. It should also prohibit the patenting of natural processes, whether these are biological or microbiological, involving the use of plants, animals and micro-organisms and their parts in producing variations of plants, animals, and micro-organisms.

c. It should ensure the exploration and development of alternative forms of protection outside of the dominant Western intellectual property rights regime. Such alternatives must protect the knowledge and innovations and practices in agriculture, health care, and conservation of biodiversity, and should build upon indigenous methods and customary laws protecting knowledge, heritage, and biological resources.

d. It should ensure that the protection offered to indigenous and traditional knowledge, innovation, and practices is consistent with the Convention on Biological Diversity (i.e., Articles 8j, 10c, 17.2, and 18.4) and the International Undertaking on Plant Genetic Resources.

e. It should allow for the right of Indigenous Peoples and farmers to continue their traditional practices of saving, sharing, and exchanging seeds and cultivating, harvesting, and using medicinal plants.

f. It should prohibit scientific researchers and corporations from appropriating and patenting indigenous seeds, medicinal plants, and related knowledge about these life-forms. The principles of prior informed consent and right of veto by Indigenous Peoples should be respected.

If the earlier proposals cannot be ensured, we call for the removal of the Agreement on Agriculture, the Forest Products Agreements, and the TRIPs Agreement from the WTO.

We call on the member-states of the WTO not to allow for another round whilst the review and rectification of the implementation of existing agreements has not been done. We reject the proposals for an investment treaty, competition, accelerated industrial tariffs, government procurement, and the creation of a working group on biotechnology.

We urge the WTO to reform itself to become democratic, transparent, and accountable. If it fails to do this we call for the abolition of the WTO.

We urge the member nation-states of the WTO to endorse the adoption by the U.N. General Assembly of the current text of the U.N. Declaration on the Rights of Indigenous Peoples and the ratification of ILO Convention 169.

We call on the peoples' organizations and NGOs to support this "Indigenous Peoples' Seattle Declaration" and to promote it among their members.

We believe that the whole philosophy underpinning the WTO Agreements and the principles and policies they promote contradict our core values, spirituality, and worldviews, as well as our concepts and practices of Development, trade and environmental protection. Therefore, we challenge the WTO to redefine its principles and practices toward a "sustainable communities" paradigm, and to recognize and allow for the continuation of other worldviews and models of development.

Indigenous Peoples, undoubtedly, are the ones most adversely affected by globalization and by the WTO Agreements. However, we believe that it is also us who can offer viable alternatives to the dominant economic growth, export-oriented development model. Our sustainable lifestyles and cultures, traditional knowledge, cosmologies, spirituality, values of collectivity, reciprocity, respect, and reverence for Mother Earth are crucial in the search for a transformed society where justice, equity, and sustainability will prevail.

INDIGENOUS PEOPLES' ORGANIZATIONS PARTICIPATING IN THE SEATTLE WTO THAT SIGNED ON TO THIS DECLARATION

Tom Goldtooth, Indigenous Environmental Network, USA/Canada

Chris Peters, Seventh Generation Fund, USA

Antonio Gonzales, International Indian Treaty Council, International

Margarita Gutierrez, Social Commission for the Development of the Nanhu, Mexico

Debra Harry, Indigenous Peoples Council on Biocolonialism, USA

Clemencia Herrera Nemarayema, National Indigena Organization of Colombia, South America

Chief Johnny Jackson, Klickitat Band of Yakama, Elder Committee of Indigenous Environmental Network, USA/Canada

Carol Kalafatic, International Indian Treaty Council, International

Dune Lankard, Eyak Alaska Preservation Council, USA

Chief Arthur Manual, Interior Alliance of First Nations, Canada

Alvin Manitopyes, Cree Strong Heart Environmental and Wellness Society, Canada

Jim Main Sr. Gros Ventre White Clay Society, USA

Jose Matos, Indigenous Alliance Without Borders, USA/Mexico

Esther Nahgahnub, Anishinabeg Treaty 1854 Committee, USA

Priscilla Settee, Indigenous Women's Network, USA/Canada

Taita Stanley, Movimiento de la Juventad Kuna, Panama

Chaz Wheelock, Great Lakes Regional Indigenous Environmental Network, USA/Canada

Clemente lbe Wilson, Movimiento de la Juventad Kuna, Panama

Nilo Cayuqueo, Abya Yala Fund, USA

Victoria Tauli-Corpuz, Indigenous Peoples Network for Policy Research and Education, Philippines

CLOSING ADDRESS

Phillip Deere

At this time I will bring a short message coming from my ancient ancestors that has never been mentioned because the message had remained with the traditional Indian people.

The prophecies of my people have come about. This is what we have witnessed. Many of the traditional people here understand this. That the Russell Tribunal here is a part of the prophecies within my own people; it was said that this could come about within these prophecies. It is hard to translate into the borrowed language; however, I would like to bring this to your attention that we too had prophets who told my people that there is a white room leaning up against the western skies. This will sweep across our country; and from the north the white bear would come to us. From the east we will see a man in a red coat that will come to us. From the south, there will be a feeling of warm air and we will hear the winds coming through the forest blowing against the reeds and bamboos. We'll be able to hear music in this wind. It is to be remembered that when these prophecies begin to fulfill, that the Indian people will go somewhere known to us, as King of Kings, leaders of leaders will assemble. The Indian people will sit somewhere as if though they are criminals. Around this time when these prophecies are beginning to happen among the Indian Nations, there will be found a boy perhaps an orphan boy with raggedy clothes. Around his neck will be the identity of the Indian people—on his chest the identity of the Indian people will be there. The young boy will have eyes of an eagle. The eagle that can see direct into the sun. With the clear eyes he will lead the people.

Beyond the black smokes he will be able to see beyond the sun. He will be able to see and those that follow will find life there. These are the prophecies of our ancient ancestors. Here, in the Russell Tribunal we find many nations of people. It is now time that we search out who this leader is. That as Native people we must have a clear understanding of these prophecies. That our eyes be not glazed to the spiritual leaders and medicine people. These they have preserved in their minds from one generation to the other.

There are instructions that you fix your feathers. The birds of the night who do not sleep at night—certain people must pick up these feathers that they will be able to sit-up all night and to overcome. I thought of this last night when the jury sat—working continuously until 6:00 this morning. It is the fulfillment of these prophecies that their eyes must be strong at certain times. Therefore, I sat with them till this morning. This is no accident, no coincidence that we are here. The people of the red clay of Americas will always continue to go on. The religion, the prophecies, no government will ever stop it—no human being can prevent it that these prophecies will come about. And in time to come we will see from the Russell Tribunal, and time will tell us that these prophecies will be fulfilled. The spiritual connections that we have with our brothers from the south are also connected with the countries throughout the whole universe. And at this time, conclusion of this Russell Tribunal, we felt that warm air, we felt that wind from the south, perhaps all over the world we have felt that warm air. During this time, it is now time that we hear the winds blowing through the forest of Brazil, it is time that we hear the winds blowing against the reeds and bamboos, that is music, that has a sound that has a rhythm that has been handed down for thousands and thousands of years. We are people that are made and placed here for a purpose. Through many struggles, through many years of struggle and sufferings we refuse to die— Thank you.

MESSAGE FOR THE WORK AHEAD

John Mohawk

I think we're gathered here today, that we're witnesses to that which must become a significant and an historical event. The process, the big process, which we've heard described has its origins at the beginning of the modern world. When the first Europeans contacted the Americas, they were confused about where they had landed and about the peoples they had encountered.

They debated whether or not the Native Peoples whom they met were actually to be considered human beings at all. Spanish conquistadores offered up a position, offering to the world that the Native Peoples were somehow a subhuman race. Somehow related to Aristotle's theory of the universe, which could be interpreted as explaining that there were animals and there was civilized man; there were gradiations of man, culminating in animals. And in that terminology, that understanding of the world, that [Aristotelian] thought, came the roots of modern racism, wherein European peoples determined, first, that Native People of the Western Hemisphere were not fully human beings; and second, they determined that they were not to be treated as equal counterparts; that they could not form governments; that they could not possess religion; and that they were incapable of coming to the civilized arts.

The beginning of oppression in the modern world began in the Americas. Racism began in the Americas. It defines the period we know as the modern world. Nearly 500 years have passed since Columbus first noted in his notebook that these people whom he had encountered might make good slaves. Nearly five centuries have passed; and the original thoughts of Columbus about the possible utilization of Native Peoples has little changed in the legal system of the world.

Columbus did not recognize the legal existence of Native Nations, and peoples of the world do not recognize the existence of Native Nations. We are here today—we are witnessing a step which is leaning toward the process which will bring a fundamental change in that relationship between European peoples and Nations, and Native peoples and Nations of the world. It is a fundamental step because European peoples did not steal the lands of individuals—European conquistadores destroyed NATIONS. European invaders did not destroy the civil rights of personalities, they destroyed enmass the whole rights of Peoples to exist as Peoples. And that is the fundamental wrong which we must move to correct.

We are entering into the 21st Century and the 21st Century is certain to be a period of time which will be different from [that] which preceded it. In the five previous centuries there was room enough for expansion of economics which brought to the world of Western Europe great material advantages. There was material enough—raw materials, enough to sustain a world-wide economy of colonialism and extraction. And we have seen the results of those policies of colonialism and extracted economy. They must have hand-maidens with names like Genocide and Ethnocide. And the processes of genocide and ethnocide are processes directed at whole Peoples.

Now we enter the 21st Century. It is a time for a new era. It is a time of the end of the process of gross extractions of materials from what you call the Third World countries because we are at a period of crisis in which the amount of materials necessary to sustain the world's economies is not available at the present rates of consumption. We enter a century in which one of the probable results will be mass starvation of peoples, mass relocation of people, certainly the darkest future century to have occurred of the last five. We can enter that century as opposing groups, one exploiters, the other the exploited. We can approach it as peoples scrambling for the last vestiges of the energy resources that built a former empire. We can approach it as antagonists scrambling for crumbs on the world's table, or we can begin to set the foundation that would create a world unity of human objectives.

The beginning of the concept of the unification of peoples, the idea that the world could be somehow governed by one world moral order, that the world could somehow find ways in which cultures of people can assist one another—that begins with the visions that the International Laws of the world will protect all peoples of the world as one.

We can enter the next Century in a cooperative way. It is possible. We can meet the needs of humanity by sharing the wisdom of one another's culture and we can do it by recognizing the dignity of nationhood of peoples of the world who possess the knowledges who would make that a possibility. It can be that way! We can't do it scolding Nation-States about their inability to maintain proper civil rights within their boundaries; we can't do it by standing idly by and watching countries destroy whole nations of people within their boundaries and saying that's simply the cultural affairs of the country. The destruction of people of the world is the concern of all the peoples of the world.

We can bring a new international order. A real order. Not quietness and subservience to force, but the possibility of freedom based on International Law protecting everyone's rights. We can bring that kind of order, but we can only bring it if we call the peoples of the world to unite to reject the oppressors, the genocidal perpetrators, the ethnocidal perpetrators. We can do it only when world consciousness can come to bare the crimes against humanity that take place, and right now those crimes take place in the Western Hemisphere, in the Nations of Latin America, in the nations of North America, where peoples are being subjected to the machine gun, and not to the moral code of the world.

I offer this to you in conclusion, that the strategy that we adopt call upon the Nations of the world—all the world's Nations—and the peoples of the world to take action. We do not call upon them to feel bad that the Indian is disappearing. We can't call upon them to wish that something could be done. We don't call upon the people of the world to stand by and watch as spectators. We call upon the people of the world to begin to unite and the place where they need to begin to unite is in those world organizations where the rights of indigenous people can become entrenched in a whole new body of international law. We call upon them for that action, we need to have you call upon them for that action, we need there to be a voice to rise up in Western Europe as there needs to be voice rising up all over the world. We call upon you to help us to entrench the principles that must be entrenched in order that we can begin to try to build the kinds of codes of behaviour which will actually at some day in the future begin to guarantee the rights of people throughout the world. That's the goal that we have, that's the only goal that really makes any sense to us. We call upon you to help us, to support us, to move with us and to understand what it is that our objectives are. And for that and for this gathering for the convention of the Tribunal, for the work of everybody, and the goodwill of everybody, for all of that on behalf of all the peoples who came here—for this Tribunal, I thank you.

Wilverna Reece, a Karuk basket weaver from the Klamath River region of northern California, participates in the annual gathering of the California Basket Weavers Association. Such events have contributed to the revitalization of basket weaving traditions.

PART REVIEW

DISCUSSION QUESTIONS

Tom LaBlanc, *Indianismo!*
1. What do you think the poet means by the term *Indianismo?*

Oren Lyons, Ingrid Washinawatok-El Issa, and José Barreiro, *Voices of Indigenous Peoples*
1. Why did Chief Oren Lyons say that December 10, 1992, was "historic for indigenous peoples of the world"?
2. Describe two of the ongoing struggles waged by contemporary U.S. Indians that are enumerated in the report to the conference by Ingrid Washinawatok-El Issa.
3. How do the current political status and struggle of Mexican Indians differ from those of Native American groups in the United States?
4. Describe two of the recent or ongoing struggles of Native peoples in Central and South America, as enumerated in the report by José Barreiro.

Joane Nagel and C. Matthew Snipp, *Ethnic Reorganization*
1. What do the authors mean by ethnic reorganization?
2. Name and briefly explain the four types of ethnic reorganization discussed in the article.
3. What is meant by the statement that these different forms of ethnic reorganization are "mechanisms of ethnic survival, reconstruction, and creation"?

Russel Lawrence Barsh, *Aboriginal Peoples and Quebec*
1. The province of French-speaking Quebec and possibly, also, the Acadians may separate from Canada in the near future. What are the implications of these developments for the Aboriginal Peoples?
2. What are some of the problems facing the new Inuit province of Nunavut?

Lanada Boyer, *Reflections of Alcatraz*
1. Why did the Indian students occupy Alcatraz Island in 1969?
2. Describe the author's spiritual experience on Alcatraz.
3. How did the government negotiator, Bob Robertson, try to divide the Indians and weaken support for the occupation?

Troy R. Johnson, *Roots of Contemporary Native American Activism*
1. What is the significance of the Alcatraz occupation to the Indian activism of the 1960s and 1970s?

Leanne Hinton, *Hawaiian Language Schools*
1 Why did a small group of Hawaiian educators establish the Pūnana Leo preschools in 1983?
2. The author concludes that the Hawaiian language immersion program is the most successful language revitalization program in the United States. Explain why it is so successful. Give several examples.

Maya Indian Rebellion
1. What action did the Mexican government take in 1992 that precipitated the Zapatista (EZLN) rebellion?
2. What was the status of the struggle as of 1998–1999?

Russel Lawrence Barsh, *A "New Partnership" for Indigenous Peoples*
1. What events or developments at the United Nations led to the drafting of the Declaration on the Rights of Indigenous Peoples?
2. Why did the representatives of indigenous organizations at the United Nations argue that the term *peoples* should be used in the draft declaration instead of *populations?*
3. What is so "dangerous" about the current draft that led some member states of the United Nations to oppose it ?

Indigenous Peoples' Seattle Declaration
1. What is the World Trade Organization?
2. Why do indigenous peoples oppose the WTO?

KEY TERMS

aboriginal rights
CONAIE (Indigenous Confederation of Ecuador)
Doctrine of Discovery
ethnic reorganization
Hawaiian Pūnana Leo preschools
Indianismo
Indians of All Tribes
International Year of the World's Indigenous People (1993)
James Bay
Johnson v. McIntosh (1823)
Kula Kaiapuni Hawai'i schools

language immersion
National Congress of American Indians (NCAI)
nongovernmental organizations (NGOs)
Nunavut
revitalization
Rigoberta Menchú Tum
self-determination
sovereignty
treaty federalism
United Nations Declaration on the Rights of Indigenous Peoples
Working Group on Indigenous Populations
World Trade Organization (WTO)

SUGGESTED READINGS

BARINGER, SANDRA K. "Indian Activism and the American Indian Movement: A Bibliographical Essay." *American Indian Culture and Research Journal,* 21, no. 4 (1997): 217–250.

BARSH, RUSSEL, and JAMES YOUNGBLOOD HENDERSON. *The Road: Indian Tribes and Political Liberty.* Berkeley: University of California Press, 1980.

BURGOS-DUBRAY, ELISABETH, ed. *I, Rigoberta Menchú: An Indian Woman in Guatemala.* Trans. Ann Wright. New York: Verso, 1984.

CHAMPAGNE, DUANE. "Self-determination and Activism among American Indians in the United States 1972–1997." *Cultural Survival Quarterly* (Summer 1997): 32–35.

CHURCHILL, WARD. *Struggle for the Land: Indigenous Resistance to Genocide, Ecocide and Expropriation in Contemporary North America.* Monroe: Maine: Common Courage Press, 1993.

CHURCHILL, WARD. "The Tragedy and the Travesty: The Subversion of Indigenous Sovereignty in North America." *American Indian Culture and Research Journal,* 22, no. 2 (1998): 1–69.

CHURCHILL, WARD, and JIM VANDER WALL. *Agents of Repression: The FBI's Secret Wars against* the Black Panther Party and the American Indian Movement. Boston: South End Press, 1988.

COHEN, FAYE G. *Treaties on Trial: The Continuing Controversy over Northwest Indian Fishing Rights.* Seattle: University of Washington Press, 1986.

CORNELL, STEPHEN. *The Return of the Native: American Indian Political Resurgence.* New York: Oxford University Press, 1988.

CROZIER-HOGIE, LOIS, and DARRYL BABE WILSON. *Surviving in Two Worlds: Contemporary Native American Voices.* Austin: University of Texas Press, 1997.

DELORIA, VINE, JR. *Behind the Trail of Broken Treaties: An Indian Declaration of Independence.* Austin: University of Texas Press, 1985.

DELORIA, VINE, JR. *Custer Died for Your Sins: An Indian Manifesto.* Norman: University of Oklahoma Press, 1969.

DUDLEY, MICHAEL KIONI, and KEONI KEALOHA AGARD. *A Hawaiian Nation II: A Call for Hawaiian Sovereignty.* Honolulu: Naa Kaane O Ka Malo Press, 1990.

EWEN, ALEXANDER, ed. *Voice of Indigenous Peoples: Native People Address the United Nations.* Santa Fe: Clear Light Publishers, 1994.

FORBES, JACK D. *Native Americans and Nixon: Presidential Politics and Minority Self-determination.* Los Angeles: UCLA American Indian Studies Center, 1981.

ISMAELILLO and ROBIN WRIGHT, eds. *Native Peoples in Struggle: Cases from the Fourth Russell Tribunal & Other International Forums.* Bombay, N.Y.: Anthropology Resource Center and E.R.I.N. Publications, 1982.

JAIMES, M. ANNETTE, ed. *The State of Native America: Genocide, Colonization, and Resistance.* Boston: South End Press, 1992.

JOHNSON, TROY, JOANE NAGEL, and DUANE CHAMPAGNE. *American Indian Activism: Alcatraz to the Longest Walk.* Urbana: University of Illinois Press, 1997.

JORGENSEN, JOSEPH. "A Century of Political Effects on American Indian Society, 1880–1980." *Journal of Ethnic Studies,* 6, no. 3 (1978): 1–82.

LYONS, OREN, and JOHN MOHAWK. *Exiled in the Land of the Free: Democracy, Indian Nations, and the U.S. Constitution.* Santa Fe: Clear Light Publishers, 1992.

MATTHIESSEN, PETER. *In the Spirit of Crazy Horse.* 2d ed. New York: Viking Press, 1991.

MOHAWK, JOHN. *A Basic Call to Consciousness, Akwesasne Notes.* New York: Mohawk Nation via Rooseveltown, 1978.

NAGEL, JOANE. *American Indian Ethnic Renewal: Red Power and the Resurgence of Identity and Culture.* New York: Oxford University Press, 1995.

NAGEL, JOANE, and TROY JOHNSON, eds. "Special Edition: Alcatraz Revisited: The 25th Anniversary of the Occupation, 1969–1971." *American Indian Culture and Research Journal,* 18, no. 4 (1994).

"Native Rebellion and U.S. Intervention in Central America." *Cultural Survival Quarterly,* 10, no. 1 (1986): 59–65.

NIEZEN, RONALD. *Defending the Land: Sovereignty and Forest Life in James Bay Cree Society.* Needham Heights, Mass.: Allyn and Bacon, 1998.

ROSS, JOHN. *Rebellion from the Roots: Indian Uprising in Chiapas.* Monroe, Maine: Common Courage Press, 1995.

SELVERSTON, MELINA H. "PACHACUTIK." *Native Americas* (Summer 1998): 11–21.

STOLL, DAVID. *Rigoberta Menchú and the Story of All Poor Guatemalans.* Boulder, Colo.: Westview Press, 1999.

TALBOT, STEVE. "'Free Alcatraz': The Culture of Indian Liberation." *Journal of Ethnic Studies,* 6, no. 3 (1978): 83–96.

TALBOT, STEVE. "The Meaning of Wounded Knee, 1973: Indian Self-Government and the Role of Anthropology." Pages 227–258 in *The Politics of Anthropology.* Ed. Gerrit Huizer and Bruce Mannheim. The Hague: Mouton, 1979.

TRASK, HUANANI-KAY. *From A Native Daughter.* Monroe, Me.: Common Courage Press, 1993.

WEARNE, PHILLIP. *Return of the Indian: Conquest and Revival in the Americas.* Philadelphia: Temple University Press, 1996.

WELLS, ROBERT N., JR., ed. *Native American Resurgence and Renewal: A Reader and Bibliography.* Metuchen, N.J.: Scarecrow Press, 1993.

WEINBERG, BILL. "Mexico's Other Indian War: Fire in the Sierra Madre del Sur." *Native Americas* (Spring 1999): 48, 50–57.

WEINBERG, BILL. "La Miskitia Rears Up." *Native Americas.* (Summer 1998): 22–33.

WEYLER, REX. *Blood of the Land: The U.S. Government and Corporate War against the American Indian Movement.* New York: Everest House, 1983.

APPENDIX A
NATIVE MEDIA

JOURNALS, MAGAZINES, NEWSPAPERS

American Indian Art Magazine
7314 East Osborne Dr.
Scottsdale, AZ 85251

American Indian Culture and Research Journal
American Indian Studies Center
University of California
Los Angeles, CA 90095-1548

American Indian Quarterly
University of Nebraska Press
P.O. Box 880484
Lincoln, NE 68588-0484

Atlatl
P.O. Box 34090
Phoenix, AZ 85067-4090

The Canadian Journal of Native Studies
Department of Native Studies
Trent University
Peterborough, ON K9J7B8, Canada

The Council
122 First Ave.
Fairbanks, AK 99701

Daybreak Star Reader
United Indians of All Tribes
Daybreak Star Arts Center
Seattle, WA 98199

Indian Affairs
Newsletter of the Association of American
Indian Affairs
Box 268
Sisseton, SD 57262

Indian Country Today
1920 Lombardy Dr.
Rapid City, SD 57701

Journal of American Indian Education
Center for Indian Education
Arizona State University
P.O. Box 871311
Tempe, AZ 85287

Journal of Indigenous Studies
Gabriel Dumont Institute of Native Studies
and Applied Research
121 Broadway Ave., East
Regina, Sask. S4N026, Canada

NARF Legal Review
Native American Rights Fund
1506 Broadway
Boulder, CO 80302

Native Americas
Awe:kon Press
300 Caldwell Hall
Cornell University
Ithaca, NY 14853

Native Peoples
Media Concepts Group, Inc.
P.O. Box 36820
Phoenix, AZ 85067-6820

Native Studies Review
Native Studies Department
104 McLean Hall
University of Saskatchewan
Saskatoon, Sask. S7N0W0, Canada

Navajo Times
P.O. Box 310
Window Rock, AZ 86515

News from Indian Country
The Nations Native Journal
Rte. 2, Box 2900-A
Hayward, WI 54853

News from Native California
P.O. Box 9145
Berkeley, CA 94709

Red Ink
American Indian Graduate Center
1610 E. Seventh Street
Tucson, AZ 85719

Treaty Council News
54 Mint St., #400
San Francisco, CA 94103

Tundra Times
P.O. Box 92247
Anchorage, AK 99509-2247

Turtle Quarterly
Native American Center for the Living Arts
25 Rainbow Mall
Niagra Falls, NY 14303

Wacazo Sa Review
The Red Pencil Review
Department of American Indian Studies

102 Scott Hall
University of Minnesota
Minneapolis, MN 55455

Winds of Change
American Indian Science and Engineering Society
AISES Publishing, Inc.
5661 Airport Blvd.
Boulder, CO 80301-2339

Wind Speaker, Canada's National Aboriginal
News Publication
The Aboriginal Multi-Media Society of Alberta
15001 112 Ave.
Edmonton, AB T5M2V6, Canada

RADIO AND TELEVISION

The Aboriginal Multi-Media Society of Alberta
15001 112th Ave.
Edmonton, AB T5M2V6, Canada

Confederated Tribes
Telecommunication Project
P.O. Box C
Warm Springs, OR 97761

Inuit Broadcasting Corporation (IBC)
703 251 Laurier Ave.
Ottawa, ON K1P5J6, Canada

Native American Public Broadcasting
Consortium
P.O. Box 83111
Lincoln, NE 68501

Native Communications Society of the Western
Northwest Territory
P.O. Box 1919, Aquarius Bldg.
Yellowknife, NT X1A2P4, Canada

Native Media Network
P.O. Box 848
Portage La Prairie, MB R1N3C3, Canada

National Native News
Alaska Public Radio Network
810 East Ninth Ave.
Anchorage, AK 99501

The Native Voice
200-1755 E. Hastings St.
Vancouver, BC V5L1T1, Canada

Navajo Nation Office of Broadcast Services
P.O. Box 2310
Window Rock, AZ 86515

Northern Native Broadcasting Yukon (NNBY)
4228 A Fourth Ave.
Whitehorse, YK Y1K1K1, Canada

Migizi Communications, Inc.
First Person Radio
3123 East Lake St., Suite 200
Minneapolis, MN 55406

THEATER

American Indian Community House Theatre
404 Lafayette St.
New York, NY 10003

American Indian Dance Theatre
223 East 61st St.
New York, NY 10021

Association for Native Development in the
Performing and Visual Arts
2049 St. Joseph St.
Toronto, ON M4Y1J6, Canada

Four Winds Theatre
P.O. Box 912
Hobbema, AB TOC1N0, Canada

Native Earth Performing Arts, Inc.
37 Spadina Rd.
Toronto, ON M5R2S9, Canada

Spiderwoman Theater
77 Seventh Ave., Apt. 85
New York, NY 10003

AMERICAN INDIANS ON THE WEB

There are a number of Native American
websites that are especially recommended. For
a description of and commentary on these
websites, see the review by Buffy Sainte-Marie
in *Yahoo! Internet Life* (July 1999), pp. 120–121.
They include the following:

Lisa Mitten's Native American Sites:
www.pitt.edu/Imitten/indians.html

First Nations Web site based in Canada:
www.schoolnet.ca/aboriginal

Karen Strom's Welcome to Hanksville!:
Hanksville.phast.umass.edu

Paula Giese's Native American Indian:
Indy4.fdl.cc.mn.us/isk

Elaine Cubbins's Techniques for Evaluating
American Indian Web Sites:
www.u.arizona.edu/ecubbins/webcrit.html

Tribal College Journal:
cs.fdl.cc.mn.us/tcj

Review of books for children by Oyate:
www.oyate.org

Native American Rights Fund:
www.narf.org

Navajos.com:
www.navajos.com

Indian Pueblo Cultural Center:
www.indianpueblo.org

Buffy Sainte-Marie's Cradleboard Teaching
Project:
www.cradleboard.org

Teaching Indigenous Languages:
jan.ucc.nau.edu/jar/TIL.html

SUGGESTED MOVIES

(Many of these are available in video.)

Black Robe (Film, United States)
Clear Cut (Film, Canada)
Dance Me Outside (Film, Canada)
Dances with Wolves (uncut version) (Film,
United States)
El Norte (Film, United States)
Grand Avenue (Television miniseries, United
States)
Grey Wolf (Film, United States)
Hombres Armados (Men with Guns) (Film,
United States)
Medicine River (Film, Canada)
Pow-wow Highway (Film, United States)
Smoke Signals (Film, United States)
Thunder Heart (Film, United States)
War Party (Film, United States)
Where the Spirit Lives (Film, Canada)

APPENDIX B

INDIGENOUS PEOPLES' ORGANIZATIONS

INTERNATIONAL

Cultural Survival
46 Brattle St.
Cambridge, MA 02138

International Indian Treaty Council
54 Mint St., #400
San Francisco, CA 94103

World Council of Indigenous Peoples
555 King Edward Ave.
Ottawa, ON, KIN6NS, Canada

CENTRAL AND SOUTH AMERICA

ADMAPU
Casilla 1676
Temuco, Chile

Alianza Nacional de Profesionales Indígenas
Bilingues AC
Madero 67-60 piso
Despacho 611
México 1 D. G. CP 06000

Asociación Regional Mapuche
Nehuen-Mapu

Bulnes 699
Oficinas 309-310
Temuco, Chile

Comité de Pueblos y Communidades Indígenas
del Oriente
Boliviano (CIDOB)
Casilla 4213
Santa Cruz, Bolivia

Confederación de Nacionalidades Indígenas de
la Amazonia Ecuatoriana (CONFENIAE)
Apartado Postal 4180
Quito, Ecuador

Consejo Indio de Sur América (CISA)
Apartado 2054
Correo Central
Lima, Peru

Consejo Nacional de Coordinacion de las
Nacionalidades Indígenas del Ecuador
(CONAIE)
Apartado 4180
Quito, Ecuador

Consejo Regional Indígena del Cauca (CRIC)
Apartado Aereo 516
Popayan, Colombia

Consejo Regional de Pueblos Indígenas (CORPI)
Apartado 6979-1000
San Jose, Costa Rica

MISATAN
Puerto Cabezas
Costa Atlántica, Nicaragua

MISURASATA
Apartado 437
Paras
San Jose, Costa Rica

Movimiento Indio Tupac Katari (MITKA)
Chitakolla Centre
Casilla 20214
Correo Central
La Paz, Bolivia

Also:

Asociacion Interétnica para el Desarollo de la Selva Peruana (AIDESEP), Peru

Asociacion Nacional Indígena Salvadorena (ANIS), El Salvador

Association des Amerindiens de Guyane Francaise (AWARA), French Guyana

Comité de Unidades Campesinas (CUC), Guatemala

Confederación de Nationalides Indígenas del Peru (CONAP), Peru

Congreso de Organizaciones Indios de Centroamerica, Mexico y Panama

Coordinadora de las Organizaciones Indígenas de la Cuenca Amazonica (COICA)

Movimiento de la Juventud Kuna (MJK), Panama

Organización de las Naciones Indígenas de Colombia (ONIC), Colombia

Organización Regional Huilliche

Uniao dos Nacoes Indígenas (UNI), Brazil

NORTH AMERICA

Alaska Native Coalition
P.O. Box 200908
Anchorage, AK 99520

American Indian Science and Engineering Society (AISES)
1085 14th St., Suite 1506
Boulder, CO 80302

Americans for Indian Opportunity (AIO)
3508 Garfield St., N.W.
Washington, DC 20007

Four Directions Council
4733 no. 17th Ave. NE 37
Seattle, WA 98105

Grand Council of the Cree
24 Bayswater Ave.
Ottawa, ON K1Y2E4, Canada

Indian Law Resource Center
601 E St., S.E.
Washington DC 20003

Indigenous Survival International
Dene National Office
P.O. Box 2338
Yellowknife NT XIA2P7, Canada

Indigenous Women's Network
P.O. Box 174
Lake Elmo, MN 55402

Inuit Circumpolar Conference
429 'D' St.
Anchor, AK 99501

Inuit Tapirisat of Canada
176 Gloucester St. (3rd Floor)
Ottawa, ON, Canada

Métis National Council
116 Middleton Crescent
Saskatoon, Sask. S752W4, Canada

Mohawk Nation/Akwesane Notes
Box 196
Rooseveltown, NY 13683-0196

National Congress of American Indians (NCAI)
900 Pennsylvania Ave., S.E.
Washington, DC 20003

National Indian Brotherhood Assembly of First Nations
222 Queen St. Suite 500
Capital Square Bd.
Ottawa, ON, K1P5V19, Canada

National Indian Youth Council
201 Hermosa Dr. NE
Albuquerque, NM 87108

Native American Rights Fund (NARF)
1506 Broadway
Boulder, CO 80302

Native Women's Association of Canada
195a Bank St.
Ottawa, ON K291W7 Canada

OYATE
2702 Mathews St.
Berkeley, CA 94702

APPENDIX C

NATIVE AMERICAN STUDIES PROGRAMS
IN THE UNITED STATES AND CANADA

Website:
www.richmond.edu/rnelson/guide.html
The new guide at the website above is an attempt to update and expand a thirty-page guide published by the Association for the Study of American Literatures in 1993. This guide is being published in both hard copy and electronic form. It is a comprehensive survey of U.S. and Canadian Native American Studies programs being offered as majors, minors, and certifications at the baccalaureate level or above. The following is a list, arranged by region, of the institutions that offer such programs.

Eastern U.S.

CT: U of Connecticut

MA: Amherst C
U of Massachusetts
Hampshire College
Mount Holyoke C
Smith C

ME: Colby C
U of Maine

NH: Dartmouth C
U of New Hampshire

NC: UNC at Pembroke
UNC at Wilmington

NY: Colgate U
Cornell U
SUNY at Buffalo
SUNY at New Paltz
SUNY at Oswego

North-central U.S.

IA: Iowa S U
Morningside C

KY: Northern Kentucky U

MI: Northern Michigan U

MN: Bemidji S U
C of St. Scholastica
U of Minnesota, Twin Cities

ND: U of North Dakota

NE: U of Nebraska, Lincoln
U of Nebraska, Omaha

SD: Black Hills S U
U of South Dakota

WI: Northland C
U of Wisconsin, Eau Claire
U of Wisconsin, Madison
U of Wisconsin, Milwaukee
U of Wisconsin, Superior

South-central U.S.

OK: Northeastern S U
U of Oklahoma
Oklahoma S U
U of Science and Arts of Oklahoma
U of Tulsa

Western U.S.

AK: U of Alaska, Fairbanks

AZ: U of Arizona

CA: U of California, Berkeley
U of California, Davis
U of California, Irvine
U of California, Los Angeles
U of California, Riverside
C S U, Chico
C S U, Hayward
C S U, Long Beach
C S U, Sacramento
C S U, San Bernadino
Humboldt S U
Mills C
San Diego S U
San Francisco S U

CO: U of Colorado, Boulder
U of Denver

MT: Montana S U
U of Montana

NM: U of New Mexico
New Mexico S U

WA: Eastern Washington U
The Evergreen S C
U of Washington
Western Washington U
WY: U of Wyoming

Canada

AB: U of Alberta
U of Lethbridge

NS: U of Cape Breton
ON: Laurentian U
U of Toronto
Trent U
SK: U of Saskatchewan
Saskatchewan Federal Indian C

APPENDIX D

AMERICAN INDIAN

HIGHER EDUCATION CONSORTIUM

AIHEC—Headquarters
121 Oronoco Street
Alexandria, Virginia 22314
(703) 838-0400 Fax (703) 838-0388
e-mail: aihec@aihec.org

Bay Mills Community College
12214 West Lake Shore
Dr. Brimley, Michigan 49715
(906) 248-3354 Fax: (906) 248-3351

Blackfeet Community College
P.O. Box 819
Browning, Montana 59417
(406) 338-7755 Fax: (406) 338-3272

Cankdeska Cikana Community College
P.O. Box 269
Fort Totten, North Dakota 58335
(701) 766-4415 Fax: (701) 766-4077

Cheyenne River Community College
P.O. Box 220
Eagle Butte, South Dakota 57625
(605) 964-6045 Fax: (605) 964-1144

College of the Menominee Nation
P.O. Box 1179
Keshena, Wisconsin 54135
(715) 799-4921 Fax: (715) 799-1308
e-mail: vfowler@menominee.com

Crownpoint Institute of Technology
P.O. Box 849
Crownpoint, New Mexico 87313
(505) 786-4100 Fax: (505) 786-5644
e-mail: jmtutt@aol.com

D-Q University
P.O. Box 409
Davis, California 95617
(530) 758-0470 Fax: (530) 758-4891
e-mail: dqupres@aol.com

Dine College
P.O. Box 126
Tsaile, Arizona 86556
(520) 724-3311 Fax: (520) 724-3327
e-mail: tlewis@crystal.ncc.cc.nm.us

Dull Knife Memorial College
P.O. Box 98
Lame Deer, Montana 59043
(406) 477-6215 Fax: (406) 477-6219
e-mail: aspang@www.dkmc.cc.mt.us

Fond du Lac Tribal & Community
College
2101 14th Street
Cloquet, Minnesota 55720-2964
(218) 879-0800 Fax: (218) 879-0814
e-mail: ljbriggs@asab.fdl.cc.mn.us

Fort Belknap College
P.O. Box 159
Harlem, Montana 59526
(406) 353-2607 Fax: (406) 353-2898

Fort Berthold Community College
P.O. Box 490
New Town, North Dakota 58763
(701) 627-3665 Fax: (701) 627-3609

Fort Peck Community College
P.O. Box 398

Poplar, Montana 59255
(406) 768-5551 Fax: (406) 768-5552

Haskell Indian Nations University
P.O. Box H-1305
Lawrence, Kansas 66046
(785) 749-8497 Fax: (785) 749-8411
e-mail: bmartin@ross1.cc.haskell.edu

Institute of American Indian Arts
1600 St. Michael's Drive
P.O. Box 20007
Santa Fe, New Mexico 87504
(505) 988-6463 Fax: (505) 986-5543

Lac Courte Oreilles Ojibwa Community
College
R.R. 2., Box 2357
Hayward, Wisconsin 54843
(715) 634-4790 Fax: (715) 634-5049
e-mail: lcooccl@win.bright.net

Leech Lake Tribal College
Route 3, Box 100
Cass Lake, MN 56633
(218) 335-2828 Fax: (218) 335-7845
e-mail: Iltcoll1@mail.paulbunyan.net

Little Big Horn College
P.O. Box 370
Crow Agency, Montana 59022
(406) 638-2228 Fax: (406) 638-2229
e-mail: janine@main.lbhc.cc.mt.us

Little Priest Tribal College
P.O. Box 270
Winnebago, Nebraska 68071
(402) 878-2380 Fax: (402) 878-2355

Nebraska Indian Community
College
RR 2 Box 164
Niobrara, Nebraska 68760
(402) 857-2434 Fax: (402) 857-2543

Northwest Indian College
2522 Kwina Road
Bellingham, Washington 98226
(360) 676-2772 Fax: (360) 738-0136
e-mail: boblorence@telcomplus.com

Oglala Lakota College
P.O. Box 490
Kyle, South Dakota 57752
(605) 455-2321 Fax: (605) 455-2787

Red Crow Community College
P.O. Box 1258
Cardston, Alberta
Canada TOK OKO
(403) 737-2400 Fax: (403) 737-2101
e-mail: redcrow@upanet.uleth.ca

Salish Kootenai College
P.O. Box 117
Pablo, Montana 59855
(406) 675-4800 Fax: (406) 675-4801
e-mail: joe_mcdonald@skc.edu

Sinte Gleska University
P.O. Box 490
Rosebud, South Dakota 57570
(605) 747-2263 Fax: (605) 747-2098

Sisseton Wahpeton Community
College
P.O. Box 689
Sisseton, South Dakota 57262
(605) 698-3966 Fax: (605) 698-3132
e-mail: elden@daknet.com

Sitting Bull College
HC 1, Box 4
Fort Yates, North Dakota 58538
(701) 854-3861 Fax: (701) 854-3403

Southwestern Indian Polytechnic
Institute
Box 10146-9169
Coors Road NW
Albuquerque, New Mexico 87184
(505) 897-5347 Fax: (505) 897-5343
e-mail: ce@native.sipi.bia.edu

Stone Child Community College
Rocky Boy Route, Box 1082
Box Elder, Montana 59521
(406) 395-4313 Fax: (406) 395-4836

Turtle Mountain Community
College P.O. Box 340
Belcourt, North Dakota 58316
(701) 477-5605 Fax: (701) 477-5028
e-mail: cartym@aol.com

United Tribes Technical College
3315 University Drive
Bismarck, North Dakota 58504
(701) 255-3285 Fax: (701) 255-1844
e-mail: dmgipp@aol.com

American Indian College Fund
(a separate, non-profit, fundraising organization
for the tribal colleges)
1111 Osage Street
Bldg. D, Suite 205-A
Denver, Colorado 80204
(303) 892-8312
fax (303) 572-0650
e-mail: aicf@aol.com

CREDITS

Cover	"Icon Indigena–Locus #1" © 1989 Parris K. Butler
Page 1	"Untitled" © Parris K. Butler
Page 69	"Full Moon Obscured by Spring Foliage" © 1997 Parris K. Butler
Page 125	"Comet" © 1997 Parris K. Butler
Page 168	"1491" from the "Feather" series © 1992 Larry McNeil
Page 169	"Would I Have Been a Member of the Nighthawk Snake Society or Would I Have Been a Half-Breed Leading the Whites to the Full Bloods?" © 1991 Hulleah J. Tsinhnahjinnie
Page 171	"Footprints" from the "Imprint" series © 1994 Pamela Shields
Page 184	Untitled © 2000 Parris K. Butler
Page 207	Library of Congress
Page 209 *(left)*	Library of Congress
Page 209 *(right)*	Carl Mydans/Hulton Getty/Archive Photos
Page 227	"Untitled" © 2000 Parris K. Butler
Page 258	Corbiss
Page 266	© Charles Bill
Page 284	"Untitled" © 1997 Parris K. Butler
Page 327	© 1992 Victoria J. Bomberry
Page 344	"New Moon Rising" © 1997 Parris K. Butler
Page 399	"Mike Yamashita/Woodfin Camp & Associates
Page 412	"Untitled" © 2000 Parris K. Butler
Page 466	"Sunrise" © 1997 Parris K. Butler
Page 513	© 2000 Ilka Hartmann
Page 514	© 2000 Ilka Hartmann
Page 519	AP/Wide World Photos
Page 531	© Michelle Vignes. Permission granted by the California Indian Basketweavers Association (CIBA).
Page 535	International Indian Treaty Council © 1984. Reprinted with permission.

All other artwork and photographs are credited where they appear in the text.

INDEX

The indigenous peoples—nations or tribes discussed in this book—and their subjects and page references are set boldface in this index.

© 1997 H. J. Tsinhnahjinnie